S0-BRO-305

320
P75

74592

DATE DUE			
Sep 24 '71			
GAYLORD M-2			PRINTED IN U.S.A.

WITHDRAWN

POLITICS AND EXPERIENCE

Essays presented to

MICHAEL OAKESHOTT

Politics and Experience

ESSAYS PRESENTED TO
PROFESSOR MICHAEL OAKESHOTT
ON THE OCCASION OF
HIS RETIREMENT

EDITED BY

PRESTON KING

Lecturer in Political Theory and Institutions, University of Sheffield

AND

B. C. PAREKH

Lecturer in Politics, University of Hull

CAMBRIDGE
AT THE UNIVERSITY PRESS
1968

CARL A. RUDISILL LIBRARY
LENOIR RHYNE COLLEGE

Published by the Syndics of the Cambridge University Press
Bentley House, 200 Euston Road, London N.W.1
American Branch: 32 East 57th Street, New York, N.Y. 10022

© Cambridge University Press 1968

Library of Congress Catalogue Card Number: 68 24482
Standard Book Number: 521 07333 2

320
P75

74592

July, 1971

Printed in Great Britain
at the University Printing House, Cambridge
(Brooke Crutchley, University Printer)

CONTENTS

ACKNOWLEDGMENTS

There are many persons to whom the editors are obliged for their assistance in the compilation of this volume. Foremost among these are Professor Elie Kedourie, Mr Maurice Cowling, and Mr Maurice Cranston. The support of Professor G. R. Elton has been invaluable, and so has the advice we have been fortunate to receive from Professor W. H. Greenleaf, Professor G. R. G. Mure and Professor A. H. Birch. We must also thank a close friend, Mr James Moore, who supported and advised on the project from its inception.

In the nature of things, a volume of this kind progresses from idea to reality in a slow and halting manner, requiring the cooperation of many persons and several changes of course. In this connection the Cambridge University Press has displayed considerable patience and understanding: to neglect to say so would reveal in us a lack of proper gratitude. Finally, we must thank Pramila Parekh and Hazel King, who have helped in a variety of practical ways to make this publication possible.

P. K.
B. C. P.

CONTRIBUTORS

SAMUEL COLEMAN   *Lecturer, Department of Philosophy, Columbia University*

DONALD DAVIE   *Professor, Department of English Literature, University of Essex*

W. H. DRAY   *Professor, Department of Philosophy, University of Toronto*

M. M. GOLDSMITH   *Assistant Professor, Department of Government, Columbia University*

W. H. GREENLEAF   *Professor, Department of Politics, University of Swansea*

PRESTON KING   *Lecturer, Department of Political Theory and Institutions, University of Sheffield*

DOROTHEA KROOK   *Associate Professor, Department of English, University of Jerusalem*

K. R. MINOGUE   *Reader, Department of Politics, The London School of Economics and Political Science*

B. C. PAREKH   *Lecturer, Department of Political Studies, University of Hull*

R. S. PETERS   *Professor, Institute of Education, University of London*

J. G. A. POCOCK   *Professor, Department of History, University of Washington, Missouri*

W. H. WALSH   *Professor, Department of Logic and Metaphysics, University of Edinburgh*

SHELDON S. WOLIN   *Professor, Department of Political Science, University of California, Berkeley*

EDITORS' INTRODUCTION

It is perfectly possible for any mode of reflection to die out, whether it be theological, historical, philosophical, scientific or otherwise. Whether any particular variety of thought, such as political philosophy, is dead or not merely depends upon whether it is practised—although the more serious question, as to whether it should be practised, remains. An answer to this question cannot be rendered abstractly; everything must turn on how well the practice is displayed; inevitably, every reader will judge the quality of the performance for himself.

A fairly wide variety of essays are collected together in the present volume. They all broadly reflect an interest in politics and philosophy, bearing upon the nature of political philosophy, tradition, revolution, history, ideology, rationalism, education and literature. They have been written especially for this volume, and are published in honour of one of the most eminent of contemporary political philosophers, Professor Michael Oakeshott.

One of the most interesting aspects of Professor Oakeshott's work, despite its relatively limited bulk, is the attempt he makes within it to achieve the most comprehensive understanding of experience possible. It is this attempt at comprehensiveness which renders his writings both genuinely interesting and genuinely philosophical. In his intellectual history, three principal works stand out: *Experience and its Modes* (1933) and *Rationalism in Politics* (1962), which included *The Voice of Poetry in the Conversation of Mankind* (1959). The essays which are newly published here all reveal a common concern with some of the basic themes which figure prominently in the work of Professor Oakeshott. We have, in fact, expressly taken the opportunity provided by this occasion for further, independent exploration of these themes.

In *Experience and its Modes* Professor Oakeshott argues that experience can be perceived from at least three fundamental standpoints: history, science and practice. In *The Voice of Poetry in the Conversation of Mankind* he provides an account of aesthetic experience. In *Rationalism in Politics* we are confronted with a collection of essays which attempt to locate the character of political experience within the practical world. Underlying these analyses is the assumption that philosophy involves the perception of experience as a whole. Professor Oakeshott's concern with comprehensiveness tends to render his work philosophical; and from this perspective one can appreciate his interest in Hobbes. But, equally, his concern with historical experience tends to generate an interest in tradition; and from this perspective one can understand his considerable esteem, not for Burke, but for Hegel.

Two principal areas of interest emerge out of Professor Oakeshott's work for the student of politics. One relates to the nature of politics conceived empirically, in time, historically; and the other relates to the nature of politics conceived rationally, out of time, or logically. Michael Oakeshott is not satisfied to see these two matters entirely divorced from one another. He attempts to define the logic of tradition or history; and to indicate the historicity or traditional character of logic. He has an historical sense, and a logical sense, as well as the common sense never to want to see (within the realm of practical experience) the first two separated from each other; hence springs an equal distrust of the supposed reality of 'brute' facts and of 'pure' ideas. It is such considerations as these which have influenced the planning of the present volume, as well, of course, as its title.

It would be out of place for us to attempt to provide an overall summary of Professor Oakeshott's position. Those who desire this may profitably consult Professor Greenleaf's *Oakeshott's Philosophical Politics* (Longmans, 1966). All that we immediately seek to do is to relate the essays presented here to some of the major themes which dominate Professor Oakeshott's work. These essays bear with varying degrees of directness upon the positions explicitly advanced by him. Professors Walsh and Dray, for example, deal directly with Professor Oakeshott's understanding of history. Professor Peters deals with his philosophy of education. In these first three essays the authors provide statements and critical assessments of certain aspects of Professor Oakeshott's work. In the fourth essay this concern is broadened. Dr Goldsmith provides a comparative analysis of three important interpretations of Hobbes which should help to put Oakeshott's own interpretation into better perspective. The next three essays become increasingly general in scope, all being concerned with the nature and function of political philosophy. The second half of the book—chapters eight to twelve—is devoted, by contrast, to the independent treatment of a cluster of related problems: on the one hand, tradition and revolution: on the other, rationalism and ideology. Professor Pocock and Dr Coleman are primarily concerned to explore the nature of tradition; Mr Minogue is primarily concerned with the nature of revolution; Mrs Krook is concerned to demonstrate that certain types of rationalism may generate beneficial institutional results; while the next essay, on ideology, seeks to draw attention to some of its logical inadequacies. It will be clear that this volume does not express a single coherent argument, and therefore that the essays which it contains are not intended to be read in sequence, but according to the mood and inclination of the reader.

We have attempted to impose upon the volume a certain coherence; but coherence is a phantom whose presence can never be truly and satisfactorily secured. There are nonetheless two major inadequacies for which we offer apologies. The first relates to our failure to obtain a thoroughly modern analysis of Hegel. In the case of the second, although we have been fortunate in receiving from Professor Davie an essay touching upon a particular case of the relationship between politics and literature, we regret that we were unable to obtain as well a more general treatment of this theme.

In conclusion, we may be permitted to remark that we do not believe that a volume of this kind, if it has any merit, will fail to have some influence upon those who read it. But the nature of that influence we believe it impossible to predict. All that we hope for, and expect, is a truly critical appreciation of these essays. It is in this spirit that they have been written and are presented. The overall spirit of this volume, following the lead offered by Professor Oakeshott's own writings, is explanatory rather than recommendatory. It is our hope that the essays collected here will throw further light upon certain central problems with which he has been vitally concerned throughout his academic career. Ultimately, this is the only way in which a truly distinguished scholar can be praised: not by praising him, but by being critically attentive to those problems which have absorbed so great a part of his time and attention. All of the contributors to this volume can be expected to have marginally divergent practical commitments and intellectual interests. The only fundamental tie that binds them within these covers is their shared interest in the work of Michael Oakeshott, whom they view from various perspectives, but from whom they have all learned much that is valuable.

THE PRACTICAL AND THE HISTORICAL PAST

W. H. WALSH

Both in *Experience and its Modes* and in his important and challenging essay 'The activity of being an historian'[1] Professor Oakeshott distinguishes sharply between what he calls 'the practical' and 'the historical' attitude to the past. Concern with the past is, of course, a very common feature of human experience, but it is a mistake to think that such concern is always, or even often, historical. On the contrary, what might be called the normal or everyday approach to the past, the approach of the relatively unsophisticated, is to see it as something which exists in relation to, and explains, the present. The past thus regarded is thought of as worth knowing not for its own sake, but only 'in relation to ourselves and our own current activities';[2] it is accordingly not so much *the* past as *our* past. Our interest in it is limited, as Oakeshott illustrates from the lawyer's concern with a will, to what bears directly on present hopes, fears or aspirations; we see it most commonly as leading up to, making intelligible, often as justifying or condemning what we take to be happening now. That is to say, we read events, so long as we persist in this practical attitude, backwards; we are not concerned to consider them as they truly were in themselves. By contrast, it is the aim of historians, in the proper sense of that term, to study the past for its own sake, to treat it as something which exists independently of themselves and deserves investigation in its own right. Oakeshott does not deny that the emergence of this attitude towards the past has been gradual and is even now by no means complete; he allows that those who call themselves historians are under constant temptation to fall back into the practical way of thinking, and that their ability to resist the temptation can by no means always be counted on. But he argues, even so, that we are justified in speaking of a specifically historical attitude to the past on the ground that we find such an attitude manifested in the writings of historians and, 'generally speaking',[3] only in the writings of historians. To pass from, say, the reflections of an active politician on British rule in India or the account of the medieval church given by one who wants to defend or denigrate Catholicism to the treatment of the same subjects by a trained historian

---

[1] *Rationalism in Politics and other Essays* (abbreviated as *R.P.*), pp. 137–67; first published in *Historical Studies I*, ed. T. Desmond Williams, 1956.　　[2] *R.P.* p. 147　　[3] *R.P.* p. 153.

is to pass to another world altogether, one in which a different way of thinking and a different idiom prevail. The vocabulary appropriate to the former, a vocabulary of utility and disutility, praise and blame, justification and abuse, gives way to a manner of speaking which is suited primarily to saying precisely what occurred. The true historian may explain by writing a full narrative of events and showing how one led naturally to another, but he will never seek to explain by arguing that what happened then makes sense because it led on to what is happening now. Still less will he explain by finding causes, the discovery of which will enable us to take practical steps now. The language of causes, along with that of moral praise and blame, will be quite foreign to him as an historian.

This doctrine was originally put forward in a context where Oakeshott was not merely expounding the historical point of view, but also assessing its philosophical adequacy, and this led him to distinguish between the past as it is 'for history' and the past as it is 'in history'.[1] Contrary to what the working historian supposes, the past cannot have real existence in itself; in all its forms it is a construction out of present experience. Oakeshott does not retract this view in his later essay, but I propose to set it on one side for the purposes of the present discussion. I suspect that a refusal, warranted or unwarranted, to treat Oakeshott's metaphysical position seriously has distracted attention from the full importance of the points he has to make in this area of thought. And I believe that we are entirely justified in considering Oakeshott's main distinction in abstraction from his further metaphysical discussion, for even if we have to agree that, ultimately, the past has no existence except in relation to present experience, there will still be two ways of taking it, practical and properly historical, and the differences outlined above will still stand.[2]

The first point I should like to make about Oakeshott's distinction between the practical and the historical past is simply to endorse it and reiterate its importance. In calling attention to this feature of historical thought Oakeshott has put his finger on a truth which is both very simple and of central significance: that history is, or at least aspires to be, a branch of knowledge, and that it accordingly presupposes in its exponents the attitude appropriate to knowledge, which is that they shall let their thinking be guided not by personal considerations, but by the needs of their subject-matter. This of course involves treating

[1] *Experience and its Modes*, p. 107.
[2] In his 1956 essay Oakeshott mentions a third way of taking the past which he describes as 'contemplative' and illustrates from the procedure of historical novelists. But this too can be set aside without loss here.

that subject-matter as having a character of its own to which our think-ing must conform, and this in turn is to endow it with independence and autonomy. It may seem that these points are so obvious as not to be worth making. But though the main characteristics of knowledge were already clear to Plato, the fact is, as Oakeshott brings out in passing, that the dispassionate attitude which goes with its pursuit was very slow to develop. Even in the field of physical science the understanding of astronomical phenomena was long bedevilled by the belief that the stars in their courses have an influence on our lives; what men wanted to find out was not the true state of affairs in all its detail, but rather the interesting facts, i.e. those which were to affect them for good or ill. It was comparatively late in the Christian era that the notion of a truly scientific attitude, one in which we set aside our hopes and fears and simply investigate the phenomena for their own sake, won anything like general acceptance, though it would be false to suggest that it was entirely unknown at a much earlier date. It is significant, however, that the field in which it was first practised was that of mathematics, whose objects can seldom have been of much emotional concern to human beings. Conversely subjects such as history whose findings can move men deeply were extremely slow to develop. As late as the eighteenth century history was being described as 'philosophy teaching by ex-amples', and the idea that the centre of historical study lay in some practical purpose was widely accepted throughout that supposedly scientific period. Even in the following century the notion that a main task for history was to search out the origins of what interests us now was extremely widespread; 'Whig' history, which demonstrated that the march of events inevitably culminated in the glories of the present, was very much in fashion, and many of those who rejected it did so only to embrace an alternative view which saw the past as vastly superior to the present and therefore treated it as a refuge from real or imagined evils. Oakeshott's emphasis on the distinction between the historical and the practical past is intended as a corrective to all these mistakes; it is part of an attempt to think out the theory which lies behind modern 'scientific' history, and deserves the closest attention just because of that fact.

If anything is clear in the practice of history today, it is that the historian regards himself as occupied in an investigation which is, or at least ought to be, pursued in a wholly impersonal manner. His business is to establish and understand the facts, whether he likes them or not. By making that feature central in his account of historical thought Oake-shott has clearly seized on a point of vital importance. But he has not, of course, been content to make this point in a general way; he has gone further and spelled out its corollaries with a boldness and clarity of mind superior to that of any other contemporary theorist of history. It is to what he has to say in establishing these corollaries that I now wish to turn.

According to Oakeshott, 'scientific'[1] history or history proper involves the following. First, as already stressed, that we investigate the past for its own sake, which means that we do not restrict our attention to those parts of it which obviously connect or contrast with the present, but try to find out as much as we can without any *arrière-pensées*. Sheer desire to know must be our guiding motive here; to study the past with the idea of pointing a moral or supporting a cause is altogether foreign to this point of view. Closely connected with this first requirement is a second, that we cease to look at history from the vantage point of the present and so read it backwards. Many studies have been produced with titles like 'The Evolution of Parliament' and 'The Origins of the Tory Party', but Oakeshott argues that, in so far as they live up to their pretences, they cannot be treated as strictly historical. If we are to give our attention to the past for its own sake, we must pay it the compliment of regarding it as interesting in itself and not just because it led on to something else. In concerning themselves with 'origins' or 'developments' historians relapse into the practical attitude and so show their thinking to be pre-scientific. But the effects of that attitude come out not merely in the aspirations of historians, but above all in their language. And this leads Oakeshott to formulate a third requirement in scientific history, that historians refrain from using terms with practical overtones. The effects of this demand are far-reaching, for it emerges that historians are to eschew not just the vocabulary of praise and blame (a conclusion already drawn by earlier theorists such as Butterfield), but also any terminology which reflects or implies personal involvement. So, says Oakeshott,[2] we must expunge from our histories such statements as the following:

'He died too soon.'
'The death of William the Conqueror was accidental.'
'He dissipated his resources in a series of useless wars.'
'The Pope's intervention changed the course of events.'
'The effect of the Boer War was to make clear the necessity for radical reform in the British Army.'

Let us begin by considering this last point. Oakeshott develops his view in a passage from which I will quote at length:[3]

[1] Oakeshott does not himself use the phrase 'scientific history'. But it is clear that what he has in mind is identical with what Collingwood understood under this description and what J. B. Bury advocated in his lecture on 'History as a Science'. Scientific history in this sense does not necessarily make any appeal to the results of natural or even social science; it is scientific in its attitude to its subject-matter rather than in its particular methods.

[2] *R.P.* p. 148.   [3] *R.P.* p. 154.

In the specifically 'historical' attitude...the past is *not* viewed in relation to the present, and is *not* treated as if it were the present. Everything that the evidence reveals or points to is recognised to have its place; nothing is excluded, nothing is regarded as 'non-contributory'. The place of an event is not determined by its relation to subsequent events. What is being sought here is neither a justification, nor a criticism nor an explanation of a subsequent or present condition of things. In 'history' no man dies too soon by 'accident'; there are no successes and no failures and no illegitimate children. Nothing is approved, there being no desired condition of things in relation to which approval can operate; and nothing is denounced. This past is without the moral, the political or the social structure which the practical man transfers from *his* present to *his* past, The Pope's intervention did not change the course of events, it *was* the course of events, and consequently his action was not an 'intervention'. *X* did not die 'too soon'; he died when he did. *Y* did not dissipate his resources in a series of useless wars: the wars belong to the actual course of events, not some imaginary illegitimate course of events.

Despite the explanation, it must be confessed that much of this doctrine has an air of paradox. The paradox derives, if I am not mistaken, primarily from what is said about there being no successes or failures in history. On the contrary, we want to protest, history is the record of men's successes and failures, whether achieved individually or collectively; it derives its unique interest precisely from that fact. History is concerned with what men have achieved or tried to achieve, or again it is concerned with obstacles and shortcomings, weaknesses of will and the like, which led them to lose their grip and fall back in confusion and failure. To think otherwise is to suggest that historians should have nothing to say about agents, actions and activities, when these are the very stuff of the subject. If an historian is not to be allowed to talk of success or failure, by what right will he employ verbs of action of any sort? Or is he to be permitted to say that the Pope sent an emissary or despatched forces, but not to mention what the effect was of the action he took? It is hard to see by what right one could justify the first and rule out the second, especially if it happened to be true that the Pope intended his action to have the result in question. If we are to investigate what happened in the past for its own sake, we must surely specify more than what men did in the most immediate of terms; we must make clear their intentions and indicate the extent to which they succeeded in carrying them out.

Oakeshott's objection to this is presumably that as soon as we begin to talk of success or failure we presuppose a point of view which must be that of some particular agent; we identify ourselves with some cause or project, and so relapse into the practical attitude. Similarly when we say that *X* died too soon or that the Pope intervened: a man dies too soon, or intervenes, from the point of view of some particular purpose, and it is not the business of the scientific historian to commit himself about anyone's purposes. The aim of history is to discover or understand, not to get anything done. But does this mean that it is illegitimate for the historian to speak in terms of purposes at all? There is a passage in *Experience and its Modes* where Oakeshott says that we should 'reject any notion of a "plot" or "plan" in history, in the sense of an outline skeleton of important events, the abstract story without the details. History and the plot of history are the same thing, to know one is to know the other.'[1] One could, however, agree with this and still argue that history is full of plots and plans, attempted if not always successfully carried out. Is the historian not to recognise this fact? Or is Oakeshott wanting to point out, like Tolstoy, that many of the successes men pride themselves on result from good fortune rather than good organisation, and cannot be seen as the rational achievements they are made out to be? If that were his intention, it would still remain true that men cherish long-term aims which get carried out in some fashion or other; to specify these aims and trace the steps in their realisation would still be a proper task for the historian. And even if all talk of long-term aims in history were precluded, it would still be proper to speak of short-term projects such as outwitting an opponent in parliamentary debate or taking a (limited) objective at a certain point in battle.

What then of the suggestion that, as soon as one speaks in terms of purposes, one *identifies* oneself with a particular project and so abandons the scientific for the practical attitude? It seems to me that there are two things to be said. First, that one can speak from a point of view without embracing that point of view. It is possible, for instance, to give an account of a political campaign as seen through the eyes of one of the leading contenders without any implication that he *ought* to have succeeded. I do not deny that there are difficulties here: it is obvious that popular historians in particular readily identify themselves with a certain standpoint and so construct narratives which are open to Oakeshott's strictures. But one way in which the modern professional historian is superior to his amateur predecessors is just in his appreciation of the complexity of the facts he has to investigate, a complexity which comes out when he makes clear that many different individuals and bodies were pursuing many different purposes. What he will aim to do is describe the situation as seen by the main agents in turn, not concentrate on one at the expense of the others. But if it is suggested that it would be better if he avoided even the temporary taking up of a standpoint, the reply to this must be to ask what the correct frame of

[1] *Experience and its Modes*, pp. 143–4.

mind for him is supposed to be. Is he to be so impartial that he refrains from mentioning that men were engaged in forwarding their particular purposes? Is he to remain so strictly on the theoretical level that he loses sight of the fact that history is the sphere of the practical, and hence cannot be properly described in a language which eschews practical terms altogether?

I cannot believe that Oakeshott intends any such consequence. Nor can I understand how he can maintain, at least in an unqualified way, that in history 'the place of an event is not determined by its relation to subsequent events'.[1] He is thinking here, of course, of the 'Whig' practice of seeing past happenings in their relationship to the present; to read history backwards, on this view, is to see it as a process culminating in what engages our attention and stirs our emotions now. But it is possible to locate events as part of a continuing process, and so to relate them to what happened subsequently, without falling into any such errors. If 'the Evolution of Parliament' is a suspect phrase, on the ground that it presupposes the standpoint of the present, 'the Rise of the Gentry' is surely quite unobjectionable. There was indeed a time, or so it is argued, at which the Gentry exercised an all-important influence on English political life, but it is not the present time, and an historian who speaks of the rise of the Gentry is not claiming that history makes sense because it led up to that particular state of affairs. What he is doing, on the contrary, is offering guidance through the tangle of particular events by identifying an important trend or development. It seems to me to be an obvious and central task for the historian to identify trends and developments in this way; part of his job, as I have expressed it elsewhere, is to 'colligate' events under appropriate concepts, thus explaining how they go together and making possible a clear view of a period or age. I realise of course that there are historians who view this process with suspicion, on the ground that any continuing pattern we claim to descry in the particular facts must be imposed by ourselves. But I can see no justification for this extreme nominalism, which conflicts with the plain fact that men carry out policies and work for causes over long periods of time, with the result that their different actions are internally related to one another. In such cases it is certainly true to say that the place of an event is determined by its relation to subsequent events: in the simplest sort of instance, a man did A because he had it in mind to do B, and doing A was a necessary condition of being in a position to do B. But even when, as most often happens, things are less tidy than this, it still makes sense to speak of events which are widely separated in time as forming parts of a single development, and thus to treat the earlier members of the series as standing in essential relation to

[1] *R.P.* p. 154.

the later. We do this whenever we have to do with processes which can be initiated, forwarded or impeded by human effort, processes in whose outcome men take a strong interest. The peculiarity of history is that the historian knows the outcome of the processes with which he deals and is therefore in a position to say what the persons he writes of have achieved or failed to achieve. My thesis is that this is something we expect historians, even 'scientific' historians, to do for us, and that it cannot be done without viewing what happened from the standpoint of subsequent developments.

If this is correct, it follows that there is nothing wrong in principle with reading history backwards. Every historian will read history backwards in some degree, in so far as he identifies continuing trends or processes. And he will be justified in doing so, because he has the advantage over those whose deeds he narrates in possessing the power of hindsight: he knows, as those alive at the time could not, what the outcome of actions was, and so can specify what was *really* happening with a sureness which was not possible for contemporaries. There are historians and theorists of history who speak as if it were a regrettable fact that the historian possesses hindsight; for them the ideal situation would be for the historical investigator to see things precisely as the agents with whom he is concerned saw them. But this is to close one's eyes to the realities of history, and forget that, in favourable circumstances, an historian can know more of what was going on at a particular time and can get it into better perspective than any person living in the period possibly could.

It should scarcely be necessary to reiterate that this is not to reinstate 'Whig' history or any variant of it. To identify historical developments is to see events in the light of their outcome, but that is something quite different from viewing them as the background or justification of the present. The distinction between the practical and the historical past is preserved on this view as much as it is on that which it counters, for it still remains true for those who hold it that the primary task of the historian is to say what happened, to investigate and delineate the facts for their own sake. The only difference involved—though it is certainly a significant difference—is that it is recognised that 'saying what happened' amounts to more than merely detailing events one after another. As well as detailing events historians have to sum them, and this means that they must see how they go together to constitute recognisable developments or processes (including, of course, processes of decline). But all this is a matter of truth or falsehood; its object is understanding, not the advancement of some practical cause or the strengthening or weakening of someone's will, whether the historian's or anyone else's.

A further deduction which Oakeshott draws from his distinction between the historical and the practical attitudes to the past is that the search for causes forms no part of history proper.[1] This is a highly complex subject, which I can discuss only briefly here.[2] Oakeshott's suspicion of historical causes springs partly from the belief that cause is either a practical notion or a concept belonging to natural science, partly from the claim that history can be rendered intelligible without invoking any sort of causal connections. Now in so far as Oakeshott's general objection to the use of practical language in history has been discounted by the arguments set out above, it seems to me that his case for excluding at least some practical types of causation from history falls to the ground. For instance, if it is agreed that an historian, without compromising his scientific integrity, can speak of the Pope's intervening in a dispute, it must equally be agreed that he can legitimately say that the intervention was instrumental in producing a certain result. Assuredly in making such a statement—in singling out what is thought of as the crucial circumstance but for which the result would not have ensued—he speaks from a particular point of view; he looks at the situation as it presented itself to a particular agent or group and indicates what to him or them must be said to have caused what came about. He could, and for that matter quite often does, look at the same events from the point of view of a different set of agents, in which case he might very well assign causes quite differently.[3] But the fact that there is no single answer to the question what brought something about need cause no more confusion in history than it does in everyday life, nor in fact does it seem to me that readers of history are in practice confused on this point. They are well used to a narrator's appearing now in one guise and now in another, and are certainly not tempted to think that he has said the last word when he first begins to pronounce on causes.

The difficulties about cause in history, difficulties which give some plausibility to a conclusion like that of Oakeshott, lie elsewhere. They spring in the first place from the complexity of the concept of historical causation, the many different senses in which words like 'cause' are used in history. The sense we have considered so far, in which a cause is, roughly, an eliminable necessary condition, is by no means the only sense invoked by historians. Sometimes, as Collingwood pointed out,

---

[1] This deduction is explicit in *Experience and its Modes*, where the subject is discussed at length, but is not brought out in Oakeshott's later essay. But equally there is nothing in the latter to indicate a change of view.

[2] For the general view taken in the following discussion see also my paper on 'Historical Causation', *Proceedings of the Aristotelian Society* (1962–3), reprinted in the 1967 edition of my *Introduction to Philosophy of History*.

[3] This doctrine of the relativity of (practical) causes derives from Collingwood's discussion in his *Essay on Metaphysics*.

they mean by 'cause' a motive: when someone is caused to take or refrain from action in this sense he is given a motive for acting or not acting. Causation thus understood is a rational notion, whose application is entirely consistent with the maintenance of free will. And even if it is maintained that causes as motives are only a sub-species of causes as necessary conditions (which seems to me untrue), there are yet other kinds of historical cause to take into account. One thing that historians often find themselves attempting is to estimate the long-term effects of a movement or personal career; they want to assess the 'contribution' of the Quakers to English public life or to determine the 'influence' of Benjamin Jowett on the social and political status of British intellectuals. The notion of causation here involved is closely connected with that of answerability; it is, no doubt, an extension of the primitive sense in which to ask who caused something is to ask who was responsible, i.e. to whom the blame or merit should be imputed. Mr Dray has argued[1] that this moral conception of causation is still widely used by historians: in arguing about the causes of the American Civil War, for instance, they are sometimes disputing about who was ultimately responsible. But whether or not this contention is accepted, responsibility in the weakened sense illustrated by the above examples is constantly talked of by historians.

Oakeshott, in my view, has given no sufficient reason for excluding any of these types of causation from history, except perhaps for Dray's moral sense. It is true that in *Experience and its Modes*[2] he puts forward a general objection to the use of the category of cause and effect by historians, arguing that it is

fundamental to this conception...that we should be able to separate the cause and its effect, and endow each with a certain degree of individuality;

and adding

but it is just this which is impossible while we retain the postulates of historical experience. It cannot be achieved by selecting some single event and attributing to that any subsequent event or the whole course of subsequent events. No single event in history is isolable in this manner, and if it were there would be no more reason to isolate *this* event rather than *that*.

The answer to this is first that we constantly identify single events, both in history and in everyday life, and second that we do have reasons for picking on one event as a cause rather than another, for example when we assign causes in the necessary condition sense. Oakeshott would not be impressed with the answer, since he would see both the isolation of particular events and the singling out of some of them as causes as

[1] In his chapter on 'Causal Judgment in History' in *Philosophy of History* (Englewood Cliffs, 1964), which is based on an article published in *Daedelus* (1962).
[2] Pp. 131–2. The quotations that follow appear on p. 132.

evidence of the intrusion of the practical attitude into history proper. But, for reasons already given, I believe this conclusion to be mistaken. The historian, in my view, just because of his concern with action, cannot avoid talking in the terms of practical life, though he can do so without pursuing any direct practical purpose. Nor indeed could he believe history to be the seamless web Oakeshott makes it out to be without forfeiting the right to speak of particular events of any sort. But is the word 'event' to be excluded from history, as well as the word 'cause'?

A second reason why the subject of historical causation is so difficult is that, over and above the comparatively familiar causes already mentioned, historians are apt to invoke other types of causal factor altogether, attributing a particular development to the effect of economic conditions, for example, or explaining it in terms of national character. Oakeshott has no sympathy whatever with any such move. History, he writes,[1]

has no use for abstractions such as climate, geographical conditions or national character as the sole causes of events. When Lessing ascribes the eminence of Greek art to the climate and government of Greece, he has quitted altogether the region of historical thought. Or again, to say of an event that it is due solely to 'economic causes' is not bad history; it is not history at all...A cause in history must belong to and be consonant with the character of the world of history.

I take it that the point here is that to locate the moving forces in history in factors over which men have no control is to go against a fundamental presupposition of historical thought, that men are at least in some degree in a position to make their own history. But if this is the view taken, the presupposition can be preserved with only a minor change in the position Oakeshott attacks: namely, that we do not regard the conditions mentioned as the *sole* causes of anything in history. And in fact I very much doubt whether any historian who stresses factors of this kind has ever intended to make them solely responsible for what happened; he has wanted to single out, not the sole causes, but the basic causes. The point he has to make is that, if you want a real explanation of, say, the virtual disappearance of the Liberal party in British politics since the first war, you must look to a combination of economic circumstances with standing political conditions such as the electoral system, which precluded any true revival of the party's fortunes. Reference to factors of this kind indicates the conditions in which men acted at the time; it shows why they chose as they did, by making clear what they were *not* in a position to choose. But this is not to sell the pass to determinism, or to quit the field of history for that of natural science. It is not even, as Oakeshott seems to suggest, to invoke an odd species of efficient

[1] *Experience and its Modes*, p. 128.

cause which less sophisticated historians have not dreamed of. For the causes in question, as I have claimed elsewhere, function not as efficient but as formal causes in the Aristotelian sense of the term. They specify the more or less permanent framework inside which men had to act, but do not by themselves directly explain anything they positively did.

It is disappointing that Oakeshott, who shows himself so sensitive to the special character of history in its modern form, should have paid no attention to the analytic type of history, found in but by no means confined to the writings of Marxist sympathisers, in which 'abstractions' of the above kind are most commonly invoked. The practitioners of this type of history would claim to explain historical events at a deeper level than their shallower or more ignorant predecessors, who made do with the causal apparatus of everyday life. This claim certainly deserves examination, but does not get it from Oakeshott, even though he censures Thucydides for making 'personal character and motive... a first cause behind which, as a general rule, he does not press'.[1] If we ask for the reason for this omission, part of it may lie in a distaste for the work of modern analytic historians, who may well strike Oakeshott as wanting to make history scientific in a quite indefensible sense. In both his main pronouncements on history the idea that general laws about human behaviour can be brought to bear in historical thought is treated with, at best, deep scepticism. But another factor seems to come into the matter as well, namely Oakeshott's conviction that there is no reason to think that history makes sense in any fundamental way at all.

The historical past, he writes at the end of his essay on 'The activity of being an historian',

is a complicated world, without unity of feeling or clear outline: in it events have no over-all pattern or purpose, lead nowhere, point to no favoured condition of the world and support no practical conclusions. It is a world composed wholly of contingencies and in which contingencies are intelligible, not because they have been resolved, but on account of the circumstantial relations which have been established between them: the historian's concern is not with causes but with occasions.[2]

That is why

for the 'historian', for whom the past is dead and irreproachable, the past is feminine. He loves it as a mistress of whom he never tires and whom he never expects to talk sense.

Behind this pessimism there seems to lie the idea that history has either got to make sense overall, as it was supposed to do on the various versions of the doctrine of progress, or that it cannot be said to make sense

---

[1] *Experience and its Modes*, p. 131.
[2] *R.P.* pp. 166–7; the following quotation comes from p. 166.

at all. But one can agree with Oakeshott in rejecting the first alternative without following him in thinking we are therefore committed to the second. History may well be 'leading nowhere', without its being true that it consists of nothing but lightly mediated 'contingencies'. In the penultimate sentence of his essay Oakeshott speaks of history as

an activity in which a writer, concerned with the past for its own sake and working to a chosen scale, elicits a coherence in a group of contingencies of similar magnitudes.[1]

One does not know quite what to make of this mention of 'coherence', but Oakeshott's general position about historical explanation is such that it cannot amount to much. The probability is that he thinks of it on roughly the same lines as did Professor W. B. Gallie when, in his book on *Philosophy and the Historical Understanding*, he argued that it is the business of an historical narrator to reduce the element of surprise in his story, by showing that the several events he recounts had conditions in what went before, but not to eliminate contingencies by demonstrating that the outcome could have been predicted.

For reasons which will be apparent from the foregoing pages I believe that this cannot be an adequate account of historical coherence. Aside from the fact that by no means all history, particularly in its modern professional form, is presented as narrative, it must be insisted that even a narrative historian has the duty of making clear the general pattern of his story, as well as the transitions within it. He has to say in general what was going on, not merely explain how things got from one point to another. That he can do this at all connects directly with the fact that concepts like process, trend and development have application in history. Historians can find patterns in history, though patterns of a limited sort, thanks to the fact that men pursue policies, singly or collectively, over long periods of time; their achievements may not always, or even often, correspond to their aspirations, but are nevertheless such that the whole chain of events which culminates in them can be treated as a single process or development. And a process of this sort is rightly viewed as intelligible from two points of view: internally in so far as its various parts belong together in an intimate way, having something of the coherence which Idealist philosophers tried to express through the notion of unity in diversity, externally in so far as it is possible to reconstruct the setting in which the development took place and to produce a coherent account, in terms of some accredited social theory, of its effect on what took place. I am not claiming that historians are always able to produce such an account, but I think it obvious that in favourable cases, those which arise in the field of

[1] *Ibid.* p. 167.

economic history for instance, they can. In view of these facts I cannot believe that the pessimism expressed by Oakeshott on the subject of historical contintengy is justified. There is contingency enough in history, but there are stretches of intelligibility too.

I have been concerned in the above discussion only with some of the consequences which Oakeshott deduces from his distinction between the practical and the historical past. The distinction itself I regard as entirely sound; it was, in my view, an important, if largely unappreciated, achievement on Oakeshott's part to have seized on it and made it central in his account of 'scientific' history. But I do not see that accepting it commits us to the view that all practical language must be abjured by the historian, to arguing that cause is a concept which must be banished from history or to believing that there is no sense in which an historian can legitimately use his hindsight in recounting the course of events.

There is another, larger issue which I might have taken up but shall not do here. We can ask whether, granted that history is first and foremost a branch of knowledge and thus that the aim of the true historian must be to investigate the past for its own sake, it follows that it is, as Bury put it, 'a science no less *and no more*'. Oakeshott subscribes to Bury's position, as do many practising historians, in Britain at least; but I do not agree that there is no alternative to this view. For it seems to me that an historian would not forfeit his claim to be called scientific in the broad sense of that term if his investigation of the past was undertaken with other motives besides the mere desire to find out the truth. It might be that he spoke from a point of view which must be described as extra-scientific, even though his enquiries were conducted in a wholly scientific way; it might be, again, that he wished to use the results of disinterested investigation to answer further questions which were not strictly questions about truth or falsehood. I hold myself that both of these things are true of history as we have it today, and I should not agree that the fact that they are is evidence of the imperfect character of the subject as currently pursued. It seems to me on the contrary that much of the fascination and a large part of the instruction to be derived from history come from its being neither a straightforward branch of knowledge nor a straightforward practical activity, but a subtle mixture of both. But I have given such arguments as I have in favour of this conclusion in other essays,[1] and I shall not repeat them now.

---

[1] Especially in my paper 'The Limits of Scientific History', published in *Historical Studies III*, ed. James Hogan, and reprinted in the 1967 edition of my *Introduction to Philosophy of History*. This, incidentally, was written before I had read Oakeshott on 'The activity of being an historian'.

MICHAEL OAKESHOTT'S
THEORY OF HISTORY

WILLIAM H. DRAY

I

By contrast with those of his fellow idealist, R. G. Collingwood, the views of Michael Oakeshott about the nature of historical knowledge have not been much discussed. This is surprising as well as unfortunate. It is surprising, not only because of Oakeshott's own eminence as an historian and political theorist, but also because of the high esteem in which Collingwood himself held Oakeshott's philosophical work, especially the relevant parts of *Experience and its Modes*, which he once hailed as representing 'the high-water mark of English thought upon history'.[1] It is unfortunate because Oakeshott's analysis, in spite of the opposition to 'positivism' which it shares with Collingwood's, and some doctrinal agreements of a more specific nature, actually orients the philosophical discussion of history in directions no more than hinted at by the latter. For anyone interested in the contribution of English idealism to the philosophy of history, Oakeshott's writings are an indispensable source.

The differences between Oakeshott's and Collingwood's theories of history in fact extend beyond mere differences of emphasis. Oakeshott, for example, denies outright the well-known Collingwoodian doctrine that the task of the historian is to revive or re-enact the past. It is central to his own position that the historical past is dead, not 'living in the present', and that any attempt to revive it would be, not history, but 'a piece of obscene necromancy'.[2] Oakeshott rejects also the Collingwoodian limitation of history's subject-matter to the reflective actions of human beings; for he finds 'nothing in the human to distinguish it absolutely from the non-human past'.[3] Again, where Collingwood represents historical knowledge as yielding, if not prediction and control on the model of the natural sciences, then at least a kind of practical wisdom, Oakeshott roundly declares that history is 'wholly without relevance to practical life'.[4] And where Collingwood regards the

[1] R. G. Collingwood, *The Idea of History* (Oxford, 1946), p. 159.
[2] 'The activity of being an historian', in Michael Oakeshott, *Rationalism in Politics and other Essays* (London, 1962), p. 166.
[3] *Experience and its Modes* (London, 1933), p. 102.
[4] *Ibid.* p. 157.

explanatory concept of causation as having a peculiarly satisfactory historical use—its role in natural science being somewhat more dubious—Oakeshott rules the concept out of historiography altogether as an inappropriate intrusion of scientific ways of thinking. Against such a background of disagreement, Oakeshott's remark, in reviewing Collingwood's posthumous *Idea of History*, that only its author's bad health and early death prevented his doing for history what Kant had done for natural science in his day, was a generous one.[1] Nor can it simply be assumed that Oakeshott came eventually to adopt a more Collingwoodian position. For in his later essay, 'The activity of being an historian', he appears to retract nothing of importance from his earlier account of history in *Experience and its Modes*. And his reviews of historical books have continuously applied—if necessarily in a piecemeal way—his original leading ideas.

That Oakeshott should have held a distinctive and thoroughly challenging view of history so consistently and for so long makes it the more regrettable that he never set himself the task of its full-scale critical elaboration. For although elegantly and powerfully expressed, both the chief sources cited are also, for the most part, frustratingly sketchy, and often downright mysterious as well. The present paper, in taking issue with some of Oakeshott's *ipissima verba*, will not contribute directly to the needed elaboration. It will endeavour nevertheless to direct attention to some points at which such elaboration would be fruitful. The chief focus of discussion will be upon the very sharp contrasts which Oakeshott draws between historical modes of thought and what he regards as scientific and practical ones. Examination of these contrasts will be prefaced by a short summary of Oakeshott's theory as a whole, and followed by a consideration of the way he uses his fundamental contrasts to debar concepts like cause and chance from historical work. It will be conceded that much of what Oakeshott says expresses recognizable attitudes of historians toward their work. It will be questioned, however, whether the theoretical basis on which he argues for the distinctiveness of historical enquiry can be maintained without substantial modification.

II

The context of Oakeshott's discussion of history in *Experience and its Modes* is a quasi-Hegelian examination of the forms of experience, their relationship, status, and degree of internal coherence. History is regarded as one of those forms: a 'world of ideas', which, as such, has its own system of postulates or structural categories. Of these Oakeshott discusses, in particular, those of 'the past', 'fact and truth', the 'indi-

[1] *English Historical Review*, January 1947, p. 84.

vidual' and 'explanation'. Let me sketch briefly some typical claims of his with respect to each.

According to Oakeshott, the whole of present experience is historical in so far as it is brought under the category of the historical past, i.e. in so far as what is perceived is regarded as evidence for a past of the appropriate sort.[1] This past is to be distinguished from the past as merely remembered, as fancied, as what must or might have been, or as what merely happens to interest us. But it is also to be distinguished from the past 'as it actually happened', if by this we mean anything more than 'what the evidence obliges us to believe'.[2] Oakeshott's is a radically constructionist theory of history: it denies the intelligibility of any distinction between history and historiography, between the actual course of events and what the historian constructs in accordance with the categories of historical thought.[3] History is not, of course, a *free* construction. It is nevertheless the historian's 'creation' rather than his discovery.[4] It follows that an historical account cannot be said to be a 'revival' of a 'fixed and finished' past. It follows also that the historical series is really present—the historian's present constructive experience—although it is regarded by him as past. The ultimate incoherence of regarding it this way leads Oakeshott to charge that, from the higher standpoint of philosophy, history is a defective form of experience—an 'arrest' as he calls it. It mistakes the nature of its object.[5]

The difference between the historian's own concept and the one the philosopher sees really to be implicit in his enquiry is characterized by Oakeshott as the difference between the past *for* history and the past *in* history. A similar distinction between standpoints seems to be relevant to his account of the notion of historical fact or truth. Facts, Oakeshott insists, are not the data of historical interpretations, they are their conclusions; and the criterion of truth employed in reaching them is coherence. This appears to be said from the standpoint of elucidating the idea of the past *for* history. From the higher standpoint, truth can be said simply to *be* coherence. In either case, what is meant by the coherence of historical construction appears to be more than mere logical compatibility, whether of the component facts with each other or of the facts with the evidence on which they are asserted. For, according to Oakeshott, there can be no 'isolated' facts. To be a fact is to find

[1] *Experience and its Modes*, pp. 102 ff.
[2] *Ibid.* pp. 107 ff.   [3] *Ibid.* p. 94.
[4] Problems arising out of Oakeshott's constructionism will not be discussed in this paper directly. This aspect of his theory has been examined and developed by J. W. Meiland in *Scepticism and Historical Knowledge* (New York, 1965), which distinguishes Oakeshott's reduction of past to present from those of Croce and Collingwood.
[5] *Experience and its Modes*, pp. 110–11, 146, 148.

a 'necessary' place in an 'integrated' historical world.[1] Further light on what finding such a place entails is presumably to be sought in Oakeshott's account of historical explanation. For it would be strange, in elucidating the concept of historical truth, to insist on a type of connection between evidence and fact which was utterly unlike that obtaining between the incidents of historical narratives themselves.

Very important for Oakeshott's eventual contrast between historical and other (especially scientific) forms of experience is his account of the concept of the historical individual.[2] The subject-matter of history, he says (apparently here ignoring his own claim that history is not limited to the human past), concerns events, institutions and persons: such things as the French Revolution, the Roman Empire and Frederick the Great. Such individuals are identified as relative continuities separated from their environment by relative discontinuities, and in a manner in which physical location may be relatively unimportant. At various times, for example, East and West maintain the continuity of the Roman Empire. Such individuals, Oakeshott observes, are themselves, in a sense, the products of generalisation; for they are syntheses of historical materials.[3] But they are not, he claims, subject to further generalisation—for example, of the scientific sort. To subject them to this would be to deprive them of their specifically historical character. Once again, a defectiveness of sorts is discerned in the historian's enquiry, this time in a certain artificiality and instability in historical individuation, which Oakeshott represents as falling somewhere between 'definition' and 'mere designation'. The only fully coherent individual, he says, would be 'the whole'. But such an individual would transcend the postulates of historical experience.

Equally important for the distinctiveness of historical experience, according to Oakeshott, is its category of explanation.[4] The problem which gives rise to the demand for explanation is change. The specifically historical way to account for change, Oakeshott maintains, is to give a full account of it: 'The relation between events is always other events.'[5] Thus 'to see all the degrees of change is to be in possession of a world of facts which calls for no further explanation'. Oakeshott locates the criterion of intelligibility in history in what he calls the principle of the unity and continuity of history—a 'structural presupposition' with a role in historical experience analogous to that which he conceives the principle of mechanism to play in the world of science.[6] The continuity at issue, he adds, is not that of a series related by links of necessary and sufficient conditions as scientists understand these

---

[1] *Ibid.* p. 111.
[2] *Ibid.* pp. 118–24, 144, 148.
[3] *Ibid.* pp. 154, 160.
[4] *Ibid.* pp. 125 ff.
[5] *Ibid.* p. 143.
[6] *Ibid.* p. 144.

notions; nor is it to be discovered by causal analysis. The historian's events are through and through contingent.

In 'The activity of being an historian' Oakeshott's views are presented without direct reference to the epistemological and ontological issues which make the earlier work so difficult at times. Here his chief concern is to distinguish and characterize what he regards as a specifically historical attitude to the past from three other attitudes which we may take to it, which he calls the contemplative, the practical and the scientific. Each is said to express itself in a characteristic idiom, and to be recognizable by its typical questions and statements. About the contemplative attitude, which is the one proper to an artist or poet, Oakeshott has comparatively little to say. From its standpoint, events are seen merely as 'causeless "images" of delight, which provoke neither approval nor disapproval, and to which the categories "real" and "fiction" are alike inapplicable'.[1] Typical of adopting such an attitude are the works of historical novelists like Tolstoy or historical dramatists like Shakespeare.[2] Whether or not we are to regard the object of the contemplative attitude as an artistic past properly so-called, Oakeshott does not unequivocally say. He does point out, however, that contemplative construction is parasitic upon other attitudes to the past for its materials. The contemplative attitude thus seems not to be restricted to what Oakeshott called the 'fancied' past.

The practical attitude requires us to ask precisely the questions the contemplative considers unimportant: the enquirer has an 'objective' interest. But in another sense this second attitude is not objective. Its concern is not with what happened as fact, but with the extent to which it makes the world 'habitable'. Such an attitude is betrayed by the use of terms like 'cheap' or 'useful', 'dangerous' or 'reprehensible'.[3] Whenever we adopt it, Oakeshott maintains, we 'read the past backwards'; we see it, perhaps, as an authority for some present practice, as the justification of some present state of affairs, or as a source for solving some present problem. In all such cases we are concerned to take just so much out of the past as we can *use*. We study the past in relation to the present.[4]

By contrast, when we take up a scientific attitude we endeavour to regard past events independently of their relation to us and our desires and interests: we are concerned with events rather in their relationship to each other. We shift from a practical to a scientific attitude to the present, thus conceived, for example, when we report the temperature, not as 'hot', but as '90 degrees F'; and any construction of a scientific past will display similar shifts.[5] But the scientific attitude

[1] 'The activity of being an historian', p. 143.   [2] *Ibid.* p. 149.
[3] *Ibid.* pp. 144–5.   [4] *Ibid.* p. 147.   [5] *Ibid.* p. 145.

involves more than 'objectivity' in this further sense; it seeks to relate events through the notion of necessary and sufficient conditions; and this entails our regarding the past as exemplifications of general laws. As in the case of the contemplative attitude, Oakeshott hedges a bit on whether it is strictly possible to regard *the past* that way.[1] The scientific approach, he observes, diverts attention from actual events (here 'actual' seems to mean only 'individual') toward the 'hypothetical situations' specified by the explanatory laws—these being the real subject-matter of science. In concluding from this that there is thus really no scientific past, Oakeshott may appear to be generating un-necessary paradoxes. But the source of his concern is at any rate clear: that any scientific construction of past events will be limited to what can be grasped as 'instances'.

The historical approach to the past, like the scientific, is concerned with events as independent of ourselves.[2] In its concern for objectivity in this sense, Oakeshott declares, it is a partner of the scientific attitude, and it has in fact emerged in conjunction with it in Western culture. Indeed, according to Oakeshott, the battle both had to wage against primordial practical and contemplative attitudes has led to some con-fusion between them, and even to the diverting of historical develop-ment, especially in the nineteenth century, into a *cul-de-sac*—the self-conscious attempt to 'raise history to the rank of a science' (he seems to be thinking especially of classical attempts to discover specifically historical laws). Between the two attitudes there is this fundamental similarity: like the (so-called) scientific past, the historical must be 'the past for its own sake', and hence not practical. But history, according to Oakeshott, does not render its past intelligible through appeal to general-isations or laws. There is, of course, a familiar sense in which history is properly called a science. But this entails only its demanding accuracy, excluding prejudice and arguing critically from evidence.[3]

III

The contrast Oakeshott draws between history and science thus turns chiefly on his claim that they employ quite different concepts of explanation. If we try to make historical facts intelligible as 'exempli-fications', Oakeshott declares, 'history is dismissed'.[4] It is far from a simple matter, however, to determine exactly what he means by this, or precisely what the arguments are which he thinks warrant this con-clusion. He may be interpreted, for example, as claiming only that to offer explanations of the scientific kind would be unhistorical in the

---

[1] *Ibid.* p. 149.   [2] *Ibid.* pp. 152–3.
[3] *Experience and its Modes*, p. 159. [4] *Ibid.* p. 154.

sense of going beyond a distinctively historical treatment of what is studied. History would be 'dismissed' in the sense of being replaced by something else, as Oakeshott defines 'the historical'. But it often seems as if considerably more than this is claimed, as when we are told that 'in history there *are* no "general laws" by means of which historical individuals can be reduced to instances of a principle'.[1] Here Oakeshott appears to argue that a scientific understanding of historical events is impossible because what the historian is concerned with simply does not fall under generalisations. Perhaps in a constructionist theory of history the distinction between what is inappropriate and what is impossible for the historian is not of ultimate importance. Let us nevertheless try to consider the two claims separately, beginning with the second.

Why cannot historical individuals be generalised about? Oakeshott's claim, unlike that of some other theorists who draw the same conclusion, is not based upon the well-known practical difficulties of discovering plausible general laws governing social conditions and events. Neither is it a derivation from an indeterministic theory of human action (as Collingwoodian-type views sometimes are). It is based on the alleged peculiarities of the historical individual which Oakeshott traces to its being only 'designated' and not 'defined'. Historians, like scientists, employ general classificatory terms; they write, for example, of the French 'revolution'. But in history, Oakeshott maintains, such terms are mere 'conveniences'.[2] And by this he does not just mean that in the hands of historians they are used vaguely or unconscionably—as we might be tempted to conclude from the remark that Gibbon's conception of 'barbarism and religion', although useful for his purposes, was not 'clear and concise'.[3] It is rather that, in view of the way the referents of such classificatory terms are constructed—i.e. on the criterion of relative continuity between relative discontinuities—there is no assurance that there will be enough similarity between any two of them for a generalisation to be applicable. We are referred, in this connection, to Huizinga's observation that historical terms like 'Carolingian', 'feudal', 'Christian' and 'humanist' are not 'foundations upon which large structures may be built'.[4]

But Oakeshott goes further: he declares it to be a 'postulate', not just a fact, of history that no generalisations will be applicable to its individuals. Historical understanding, he says, 'excludes identity'. 'Whenever the historian is presented with an apparent identity, not merely are his suspicions aroused, but he knows that he is passing beyond

[1] *Ibid.* p. 161 (my italics).   [2] *Ibid.* pp. 119, 148.
[3] *Ibid.* p. 120.
[4] 'The activity of being an historian', p. 162 n. 1.

his own presuppositions; for it is posited from the beginning that the
world of history is a world from which identity has been excluded.'[1]
Historians treat their individuals as unique processes of change. Not
unique in any sense which would exclude their being talked about;
but unique, apparently, at least in a sense which would rule out identical
descriptions of different historical events which have been individuated
by means of the same classification term. This is a very strong statement
of a view which is familiar enough. The interest of scientists, we are
often told, is in the similarities between events. By contrast, 'history is
regulated by the pursuit of differences'. It follows, Oakeshott adds,
that the question whether or not history repeats itself is not one to be
decided by examining the course of events itself. It is answered in the
negative by the 'postulates' of history.[1]

Now it can scarcely be denied that Oakeshott here calls attention to
a *characteristic interest* of historians. It might plausibly be held, for example, that a book on 'the anatomy of revolutions', looking only, or
even chiefly, for what they had in common, would lack a specifically
historical interest. It is characteristic of historical practice, too, that
gross classification terms should be used only to refer initially to what
is to be explained, the explanation going on to treat what is referred
to as different from other members of the indicated class. An historian,
for example, is not likely to be satisfied with an explanation of the French
Revolution simply *as* a revolution; he will want to explain its having
features which it does not share with the Russian, American and English
revolutions. Yet it is hard to see how all this can legitimately be given
the status of a 'postulate' yielding *a priori* truths about history. We
would surely not charge an historian with having 'deserted history',
for example, because he happened to have dealt with a certain event
under a description which, in fact (with a change of proper names and
spatio-temporal references), applied also to another. It is one thing to
say that no historical individual can be *assumed* to be like any other in
all those respects which made it worthwhile distinguishing it from its
environment—still less all the further respects which may subsequently
turn out to be historically interesting; it is quite another to say that
a proper historical attitude requires the affirmation that two individuals
never *could* be alike in these respects. Even the 'postulate' of physical
determinism in scientific enquiry is now seldom interpreted in such
terms. It is far more likely to be treated as an expression of the aims
(and perhaps even just the hopes) of scientists.

A further difficulty in Oakeshott's account arises out of an apparent
confusion in it between the thesis that historical events cannot be subsumed under generalisations and the thesis that historical events never

[1] *Experience and its Modes* p. 167.

repeat themselves. For a positivist opponent might well agree that *in fact* no two historical events are ever given identical descriptions by historians, so that history in that sense never repeats itself, while still maintaining that each event can be explained under its own description in what Oakeshott calls the scientific way. For no matter to what level of detailed description the historian is driven by his characteristic interest in the individuality of events, if what he in the end claims to explain is an event under any definite description whatever, then it is surely logically possible, at least, that he should explain its having each of the characteristics mentioned in that description by reference to general laws—the whole event being explained by subsumption under a vast variety of laws or generalisations. Only the thesis that historians study events as absolutely unique—i.e. as lying beyond reach of any definite description at all—would close off this possibility; and this is a move from which Oakeshott, after observing that there was 'some truth' in it, prudently drew back.[1]

He may, in any case, have conceded the essential point when he allowed that, if not universal generalisations, then at least summative or enumerative ones are possible in history: generalisations like 'All the Reformation Parliaments were packed' or 'No matriarchy has ever given rise directly to a full civilisation' (anthropology being, for him, an historical discipline).[2] For if the referents of the general terms 'parliament' and 'matriarchy' are not prevented, by having been individuated in the specifically historical way, from being incorporated into such limited generalisations, it is difficult to see any *theoretical* reason why they should not be incorporated into unlimited ones. In this connection, it is interesting to note that Oakeshott himself feels obliged to set some limit to the extent to which the historical past must be unlike the present. For although he claims that the very '*differentia* of the historical past' lies in its 'disparity from what is contemporary', he allows that 'a general similarity between the historical past and the present' must be postulated by the historian 'because he assumes the possibility of understanding what belongs to the historical past'.[3] Insisting that the historian's proper business is with the 'detailed dissimilarity' rather than 'this bare and general similarity' will not entirely remove the suspicion that Oakeshott here implicitly accepts some form of what he calls the scientific view of explanation after all. For whatever the historian's 'business' is said to be, discerning similarities seems to be a *sine qua non* of his understanding anything.

But if Oakeshott fails to give convincing reasons for holding that subsumption under law is an impossible form of explanation in history, has he anything of interest to say about its inappropriateness? Central

---

[1] *Ibid.* p. 119.   [2] *Ibid.* pp. 161, 164.   [3] *Ibid.* p. 106.

to his case here is the claim that historians seek an entirely different kind of understanding from that which is achievable through such sub-sumption—a kind arising out of their interest in a 'particular' past, which is conceived as an 'integrated world' containing no 'absolute *hiatus*'. The historian's principle of intelligibility is 'the unity and continuity of history'. More specifically, the historian understands historical change by filling in apparent gaps; his method 'is never to explain by means of generalisation, but always by means of greater and more complete detail'.[1]

The chief kind of difficulty raised by this positive account of historical explanation is the unclarity of the notion of continuity which it employs. This is crucial, since many of Oakeshott's opponents will hold that the only viable criterion of two events being continuous is precisely what he is trying to reject: namely, their being connected by a law. We speak of a *dis*continuity, it will be argued, when one event's following another cannot be seen as natural or inevitable; we establish continuity by showing, through reference to laws or generalisations, that the sequence was natural or inevitable after all. Such an explication of historical continuity would obviously be unacceptable to Oakeshott, but his alternative to it is unfortunately no more than hinted at—generally in highly metaphorical terms. Historical explanation, he says, seeks to 'transform what is given into what is satisfactory';[2] it points to events which 'mediate one circumstance to another'; it shows that what happened, although 'contingent', was not 'a tissue of mere conjunc-tions', but rather 'an intelligible convergence of choices and actions'.[3] One looks in vain to the passage in *Experience and its Modes* in which Oakeshott offers his most extended exposition of specifically historical understanding for further light on all this.[4] History, he says there, accounts *for* change by means of a full account *of* change—as if the appropriateness of this were plain to see; the historian tolerates no *lacuna*—as if what constituted one for historical purposes needed no further explication; the explanatory task is to display *all the degrees* of change—as if 'all' here had some clear sense. The difficulty is only compounded when we are assured that 'change in history carries with it its own explanation'. Is historical change in some intelligible sense *self*-explanatory? How much would have to be built into the notion of a specifically historical type of change to make it at all plausible to say so?

It might be thought that we could at any rate come to grips with Oakeshott's positive doctrine through examining what he considers to

---

[1] *Ibid.* p. 143.   [2] *Ibid.* p. 98.
[3] *Ibid.* p. 89; 'The activity of being an historian', p. 157.
[4] *Experience and its Modes*, p. 143.

be good historical practice: for example, the lengthy citation from
Maitland, in 'The activity of being an historian', which explains how
the notion of land being held of the king became the theory of English
law at the Norman Conquest.[1] Certainly here we get an 'account',
a detailed tracing of a process of change. But the story is noticeably
punctuated by a series of 'of courses' which invite an analysis which
Oakeshott makes no attempt to provide. In Normandy, Maitland
points out, lands were held of the duke, who in turn held of the king—
and he adds: 'of course it was the same in England; no other system
was conceivable'. Are there no assumptions, shared by historian and
reader, guaranteeing this inconceivability, and giving force to this 'of
course'? The justification for Oakeshott's denial that these would include the assumption of explanatory laws has to be eked out of such
vague notions as 'intelligible convergences of choices and actions'.
Perhaps the development of such a notion would have led to an
explication of historical continuity in terms of the *rational appropriateness*
of actions to their circumstances rather than their subsumability under
laws, bringing Oakeshott's theory of history into closer relation with
Collingwood's at this point. Oakeshott himself, however, leaves the
notion undeveloped.

A second difficulty in Oakeshott's account of historical understanding
—a potential one, at least—centres on the relation he conceives to hold
between historical explanation and historical individuation. Both,
according to him, involve the discerning of continuity in the course of
events; but on the face of it at least, this generates a paradox. For to
individuate is to discover *dis*continuity as well as continuity: it is to
recognise a 'hiatus' between an individual and its environment or
other individuals—the very thing historical explanation eliminates. To
explain historically seems thus destined to undo individuation's work.
As Oakeshott himself puts it, in discussing the 'defectiveness' of the
historical individual, it is characteristic of historical thought that 'its
movement tends to supersede the conception of individuality upon
which it is based'.[2] The only obvious solution to the paradox—suggested
by Oakeshott's remark that the only fully intelligible individual is the
whole—is ruled out by him as contrary to the postulates of history. For
otherwise the historian's goal might have been taken to be *total* explanation, which would at the same time have involved the elimination
of all individuals except the historical process as a whole. If there is any
other way out of the paradox, it is presumably to be sought through the
notion of kinds and degrees of continuity, and even judgments of continuity from varying standpoints and for varying purposes. In the light

[1] 'The activity of being an historian', pp. 157–8.
[2] *Experience and its Modes*, p. 123.

of what Oakeshott goes on to say about the incompatibility of historical and what he called 'practical' thinking, however, it appears unlikely that he would accept any such 'relativistic' solution.

IV

Let us turn then to Oakeshott's contrast between history and practice.[1] We construct a practical rather than historical past, he observes, whenever we view what happened in relation to present interests and activities, and especially if our account is designed to serve 'either of two masters—politics or religion'. And perhaps few would quarrel with the conclusion that to write history on such a principle would fail to express a specifically historical attitude. We distinguish ordinarily between history and a *use* we may make of historical knowledge; and we would expect the two approaches to yield accounts differing radically in selection, arrangement, mode of description, and perhaps even explanation. When we look at how Oakeshott elaborates the distinction, however, his contrast between history and practice begins to look less innocuous. And when we see what he would sweep out of historical accounts in consequence of it, some further theoretical justification becomes necessary

According to Oakeshott, there are many ways in which we can construct a practical rather than an historical past. We do this whenever the significance of what happened is taken to lie in its warranting our 'practical beliefs about the present', in its being a 'storehouse of political wisdom', in its providing the 'authority for religious beliefs', in its offering 'raw materials of literature' or 'a mode of expressing a philosophical system'—even in its being simply a 'reflection' of the present, or perhaps a 'refuge' from it.[2] It is similarly practical if we look in it for what has been 'influential in deciding the present', or if we allow ourselves to impose moral judgments upon it, treating it, he observes, as 'a field in which we exercise our moral and political opinions, like whippets in a meadow on Sunday afternoon'.[3] All these involve viewing the past 'in specific relation to the present'. Oakeshott adds that what he distinguishes here is not what has generally been referred to as 'bias' in history. For 'a wide sympathy for all the persons and interests engaged in a situation' would not, he claims, transmute a practical, present-oriented account into a specifically historical one.[4] Nor should we confuse it with the kind of present-orientation which follows from Oakeshott's 'constructionist' account of historical know-

---

[1] *Ibid.* pp. 103 ff.; 'The activity of being an historian', pp. 147 ff.
[2] *Experience and its Modes*, pp. 103–5; 'The activity of being an historian', pp. 147, 153–4.
[3] *Ibid.* p. 165.   [4] *Ibid.* p. 161.

ledge generally. For this represents history as necessarily relative to the present only in the sense of *being* present, i.e. what the evidence presently obliges us to believe. To seek freedom from present-orientation in the latter sense, Oakeshott points out, would be to seek 'freedom from experience'.[1]

Oakeshott's list nevertheless remains an astonishingly miscellaneous one; and the relevance of some of his considerations to the notion of 'treating the past as if it were present' is much less obvious than that of others. For example, while we might indeed regard interpretations aimed at finding excuses, exemplars, authorities, incentives, materials or refuges as 'views' of the past serving an ulterior practical purpose, it would surely be strange to regard an account as practically oriented in the same sense simply because it did contain some moral judgments. It would be even stranger to regard it as so oriented because its aim was to *explain* the present: that problem would surely be characterised more naturally as a theoretical than as a practical one. For Oakeshott, both evaluation and explanation in history appear necessarily to involve 'reading the past backwards'; yet the sense in which these are relative to the present are not only different from 'uses', but different from one another. Evaluative history, for example, need be present-oriented only in the sense that the historian employs standards judged by him in the present to be valid (and surely does not *have* to be treasured as a moral exercise!). Explanatory history is present-oriented also in the sense that it must take certain present states of affairs as a datum, as an explanandum.

The full force of Oakeshott's conception of the practical approach to the past may not become apparent, however, until we look at some of the examples he gives of what would have to be banished from historical narrative if historians consistently adopted a specifically historical attitude. We should not, he says, be able to say such things as that the death of William the Conqueror was accidental, that a certain ruler dissipated his resources in useless wars, that an intervention by the pope changed the course of events, that defeats in Africa made clear the necessity of reforming the British Army, that the most serious consequence of the Napoleonic wars for Britain was loss of continental markets, or that the Factory Acts culminated in the modern Welfare State.[2] All such familiar types of statements, Oakeshott maintains, are in the idiom of practice and betray a practical concern. In history proper things simply happen. Deaths are neither accidental nor necessary, wars are neither useless nor useful, consequences are neither serious nor trivial. Interventions do not change the course of events; they are

---

[1] *Experience and its Modes*, p. 94.
[2] 'The activity of being an historian', pp. 148, 154; *Experience and its Modes*, p. 140.

that course. And there are no culminations, main movements, turning points or catastrophes: only a world of interrelated events.

Such examples, and Oakeshott's comments on them, show how very broadly we are to interpret the notion of relativity to the present as a mark of the practical past. Oakeshott has already been observed to extend the application of this notion from the obvious case of the historian's making judgments of present utility to cases where he simply explains the present in terms of the past or evaluates the past in terms of presently accepted values. We now find him extending it to cover cases where relativity to *any* subsequent state of affairs, and not just the historian's own present, is regarded as unhistorical—e.g. to all tracing of consequences and all explanation of a later in terms of an earlier state of affairs. We find the notion extended also to disqualify even those judgments of utility and value made from the standpoint of the historical period under study—this in spite of the fact that an attempt to reconstitute a period's own outlook and way of life, by contrast with a mere elaboration of the way the age appears from the vantage point of our own present, has often been taken as the mark of a specifically historical approach. Historical construction, Oakeshott observes, involves a way of thinking about the past 'which would have been impossible for anyone who lived in that past'.[1] The historical past lacks 'the moral, the political or the social structure' of a past seen 'practically', whether from its own vantage point or some other one.[2] In this connection Oakeshott's theory differs most markedly from Collingwood's and all theories of historical understanding as re-thinking or re-experiencing.

Oakeshott's final claim here might be resisted either on the ground that his exclusions are inappropriate, or on the ground that they are impossible. In support of the first sort of objection it should be observed that, in elaborating the notion of the practical past and the practical attitude to the past, what Oakeshott is really supposed to be doing is elucidating the notion of 'disinterestedness' which, in discussing the postulates or categories of historical experience, he had said was implicit in a properly historical attitude; he is showing what is involved in the notion of the historical past as the past *for its own sake*.[3] Now the latter is a tricky notion. It has led Carl Becker, for example, to imply (presumably with a straight face) that historians, in order to be disinterested, would have to study an object of historical interest like Magna Carta for *its* sake, not their own.[4] And it leads Oakeshott

[1] Review of W. H. Walsh, *Introduction to Philosophy of History* (London, 1951), *Philosophical Quarterly*, July 1952, p. 277.
[2] 'The activity of being an historian', p. 154.   [3] *Experience and its Modes*, p. 106.
[4] 'What are historical facts'?, in Hans Meyerhoff, *The Philosophy of History in Our Time* (New York, 1959), p. 121.

himself to attribute to the historian an 'adoration' of the past: he is said to 'love it as a mistress, of whom he never tires and whom he never expects to talk sense'.[1] But surely all that need be meant, and all historians ordinarily mean, by insisting that in history the past must be studied for its own sake is the impropriety of a practical interest in the sense of seeking to *use* one's results for an ulterior purpose, i.e. a practical interest in the ordinary rather than the extended Oakeshottian sense. Oakeshott's general definition of the practical attitude requires the historian to approach the past without regard to its 'habitability'.[2] This turns out to mean habitability, not just from the standpoint of the historian, or those for whom he writes, but also from that of contemporaries, and even (one suspects, in the end) of anyone at all. Such 'disinterestedness' would seem certain to extrude all the human interest from historical accounts, and it may surely be questioned whether this is really a proper way to seek historical understanding.

But is Oakeshott's proposal, in any case, really possible of implementation? One may wonder whether he was not himself occasionally caught by his own criterion. Thus, on on one occasion, after hailing Roseberry's *Napoleon, The Last Phase* as an 'historical masterpiece', which 'releases us from the burden of history as the intellectual and moral preface to the contemporary world', he was incautious enough to go on to imply that a history book should be read 'not because it is important but because it is fascinating'.[3] One might wonder, too, whether Oakeshott's claim, if taken literally, would not lead to the following paradox: that since, according to him, serving a present theoretical interest is itself an expression of a practical attitude, a person who sought a specifically historical understanding of the past would necessarily have his findings disqualified as practical rather than historical.

Paradoxes apart, the question is how the historian can be conceived as doing what Oakeshott says is central to his enquiry—individuating and explaining—under the prohibitions imposed upon him. For the mistress *is* expected to talk sense in her own idiosyncratic way. The historian, we are told, proceeds by detecting and filling in 'gaps'. But Oakeshott has made it clear that historical gaps are not merely spatio-temporal. He has denied, too, that they are breakdowns of sequential inevitability, as determined by the application of laws or generalisations. What then will count as historical gaps? Surely sequences which, on the face of it, are puzzling because they involve noticeable changes of quality or mode of life—changes in the 'normal course of events', humanly speaking. It is hard to see how such gaps could be

---

[1] 'The activity of being an historian', p. 166.   [2] *Ibid.* p. 153.
[3] Review of K. B. Smellie, *Why we read History'*, *Cambridge Journal*, September 1948, p. 766.

characterised except in what Oakeshott would regard as practical terms: they involve questions of 'habitability'. On what other sorts of criteria, once spatio-temporal and causal ones have been excluded, could the Renaissance be judged discontinuous with the Middle Ages? Or the Tennis Court Oath be judged continuous with the Terror? As deployed by historians, in other words, the allegedly structural notions of continuity and coherence seem themselves to be quasi-'practical'. Oakeshott denies that the historical past has 'the moral, political and social structure of the present'. If by this he means only that it will have a different structure of the same sort, then we shall still have to make 'practical' judgments to determine what it is. If he means that it has *no* such structure, it is hard to see how the notion of an historical gap itself can have any meaning.

It might be noted that, just as Oakeshott, in the end, when distinguishing history from science, wavers somewhat about the past being utterly dissimilar from the present, so he wavers, in distinguishing history from practice, over the impropriety of making moral judgments about it. Past conduct, he concedes at one point, may have to be described in 'generally speaking, moral terms'.[1] It should be noted, too, that he produces no examples of histories which succeed in eliminating the 'practical' idiom. Geoffrey Barraclough's essay on 'The Mediaeval Empire', which Oakeshott praises as a model of historical reinterpretation,[2] is rich in 'curious outcomes', 'wearisome negotiations', 'needed but costly wars' and 'unexpected interventions'. Duncan Forbes's *The Liberal Anglican Idea of History*, which, according to Oakeshott, goes a long way toward replacing the nineteenth century's self-understanding with a specifically historical understanding of it, really only places alongside the already articulated view of the majority an equally 'practical' account from the standpoint of a minority.[3]

Oakeshott's explanation of this would be that the distinctive historical attitude is, as yet, only a discernible direction of enquiry; there are only approaches to it in actual historical writing.[4] Most so-called history, he says, is written in the practical idiom, the century-long struggle to escape from the scientific modes of thought having been more successful than the much longer struggle against the 'primordial' practical viewpoint. Oakeshott's notion that historical disinterestedness requires translation of records from the language of self-understanding into something less parochial does indeed call attention to the realities of historical work. It is difficult to see, however, that he has shown how the movement toward a properly historical attitude can sensibly involve more

[1] *Ibid.* pp. 162–3.
[2] Review of *History in a Changing World*, *The Spectator*, 17 February 1956, pp. 220–1.
[3] Review in the *Cambridge Journal*, January 1953, p. 248.　　　[4] *Ibid.* pp. 157, 151.

than an attempt to understand the past from *many* points of view, none of them being, from some special standpoint—even a special one to be called the historical—the 'right' one; and all of them involving judgments of the sort which Oakeshott's very broad sense of 'practical' seems to rule out. The idea of successive approximation to a specifically historical interpretation of the past, as Oakeshott describes it, looks very much like the pursuit of an unrealisable, because unintelligible, ideal.

v

Oakeshott's claim that historical understanding is neither scientific nor practical obtains its most extended theoretical application in his discussion of the notions of cause and chance as explanatory historical categories.[1] Taking the views of the English historian J. B. Bury as his point of departure, he argues that, although they are clearly embedded in accepted historical writings, the use of such concepts is actually inconsistent with the presuppositions of historical experience—they are not 'relevant to the character of the historical world'.[2] He therefore urges their abandonment. While few new issues arise out of this discussion, it has some independent interest. And it shows again how far Oakeshott was willing to press the leading ideas we have been examining.

The case against the concept of causation begins with a distinction between three ways this concept might be employed by an historian. The first, Oakeshott says, yields 'general' causes, by which he seems to mean attempts at explanation of the course of history of a speculative or religious kind ('the Stars', 'Fate', 'Fortune', 'God').[3] The main thrust of his argument here, however, is not entirely clear. The comment 'what can be used indifferently to explain everything, will in the end explain nothing', surely does not dispose of all the proposed causal conclusions of this kind; for speculative and religious theories of history have generally been offered in explanation only of *certain* events—the ones of speculative or religious importance. It is easier to agree with Oakeshott's claim 'an event without a cause (other than God) is not in any sense an historical event'. And still easier if this merely means— as it seems to—that we do not achieve anything deserving to be called specifically historical understanding of an event through attributing it to such an 'external' origin.

Oakeshott's second class of cases, which he regards as expressing a scientific attitude, he calls 'sole' causes. These are defined as 'the minimum conditions required to account for any example of an observed result', and he instances alleged explanations in terms of such

---

[1] *Experience and its Modes*, pp. 126 ff. [2] *Ibid.* pp. 126, 41. [3] *Ibid.* pp. 126–7, 133.

'abstractions' as climate, geography, national characteristics or economics.[1] 'To say of an event that it is due solely to "economic causes"', he observes, 'is not bad history; it is not history at all.' Once again, however, Oakeshott's claim cannot be assessed without further analysis. For his objection to 'sole' causes is not just that they claim to be minimum sufficient antecedent conditions: it seems to be his assumption that what will be so designated will always be factors of some restricted range. As a reaction against single-factor theories of historical causation, Oakeshott's objections will generally be accepted as sound; but the temptation to regard conditions of this sort as sufficient is surely not now very great. Some of Oakeshott's other specific criticisms appear to have even less force. For example, to argue that a sufficient condition approach either limits historical understanding, unacceptably, to immediate antecedant conditions or draws the historian into 'an infinite regress of abstractions in search of an absolute beginning' is just to repeat an old fallacy about explanation. It is to ignore the truism that, having been given an explanation, we can always ask for more. This principle is as applicable to an Oakeshottian account of historical explanation as it is to the ones he attacks.

The most fundamental objection made against causes as sufficient conditions, however, is that they require explanation in terms of 'abstraction'—to which Oakeshott appears to add (without specifically saying so) that the events explained by abstractions are themselves necessarily regarded as abstract, i.e. as mere 'instances'.[2] The way Oakeshott puts this point sometimes makes it difficult to take it seriously. For he seems to imply, misleadingly, that a sufficient condition explanation could never be considered the explanation of a *particular* event. This is his reason, in 'The activity of being an historian', for doubting whether there can, strictly speaking, be a 'scientific past'; for the scientists' world, he says, is a 'world not of actual events, but of hypothetical situations'.[3] For Oakeshott, it seems, to regard an event as an 'instance', even though it actually occurred, is to treat it as a 'hypothetical situation'. The issue is not made clearer by his giving, as an example of an attempt at scientific explanation in history, not an allegedly law-subsuming account of a particular occurrence, but rather the general claim, derived from Valery, that 'all the revolutions of the 19th century had as their necessary and sufficient conditions the centralised institutions of power...'.[4] For this may quite wrongly give the impression that it would be impossible to judge, through appeal to general laws, that a specific historical event had a set of sufficient conditions peculiar to it. It is as if any employment of laws in an explanation changes the

[1] *Ibid.* pp. 127–8.   [2] *Ibid.* pp. 128–9.
[3] 'The activity of being an historian', p. 149.   [4] *Ibid.* p. 149.

subject of the explanation from the actual event to which they are ostensibly applied to the class of events of which it is supposed to be a member.

Oakeshott returns to the problem, on a slightly different tack, in a general discussion of causation. All causal judgment, he says, requires us 'to separate the cause and its effect and endow each with a certain degree of individuality', thus involving us in 'abstraction' in a rather different sense.[1] According to Oakeshott, 'no single event in history is isolable in this manner, and if it were, there would be no more reason to isolate *this* event rather than *that*'. Trying to escape this difficulty by taking 'the *complete* antecedent course of events' as cause, he adds, destroys the causal concept altogether. Oakeshott himself anticipated the most likely objection to this, namely, that he has already allowed the necessity of 'breaking up' the continuity of history by insisting that historical thinking cannot proceed without the designation of individuals.[2] But he can scarcely be said to have answered it. To distinguish cause and effect is surely no more to introduce 'false and misleading interruptions' into the continuity of history than to recognise historical individuals is. And to speak of the former as 'forcing one of the pieces outside the whole itself' is surely too metaphorical to count as a serious objection.

The third type of cause which Oakeshott distinguishes he calls 'decisive' causes; and here it is clear that what he is criticising is a kind of judgment very commonly made in much that passes for historiography.[3] His examples include the causal attribution of the spread of Christianity to the escape of St Paul from Damascus, at least partly on the ground that if he had been captured and killed, the prospects of the new religion would have been dim. Oakeshott's reaction here is similar, although not identical, to Collingwood's when the latter objected to a 'Cleopatra's Nose' conception of historical causation 'which in despair of genuine explanation acquiesces in the most trivial causes for the vastest effects'. Although he does not use this language, Oakeshott's 'decisive' causes are obviously suspect partly because they are merely necessary conditions of their effects. But his chief complaint is that in history, provided we take the specifically historical standpoint, 'it is impossible to distinguish between the importance of necessities'.[4] In history, every condition is 'positive'; nothing is 'non-contributory'.

Oakeshott denounces this third type of cause as 'a monstrous incursion of science into the world of history'. In his own terms, since it involves the deployment of necessary, if not sufficient, conditions, this is true. But it is even more an incursion of what he called the practical,

---

[1] *Ibid.* p. 152. [2] *Experience and its Modes*, p. 144.
[3] *Ibid.* pp. 128–30. [4] *Ibid.* p. 129.

as his subsequent remarks show he was well aware. For we shall be unable to distinguish between the importance of necessities only as long as we are prevented from applying some standard of importance to what we call the necessary conditions of what we are explaining. Oakeshott's claim here is thus only made plausible by his sharp exclusion of the practical from the historian's concern. As many recent writers have pointed out, the selection of important conditions out of sets of sufficient ones is a common feature of most causal thinking. It might even be claimed that the contrast of cause with mere background condition on some criterion of importance is as basic an aspect of causal judgment as the assertion of a connection between cause and effect. Oakeshott is certainly consistent in ruling such causal judgments out of history. His more empirically minded opponents will doubtless be more inclined to take the historian's causal enquiries as a datum for theorising here, and then ask what this entails for a specifically historical attitude to the past.[1]

The case which Oakeshott makes against the notion of chance as a category of explanation in history is elaborated in response to a discussion by Bury of some apparent examples of the important role played by accidental events in history.[2] The most interesting of these concerns the gradual decline of the Roman Empire in the West as the barbarians succeeded in penetrating and founding states within it. What happened, Bury contends, cannot be accounted for by any 'general cause' which made the decline 'inevitable'. When historically explained it is seen to involve a series of sheer 'contingencies' or 'coincidences', like the surprising appearance of the Asiatic Huns, driving the Goths before them; the rashness of the Emperor Valens, which allowed the fleeing Goths to defeat a Roman army which barred their path; the premature death of Valens' able successor, Theodosius, before he could deal effectively with the problem posed by the subsequent settlement of the Visigoths within the imperial frontiers; the unfortunate mediocrity of both the sons who then divided the empire between them; and the mysterious character of Stilicho, who used his influence with one of them to have barbarians admitted wholesale, until total disaster ensued. The story seems a paradigm case of a course of events which, with any luck, might well have gone otherwise.

Oakeshott interprets Bury as arguing, on the basis of such examples, that some historical events, at least, cannot be fully accounted for in terms of cause and effect; we need also the 'co-operative' concept of

---

[1] Oakeshott also considers the causal credentials of events which have 'a high degree of individual completeness', like the fall of the Roman Empire or the Reformation (*Experience and its Modes*, p. 129), and of events expressing individual human wills (*Experience and its Modes*, p. 130).

[2] 'The activity of being an historian', pp. 133 ff.

MICHAEL OAKESHOTT'S THEORY OF HISTORY

accident or coincidental occurrence. The resulting conception of history, he goes on to claim, is of a collection of causal sequences, every event having a place in one or other of them, but 'accidents' from time to time arising out of a 'collision' of otherwise independent sequences, resulting in at least one of them being diverted from its 'natural development'. Oakeshott has little difficulty disposing of such a view, from the standpoint of his own analysis of a properly historical attitude. For in retaining the notion of causation, Bury's account is open to all the objections already raised against the employment of a practical-scientific category. And in adding that of accident it obliges the historian to make further judgments of events from the standpoint of practice, i.e. as 'abnormal', 'surprising' or 'untimely'. The notion of a 'normal course of development' is itself foreign to historical thought, Oakeshott claims. When an alleged legal historian, like Dicey, makes reference to such, he speaks as a lawyer, not as an historian.[1]

Worse still, Oakeshott claims, Bury's theory not only contradicts the postulates of historical thought, but is itself self-contradictory. For in so far as we take the notion of cause seriously, then events which are said to lie at the intersection of causal chains are as much caused, and therefore not accidental, as any others. Indeed, if anything, they are more so, since they have two causal antecedents rather than one. But in so far as we take the notion of accident seriously, we must deny that an accidental event is caused. Further, since any allegedly rigid causal sequence can, upon analysis, be shown itself to be 'an unrecognised conflux of coincidencies', we must go on to deny that any events are caused.[2] Far from being 'co-operative' categories, Oakeshott maintains, the notions of cause and accident exclude each other. The supposed distinction between historical events which are caused, and those which are accidental, turns out to be a 'meaningless' one.

But this latter objection, at least, seems to rest upon a very strained interpretation of Bury. The point his example is making is surely that the fall of the Empire, although it is to be interpreted in terms of causes, must employ 'causes which had nothing to do with the condition of the Empire'. In denying the explanatory efficacy of 'general causes' it is these (and not general causes in the sense Oakeshott himself previously used that term) which Bury has in mind.[3] And the denial that the fall of Rome was 'inevitable' turns similarly upon a distinction between two kinds of causes which events may have, not between caused and uncaused events. Bury contrasts events which are 'the product of accident' with those which have 'general causes'; he does not, as Oakeshott apparently believes, contrast them with events which have 'specific' causes. A similar consideration may be applied to the interpretation of

---

[1] *Experience and its Modes*, p. 139.   [2] *Ibid.* p. 138.   [3] *Ibid.* p. 134.

the term 'inevitable'. What is inevitable, for Bury, is what has its cause in the whole structure of the social whole under examination; what is accidental has only 'specific' causes. It might be noted that this corresponds at least roughly to the way the term 'inevitable' and 'accidental' are normally used in historiography. Oakeshott, of course, would not recognise any force in such an empirical consideration. And he would rightly suspect that the distinction between inevitable and accidental just suggested betrays what he himself would call the practical standpoint.

If it were not *a priori* excluded by Oakeshott's view of the postulates of history, the interest of the philosopher would surely at this point be to try to see exactly how the notion of accidental or chance event (as in the case of 'decisive' cause) is standpoint-relative in history. It might be observed, for example, that regarding an event as a matter of accident or chance, though caused, seems to retain at least an analogy with the straightforward case of an event's having no cause at all. In the case of the emperor's untimely death, for example, one of the 'colliding' causal chains—the biological one—lies beyond the scope of the historian's kind of enquiry: it might be said to have no specifically *historical* cause.[1] What happened may consequently be represented as something unforeseen, perhaps even as an 'intrusion' into the course of events at this point. A further extension of the notion of historical 'chance' which is commonly made, and which is also illustrated by Bury's example, is to events whose causes, although not beyond the range of historical enquiry, are beyond the range of the immediate interests of the particular history being constructed. The appearance of the Huns, for example, was a matter of chance because its causes simply lie outside the story the historian of the Roman empire is telling. The judgment that an historical event happened by chance thus seems to be a function of what the historian (and perhaps his readers) are concerned about: their interests and viewpoints appear to have a structural role to play. It follows that from one standpoint an event may properly be judged to be a chance occurrence, while from another it could not be: the activities of the Huns, for example, were scarcely a matter of chance from their own standpoint. The issues raised by such analysis are of importance for any general account of historical thinking which takes the historian's own performances as a datum. There is no room for them, however, within the system of postulates which, for Oakeshott, define historical experience.

[1] I have discussed Bury's example in a similar way in 'Determinism in history', in *The Encyclopedia of Philosophy* (New York, 1967), vol. 2, p. 376.

VI

Oakeshott was praised by Collingwood for having 'completely vindicated the autonomy of historical thought': for having shown that the historian is 'master in his own house' and 'owes nothing' to anybody else.[1] Much of what he said does make it look as if something like that was indeed his goal. The foregoing discussion of the contrasts drawn between history and science and history and practice have given reasons for thinking that Oakeshott failed to achieve this goal. They make it doubtful, too, whether such a goal, strictly conceived, was either a desirable or a feasible one.

Oakeshott himself occasionally betrays uncertainty about his own theory of historical understanding. He confesses in the later paper, for example, that such understanding achieves, at best, 'a peculiarly tentative and intermediate kind of intelligibility',[2] which, he says, often provokes us to seek something else, perhaps 'a more comprehensively "scientific" understanding of the world'. He admits elsewhere that historical analysis, as he conceives it, actually leaves the past 'incompletely intelligible'.[3] More surprisingly, he even suspects, at one point, that history itself 'exhibits an elementary scientific character', which may 'point toward' a fuller development to come. Oakeshott's more characteristic doctrine is that the further development of an emerging, and not yet fully formed, historical approach to the past will separate it even more clearly from those of science and practice. But he has doubts, which often seem to arise out of the very sorts of difficulties which have been surveyed here.

One could wish that Oakeshott's emphasis had been less on the establishment of strict historical autonomy, and more on a positive account of the way historical construction actually proceeds: an approach which might well have revealed distinctiveness without the kind of separateness which turns out to be so difficult to maintain. For that distinctiveness might have been found to lie in the way elements from other attitudes are combined in the attempt to make an actual course of events intelligible from standpoints of human interest. After admitting a practical element in historical accounts in the form of some human concern of structural significance, the task would still have been to distinguish between legitimate and illegitimate types of such concern—the sort of thing which presumably underlies the contrast we draw between history and propaganda or escape literature. And after admitting a scientific element, at least in the form of a need to find some likeness between past and present, the task would still have been

---

[1] *The Idea of History*, p. 155.
[2] 'The activity of being an historian', p. 159. [3] *Ibid.* p. 138.

to distinguish between relevant and irrelevant likenesses—those, for example, which allow us to represent a past form of life as a recognisably human activity and those which result in anachronism or history written to a thesis. Yet in spite of such criticisms, it must be conceded that a reading of Oakeshott is far more likely to stimulate profitable and relevant reflection about the nature of history than a perusal of most of the more analytical accounts of it which have been produced by English and American philosophers in recent years. It is thus greatly to be hoped, regardless of the view he may adopt toward the sort of criticism presented in this paper, that Oakeshott will find opportunity to undertake the critical elaboration of his theory himself.

MICHAEL OAKESHOTT'S
PHILOSOPHY OF EDUCATION

R. S. PETERS

There will always remain something of a mystery about how a
tradition of political behaviour is learned... *M. Oakeshott*

INTRODUCTION

On reading much modern analytical philosophy one is often tempted
to reflect that there is too much technique and too little judgment, to
use one of Oakeshott's cardinal distinctions. Technical competence is
shown in making distinctions, but what is often lacking is a 'nose' for
the distinctions on which anything of philosophical importance depends.
Oakeshott's 'style' of philosophy exemplifies the obverse combination
of virtue and vice. He almost always has something to say which is
interesting and important; but his impressionistic and rather literary
approach to philosophical analysis often leaves what he has to say in
a somewhat shadowy state. Few modern philosophers, of course, write
with Oakeshott's literary skill; their articles read like work-notes rather
than pieces prepared for others to read. But Oakeshott's literary vir-
tuosity sometimes involves a systematic elusiveness when he touches
upon situations covered by his key concepts.

This elusiveness applies particularly to his concept of 'tradition', on
which I have had occasion to comment elsewhere.[1] It applies also to
certain key concepts in his philosophy of education such as 'judgment'
and 'imparting', with which I shall be concerned in this chapter.
Nevertheless Oakeshott almost always raises fundamental philosophical
issues in an exciting way, and stimulates others to further thought about
them. This is particularly true of his philosophy of education with most
of which I have great sympathy; indeed my own views have been much
influenced by his writings, though he would be the last person to
demand much in the way of acknowledgment.

OAKESHOTT'S GENERAL CONCEPTION OF EDUCATION

In talking about education Oakeshott always starts, as is fitting for
a philosopher of the idealist school, for whom history is of cardinal
importance, with the civilized heritage of a people, with Hegel's

[1] See S. I. Benn and R. S. Peters, *Social Principles and the Democratic State* (London: Allen
and Unwin, 1958), pp. 312–18.

'second nature' composed of 'a stock of emotions, beliefs, images, ideas, manners of thinking, languages, skills, practices, and manners of activity'[1] out of which the 'things' which confront us in our environment are generated. Education consists in the initiation of a new generation into this civilised heritage. But Oakeshott never views this initiation as a process of moulding people or of transmitting this heritage in an undiscriminating or routinised way. He usually draws attention to the activity of the learner by using homely phrases which avoid the jargon of 'self-realisation' and 'the development of individual potentialities'. A typical way of putting it is as follows:

Education I will take to be the process of learning, in circumstances of direction and restraint, how to recognize and make something of ourselves. Unavoidably, it is a two-fold process in which we enjoy an initiation into what for want of a better word I will call a 'civilisation', and in doing so discover our own talents and aptitudes in relation to that civilisation and begin to cultivate and to use them. Learning to make something of ourselves in no context in particular is an impossibility; and the context appears not only in what is learned but also in the conditions of direction and restraint that belong to any education.[2]

This civilised heritage, within which the individual has to learn to make something of himself, Oakeshott sometimes discusses in terms of a conversation. 'If, then, we recognise education as an initiation into a civilisation, we may regard it as beginning to learn our way about a material, emotional, moral, and intellectual inheritance, and as learning to recognise the varieties of human utterance and to participate in the conversation they compose.'[2] He uses this metaphor in order to stress three points: first of all the fact that there are different 'voices'— e.g. that of science, poetry, history, morals—and secondly the necessity for communication between those who, without opportunities for cross-disciplinary conversation, are in danger of confining their discussions to one mode of thought. He thinks that the main function of a university, as distinct from a graduate school or a technical college, is to provide the occasions and the facilities for a sustained conversation of this sort. This is his way of stressing the importance of what educationalists refer to in their jargon as 'developing the whole man'. He thinks, thirdly, that the metaphor of a conversation is appropriate because the relation between the voices are not those of assertion and denial 'but the conversational relationships of acknowledgement and accommodation'. By this, presumably, he means things such as that in a discussion of, for instance, a moral problem, a scientific generalisation can never of itself constitute a refutation of a moral assertion but can be relevant to it in

[1] M. Oakeshott, 'The study of politics in a university' in *Rationalism in Politics and other Essays* (London, 1962), p. 304.   [2] *Ibid.* p. 304.

certain ways. Arguments, or discussions, on the other hand are structured in terms of one mode of thought.

Each of these 'voices' or modes of experience has what Oakeshott calls (perhaps somewhat misleadingly) a distinctive 'language' and 'literature' of its own. The language is for example 'the manner of thinking of a scientist'; the 'literature' is for example 'a text book of geology or what may be called the current state of our geological knowledge'.[1] This distinction enables him to demarcate, in a rough and ready way, school, vocational, and university education.

TYPES OF EDUCATION

School education

School education is concerned, in Oakeshott's view, mainly with initiation into the different literatures. After acquiring basic skills the child begins to enjoy and even to use the intellectual capital of a civilisation. Much, however, is acquired that the child does not really know how to use. It is a capital which generates something valuable on its own account. 'Learning here is borrowing raw material the possible uses of which remain concealed.'[2] Oakeshott assigns a very specific function to school education which would shock most educationalists. He regards it as

learning to speak before one has anything significant to say; and what is taught must have the qualities of being able to be learned without necessarily being understood, and of not being positively hurtful or nonsensical when learned in this way. Or, it may be said, what is taught must be capable of being learned without any previous recognition of ignorance: we do not begin to learn the multiplication tables because it suddenly dawns upon us that we do not know the sum of nine eights, nor the dates of the kings of England because we do not know when Edward I came to the throne: we learn these things at school because we are told to learn them. And further, school-education is without specific orientation; it is not yet concerned with individual talents and aptitudes, and if these show themselves (as they may) the design in school education is not to allow them to take charge. At school we are, quite properly, not permitted to follow our own inclinations.[3]

So much for 'discovery' methods and following the interests of each child!

Actually Oakeshott puts his position more strongly and starkly than is really either defensible or necessary; for given that school education is all that over two-thirds of the population get at the moment, Oakeshott's view of education as consisting in 'making something of oneself' could only therefore apply to an élite if no account is to be taken, at the school level, of individual aptitude and talent. Also from the point of

---

[1] *Ibid.* p. 308.   [2] *Ibid.* p. 305.   [3] *Ibid.* p. 306.

view of successful initiation some account must be taken of the inclinations of individuals and of their aptitudes; for motivation is the key to effective initiation. And though it is sheer dogma to assert that learning is only possible if what is to be learnt is closely related to the contingent concerns of the individual, it is equally dogmatic to assert that at school the individual is not allowed to follow his own inclinations, or to deny that a child may learn when Edward I came to the throne because he becomes aware of a gap in his knowledge. Perhaps all that Oakeshott means is that at the school level the content of a curriculum cannot be determined by individual interest or inclination and that at least a 'core' of our common heritage must be transmitted to all. That is reasonable enough. But within this common heritage there is plenty of room for individual aptitudes and it can only be handed on effectively if some account is taken of individual attitudes. Again though I think that Oakeshott is right, as against many modern educationalists, in insisting that at school much has to be learnt before it can be properly understood or the point of it grasped (e.g. moral rules, spelling, reading, poetry) nevertheless it does not follow that there is no place for the type of learning advocated by followers of Dewey or by adherents of 'discovery methods'. There was, after all, some point in Whitehead's polemic against 'inert ideas'.

Vocational education

There are two ways, according to Oakeshott, in which education can branch out after school, which he calls vocational and university education. In vocational education a literature is acquired which is relevant to the performance of some skill or to fitting a man for a specific place in a manner of living. A specific body of knowledge has to be acquired and the individual has to be able to move about within it with ease and confidence and to use it. The history of such a body of knowledge, and the errors and struggles of the past, however instructive, are of no account; what must be handed on is only the current achievement of a civilisation in respect of a skill or practice needed in the contemporary world. No provision need be made for 'teaching people how to be ignorant'.

This account of what is distinctive of technical education is acceptable in a general sort of way, though some of the details are debatable. For instance it could be argued that Oakeshott has given a delineation of technical training rather than of technical education. Education surely implies some understanding of principles, not just the amassing of information relevant to the practice of a skill or to fitting a man for a place in society. Education also implies some breadth of understanding. On his criterion we would have to say that the Spartans were professionally educated. And surely that is the last thing we would say about them; we would surely say that they were highly trained. We could, however, describe an engineer as educated if he appreciated what was intrinsic to engineering, if he had an understanding of principles and not just a mastery of information relating to engineering, and if he was also capable of appreciating aspects of life other than those intimately connected with engineering.

University education

A university education, according to Oakeshott, has a quite different sort of emphasis; for it is an education in 'languages' rather than in 'literatures'. 'It is concerned not merely to keep an intellectual inheritance intact, but to be continuously recovering what has been lost, restoring what has been neglected, collecting together what has been dissipated, repairing what has been corrupted, reconsidering, reshaping, reorganising, making more intelligible, reissuing and reinvesting.'[1] The direction of study is determined by academic considerations alone, not by extrinsic pressures and demands. The various modes of thought are not taught as literatures to be assimilated but as languages in which different types of exploration can be conducted. What is characteristic of a university education, however, as distinct from that of a graduate school, or a technical college, is that students are given the run of the place where these languages are being used. They do not have to assimilate a body of knowledge to apply for a practical purpose, nor do they have to engage, at the undergraduate level, in research. University teachers, therefore, are not simply frontiersmen on the boundaries of knowledge; they also have to teach from those texts which experience has shown to be most effective in conveying the 'language' of a mode of thought.

Nevertheless, Oakeshott argues, though the main function of a university is to initiate students into the 'language' of a mode of thought, this cannot be done effectively without a study of the appropriate 'literature'. Science as a way of thinking can only be acquired by studying some science; it is no substitute to study some so-called 'scientific method'. Learning to think historically is to be achieved only by observing and following an historian at work on a particular aspect of the past. A 'literature' is studied, therefore, not, as in vocational education, to use for any practical purpose but as the paradigm of a 'language'.

There is much to be said in favour of Oakeshott's account of university education, especially as a corrective to the views of those who demand that universities should become centres of the 'knowledge industry' and should be concerned mainly with providing the theory to solve the practical problems of the community. But it might be

[1] *Ibid.* p. 310.

criticised in that he makes a university seem much too much like a Liberal Arts College. In countries where Liberal Arts Colleges have not been separated from Graduate Schools and Institutes of Technology, a university is surely an institution where 'conversations' and teaching are essentially conducted within the context of research. He places too little emphasis on the distinctive character given to such activities by the fact that those who provide most of the talking points are themselves exploring the frontiers of knowledge as well as teaching. On his account a good Adult Educational Settlement, where no one is actively engaged in research, and where no one is a real authority on a subject, would be indistinguishable in its essence from a university. The main difference would be that students do a three-year course—e.g. in philosophy or history—for love and without getting a degree for it. Indeed the absence of a degree would make his notion of contributing to a conversation more applicable; for the fact is that in universities there are sharp-eared men around who listen to the sallies of students and grade and assess them on criteria within one form of thought. This would be very bad form in a real conversation.

PROCESSES OF EDUCATION

Technical and practical knowledge

When Oakeshott addresses himself to the question of how the capital of a civilisation is handed on he makes the same type of distinction as that between a 'language' and a 'literature' but deploys it for a different purpose. He distinguishes *technical* knowledge which can be formulated in rules, which are, or may be, deliberately learned, remembered and put into practice, and *practical* knowledge which exists only in use and which cannot be formulated in rules. This does not mean that it is some esoteric sort of knowledge; it only means that the method by which it may be shared and becomes common knowledge is not the method of formulated doctrine. It is what we might call traditional knowledge, and is involved in every kind of activity. Oakeshott's favourite examples, which can be found both in his early article on 'Rationalism in Politics'[1] in the *Cambridge Review* and in his later 'Political Education',[2] are cookery, science and politics. There is a body of knowledge in each and recipes for proceeding with the activity; but no one supposes that the knowledge necessary for being a good cook, scientist, or politician can be written down in any book. Technique may tell a man *what* to do, but it is only practice that will tell him *how* to do it. Techniques, rules, information can be written down; instruction can be given in them; it

---

[1] See 'Rationalism in Politics' reprinted in *Rationalism in Politics and other Essays*, pp. 8–11.
[2] Also reprinted in *Rationalism in Politics and other Essays*, pp. 119–23.

can even be learned by correspondence. Practical knowledge, on the other hand, can only be shown. It cannot be taught or learnt; it has to be acquired or imparted. 'It exists only in practice, and the only way to acquire it is by apprenticeship to a master—not because the master can teach it (he cannot), but because it can be acquired only by continuous contact with one who is perpetually practising it.'[1]

Instructing and imparting

In a recent lecture delivered at the University of London Institute of Education on 'Learning and Teaching'[2] Oakeshott attempts to make more explicit the distinction he has in mind between 'instructing' and 'imparting'. He argues that we carry around with us what we may be said to know in the form of countless abilities, which is an equipment which we possess in terms of what it enables us to do or understand. These abilities are of different kinds and cannot be assimilated to each other—e.g. the ability to understand and to explain cannot be assimilated to the ability to do or to make. Each of these abilities are conjunctions of 'information' and 'judgment'. 'Information' is impersonal and consists of facts that can be written down; it is the answer to the questions 'who? what? where? which? how long? how much?', etc. It may be useful or useless depending on whether the facts in question are or are not related to a particular skill or ability. Its importance depends on the extent to which it provides rules or rule-like propositions relating to abilities.

There are two ways in which such rules may be related to knowledge. Either they must be known as a condition of being able to perform (e.g. the Morse code) or they are rules for assessing performances in terms of correctness or incorrectness (e.g. grammatical rules). The latter types of rules are observed in the performance and are capable of being known; they provide the criteria for detecting an incorrect performance, but a knowledge of them is not a condition of a laudable performance. There is also a third type of rules, which may be called principles, which are propositions advanced to explain what is going on in any performance, which supply its 'underlying rationale'. These are never components of the knowledge which constitutes the performance. They belong to the performance of explaining a performance— e.g. in the case of riding a bicycle, the principles of mechanics, in the case of moral conduct Aristotle's doctrine of the mean, which are unrelated either to learning the form of behaviour in question or to a good performance.[3]

---

[1] *Rationalism in Politics and other Essays*, p. 11.
[2] Published in R. S. Peters (ed.), *The Concept of Education* (London: Routledge and Kegan Paul, 1966).   [3] *Ibid.* p. 166.

KPA

There is, then, in all knowledge an ingredient of information which may vary from an indeterminate awareness of facts to rules or rule-like propositions of the first or second sort which inform the skills and abilities in which we carry around what we may be said to know. But this ingredient of information never constitutes the whole of what we know. It must also be partnered by 'judgment'. 'Knowing *how*' must be added to 'knowing *what*'. This is not merely unspecified in propositions; it is unspecifiable in propositions. It does not and cannot appear in the form of rules. This is an ingredient of all genuine knowledge and not a separate kind of knowing specified by an ignorance of rules; for information has to be used, rules have to be applied, and it does not itself enable us to interpret it, to decide upon its relevance, to recognise what action permitted by the rule should, in the circumstances, be performed. 'For rules are always disjunctive. They specify only an act or a conclusion of a certain general kind and they never relieve us of the necessity of advice. And they never yield anything more than partial explanations: to understand anything as an example of the operation of a rule is to understand it very imperfectly.'[1]

Judgment, then, is not revealed just in skills like riding a horse or diagnosing a disease; it is involved also in the practical relationships between human beings. Maxims and interpersonal rules require interpretation; where there is a conflict between precepts it cannot be resolved by the application of other rules. Each individual has a 'style' of his own which relates to the way in which his judgment is exercised. 'Not to detect a man's style is to have missed three-quarters of the meaning of his actions and utterances, and not to have acquired a style is to have shut oneself off from the ability to convey any but the crudest meanings.'[2] In brief, unless a man has developed judgment he has acquired neither skills nor the different 'languages' characterising the modes of thought of a civilisation. A mere knowledge of the 'literature', of the information and rules, is insufficient; they may help in telling us what not to do but they provide no prescriptions for their own application.

What conclusions, then, does Oakeshott draw for teaching from this analysis of what has to be passed on? First that the two components of knowledge ('information' and 'judgment') can both be communicated and acquired, but not separately. Secondly that they cannot be acquired in the same manner. Indeed Oakeshott confesses that the distinction which he makes is the result of reflection upon teaching and learning rather than upon the nature of knowledge. Thus teaching consists in a two-fold activity of 'instructing' (or communicating 'information') and imparting (or communicating 'judgment') and learning is similarly a two-fold activity.

[1] *Ibid.* p. 168.   [2] *Ibid.* p. 169.

The teacher as instructor is confronted by a pupil who is familiar with the activity of acquiring information, particularly information of immediate use. His task is to introduce pupils to facts which have no immediate significance. He has therefore to decide the part of our inheritance which has to be transmitted and to make it more readily accessible by giving it an organisation in which the inertness of its component facts is modified. 'The organisation provided by an immediate application to the life of his pupil is spurious; much of the information he has to convey has no such application and would be corrupted by being turned in this direction.'[1] Dictionaries and encyclopaedias are no good either; for they are not designed for the purpose of learning. Organisation in terms of 'languages' is altogether too sophisticated. The instructor perforce must settle for more or less arbitrarily designed 'subjects', which compose a curriculum; these are convenient organisations of information, not modes of thought. But they permit facts to reveal their rule-like character as tools to be used in doing, making, or understanding and thus throw off some of their inertness. The teacher as instructor also has to decide on the order in which to present this organisation of facts and to exercise his pupils so that they recognise them in forms other than those in which they were first acquired. Accuracy is vital in this operation and readiness to recall.

In addition to acquiring information from the teacher it is hoped that the pupil is also acquiring judgment. This begins to emerge whenever the pupil perceives that information must be used and perceives the possibility of irrelevance. The organisation of information may help in this development; for the pupil begins to be able to do, make, understand, or explain in the mode of thought which underlies the information. The pupil cannot be instructed how to think in these different ways; it is a by-product of acquiring information and is imparted obliquely in the course of instruction. This can only be done if the information and maxims are constantly related to concrete situations. Also to be imparted are the intellectual virtues that go with judgment—disinterested curiosity, patience, honesty, exactness, industry, concentration, and doubt. Most difficult of all for the pupil to acquire is the ability to detect the individual intelligence at work in every utterance and act, the style which each individual brings to his thought and action. 'We may listen to what a man has to say, but unless we overhear in it a mind at work and can detect the idiom of thought, we have understood nothing.'[2]

Judgment is not imparted in the abstract or separately; it is never explicitly learnt and it is known only in practice; but it may be learned in everything that is learned. 'If it is learned, it can never be forgotten,

[1] *Ibid.* p. 171.　　　　　　[2] *Ibid.* p. 174.

and it does not need to be recollected in order to be enjoyed. It is, indeed often enough, the residue which remains when all else is forgotten; the shadow of lost knowledge.'[1] How then is judgment imparted?

It is implanted unobtrusively in the manner in which information is conveyed, in a tone of voice, in the gesture which accompanies instruction, in asides, and oblique utterances, and by example. For 'teaching by example', which is sometimes dismissed as an inferior sort of teaching, generating inflexible knowledge because the rules of what is known remain concealed, is emancipating the pupil from the half-utterance of rules by making him aware of a concrete situation. And in imitating the example he acquires, not merely a model for the particular occasion, but the disposition to recognise everything as an occasion. It is a habit of listening for an individual intelligence at work in every utterance that may be acquired by imitating a teacher who has this habit. And the intellectual virtues may be imparted only by a teacher who really cares about them for their own sake and never stoops to the priggishness of mentioning them. Not the cry, but the rising of the wild duck impels the flock to follow him in flight.[2]

The thesis as a conceptual truth or as an empirical generalisation

Oakeshott's distinction between 'instructing' and 'imparting' is obviously a very important one, but the details of it are not altogether clear. So it is necessary to probe a bit further into it. He seems to maintain, first, that things like judgment, taste, and discernment can only be imparted; they can never be the result of mere instruction. Information and rules, on the other hand, are fit material only for instruction. Secondly 'imparting', on Oakeshott's view, must involve the example of the teacher; things like 'judgment' can only be 'shown', and this is how they are picked up. The rule book will not do, because the rules have to be applied, and we can only learn to apply them by working with somebody who knows how to apply them.

The first part of this thesis seems to be partly a *conceptual* truth in that 'impart' rather than 'instruct' is the word which we use when we wish to indicate that something has been successfully learnt from a teacher, as well as when we wish also to suggest some sort of mystery about how this has been accomplished. 'Impart', in other words, is what Ryle calls an 'achievement' word.[3] It implies, surely, not necessarily that the teacher has been engaged in some activity additional to instructing but that he has somehow achieved success in his task. Thus, contrary to Oakeshott's thesis, information or rules can be imparted, as well as judgment and discernment. As, however, it is desirable that information should be used and rules applied, judgment would usually be

---

[1] *Ibid.* p. 175.   [2] *Ibid.* p. 175.
[3] See G. Ryle, *The Concept of Mind* (London: Hutchinson, 1949), pp. 149–53.

regarded as a criterion of success, rather than the mere acquisition of information. The pupil should emerge with judgment and discernment rather than just be stuffed with 'inert' ideas. It is, therefore, not surprising that Oakeshott associates 'imparting' with 'judgment'; for this is the word which we use when we wish to point to the teacher's success. But it is not the case that only judgment can be imparted. It is merely a contingent fact that we do not regard the mere passing on of information as sufficiently important to grace it often with a 'success' word.

But is it also true—and this, too, might be a conceptual truth or it might be an empirical generalisation—that such successful results only occur when the teacher 'shows' or exemplifies the proper performance? Must there be some sort of mystery about the transaction which the term 'impart' also suggests? Could not, or cannot, mere instruction be sufficient? This is a much more complicated question to answer; for Oakeshott maintains that all passing on of knowledge and skill must involve the imparting of judgment if it is to be successful. But to maintain such a general thesis he uses the word 'judgment' in several different ways, at least three of which must be distinguished.

(i) There is, first of all, a general sense of 'judgment' used by idealist philosophers such as Bradley to speak of any situation in which a concept or rule is applied to a particular case. Thus recognising something as red or as a cat or as a breach of the Highway Code involves 'judgment' in this sense, just as much as recognising someone who is in disguise or determining whether someone was driving with due care and precaution. Does 'judgment' in this very general sense have to be imparted by processes such as imitation or identification in which acts or noises are copied or attitudes, interests, and wants are 'taken in' from the example of a teacher?

The answer is that, in this sense of judgment, examples are necessary for learning but not necessarily example. To be able to perceive or think is to be able to use concepts, and learning a concept involves both learning the rule which binds together the instances and learning by examples what counts as an instance. That is why a colour-blind man could not have a full concept of 'red'. But this process of producing an example to teach a concept or a rule is the most typical case of *instruction*. If we say 'cat' to a child and point to the animal in question that is a case of instruction. If we say later that 'the cat is on the mat' and again point, that again is a piece of instruction. If the instruction is successful, either in the sense that the child can go on to use the words correctly in this and in different situations, or in the sense that he remembers the piece of information, then we might say that we had taught the child a concept or imparted some knowledge to him. Judgment in its most general idealist sense would be involved; but though, at some stage, the use of examples would be necessary, the example of the teacher would not. After all, a great deal of instruction of this sort can be carried out by teaching machines. The rules, for instance, for the use of a concept like that of 'conditioning' could be roughly formulated and instances could be described in detail from the classical experiments to illustrate the use of the concept. A student could learn how to use such a concept if the relevant features of this situation were clearly made explicit by the programme of the machine. The student could then be given other examples so that he would quite quickly learn how to apply such a concept to unfamiliar situations.

Now 'judgment' of the idealist sort is involved here. But it is obviously something much more mundane than the 'judgment' of a judge, and situations can be controlled and structured in such a way that the learner can grasp the concept by instruction. He has, of course, to be brought to grasp the rules involved; but instructions can be formalised for bringing students of average intelligence to grasp such rules. Example, as distinct from examples, only becomes important when something aproximating to a skill is involved. It might be argued that in the early stages of learning an embryonic sort of skill is involved; for rules and concepts at this stage are necessarily presented in unstructured and unfamiliar types of situations where the child has to discriminate between possible types of application. Even in learning 'blue', for instance, the child has to grasp that this is an information-conveying type of word rather than an order, and that it is a colour-word within the general class of information-conveying types of word. Unless he had picked up a lot about the use of language from the example of his parents he would not be in a position to benefit from instruction by examples. Once he has become a language user instruction can accomplish a lot merely by examples because he has 'picked up' the general skills involved in using language in different ways by following the example of others. This may well be true; but what it also shows is that there is a great deal of 'judgment' in the idealist sense which can be learnt by instruction once the general skill of using a language has been acquired.

(ii) The general skill of using a language may exemplify a second and more specific sense of 'judgment', the paradigm case of which is the type of task performed by a judge. He is faced by a complex situation where many rules might apply to a set of facts and he has to determine which rule does apply. Judgment of a similar sort is involved in diagnosis, in tact, in deciding which golf club to use, or in dealing with non-routine types of situation in war, business and politics. This is surely the type of situation with which the term 'judgment' is usually associated. 'Judgment', in Oakeshott's thesis, is above all a term of approval. But we do not give a person a merit mark for judgment in the first sense—i.e. if he recognizes an obvious breach of the Highway Code or if he straightaway follows some instructions correctly for getting to Piccadilly. If he failed in such elementary applications of rules or use of information we might think him a fool. But we certainly would not praise him particularly if he was successful or ascribe judgment to him. It may well be the case that the difference between 'judgment' in the first and second senses is a difference in degree; it may well be the case also that judgment in the first idealist sense is only possible if some skill has been mastered which once involved judgment in the second sense. But the fact is that we do not normally use the word 'judgment' for straightforward cases of applying rules or using information. We reserve it for the special cases where applying rules or interpreting information presents a problem.

Could people only learn judgment in this second value-laden sense by serving their apprenticeship under somebody who already has it? That this is the only way in which it could be learnt seems to be the burden of Oakeshott's political and educational writings, in which he usually contrasts this way of picking it up with formalised instruction or the use of manuals and guides. No doubt some kind of apprenticeship system is the most effective and the quickest way of learning judgment of this sort. But it is questionable whether it is the only way. Oakeshott has a contempt for self-made men; but though they may learn judgment the hard way, it has to be demonstrated that they cannot learn it on their own, which seems to be his thesis. Oakeshott also has a contempt for method; yet method at least provides canons laying down what should not be done; it provides boundary fences within which the learner can try out things for himself. And here we come to the core of the matter, which is insufficiently emphasised in all Oakeshott's writings: *practice*, in which the learner methodically works at some task until he has more or less mastered it and is able to rest on a solid basis of habit in tackling some novel situation. Of course what we call 'training' usually involves practice under the supervision of some skilled performer. But it is a disputable empirical thesis that this is the only way to develop skill and judgment. Who, after all, was the master whose philosophical 'judgment' rubbed off on Socrates?

Of course those who are self-taught must learn 'judgment' in the first idealist sense from others; they have to learn to speak and to apply rules in paradigm situations before they can carry on their own; they have to be familiar with a literature from which problems or incoherences arise which puzzle them. But, given such a start, practice, intelligence, and method can take a man a very long way more or less on his own. Dewey's account of the development of critical thinking certainly pays too little attention to the role of the teacher as a paradigm of a form of thinking; it is *too* biased in favour of the do-it-yourself ideology of the frontier. But it would be odd if this rationalistic type of account applied to *no* cases in which people gradually learned to think for themselves and if *all* people who were more or less self-taught necessarily lacked judgment. Could it not be the case, too, that a man who was not a very good philosopher or scientist himself might be very good at initiating others in the early stages? He might have the ability to exhibit and convey to others the essentials of a form of thought in a crude but exciting way. He might lack the judgment to progress very far with it himself, to be an acknowledged master; but he might be very good at initiating others at the undergraduate level.

Oakeshott's emphasis, too, on picking up a skill by watching a master overlooks a very common learning situation that is not to be despised— that in which a learner practises a skill with a coach who is not himself particularly proficient at the skill in question. Some of the best teachers of golf or cricket, for instance, are not themselves superlative performers. What they have mastered is the art of commenting on and encouraging the performances of others. And they often do this by the reiteration of rules which are anathema to Oakeshott. They say things like 'Keep your right elbow in' or 'Don't hit from the top of the swing'. The performer gradually improves in response to such discerning instructions. There are, perhaps, many who learn much better by imitation which lacks such rule-ridden self-consciousness; but, on the other hand, others may not be particularly imitative and may learn better if coached by one who knows what a good performance looks like without himself being a superlative performer. Could it not be that Oakeshott's thesis about learning by example is merely a generalisation of his own favoured way of learning? Oakeshott produces no empirical evidence for his general thesis. But, perhaps, like Hobbes he reached it by reading in himself 'not this or that particular man; but mankind'.

Perhaps Oakeshott conflates under the general heading of 'teaching by example' two features of a situation which do not always go together. There is first of all that of the exhibition of the performance in question by the teacher and there is secondly the imparting of a skill or judgment not just by examples but by on the spot correction of the pupil's efforts towards mastery of it. It is conceivable that a learner could achieve considerable expertise in some skill like golf or shooting without reliance on *either* aspects of such an apprenticeship situation. For this would be a situation where the goal is more or less unambiguous and skill in hitting a target could be achieved by trial and error and constant practice. But in fields like that of the law or politics, where the notion of an overall 'goal' is rather out of place and where what constitutes success in a given case depends upon multiple criteria, it is almost inconceivable that a person could become proficient without one or other aspects of the apprenticeship system being present. For as Aristotle put it 'the decision lies with perception'. There may be ninety-nine ways of going wrong and only one way of going right. If judgments of this sort could be formalised in rules there would be no need to have judges for applying the rules of a legal system. A man could not, in such situations, learn 'judgment' on his own because he could never know what was constitutive of success. In shooting or golf, on the other hand, he might do this because he would know that success consisted in hitting the bird or getting the ball into the hole in as few shots as possible. It is only if an activity like politics is viewed as the pursuit of an overall end such as power that the do-it-yourself form of learning begins to look appropriate. Hence Oakeshott's strictures on books like Machiavelli's *The Prince* and on the general conception of politics as the taking of means to independently premeditated ends.

The upshot of this analysis would be, then, that in so far as an activity approximates to a skill which could be said to be 'goal-directed' in a fairly determinate way, there would be a correspondingly open possibility of do-it-yourself methods of learning, given a preliminary period of initiation into the rudiments of the activity. In so far, however, as 'success' in an activity is impossible to characterise without concrete interpretations or implementations of general principles, the possibility of do-it-yourself methods would become correspondingly more remote. But though apprenticeship would be necessary for the attainment of skill or judgment in such complex activities it need not take the form of learning from the example of the master; it might be sufficient for the master to correct the performances of his pupils on the spot. One of the best swimming coaches in recent times was a man who could not swim.

(iii) Oakeshott also refers on occasions to a third sort of thing, the 'style' of the individual performer. By this he means to draw attention not just to individual acts of judgment in the second sense but to the individual intelligence at work in every utterance and performance. It is necessarily the case that in so far as this can be passed on it must involve example; for as it is, by definition, individual to the person concerned, comprising a characteristic manner of thinking and acting, it would have to be shown to be both detected and imparted.

When talking about 'style' Oakeshott seems to conflate together the possibility of detecting it in another and the possibility of acquiring it from another. But the two do not necessarily go together. There are many philosophers of discernment who can detect Wittgenstein's characteristic 'style' of philosophy; but, though their own mastery of the 'language' might lead them to recognise the importance of many of his insights, they might well shudder at the 'style' with which they were delivered, Others, however, might admire the performance as a whole and might model themselves on it—mannerisms and all. This brings out that 'style' for Oakeshott is a term of approval which is associated only with desirable traits. But much of a person's 'style' may be an unnecessary and perhaps trivial or distracting adornment. There was a time when one could almost tell where an English philosopher was trained by observing the mannerisms and gestures which had been imparted to him!

Oakeshott, I feel sure, would deplore too much absorption of the 'style' of another. For that would be inconsistent with his insistence that 'making something of ourselves' is an important aspect of education. Presumably he means that it is judgment in the second sense, which is to be acquired from masters of the different languages; their individual style (including its superfluous idiosyncrasies) is to be 'detected' and admired but not slavishly copied.

When Oakeshott speaks about the imparting of judgment his own style of writing intimates somehow that we are confronted with a mystery. Indeed he perhaps chooses the word 'impart' because of its association with recondite matters. He cites no mundane empirical studies of apprenticeship and the transmission of skills; he indulges in no speculation about the psychological processes involved. Theories about roles, imitation or identification are never mentioned. He leads his readers to the uncharted region between the logical and psychological and there he leaves them. Omne ignotum pro magnifico.

There are others, however, for whom a mystery is not something that is to be hinted at and enjoyed, especially when it is alleged to pervade every situation in which a new generation is being initiated into skill, task, and judgment. On the contrary it provides a splendid occasion to satisfy all those rationalistic yearnings for clarity and problem-solving that Oakeshott so deeply deplores. Any mundane fellow who is set on exploring this uncharted region will first of all have to map the concepts which criss-cross the region. He will then need a spade to dig into psychological and sociological theories in order to unearth some relevant generalisations about social learning. My guess is that he will not find himself working alone but will find that he is helping to open up a region which will prove to be one of the most fertile for the growth of educational theory during the next decade. More understanding of these apprenticeship situations may dispel the mystery a bit, but not the wonder. It may even help us to teach a bit better.

MORAL EDUCATION

Oakeshott's account of moral education depends largely on the distinction which he makes between the 'habit of affection and behaviour' of the person brought up in a settled tradition and the 'reflective morality' of the person brought up to pursue ideals and to implement principles. It depends, too, on the rather idiosyncratic understanding which he has of 'principles' and of the lack of connection between them and behaviour. On the one hand he argues[1] that there is (or perhaps was) a form of moral life which consists in a 'habit of affection and behaviour'. People do not reflect upon alternative courses of action, and make choices determined by principles or ideals; they simply follow unreflectively the tradition in which they have been brought up. They acquire this in the way in which they learn to speak their mother tongue, by living with others who practice this morality. No doubt what they learn can be formulated in rules; but there is no need for it to be. People can learn to speak grammatically without their having also to be able to formulate rules of grammar. This sort of education, therefore, gives people the power to act appropriately without hesitation in a whole range of situations; but it does not give them the ability to explain or defend their actions as emanations of moral principles. A man has acquired what this type of education can teach him when his moral dispositions are inseparably connected with his *amour-propre*. This form of behaviour, though traditional, is not fixed; for it evolves in the way in which a living language evolves.

On the other hand there is reflective morality, which is determined not by a habit of behaviour but by the reflective application of a moral criterion. It takes the form either of the self-conscious pursuit of moral ideals or of the reflective observance of moral rules. A man must first formulate his rule of life or his ideal in words; he must also have the ability to defend these formulated aspirations against criticism. And, thirdly, he must learn to apply them in current situations in life in problem-solving behaviour. Moral education, therefore, must consist first of all in the detection and appreciation of ideals and principles. Secondly there must be training in the art of their intellectual management and thirdly training in the art of their application to concrete circumstances. The danger of this form of morality is that uncertainty in action is more or less proportionate to certainty in thinking about these ideals; moral reflection may undermine moral habit. It will make people miserable because of its demand for perfection and will suffer from inelasticity and imperviousness to change.

Oakeshott realises, of course, that these two sorts of morality are

[1] See 'The Tower of Babel' in *Rationalism in Politics and other Essays*, pp. 61–70.

really 'ideal types'. In most actual moralities there is a blend of the two. His concern is to attack a way of life in which the latter rather than the former type of morality predominates.

Before discussing the dichotomy it is necessary to clarify Oakeshott's conception of 'principles'. He regards them as 'abstracts' of practice. His frequent use of the word 'ideology' in this context is significant; for Oakeshott regards principles as being somehow spurious in relation to justification and, causally speaking, as by-products of activity. Indeed I think that it is his relativistic conviction that they cannot be justified that leads him to speak of them as 'explaining' conduct in the above passage in which he contrasts 'principles'[1] with rules of correctness implicit in conduct as well as in the grammar of a language. He exemplifies Aristotle's doctrine of the mean in the case of conduct being on a par with the principles of mechanics in the case of riding a bicycle.

There may be something rather special about the status of Aristotle's doctrine of the mean. But, whatever one makes of Aristotle's doctrine, this is really a very odd use of 'principle' in the run of the mill moral case. When speaking of principles Oakeshott always quotes something pretty abstract like 'natural rights' or 'justice', but surely, in the moral sphere, all we mean by a 'principle' is something that provides backing to a rule or which makes reasons relevant. Whether or not fundamental principles such as 'justice' or 'the minimization of avoidable suffering' can themselves be justified is a very complicated question;[2] but certainly the relationship between rules of conduct and principles is one of justification. In a moral context a principle just *is* a higher order rule that is appealed to when justification is required for one at a lower order. Thus if someone like Mill claims that divorce is wrong if the married couple have children, because of the probable suffering that it will cause them, then the avoidance of suffering is functioning as a principle. 'Judgment' is, of course, needed in order to apply such a principle; for what counts as suffering in a particular case and whose suffering is to be given most weight? Much of what Oakeshott says about 'judgment' is most pertinent to the application of principles. But it is his bizarre account of them that leads him to say that an appeal to them is a rationalist aberration. Indeed his own account even of 'practical' or 'traditional' knowledge is unintelligible without assuming a background of principles; for without such a background how are any reasons for action relevant? Oakeshott's account of the politician keeping the ship of state on an even keel and dealing with 'incoherences' which arise in a developing tradition presupposes not only that 'coherence' is good (whatever this amounts to in practice!) but also that considerations

---

[1] See above, p. 49.
[2] See R. S. Peters, *Ethics and Education* (London: Allen and Unwin, 1966), chapters III–VIII.

relating to security and stability are relevant. And if 'salus populi suprema lex' is not a 'principle' I do not know what is.

Oakeshott, too, seems to think that principles are really 'abstracts' from practices, whereas he caricatures rationalists as thinking that they are rules that are formulated as guides to practice. But why should they be either? Some principles, for instance, might be presuppositions of a practice. They need not be formulated beforehand by those who indulge in it, neither need they be abstracts from it. The principle, for instance, that truth matters need not be formulated beforehand by people discussing some scientific problem. It need only be appealed to if a participant in the discussion starts introducing irrelevant personal remarks or disregarding some evidence. Neither is it necessarily an 'abstract' of the practice of discussion; for such a discussion would surely be unintelligible unless the participants were already committed to it. For they have to conceive the situation in a certain way in order to make it a practice of this determinate sort. In a similar way the concern for health is a presupposition of, not an abstract from, the practice of medicine. There is therefore a sense in which Oakeshott's account of 'practices' is as inadequate as his account of 'principles'.

To probe further into the relationship between principles and practices would take us too far away from Oakeshott's philosophy of education. It must also be remarked that though Oakeshott's ideal types of morality provide two fascinating models that might have had application to classes of people within our society at some distant time in the past, they have little application to adults in modern industrial societies in the West. This is admitted by Oakeshott when he claims that nowadays the two are blended and that his main purpose is to attack a way of life which includes too much of the reflective and too little of the traditional style of behaviour.

From the point of view of moral education, however, both his dichotomy and his emphasis on tradition are instructive, as I have argued elsewhere.[1] Given that we live in a changing society with a fair degree of differentiation at a certain level in moral standards, young people are bound to be forced to reflect from time to time on where they stand. They have, therefore, to develop the elements of what Oakeshott calls a reflective morality, though his account of it, with the bizarre role accorded to principles in it, would have to be modified. But, for a variety of reasons, it is out of the question for young children to acquire such a morality until they pass out of what Piaget calls the 'transcendental stage' of moral judgment. At an early age, therefore, their morality will have to approximate to Oakeshott's 'habit of affection and behaviour'.

[1] See R. S. Peters, 'The paradox of moral education' in W. R. Niblett (ed.), *Moral Education in a Changing Society* (London: Faber, 1963).

The crucial task of moral education is to initiate them into this in such a way that they can gradually come to grasp the principles underlying what they have picked up from their parents and teachers, so that they will be able to act with understanding and adapt their practice to moral situations, make sensible choices and perhaps even challenge some practices as no longer defensible. The palace of reason has to be entered by the courtyard of habit. There are too many 'progressive' educators and parents who place too little emphasis on the enormous importance of habit and tradition in moral education. Oakeshott's brilliant sketch of traditional morality is a healthy corrective to such rationalistic excesses.

CONCLUSION

It is a recurrent theme in Oakeshott's writings that a man who is skilled at something such as cooking may not have the additional skill of being able to make explicit what he is about. Oakeshott himself provides a clear case of a person who combines both sorts of gifts. He is a gifted teacher and administrator whose unpretentious concern both for his subject and for his students is immanent in everything that he does. And I have never known a man with such a contempt for conscience discharge his duties so conscientiously. So when he reflects and writes, one feels that it is a genuine reflection of his experience and view of the world. Above all writers on politics and education today he has a style, an idiom of his own, and this is inseparable from his conduct of affairs. There is nothing second-hand or spurious about it or him. One may not agree with him—or, to put it more accurately, one agrees with him so much at first that it is particularly infuriating when he proceeds to what one thinks is the wrong conclusion! But he is there, all of a piece, to remind us perhaps of values that we are in danger of forgetting in the present gimmickry which passes for politics and in the present escalation of education, with its emphasis on quantity rather than quality.

It has not been until recently the fashion for university teachers outside education departments to write much about education. They thought they knew about it, of course; for are they not teachers themselves and have they not been to school? But their reflections about it were about as informed as a farmer's reflections about the weather. Recently, however, since it has been widely recognised that education is both an investment for the community and a means of social ascent for the individual, there have been many academics who have given forth on the subject of the organisation and distribution of education. Oakeshott, however, is one of the few who have consistently reflected and written on what the business is really about. Indeed he confesses that his views about knowledge derive from his reflections on teaching.

And when he writes about education it is manifest that he knows what it is about. He knows too that matters of organisation and distribution are of secondary importance compared with the heart of the matter—the living contact between a teacher and his pupils. This article has only attempted to convey the main contours of his thought. There have, too, been criticisms and queries—mainly on points of detail. But what cannot be adequately conveyed in such an abstract of a way of thinking is the overall impression of an extremely civilised man writing with acuteness, elegance and conviction about a matter which is of no small account—the passing on of a civilisation.

A CASE OF IDENTITY

M. M. GOLDSMITH

To yearn for that blissful time when each man knew, intuitively and effortlessly, his own identity, is futile. Identities have become slippery, problematical entities which can be changed, assumed, shed, lost, discovered, and even split—perhaps infinitely. But, by relying on the devices—a quick glance at a passport or driver's licence, or fingering some money or keys—recommended by Nigel Dennis in *Cards of Identity*, one can preserve an identity.

Although the identity problem has become more severe and more widely known in this century, it is not a modern invention—but rather a modern discovery. Although the solution of an identity problem is ordinarily a therapeutic technique, it is legitimate, and sometimes interesting, to investigate a case of identity even though the subject—being dead—cannot be a patient.[1] Furthermore, Mr Dennis has shown that it is by no means necessary to restrict the subject of identity problems to actual human beings; members of the identity club found fictional cases most revealing—perhaps because their theories of identity could be illustrated in them so much more neatly.

The case of identity I wish to discuss is that of Thomas Hobbes. It is a much-disputed case about which there has never been general agreement; the dispute about Hobbes began in his own time and it has recently been intensified.[2]

In a case so disputed by so many experts in identity, it is wise to begin with some facts undisputed. Despite the paucity of information about

[1] For an example, see E. H. Erikson, *Young Man Luther* (New York, 1962).
[2] Some modern contributions to the discussion of Hobbes are: F. Tönnies, *Hobbes—Leben und Lehre* (Stuttgart, 1896); G. C. Robertson, *Hobbes* (Edinburgh, 1901); L. Stephen, *Hobbes* (London, 1904); A. E. Taylor, *Hobbes* (London, 1908); and 'The ethical doctrine of Hobbes', *Philosophy*, XIII (1938), 406–24; G. E. C. Catlin, *Thomas Hobbes as Philosopher, Publicist, and Man of Letters* (Oxford, 1922); J. Laird, *Hobbes* (London, 1934); F. Brandt, *Hobbes' Mechanical Concept of Nature* (Copenhagen, 1928); L. Strauss, *The Political Philosophy of Hobbes: its Basis and its Genesis* (Oxford, 1936). Professor Oakeshott's introductory essay to *Leviathan* (Oxford, 1946) turned the flow of commentary into a flood of dispute about the problems he raised concerning Hobbes's moral and political thought. See R. Polin, *Politique et philosophie chez Thomas Hobbes* (Paris, 1953); R. Peters, *Hobbes* (Harmondsworth, Middlesex, 1956); H. Warrender, *The Political Philosophy of Hobbes: his Theory of Obligation* (Oxford, 1957); C. B. Macpherson, *The Political Theory of Possessive Individualism* (Oxford, 1962); F. C. Hood, *The Divine Politics of Thomas Hobbes, an Interpretation of Leviathan* (Oxford, 1964); J. W. N. Watkins, *Hobbes's System of Ideas* (London, 1965); K. C. Brown (ed.), *Hobbes Studies* (Oxford, 1965); M. M. Goldsmith, *Hobbes's Science of Politics* (New York, 1966). Upon the flood a number of paperbacked Leviathans, most of them mutilated, flounder about.

the subject's life and activities,[1] enough is known for a brief statement of the external facts of the subject's identity:

Thomas Hobbes:

born: Westport near Malmesbury, 5 April 1588;

physical description: tall, black hair (greying with age), hazel eyes, moustache, and a small beard from his lower lip—otherwise clean-shaven;

education: Malmesbury School, Mr Robert Latimer; Magdalen Hall, Oxford (B.A. 1608);

occupations: secretary, librarian, tutor (later companion) to the Cavendish family, Earls, later Dukes, of Devonshire; occasionally guided youths around the continent; tutor (in mathematics) to Charles Stuart; humanist; scientist; mathematician; philosopher; wit; author;

addresses: c/o Cavendish, Hardwick Hall, Derbyshire, or c/o Crooke, bookseller, Green-Dragon, St Paul's Churchyard, London;

military service: none;

religion: professes to be of the Church of England;

political affiliation: royalist;

died: Chatsworth, 4 December 1679; buried at Ault Hucknall, near Hardwick.

The problem of Hobbes's identity is not a superficial one—one requiring only that the subject, like an amnesiac, recognise his identity; it is a more complicated problem requiring a deeper analysis.

The simpler solutions to the problem of Hobbes's identity—some of them proposed while he was still alive—are inadequate. That Hobbes was a secret Cromwellian who had written *Leviathan* to justify Oliver's claims to power (for example) is sufficiently refuted by the fact that *Leviathan* was published three years before Oliver became Protector; even Hobbes did not claim that kind of prescience.[2]

Another simple solution first proposed in the seventeenth-century is that Hobbes was extraordinarily timid, obsessed with fear—fear of the dark, fear of death, fear of ghosts, fear of others, even fear of his own shadow.[3] He did not fight for the royalist cause in the Civil War; he escaped to France at the beginning of the Long Parliament—'the first of all that fled'.[4]

[1] Most of our information about Hobbes's life comes from John Aubrey's '*Brief Lives*', *chiefly of Contemporaries*, ed. A. Clark, 2 vols. (Oxford, 1898). S. I. Mintz is writing a biography of Hobbes.

[2] See John Wallis, *Hobbius Heauton-timorumenos* (Oxford, 1662), p. 5. Cf. Hobbes's refutation of Wallis on this point: *Considerations on the Reputation, Loyalty, Manners, and Religion of Thomas Hobbes* in *The English Works of Thomas Hobbes of Malmesbury*, ed. Molesworth, 11 vols. (London, 1839–45) (abbreviated as *EW*), IV, 415.

[3] S. I. Mintz, *The Hunting of Leviathan* (Cambridge, 1962), p. 1.

[4] Hobbes, *Considerations*, *EW*, IV, 414.

Yet the identification of Hobbes as a timid, frightened man seems curiously inadequate. That he was afraid of ghosts, which are, in his philosophy, the mere distempered imaginings of men unable to distinguish between dreams and ordinary sensation, seems most unlikely. Men

if they be timorous, and supperstitious, possessed with fearfull tales, and alone in the dark, are subject to the like fancies; and believe they see spirits and dead mens Ghosts walking in Church-yards; whereas it is either their Fancy onely, or els the knavery of such persons, as make use of such superstitious feare, to passe disguised in the night, to places they would not be known to haunt.[1]

Hobbes would really have had to be timid to fear his own imagination. Aubrey reports that Hobbes was not afraid of ghosts:

I have often heard him say that he was not afrayd of *sprights*, but afrayd of being knockt on the head for five or ten pounds, which rogues might thinke he had in his chamber.[2]

Hobbes himself contributed to this false identity. He admitted that he fled because he did not know how the Long Parliament would treat him. He was no Strafford, but he had written a treatise, *The Elements of Law, Natural and Politic*, in defence of the king. He did not return during the Civil War to fight for King Charles. Nevertheless, he was fifty-two and a scholar; only Sir John Falstaff would not have hesitated over such a recruit.

In his political thought Hobbes emphasises the motivating utility of fear. Fear of a common power was necessary if men were to live in society. A man would submit to a conquering power because he feared the conqueror, or join others to construct an artificial power for fear of what would happen if they did not.[3] Fear could be relied on; fear of death provides a common basic motivation because to go on living is a primary condition of achieving any other end.

Not only did Hobbes rely upon fear as the basis of the state, but he also promoted the notion that he and fear were identical, indeed he himself tells us that he and fear were born twins.

> *Fama ferebat enim diffusa per oppida nostra,*
> *Extremum genti classe venire diem.*
> *Atque metum tantum concepit tunc mea mater,*
> *Ut pareret geminos, meque metumque simul.*[4]

---

[1] Hobbes, *Leviathan* (2) (Oxford, 1909), p. 17. (All subsequent references to *Leviathan* in this chapter are to the 1909 edition.)

[2] Aubrey, *Brief Lives*, I, 353.   [3] *Leviathan* (20), pp. 152–3; *De Cive* (i, 14), *EW*, II, 12.

[4] *Vita Carmine Expressa*, in *Thomae Hobbes Malmesburiensis—Opera Philosophica quae Latine scripsit Omnia*, ed. Molesworth, 5 vols. (London, 1839–45) (abbreviated as *LW*), I, lxxxvi.

    A contemporary translation, *The Life of Mr Thomas Hobbes of Malmesbury. Written by himself in a Latine Poem. And now translated into English* (London, 1680) has (p. 2):

'Fear and I were born twins for my mother was brought to bed prematurely by reports of the Spanish invasion.' It is a good story; no wonder Hobbes was fond of it. But it cannot be true in this form. The Duke of Medina-Sidonia, commander of the Armada, received the standard for the expedition in the cathedral of Madrid on 25 April. He sailed on 29 May, but bad weather forced him to put back into port to refit his unwieldy fleet. Consequently, the Armada was not sighted in England until 29 July.[1] Hobbes was already nearly four months old, for he had been born on Good Friday, April 5th. The reports of the approach of the Armada which reputedly frightened Hobbes's mother into premature labour then, were themselves premature.

Hobbes's personal timidity is very doubtful. Charles II used to call him 'the beare'—'Here comes the beare to be bayted!'[2] Hardly the epithet or the remark a king who 'never said a foolish thing' would apply to a timid man.

But Hobbes's courage is not supported merely by the fact that he was a dangerous antagonist for the wits at court. Hobbes published. Reacting to Galileo's trial, Descartes locked his treatise on the world in a drawer; he published his *Discourse on Method* anonymously and only reluctantly admitted that he had written it. The only work Spinoza published under his own name during his life was an exposition of Descartes' philosophy; his *Tractatus Theologico-Politicus* was published anonymously, the *Ethics* posthumously. Locke finally acknowledged his authorship of *Two Treatises of Government*—two weeks before he died; in a codicil to his will he gave it, with his other anonymous works, to the Bodleian Library.[3] But Hobbes published. He published heterodox opinions under his own name, published while he was alive, published in Latin, in English, in French, and in Dutch. He was not too timid to risk that.

Perhaps the profounder analyses of Hobbes's identity are more adequate. Unfortunately the experts, like the members of Mr Dennis's identity club, do not agree. Some think that Hobbes's political theory is part of his scientific philosophy, some deny it. He has been identified with Bacon, Galileo, Aristotle, and the scholastics. He has been described as an evil atheist and as a moral rationalist. But we have

> For Fame had rumour'd, that a Fleet at Sea,
> Wou'd cause our Nations Catastrophe;
> And hereupon it was my Mother Dear
> Did bring forth twins at once, both Me, and Fear.

Aubrey dutifully repeats this story, *Brief Lives*, 1, 327–8.

[1] See Garrett Mattingly, *The Armada* (Boston, 1959), pp. 215, 250–65.
[2] Aubrey, *Brief Lives*, 1, 340.
[3] See John Locke, *Two Treatises of Government*, ed. Laslett (Cambridge, 1960), p. 4.

recently been told that Hobbes was neither Satan nor Kant. He was
a traditional Christian natural law theorist—apparently he was either
Richard Hooker or Thomas Aquinas. (Actually he must be Hooker, for
those who make this identification seem unaware of Hobbes's Italian
connections.) To be told that a man frequently accused of atheism was
really a traditional orthodox Christian might astonish us—until we
remember that we have also been told that Locke was really Hobbes by
those who do not seem to know that Hobbes was really Hooker.

One of the most influential analyses of Hobbes is that of Leo Strauss;
The Political Philosophy of Hobbes (in 1936) identified Hobbes as the
originator of modern political philosophy.[1] Strauss argued that (1)
Hobbes's political philosophy involved a radical break with traditional
philosophy, i.e. the classical tradition of Aristotle, natural law, and
scholasticism. (2) The real basis of this break with tradition is not his
adoption of scientific or of geometric method. (Hobbes's discovery of
geometry—at forty!—can hardly be described as a crisis of identity.)
The true basis of Hobbes's break with tradition is a new moral attitude,
an attitude merely obscured by the 'scientific' formulation of Hobbes's
thought. (3) Both the evidence for this break and the meaning of it may
be discovered in the development of Hobbes's thought.[2]

Strauss discovered in Hobbes two moralities: a morality of pride or
vanity and a morality of fear. The second gradually came to dominate
Hobbes's moral thought.[3] To establish the moral superiority of fear over
pride Hobbes thought it necessary to ground that superiority in
materialism. Men are naturally vain; they regard themselves as superior
to other men and demand recognition from others of this imaginary
superiority. The recognition denied, a struggle for supremacy results;
but that struggle, a real physical struggle, subjects the naturally vain
man to physical pain, and the sudden fear of violent death. The struggle
for supremacy thus becomes a struggle for life.[4]

Such is Strauss's reading of Hobbes. According to his reading vanity
or vainglory stands for imaginary pleasure; fear for real bodily pain.

[1] Professor Strauss has revised his opinion; he now accords that distinction to Machiavelli.
See Strauss, *The Political Philosophy of Hobbes*, pp. vii–ix, xv; *Natural Right and History*
(Chicago, 1953), especially pp. 166–202; *Thoughts on Machiavelli* (Glencoe, Ill., 1959), pp.
9–14. Yet Hobbes's claim to be the 'originator of modernity' must be taken seriously;
see 'On the basis of Hobbes's political philosophy', in *What is Political Philosophy?*
(Glencoe, Ill., 1959), p. 172.
[2] This formulation is based on Michael Oakeshott, 'Dr Leo Strauss on Hobbes', *Politica*, II
(1937), 366 ff.
[3] The evidence for such a development is weak. Only the 'Introduction' to Thucydides'
History predates Hobbes's 'scientific' works—and that not only offers little evidence of
a moral philosophy but also can hardly be called early. The references collected into
a morality of vanity occur throughout Hobbes's life. See Oakeshott, 'Dr Leo Strauss on
Hobbes', *Politica*, II (1937), 371–2; Polin, *Politique et Philosophie chez Thomas Hobbes*, pp. 153–5,
159–64.   [4] Strauss, *The Political Philosophy of Hobbes*, pp. 18–23.

Vanity is irrational, fear rational; vanity is immoral, fear moral. To justify this polarity, Hobbes relies upon his materialism:

Hobbes seems to have thought that this view [that what is not body is nothing] supports sufficiently his contention that only the pleasures and pains of the body are genuine, whereas the pleasures and pains of the mind are vain or fantastical; cf. *De Cive*, I, 2 [*EW*, II, 5] and *Leviathan*, ch. 27 [p. 230] with *Leviathan*, ch. 6 [p. 42]. Or, in other words, he seems to have thought that his corporealism legitimates the polarity of reasonable fear and unreasonable glory.[1]

But Strauss believes that Hobbes's materialism is not a morally neutral, scientific position. For that scientific mechanical materialism itself expresses a moral position; by relying on motion and endeavour, material pushes and pulls, to explain events, including perception, it thereby prefers the sense of touch over the higher senses, a preference also implied in the antithesis of vanity and fear.[2] Far from being a neutral ground for Hobbes's moral position, his science was merely an attempt to reinforce that position. To put it another way, Hobbes's rejection of classical—Aristotelian—political philosophy was not based on his rejection of classical—Aristotelian—natural science, but rather his denial of the validity of teleological natural science is a consequence of his rejection of classical political philosophy. Strauss seems to think that Hobbes rejected Aristotle and the classical tradition because classical philosophy supported aristocracy and therefore subversion of monarchy and Hobbes intended to support monarchy.

According to Strauss, Hobbes suffered from a modernity complex: the rejection of teleological political philosophy, the illusion of non-evaluative natural and political science, the attempt to disguise moral preferences as objective choices, the displacing of reason by passion as the dominant element in human nature.

It is an interesting and suggestive analysis, but it contains very great difficulties. Hobbes did indeed prefer monarchy, but when he constructed his political philosophy he recognised that he could not demonstrate its superiority to other forms of government. He could prove, he thought, that a sovereign was necessary, that *mixarchy* was nonsense, that all sovereigns must possess certain powers; he could only argue that the inconveniences alleged to exist in monarchies also existed in popular states and that monarchy had fewer inconveniences and was less subject to them than was a collective sovereign.[3] Monarchy was merely desirable; sovereignty was scientifically necessary.

[1] Strauss, 'On the basis of Hobbes's political philosophy' in *What is Political Philosophy?*, p. 178, n. 4.   [2] Strauss, *The Political Philosophy of Hobbes*, pp. 27, 165.
[3] *Leviathan* (19), pp. 142–52; *De Cive* (Preface, x, 1–19), *EW*, II, xxii, 114–42; *The Elements of Law, Natural and Politic* (II, v, 1–8) ed. Tönnies (London, 1889), pp. 137–43. See Watkins, *Hobbes's System of Ideas*, pp. 27–46.

The basis of Strauss's interpretation of Hobbes is the polarity of imaginary vanity and real bodily fear, that polarity which Hobbes is supposed to have thought justified by his materialism. But Hobbes did not regard fear as a bodily reaction; fear is not simply an aversion, but an aversion based upon the opinion of a future hurt. Fear itself is an imagination and it, like all mental acts, is to be explained by bodily motion.[1] Hobbes did not think that materialism implied the unreality of imaginary pleasures or imaginary pains. The pleasures and griefs of the mind are no less real and no less motion in a body than is that pleasure or pain 'that seemeth to affect the corporeal organ of sense'.[2] Imagination is, after all, nothing but decaying sensation.

Moreover, Hobbes admitted the existence of vain fear and of real glory. Some men are excessively fearful; insanity may proceed not only from excessive pride but also

from too much vain fear and dejection: as in those melancholy men that have imagined themselves brittle as glass, or have had some other like imagination; and degrees hereof are all those exorbitant and causeless fears, which we commonly observe in melancholy persons.[3]

Not all fear is rational, nor is all glory irrational or vain. Glorying is enjoying the thought of one's own power; if this imagination is grounded on past experience and if it leads to further action it is not vain.[4] Even the desire for fame after death may dispose men to laudable actions.

And though after death, there be no sense of the praise given us on Earth, as being joyes, that are either swallowed up in the unspeakable joyes of Heaven, or extinguished in the extreme torments of Hell: yet is not such Fame vain; because men have a present delight therein, from the foresight of it, and of the benefit that may redound thereby to their posterity: which though they now see not, yet they imagine; and any thing that is pleasure in the sense, the same also is pleasure in the imagination.[5]

Hobbes held neither that all glory was vain, 'imaginary', and irrational nor that all fear was sensible, real, and rational. But if Hobbes's science presupposes the moral antithesis of vanity and fear, he would not be entitled to hold that position; he would have been inconsistent in erroneously believing that he could hold it.

The argument that Hobbes's mechanical materialism involves a preference for the sense of touch over the higher senses, that this preference is a moral preference, and that the position involves a polarity of vanity

---

[1] *Leviathan* (6), pp. 41–3; *Elements of Law* (I, vii, 2), pp. 28–9.
[2] *Elements of Law* (I, vii, 9), p. 31.
[3] *Elements of Law* (I, x, 11), pp. 52–3. See also *Elements of Law* (I, xi, 2), p. 38, and *Leviathan* (6, 8), pp. 44, 57.
[4] *Leviathan* (6), pp. 44–5; *Elements of Law* (I, ix, 1), pp. 36–8.
[5] *Leviathan* (11), p. 76.

and fear is a curious one. It is curious because examining it yields some odd results. In the seventeenth century mechanical materialism meant a causal explanation of events. Such an explanation rigidly excludes occult forces, i.e. invisible, unobservable influences of one thing upon another thing. Action of one body upon another body must always occur through observable, causal, mechanical links. The 'preference for the sense of touch' is equivalent to the exclusion of action at a distance. The central problem involving action at a distance for seventeenth-century physics was the problem of the transmission of light. It is light and sight which must be explained, and they must be explained scientifically and causally and without relying on action at a distance; Hobbes was only one of many scientists intensely interested in optics.

The exclusion of action at a distance (the preference for touch) is far from being peculiar to Hobbes; it is common to seventeenth-century scientists and natural philosophers.

Tis unconceivable that inanimate brute matter should (without ye mediation of something else wch is not material) operate on & affect other matter without mutual contact; as it must if gravitation in the sense of Epicurus be essential and inherent in it. And this is one reason why I desired you would not ascribe innate gravity to me. That gravity should be innate inherent and essential to matter so yt one body may act upon another at a distance through a vacuum without the mediation of anything else by & through wch their action or force may be conveyed from one to another is to me so great an absurdity that I beleive no man who has in philosophical matters any competent faculty of thinking can ever fall into it.[1]

No less than Thomas Hobbes, Isaac Newton denied the possibility of action at a distance. Any mechanical explanation of natural phenomena that denies action at a distance, i.e. all seventeenth-century science, explains the higher senses by the sense of touch—sight is produced by particles touching the sensitive organ or by vibrations in a medium touching it.

Hobbes's science, then, was not idiosyncratic. Here Strauss's analysis applies to all mechanical science and not only to Hobbes's science. Strauss, who regards the issue between the teleological and the mechanical views of the universe as important,[2] seems to criticise the mechanical explanation from the standpoint of one who accepts the teleological, or Aristotelian, position. From this standpoint, Hobbes appears as a typical case of modernity.

Another deep analysis of Hobbes emphasises men's competitiveness. Nor need this competitiveness be based on a universal vanity, the desire

[1] Isaac Newton to Richard Bentley, 25 February 1692/3, in *The Correspondence of Isaac Newton*, ed. H. W. Turnbull (Cambridge, 1961), III, 253–4.
[2] See *Natural Right and History*, pp. 7–8.

of every man for unlimited power. It is not necessary that all men desire power immoderately: if some men desire unlimited power, moderate men will be compelled to contend for more and more power in order to secure their continued existence and their continued enjoyment of the fruits of their moderate power.

This element of competitiveness, C. B. Macpherson holds, is not inherent in Hobbes's Galilean resolution of society into its constituent individual men, nor in the resolution of human nature into its causal elements. Why should the rather complicated power-seeking automata called men be competitive?

Professor Macpherson's answer is that Hobbes introduces an implied social postulate into his discussion of power. Hobbes first describes power as the ability to effect some result, but he later says that power must be measured comparatively: power is not the simple ability to do but rather the comparative quantity by which the power of one man exceeds that of another. Each man's power is to be conceived as opposed to that of other men; equal powers offset each other and thus nullify each other. Thus the notion that power is comparative involves the assumption that men exist in a competitive social situation: 'society is so fluid or fragmented that the behaviour of the immoderately desirous men compels all the others to enter the contest for power over others.'[1]

Hobbes thought that analysis would reveal not primitive man but the principal elements of human nature. What it actually reveals is not human nature in itself but seventeenth-century human nature without the restraints of seventeenth-century society. In other words, Hobbes gives an account of human nature as it was formed by the society he lived in. And Professor Macpherson contends: (1) that England in the seventeenth-century was a possessive market society; and (2) 'Hobbes was more or less consciously taking that society as his model of society as such'.[2]

Macpherson distinguishes three models of society: customary or status society; simple market society; and possessive market society. The customary or status society is one in which the burdens and rewards are fixed: (1) Work is authoritatively allocated. (2) Every individual and social group is assigned by law or custom to a mode of life—a way of working and an appropriate socially assigned reward. (3) The right to use land is conditioned upon performing services or functions; there is no private ownership of land. (4) The labour force is tied to performing services, attached to the land, or in bondage to masters: men are not free to sell their labouring power.[3] This model of society, Macpherson

---

[1] Macpherson, *The Political Theory of Possessive Individualism*, pp. 33–41.
[2] *Ibid.* p. 46. For Macpherson's argument, see *ibid.* pp. 46–70.
[3] *Ibid.* p. 29.

explains, allows for conflict among the lords or masters for increased power, honour, or wealth. It is also conceivable that the labourers may rebel against their condition—a slave revolt. But it excludes universal competition, the attempt of each individual to get a larger share of the benefits of society.

I can think of no society which conforms completely to Macpherson's model; even 'primitive', 'customary', or 'feudal' societies are too fluid. But Plato's description of the timocratic state in the *Republic* is close. The timocrats enslaved the labouring classes which were free in the best state; they no longer allow children to be reclassified; they engage in competition for wealth and power.[1]

The second of the models is the simple market society. In this society: (1) Neither work nor rewards are authoritatively allocated. (2) Contracts are enforced. (3) All individuals attempt to maximise their utilities, or get the maximum satisfaction from the minimum expenditure of energy or goods. (4) All individuals have land or other resources on which to labour. (5) So that there can be no market in labour, it is postulated that the satisfaction of retaining control of one's own labour outweighs any difference between expected wages and expected returns as an independent producer.[2] Thus the simple market society provides for a system of free and self-regulating exchange among permanently independent individual producers. It corresponds to no society that has ever existed in fact or in theory, but some anarchists, especially Max Stirner and, to some degree, Proudhon, come close to this model.

By retaining the first three assumptions of the simple market society, a possessive market society may be constructed by adding: (4) Men may alienate their capacities to labour. (5) Land and resources are similarly individual property. (6) Some individuals want more goods than they have. (7) Some individuals have more energy, skill, or possessions than others.[3]

In a possessive market society men desire not only to do as well as they can with what they have, but also they desire to get more. They are acquisitive, perhaps even greedy. Furthermore, they are allowed by the rules of the society to acquire more than they have; they may own land and other capital. In addition to the desire to acquire and the right to own, they also have the ability to get more. Even if men were initially equal in possessions, differences in energy and skill would enable some to get more than others. In a possessive market society then, in which men have the desire, the ability, and the right to acquire

---

[1] *Republic*, 544 ff. The ideal society of the *Republic* and the societies described in Plato's *Laws* also resemble Macpherson's model. Perhaps some actual societies marked by rigid caste systems, e.g. India, ancient Egypt, also do.

[2] Macpherson, *The Political Theory of Possessive Individualism*, pp. 51–2.

[3] *Ibid.* pp. 53–4.

wealth, some men will come to own land and resources and other men will find it necessary to sell their capacity to labour.

If all men desire limitless power and are therefore competitive, a model of society is required which allows peaceful competition; and if only some men are insatiably power-hungry, a model of society is required which permits competition and compels the moderate men to compete. Macpherson contends

that the only model which satisfies these requirements is the possessive market society, which corresponds in essentials to modern competitive market societies; that Hobbes's explicit postulates (notably, that labour is a commodity, that some men want to increase their level of delight, and that some have more natural power than others) are essentially those of a possessive market society; that the model of society which Hobbes constructed in his analysis of power, valuing, and honouring, and confirmed in his analysis of commutative and distributive justice, corresponds essentially to the possessive market model; and that although Hobbes was not fully conscious of such correspondence, there is some evidence to suggest that he was aware of the peculiar suitability of his analysis to seventeenth-century society.[1]

To understand Macpherson's analysis of Hobbes rightly, it is necessary to see what is involved in his three social models: customary society, simple market society, possessive market society. If a single presupposition is added to the argument, the differences among the models become quite sharp. The presupposition to be added is that only labour can create value. That Professor Macpherson, who is a trained economist, is aware of the various forms the labour theory of value takes in the writings of Locke, Ricardo, and Marx, can scarcely be doubted; nevertheless, the utility of presupposing it does not depend on his conscious acceptance of that theory in any of its forms. Even if Macpherson consciously rejects the labour theory of value, it may have influenced the construction of his models—at any rate, presupposing it does clarify certain aspects of them.

Customary society, with its authoritative allocation of duties and rewards, limits as it provides for the expropriation of value created by the labourers, serfs, and slaves. Although members of the upper class may compete for more rewards, and although the lower class may revolt against the expropriators, the distribution of values is relatively fixed and universal competition to increase one's share does not exist. In short, the society provides that value produced by one class or group shall be expropriated (in some certain proportion) and distributed to another class or group.

The simple market society provides us with a rather different situation. Here each man owns land or resources and works on them himself.

---

[1] *Ibid.* p. 68.

In this society each man would appropriate only the value he produced with his own labour. Expropriation cannot exist.

In a possessive market society, however, the idyllic conditions in which the labourer receives the full product of his labour no longer exist. Some will own tools, land, and other resources and others must sell their labour for wages in order to live. Since each desires to maximise his utilities, the more powerful, the owners, will be able to hire the capacity of the workers to labour in exchange for the means of life. The worker will therefore create more value in production than he appropriates in wages; the difference, the surplus value, will be appropriated by the capitalist.

Professor Macpherson's analysis asserts that 'Hobbes's explicit postulates...are essentially those of a possessive market society' and 'the model of society which Hobbes constructed in his analysis of power, valuing, and honouring, and confirmed in his analysis of commutative and distributive justice, corresponds essentially to the possessive market model'.[1] Taking into account Macpherson's remark that 'Hobbes was not fully conscious of such correspondence' (i.e. the correspondence of his model, the possessive market model, and modern competitive societies) and with the addition of that single added presupposition, Macpherson's analysis has been clarified: Hobbes had subconscious Marxist tendencies.

In this analysis, Hobbes has been identified as the man who saw most deeply into the nature of the society in which he lived and in which we still live. He recognised the essentials of the possessive market society in seventeenth-century England: and by our fascination with him we acknowledge that he penetrated to the core of our society in that recognition. However strange it may seem, Hobbes was a great thinker because he arrived at the fundamentals of the liberal society and the modern state.

Because of its emphasis, Macpherson's account pin-points one familiar characteristic of Hobbes's thought (a commonplace of interpretation), his individualism: Hobbes argued that society must be understood by dissolving it into dissociated individuals and reconstituting society from them. Hobbes's understanding of society thus involved the use of two explicit social models: (1) the state of nature and (2) commonwealth or civil society.

The state of nature, or 'naturall condition' of men, is Hobbes's model of non-society. It is that condition which exists if society is imagined taken insunder in a Galilean thought-experiment.[2] In the state of nature, 'men as if but even now sprung out of the earth, and suddenly, like mushrooms come to full maturity, without all kind of engagement

[1] *Ibid.*   [2] *De Cive* (Preface), *EW*, ii, xiv.

to each other' are without the bonds and benefits of any sort of social organisation.[1] In such a condition there can be no agriculture, no industry, no navigation, no property, no laws, no sciences, and no arts.[2] Free of all bonds and equal to any other man, each individual in the state of nature is at liberty to do, and to do with right, whatever he judges necessary for his own preservation. Because men's desires conflict (they have divisive desires for scarce or unsharable things), because some men may desire to dominate others (triumph is sweet and power over others is useful), because each man must suspect that every other man intends to harm him (the other may believe he needs what the first man has or he may decide to protect himself by striking first), 'the estate of men in this natural liberty is the estate of war'.[3]

Hobbes's second model is commonwealth or civil society.[4] Commonwealth exists when a group of men has a sovereign, some man or council, empowered to act for that group in whatever way the sovereign decides. The sovereign is the supreme legislative authority in the society just as it is the supreme military, judicial, executive, religious, and administrative authority. The sovereign decides, acts, and judges in the name of the whole society and for the whole society; to its powers there are neither legal limits nor legal exceptions. Hobbes contended that only with a sovereign so empowered could peace be assured. Unless such a sovereign existed, a return to the war of all against all, or at least to some sort of civil war, was always possible—and Hobbes would have had his contemporaries believe that this possibility would occur. Either there was a sovereign and a peace in which all the commodities of civilisation could exist or there was no sovereign and thus no peace and at best a mere truce in the fighting.

Neither of Hobbes's two explicit models is a 'possessive market society'. The state of nature cannot be one, for, although it permits universal competition, it supposes that universal competition to be utterly unrestricted. The possessive market society requires property and laws to defend it. In the state of nature there is no authority to enforce laws or contracts:

It is consequent also to the same condition, that there be no Propriety, no Dominion, no *Mine* and *Thine* distinct; but onely that to be every mans, that he can get; and for so long, as he can keep it.[5]

---

[1] *De Cive* (viii, 1), *EW*, II, 109. For Hobbes's description of the state of nature, see *Elements of Law* (I, xiv, xix), pp. 70–4, 99–105; *De Cive* (i), *EW*, II, 1–13; *Leviathan* (13), pp. 94–8
[2] The most famous version of this passage is *Leviathan* (13), pp. 96–7, but see also *De Cive* (i, 13), *EW*, II, 12 and *Elements of Law* (I, xiv, 12), p. 73.
[3] *Elements of Law* (I, xiv, 11), p. 73.
[4] See *Elements of Law* (II, i–ix), pp. 107–84; *De Cive* (v–xiv), *EW*, II, 63–202; *Leviathan* (Part II, 17–381), pp. 128–285.
[5] *Leviathan* (13), p. 98.

Moreover, 'every man has a Right to every thing; even to one anothers body' as long as the condition of universal unlimited competition, the war of all against all, exists.[1] This state then cannot be a possessive market society.

Hobbes did use a second model—civil society, or commonwealth. Some of its characteristics are consistent with a 'possessive market society': protecting life, securing property, and enforcing covenants are functions performed by the sovereign or its officers. Had Hobbes aimed at a society on the 'possessive market' model he could have rested content with these limits, or perhaps a few additional ones; it may be merely anomalous that Hobbes allows the sovereign to determine where and for what commodities the subject may engage in foreign trade (as well as to define the rights of property and the terms of contracts), that he recommends taxation on expenditure, and that the sovereign is to promote industry of all sorts for the able-bodied and provide public charity for the unfortunate.[2] It might be arguable that the powers of the sovereign over the lives and property of the subjects are necessary to provide the framework of order and security within which men may contend. But it is hardly consistent with the 'possessive market society' for the sovereign to assign to each man his place and degree of honour and dignity.[3] Hobbes's second model may be consistent with the 'possessive market society' in some respects, but it is, in just those respects, consistent with any sort of system of law and with any system of ownership whether individual, familial, or societal. The two models are incongruous in other ways because Hobbes's civil society is a model that provides for peace, even at the expense of all competition in order to avoid contention, whereas Macpherson's 'possessive market society' is organised for a limited, if universal, competition.

Recognising that neither of Hobbes's two explicit models is consistent with the 'possessive market society', Professor Macpherson finds this third model implicit in Hobbes's discussions of valuing and of justice; he finds it primarily in Hobbes's explanation of human nature before he introduced his explicit models.

Not the least of the difficulties presented by this analysis is that it requires us to believe that the 'possessive market society' accurately describes what were, or were coming to be, the realities of English life. But were I looking for an example of a commercial society in the seventeenth century, I should not choose England, but the Low Countries (or even some parts of France or Italy), where at least political and social life was dominated by an urban commercial oligarchy (a *bourgeoisie*) rather than by a landed aristocracy. Although seventeenth-century Englishmen complained that the social order (the finely graded

---

[1] *Ibid.* (14), p. 99.   [2] *Ibid.* (24, 30), pp. 188–93, 266–7.   [3] *Ibid.* (18), p. 139.

pyramid that rose from pauper, cottager, and labourer to the landed gentry and its tiny aristocratic peak, the peerage) was breaking down, the observer, noting how consistently those successful in trade, commerce, manufacture, law, or administration, put their gains in land and assimilate to the gentry, must doubt the accuracy of the cluckings of these social chicken-littles.[1]

Did Hobbes draw a model of a possessive market society from his observations in England? Or did he perhaps discover the elements of this model in the Netherlands, in France, in Italy, or even, since Athens was, slavery apart, as egalitarian as any seventeenth-century European society, from reading about classical antiquity?

The 'possessive market society' describes some legal institutions appropriate to a commercial society (a market in land, labour, and commodities and the enforcement of market agreements—contracts) and it stipulates a psychological motivation that will ensure market transactions—greed. If men are greedy, differentially endowed with ability, intelligence and energy, and allowed to utilise their different capacities freely, then (even supposing an initial equality in the goods of fortune) the free operation of the market will produce an unequal distribution of wealth.

For England, as well as for the other societies mentioned, the 'possessive market' model is too commercial and too egalitarian. It takes no account of social and legal privilege; it ignores the elaborate social hierarchy of graded ranks and orders: each man deferring to superiors and expecting deference from his inferiors according to his position in the social order.[2]

To be perverse, one might easily argue that the model of the 'deferential society' rather than the 'possessive market society' is to be discovered in, or extracted from, the parts of *Leviathan* in which Hobbes discusses valuing. Deference or honouring manifests the value at which one man rates another. 'To Value a man at a high rate, is to *Honour* him; at a low rate, is to *Dishonour* him. But high, and low, in this case, is to

---

[1] For descriptions of seventeenth-century English society, see P. Laslett, *The World we Have Lost* (London, 1965), especially pp. 22–52, and Lawrence Stone, *The Crisis of the Aristocracy, 1558–1641* (Oxford, 1964), pp. 21–270.

[2] See Lawrence Stone, *The Crisis of the Aristocracy*, pp. 21–64. For the political theory of order see W. H. Greenleaf, *Order, Empiricism and Politics: Two Traditions of English Political Thought, 1500–1700* (London, 1964), pp. 14–57, and J. G. A. Pocock, '"The onely politician"; Machiavelli, Harrington and Felix Raab', *Historical Studies: Australia and New Zealand*, XII (1966), 265–96.

But although wealth may (ultimately) buy social status, position and power in society may procure riches; see R. Dahrendorf, 'On the origin of social inequality', in P. Laslett and W. G. Runciman (eds.), *Philosophy, Politics and Society II* (Oxford, 1962), pp. 100–5.

For a thorough discussion of the social significance of Hobbes's thought, see Keith Thomas, 'The social origins of Hobbes's political thought', in K. C. Brown (ed.), *Hobbes Studies*, pp. 185–236.

be understood by comparison to the rate that each man setteth on himselfe.'[1] In addition to the state's valuing of a man, indicated by his offices, titles and decorations, Hobbes describes an extensive list of ways in which men can honour or disparage others.[2] Some are peculiarly appropriate for deferring to a superior: asking for aid, imitating, giving place, obeying. Others are ways in which superiors can show their appreciation for inferiors: employing them, listening to them, promoting their good, giving them large, rather than trifling, gifts.

Gifts and gratuities are indeed one way in which a deferential society differs from a market society. In the former, the great distribute largesse to their inferiors and gifts to their equals; in a market society these actions simply squander capital (except when charitable donations reduce one's taxes or when bribes are part of the bargain—but in this case the briber must account the bribe part of the purchase price rather than a gift). A commercial gift, or bribe, is the amount sufficient to secure the benefit sought, but a deferential society requires a more elaborate calculation which takes into account the relative social positions of donor and recipient.

To have received from one, to whom we think our selves equall, greater benefits than there is hope to Requite, disposeth to counterfeit love; but really secret hatred; and puts a man into the estate of a desperate debtor, that in declining the sight of his creditor, tacitely wishes him there, where he might never see him more. For benefits oblige; and obligation is thraldome; and unrequitable obligation, perpetuall thraldome; which is to ones equall, hatefull. But to have received benefits from one, whom we acknowledge for superiour, enclines to love; because the obligation is no new depression: and cheerfull acceptation, (which men call *Gratitude*,) is such an honour done to the obliger, as is taken generally for retribution. Also to receive benefits, though from an equall, or inferiour, as long as there is hope of requitall, disposeth to love: for in the intention of the receiver, the obligation is of ayd, and service mutuall; from whence proceedeth an Emulation of who shall exceed in benefiting; wherein the victor is pleased with his victory, and the other revenged by confessing it.[3]

Competition—often literally cut-throat—prevails in a deferential society, as Pastons, Cavendishes, Bacons, or what you will, try to claw their way to the top of the heap.[4] The successful social climbers acquire titles of honour in the process; honorific embellishments which no longer designate public officers but which serve 'to distinguish the precedence, place, and order of subjects in the Common-wealth'.[5]

---

[1] *Leviathan* (10), p. 68. N.B., the comparison is to the individual's conception of his due and not to his market price.   [2] *Ibid.* pp. 68–9   [3] *Ibid.* (11), pp. 76–7.

[4] See J. Gairdner (ed.), *The Paston Letters* (4 vols.; Westminster, 1900), *passim*; Stone, *The Crisis of the Aristocracy*; Alan Simpson, *The Wealth of the Gentry, 1540–1660* (Chicago and Cambridge, 1961).   [5] *Leviathan* (10), p. 74.

From *Leviathan* the model of a deferential society can be extracted. (1) Society is an ordered and continuous chain of status positions. (2) Each position has a known relation to other positions in the order, and each position is recognizable by its occupants and by others. (3) Recognition of another's superiority is outwardly expressed in deference; the social order is an order of honour. (4) Favour will be sought, and service rewarded, with gifts and gratuities which must be proportioned to the positions of the donor and the recipient as well as to their purpose. (5) No absolute barrier to rising or falling in the social hierarchy exists. The society is graded but it is not a caste system; the barriers may be high or low. For example, a wealthy yeoman needs merely to change his style of life to become a gentleman; the cottager may in favourable circumstances become a husbandman or even a farmer; the peerage is recruited from the gentry and is intermarried with it. But wealth alone is not enough: Eliza Doolittle with money would be nothing but a wealthy flower-seller. Partly because of their wealth and power, upstarts like Cardinal Wolsey and Archbishop Laud were objects of social snobbery. The folklore of a deferential society will celebrate Dick Whittington, a proto Horatio Alger hero, but it may inculcate social quietism as well—the fisherman discovered that his wife, discontented with her fish-wife's life, was equally discontented as duchess, queen, or empress.

To extract the model of a deferential society from Hobbes's *Leviathan* does not demonstrate that the 'possessive market society' is not to be found there too. But if the discovery of the 'deferential society' in this part of *Leviathan* is convincing, then any claim that the 'possessive market society' is the exclusive, sole, and singular model Hobbes used is untenable.

The 'deferential society' is a dubious structure extracted by a doubly partial reading of the text—it is derived from a few passages read with the intent of confirming that hypothesis. But the 'possessive market society', however monolithic it seems, is also founded upon this shaky rock.

The *Value*, or WORTH of a man, is as of all other things, his Price; that is to say, so much as would be given for the use of his Power: and therefore is not absolute; but a thing dependant on the need and judgement of another... And as in other things, so in men, not the seller, but the buyer determines the Price. For let a man (as most men do,) rate themselves at the highest Value they can; yet their true Value is no more than it is esteemed by others.[1]

This passage does not establish a market in labour. It is ambiguous; for in a truly competitive market a man's price is not dependent on the need and judgment of another; it is not the price the buyer will give

[1] *Leviathan* (10), p. 67.

but the market price—established for each buyer and seller independently of their individual desires by the impersonal mechanism of the market composed of many buyers and sellers. A bargain about a price struck between buyer and seller does not make a market; it is merely a single contract. Furthermore, in a 'possessive market society' the objective exemplification of value is price. Nevertheless Hobbes goes on to say not that the manifestation of each man's value is price but rather, 'The manifestation of the Value we set on one another, is that which is commonly called Honouring, and Dishonouring'.[1]

Did Hobbes then assume, perhaps unconsciously, the model of a 'deferential society' in addition to or instead of that of a 'possessive market society' in the discussions of man prior to the introduction of the model of the state of nature? I doubt that an exclusive and consistent model of society was used by Hobbes in that discussion. It seems to me to be an attempt to cover as extensive a range of human behaviour as possible.[2]

The theory that Hobbes assumed a possessive market society which he then resolved into a model of non-society, the state of nature, would be strengthened if some elements of possessiveness remained after Hobbes's Galilean analysis or if some were introduced in the reconsitution of society.

Hobbes's accounts of the laws of nature and of the institution of society in *De Cive* and *Leviathan* are dominated by his insistence on the necessary equality of men and their complete submission to the sovereign. They are lucky to get out of the state of nature with a whole skin; they seek continued life rather than the security of any natural rights to property.

If only Hobbes had provided a natural right to acquire property rather than the barren right to all things, if only he had included some rule about commerce among the laws of nature, would not the case that he assumed a 'possessive market society' be improved?

But Hobbes explicitly provided both these things. Both are to be found in the earliest extant version of what later became *De Cive* and *Leviathan*, viz. *The Elements of Law, Natural and Politic*. There he says:
'It is also a law of nature, *That men allow commerce and traffic indifferently to one another.*'[3]

The reason Hobbes gives is that denial of equal treatment declares hatred and war. Whatever its justification, the rule provides one of the classic elements of the free market: trade is open to all comers.

---

[1] *Ibid.* p. 68. Cf. Macpherson, *The Political Theory of Possessive Individualism*, pp. 37–40.

[2] Compare *De Corpore* (xvi, 1–5), *EW*, I, 218–27, where Hobbes gives formulae for a series of possible varieties of accelerated motions only one of which will later be used as the mathematical formula for falling bodies.

[3] *Elements of Law* (I, xvi, 12), p. 87. Macpherson does not seem to mention this passage or the following one.

But in later versions this rule has been absorbed into the more general rule that men are not to indicate hatred or contempt by word, deed, countenance or gesture.[1]

Moreover, Hobbes at one time believed that men could rightfully acquire different amounts of property in the state of nature—and that they would bring this property into society with them. The earliest version of the *Elements of Law* provides just such a possessory right among the laws of nature:

Of the law of nature also it is: that entering into peace every man be allowed those rights which he hath acquired by the covenants of others. That is to say, right against him that hath covenanted. And this law is no more in effect, but that the peace which a man entereth into, discharge not the covenants made unto him by others; else is not that equality kept which the law of nature requireth. And men had rather keep their own advantages with the hazard of war, than lose them by unequal peace, unless all others do the like. And therefore in the first making of peace, the law of nature teacheth, that every man ought to hold that which he once hath lawfully and without controversy possessed, or solely used.[2]

Hobbes struck out this passage. He replaced it with a briefer statement in another version: 'Another, that men entering into peace retain what they have acquired.'[3] But this passage too was struck out, leaving only a provision for equal right: each is to allow others what he demands for himself. The only irreducible claim of right each man brings into society is the right to defend his life with its consequent rights to air, water, fire, and place to live—the necessities of life.[4] And in the final version of this passage in *Leviathan* men are forbidden rights they will not allow to others, but allowed to retain the right to the necessities of life.[5]

The course of Hobbes's thought exhibits a process of abstraction until he arrived at a formulation of the rule so general that it is impossible to tell whether men legitimately acquire things in the state of nature or not. The radical dissolution of position and property into the equality of the state of nature has as its counterpart the absolute power of the sovereign both as the source of property and the fountain of honour.[6]

---

[1] See *De Cive* (iii, 12), *EW*, II, 38, and *Leviathan* (15), p. 117. For a brief comparison of Hobbes's various formulations of the laws of nature, see my *Hobbes's Science of Politics*, pp. 245–7.

[2] *Elements of Law* (I, xviii, 3), p. 89 n. This copy, which Tönnies called 'H' is now catalogued 'A₂B' in the Hobbes papers at Chatsworth.

[3] *Ibid.* This is Tönnies 'A', British Museum Harleian MSS, 4235.

[4] *Ibid.* (I, xvii, 2), p. 88.   [5] *Leviathan* (15), p. 118. See *De Cive* (iii, 14), *EW*, II, 39–40.

[6] *Leviathan* (18), pp. 137, 138–9. The only contradiction to the sovereign's power over property rights occurs at *Leviathan* (24), p. 191: the sovereign may not redistribute the land it has already parcelled out. But this passage is dropped in the later Latin version: *LW*, III, 186–7.

The analysis of Hobbes, which sees him having unconscious Marxist tendencies because he assumed the model of a possessive market society, is a difficult one to sustain. The possessive market model cannot be regarded as unique or exclusive for at least one other social model can be constructed from the same materials. The history of Hobbes's mental development seems to support the view that he lost or sublimated the tendencies toward possessive individualism he once possessed.

If Hobbes did not suffer from a modernity complex and if he was not subject to unconscious Marxist tendencies, how is he to be explained? A third deep analysis has been proposed by Howard Warrender.

Warrender takes up one of the knottiest of Hobbes problems, that of obligation. A simple brief outline of Hobbes's argument exhibits the problem: stimulated by their fear of each other and by desire for a better condition, men are motivated to seek a way out of the state of nature. Discovering the laws of nature, men agree, covenanting each one with every other, to give up their natural right to all things and to nominate and to obey a single authorised representative of them all, an individual or a collective sovereign. (Alternatively, each may submit to a conqueror as an individual.) The sovereign promulgates laws, specifies punishments, and appoints officials to adjudicate disputes, enforce the laws, and punish violators of them. Thus social standards of conduct are enforced: conforming subjects are protected in their rights against violators of these norms.

To the question of any subject 'why should I obey the laws or the sovereign?' Hobbes seems to give several answers. First, obey because it is better for you to do so. Disobedience will be followed by punishment; disobedience, if general, would return men to the state of nature. Both consequences are undesirable, therefore obey. Second, obey because in your covenants to your fellow-citizens or in your covenant of submission to the sovereign, you have promised to obey. Third, obey because God has commanded you to obey, for the laws of nature are the laws of God; moreover, obedience is commanded in Scripture. (Hobbes carefully showed that his doctrines were consistent with and confirmed by Scripture.)[1]

On Professor Warrender's view, this account is inadequate. The first reason (it is beneficial to obey) describes not a moral obligation but a prudential calculation. The second is inadequate because it describes the instruments for undertaking obligations but not the grounds of the obligations undertaken. What makes covenants and laws oblige? The laws of nature. Then why aren't these laws obliging in the state of nature? Warrender argues that they are obliging but that their opera-

[1] *Elements of Law* (i, xviii, ii, vi, vii), pp. 95–9, 144–67; *De Cive* (iv, xi, xv–xix), *EW*, ii, 50–62, 143–9, 203–319; *Leviathan* (32–47), pp. 286–546.

tion is suspended whenever certain validating conditions have not been met. Only the second reason (as revised) and the third reason indicate possible grounds of moral obligation.[1]

Unless Hobbes is identified as Spinoza, unless he held that moral obligation and self-interest are the same and that one's right is equal to one's power, and excluding the possibility that he was utterly confused, Hobbes must have had some moral theory. Hobbes's moral theory must account for men's obligations to obey civil laws, the civil sovereign, the laws of nature, and even God. Warrender will not allow a miraculous appearance of obligation only in civil society, for obligations in civil society are clearly dependent on a prior obligation to follow the laws of nature. At every level of Hobbes's discussion obligation is the central problem: Hobbes had an obligation fixation.

According to Professor Warrender, there are three possible explanations of the ultimate ground of obligation which are to some degree supported in Hobbes's discussion: obligation may be based upon salvation, on the will of God, or upon a self-evident natural law.[2] The first alternative is that the laws of nature are to be obeyed because men ought to act in the manner best calculated to attain salvation. To obey in the hope of this promised reward is a form of self-interest, but it is the highest form.[3]

The second alternative is that the laws of nature are to be obeyed simply because it is the will of God that they be obeyed.[4] God is our supreme sovereign and his commands are to be followed.

The third possibility is that the laws of nature are to be obeyed simply because they are rationally necessary. That Hobbes regarded them as the commands of God merely provides a formal termination to his theory in which every law must have some commander. Since Hobbes did not recognise the laws of nature as ultimate moral principles, self-evidently authentic, this alternative is the weakest of the three.[5] It seems that we must accept one or the other of the first two explanations: Hobbes's identity has been revealed—he is a traditional natural law theorist and perhaps an orthodox Christian.[6]

Before we accept this curious result perhaps we could devise some test to check it. Since Hobbes has been more commonly described as an atheist than as a Christian natural law theorist, I propose to examine the answers to a variation on the obligation question: 'Why should one obey God?' Three answers have been suggested:

(1) 'Obey God because the sovereign has ordered you to.' The

---

[1] See Warrender, *The Political Philosophy of Hobbes*, especially pp. 13–29, 266–329.
[2] *Ibid.* p. 311.   [3] *Ibid.* pp. 278–98.
[4] *Ibid.* pp. 299–311.   [5] *Ibid.* pp. 251, 311.
[6] See Hood, *The Divine Politics of Thomas Hobbes*, pp. 13, 22–40.

sovereign has established by law a church, promulgated and interpreted the laws of nature, and formulated a profession of faith. Since
the subject is obliged to obey the sovereign, he is obliged to accept the
sovereign's determination about religion, opinion, and worship. Hobbes
specifically mentions the sovereign's right to regulate these things.[1]

The solution is attractive—partly because Hobbes occasionally seems
to adopt it. He at least urges men to accept the religion established in
their states. Adopting this form of extreme Erastianism involves allowing
Christianity no greater respect than any other religion; Hobbes would
have to deny that a Christian has a right to refuse obedience even to
a command to abjure his religion. Although Hobbes comes close to
this position when he holds that a Christian has the liberty to conform
his actions while retaining his inner belief, he grudgingly recognises that
some few men may have a revealed duty to preach to infidels which
conflicts with their duty to obey the civil laws. (Such a conflict cannot
exist in a Christian society, for there church and commonwealth are
identical.)[2]

Even if Hobbes's recognition of the special position of Christianity is
disallowed as disingenuous or as inconsistent with his general principles,
this first solution would leave an obligation problem unresolved. It
would require an account of why subjects are obliged to obey the civil
sovereign which did not rely on an obligation to obey God.

(2) 'Obey God because you are obliged by your own higher self-
interest in attaining eternal rewards and avoiding eternal punishments.'
There is at least one passage in Hobbes which seems strongly to support
this solution.

Every man by nature (without discipline) does in all his actions look upon,
as far as he can see, the benefit which shall redound to himself from his
obedience. He reads that covetousness is the root of all evil; but he thinks,
and sometimes finds, it is the root of his estate. And so in other cases, the
Scripture says one thing, and they think another, weighing the commodities
and incommodities of this present life only, which are in their sight, never
putting into the scales the good and evil of the life to come, which they
see not.[3]

If one's obligations are grounded upon considering the consequences
of one's actions for a future life (salvation or damnation), one must first
know what those consequences will be. Knowledge of a future life could
be either naturally acquired in the same way that men acquire knowledge about the other consequences of their actions or it could be revealed to men through some divine agency. Although some eminent

---

[1] *Leviathan* (18, 26, 42), pp. 136–7, 220–2, 421–8.
[2] *Leviathan* (31, 39, 42), pp. 283, 362, 387–90.
[3] *Behemoth*, ed. F. Tönnies (London, 1889), p. 54.

thinkers have asserted that men could know naturally of a future life or have found a proof of the soul's immortality convincing, Hobbes is not one of them. He quite explicitly denies the possibility of any natural knowledge of future rewards and punishments.

> There be some that proceed further; and will not have the Law of Nature, to be those Rules which conduce to the preservation of mans life on earth; but to the attaining of an eternall felicity after death...But because there is no naturall knowledge of mans estate after death; much lesse of the reward that is then to be given to breach of Faith [the example being discussed]; but onely a beliefe grounded upon other mens saying, that they know it supernaturally, or that they know those, that knew them, that knew others, that knew it supernaturally; Breach of Faith cannot be called a Precept of Reason, or Nature.[1]

Natural knowledge of any sort of eternal rewards and punishments being excluded, any obligation to act for salvation and to avoid damnation must be based on revealed knowledge. All Hobbes's references to future rewards and punishments, heaven and hell, and the life to come (as in the quotation from *Behemoth* above) explicitly rely on and interpret what is revealed in Scripture. But revelation is not binding on all men; it binds only those to whom it is revealed, members of God's prophetic (not natural) kingdom.[2]

If men's obligation to obey God and God's laws is grounded on a revealed knowledge of future rewards and punishments, then those who have not received any such revelation (viz. all but Christians, Jews, and perhaps Moslems) would not be bound; they would stand outside natural law. (Even St Thomas did not believe this.)

Hobbes did not argue that those outside a revealed religion could have no obligations to obey natural law and their sovereigns. On the contrary, he emphasises the continued rights of civil sovereigns to their subjects' obedience after they have become Christian.[3]

By emphasising the duty of subjects not to accept the claims of preachers unauthorised by the sovereign, and by emphasising the right of Christians to scrutinise closely enthusiastic pronouncements and pretended miracles, Hobbes encourages scepticism about all claims to

---

[1] *Leviathan* (15), p. 113.

[2] *Leviathan* (31, 35, 36, 40, 41, 42), pp. 275, 314–5, 317, 319–20, 334–7, 369–74, 377–8, 386–8. Hobbes discusses the prophetic kingdom of God in Parts III and IV of *Leviathan*. The Kingdom of God is a kingdom properly so called, originally constituted by a covenant of the Jews and later renewed with Christians. The subjects of this kingdom were bound to obey first Moses and his successors who possessed complete civil and religious sovereignty and later, after Christ, their civil sovereigns. Men are obliged to acknowledge as authentic whatever revelation the Christian sovereign commands and they are never obliged to acknowledge as authentic any private man's supposed revelation. See also *Leviathan* (40, 42), pp. 368, 386–90, 401, 421–5, 427–8.

[3] *Leviathan* (42), pp. 421–2.

revelation. How can one be sure of another's revelation which is most likely to be a self-delusion or an attempt to delude others?

One possibility remains open. If others' revelations are unreliable, what about a general revelation to each individual. But Hobbes excludes this possibility too.

As for Sense Supernaturall, which consisteth in Revelation, or Inspiration, there have not been any Universall Lawes so given, because God speaketh not in that manner, but to particular persons, and to divers men divers things.[1]

Obligation to God cannot be based on salvation and damnation. God's eternal rewards and punishments are not known naturally, nor are they known to each man by an individual revelation. They are known only in God's prophetic kingdom—that is, they are known only to men who are obliged to accept some interpretation of God's word because they have covenanted into that society.

(3) 'Obey God because he is God and you are men.' It is God's will that men obey and God's right is established by his irresistible power.

This may seem to be no explanation at all, but a merely circular reassertion. 'Why am I obliged to obey God? Because he is God.' Nevertheless Hobbes commends the argument of the book of Job and bases God's right on his irresistible power.[2]

However close Hobbes comes to this position, he does not in the end accept it. Irresistible power is the basis of God's right. But God's right does not imply any obligations of men to obey, for, as Professor Warrender has shown, rights and duties are not correlative in Hobbes.[3] If all men were obliged to obey God simply because he is God all men would be God's subjects and those who disobeyed would be subject to punishment. Hobbes did not think that all men are God's subjects. Atheists deny that they are God's subjects, for they do not even recognise his existence. And Hobbes accepts their denial of subjection while rejecting their claim to escape punishment. Atheists are legitimately afflicted not as subjects but as enemies of God.[4]

Since some men (atheists) are not obliged to obey God—even though they are subject to his power, men are not obliged to obey God simply because he is God, nor are they obliged to obey his commands simply because he so wills it.

If these three explanations are inadequate, they why should one obey God?

Hobbes does give an answer to these questions. By closely examining the universe, using the correct Galilean method, men may discover

---

[1] *Leviathan* (31), p. 275.   [2] *Ibid.* pp. 276–7.
[3] Warrender, *The Political Philosophy of Hobbes*, pp. 18–20.
[4] *De Cive* (xiv, 19), *EW*, II, 198–9; cf. *Leviathan* (31), pp. 274–5.

that it is a world of uniformly necessary causation. Science shows men a causal world. Although they cannot think their way back through the chain of causes to the first cause, and although they cannot imagine the nature of that first cause, yet men can arrive at the necessity of a first, eternal moving cause. Men can know that there is a God who is the guarantor of a necessary causal system.[1]

On this theory the laws of nature are more than merely moral injunctions. The laws of nature are hypothetical statements relating causes to effects; they may be invoked like statements in any other science to predict the consequences of actions under certain circumstances. Similarly the sanctions for 'violating' these laws are like the sanctions for 'violating' the other causal laws. If you don't want to take a nasty tumble, you don't step off a cliff. If you don't want to be killed in the general mêlée, you make sure that the laws of nature are followed by establishing a society. The sanctions for not obeying the laws of nature are the caused consequences of one's own actions.

There is no action of man in this life, that is not the beginning of so long a chayn of Consequences, as no humane Providence, is high enough, to give a man a prospect to the end. And in this Chayn, there are linked together both pleasing and unpleasing events; in such manner, as he that will do any thing for his pleasure, must engage himselfe to suffer all the pains annexed to it; and these pains, are the Naturall Punishments of those actions, which are the beginning of more Harme than Good. And hereby it comes to passe, that Intemperance, is naturally punished with Diseases; Rashnesse, with Mischances; Injustice, with the Violence of Enemies; Pride, with Ruine; Cowardise, with Oppression; Negligent government of Princes, with Rebellion; and Rebellion, with Slaughter. For seeing Punishments are consequent to the breach of Lawes; Naturall Punishments must be naturally consequent to the breach of the Lawes of Nature; and therfore follow them as their naturall, not arbitrary effects.[2]

God, the first cause, does not need the arbitrary effects of heaven and hell to enforce the laws of nature; his natural punishments are built into the causal order.

When men understand that the world is an order of necessary causes, then they realise that they cannot escape from God's power no matter what they do. 'Whether men will or not, they must be subject alwayes to the Divine Power. By denying the Existence, or Providence of God, men may shake off their Ease, but not their Yoke.'[3]

Those who deny God's existence or providence do not understand the nature of the world. The atheist is a fool who cannot escape God's

---

[1] *Leviathan* (11, 12), pp. 80–1, 83; *De Corpore* (xxvi, 1), *EW*, I, 411–12; *Elements of Law* (I, xi, 2), pp. 53–4. [2] *Leviathan* (31), p. 284.
[3] *Ibid.* p. 274; cf. *De Cive* (xv, 2), *EW*, II, 204–5.

power although he has no obligation to him, for '*he never submitted his will to God's will*'.[1]

When a man understands the nature of the universe, he realises that he cannot escape God's power. His comprehension of his own weakness in relation to God amounts to an intellectual submission in which he acknowledges God's power. Hobbes calls this the kind of natural obligation where liberty

is taken away by hope or fear, according to which the weaker, despairing of his own power to resist, cannot but yield to [*non potest non obedire*] the stronger. From this last kind of [natural] obligation, that is to say, from fear or conscience of our own weakness in respect of the divine power, it comes to pass that we are obliged to obey God in his natural kingdom; reason dictating to all, acknowledging the divine power and providence [*dictante scilicet ratione omnibus Dei potentiam et providentiam agnoscentibus*], that there is no kicking against the pricks.[2]

By understanding the nature of the world, a man becomes conscious of his own weakness in relation to God and his causal order. His realisation that he is subject to God and to God's natural laws and natural punishments is an act of submission to God. Men are obliged to obey God in the same way they are obliged to a sovereign, to keep a covenant, or gratefully to requite benefits accepted—in every case they are obliged by their own acts of covenanting, submitting, or accepting, 'there being no Obligation on any man, which ariseth not from some Act of his own'.[3]

The ground of obligation in Hobbes then is: One can only be bound by one's own act. The act may be one of covenanting, of accepting a benefit, of submitting to a conqueror (or to his society), or of making an intellectual submission to God.

There is one more objection to identifying Hobbes primarily as a victim of an obligation fixation. Hobbes did contend that more than

---

[1] *De Cive* (xiv, 19), *EW*, II, 98.

[2] *De Cive* (xv, 7), *EW*, II, 207, *LW*, II, 336–7. And see Hobbes's interpretation of this passage in *An Answer to Bishop Bramhall*, *EW*, IV, 294–5: 'In the seventh paragraph of chapter xv. of my book *De Cive*, he found the words in Latin, which he here citeth. And to the same sense I have said in my *Leviathan*, that the right of nature whereby God reigneth over men, is to be derived not from his creating them, as if he required obedience, as of gratitude; but from his irresistible power. This he says is absurd and dishonourable. Whereas first all power is honourable, and the greatest power is most honourable. Is it not a more noble tenure for a king to hold his kingdom, and the right to punish those that transgress his laws, from his power, than from the gratitude or gift of the transgressor. There is nothing therefore here of dishonour to God Almighty. But see the subtilty of his disputing. He saw he could not catch *Leviathan* in this place, he looks for him in my book *De Cive*, which is Latin, to try what he could fish out of that: and says I make our obedience to God, depend upon our weakness; as if these words signified the *dependence*, and not the *necessity* of our submission, or that *incumbere* and *dependere* were all one.'

[3] *Leviathan* (21), p. 166.

moral obligation was necessary were men to live in peace and comfort. Merely moral obligation left them in the state of nature; they had to be tied to their obligations by the coercive power of the sovereign.

None of the three deep analyses of Hobbes's identity has proved satisfactory. Each identification turned out to be markedly peculiar to the analyst. By emphasising a particular characteristic, each imposed a strange and narrow consistency upon Hobbes. Nevertheless, examination of these interpretations does support some conclusions. Hobbes's acceptance of science was not merely superficial; analytic-synthetic method, with its concomitant mechanical materialism, was the basis of his philosophic system. He applied this method to the explanation of man and society as well as to the explanation of nature. It underlay his analysis of society into the state of nature and his synthetic reconstitution of it by means of 'scientific' laws of nature. It provides the basis not only for his account of political obligation but also for his explanation of men's obligations to God.

However, I do not think that interpreters of Hobbes are entirely like the members of Mr Dennis's identity club; at least they have not begun to make up their cases merely to illustrate their theories. By examining their analyses, and especially by discovering where they have gone wrong, we can learn about Hobbes. The interpreters contribute to our understanding of Hobbes, but only if we take the trouble to listen to what they have to say about him. Then we realise that the discussion is not a debate which some win and others lose, but a conversation in which all who participate gain.

IDEALISM,
MODERN PHILOSOPHY
AND POLITICS

W. H. GREENLEAF

In one of his notebooks, Wittgenstein wrote that it is possible to try to jump over too wide chasms of thought and so to fall in. This essay is in the nature of such a leap, for it follows up the suggestion that there is a certain affinity between philosophical idealism and modern linguistic philosophy, two manners of thinking that are usually supposed to be far apart. The main area of comparison is political ideas and the analysis will concentrate on the work of Oakeshott and Weldon, who are taken to represent the two styles of thought as applied to this field. This examination is followed by some scattered observations of similar but more general aspects of the parallel. It is all, I confess, a little sketchy, but may lead to fuller enquiry elsewhere.

First, I must state, baldly, how the more important terms of the discussion are used and say a little about the nature of the gulf said to exist between contemporary philosophy and idealism.

By idealism I mean the manner of thinking most fully elaborated by Hegel and which, in this country, has been reflected in the writings of, for example, Green, Bosanquet, Bradley, Muirhead and Collingwood. The reason each exponent had for espousing this mode of thought varied. Often it was the possibility of restating in what seemed to be satisfactory philosophical terms the truths of religion, or of art, or sometimes of history. Basically, the appeal of idealism was that, while not denying the significance of science or the pragmatic maxims of everyday life, it also found a place at least as, if not more, important for these other categories. In the same fashion, the exact way in which this style of thought was developed in each case was never the same. Green's preoccupation with moral absolutes hardly appears in, say, Bradley or Collingwood; and Oakeshott's great concern with the autonomy of history is not shared by McTaggart. Nevertheless, amid all the diversities there is a certain unity of manner which is really a theory of judgment, knowledge, and experience, and a conception of rationality which envisages the cumulative achievement of successive levels of understanding which are at once wider, deeper, and more coherent than any which have gone before.

By contemporary or modern philosophy, I mean the various current styles of linguistic analysis which, on the whole, now dominate professional philosophy in this country.[1] As with any so-called 'school' of philosophy, there is no absolute conformity or norm and it embraces men who often differ markedly in their manner and interests. But, of course, I take the term to cover the writings of people like Wisdom, Ryle, Wittgenstein, Austin, Hampshire and Hare. And I imagine they would agree, despite their often significant differences, that many of the traditional problems of philosophy arise from certain features of our language and from its misuse (being misled by words, being trapped into empty verbal argument, failing to make proper distinctions or to observe ambiguities, looking for 'things' behind words where none exists, and so on). The first task of philosophy (seen in these terms) is to lay bare and eliminate such confusions by an examination of ordinary concepts and their logic, a job which is not so simple as it might seem, because the conventions of everyday speech are so very complex. Beyond this intellectually therapeutic level, more systematic examination of the same kind may be undertaken for its own sake. It is true that there are present-day thinkers who are not (in the sense here stated) 'modern philosophers' and who do not adhere wholly or at all to one or other of the dominant points of view, but (in Britain at least) they are few in number, their voices are either little heard or heeded, and they are invariably dismissed as eccentric or out-dated.

Indeed, one opinion shared by a good many modern philosophers is that idealism (the philosophical orthodoxy of the day before yesterday) is a mode of thinking to be firmly, even vituperatively, rejected. A typical reflection of this critical and depreciatory spirit can be found in Mr G. J. Warnock's *English Philosophy since 1900*. His comments upon idealism are put in remarkably careless form and indicate an almost complete lack of historical sense and sympathy, but there is little doubt that they typify the usual present-day reaction.[2] I recall, too, the foolish

---

[1] Modern philosophy in this sense is to be distinguished from logical positivism, for it is not explicitly wedded to the 'verification principle' as a criterion of meaning. Indeed, a distinguishing feature is the rejection of the central positivist doctrine that to be meaningful is to be either factually descriptive or analytic.

[2] Some contemporary philosophers, though sensitive to outspoken criticism of themselves, are often not very guarded in the language they use about others. While conceding that idealism did not exactly perish by refutation, Mr Warnock manages to suggest that it was a misleading, if not improper, style of thought. Yet:

(a) His accusation of high-flown metaphysical ambitions fails to draw the elementary distinction between (to use Professor Walsh's terms) a transcendental and an immanent metaphysics; the idealists are as critical as most of dogmatic rationalist metaphysics of the former kind.

(b) His suggestion that idealism is dissatisfied with common and current ways of thinking is deceptive. These modes are only rejected as the sole and exclusive categories of thought.

(c) His characterisation of idealists as concerned to establish some 'ultimate unshake-

remark (attributed to Professor Ryle) that Hegel does not deserve study even as error.

But this situation and attitude are misleading, for they obscure most manifest similarities between the manner of the modern philosophers and that of the despised idealists. As Mr Mure put it, this manner bears the bar sinister on its escutcheon. The rest of this essay is devoted to observing this affinity in one or two respects. It is not, of course, that there are no differences; but these have been observed to excess and it is time to shift the focus of attention to the areas of similarity and common assumption.

I

A start may be made by looking at the ways in which, in the context of each attitude, analysis of political activity and thought is carried on. For the purpose of this comparison, I take the writings of the late T. D. Weldon to embody a general statement of the appropriate stance to adopt in the light of linguistic analysis, and those of Professor Oakeshott to reflect the idealist point of view. Perhaps something should be said about this choice of instances because their representative character may be queried.

With the modern philosophers, there is the difficulty that, on the whole, they do not discuss the practical problems of everyday life which ordinary language reflects nor do they seem very interested in trying to isolate the logical form of a political judgment. From time to time, as if in an access of bad conscience, some of them do wonder about the causes of this neglect (though some of the reasons proposed are distinctly odd) and if and how it might be remedied.[1] Yet, whatever factors are at work, it clearly remains the case that there are few modern philosophers who have dealt at any length with the logic of political discourse as a

---

able [sic] basis for ethics' is true of some, but not of all of them; not, for instance, of Bradley or Collingwood or Oakeshott. Idealists have had a great deal to say about the logic of ethical understanding and the various levels which ethical reason achieves, but I would have thought that, in this way, the flexibility, the relativity even, of their conclusions was most noticeable.

(d) His dislike of their literary style is a matter of taste: in this respect I personally prefer, say, Collingwood to Mr Warnock and certainly do not think that most modern philosophers are outstandingly lucid.

(e) Mr Warnock is right about the novelty of philosophical idealism but, typically, misses the point: it could hardly have emerged until the conditions for its cultivation (in particular the growth of genuine historical understanding) were present; and it was not so alien a growth as he implies—both Green and Oakeshott, for instance, often remind one of Hume.

No, Mr Warnock's critical review of idealism is hardly well-conceived. May we dispense with this kind of attack in future? May we?

[1] See, e.g., I. Murdoch, 'A house of theory', in N. Mackenzie (ed.), *Conviction* (London, 1958), pp. 224–5; R. Wollheim, 'Philosophie analytique et pensée politique', *Revue française de Science Politique*, XI (1961), 295–308; B. Williams and A. Montefiore (eds.), *British Analytical Philosophy* (London, 1966), intro., pp. 14–16; D. F. Pears (ed.), *The Nature of Metaphysics* (London, 1962), pp. 159–62.

whole and its problems. Of course, Mr Hare has discussed the matter of moral utterance (and raised some very interesting questions in so doing);[1] Professor Hart, and others, have examined in detail the concept of law and cognate topics; and various piece-meal analyses of specific ideas have been undertaken, of sovereignty and the state, of freedom, equality, democracy, justice, rights and so on. Nevertheless Mr Weldon's treatment is, I fancy, the only *general* inquiry into the vocabulary of politics and the logic of its concepts, and it is because of this that I here deal with it as such. His work has indeed been received as a key statement of the modern style of philosophy as applied to politics;[2] and his commitment to the new techniques of inquiry is undoubted. Thus, he begins his best-known book by stating that its theme is essentially bound up with the development of modern philosophy and its preoccupation with the way in which problems arise from 'the eccentricities of the language in which we try to describe the world'.[3] Weldon holds that the basic mistakes made in 'classical' (that is, traditional-type) political philosophy were caused by 'carelessness over the implications of language' and by adherence to an erroneous 'central doctrine' about the meaning of words.[4] So his analysis of political discourse is explicitly founded on the advance in linguistic understanding which constitutes the revolution in thought associated with modern philosophy.

Although, therefore, my choice is to some extent forced by the paucity of material, I feel justified in taking Weldon as representative of the dominant contemporary view.

So far as the modern idealists are concerned, there is also little choice, but for the quite different reason that there are now so few who adhere to this style of thought. Its major figures have nearly all disappeared from the scene and have not been replaced. Bradley, Bosanquet and McTaggart died in the 1920s, Muirhead and Collingwood during the last war, and there remain only a few lone figures among whom are Sir Malcolm Knox and G. R. G. Mure. But Oakeshott is pre-eminent among this dwindling band. He has explicitly stated that, in the formation of his views, he owed most to the idealist tradition, specifically to Hegel and Bradley;[5] and I have suggested elsewhere that every aspect of his thought is most appropriately seen in this intellectual context.[6]

---

[1] See below, pp. 122–3.
[2] See, e.g., A. Quinton, 'Linguistic analysis', *La Philosophie au Milieu du xxᵉ Siècle*, II (1958), 194–5, and Murdoch, *loc. cit.* p. 225.
[3] T. D. Weldon *The Vocabulary of Politics* (London, 1953), p. 9.
[4] *Ibid.* pp. 11, 17–20. Cf. 'Political principles', in P. Laslett (ed.), *Philosophy, Politics and Society* (1st ser., Oxford, 1956), pp. 22–3.
[5] *Experience and its Modes* (Cambridge, 1933), p. 6.
[6] See my *Oakeshott's Philosophical Politics* (London, 1966), esp. chapters I–II.

Indeed, with the exception of the works of Collingwood, Oakeshott's writings constitute the most recent wide-ranging statement to appear in this country of the idealist philosophy and its political and other implications.

For this kind of reason, then, I shall treat the works of Oakeshott and Weldon as representative of these two points of view and compare them in their political aspects. And I shall suggest that, despite the supposed gulf between these attitudes, there are certain important points of affinity. Naturally there are many differences, the variation in depth and thoroughness of treatment being particularly marked. But on some basic issues, the two men expound remarkably similar views.[1] The two major themes in respect of which I want to undertake the comparison are their discussions of political activity and of political philosophy.

For both Oakeshott and Weldon, politics is essentially a practical activity, part of the process of dealing with the difficulties of public life as these arise in the ordinary conduct of affairs.[2] And one of the most important questions which can arise in the analysis of this field concerns the type of judgment which is appropriate to the activity. In politics people are confronted by obstacles that have to be surmounted, by alternative policies or courses of action between which a choice has to be made, and so on. In what terms is such a situation properly appraised? In the light of what rules or principles of action may the most effective and intelligible decision be reached? Here both men agree that theoretical or transcendental thinking is irrelevant to practical judgment and may be misleading as well. Their point of view appears to have a common origin in Hume's and Kant's attack on metaphysical rationalism and asserts that it is a fundamental error to try to give proofs in support of political actions, principles, policies, decisions, when only reasons are appropriate or possible. Neither believes in absolute standards or in the universal applicability of a single rational method capable of reaching certain conclusions about these practical affairs. Both repudiate such intellectualist fallacies and the doctrinaire or ideological politics to which they lead. The terms of analysis employed by each vary, but the general likeness of manner and purpose is evident.

Wittgenstein writes that philosophy cannot give the actual use of language any 'foundation'.[3] Weldon's view is similar: that it is not

---

[1] Of course, I am not the first to observe this kind of similarity: see the comments of E. Gellner, 'Contemporary thought and politics', *Philosophy*, xxxii (1957), 336, 340; Murdoch, *loc. cit.* pp. 225–6; and W. J. M. Mackenzie, 'Oakeshott's conversational engineering', *Universities Quarterly*, xvii (1962–3), 82–3. But these references are only very brief and I think the matter has not so far been adequately examined.

[2] E.g. Oakeshott, *Rationalism in Politics and other Essays* (London, 1962), pp. 112, 123, and his 'Political laws and captive audiences', in G. R. Urban (ed.), *Talking to Eastern Europe* (London, 1964), p. 291; Weldon, 'Science and politics', *Arist. Soc. Suppl.* xxiii (1949), 141, 148–50.   [3] *Philosophical Investigations* (2nd. ed., Oxford, 1963), i, § 124.

possible to provide any certain or essentialist underpinning for a set of political institutions or opinions. Specifically, he attacks the search for 'theoretical foundations' in politics, that is, for some objective principle by which the value of a political system can be assessed, the belief that indubitable axioms and arguments can be invoked in support of given practices.[1] An example is the case so often made out for 'democracy':[2] that all human beings must be respected because they are rational and have rights as such, and so must be treated as ends and are bound only by laws they have agreed to, and so on.[3]

Weldon's arguments against foundational thinking in politics are directed against the search for 'proofs' of either an a priori or scientific kind. Basically his case rests on the logical fork much employed by positivists and which goes back at least to Hume: if a conclusion is supposed to be deductively proved then it is tautologous and has no necessary empirical connection, while if its essential elements concern relations of matter of fact then it cannot be incorrigible. Thus, in the first respect, Weldon is critical of the view that such words as justice or state or law have ontological correlates, the nature of which may be determined by the deductive analysis of appropriate self-evident axioms and that, once achieved, knowledge of such immutable concepts may be used to judge actual behaviour and institutions. For, in addition to the general point about the empirical irrelevance of postulational thinking, it is difficult to know when the essential meaning of the concept, the indubitable proof, has been achieved. Moreover, no detailed conclusion flows from such a generalised notion, or anything does: whatever is read into it. To be of practical use, a theoretical foundation of this sort needs to be interpreted, given a concrete content, used; and this can only be done by calling on a kind of knowledge it does not itself provide.[4] And when this foundation is qualified and made practically precise, it will not be universally applicable or acceptable.[5] And, in the second respect, where what is sought is a scientific law or standard of numerical grading (like that perhaps which the utilitarians had in

---

[1] *The Vocabulary of Politics*, pp. 9–12 and coverpiece. Cf. *States and Morals: a Study in Political Conflicts* (London, 1946, repr. 1962), pp. 22, 234–5, 271–2.

[2] *The Vocabulary of Politics*, pp. 95, 97. There is a certain confusion in Weldon's analysis of 'democracy' because he usually fails to distinguish effectively between (what might be called) 'transcendental' and 'traditional' democracy. The former is based on metaphysical foundations of the kind he rejects while the latter is an actual, historical manner of living (cf. Oakeshott's distinction between 'popular democracy' and 'parliamentary government').

[3] Weldon also examines Hegelian and Marxist foundations though his discussion is curious. He seems, for instance, to equate Hegelianism in its political aspect with the organic theory of the state and with totalitarianism and to assume that its philosophical basis is of the same logical kind as that of (transcendental) democracy.

[4] *The Vocabulary of Politics*, pp. 97–8, 138, 173–4, 180.

[5] 'Political principles', p. 30.

mind), Weldon observes that making a political decision is not simply like solving a puzzle or problem that has a definite answer: you cannot just apply a given technique, and learning about politics is not like learning conic sections. It is not the case that calculation will solve all practical problems, for 'it is judgment and not scientific knowledge of the probable consequences of actions' which is required in a ruler.[1] Neither deductive nor scientific thinking, therefore, can provide a certain standard of judgment. And the conclusions supposed to be reached in either way cannot be 'proofs', though they may be rules or guides which it is reasonable to recommend.[2]

To anyone who knows the writings of the idealists this is, in general, all very familiar. For example, one of the main purposes of Bradley's *Ethical Studies* was to demonstrate the failure of any abstract morality and to show in what way it should be completed or given practical form. With the work of Oakeshott himself there is a very close parallel. Weldon's rejection of theoretical foundations, of 'doctrinaire adherence to abstract principles',[3] is very like Oakeshott's criticism of naturalism and of rationalist ideologies, doctrines too abstract to provide practical guidance. It is not necessary to offer here more than a definition of Oakeshott's view.[4] But, by naturalism, Oakeshott means the attempt to reduce political judgment to the categories of natural science and thus to render political decisions a matter of exact calculation; while rationalism is the belief that all the knowledge relevant to any activity may be formulated and reduced to rules and that action is only rational if in accordance with such criteria (which are taken to be independently proved and absolute). Such standards are not as helpful as they are supposed to be because they ignore the imponderables of experience and provide a specious certainty foreign to the real character of the activity concerned.

But, of course, if political activity is not properly to be seen as guided by foundations or ideologies, how is it to be made intelligible and in what terms are practical appraisals to be made? How should political problems be tackled? These questions raise a number of issues about political principles and moral rules. And again the answers given by Oakeshott and Weldon are remarkably alike. They both reject the idea that to repudiate ideological abstraction or foundations is necessarily to leave the field clear to subjectivism. Oakeshott argues that to see politics in terms of individual caprice is unsatisfactory both because it leaves the activity rationally unintelligible and because caprice is, in any case,

[1] *The Vocabulary of Politics*, pp. 75–83, 150–1; 'Science and politics', pp. 146, 151.
[2] Cf. 'Science and politics', pp. 143, 151–2.
[3] *The Vocabulary of Politics*, p. 127.
[4] For a fuller summary see my *Oakeshott's Philosophical Politics*, index, sub 'naturalism' and 'rationalism'.

never absolute or complete. Similarly, Weldon goes to great lengths to deny that political judgment (if it is not based on foundations) is, therefore, a matter of personal interest, impulse, preference or habit. 'I do not believe', he writes in one place, 'that by discarding political foundations or ideologies I am logically committed to political scepticism.' And again, 'it is an abuse of language to say that appraisals are simple statements of baseless prejudices.'[1] It follows that lamenting over lost political principles is quite inappropriate; any supposedly necessary link between the repudiation of objective standards and subjectivism in politics is quite false. To discard political foundations is simply to get rid of 'metaphysical lumber'; it does not of itself lead to 'cynicism, scepticism, or the rejection of moral or political evaluations'. For instance, whenever we say of something that it is wicked, we are not describing merely our own emotional state or simply making an exclamation. For appraisal words do involve trying to make a reliable report about the world.[2]

But how should such a report be made? In what way is a political judgment achieved if it is to be based on neither some abstract rationalist standard (a theoretical foundation) nor mere habit, personal feeling or idiosyncracy (subjectivism)? How is it possible to have principles for which sensible and legitimate reasons can be given?[3] And here it must be said that, although both men are in general agreement, Oakeshott's consideration is much more satisfactory in that he makes explicit and deals more fully with what Weldon only tackles rather superficially but on which his case nevertheless depends: the logic of tradition.

In this respect, then, what is wrong with Weldonism (if the point of view may so be called) is not so much its attack on 'classical political philosophy' as its failure to make explicit, or rather to explore adequately, the alternative form of political appraisal and the kind of experience on which this must be based. Only an outline is presented, for Weldon contents himself with a few hints about this issue. Partly, of course, he is concerned more to knock down the case for trying to establish theoretical foundations of any sort than to develop his own understanding of the kinds of reason which may legitimately be put forward in support of political preferences; nevertheless this part of his case is manifestly vital and equally clearly deficient as he recounts it.

Weldon's main suggestion here is an analogy between the process of forming a political judgment and that by which, say, a selection committee reaches a decision about the suitability of the candidates before

[1] *The Vocabulary of Politics*, pp. 160, 170. See also, *ibid.*, coverpiece and pp. 144–60; *States and Morals*, pp. 272–3; and 'The justification of political attitudes', *Arist. Soc. Suppl.* XXIX (1955), 117.
[2] *The Vocabulary of Politics*, pp. 13–16, 43.
[3] Cf. 'The justification of political attitudes', p. 118.

it: it establishes the relevant dispositions (honesty, assiduity, intelligence, particular skills, etc.), assesses their relative importance in respect of the job in question, and then tries to apply these considerations to the applicants.[1] This is not a matter about which it is possible to be exact or certain and there is no single or infallible test which can be applied, but it is one about which intelligent discussion and a measure of agreement are possible. Moreover the considerations are referable to a factual context; and reasons can be given for the views expressed though these opinions cannot be proved. In this process there is no reference to absolute standards and conclusions are not deduced from general principles; but at the same time, more than personal prejudice can be involved. This parallel with a selection committee is a practical and amusing way of putting the problem (rather like Oakeshott's examples of bloomers and the question of throwing in cricket) and the suggestion is that political judgments are of the same kind. Weldon also draws an analogy between the process of making appraisals in politics and and the way in which the aesthetic critic assesses the value of a work of art. The purpose of this similitude is the same: to suggest that reasonable opinions may be achieved on the basis of experience of the medium but not incorrigible judgments based on some objective and abstract standard.[2] So that, for Weldon, 'governing at any level is essentially a matter of judgement and decision...and not a matter of theoretical reasoning'. In politics there is no possibility of reaching an ultimate goal in terms of a timeless or spaceless test. It is a continuous activity of search for improvement. It is a question of making appraisals and recommendations on the basis of experience, assessments that are not incorrigible.[3]

But, apart from these relatively brief and somewhat superficial references to the work of selection committees (and artists and their critics) Weldon says little about the rationale of this process and how it appears in detail in the realm of political judgment. He often refers to the empirical context in which practical appraisals are made, to rules of behaviour which are 'generally regarded' in particular countries.[4] But this continual skirmishing around the main theme is irritating, for Weldon fails in *The Vocabulary of Politics* to go on to consider the nature of such traditions of conduct (for this is in fact what he has in mind), how they grow up, the extent of their consistency, how they alter, and so on. Nor is this an isolated instance: the same unfortunate deficiency is revealed also in Weldon's other writings. It is true of his paper on 'Appraisals', where he considers and rejects 'subjectivist' and 'objectivist' theories of ethics but fails to step much beyond this negative and,

[1] *The Vocabulary of Politics*, pp. 151–6.   [2] *Ibid.* pp. 160–1, 164–70, 178.
[3] *Ibid.* pp. 166–7, 170, 172; 'Science and politics', pp. 151–2.
[4] E.g. *The Vocabulary of Politics*, p. 158.

CARL A. RUDISILL LIBRARY
LENOIR RHYNE COLLEGE

nowadays, rather ordinary conclusion. He explicitly recognises that 'Disapproval, it must be insisted, involves a whole complex of behaviour'.[1] Yet he does not think it necessary to explore this understanding further. And, again, in *States and Morals*, he repudiates the idea of universal ethical rules as a basis for political obligation, denies that this necessarily leaves the field open to moral subjectivism and political anarchy, and says that genuine moral and political obligations only arise from particular relationships between individuals. This is to say that moral and political rules arise in a specific social context. But the process of justification is not something which, in its concrete detail, Weldon really bothers to consider; yet the remarks he does make[2] clearly show that it is a tradition of activity which he has in mind. And while he is very critical of, say, Bosanquet, his own opinions about the overlapping groups of individuals and the sense of different responsibilities to which these give rise remind me of nothing so much as the position set out (more satisfactorily and broadly) in *The Philosophical Theory of the State*.

Weldon's indebtedness to the concept of tradition may be illustrated in a number of ways. Thus, in his paper on 'Science and Politics', he makes some remarks about the importance of custom and conventional rules and how these accepted ways of activity become formalised for one reason or another in laws and institutions and how in time these acquire 'a sort of privileged and mystical status'.[3] Again, in another paper presented to the Aristotelian Society on 'The Justification of Political Attitudes', Weldon remarks how political principles 'are built into a way of life or customary pattern of behaviour'. And he observes, too, how they may have a limited application and are not necessarily consistent with one another: a way of life is 'a complicated pattern of different but interlocking activities'.[4] In a most revealing passage of this essay, which clearly indicates the affinity of the political implications of modern philosophy with idealism in general (and specifically with the attitude reflected by Oakeshott), he writes:

Provisionally, then, to justify my political attitudes is to give the reasons for my political principles or rules of conduct; and the *only* way in which this can be done is by expounding the way of life which these rules, taken as a whole, are designed to maintain or to alter for the better.[5]

But there is so much he does not explain: such as, by what criterion derived from or immanent in this way of life we know in what direction

---

[1] *Philosophy*, xxv (1950), 324.   [2] *States and Morals*, pp. 272–9.

[3] 'Science and politics', pp. 146–8. Weldon also uses the favoured analogy with games, *ibid.*

[4] 'The justification of political attitudes', pp. 119–20. Cf. p. 121 on the degree of coherence achieved.   [5] *Ibid.* p. 120 (my italics).

to advance, to improve things; what to do in the case of contradictory indications; and the like. Summing up his point of view, he says:

To justify a political principle is to describe the way of life accepted by all or nearly all the members of a particular State at a particular time. Political principles differ within a State because people see their State in different ways—it looks different to different people...Such differences may not be capable of adjustment by discussion, but they can at least be understood and discussed, and disputants *may* reach common ground for agreement or disagreement provided that their way of looking at things in general is more or less identical...This condition is not satisfied unless there is a common language or idiom in which discussion can take place.[1]

It is not surprising that Weldon writes in terms that can easily be described as 'the pursuit of intimations'.[2] What else, indeed, could or should be done? Very frequently, then, Weldon writes of political appraisal in the only possible and relevant context: that of a traditional way of life, the implications of which are being followed.[3]

Weldon says that this position involves difficult and complicated questions. But his failure to consider in detail their logical character is a considerable weakness in his position. A full defence and adequate explanation of his point of view requires a satisfactory examination of this problem. He explains (what is obvious) that somewhere explanation has to come to a stop; when considering the reason for any form of conduct it is, in the last resort, only possible to say 'Well, this is Great Britain, isn't it?'[4] But what he does not try to do—which is surely possible?—is to say something more of what this position implies.

It is surely relevant, too, that others who adopt the same style of philosophy may be detected in a similar shortcoming. For instance, Miss Margaret Madconald, in her well-known essay on 'The Language of Political Theory', rejects (like Weldon) the possibility of a certain foundation as a standard of political judgment: 'no general criterion of all right actions can be supplied', no answer that is 'always and infallibly right' is possible.[5] She then goes on to outline briefly her idea of a feasible mode of decision, one that is neither based on such a 'foundation' nor merely arbitrary. The standard indicated is variable and by no means exact and is acknowledged as such: it is a changing amalgam of consent, tradition and the objects promoted by govern-

---

[1] *Ibid.* p. 130.
[2] See, e.g., *The Vocabulary of Politics*, pp. 31–3, 54.
[3] *Ibid.* pp. 45, 57, 59, 61, 178–9, 186–91, esp. 188–9; and 'Political principles', p. 30.
[4] *The Vocabulary of Politics*, p. 57. Cf. the interesting parallel in Wittgenstein's *Philosophical Investigations*, I, §§ 1, 217, 381–2; II, p. 226; also Toulmin, *An Examination of the Place of Reason in Ethics* (Cambridge, 1950), pp. 145–6.
[5] A. G. N. Flew (ed.), *Logic and Language* (1st ser., Oxford, 1951), pp. 183–4.

ment.[1] Yet, like Weldon, Miss Macdonald completely fails to discuss this concept in any satisfactory detail. And, of course, the idea can only become fully meaningful when given concrete context and this can only be derived from the way of life of those concerned, that is, from an actual tradition of behaviour, and what is implicit in this tradition. The same is true of Miss Macdonald's analysis in her paper on 'Natural Rights' where she also argues that practical evaluative utterance is neither capable of proof or certain nor something based on the procedures of the natural sciences. It is the outcome rather of a process like that of argument in a court of law or by which an art critic reaches a considered opinion. But, again, what is implied in this appeal to practical recommendation and the 'system of evaluation' it involves is not followed through.

This is why Oakeshott's statement of the matter is so much more satisfactory: it makes clear what Weldon (and the others) should have made explicit but leave largely unsaid. I say 'largely' because it is not (as we have seen) that Weldon is wholly unaware of what is involved: he has a number of relevant remarks to make about conventional rules and the way of life from which they derive and to which they refer. But these comments he leaves unprobed and unconnected such that they fail to constitute a coherent whole.

Oakeshott's position on these matters (which in many ways is very like that of Hume) is, briefly, that institutions, customs and rules of behaviour exist, but not in a completely consistent fashion. There may be conflicts and contrasting pressures in this world of 'what is'. There is implied and envisaged, therefore, another world more uniform and desirable in which these differences are seen to be eliminated: this is the world of 'what ought to be'. And the life of practice, of morals and politics, consists in the never-ending attempt to transform the one into the other. An existing tradition of behaviour intimates lines of development, how it might be improved or made more coherent. And these possible lines of improvement are derived neither from outside the tradition (by reference to some independently premeditated standard), nor from personal prejudice simply, but from the mode of behaviour, the way of life itself. Practical action (political decision, for instance) involves neither following a superior or transcendental law nor doing what one likes or what one's mere conscience dictates: it is action in accordance with not simply established rules (this would be reactionary or invite a state of *stasis*), but established rules and what they, and the inconsistencies they contain, imply. Thus 'politics' is the activity of attending to the arrangements of a society by 'the amendment of existing arrangements, by exploring and pursuing what is intimated in them'.[2] Such is, indeed, the way changes take place in the design of anything:

[1] Flew, *Logic and Language* (1st ser.), pp. 185-6.   [2] *Rationalism in Politics*, pp. 123-4.

furniture, motor cars, moral rules, political activity, university sylla-
buses, etc., and a particular kind of knowledge, experience and education is involved. This is not, perhaps, an uncontentious view. But it is
the view (or so I understand it) implied in the standpoint established
by Weldon—selection committees call upon this kind of traditional
experience (which is indeed like that of the politician and statesman).
But Oakeshott, and not Weldon, is the one who elaborates in detail
what it means and implies, and who relates it, too, to a view of experience
as a whole expounded in considerable detail.

Moreover, Weldon's failure to analyse deeply his own understanding
of political judgment helps to conceal the affinity of his view to that of
Oakeshott, and therefore to that of the idealists. At the same time, in
one way his failure to go very far saves his case (as he presents it): if he
had probed deeper in the way I suggest he would have realised that the
'classical' themes and writers he lumps together are basically very
different. Here he is involved in a basic failure of historical interpretation.

The second major, and not unrelated, theme concerns Oakeshott's
and Weldon's views of political philosophy and so of philosophy as such.

There is a certain difficulty in Weldon's understanding of these
matters (to take his position first), an ambivalence which arises because
he does not seem sure about what doing philosophy is. Very often, perhaps characteristically, he expresses the view that philosophy is a second-
order subject dealing with the clarification of the language in which
first-order activities (like science, politics or moral judgment) are carried
on and discussed. In his essay on 'Political Principles' he writes:

> It is not the job of philosophy to provide new information about politics,
> biology, physics or any other matter of fact. Philosophical problems are
> entirely second-order problems. They are problems, that is, which are
> generated by the language in which facts are described and explained by
> those whose function it is to construct and defend scientific, historical and
> other types of theory.[1]

Thus philosophy reveals no new facts about the world but rectifies the
logical geography of the knowledge of the world we already have. Its
job is solely to expose linguistic muddle. And, of course, this is a view
typical of contemporary philosophical opinion.[2]

But in a number of passages, Weldon says that philosophy is somewhat more than this[3] and in two respects. First, he often acknowledges

---

[1] 'Political principles', p. 22. Cf. *ibid.* p. 33 and *The Vocabulary of Politics*, pp. 9–11, 44, 160, 172, 175, 176.

[2] Cf. G. J. Warnock, *English Philosophy since 1900* (London, 1958), p. 167; G. Ryle *The Concept of Mind* (London, 1949), p. 7; Wollheim, *art. cit.* pp. 296–8.

[3] Cf. the interesting remark that 'if we say that political philosophy is concerned solely with linguistic usage' we may be convicted of talking nonsense (*The Vocabulary of Politics*, p. 42).

that if philosophy is the clarification of language then it necessarily involves in itself a considerable first-order knowledge.[1] Thus to study a language and its concepts (which are entirely conventional symbols) requires knowledge of the nature and history of the activity to which these relate and from which they spring. This is because the analysis of language cannot be conducted in a vacuum and unless this knowledge is acquired the essential context of understanding is absent and the philosophy will be abstract and without content. It may be agreed that words do not have essential meanings but only uses: and that to 'know their meaning is to know how to use them correctly'. But 'it is senseless to attempt an inquiry into the use of any language without knowing what that use is, for second-order talk presupposes at least competence to handle first-order talk'.[2] So, the study of scientific discourse needs the perspective of scientific experience and a knowledge of scientific practice.[3] Similarly, it is essential to know something about history and actual political organisation before adequate analysis of political thought is possible. And an account, for instance, of the concept of ownership assumes a system of social relations and a means of their protection.[4] Again, the study of political language needs to be supplemented by an examination of the ideological context and climate of opinion in which alone that language can be adequately comprehended.[5] This kind of framework must be understood if analysis is to be adequate even though its presence may be hidden in presenting the results of any inquiry. Yet, while recognising that philosophy involves such contextual studies, Weldon's own discussions show that he had little of the historical sense or imagination required. And, somewhat paradoxically, he went so far as to suggest that it was impossible ever to enter into the mind of those who lived and worked with quite different *Weltanschauungen* from his own.

Then, secondly, Weldon does not always seem sure that philosophy is a practically neutral exercise.[6] At times he recognises that philosophy,

[1] Cf. Miss Macdonalds' view that 'completely to understand ethical problems and theories, more than linguistic considerations are required [and if] this is true of ethics, it is even more true of politics' (*Logic and Language*, 1st ser., ed. Flew, pp. 171–2). See also J. L. Austin, *Philosophical Papers* (Oxford, 1961), pp. 130, 134–7.

[2] *The Vocabulary of Politics*, p. 19; 'Political principles', p. 24.

[3] E.g. *Mind*, LVII (1948), 252.

[4] *The Vocabulary of Politics*, pp. 26–7.

[5] *Ibid.* pp. 28–9, 172; 'Political principles', p. 32; 'The justification of political attitudes', pp. 124–8.

[6] Other linguistic philosophers clearly feel the same; it must be significant that the following passage from Hume's *Enquiry concerning Human Understanding* (1, 5) is cited as the epigraph to the second series of essays on *Logic and Language*: 'And though a philosopher may live remote from business, the genius of philosophy, if carefully cultivated by several, must gradually diffuse itself throughout the whole society, and bestow a similar correctness on every art and calling.'

although ostensibly concerned only with linguistic clarification, can, even as such, have a considerable effect on actual belief and conduct:

> ...though second-order talk is not directly concerned with the validity of the first-order principles whose logical force it examines, it is a serious over-statement to say that the psychological attitude of those who adhere to such principles is quite unaffected by such examination. To say that political philosophy is concerned with linguistic analysis and with nothing else at least suggests that, since it has no aim except clarification, it can have no effect on actual political beliefs. And this is not true.[1]

Thus, his own attack on the linguistic confusions which underlie the essentialist search for theoretical foundations in politics, if found per-suasive, is bound to affect political activity and thinking. In particular, this line of criticism undermines the cogency of universal and absolute standards in morals and politics: for instance, the kind of criteria often invoked to justify fundamental or rapid change in the existing social or political structure. In such a way, linguistic analysis may have 'a strong deflating tendency'.[2] This is one reason, perhaps, why con-ceptual philosophy is treated in so hostile a fashion by those with radical or ideologically based political opinions. In the same sort of way, the doctrine that philosophy entails no logically necessary practical conse-quences and is irrelevant to the conduct of everyday life is bound to affect the status of, say, moral, religious or political beliefs and the way in which these are discussed. Another important effect arises from the way in which philosophy can reveal invalid forms of argument. By critically examining political beliefs it might suggest, for instance, that an evaluative conclusion is falsely derived from premises which do not themselves contain an evaluative element. And while it is true that the validity of a political principle or belief does not necessarily depend on the case which may from time to time be put forward in its support, in practice political arguments and convictions are intimately connected. The former provide the frame by which the beliefs are sustained or the basis on which it is considered reasonable to put the convictions forward. At the least, therefore (and even considered as a second-order activity only), philosophy can make an important negative contribution to political thought and conduct by invalidating or clarifying political convictions.[3] In addition, the philosophical problems that arise in such areas as politics necessarily reflect the actual issues which emerge in the world. Philosophy does not discuss anything, but only what is significant in the realm of discourse concerned.

---

[1] 'Political principles', p. 24. Cf. *States and Morals*, pp. xii–xiii, 4–14; also M. Macdonald 'The language of political theory', *Logic and Language* (1st ser., ed. Flew), p. 170.
[2] 'Political principles', pp. 24–5, 32–3.
[3] See R. Wollheim, 'Philosophie analytique et pensée politique', *loc. cit.* pp. 304–8.

The interesting parallel here is that Oakeshott's thought embodies an exactly similar ambivalence: which is to say that his view of philosophy somehow seems incomplete. He does not admit that philosophy (second-order explanation) contributes anything to the conversation of mankind among the modes of experience (first-order knowledge) and holds that to discuss politics philosophically is to consider politics in terms which are irrelevant to practical conduct. Yet at the same time he applies his philosophical manner of thought to matters of practical judgment. Really neither Oakeshott nor Weldon can bring themselves to accept a merely intellectual role for what, in theory, they cast as a neutral, practically irrelevant, style of thought. And so they cannot provide a coherent conception of philosophy. In Weldon's case, the reason is simple enough; he was hardly a profound or systematic thinker and never probed or developed his ideas sufficiently. With Oakeshott, the matter is very different. His first major work, *Experience and its Modes* (1933), constituted a detailed and extensive elaboration of his general point of view, a perspective to which, despite some changes, he has basically remained true ever since. Nevertheless, the same sort of difficulty arises as in the case of Weldon's more superficial view. And the tension in Oakeshott's work derives from a failure to distinguish sufficiently between two distinct ideas of philosophy: between philosophy as a manner of thinking or attitude, and philosophy as what is achieved (the highest possible abstract and universal level) as a result of this style of analysis. Oakeshott sometimes speaks of philosophy as the 'perpetual re-establishment of coherence', the continual and critical examination of inconsistency with a view to its resolution in a more intelligible understanding. Seen thus, philosophy is a method of thought; and it is apparent that this critical mode of analysis, this ever-lasting search for a more satisfactory perspective, is capable of application in any area of experience whatsoever. Whether the subject-matter is scientific discourse or the world of politics, the question of university education or the nature of the British political tradition, a 'philosophical' point of view is established by the adoption of this approach whatever the level of abstraction achieved; and so it seems that philosophy can, by virtue of its methodology, have much to contribute to practical or any first-order matters. But, on the other hand, Oakeshott resolutely maintains that philosophical explanation has nothing to offer to the conduct of modal affairs. And the rationale of this view derives, I think, from the other, rather different, conception of philosophy implicit in his works. This is that philosophy is not merely a method of trying to achieve the most inclusive and concordant point of view, but the understanding of experience as a whole that is actually achieved in this way. The picture that Oakeshott presents is familiar enough: the various modes of experience, their nature, limitations, and so on.[1] And as philosophy *is* this view of experience as a whole, this abstract 'world' which encompasses and transcends the limitations of modal experience, it is necessarily different and distinct from them. So, its perceptions must be irrelevant to the conduct of the various modal activities because these are, in philosophy, wholly transformed: they are categories of abstract explanation and not of persuasion, delight, historical continuity or objective law. Of course, in Oakeshott's case these two conceptions of philosophy are related: the perspective of experience as a whole is achieved by means of the pursuit of coherence. Yet they are notionally distinct. Moreover, it is apparent that the view of the totality of experience which Oakeshott presents is itself incomplete. For he fails to show how modal experience arises, accepting each independent 'arrest' as merely given, and, as it were, arbitrary. Whereas, what the philosophical method requires is a further step, a wider coherence, which will encompass these differences in a higher unity, a view of experience in which each mode is seen as necessary and as related to the others in a rational fashion. Indeed, the existence of this greater coherence is implied in Oakeshott's admission that an individual can change from one modal point of view to another and also to the philosophical frame of mind. For, while each of these attitudes may be distinct, the individual himself and his experiential development provide an element of continuity, the unity within which these differences of perspective appear. So here, too, it is impossible to rest content with a divided self or with anything but a complete and rational account of all the various forms of experience and of the links between them: together they constitute a world with its own logic of development and completeness. A conception, like that of Hegel and Collingwood, of a linked series or scale of forms is surely involved, though Oakeshott (following Bradley) is, I suppose, content to take refuge from the task in a sceptical denial that this achievement is possible.

Both men, therefore, overlook something essential about the relation between philosophy and practical activity. If (as for Weldon) philosophy shows us that we have been confused about the vocabulary of politics or the nature of political principles; and if (as for Oakeshott) philosophy shows us that ideology (or technical knowledge) is by itself inappropriate as a guide to political activity, then, in each case, the philosophical thesis is itself a contribution to the conduct of practical life. At the very least this must be so because when the philosopher himself turns from his professional preoccupation to political activity (in the wide sense of dealing with political problems) then he cannot, being the same person,

[1] See the account in *Rationalism in Politics*, pp. 197 ff., and the summary in my *Oakeshott's Philosophical Politics*, chapters II and III.

simply forget what his philosophy has taught him; he does not change when he changes his hat or alter simply because he turns and faces another way.

One conclusion that certainly follows from all this is that modern philosophy is by no means merely neutral, trivial or sceptical from the practical point of view, though its practitioners do their best to hide this. It has important practical implications for the philosopher's own conduct and intellectual pursuits and in its effect on the views of others. I do not suggest for one minute, however, that a particular set of political views is involved; it is clear, on the other hand, that, by virtue of the criticisms of theoretical foundations, etc., the net effect must be (in a general sense) dampening and 'conservative'.[1] I personally have no objection to this, indeed I welcome it. But I also think that critics of modern philosophy do have a valid ground for complaint when its exponents are loath to concede this kind of thing and to work out what is (in such a fashion) implied in their point of view. It is thus most unfortunate that they pay little or no attention to the style of practical political appraisal that their philosophical attitude involves. One of the objects of this essay is to be therapeutic: to show the conceptual philosopher that if he would only turn round, alter his perspective, he would find that the door he thought was firmly closed behind him had been open all the time. He should get out into the clear the implications of the kind of philosophical activity he undertakes. At least the idealist (for all his faults) knows consciously what he is doing and can write better about his enterprise as a result.

II

My second main theme is that the affinity between the political implications of idealism and modern philosophy (as reflected in the writings of Oakeshott and Weldon) may be paralleled by a still more fundamental likeness of doctrine. So despite their contumacious repudiation of idealism, the contemporary philosophers are nevertheless linked to what they reject, and this not at all in superficial appearance or form but in basic manner. This suggestion may be examined from two angles. First, in connection with their respective views of what it means to do philosophy; secondly, with reference to the link envisaged between language and tradition. Likenesses of this kind show that to stress a simple antithesis between idealism and contemporary philosophy is very wide of the mark, though no more so perhaps than is usually the case with

[1] Cf. W. H. Walsh, *Metaphysics* (London, 1963, repr. 1966), p. 197. Further, there seems to be some similarity between the specific political opinions of Oakeshott and Weldon. They share a whiggish and pluralist conception of society and stress on individualism. Though, again, Oakeshott has said much more about what is involved in this point of view.

intellectual (or other) 'revolutions' in which the links of continuity are always greater in number and strength than those who claim to be innovating usually like to imagine.[1]

First of all, there are certain negative connections. Both share a certain anti-positivism, and also reject abstract speculation of the transcendental kind, so subscribing to a sort of 'metaphysical agnosticism'. Again, there is the idea that philosophy should not try to construct a massive speculative system about the world but rather inquire critically into language and concepts of various kinds. (Though, as I have already indicated, certain confusions can arise about the nature of this philosophical analysis.)

But beyond this kind of thing there are sometimes hints of more positive parallels. Idealists have tended to discuss different worlds or levels of knowledge: as Collingwood wrote of history, art, religion, science and philosophy and Oakeshott of the various modes of experience. And, interestingly enough, modern philosophers can be found speaking in similar terms. For instance, Wittgenstein refers[2] to different 'languages', each of which reflects (and is 'woven to') a specific form of activity and understanding. Thus, 'this is red' and 'this is good' have the same grammatical form but are nevertheless very different: the logics of the descriptive and evaluative jobs performed by language are not the same. The rules of each mode of thinking and talking have to be distinguished and described; so that to show the logic of a word like 'good' is to describe the world of concepts appropriate to moral evaluation.[3]

Naturally, the degree to which the real nature of this kind of classificatory analysis is recognised varies from one modern philosopher to another. Some deny altogether the validity of the exercise while others regard it as an essential part of philosophical inquiry.[4] In many cases, the doctrine of basic and independent categories is present but only implied. But some do consider it explicitly. Mr Strawson, for instance, in a discussion of what he takes philosophy to involve, suggests that beyond therapeutic analysis (the diagnosing and correction of specific

[1] Though see the remarks of Mr D. F. Pears in G. Ryle (ed.), *The Revolution in Philosophy* (London, 1956), pp. 41–3, 54–5, and of Professor J. Wisdom in *Paradox and Discovery* (Oxford, 1965), pp. 71, 74–5. Brief notice of this general affinity has been taken by Professor Gellner, e.g. *Words and Things* (London, 1959), p. 145, and in his contribution to J. H. Plumb (ed.), *Crisis in the Humanities* (Harmondsworth, 1964), pp. 56, 58, 61 n., 62, but his tone in making these comments is unfortunately pejorative and he is too out of sympathy with either component of the comparison to carry much conviction.

[2] E.g. *Philosophical Investigations*, I, §§ 19, 23. Cf. the comments of Professor Walsh in his *Metaphysics*, pp. 122–3.

[3] Sometimes, too, Wittgenstein makes a remark that recalls the way some idealists had of arranging these various forms of experience in a hierarchy, e.g. *The Blue and Brown Books* (Oxford, 1964), pp. 44–5.

[4] Cf. Warnock, *English Philosophy Since 1900*, pp. 152–3.

and recognised philosophical disorders) there is the possibility of inquiry
of a more systematic kind, research for its own sake into speech forms,
types of concepts and discourse, and their systematic ordering and
description. In this context he refers to the work open to what he calls
the 'inventive philosophical imagination', considering how the nature
of the world can be viewed through different conceptual apparatuses,
how it might be discussed in different forms of discourse. This task, he
thinks, might even be called metaphysical.[1] Mr Hampshire has made
a similar point. Naturally (he thinks) no philosopher would to-day
attempt to base a metaphysical system on a foundation of pure deduction and *a priori* reasoning. (Idealists would, of course, agree.) But even
if a particular method of discussion is thus rejected, 'some general view
of the scope of human knowledge, of its divisions into different types' is
still required to provide us with 'the outlines of a map of human knowledge' and its limits. Hampshire then goes on to talk (in very idealist
manner) of how we distinguish 'different levels of comprehensiveness
and objectivity in our actual knowledge' and of how knowledge becomes more genuine 'the more comprehensive it is'. 'Therefore, at the
top of the scale, perfect knowledge would be absolutely comprehensive'
and the knowing subject 'would know things as they are in their own
true, objective order', though it is unlikely that such a state can ever
be achieved, so that truth always lies ahead. This is, of course, very like
Bradley on the Absolute or Oakeshott on 'experience as a whole'. And,
echoing the conception of different modes, Hampshire says: 'Perhaps
no one would now claim that there is just one, finally correct way of
exhibiting this systematic connection. Rather there is room for a variety
of different tentative systems, none of them claiming finality, but each
bringing into prominence some very general feature of our discourse.'[2]

This type of viewpoint seems quite pronounced in Professor Wisdom's
works. Thus he has written that the point of philosophical statements is
'the illumination of the ultimate structure of facts, i.e. the relations
between different categories of being or (we must be in the mode) the
relations between different sub-languages within a language'.[3] Specifically in his essay on 'The Logic of God', he appears to attach considerable importance to understanding the nature of different apprehensions
of reality, different forms of perspective or reflection.[4] Again, the same

---

[1] 'Construction and analysis' in *The Revolution in Philosophy* (*ed. cit.*), pp. 105–9. Also see
Warnock on 'Analysis and imagination', in the same volume, pp. 111–26, esp. p. 122.

[2] 'Metaphysical systems' in *The Nature of Metaphysics* (*ed. cit.*), pp. 31, 32–4, 35. Cf. the
similar references to different categories of knowledge in *Thought and Action* (London, 1959),
e.g. pp. 9, 14, etc., and also in the discussion on 'Philosophy and beliefs', *The Twentieth
Century*, CLVII (1955), 511–12.

[3] J. Wisdom, *Philosophy and Psychoanalysis* (Oxford, 1953), p. 37. Cf. *ibid.* pp. 39, 42, 263–6.

[4] *Paradox and Discovery*, ch. 1. Cf. the references to 'varieties of thought', etc., *ibid.* pp. 104–5.

theme is hidden in Professor Austin's writings. It is true he was mainly and explicitly concerned with different classes of utterance distinguished only in grammatical terms. But he does make references of somewhat wider import to the possibility of different perspectives, seeing things in different ways.[1] And he observes the distinction between ordinary language and the scientific mode of discourse,[2] though he was not curious (or sophisticated) enough to inquire whether this simple, two-fold differentiation of modes was exhaustive. Finally, there are Professor Ryle's remarks about this issue. There are passages in which he explicitly, and somewhat rudely, rejects the type of categorisation accepted by idealists or, at least, is somewhat sceptical about it.[3] Yet, he can speak well (though with only the conventional sympathy of the occasion?) of Collingwood's analysis of various forms of perception,[4] or even, in one place, define philosophy as the 'systematic restatement' of various syntaxes in order to exhibit 'the forms of the facts into which philosophy is the inquiry'.[5] And one of the Tarner lectures (naturally, perhaps, in view of the scope of the foundation) is devoted to a discussion of the worlds of science and of everyday life as two different ways of seeing, both of which are true. The language and ethos of all this is quite like that of the idealist. These are, Ryle says, 'two different but complementary ways of giving information of very different sorts'. They are not rivals and neither is true or false at the expense of the other. The picture is further elaborated in the same manner: 'The nuclear physicist, the theologian, the historian, the lyric poet and the man in the street produce very different, yet compatible and even complementary pictures of one and the same "world".' And Ryle stresses that the thought-processes of each point of view are different and independent, though we can switch from one conceptual apparatus to another. But then, having outlined an idealist-type doctrine of this sort (it might be Oakeshott talking about the voices in the conversation of mankind), Ryle draws back and clearly shows his doubts.[6] The result is that one is not sure what his view is; and it is not really clear when, in *The Concept of Mind*, he writes of categories, whether he is talking of linguistic–logical modes, or ontological or factual areas.[7]

---

[1] E.g. *Sense and Sensibilia* (Oxford, 1962), pp. 100–1. Cf. p. 68.

[2] *Philosophical Papers*, pp. 36, 133.

[3] 'Categories', *Logic and Language* (2nd ser., ed. Flew, Oxford, 1953), p. 75; *Dilemmas* (Cambridge, 1954, repr. 1964), pp. 8–9.

[4] *Philosophical Arguments* (Oxford, 1945), pp. 3–4. Cf. the reference to the need to map systematically the geography of the logical powers of ideas, *ibid.* pp. 10–11.

[5] 'Systematically Misleading Expressions', *Logic and Language* (1st ser., ed. Flew), p. 36.

[6] *Dilemmas*, chs. v and vi, esp. pp. 78, 80–1, 89–90, 91–2. Cf. the indecision of pp. 8–11.

[7] E.g. *The Concept of Mind*, pp. 8 and 17. Cf. the comment of G. J. Warnock, *op. cit.* pp. 96–7. Mr Mure is sure Ryle is a straightforward linguistic phenomenalist (*Retreat from Truth* (Oxford, 1958), p. 146), but I am not so certain.

From such a viewpoint as this, it naturally follows that one main concern must be to prevent any confusion of different modes or languages. Idealists always respected the differences between the various realms of appearance or determinations of thought (or whatever the term was) just as the conceptual analyst has. Throughout *Experience and its Modes*, for instance, Oakeshott is concerned to expound the point of view, that philosophy is the analysis of the different modes of experience (the concepts and activities called science, history and practice—later he added poetry, i.e. art in general) and that the greatest error it is possible to commit is that of irrelevance, an *ignoratio elenchi*, a confusion or assimilation of the concepts appropriate to one mode with those of another. Ryle's concern with the 'category-mistake', that is, 'the presentation of facts belonging to one category in the idioms appropriate to another'[1] may be relevant here; though it is difficult to know, from his examples, whether he really means to refer to linguistic error simply or to (what the term implies) knowable areas of experience. Wittgenstein certainly spoke of misunderstandings concerning the use of words which could be caused 'by certain analogies between the forms of expression in different regions of language'. Indeed, not knowing one's way about is the result of mixing up forms of language. He also referred specifically to the danger of confusing the scientific mode of speech with that of the ordinary world of common speech and to the errors to which this leads.[2] Professor Flew has expressed a similar concern: for if, he says, questions are asked about one kind of language which are not appropriate to it, only 'nonsense and paradox will result'. Indeed, he attributes to the insight that grammatical similarities or differences may be misleading, in respect of questions of logical confusion, the foundation and success of modern philosophy.[3] Finally, Professor Wisdom writes of the dangers of 'inappropriateness', of overlooking differences in the 'style of functioning' of, say, poetic and scientific statements.[4]

The second important point of comparison concerns language and tradition. The way in which many contemporary philosophers look at language games, or, specifically, at ordinary language, is very like the way in which an idealist considers established or traditional modes of activity. In each case, it is supposed that there is immanent in the language or tradition a rationale which in a sense justifies its existence or present form. It has indeed, and not unreasonably, been suggested

---

[1] *The Concept of Mind*, pp. 7–8, 16–17. Cf. *Philosophical Arguments*, pp. 10–11; 'Categories' in *Logic and Language* (2nd. ser., ed. Flew), pp. 75–6.

[2] *Philosophical Investigations*, I, §§ 90, 123 (cf. § 194 *ad fin.*); *The Blue and Brown Books*, pp. 45–6. Presumably another aspect of this wish to prevent confusion is the desire to avoid untenable universalisation or general definition.

[3] *Logic and Language* (1st ser., ed. Flew), pp. 7–8.   [4] *Philosophy and Psychoanalysis*, p. 53.

that the manner in which the modern philosopher talks about this theme bears at least a close family resemblance to Hegel on the concrete universal.[1]

The aspect of modern philosophy under consideration may be made clear by a few examples. First of all, what Wittgenstein has to say about this. In the *Tractatus*, he writes that, in fact, 'all the propositions of our everyday language, just as they stand, are in perfect logical order'. And this view is exactly repeated in the *Philosophical Investigations*.[2] In a picturesque, literary metaphor, Wittgenstein observes the historical growth of language, describing it as 'an ancient city: a maze of little streets and squares, of old and new houses, and of houses with additions from various periods; and this surrounded by a multitude of new boroughs with straight regular streets and uniform houses' (by the latter he seems to mean the symbolisms of the exact sciences).[3] The suggestion seems to be that existing language, because it has grown up over so long a period in response to the actual needs of men, is much more likely to provide a satisfactory (because subtle and flexible) way of thinking and communicating than any artificial or ideal terminology. A purely invented language or a stress on only one aspect of our discourse must be an abridgement of traditional or common speech and unable fully to represent its complexities. It would be abstracted from the real-life situations in which language works: it would be to sublime our language, and this is why a purely private language is impossible. In this connection, it is instructive to note that Keynes (in his essay on 'My Early Beliefs') refers to Wittgenstein in the context of a passage deploring his own (Keynes's) failure when young to appreciate the value of traditional wisdom and the restraints of custom, a passage which likewise attacks a thin and superficial rationalism. Wittgenstein seems to have criticised the lack of respect and reverence for inherited wisdom which characterised the group around Keynes.[4]

A similar view is also expressed by other modern philosophers. For instance, Professor Austin, in his presidential address to the Aristotelian Society, wrote:

[1] Walsh, *op. cit.* p. 153 n. 1. Wisdom on 'unity within variety' is a good instance of this trait in the modern philosopher: see his *Paradox and Discovery*, pp. 57–8, 70, 87–9, 105, 143–5. Professor Walsh also draws an interesting parallel between Wittgenstein and Burke, *op. cit.* pp. 16, 123–4, 130–2. One sees exactly what he has in mind, even though his understanding of Burke seems incomplete: Burke was basically a natural-law theorist, and a better example of 'traditionalist' political thought might be that of Hume—or Weldon or Oakeshott. Cf. p. 120 n. 5 below.

[2] *Tractatus Logico-Philosophicus* (tr. Pears and McGuinness, London, 1963), 5.5563; *Philosophical Investigations*, I, §§ 97–8; cf. *The Blue and Brown Books*, p. 28.

[3] *Philosophical Investigations*, I, § 18.

[4] Keynes, *Two Memoirs* (London, 1949), pp. 99–103; cf. L. Woolf, *Sowing* (London, 1960), pp. 153–4.

our common stock of words embodies all the distinctions men have found
worth drawing, and the connexions they have found worth making, in the
lifetimes of many generations: these surely are likely to be more numerous,
more sound, since they have stood up to the long test of the survival of the
fittest, and more subtle, at least in all ordinary and reasonably practical
matters, than any that you or I are likely to think up in our arm-chairs of
an afternoon—the most favoured alternative method.

So, while ordinary language cannot, as it stands, be the last word, it
must be the first, for it does embody 'the inherited experience and
acumen of many generations of men' and so cannot mark merely
nothing.[1] In another paper, Austin stressed that language 'develops
in tune with the society of which it is the language' so that, for example,
'the social habits of the society may considerably affect the question of
which performative verbs are evolved'.[2] Austin's famous concept of
performative utterance must presuppose a moral system: to do an act
by saying 'I promise' cannot take place in a moral–social vacuum. As
Austin said, the circumstances of the performative utterance have to be
appropriate, and among the conditions are 'an accepted conventional
procedure' about the utterance. And the other conditions depend, in
effect, on these conventions.[3] Similarly, his general discussion of 'in-
felicities' in usage is remarkably like a review of the problems arising in
the course of behaving in a traditional manner as an idealist would discuss them: Oakeshott on 'incoherence', for example. In much the way,
too, that Austin's remarks about the untoward effects of 'tampering
with words'[4] are like, say, Burke on the pernicious practical effects of
abstract 'reason' or Oakeshott on 'rationalism'. Further, he seems to
envisage the growth or development of concepts as a sort of pursuit of
intimations appropriate in the circumstances obtaining.[5]

Summing up this viewpoint, Mr Warnock (using terms which again
remind me of an idealist, like Oakeshott, talking about the need to
reject rationalist abstraction in favour of the fullness of a concrete
tradition of behaviour) says: 'There is no one pattern to be revealed, no
single account to be offered, no small set of definite rules. On the contrary, the forms and uses of language are inexhaustibly flexible and
various.' In all its variety, language 'is, as it were, a storehouse of

[1] *Philosophical papers*, pp. 130–3. Cf. *ibid.* pp. 31 ff. and his remarks reported in *La Philosophie
Analytique* (Cahiers de Royaumont, Philosophie, No: IV, Paris, 1962), p. 335. See Mr Hampshire's comments on this view of Austin's which he calls 'The principle of sufficient linguistic reason', *Proc. Arist. Soc.* LX (1959–60), VI.

[2] *Philosophical Papers*, p. 232.

[3] *How To Do Things with Words* (Oxford, 1962), pp. 8–9, 14, 19–20.

[4] *Sense and Sensibilia*, p. 63.

[5] Compare Austin on picking up the ball in football and running (*How To Do Things with
Words*, pp. 30–2, cf. p. 83) and Oakeshott on throwing the ball when bowling in cricket
(*Rationalism in Politics*, pp. 134–5.)

long-garnered principles and distinctions'. And (he says in another place), 'it is most unlikely' that language 'should have taken on the shapes it has' without 'very good reasons'.[1]

The general point could, I take it, be put in the following series of recommendations. In the search for the meaning of a concept:

(a) don't refer to some artificial, abstract criterion:

(b) don't assume that an expression can mean what anyone wants it to mean: but

(c) look for its use, i.e. the meaning immanent in the appropriate ordinary language and in the activity with which this use is interwoven.[2]

Of course, this is an eminently sensible way of proceeding. But we should probe deeper and ask what this acceptance of the rationality of ordinary language implies and presupposes. This is, really, the question about modern philosophy in general which parallels the particular point raised in connection with Weldon's acceptance of established standards in empirical appraisal. And it seems obvious that the issue is about the relation between language and society; or, more specifically, between language (words and concepts) and the context and rules which govern its use. When the usage of a word or the meaning of a concept is described what is indicated is the rules which make it uniform: for a series of occasions and many people are involved. Establishing a standard use implies, therefore, a social context in which alone the language is intelligible.[3]

In his memoir of Wittgenstein, Professor Malcolm reports that one of the Master's remarks struck him 'as being especially noteworthy and as summing up a good deal of his philosophy. It is "Ein Ausdruck hat nur im Ströme des Lebens Bedeutung" (An expression has meaning only in the stream of life).' He adds that Wittgenstein thought this aphorism was written down somewhere in his manuscripts, but he (Malcolm) had not seen it.[4] Nevertheless, it is certainly a characteristic opinion, and a basic one, and may be paralleled in the published works in the many references to 'a form of life', i.e. a mode of behaviour and the conventions governing it. When, Wittgenstein said, you come down to conventions, then you have struck rock bottom in your inquiry. To

---

[1] *English Philosophy Since 1900*, pp. 72, 150–1; 'Analysis and imagination', in *The Revolution in Philosophy* (ed. Ryle), p. 119.

[2] Cf. Wittgenstein, *Philosophical Investigations*, I, § 43; *Lectures and Conversations on Aesthetics, Psychology and Religious Belief* (ed. Barrett, Oxford, 1966), 'Lectures on aesthetics', I, §§ 5–6.

[3] P. Winch, *The Idea of a Social Science and its Relation to Philosophy* (London, 1958, repr. 1965), pp. 25–35, 40, 44, 123. Cf. the passage from Tolstoy's *War and Peace* (XII, 13) cited in Toulmin, *Reason in Ethics*, p. 68.

[4] N. Malcolm, *Ludwig Wittgenstein: a Memoir* (London, 1958, repr. 1962), p. 93. There is a sentence like the one Malcolm cites in *Zettel* (ed. Anscombe and von Wright, Oxford, 1967), § 173.

'imagine a language means to imagine a form of life'. The '*speaking* of language is part of an activity, or of a form of life'. It is 'as much a part of our natural history as walking, eating, drinking, playing'. 'What has to be accepted, the given, is—so one could say—*forms of life*.'[1] This point is shown, too, by the examples of language games which Wittgenstein invents: they involve such activities as buying from a shopkeeper, building and so on.[2] Thus, linguistic activity implies a 'culture'; to say one understands a word implies 'the whole environment of the event of saying it'.[3] Even the single act of naming an object cannot make sense unless 'a great deal of stage setting in the language is presupposed'.[4] Stressing the importance, in using words, of practice and custom, Wittgenstein says (exemplifying the point by reference to specific activities) that 'To obey a rule, to make a report, to give an order, to play a game of chess, are *customs* (uses, institutions)'—each, it is understood, with its own appropriate language conventions.[5] Language is 'founded on convention'.[6] And so, for instance, entirely different language games are played at different historical periods.[7] All this kind of thing lies in the background of using ordinary language. And to say that the various activities and types of discourse are governed by conventional rules is to indicate that they are not a matter of individual idiosyncracy or opinion: a society of individuals is involved and this makes possible an objective check, though not one referring to any abstract or ideal standard. For 'There is no outside; outside you cannot breathe'; there is only the standard immanent in the activity of language itself. Yet it is, of course, not an easy matter to determine what, in any given case, the conventional rules are. Thus, 'Language is a labyrinth of paths'—like any traditional form.[8] Mr Hampshire is one of those who have stressed the importance of this background of human activities and purposes when he describes the central lesson of Wittgenstein's later work, and of his repudiation of merely formal, systematic philosophy, as the view that

we fall into nonsense, mere idle words, if we consider questions or statements apart from the actual context of human life in which the questions would ordinarily be asked or the statements made. In order to achieve sense in

---

[1] *The Blue and Brown Books*, p. 24; *Philosophical Investigations*, I, §§ 19, 23, 25; *ibid.* II, p. 226e. Cf. Weldon's use of the concept throughout 'The justification of political attitudes'.

[2] Cf. *Philosophical Investigations*, I, § 6.

[3] *The Blue and Brown Books*, pp. 134, 157, Cf. 'Lectures on aesthetics', I, §§ 25–6, 35; also the comment of Gellner in *The Crisis in the Humanities* (ed. Plumb), pp. 56, 64, 71, 79–81.

[4] *Philosophical Investigations*, I, § 257; cf. *Zettel*, §§ 176, 387.

[5] *Philosophical Investigations*, I, § 199 (italics in original). See generally I, §§ 197–208; also the comments in D. Pole, *The Later Philosophy of Wittgenstein* (London, 1958), esp. pp. 2–3, 52, 75 and Warnock, *op. cit.* pp. 72–3.   [6] *Philosophical Investigations*, I, § 355.

[7] 'Lectures on aesthetics', I, §§ 25, 29, 31. Wittgenstein apparently thought it reasonable to talk of 'deterioration' (and so of 'progress'?) in an activity over time, *ibid.* I, §§ 33–4. Interesting possibilities are opened up by these opinions but are not pursued.

[8] *Philosophical Investigations*, I, §§ 103, 203, 238, 241.

thought and language, it is not enough merely to observe the dictionary definitions of words, the rules of grammar and the laws of logic. The significance of any statement whatever, together with its grammar and its logic, presuppose some constant background of ordinary human interests and purposes and of ordinary human experience

So, in any study of the scope and nature of human knowledge, we must ('as Kant and Wittgenstein suggested'), 'start on this explanation from the actual human situation which conditions all our thought and language'.[1]

What is involved is made even clearer by Professor Hart, as is perhaps to be expected by the nature of his subject. Introducing his analysis of the concept of law, he writes that

the suggestion that inquiries into the meanings of words merely throw light on words is false. Many important distinctions, which are not immediately obvious, between types of social situation or relationships, may best be brought to light by an examination of the standard uses of the relevant expressions and of *the way in which these depend on a social context, itself often left unstated.*

It is because he adopts this view that Hart can describe his study as 'an essay in descriptive sociology' and its aim as 'to further the understanding of law, coercion, and morality as different but related social phenomena'. And elsewhere Professor Hart writes that our notions of, say, an action or of property are very complex social concepts 'and logically dependent on accepted rules of conduct'.[2] Similarly, in a recent discussion of the concept of 'democracy', Professor Wollheim has suggested that the differences of meaning which can be detected are not arbitrary, as can be seen when they are considered in 'the whole context' in which the word is 'habitually used'. When placed 'in this wider setting,... the air of arbitrariness will tend to disappear'.[3] Reference has already been made to Professor Austin's emphasis on the study of actual language as it has grown up,[4] and there are many passages in which he stresses the importance of studying words in their concrete context.[5] In a couple of places, he explicitly indicated that he thought it useful to do some history in order to determine the meaning of an expression. But these open references are exceptional; the need is more often implied; and he facetiously referred to this kind of exercise as 'trailing clouds of etymology'.[6] Yet despite this, and even though he speaks about

[1] 'Metaphysical Systems', in *The Nature of Metaphysics* (ed. Pears), pp. 26–7, 31, cf. p. 34.
[2] *The Concept of Law* (Oxford, 1961), p. vii (my italics); 'The ascription of responsibility and rights' in *Logic and Language* (1st ser., ed. Flew), p. 161.
[3] R. Wollheim, 'On the theory of democracy', in *British Analytical Philosophy* (ed. Williams and Montefiore), p. 253.   [4] See above, pp. 115–16.
[5] E.g. *Philosophical Papers*, pp. 32, 124, 134–7, 198, 224–5, 231.
[6] *Ibid.* pp. 111–13, 149–51.

prising words off the world to examine them closely in respect of their inadequacies and arbitrariness, it is difficult to see how this can be attempted without due consideration of their context, especially as he goes on to refer to the place of words in the traditional life of mankind in specific situations and as leading us to the realities they represent.[1]

This really is the issue. If to study a language and its concepts is to know also an activity or form of life to which that language is intimately linked, is it possible to separate the two aspects involved? Is it not necessarily true that the analysis of concepts and categories as they are actually used[2] must partake also of a sort of historical or sociological inquiry? To try to settle puzzles about, say, 'the mind' or 'the state' by seeing how such words are used involves questions about the context and purposes of use, about, too, developments and changes in the use of words over time. After all, a language is an aid to social activity and a means of communication:[3] that is, it is a part of a larger complex of developing human relationships. And like any 'text' its meaning can only be unravelled in the correct 'context'. So it is impossible to study usage in any meaningful sense without taking this framework into account, this continually growing 'system of social activity'[4] of which language is a part.

Determining the use of a word, understanding concepts in any full or concrete sense, necessarily involves, therefore, embarking on the widest kind of historical inquiry into which philosophy (in the narrow, linguistic sense) is absorbed. It is never made clear, but it is apparent from this, that if modern philosophy repudiates the principles of positivism, then it replaces the categories of 'science' with those of 'history': and this is what, basically, allies it to the idealists.[5]

And in this connection, it must be observed that those opponents of modern philosophy, such as Professor Gellner,[6] who suggest that, on the terms of that philosophy, the status quo must be accepted for no criticism of what exists is possible, are quite wrong. Gellner, and those of similar mind, observe the modern philosopher's rejection of any

---

[1] *Philosophical Papers*, p. 130.

[2] *Philosophical Investigations*, I, § 124; Strawson, 'Construction and analysis', in *The Revolution in Philosophy* (ed. Ryle), pp. 103-4.

[3] *Philosophical Investigations*, I, § 491.

[4] Cf. Hart, *The Concept of Law*, p. 239 (note to p. 28 *ad fin.*); and *ibid.* pp. 234-5 where Hart stresses the importance, in discriminating between varieties of usage, of referring to contextual social situations'.

[5] It is, however, symptomatic of the manner of modern philosophers that they have paid little attention to the general history of their own subject. Yet their own suggestion that traditional philosophical problems are often confusions about language would, one might think, have required a detailed attention of this kind. But, of course, to investigate these matters would bring the student slap up against the problems of historical continuity, context and interpretation.

E.g. in *Crisis in the Humanities* (ed. Plumb), pp. 65, 68 and n.

transcendentally or similarly objective standard and seem to suppose that, therefore, in order to avoid the anarchy of subjectivism it is necessary simply to accept whatever standards are established, just as ordinary language is accepted as it stands. Yet this view overlooks the possibility of an immanent criterion, like that pursued by the idealists, and to which, in fact, the modern philosophers refer. This emerges when they discuss difficulties in ordinary usage and how it might be improved. They cannot refer to the criterion of a rationally ideal language, for this is rejected; the question is not of doing what one pleases; and the standard involved is that inherent in the usage itself which is being examined. Austin is looking in this direction when he writes 'Although it will not do to force actual language to accord with some preconceived model: it *equally* will not do, having disovered the facts about "ordinary usage" *to rest content* with that, as though there were nothing more to be discussed and discovered.'[1]

That modern philosophers appeal to a standard immanent in ordinary language is also revealed by their procedure. The ordinary man (even if he is 'educated') uses terms quite loosely and without differentiating as precisely as he might and as exactly as the linguistic philosopher does. He may in a way be wrong in being thus imprecise; but this does mean that ordinary language *as actually spoken and used* may be a rather different and more blunt medium than the ordinary language of the philosopher.[2] That this is possible is, of course, the result of convention, situation, tone of voice, gesture and other factors which make actual meaning precise enough.[3] But it does imply that the ordinary language of the philosopher is a sort of construct derived from actual speech. For example, in *Sense and Sensibilia*, Austin probes the distinctions between 'illusion' and 'delusion', and between 'like', 'seem' and 'appear', and employs this analysis (most of the time anyway) to significant philosophical purpose. But, in his everyday use of the words, does the ordinary man always distinguish so precisely? I doubt it. Indeed, terms that the philosopher likes to differentiate clearly the ordinary man may prefer to use as synonyms. The philosopher does not simply *describe* ordinary usage, as Wittgenstein was fond of asserting; he selects and refines. Ordinary language, then, is to be distinguished from 'Ordinary Language'. Concerned with the latter, the modern philosopher concentrates on standards and distinctions only implicit in the former.[4]

---

[1] *Philosophical Papers*, p. 37 (italics in original). Cf. *ibid.* p. 133 and *Sense and Sensibilia*, p. 63.
[2] Cf. Austin's reference to the looseness of 'colloquial speech', *Sense and Sensibilia*, p. 35 n.
[3] See e.g. *Zettel*, §§ 17, 144, 173, 176.
[4] Cf. Ryle, 'Systematically misleading expressions', in *Logic and Language* (1st ser., ed. Flew), pp. 11–14; P. L. Heath 'The appeal to ordinary language', *Philosophical Quarterly*, II (1952), 6–8. F. P. Ramsey said somewhere that the chief danger to philosophy was 'scholasticism ...which is treating what is vague as if it were precise'.

But the main point (about the relationship between the apparently neutral and abstract discussions of the modern philosopher and an actual form of life) may be reasserted by looking at the contemporary analysis of moral discourse.

Some modern philosophers have held the so-called emotive theory of ethics, that is, the view that the activity of valuing is essentially a statement of the individual's own feelings. To expound a moral point of view involves not a judgment but an exclamation. Yet this view raises certain difficulties of a kind relevant in the present context. In particular, it might be asked whether the feelings involved are entirely arbitrary: will they not be conditioned, derived from an already existing tradition of moral conduct? Emotional expression (of praise or condemnation, for instance) is intimately connected with a set of conventional behavioural attitudes. So that a moral statement (seen in emotional terms) presupposes a pre-existing ethical code.

Again, other modern philosophers, who are not emotivists, hold that ethics is the logical study of the language of morals and does not, therefore, involve commitment to a specific ethical point of view. Yet, although this looks nice and neutral in the best modern manner, a similar sort of cultural reference is involved. This is true, for instance, of Mr Hare's examination of moral action and the sensible choices of which it consists which has, most perceptively, been characterised as 'on the whole a satisfactory representation of the morality most commonly held in England'.[1] As I understand his point of view, it is that moral principles are both universalisable and practical in the sense that they are not simply capricious (reasons, albeit not of transcendental reference, can be given for them) and they can be used to guide action. At the same time, such principles are not incorrigible so it must follow that a rational moral judgment is one which is tolerant of other, different, points of view and which tries to arbitrate between conflicting interests and ideals. Consequently, although the analysis is cast in the apparently objective guise of second-order analysis of moral language, such terms as 'good', and 'right', it seems to result in, or itself rest on, a specific moral attitude, that of tolerant liberalism. It implies the existence of reasonable, mature individuals who do not press their opinions or interests too far; as also, I imagine, it implies the existence of rules and rulers of a certain type adequate to control any excess that emerges. I do not myself find this built-in model of traditional British liberalism either surprising or reprehensible: quite the contrary. But this kind of premise is best articulated. If it is not brought out into the open, explicit moralising is perhaps

[1] Iris Murdoch, 'Metaphysics and ethics', in *The Nature of Metaphysics* (ed. Pears), p. 111. Cf. her contribution to the discussion on 'Philosophy and beliefs', *The Twentieth Century*, XLVII (1955), 504, 516.

avoided, but it is nonetheless there, done 'unconsciously'.[1] And the vital task of examining satisfactorily actual traditions of moral conduct is perforce neglected. Interestingly enough, there seems to be a measure of agreement among some modern philosophers about this deficiency in correct ethical thinking.[2] I suppose Mr Toulmin has come closest to trying to overcome this defect and his attempt involves an explicit recognition of established ethical rules. Most interestingly, too, the way in which he describes the development of ethical understanding is very like that of the idealists. He considers and rejects the views that 'good' is either a sort of objective property or simply a report on one's own feelings or a concept used for persuasion. He then suggests that the question to be asked is not 'What is good?' but 'What is a good reason in ethical discussion?'. This leads him to his analysis of moral under-standing and to the view that it is a developing thing and that an essen-tial phase of its growth is embedded in obedience to the moral obliga-tions of the society in which one lives; though this must lead to a further phase of criticism about this system of obligation.[3] How very like Bosanquet or Bradley this is! Indeed the latter is specifically cited (though there are also some Popperite naïveties comparing this process of moral growth to engineering). The final passage, quoted from Lowes Dickinson, has obvious similar affinities.[4]

Modern philosophers, then, fail to probe adequately enough into the presuppositions and implications of their own procedures. In particular, they do not appreciate (except in an occasional and partial way) the nature of the contextual, historical considerations that the analysis of language really demands. They might say this is not their job; but then, if this is so, what we need is (in the old-fashioned sense) a philosophy of philosophy (as linguistic analysis). I would not for one moment agree with those who suggest that the approach of modern philosophy is necessarily trivial or useless; and it clearly demands a very high degree of intellectual acumen and sophistication. But it does set aside matters of considerable and fundamental significance in what (until recently) was regarded as the philosophical field: not only its own foundations but other interesting areas of discussion. Further, the range of application of its techniques seems limited; and everything is seen in the mirror of standard English which is used as an authoritative philosophical guide.[5]

The linguistic attitude clearly implies a *Weltanschauung*, a view of all

[1] I. Murdoch, 'Metaphysics and ethics', p. 121.
[2] See M. Warnock, 'Final discussion', *The Nature of Metaphysics*, p. 163; A. Montefiore, 'Fact, value and ideology', in *British Analytical Philosophy* (ed. Williams and Montefiore), pp. 183, 186, 201, 202.
[3] *Reason in Ethics*, pp. 170-1, 223.
[4] *Ibid.* p. 225.
[5] Cf. Bradley, *Ethical Studies* (2nd ed., Oxford, 1962), pp. 1-3.

sorts of facts seen as a whole,[1] a recommendation that we should regard them in a certain way. But it is curiously lop-sided; a pattern of connections is missed. And the type of affinity briefly examined here suggests that an adequate rationale of the wider perspective that is implied and which might be achieved lies in the idealist tradition. Close and sympathetic attention to the insights this tradition can offer, and less facile denigration, would constitute a valuable change of direction, not least in respect of the philosophical analysis of such practical thought and activity as politics.

[1] Wittgenstein, *Philosophical Investigations*, I, § 122. The puzzlement evident in this passage is slurred over in the translation. 'Die übersichtliche Darstellung' is not merely 'A perspicuous representation' but rather 'The overall view', which, as Wittgenstein sees, produces understanding by seeing connections. Nor perhaps was he elsewhere wholly unsympathetic to such a 'metaphysical' enterprise: see *ibid.* I, § 111.

PARADIGMS AND POLITICAL
THEORIES

SHELDON S. WOLIN

The status of political theory has been a perennial subject of controversy. In recent years the debate in the United States has focused upon
methodological considerations. This was probably inevitable, given the
intention of a sizable group to transform the study of politics into a 'science
of politics modelled after the methodological assumptions of the natural
sciences'.[1] In pointing to the model of scientific inquiry as the appropriate one for political and social science; by claiming that reliable
political knowledge was to be acquired only by emulating scientific
procedures of observation, data-gathering, classification, and verification; and by insisting that precise knowledge was identical with the
transformation of 'metaphysical' or 'normative' statements into empirically verifiable ones, the exponents of science succeeded in restricting
the debate to procedural matters. On this ground they encountered
only scattered opposition. An occasional critic might charge social
scientists with the mistake of treating philosophical questions as empirical ones,[2] but as resistance dwindled it was increasingly assumed
that the case had been proven for applying scientific methods to the
study of politics, that it was indeed science that was being applied, and,
consequently, that the time was not distant when political science would
enjoy the two main benefits of science, precise and cumulative knowledge. It is now commonplace to encounter in the literature of political
and social science a statement like the following which occurs almost
as an afterthought: 'Everything we have said already has been based
on the assumption that social science is not only possible but even essentially the same as natural science.'[3]

There are two features of the case for a scientific politics which I wish
to examine here. As suggested above, the advocates of science have set
for themselves the objective of developing a theory which will serve as
a guide for empirical inquiry. They state explicitly that this theory is
intended as a substitute for 'traditional' (i.e. pre-scientific) theory. The
nature of the substitute has two aspects: it involves the application of

[1] D. Easton, *A Framework for Political Analysis* (Englewood Cliffs, New Jersey: Prentice-Hall,
1965), p. 8.
[2] P. Winch, *The Idea of a Social Science* (London: Routledge and Kegan Paul, 1956), *passim*.
[3] B. Barber, *Science and the Social Order* (New Tork: Collier Books, 1962), p. 311.

a different method, that of science, and a different set of questions. The idea of a substitute presupposes a critical judgment about the shortcomings of traditional theory. A representative example of such a judgment would be the following: 'Theorizing, even about politics, is not to be confused with metaphysical speculation in terms of abstractions hopelessly removed from empirical observation and control.'[1] This is the first feature of the case which I propose to examine. It will be my contention that the nature of traditional theory has been misunderstood and that this misunderstanding has been read back so as to mislead the political scientist about the nature, consequences, and possibilities of his own enterprise.

The second feature is closely connected with the first. The scientific critique has charged that traditional political theory has failed to produce cumulative knowledge. The response of the defenders of the tradition has been surprisingly weak. Sometimes they have contended that it is no longer possible to produce an original theory about politics. Most of the important things, it is alleged, have already been said. Other times the defenders of the tradition have argued that each age or society has been concerned with its own peculiar political problems, and hence political knowledge has been and always will be local and restricted. The political scientist has taken advantage of these uncertainties and, by pointing to the successful example of science, has argued that one of the boons of scientific methods is the promise of creating an expanding body of reliable knowledge. Under this heading, I wish to examine the possibility that the idea of scientific progress has been misconceived.

To a considerable extent, the two aspects are related. The political scientist[2] contends that *because* traditional theory was preoccupied with metaphysical or 'normative' concerns, it was unable to produce a cumulative body of knowledge. In addressing questions about the nature of justice, authority, rights, and equality and in formulating these questions in terms of projective models of a good society which were supposed to embody the true form of justice and authority, traditional theory saddled itself with a type of inquiry in which it was impossible to progress, or, indeed, even to specify what a cumulative advance would look like. The usual objection made by political scientists is that traditional theory abounds in assertions which are in principle untestable. In those cases, such as in the writings of Machiavelli, where the statements are amenable to empirical proof, theorists

[1] H. D. Lasswell and A. Kaplan, *Power and Society: a Framework for Political Inquiry* (New Haven: Yale University Press, 1950), p. x.

[2] I use interchangeably the words 'political', 'social', and 'behavioural' science. Inasmuch as most political scientists aspire to be 'social' or 'behavioural' scientists, my usage is not arbitrary. My comments are directed primarily at American political science.

have been satisfied with examples or illustrations rather than systematic evidence.

The contemporary political scientist is determined to avoid these pitfalls by following a different prescription: 'Whether [a] proposition is true or false depends on the degree to which the proposition and the real world correspond.'[1] If theory is to produce reliable political knowledge, it must subject its assertions to systematic testing. In the past the failure to develop methods of empirical verification and to formulate statements which, in principle, are testable, has deprived theory of the means for resolving conflicting assertions about politics or for establishing a reliable foundation of knowledge upon which succeeding research might build. By rejecting scientific procedures, earlier theorists had closed off the possibility of cumulative knowledge and had condemned the enterprise to an anarchic condition in which no problem is ever solved, no issue ever closed, and no assertion, however bizarre, ever refuted. Although on occasion the dissenting voice of a Hobbes might protest the scandalous contrast between the static condition of theory and the progressive course of science, the situation remained unremedied for centuries. A few decades ago, a contemporary political scientist expressed exactly the same judgment as Hobbes: that political science had not as yet advanced beyond the stage of Aristotle.[2]

According to its critics, the non-cumulative character of traditional theory is inherent not only in its preoccupations and methods but in its strategy as well.

A science of politics [we are told], which deserves its name must build from the bottom up by asking simple questions that can, in principle, be answered; it cannot be built from the top down by asking questions that, one has reason to suspect, cannot be answered at all, at least not by the methods of science. An empirical discipline is built by the slow, modest, and piecemeal cumulation of relevant theories and data.[3]

The history of science is said to demonstrate that cumulative knowledge has been the result of cooperative effort. Ideally, therefore, theories should be akin to battle-plans which permit numerous researchers to push ahead, each adding his own advance to the previously consolidated position and preparing the way for a fresh push after his own assignment has been completed. Traditional theory, in contrast, has produced its solitary heroes, inspired by the dream of creating *the* theory which would stand perfect and complete for all time, consciously designed not to encourage modifications or improvements. Our contemporary

---

[1] R. Dahl, *Modern Political Analysis* (Englewood Cliffs, New Jersey: Prentice-Hall, 1963), p. 8.
[2] H. Simon, '"The decision-making schema": a reply', *Public Administration Review*, vol. 18 (1958), p. 63.
[3] H. Eulau, *The Behavioral Persuasion in Politics* (New York, Random House: 1963), p. 9.

conception of the strategic implementation of theory was first announced by Bacon, who had mocked classical philosophy—'it can talk,
but cannot generate'—and had spread before men's eyes a vision of
organised and strategically directed research that is now taken for granted:

For I well know that axioms once rightly discovered will carry whole troops
of works along with them, and produce them, not here and there one, but in
clusters...Consider what may be expected...from men abounding in
leisure, and from association of labours, and from successions of ages: the
rather because it is not a way which only one man can pass at a time (as is
the case with that of reasoning) but one in which the labours and industries
of men (especially as regards the collecting of experience) may with the
best effect be first distributed and then combined. For only then will men
begin to know their strength, when instead of great numbers doing all the
same things, one shall take charge of one thing and another of another.[1]

The case for the scientific study of politics is based on the contention
that traditional theory was 'trans-empirical',[2] more concerned with
transcending the world of facts than with formulating propositions
which could be tested against the world of facts. This misunderstanding
of the nature of theory has foreclosed the possibility of cumulative
knowledge. One solution, which has met with widespread approval, is to
distinguish 'normative theory', which would comprise the traditional
preoccupations with 'values', ideal political orders, and the history of
political theory, from 'empirical theory' which would concentrate upon
employing scientific procedures in the acquisition of reliable knowledge
and building a growing body of steadily more inclusive generalisations.[3]

The view of science and scientific progress held by political scientists
is not unwarranted by prevailing conceptions of science. According to
one authority, '...the most dynamic, distinctive, and influential creation of the western mind is a progressive science of nature. Only there in
the technical realm does the favorite western idea of progress hold any
demonstrable meaning.'[4] The question which I wish to raise is whether
these prevailing conceptions are the only ones. Are there other conceptions of science and scientific progress which present more striking

---

[1] *The Great Instuaration* (from 'The plan of the work'; *Novum Organum*, Bk. I, cxiii. Quotations
are from the edition by H. G. Dick, *Francis Bacon: selected Writings* (New York: Random
House, 1955), pp. 447, 525.
[2] See Dahl, *op. cit.* p. 102.
[3] This distinction is defended by Dahl, *op. cit.* pp. 101 ff. and W. C. Runciman, *Social Science
and Political Theory* (Cambridge, 1963), p. 2. Some of the implications of this distinction
had been anticipated by Bacon's contrast between 'one method for the cultivation, another
for the invention of knowledge'. The former referred to the 'received philosophy' and was
useful 'for supplying matters for disputations or ornaments for discourse,—for the professor's
lecture and for the business of life'. The latter was for exploring the 'untried and unknown'.
Novum Organum, Preface. *Selected Writings*, pp. 458–9.
[4] C. C. Gillespie, *The Edge of Objectivity* (Princeton, 1960), p. 8.

analogies, not with scientific political inquiry as it is now understood, but with traditional political theory as it used to be practised? Are there conceptions which assign a different role to theory and research and which, as a consequence, cast a different and even disturbing light on the understanding of scientific progress and, more significantly, on the intellectual and material conditions necessary to promote scientific knowledge? Is the particular relationship between fact and theory, which seems to lie at the basis of the hopes for a scientific politics, so straightforward a matter in science? If there are disturbing complexities, what is their import for the relationship between political theories and political facts?

It may seem bizarre to suggest parallels between scientific theory and traditional political theory,[1] yet this objection may be overcome if one consideration, which is apt to be forgotten by political scientists, is recalled. To describe science as a cumulative body of knowledge, that is, knowledge acquired incrementally over time, is to suggest that important things can be learned about the practice of science when it is interpreted as an historical enterprise. This is the assumption of the historian of science who attempts to explain how discoveries have occurred and why some errors proved fruitful and others unproductive.[2] Until very recently the historical approach was the preferred method of studying and teaching political theory. The justification of the historical method, however, was rarely that it enabled the student to become acquainted with theories which were progressively truer. A few interpretations did suggest that earlier theories had prepared the way for the truth embodied in a particular theory (e.g. Thomism or Marxism), but on the whole these interpretations have been treated as inspired by the same sort of suspicious motives which once led Christian writers to describe the ancient religions as a *praeparatio evangelica* for Christianity. Instead, the study of the major theories from the Greeks onwards is defended either as a means for improving one's understanding of politics by exposing it to the diversity of ideas embodied in the history of theory; or as a means for becoming acquainted with 'ageless' theories;[3] or, finally, as a way of analysing the relationships between a particular theory and its social, political and philosophical milieu.[4] What has not

---

[1] Throughout this essay 'traditional political theory' is intended to refer to the major writers in the Western tradition of political theory. Marx, whose writings are full of a fine ambivalence towards the older modes of theorizing, constitutes a convenient dividing line.

[2] The fruitfulness of error has been emphasised by K. Popper, *Conjectures and Refutations* (London: Routledge and Kegan Paul, 1963), especially essays 1, 3, 4, and 10. See also J. Agassi, 'Towards an historiography of science', *History and Theory*, Beiheft 2 (1963), pp. 4–54.

[3] Justifications based upon diversity and agelessness have been advanced by J. Plamenatz, *Man and Society*, 2 vols. (New York: McGraw-Hill, 1963), vol. 1, p. xxi.

[4] G. H. Sabine, *A History of Political Theory*, 3rd ed. (New York: Holt, Rinehart and Winston, 1961), pp. v–vi.

been argued is that the student of theory should investigate Plato, Aristotle, Machiavelli, and Marx in the same spirit as the student of chemistry examines the work of Boyle, Black, Cavendish, Priestley, and Lavoisier, that is, as a movement towards a progressively truer theory.

All of this seems commonplace and scarcely worth the effort of stating it, except for the fact that many of the great theorists held a different view of their work. They believed that their theories had advanced political knowledge past the point achieved by their pre-decessors. 'I depart very far from the methods of others', Machiavelli wrote, 'but since my aim is to write something useful to him who under-stands it, I have decided to concentrate on the truth of the matter rather than with any fanciful notion.'[1] The precise sense in which Machiavelli considered his own work to be an advance over the past is a complicated question and while it is easy enough to distinguish it from a claim to having added to the previous state of knowledge, it is not so easy to say whether Machiavelli considered his own theories to have superseded completely those of the past, or only some of the past theories, or only some parts of past theories. At any event, the idea of theoretical advance is present and it is stated in a way that invites historical inquiry.

If it is granted that in some as yet unspecified sense the historical dimension is relevant both to scientific theory, which has displayed cumulative advance, and to political theory, which has not, at least apparently not in the same way, then we might consider some of the unsettling possibilities which are being suggested by the newer ways of analysing the history of science. The contemporary behaviourist, who confidently entertains a hard distinction between traditional or pre-scientific political theories and contemporary scientific ones, must surely experience some uncertainty when he reads that historians of science are experiencing

growing difficulties in distinguishing the 'scientific' component of past ob-servation and belief from what their predecessors had readily labelled 'error' and 'superstition'. The more carefully they study, say, Aristotelian dynamics, phlogistic chemistry, or caloric thermodynamics, the more certain they feel that those once current views of nature were, as a whole, neither less scientific nor more the product of human idiosyncrasy than those current today. If those out-of-date beliefs are to be called myths, then myths can be produced by the same sort of methods that now lead to scientific knowledge.[2]

---

[1] *Il Principe*, ch. 15. In this context there is great relevancy to Marx's constant effort to indicate his debts to his predecessors as well as to demonstrate the precise nature of his advance beyond them.

[2] T. Kuhn, *The Structure of Scientific Revolutions* (Chicago: University of Chicago Press, 1964; first edition 1962), p. 2. This viewpoint is implicit in the earlier work of E. A. Burtt, *The Metaphysical Foundations of Modern Science* (1924); see his discussion of the Copernican revolu-tion (New York: Doubleday Anchor, 1954), pp. 38 ff.

To take one more example of special interest to those neo-Hobbesians who look upon traditional political theories as the principal reason for the non-cumulative state of political knowledge: We are told that historians of science now entertain 'profound doubts about the cumulative process' and 'rather than seeking the permanent contributions of an older science to our present vantage, they attempt to display the historical integrity of that science in its own time'.[1]

In the remaining pages I wish to consider the possible bearing of these new interpretations of science on our understanding of both contemporary and traditional political theory. The specific issues and suggestions which I wish to consider can be most readily understood by restating briefly the major argument advanced in one recent book, *The Structure of Scientific Revolutions* by Professor Thomas Kuhn. Although Kuhn's argument is addressed to historians and philosophers of science, much of what he says has a relevancy and special poignancy for the scientifically minded political scientist. Few political scientists are trained as scientists and few are interested in investigating for themselves the logical basis or the historical development of the sciences. For the most part their conceptions of science, its methods, and its history have no other basis than some view which they believe to be authoritative. Wanting nothing more than to be allowed to get on with the work of empirical investigation, they are not anxious to engage in disputes concerning the theoretical foundations which support and justify their work. Their hope is that the meaning of science has been settled. This lends a special irony to the heroic charge which Hobbes had laid on his inheritors: if words are valued 'by the authority of an Aristotle, a Cicero, or a Thomas, or any other doctor whatsoever, if but a man', they 'are the money of fools'. The value of Kuhn's book is that it takes direct issue with certain specific notions concerning scientific progress which are a vital part of the justifications accepted by political scientists.

Kuhn disputes the view of scientific progress as a form of incremental advance which is made possible because scientists scrupulously adhere to certain practices governing theorising. He argues against the notion that scientific progress results from the way that scientists build on the achievements of their predecessors; and that scientific theories are discarded when new knowledge has disproved them, or when they fail to to conform to commonly accepted standards of scientific explanation and proof. It is not Kuhn's intention to destroy these notions of scientific progress, only to object to their being identified with the whole of scientific activity and theory construction. The cumulative growth of scientific knowledge and the process whereby a particular scientific

[1] Kuhn. *op. cit.* p. 3.

theory is modified as a result of research are part of what Kuhn characterises as 'normal science'. To convey his meaning he adopts socio-
political language. Normal science is a particular form of activity carried
on by a 'community' of scientists. Students of seventeenth-century
political thought will find Kuhn's analysis of the scientific community
familiar: it is a community based on an agreement which extends not
only to the rules governing inquiry and to stipulations concerning what
shall qualify as a scientific question and count as a scientific answer, but
it extends as well to the particular theory which is accepted as true by
the members in their research and investigation. The particular theory
which dominates a scientific community is designated a 'paradigm'.
From a sociological viewpoint, a paradigm provides a consensual basis
which consolidates the loyalties and commitments of the members. Paradigms are 'universally recognised scientific achievements that for a time
provide model problems and solutions to a community of practitioners'
(p. x). As the acknowledged arbiter of what constitutes significant
scientific activity a paradigm guides the community in its choice of
problems; the community, in turn, has as its task the solution of the
puzzles set by the paradigm. Scientific progress consists in fulfilling the
promise of a paradigm. Generally, a paradigm is worked out in three
main ways. First, scientists seek to establish in rigorous fashion the class
of facts subsumed under the paradigm. Second, they test the predictions
of the paradigm with the facts disclosed by investigation: they 'match'
fact and theory to ascertain the extent of correspondence or 'fit'.
Finally, they seek to articulate the theory by undertaking factual investigations designed to clarify problems suggested by the paradigm
(pp. 24–7).

As Kuhn would have it, the crucial mark of a mature science consists
of a paradigm recognised as such by the scientific community. Recognition means not only that the community agrees to conduct research
along lines determined by the paradigm, but that it is willing to enforce the paradigm on its members. Scientific progress is critically
dependent upon the ability of a community to develop effective means
of enforcement. The achievements of science are testimony to the skill
with which scientists have solved the political problem of organisation.
'In its normal state...a scientific community is an enormously efficient
instrument for solving the problems or puzzles that its paradigms define'
(p. 165).[1] A scientific community develops means for concerting the
energy, resources, and attention of the members and directing them

[1] Compare the above with the account of a social scientist: '...science rejects the imposition
of any truth by organized and especially by non-scientific authority. The canons of validity
for scientific knowledge are also individualistic: they are vested not in any formal organiza-
tion but in the individual consciences and judgments of scientists who are, for this function,
only informally organized.' Barber, *op. cit.* p. 99.

unremittingly towards the elaboration of a designated theory. Among these means are the rules and practices entailed by the paradigm; members of the community are expected to conform to these norms of scientific behaviour and non-conformance is usually met by sanctions. Deviant behaviour, to use the current idiom, does not normally take the form of rejecting scientific methods but of directing them to problems which do not lie within the province of the accepted paradigm or of applying them in a way which suggests a view of the world different from that implied by the reigning paradigm.

Normal scientific activity, the activity in which most scientists inevitably spend almost all their time, is predicated on the assumption that the scientific community knows what the world is like. Much of the success of the enterprise derives from the community's willingness to defend that assumption, if necessary at considerable cost. Normal science, for example, often suppresses fundamental novelties because they are necessarily subversive of its basic commitments (p. 5).

Social scientists who are impressed by the seeming fertility of the scientific imagination in producing new theories may be sobered by Kuhn's emphatic assertion that one of 'the most striking features' of normal science is 'how little' it aims 'to produce major novelties, conceptual or phenomenal' (p. 35). Scientific progress, far from arising out of the concerted quest for endless theoretical novelties, seems to require the suppression of competing viewpoints.[1] The enforcement of a paradigm permits the normal scientist to get on with his work without being distracted by the need to defend the basic principles of the paradigm, its canons of inquiry, or the view of the world which it embodies (pp. 162–3). As we shall note later, novel theories have their place, but they tend to be restricted to times of trouble when the scientific community undergoes a crisis in belief regarding its paradigm. The scientific community prospers best when crisis and novelty are rare. Unlike other communities which experience a crisis in belief and seek gropingly to adjust, the scientific community rapidly adapts itself to a new paradigm, quickly redefines its membership, and efficiently disposes of the old believers.

...There are always some men who cling to one or another of the older views, and they are simply read out of the profession, which thereafter ignores their work. The new paradigm implies a new and more rigid definition of the field. Those unwilling or unable to accommodate their work to it must proceed in isolation or attach themselves to some other group (p. 19).[2]

[1] An instructive case-study of the rigidity of the scientific community is 'The politics of science and Dr Velikovsky', *American Behavioral Scientist*, vol. vii, no. 1 (September, 1963).
[2] Kuhn's phrase, a 'more rigid definition of the field', is employed in the context of a discussion of the crisis-phase when a paradigm tends to loosen and dissolve.

The enforcing power, seemingly so vital to scientific advance, presupposes a membership willing and predisposed to acquiesce in the observance of the norms of the community. Just as other communities develop means of inducting citizens into the practices and beliefs of the community and seek to internalise the values of the community, the scientific community has also understood that the exercise of coercive authority can be made cheaper, more efficient, and less obtrusive if the modes of initiation and education of the members predispose them towards the loyal behaviour needed in paradigm-workers. Kuhn describes the process of initiation as partly a matter of winning the loyalty of a new generation of scientists to the view of the world embodied in a paradigm, and partly as a matter of enforcing the authority of the paradigm and of its community of practitioners upon the initiates. The major vehicle is scientific education which trains the student in the methods and outlook of the dominant paradigm. The use of scientific textbooks plays a strategically significant part in the education of scientists; they are a major means 'for the perpetuation of normal science'. The student is made to rely upon textbooks until this third or fourth year of graduate study and, as Kuhn wryly notes, he is rarely exposed to 'the creative scientific literature' that made the textbook possible (p. 164). In its customary form, the textbook contributes powerfully to the view that the history of science is a record of cumulative advance. Textbooks 'refer only to that part of the work of past scientists that can be easily viewed as contributions to the statement and solution of the texts' paradigm problems'. 'Partly by selection and partly by distortion' earlier scientists 'are implicitly represented as having worked upon the same set of fixed problems and in accordance with the same set of fixed canons that the most recent revolution in scientific theory and method has made seem scientific' (pp. 136–7). Kuhn concludes that 'it is a narrow and rigid education, probably more so than any other except perhaps in orthodox theology. But for normal-scientific work, for puzzle-solving within the tradition that the textbooks define, the scientist is almost perfectly equipped' (p. 165).

Thus political scientists who envy the organisation of the scientific community and the results of its research, should have a special interest in Kuhn's observations on the process whereby that community institutes one paradigm rather than another. The contemporary political scientist finds himself assailed by a variety of paradigms competing for support, material as well as intellectual and emotional. Is there an objective way for deciding between the competing claims of game theory, bargaining theory, equilibrium models, systems theory, communication theory, functional theory, or structural-functional theory? Kuhn offers little comfort on this score. Up to a certain point, what matters is not which is the 'truer' paradigm, but which is to be enforced. In the early development of most sciences, diverse theories competed for acceptance; the eventual losers were not adjudged to be less scientific, nor was the winner decided by appealing to impersonal standards of observation or experience. 'An apparently arbitrarily element' operates in the selection of one paradigm over another (p. 4). 'Philosophers of science have repeatedly demonstrated that more than one theoretical construction can always be placed upon a given collection of data.' Alternative scientific theories are easy to invent, Kuhn remarks, but scientists rarely permit themselves this form of indulgence, because it diverts energy and resources from on-going work. 'Retooling is an extravagance' (p. 76).

The arbitrary element in the choice of paradigms is best revealed during crises when an existing paradigm is being challenged. When the challenge is successful and a new paradigm displaces the old, the scientific community has undergone what Kuhn characterises as a revolution. He finds this to be a recurrent experience in the development of the mature sciences. His discussion is relevant to the political scientist who finds himself in the midst of the 'behavioural revolution'. The relevance of a scientific revolution does not lie in the repetition of a word, but in what the scientific experience discloses about the relationship between fact and theory or, more precisely, about the criteria used in discarding one theory for another.

In Kuhn's view, normal science is characterised by a close 'fit' between theory and fact. In the practice of normal science, the truth or falsity of statements is determined by confronting the operative paradigm with facts disclosed or amassed by investigation and observation (p. 80). The intimate relation between theory and fact is closely connected with, and even made possible by, the kind of activity decreed in the working out of a paradigm. Kuhn describes this activity as a species of puzzle-solving. The research problems of normal science are set by its paradigm: the problems are to the paradigm as pieces are to a puzzle. The solution 'exists' but has yet to be worked out; or, stated differently, the outcome is anticipated, but the way of achieving it remains in doubt. What may be an unsolved puzzle for one paradigm may not even exist for another (p. 80).

...one of the things a scientific community acquires with a paradigm is a criterion for choosing problems that, while the paradigm is taken for granted, can be assumed to have solutions. To a great extent these are the only problems that the community will admit as scientific or encourage its members to undertake...One of the reasons why normal science seems to progress so rapidly is that its practitioners concentrate on problems that only their lack of ingenuity should keep them from solving (p. 37).

The assumption that solutions exist to the puzzles of a paradigm gives rise to expectations about what will be found through research. As long as these expectations are mostly fulfilled, science is said to proceed normally. When the expectations are frustrated; when inquiry discloses facts which cannot be squared with the paradigm, the scientific community undergoes a crisis in belief. Its confidence in the reigning paradigm is shaken. Kuhn introduces the concept of 'anomaly' to describe these findings of normal science which cannot be reconciled with the paradigm, despite efforts made at adjusting the paradigm (pp. 52–3). Kuhn finds it difficult to advance a simple explanation as to why or when a particular anomaly provokes a crisis in theory. 'There are always some discrepancies' between a theory and nature, and normal science is able to function effectively despite 'persistent and recognized anomaly'. At one time, the existence of an anomaly will prove so compelling that it 'call(s) into question explicit and fundamental generalisations of the paradigm'. At another time a crisis may develop when the anomaly appears to obstruct certain practical aims, as when astrology inhibited the design of calendars and the resulting dissatisfaction helped to prepare the way for the acceptance of the Copernican paradigm (pp. 81–2).

When anomalies reach the stage of 'crisis' the repercussions on the scientific community are profound. In the face of repeated failures to solve the puzzles set by the paradigm, the scientist feels insecure and his insecurity is reflected in a certain loosening of discipline and a relaxation of the rules governing research (pp. 67–8, 83). 'Divergent articulations' of the paradigm begin to appear and are encouraged by a growing realisation that what had been thought to be merely a particularly stubborn puzzle is something unaccountable under the terms of the old dispensation. The few scientists who had first dared to question the paradigm are joined by others who commit themselves to resolving the crisis. Soon normal science gives way to 'extraordinary' science which signifies a determination to look at the world anew and uninhibited by the frowning presence of the old paradigm. Once the old paradigm has been doubted, its authority-structure is weakened and the resultant crisis 'loosens the rules of normal puzzle solving in ways that ultimately permit a new paradigm to emerge' (p. 80).

No paradigm is overthrown unless an alternative lies at hand; but once the new paradigm has been proclaimed, the scientific community quickly institutionalises it, employing all of its means for enforcement and compliance. The rigidity of the community, which had previously discouraged novel alternatives, now becomes a powerful asset for consolidating the new theory. The fact that it truly possesses an 'establishment' enables the scientific community to make its paradigm-switch quickly and efficiently. Above all, once the decision to switch has been taken, the authority and power of the community are available for insuring compliance (pp. 164–5).

The decision itself is not easily achieved, given the formidable apparatus of enforcement behind the existing paradigm and the fact that a paradigm is maintained by destroying its rivals and suppressing alternatives. Indeed, Kuhn appears most uncertain in the matter of explaining why it is that a paradigm is ever successfully challenged. At one point he suggests that the arbitrary element inherent in the choice of any paradigm makes it likely that normal research will encounter anomalies which will eventually provoke a crisis (p. 5). Elsewhere he simply notes that the rigidity of the scientific community may prevent insiders from challenging the paradigm but since its writ does not extend to 'outside' fields, there is always the possibility of the scientific equivalent to *l'étranger* proposing a new paradigm, a possibility that has occurred frequently in the history of science (pp. 143, 164). In the face of the resistance that any challenging paradigm is likely to encounter, Kuhn's uncertainty edges towards despair and his conclusion echoes the same doubts that haunted the medieval defenders of another kind of paradigm: 'But so long as somebody appears with a new candidate for paradigm— usually a young man or one new to the field—the loss due to rigidity accrues only to the individual' (p. 165).

The question of most interest to the political scientist is, what induces the scientific community to reject its reigning paradigm and to choose another? It is not enough to suggest that a theory is discarded when it is falsified. No theory ever fits the facts completely and every theory is capable of being falsified. A theory maintains its hold over its practitioners, not because it has resisted falsification or because it fits the facts as a glove fits the hand, but because the scientific community agrees that the theory fits the facts 'better' *when* the facts are viewed from the perspective of *that* theory (pp. 144–6).

Most political scientists tend to assume that the decision to change paradigms is analogous to a fact-finding proceeding in which, *per curiram*, scientists review new 'facts' and on the basis of logic, evidence, and experiment solemnly decide that the old theory has been superseded by a 'higher' form of explanation.[1] In Kuhn's description, a decision between paradigms appears more like an adversary proceeding,

---

[1] This appears to be the assumption underlying the following statement about 'interdisciplinary' progress in social science theory: 'What some have felt to be fruitless and wasteful inquiries into the theoretical boundaries of our discipline have simply represented a groping toward at least the gross units in terms of which political life can be identified, observed, and analyzed...Slay the dragon of disciplinary redefinition as we may, it insists upon rearing its head in a new form each time and to higher levels of conceptual sophistication.' Easton, *op. cit.* p. 22.

more competitive than deliberative.[1] What is at issue are new cognitive and normative standards, not new facts. A new theory embodies a new way of looking at phenomena rather than the discovery of hitherto inaccessible data. It represents a break with the existing tradition of scientific practice and proclaims new standards of legitimate activity; it proposes somewhat different rules for inquiry, a different problem-field, as well as different notions of significance and of what constitutes a solution. Neither the new paradigm nor the old can provide neutral procedures for deciding between their respective merits, because each paradigm has its own distinctive procedures. Because 'each group uses its own paradigm to argue in that paradigm's defense', the neutrality of each is impugned and there is no *tertium quid* available.

The lack of a neutral arbiter becomes all the more intriguing if it is recalled that established facts are susceptible to diverse explanations and that no theory provides a perfect fit with the facts.[2] The 'arbitrary' element mentioned earlier should not be taken to imply a total lack of accepted criteria for judging between paradigms. At a minimum, a new paradigm must hold out the promise of being able to transform the old anomalies into new puzzles. It must also be capable of generating new puzzles for research. Above all, a further reduction in the arbitrariness accompanying the decision to switch follows from the fact that the decision will be made by those most qualified rather than by 'outsiders'.[3] After these qualifications have been duly noted, it remains the case that the decision concerning the future possibilities of a particular paradigm is one that 'can only be made on faith' (p. 157).

Kuhn's analysis may produce some anxieties in the political scientist who had believed that scientific theories were, in some simple sense, symbolic reproductions of reality. These anxieties may provoke him to protest that 'nature' represents a 'reality' that, after all is said and done, is *there*; hence it would be misleading to suggest that the enforcement of a paradigm merely proves that a theory works, not that it is true. The reality of nature sets limits to what would be considered an admissible candidate for paradigm-adoption. The way that Kuhn treats this objection is not likely to dispel the anxieties of the political scientist. He puts it in the form of a question: 'what must nature...be like in order that science be possible at all?' His answer suggests that 'nature'

---

[1] Kuhn writes: 'Competition between segments of the scientific community is the only historical process that ever actually results in the rejection of one previously accepted theory or in the adoption of another' (p. 8).

[2] Compare the following: '...Knowledge is to be a [conceptual] reproduction of the external world...' V. Gordon Childe, *Society and Knowledge* (New York: Harper, 1956), p. 54.

[3] Kuhn does not consider the question of whether these decisions may have been influenced by governmental authorities or industrialists.

does not constitute an obvious limit at all: 'Any conception of nature compatible with the growth of science...' will do (p. 172), which would seem to be tantamount to saying that it is the requirements of scientific advance, rather than anything permanent about nature, which are determining.

II

Customarily, the historical study of political theories seeks to trace the evolution of political ideas either by demonstrating how the characteristics of the theories of one age differ from those of another, or by specifying the continuities which persist from one age to another. In the pages which follow, I should like to borrow from Kuhn's discussion in order to suggest a different way of thinking about the history of political theory. In particular, I should like to draw on his conception of the role of paradigms in the history of science and to show that a comparable phenomenon has been present in the history of political theory. My purpose is not to argue that political theory is a species of scientific theory, but rather that political theories can be best understood as paradigms and that the scientific study of politics is a special form of paradigm-inspired research. Necessarily, my references to the history of political theory will be cryptic.

When the idea of paradigms is applied to the history of political theory, it is surprising to discover many theorists have considered theorising to be an activity aimed at the creation of new paradigms. One of the most familiar expressions of this sort of self-consciousness is represented by Machiavelli's boast that 'I have determined to enter upon a path not yet trodden by anyone'.[1] The path to which he refers is, of course, one which leads to a new theory. In *The Prince* his sarcastic allusion to those who 'have fancied for themselves republics and principalities that have never been seen or known to exist in reality' was clearly intended to evoke the paradigm of utopian theories and to make it obvious to all that he was offering an alternative.[2] The same pretensions were evident in Hobbes's announcement that he had distilled 'rules' for 'making and maintaining commonwealths...which rules neither poor men have the leisure, nor men that have had the leisure, *have hitherto* had the curiosity, or the method to find out'.[3] Like

---

[1] *Discorsi*, I, Pref.
[2] In the same vein Bodin wrote: 'We aim higher in our attempt to attain, or at least approximate, to the true image of a rightly ordered government. Not that we intend to describe a purely ideal and unrealisable commonwealth, such as that imagined by Plato or Thomas More...We intend to confine ourselves as far as possible to those political forms that are practicable.' *Six Books of the Commonwealth*, Bk. I, ch. 1, tr. M. J. Tooley (Oxford: Blackwell), p. 2.
[3] *Leviathan*, ch. 20, ed. Oakeshott (Oxford: Blackwell), p. 136.

Machiavelli, Hobbes was self-conscious to the point of arrogance about the novelty of his paradigm: '...how different this doctrine is from the greatest practice of the world, especially of the western parts, that have received their moral learning from Rome and Athens...'[1] Hobbes surpassed Machiavelli in his determination to destroy previous paradigms, especially those associated with the names of Aristotle, Cicero and St Thomas.[2]

Self-consciousness in paradigm-innovation was not the peculiarity of ironic iconoclasts, such as Machiavelli and Hobbes, or the result of the sharpened historical consciousness of modern writers. Thucydides had taken pains to distinguish his own methods of inquiry from the techniques of poets and chroniclers—the true rivals of the historian and philosopher in ancient Greece—and had recommended his methods to those 'who desire an exact knowledge of the past as an aid to the interpretation of the future'.[3] Polybius had explicitly taken issue with Plato's paradigm of philosophical knowledge and had proposed instead a form which would combine the knowledge of the historian and the practical statesman.[4]

When applied to the history of political theory, Kuhn's notion of a paradigm, 'universally recognised scientific achievements that for a time provide model problems and solutions to a community of practitioners', invites us to consider Plato, Aristotle, Machiavelli, Hobbes, Locke, and Marx as the counterparts in political theory to Galileo, Harvey, Newton, Laplace, Faraday, and Einstein. Each of the writers in the first group inspired a new way of looking at the political world; in each case their theories proposed a new definition of what was significant for understanding that world; each specified distinctive methods for inquiry; and each of the theories contained an explicit or implicit statement of what should count as an answer to certain basic questions. Kuhn's criterion, that a paradigm should provide 'model problems and solutions', is approximated in the way that one theorist will adopt major elements from another. When Aquinas refers to Aristotle as 'the philosopher' and proceeds to incorporate certain key Aristotelian notions, such as *physis* and *polis*, and to put them to work, we have a striking analogy with what Kuhn calls 'paradigm-adoption'. Many other instances could be introduced to show that the tradition of political theory displays a high degree of self-consciousness about the role and function of paradigms. Harrington's political ideas were

---

[1] *Ibid.* ch. 3 (p. 242).

[2] This was most strikingly illustrated in *De Cive* (Preface to the Reader). Hobbes carefully arranged his targets, beginning with Socrates ('The first who truly loved this civil science') and proceeding through the later classical authors ('After him comes Plato, Aristotle, Cicero, and other philosophers, as well Greek, as Latin').

[3] *History*, I, 21–2.   [4] *Histories*, XII, 28. 2–3.

elaborated in reference to two main paradigms, that of 'ancient prudence' as represented by Aristotle and that of 'modern prudence' by Machiavelli.[1] One could also point to the paradigmatic influence of Locke upon eighteenth-century political writers in America and France;[2] of Hobbes upon later writers such as Benthan, James Mill, and Austin; of Marx and Max Weber upon political and social writers of the last hundred years.

In pointing to the unique status of certain major political theories, I am not suggesting that later writers merely borrowed from them or were influenced by them. The point is more substantial, namely, that major theories have served as master-paradigms enabling later and lesser writers to exploit them in a manner comparable to that of 'normal science'. This was the manner in which the Aristotelian paradigm was used by medieval writers, such as John of Paris or Ptolemy of Lucca, and, if we allow paradigmatic status to the Aristotelian–Thomistic synthesis, the same can be said of Hooker and the Spanish writers of the sixteenth century, such as Victoria and Suarez. One might also point to all of the lesser Machiavellis listed in Meinecke's *Staatsräison*, in Acton's introduction to Burd's edition of *Il Principe*, or in Benoist's ponderous volumes on *le Machiavélisme*. This matter might be stated differently by saying that one of the main reasons why students of political theory continue to read Locke instead of those writers, such as Hunton of Lawson, who are reputed to have anticipated or influenced him, is that Locke spawned Lockians who set to work using his ideas to solve political problems.[3]

These examples raise the possibility that there have been important instances of cumulative knowledge in the history of political theory. What is curious is that historians of political theory have been so reluctant to explore this possibility. In most textbooks and university courses on the subject, the method of instruction is designed to produce exactly the opposite effect of texts in the natural sciences. Instead of interpreting past theories as preparing the way for the next phase of political theories, commentators and lecturers tend to underscore the differences between the great theorists. The inevitable result is an emphasis upon discontinuity and novelty. At the same time, almost no

---

[1] Bacon had acknowledged being 'much beholden to Machiavel'. *Works*, ed. Spedding, Ellis and Heath, vol. 3, p. 430. Pareto remarked that 'many maxims of Machiavelli...hold as true today as they were in his time'. *The Mind and Society*, 3 vols. (New York: Dover, 1963), vol. 4, pp. 1736–7. Finally: 'The present work is much closer to the straight-forward empirical standpoint of Machiavelli's *Discourses* or Michel's *Political Parties*.' Lasswell and Kaplan, *op. cit.* p. x.

[2] On the working out of the Lockean paradigm in America see L. Hartz, *The Liberal Tradition in America* (New York: Harcourt, Brace, 1955).

[3] C. H. McIlwain, *Constitutionalism and the Changing World* (Cambridge, 1939), ch. IX (on Hunton); A. H. Maclean, 'George Lawson and John Locke', *Cambridge Historical Journal*, IX (1947), 69–77.

attention is paid to the numerous and nearly anonymous followers who have busied themselves working out the master-theory. Instead of being considered 'normal scientists', they are dismissed as tiresome and repetitious epigoné. If we remember that theoretical originality is not the hallmark of normal science, the historian of political theory who ignores the dilative work of the under-labourers, has closed off a whole range of questions, the most interesting of which is: what sorts of intellectual operations occur when a political theory is put to work in circumstances different from those which inspired it?

One of the functions of a paradigm is to enable its users to solve puzzles generated by the paradigm when it is applied to nature. Although, as I have contended, an analogous process has been at work in political theory, most commentators have implicitly denied that this has been the case. They have generally viewed the process either as a form of mimesis and hence not deserving of attention, or as an example of distortion. The second response is interesting, because it can be related to Kuhn's point that a paradigm is not intended to solve all puzzles in advance, but to supply the means for solving them, even if they have not been anticipated. When the historian of political theory encounters the case of a paradigm being applied to unexpected puzzles, his instinctive reaction is to suspect that the paradigm is being distorted for partisan ends. For example, following the reception of Aristotle in the thirteenth century, it was the common practice of medieval political writers to press him into service in the great polemical controversies concerning church–state relationships. In the hands of a master, such as Marsilius of Padua, the Aristotelian paradigm was not applied mechanically to matters foreseen by the paradigm, but to unanticipated puzzles.[1] As is well known, Marsilius countered the papal claims to secular authority by relying on Aristotelian arguments concerning the self-sufficient nature of the political community and its possession of all necessary means for the maintenance of internal peace and order. At the outset of his great work, *Defensor Pacis*, he announced that he would investigate the major cause of disorder and that this cause was one that 'Aristotle could not have known'.[2] Like a loyal paradigm-worker, Marsilius was not put off by the fact that Aristotle had not envisaged the medieval Church, but rather proceeded on the assumption that if Aristotle were truly 'the master of those that know' his paradigm would furnish the resources for solving a new problem.

Instead of considering this practice as a form of creative adaptation,

---

[1] Without reference to the theme of this essay, Professor Ullmann has written that 'the Aristotelian orientation of the later Middle Ages can perhaps be compared with the reorientation effected through a Galileo or a Newton.' *Principles of Government and Politics in the Middle Ages* (London: Methuen, 1962), p. 244.

[2] Dictio I, cap. 1, 7

the modern scholar responds with the finicky criticism that Aristotle's conception of a *polis* had not been intended for the much larger and dualistically organised medieval political society. Of one such attempt by James of Viterbo, an early fourteenth-century papalist, Mr John B. Morrall writes that 'one would guess that the Greek philosopher himself would have regarded this development with suspicion; the medieval territories would have seemed to him far too large to fit his conception of a true political community'.[1] It is not my intention to discredit the historian's concern with deviations from the texts, but only to protest that it has closed off some potentially fruitful ways of thinking about political theories. One of these ways involves viewing the function of a theory as directing its users to new puzzles, unresolved or even unforeseen by the theory itself. In fact this conception of a theory is in accord with the practice of some historians, as is illustrated by Professor Ullmann's remark about Aquinas: '...Thomas was the one writer who not only fully understood the Philosopher, but who also, precisely because he so fully understood Aristotle, perceived the potentialities of his doctrines.'[2]

Admittedly, an Aquinas or Marsilius can hardly be classified as paradigm-workers; they are more like paradigm-creators who combined elements of the old with distinctive additions of their own. In this respect Kuhn's remark applies to them: 'new paradigms are born from old ones' and borrow much from the conceptual and manipulative apparatus of the traditional paradigm, 'although they seldom employ these borrowed elements in quite the traditional way' (p. 148). In political theory the line is not always easy to draw between paradigm-workers and paradigm-creators, as the example of the Marxian paradigm shows. Under which category does Lenin's theory of revolution fall? or Hilferding's studies on imperialism? or Trotsky's analysis of revolution in an 'underdeveloped' society? Are these examples of normal science or of extraordinary science? Whatever conclusion one might arrive at, it seems clear that in generating a wide range of problems, in supplying a distinctive world-view, in indicating criteria of significance and canons of inquiry, Marxism has been one of the most extraordinary paradigms in the history of Western political thought.

Having pressed this far with the analogy between political theory and scientific paradigms, we must next inquire whether the history of theory reveals anything comparable to the highly efficient enforcement powers of the scientific community. Once the history of political theory is examined with this question in mind, a surprising amount of affirmative evidence turns up. Plato's Academy, for example, was

[1] *Political Thought in Medieval Times* (New York: Harper, 1962), p. 88.
[2] Ullman, *op. cit.* p. 243.

instituted to extend the master's paradigm into many areas of knowledge, among which politics was one of the most important. The same
might be said for Aristotle's Lyceum, although the political motive was
less marked than in the Academy.[1] One could also mention the example
of Calvin's Geneva and the enforcement of the Puritan paradigm in the
Massachusetts Bay Colony. An outstanding modern example is the
official status of Marxism in the Soviet Union. It is also possible that
other examples might be revealed by historical research. There is some
ground for believing that certain paradigms were enforced among communities of Renaissance scholars; the circle which included Erasmus
and More might be investigated from this point of view. Or the activities
of the eighteenth-century French Encyclopedists might serve equally well.

With the possible exception of Marxism, it appears that political
theorists have had only indifferent success in generating communities
which, on an institutionalised basis, could enforce paradigms and guide
research. The question which then suggests itself is, have political
theorists sought a different way of enforcing their theories? Here the
answer is overwhelmingly affirmative, and a brief exploration of this
theme discloses significant differences between political theorists and
scientists. In contrast to the scientist, who seeks to elicit acceptance of
his theory from his fellow-scientists, the political theorist has viewed
this form of acceptance as a secondary matter. The reason is not simply
that a genuine 'community' of theorists has been a rarity, but rather
that the kind of power which the theorist seeks is to be found in the
political community itself. By means of his theory the scientist hopes to
transform the outlook of the members of the scientific community and
to gain the support and power of that community for the application
of his theory to the investigation of nature. The aim of many political
theorists has been to change society itself: not simply to alter the way
men look at the world, but to alter the world. This is the viewpoint that
tempted Plato to journey to Syracuse, where he hoped to 'capture'
Dionysius II and convert him into an instrument for changing a political
society in accordance with the principles of Plato's theory.[2] If the
authenticity of the Platonic letters is too dubious, the same preoccupation with using power to transform society reappears in the *Republic*
(v, 473) where Plato alluded to that 'one change' which might pave
the way for radical reform, the uniting of 'political power and philosophy' in one man.

A similar impulse informed Machiavelli. The Dedication to *The*

---

[1] See W. Jaeger, *Aristotle*, 2nd ed. (Oxford: Oxford University Press, 1962), pp. 54, 286, 314 ff.
Also the essay by W. Anderson on the differences between the Academy and the Lyceum
in *Teaching Political Science*, ed. R. H. Connery (Durham: Duke University Press, 1965).

[2] See Epistle VII. The story of Plato's encounter with Dionysius was transmitted to later
centuries by Plutarch. More's *Utopia* and Elyot's *Governor* made explicit reference to it.

Prince made plain his intention of 'discussing and directing the government of princes'. Machiavelli's *Discourses* was even bolder, for it not only projected a new political system but hinted that the old one would have to be overthrown to make way for the new.

A final example is provided by Hobbes. His political objectives are recognisable in the closing lines of his Introduction to *Leviathan*:

...He that is to govern a whole nation must read in himself, not this or that particular man; but mankind: which though it be hard to do, harder than to learn any language or science; yet when I shall have set down my own reading orderly, and perspicuously, the pains left another, will be only to consider, if he also not find the same in himself.

By declaring that the theory of *Leviathan* had been prepared for 'he that is to govern a nation', Hobbes was confronted with the same problem as Plato: how to persuade the ruling authority to enforce his paradigm? That Hobbes conceived the problem to be the same is verified by the way in which he invokes the *memoria Platonis*:

...considering...how much depth of moral philosophy is required in them that have the administration of the sovereign power, I am at the point of believing this my labour, as useless, as the commonwealth of Plato.

Hobbes buoyed his sagging spirits with the belief that none had succeeded before him in reducing political knowledge to a set of simple theorems and hence there was still hope that

this writing of mine may fall into the hands of a sovereign...and by the exercise of entire sovereignty, in protecting the public teaching of it, convert this truth of speculation into the utility of practice.[1]

The successors to this tradition of paradigm enforcement are too numerous to mention. One thinks of Rousseau with his constitutions for Corsica and Poland; Bentham's appeals to the despots of Europe; Saint-Simon's efforts to gain the attention of Napoleon; and the numerous attempts made during the nineteenth century to found small communities on the basis of explicit theories. If one is impressed only by the failure of these theories, he might wish to consider how successfully a theorist's paradigm has been enforced in the Soviet Union.

It would be misleading to conclude that the only possibility open to the political theorist is either to follow the model of Plato and seek to educate a ruler or to follow the model of Marx and work for a revolution. Another method of paradigm enforcement, one which is consonant with the present *locus* of political theory in universities, is a distinct alternative. Hobbes was probably the first theorist to envision these possibilities. He recommended that his own paradigm be converted into a kind of official theory and taught at the universities, which

[1] *Leviathan*, ch. 31 (p. 241).

might then become like 'the fountains of civil and moral doctrine' from which 'the preachers and the gentry' might draw such water as ought to be sprinkled upon the people.[1]

Today the modern American university offers an even more enticing prospect, for to the natural educational influence at its disposal there has been added the power of foundations. In concert they provide a powerful mechanism for enforcing paradigms and subsidising research. Until recently, one vital ingredient has been lacking in political science departments—the paradigm itself. Previously, most departments had practised a tolerant attitude, admitting a wide diversity in methods and assumptions. Now the situation has changed dramatically. The growth of social science and the successful behavioural revolution have supplied the missing element, and there appears to be a convergence between a paradigm, a mechanism of enforcement, and ample resources for carrying on paradigm-directed research. A remarkable insight into this process is furnished, perhaps unintentionally, in David Easton's recent book, *A Framework for Political Analysis*. His description of the origins of the behavioural revolution 'in political theory' seems like an echo of Hobbes's dictum that 'the first truths were arbitrarily made by those that first of all imposed names upon things...'.[2] According to Easton, behaviouralism involves 'more' than just the adoption of scientific methods for the study of politics, and 'it is only partly correct to see in it an ideological weapon lending color and vigor to the movement of a diffuse and informal group of academic rebels against tradition'. The 'name' itself, political behaviouralism, 'can be considered an accident', produced by a desire to placate a committee of the United States Senate which had been conducting hearings for a proposed national science foundation 'to stimulate and provide funds for scholarly research'. The 'representatives of the social sciences' were dismayed to learn that some senators had their own name for the social sciences, 'the socialistic sciences', and hence were understandably reluctant to underwrite this particular type of research. Accordingly, the name 'behavioural science' was coined by its supporters 'to identify those aspects of the social sciences that might come under the aegis of a foundation devoted to the support of hard science'. The tactic proved successful and when, by virtue of another 'accidental' turn of events the Ford Foundation decided 'at about the same time' to institute a Behavioural Sciences Division, the 'name' was well on the way to becoming a movement.[3]

---

[1] *Ibid.* (p. 467). [2] *English Works*, I, 91.

[3] Easton, *op. cit.* pp. 4–13. It should be added that Easton suggests that the story may be apocryphal. Inasmuch as he introduces it in order to illustrate the same theme of power being brought to support a particular form of inquiry, the literal truth of the story is not critical.

In striking ways, the behavioural movement satisfies most of Kuhn's specifications for a successful paradigm. It has come to dominate the the curricula of many political science departments throughout the country; a new generation of students is being taught the new methods of survey analysis, data processing, and scaling; behavioural textbooks are increasingly in evidence; and there are even signs that the past is being reinterpreted in order to demonstrate that the revolution is merely the culmination of 'trends' in political science over the past few decades.[1] Whether there has occurred a phenomenon similar to that reported by Kuhn—those with other loyalties 'are simply read out of the profession, which thereafter ignores their work'—will not be discussed, except to note that some of the most interesting political theories are the work of *les étrangers*, uncommitted and marginal figures, such as Eric Hoffer, Hannah Arendt, and Bertrand de Jouvenel, who are largely ignored.[2]

At a later point we shall consider briefly the kind of paradigmatic activity represented by behaviourism, but now it will be useful to fasten upon one peculiarity of the revolution by returning to some questions posed by Kuhn: why do paradigm-revolutions occur? what kinds of anomalies are apt to provoke a search for new modes of explanation in political theory? In one respect the behavioural revolution forms a close analogue with Kuhn's description of scientific crisis. The dissatisfaction which scientists are said to express over the inability of a paradigm to solve puzzles was duplicated in the severe criticism which political scientists directed at traditional political theories. The classics could not furnish the 'operational' hypotheses for investigating specific problems, such as what determines how and whether voters will vote, the sources of voter attitudes, the extent to which beliefs deemed fundamental to the persistence of the system are shared, who makes decisions in a democratic system, and the degree of control actually exercised by citizens over their governors. The results of this dissatisfaction are familiar to most readers, but what is less obvious is the contrast between the new paradigm and the theories of the past.

Many of the great theories of the past arose in response to a crisis in the world, not in the community of theorists. It was not a methodological breakdown that prompted Plato to commit himself to the *bios thereotikos* and to produce the first great paradigm in Western political

---

[1] See, for example, R. A. Dahl, 'The behavioral approach', *American Political Science Review*, vol. 55 (1961), pp. 763–72. A more ambitious claim is made by H. Eulau, *op. cit.* p. 7: '...the behavioral persuasion represents an attempt, by modern modes of analysis, to fulfill the quest for political knowledge begun by the classical political theorists.'

[2] Ironically, Arthur Bentley, who is widely regarded among scientifically oriented political scientists as one of their great forerunners, was a truly marginal figure, even to the point of eccentricity.

thought; it was, instead, the breakdown of the Athenian *polis*. Again, it was not a simple desire to replace theological with Aristotelian methods that led to the *Defensor Pacis*, but a continuing crisis in the relations of church and state. There is no need to multiply the instances: the paradigms of Machiavelli, Bodin, Harrington, Hobbes, Locke, Tocqueville, and Marx were produced by a profound belief that the world had become deranged. The intimate relation between crisis and theory is the result not only of the theorist's belief that the world is deeply flawed but of his strategic sense that crisis, and its usual accompaniments of institutional collapse and the breakdown of authority, affords an opportunity for a theory to reorder the world. This was the theme of Plato's *Republic*; of the last chapter of Machiavelli's *Prince* and the preface to Book II of the *Discorsi*; of Hobbes's *Leviathan*; and of virtually all that Marx wrote. In each case political crisis was not the product of the theorist's hyper-active imagination but of the actual state of affairs. Greek democracy *was* undergoing its final, agonising crisis; the Florentine republic was being transformed by the Medici into a personal government; the English civil wars did lead to the breakdown of authority; industrial capitalism did produce profound social and political dislocation and did raise the question of the bourgeoisie's competence to govern. In each instance the theorist's response was not to offer a theory that would correspond to the facts, or 'fit' them as snugly as the glove does the hand. Derangement in the world signified that the facts were skewed. A theory corresponding to a sick world would itself be a form of sickness. Instead, theories were offered as symbolic representations of what society would be like if it could be reordered.

If, for a moment, we were to retrace the discussion to the point where it mentioned certain historical crises which have actually occurred, it might be suggestive to consider these crises in society from the viewpoint of Kuhn's conception of 'anomaly'. It will be recalled that an anomaly presupposes a theory which is being worked out and, in the process, certain phenomena are encountered which cannot be accounted for by the theory. If we were to consider political crises as situations in which ruling authorities cannot account for certain happenings, in the sense of being unable to deal with them effectively, we might designate these situations as anomalous. But *pace* Kuhn, in what sense do they constitute theoretical anomalies? What is the theory whose expectations are being violated or contradicted?

The obvious response is to say that Kuhn's conception of paradigms seems out of place when it is applied to a context for which it had not been devised. Instead of accepting this objection I should like to try to amend the concept so that it can be made useful for analysing actual political societies. My proposal is that we conceive of political society itself as a paradigm of an operative kind. From this viewpoint society would be envisaged as a coherent whole in the sense of its customary political practices, institutions, laws, structure of authority and citizenship, and operative beliefs being organised and interrelated. A politically organised society contains definite institutional arrangements, certain widely shared understandings regarding the location and use of political power, certain expectations about how authority ought to treat the members of society and about the claims that organised society can rightfully make upon its members. In some societies many of these features are explicitly set forth in a written constitution. In saying that the practices and beliefs of society are organised and interrelated, that its members have certain expectations and share certain beliefs, one is saying that that society believes itself to be one thing rather than another, a democracy rather than a dictatorship, a republic rather than a monarchy, a directed society rather than a free one. This *ensemble* of practices and beliefs may be said to form a paradigm in the sense that the society tries to carry on its political life in accordance with them. Further, in its agencies of enforcement and in its systems of rules, a political society possesses the basic instrumentalities present in Kuhn's scientific community and employs them in an analogous way. Society, too, enforces certain types of conduct and discourages others; it, too, defines what sorts of 'experiments'—in the form of individual or group actions—will be encouraged, tolerated, or suppressed; by its complex organisation of politics through legislatures, political parties, and the media of opinion, society also determines what shall count in determining future decisions.

In the natural course of its history a society undergoes changes which impose strains upon the existing paradigm. A society may find the paradigm being challenged directly, or it may experience difficulty in coping with the results of change. New social classes may have emerged; new economic relationships may have developed; or new racial or religious patterns may have appeared. In much the same way that a scientific community will seek to adjust its paradigm to account for 'novelty', a political society will seek to adapt its system to the new developments brought by change. To the degree that a society succeeds in adapting, its efforts might even be likened to a form of puzzle-solving. For example, given the political culture of early nineteenth-century England, its professions of being a society with representative institutions and guaranteed liberties, the ways in which that society adjusted its paradigm to accommodate the growing self-consciousness among the working classes and the accompanying demands for suffrage reforms provide an example of the adaptation of a political paradigm to new

'facts'. The paradigm has to be changed, because, if there is to be
accommodation, the 'facts' must be viewed differently: in this case,
not as they had been viewed at Peterloo but as they were to be viewed
during the passage of the successive Reform Bills. Once the 'facts' are
viewed differently and the paradigm is altered accordingly, the consequence is a change in the facts themselves. In the case of the suffrage
reforms in nineteenth-century England, new voters were created and
some old grievances disappeared.

If we now shift our attention to a different political paradigm and
at the same time recall Kuhn's remark that some phenomena may not
constitute an anomaly under one paradigm but will under another, we
may consider the status of suffrage demands relative to the paradigm of
nineteenth-century Russian Czarism. In this case the rising demands
for representative institutions and the extension of the ballot appeared
as anomalies, not, as they did in England, as puzzles. Given the political
paradigm of Czarism, the demands for change could not be accom-
modated without radically altering the paradigm. In the end, the
'facts' proved to be too much for the theory.

It is also possible to think of a third type of situation which would
build on Kuhn's remark that some puzzles impugn the ability of the
scientist rather than the paradigm (p. 80). The relative failure of
liberal administrations to deal effectively with the condition of the
American Negro, at least not until very recently, can be treated as an
instance of Kuhn's point. The fault lay not with the democratic paradigm but with its 'scientists'; the most embarrassing aspect of the Negro
protest movement was its reminder that some of the basic elements of
the paradigm, such as the Constitution and the Declaration of Independence, were more consistent with the demands of the protestants
than with the actions of the guardians of the paradigm.

III

If space permitted, it would be possible to extend the discussion of
political paradigms to examine the problem of revolution as a species
of paradigm change. In the remaining pages, however, I should like to
direct attention once more at the 'normal' political paradigm. As long
as a political society can handle its 'puzzles' and make minor adjustments in the paradigm to accord with the new 'facts' brought by social
change, that society is proceeding in a way reminiscent of 'normal
science'. Now one of the interesting points made by Kuhn is that when
normal science is busily and successfully at work, it tends to be impatient of philosophy and, in fact, does not need it. Philosophy has a
tendency to question accepted assumptions and to reopen issues which

were thought to be closed. In the eyes of normal science, philosophy appears as a distraction and a potential diversion of energies away from puzzle-solving activity. Similarly, we might say that when political societies are operating normally, they will evince little interest in political philosophy, except perhaps to eye it with sceptical disapproval if it should appear interested in questioning fundamental assumptions. Society, too, is more preoccupied with resolving the practical 'puzzles' of politics in accordance with the prescriptions of its paradigm. It also finds 'retooling an extravagance'.

Society's indifference towards theory is matched by the indifference of theorists. Throughout the history of Western political theory we find that most of the major theories have been produced during times of crisis, rarely during periods of normalcy. This phenomenon suggests that the major theories resemble 'extraordinary science': they are produced when the operative political paradigm is encountering, not puzzles, but profound anomalies. Further, the major theories exhibit the same feature of extraordinary science: they seek to discredit the existing operative paradigm. One need only recall Plato's criticism of democracy, Machiavelli's strictures on princes in the *Discorsi*, Locke's indictment of royal absolutism, and Marx's critique of capitalist society. Obviously no one will pay much attention to these attacks if they do not feel bothered by the operation of the existing paradigm. People much prefer to concentrate upon enjoying the benefits or exploring the possibilities of the prevailing system. This indifference is not the expression of a choice between having a theory or living without one. A society which is operating fairly normally has its theory in the form of the dominant paradigm, but that theory is taken for granted because it represents the consensus of the society.

Thus one can think in terms of two kinds of paradigms. There is the extraordinary type represented in the major political theories and there is the normal one embodied in the actual arrangements of a political society. Earlier an analogy had been drawn between the enforcement of a political paradigm and the enforcement of a scientific one. By extending this analogy a bit further it may be possible to locate behavioural studies and to say something about their theoretical status. As we have noted, normal science works on the paradigm provided and enforced by the scientific community; in this sense, normal science is the extension of the community's paradigm into the form of research. Turning now to behavioural studies, one of the most striking characteristics among the numerous studies on voting, community power, political participation, and decision-making is their acceptance of the prevailing political paradigm as the frame of reference and as the source of research problems. Most, if not all, of these problems are only problems because the operative paradigm suggests that they are. Among the questions being investigated are: What determines the attitudes and preferences of voters? What accounts for the apathy of voters? What is the functional value of non-participation? To what extent do political élites dominate decision-making and to what degree are they responsive to the citizenry? What effect does membership in many and often conflicting groups have upon the stability of a political system?

Since it is difficult to imagine these questions as problems under any except a liberal or democratic regime, they suggest that political behaviourism, like normal science, proceeds by an understanding of the world as defined by the dominant paradigm. To be sure, the dominant paradigm does not dictate the specific methods of inquiry, but it does influence the criteria of significance and does set limits around what is to be considered useful inquiry. Thus the contrast between behavioural theory and traditional theory comes to resemble the difference between normal and extraordinary science. Traditional theory, like extraordinary science, is preoccupied with possible rather than actual worlds and, as a consequence, it jeopardises rather than repairs the regnant paradigm.

In the case of behavioural theory and traditional theory a contrast need not imply a divorce. One of the most interesting and disturbing features of behavioural findings is their subversiveness. Many of the common notions about the quality of the democratic electorate have been shaken. The same might be said about prevailing beliefs about the democratic character of politics, decision-making in American communities, and the representativeness of elected officials. Some evidence seems to suggest that a democratic system will enjoy greater stability if certain segments of the electorate did not vote; other evidence hints that the poorer elements of the population possess attitudes which might be dangerous to the political order.[1] On the basis of these findings one might speculate that normal science may be in the process of exposing anomalies rather than puzzles. If this is the case, and if the anomalies were to become more persistent and widespread, the paradigm might be in trouble; and if this should happen, then we might expect that extraordinary science would reappear.

[1] S. M. Lipset, *Political Man* (New York: Doubleday Anchor, 1963), pp. 87 ff.

THE NATURE OF POLITICAL PHILOSOPHY[1]

B. C. PAREKH

I

Human activities are not gifts of gods, or results of abstract reasoning by an isolated individual at any particular point in time, but are developed over the course of years as they come to be practised more widely. Their character and identity are thus products of time, tradition, or practice. Mere practice, however, is hardly enough, since, as an activity is practised more widely, it also tends to acquire a number of features that are not in harmony with its original features and that tend to pull in a different direction, causing concern among its practitioners as to what precisely it is that they are doing in its name. Thus if time or tradition assists in the articulation of the identity of an activity, it also contributes to its identity crisis.

It therefore becomes necessary from time to time to step outside an activity, disengage what is and what is not out of character with it, question assumptions and ideas that have mistakenly entered into it, and form a view of its identity that, while retaining its historical continuity, enables us to impose a measure of logical rigour on its practice by determining and expunging what is merely contingent, accidental or spurious. In this context and to meet this demand philosophy becomes necessary, and it is worth noting that every activity that has gone on long enough to have become a problem to itself has tended to raise philosophical problems about its identity. While reason without tradition would not know where to begin, tradition without reason would not know where to stop.

The present essay springs from the belief that we are now at a time when, under the impact of positivism, linguistic philosophy, the rise of the social sciences and the preoccupation with the immediate present in a highly volatile world, there is a general feeling of the 'decline' or the 'death' of political philosophy, and that, therefore, a self-conscious look at its nature may contribute to a clearer articulation of its identity.

The crisis that political philosophy faces *qua* philosophy is naturally not peculiar to it but is common to philosophy itself. Nor is it the first time in its history that philosophy has experienced a crisis.

[1] I have benefited from the suggestions made by Dr. R. N. Berki and Mr H. Elcock.

It experienced its first crisis when Christian theology emerged sometime during the third century of the Christian era. Christianity never
posed serious problems for philosophy, since philosophy could always
accommodate religion in its personal as well as institutional form;
religion, for its part, could come to terms with philosophy and, at worst,
could only dismiss it as too argumentative or superficial or unconcerned
with the ultimate salvation of the soul—which involves questioning the
utility of philosophy but not its distinct character and *identity*. When the
systematic Christian *theology* with its 'truths', 'doctrines', 'preaching'
and a deductive manner of reasoning developed, the battle between
religion and philosophy was joined, since philosophy has no 'truths'
to offer, no 'doctrines' to advance, is, at best, a teacher and never a
preacher, and has no access to any unique source of knowledge. The
dominant view that emerged as a consequence of this engagement was
that while theology was divine, philosophy was only human; that
therefore philosophy could only have a role that was assigned and
sanctioned by theology, and that philosophy was simply a method and
not a body of substantive doctrines and could thus be used by theology
to defend its 'truths'.[1]

The second crisis was experienced with the emergence of the natural
sciences when the question of the function of philosophy compared with
that of the natural sciences was raised. Some argued that philosophy
was a transitional discipline that dealt with questions which natural
sciences did not yet exist to handle, and that as they emerged to do so,
philosophy would disappear. Others who were unable to accept this
view reacted in one of two ways. Some maintained that all that was
involved was a change in the role of philosophy, and that henceforth it
was not to be a first-order but a second-order activity concerned with
the analysis of the concepts, statements and methods of empirical
inquiries. Others argued that science was concerned only with facts and
not with values which remained the subject matter of philosophy.
While science would describe, philosophy could prescribe.

Philosophy experienced the third identity-crisis in the nineteenth
century when history as a distinct manner of understanding and
explaining events emerged. It was believed by its champions to be not
just different from both philosophy and science but also better than
either. It came to be argued that reality was essentially historical in
character and that therefore the historical mode of examination was
the only satisfactory one. Both science and philosophy, it was suggested,
were themselves ultimately historical, since they were never excogitated

[1] It is worth bearing in mind that philosophy of religion and philosophy of theology are not
the same as theology. In both of them, unlike in theology, philosophy is the final court of
appeal and can criticise and reject theological doctrines.

by any single individual at any single point in time but were simply a result of a long historical process in abstraction from which they had no meaning and intelligibility. It was concluded that philosophy not only involved history or had a history but that it was nothing but history.

In each of these cases philosophers had to face the task of defining the character of their activity in a way that clearly distinguished it from the dominant discipline that posed a threat to its identity. Some succeeded in doing this, while others either accepted the dominant discipline as the only legitimate and fully satisfactory discipline, or worked out a role for themselves that was compatible with and subordinate to it. The result in such cases was either the suicide of philosophy or its confusion with theology, science or history.

Naturally, political philosophy, too, was confused with or defined in terms of one of the four inquiries. Some equated it with or replaced it by political theology. Others understood it as no more than the conceptual workshop of political science where models were built—individually or collectively—tools were sharpened and ancillary services provided. Yet others thought its job was to issue recommendations, whether of a general or of a particular kind, to offer new political ideals and, in general, to advise and prompt citizens to do what it considered right. Finally, there were others who maintained that it was nothing but the history of political thought. The current debate on the nature of political philosophy bears the marks of each of these crises in the sense that most participants take the view that political philosophy, principally, is either political theology,[1] or political theory[2] (of the empirical kind), or political ethics,[3] or the history of political thought.[4] The basic thesis of the present essay is that, though political philosophy may involve all of these inquiries, it cannot be identified with any one of them, and that it is a fairly distinct and distinguishable kind of inquiry.

[1] See, for example, V. A. Demant, *Theology of Society* and *Christian Polity*; N. Micklem, *The Theology of Politics*; Emil Brunner, *The Divine Imperative*; R. Niebuhr, *Moral Man and Immoral Society* and *The Nature and Destiny of Man*; C. Dawson, *Religion and the Modern State*; and various works by Pieper, Guardini, Max Picard and Jaques Maritain.

[2] Much of the current behaviourist literature reflects this view. See also David Easton on political theory in *A Dictionary of the Social Sciences*, ed. Gould and Kold (London, 1964): according to 'the most recent and most rapidly growing usage', political theory 'is a branch of the scientific enterprise'.

[3] R. M. MacIver, *The Web of Government* (New York, 1947), p. 403. For G. E. G. Catlin in *Political Theory: What is it?*, political science is descriptive while political philosophy is prescriptive.

[4] Croce, *Theory and History of Historiography*, tr. by Douglas Ainslie, (London 1921), pp. 151–5. 'Philosophy...cannot of necessity be anything but the methodological moment of historiography.' He contrasts 'philosophy as metaphysic' with 'philosophy as history'. Elsewhere, he says, 'With the resolution of philosophy into history it may be said that "philosophy is dead"'. *Philosophy, Poetry, History: an Anthology of Essays*, by B. Croce, tr. Cecil Sprigge, London, 1966, pp. 604–7.

II

For political philosophy to be possible at all it is essential that political activity must be autonomous and have a distinct character and identity of its own. This means, first, that it must not be of such a kind that the moment one begins to ask significant questions about it one finds oneself dealing with some other activity; second, that it must be capable of being fruitfully studied in terms of concepts appropriate to itself; third, that these concepts must be logically related to each other in a way they are not related to others; and fourth, that together they must constitute a complex that has a certain degree of internal unity and homogeneity. A Marxist of a certain variety might, for example, argue that politics is an epiphenomenal activity and that the moment one begins to ask important questions about it one necessarily finds oneself discussing economic activity. For him, therefore, there cannot be an independent discipline called political philosophy. Or a moralist might argue that philosophy is concerned solely with the determination and recommendation of moral values, and that there are no moral values that are peculiar to politics. What is morally desirable in one's personal life is no less so in political life. In such a view there cannot be a separate discipline called political philosophy, as it simply has no distinct subject matter and is at best only a branch of moral philosophy.

As I am concerned only to point to the formal preconditions of political philosophy, and as it is not possible here to undertake a detailed discussion of the nature of politics, I can indicate only very briefly why I take politics to be autonomous and to raise problems that are not raised by any other activity. I think it will be generally recognised that the conduct of the collective affairs of a territorially organised community is different from conducting prayers in a congregation, or managing a business concern, or conducting proceedings in a court of law, though, undoubtedly, it shares some features in common with all of these. Unlike religious organisations, political communities are not otherworldly and do not necessarily rest on a transcendental foundation; unlike economic organisations, they aspire to be permanent, do not exist merely to achieve some specific ends, and involve considerations other than those of profit and loss; unlike courts of law, political communities do not merely enforce laws but make them, and cannot be impartial in a way that judges are. Unlike judges, governments are as much involved in the 'game' of politics as their subjects and rival parties; and, though governments might listen to all the interested groups, they do not treat them as equally important; and they bring in considerations other than the objective merits of the case in arriving at a decision concerning such groups. Besides, while the impartiality of a judge consists in deciding how to apply a law already made, that of a government consists in deciding what law to make, what interests to take into account and how much importance to attach to each. In short, legal equality is different from political equality, and judicial impartiality is different from political impartiality.

Again, though political life does raise questions of value, they are not always of the same type as those which arise in a man's personal moral life. The ideas of public good, honour, justice and even equality are central to political life in a way they are not to personal moral life. Conversely, the ideas of vice, perfection, self-improvement and internal struggle are much more integral to personal morality than to politics. Broadly speaking, what is conventionally called morality and what has generally been discussed by moral philosophers in its name, is personal or private morality, and this is only one area of moral life. An almost exclusive preoccupation with it leads to the concentration on questions like why I should return a book, or keep my promise, or be kind to my children, or not steal a neighbour's car, or not commit adultery with a friend's wife. One result of this is that a narrow and uniform pattern comes to be imposed on an immensely complex and variegated moral life, preventing us from noticing that different areas of life raise different kinds of moral problems and emphasise different moral values. For example, while judicial life stresses values like impartiality, rule observance and equity, social life emphasises those like decency, good manners and general friendliness (as distinguished from friendship); again, while economic life stresses thrift and rational calculation, political life emphasises values like honour, patriotism and public good.

All this, of course, is very sketchy and tentative, but I hope it indicates the line of reasoning on which the autonomy of politics can be established. To avoid misunderstanding, it ought to be said that autonomy does not mean isolation or insularity, and that the concern with the autonomy of politics does not involve a denial or disruption of its relations with other activities. All it involves is the recognition of the fact that politics raises some problems that are peculiar to it and that call for distinct concepts and manners of analysis.

Once the autonomy of politics is established, it becomes possible to distinguish political philosophy from other kinds of philosophy. As political activity is different from moral or social or economic activity, so political philosophy is different from moral or social or economic philosophy. It differs from them not in being a philosophy, but in being political, i.e. in being concerned with a distinct and identifiable area of problems.

Though the formal possibility of political philosophy depends on the autonomy of politics, an adequate and fully satisfactory view of it depends on something else. Politics is not a simple kind of activity, but involves various sorts of activities like making laws, making policy decisions that cannot always be embodied in laws, debating what consti-tution to adopt, public discussions of what the government should do, organising public demonstrations, and starting a revolution. Now it is quite possible that a political philosopher might consider one of these activities central to politics and define politics in terms of it. When he does this he might miss out other activities or under-emphasise and distort them, and then the resulting political philosophy cannot but be unsatisfactory. Let us take a few examples.

Many philosophers since the sixteenth century have defined politics in terms of the state and have equated political philosophy with the philosophy of the state. Bodin, Hobbes,[1] and many legalistic and positi-vistic philosophers of the nineteenth century are the clearest examples. Several modern thinkers[2] also take this view, and argue that politics did not exist before the emergence of the state and that any discussion of political philosophy must begin after the state emerged in Europe. This is why many of them start with Machiavelli. This seems to me a mistake, because the state is only one form of political organisation, and has existed only during the last four or five hundred years and only in some parts of the world. Besides it cannot be taken as a generic institu-tion to cover all kinds of political organisation, since, strictly speaking, neither the Greek *polis* nor the Roman *civitas* nor the medieval common-wealth displayed such features as the centralisation of authority, sovereignty, bureaucracy and the abstraction of the state from society that we know to be essential to the state *qua* state.

For Bentham, legislation was central to politics, so much so that his principal work in politics was entitled 'The Principles of Morals and Legislation' and not 'The Principles of Morals and Politics'. Politics in Bentham centres round the legislature—the way it should be com-posed and organised, the way it should function, the laws it should pass, etc. The profound impact of this view on the British understanding of politics is seen in the fact that even to-day several commentators equate political reform with parliamentary reform and seek to solve nearly all problems of political life by reforming the parliament, as if there were no political life outside it,[3] or as if all political issues must have a legislative

---

[1] Hobbes, it will be remembered, called himself the *first* civil philosopher.

[2] See, for example, some rather questionable remarks by Mabbott in his *The State and the Citizen* (Grey Arrow Book, 1958), p 10. Though modern political life undoubtedly raises many peculiar problems, the insights of 'pre-modern' political philosophers are not irrelevant to understanding them.

[3] This is certainly not the only criticism one would be inclined to make. The other major criticism could be of the way the idea of reform is understood. Many commentators under-stand parliament on the model of a factory and think of reform in terms of increasing legis-

origin or significance. Political philosophy therefore comes to be equated with legislative philosophy.[1]

For Hobbes, politics is mainly a matter of maintaining order and securing life and property. The elements of public debate and discussion are almost ignored. This is also true of many liberal and constitutionalist thinkers who are interested principally in securing the individual against the state and not in his controlling the state by actively sharing in the conduct of its affairs. All political problems are seen in the context of the conflict between the state and the individual, and political liberty is seen as liberty *from* the state and not as liberty to shape the state. Their basic concern is with the private life of the individual and the determination and protection of clearly demarcated private spaces, and not with the public and collective life of the community and the involvement of the individual in it. Civil life is clearly analysed but political life is ignored, and it is implied that civil relationships are the only significant forms of political relationships. Here political philosophy is identified with civil philosophy, and it is not surprising that Hobbes should have called himself the first 'civil philosopher'. It might be suggested as a general thesis that while the distinction between the civil and political is nearly always clearly recognised by classically inspired political philosophers, it is generally lost sight of in empiricist political writings.[2]

In all these and other cases, political activity is identified with one specific aspect of it, and, therefore, political philosophy comes to be identified with legislative or civil or constitutional or some other narrower philosophy. This, of course, does not mean that the philosophers concerned are not political philosophers, but only that as their view of politics is truncated and inadequate, so is their view of political philosophy.

To sum up, the possibility of political philosophy requires that political activity should be distinguishable from non-political activities like religion or economics, and an adequate view of it requires that it should not be identified with any single aspect of politics. Only by drawing these distinctions is it possible to define political philosophy in terms

lative productivity; they want to rationalise and 'modernise' parliamentary procedures so that it can produce the maximum number of laws in the available time. There are, of course, several exceptions; for example, Bernard Crick's *The Reform of Parliament* (London, 1964), where the scheme for reform has the backdrop of a clear understanding of the general nature of political activity.

[1] See Henry Maine, *The Early History of Institutions* (London, 1897), p. 370: Austin's incursion into the utilitarian ethics is at its best 'a discussion belonging not to the philosophy of law but to the philosophy of legislation'.

[2] For a further discussion of the distinction between the civil and the political, see below, p. 202. It is implicit in Aristotle's distinction between mere life and good life, and is explicitly drawn by Hegel and Montesquieu.

that do not confuse it with, among other things, social, moral, economic or religious philosophy on the one hand, and the philosophy of the state or legal, civil or legislative philosophy on the other.

III

Reflection on political activity can take place at a number of levels and can take a number of forms. One may report to others a political fact one has just noticed and which they are not likely to know about for various reasons; this is political reporting. Or one may take a current political event, analyse and explain it and point out its implications and likely consequences; this is political commentary. Or one may take a political situation and cast it in a literary mould; this is political literature.[1] Or one may feel passionately about a certain political reform and write a polemical tract making a plea for or against; this is political pamphleteering. One's reflection may, on the other hand, take a more serious and lasting form; and again it can express itself in a number of ways. One may write a manual of tactics for capturing and retaining power, or of the rules to be observed for winning political friends. Or one's reflection may take a normative direction and one may make specific or highly general recommendations and thus prescribe political morality. Or one may fuse philosophy, history, science and morality and manufacture a concoction called political ideology. Or one may explore the political implications of the dogmas of one's religion and thus engage in political theology. Or one may seek to establish causal connections, formulate statistical generalisations or develop laws and thus engage in political science.

I propose to argue that philosophical thinking is different from all these and other kinds of thinking, and that, consequently, political philosophy *qua* philosophy is different from political theology, political science, political ideology, political ethics, political utopia, political sociology, etc.

By philosophy I mean a radically and self-consciously critical interpretation of the nature of any phenomenon one happens to be inquiring into. It is *radical* in that it attempts to get to the root of its subject-matter. Many of the important philosophical questions are of the form: 'what is this thing really or ultimately?' This does not mean that philosophy arises from the 'suspicion of the senses',[2] or that it involves an *a priori*

---

[1] Political literature raises some highly interesting questions such as how to resolve a tension bound to arise from the juxtaposition of the two, not always compatible, political and literary activities, and if there is any particular form of literature, for example the drama, that is a more suitable medium for handling political situations. For an interesting discussion of these and other problems, see Irving Howe, *Politics and the Novel* (London, 1961).

[2] It is interesting to see how different philosophers take philosophy to arise differently. For Plato, it arises from wonder, for Augustine from pride, for Hobbes from doubt, for Wittgen-

dismissal of familiar phenomena in favour of some suprasensuous and transcendental reality, but only that it asks the most basic questions that can be asked and aims to arrive at an understanding that raises no further questions. A scientific inquiry, for example, may establish the existence of the sub-atomic particles and treat them as the ultimate constituents of the physical universe. But philosophy goes still further; it inquires into their mode of existence and asks if they exist independently and 'out there' or if they are ideas in the mind of the scientist or of God. It also asks if the scientific thesis can be universalised to cover non-physical aspects of the universe. If it can be universalised, it is no longer a scientific but a philosophical thesis, materialism being a philosophical, not a scientific theory.

All inquiries except philosophical ones rest on some assumptions which are not questioned and which determine the range and variety of questions that can be asked. For example, science cannot entertain a thoroughgoing doubt of the veracity of sense perception or of the measurability of things observed or of the principle of causality; theology cannot doubt the existence, or at least the reality, of God and the possibility of knowing something about him; similarly, it will be suicidal for history to question the reality of time and the possibility of its division into the past, the present and the future. Philosophy, on the other hand, is the only inquiry that involves continually trying to be conscious of and critically scrutinising any assumption that may have been made unconsciously. Ideally the aim is to make *no* assumptions and to admit only what has been fully examined and found acceptable. It is this feature of philosophy that phenomenologists have highlighted by calling it a 'presuppositionless' inquiry. Of course, no philosopher can bring all his assumptions out into the open and justify them simultaneously. Assumptions are not the kind of thing that one carries in the back of one's mind and reproduces on demand. One becomes conscious of them as one goes along, and even when one thinks one has laid bare and justified all one's assumptions one may still be making several more that may later be detected by a perceptive commentator. The point of calling philosophy a radical or a presuppositionless inquiry is to emphasise its continual self-critical character.

This leads to the second feature of philosophical inquiry; it is a fully *self-conscious* inquiry. This is such a crucial characteristic of philosophy that many philosophers have defined philosophy as a persistent attempt to become conscious of what one is and what one is doing. Philosophy is the only inquiry whose very *raison d'être* is being fully self-conscious

stein and Ryle from a feeling of puzzle, for Popper from a sense of riddle (*Logic of Scientific Discovery*, Preface to the English edition), for Marcel from a feeling of mystery, and for Jaspers from a feeling of miracle.

and urging the practitioners of other inquiries to recognise the nature and limits of their inquiries. A scientist, for example, knows how to formulate a hypothesis, how to test it and how to set up and conduct his experiments. Likewise, a historian knows how to collect and interpret his data and reconstruct and explain a particular past event in a certain well-established manner. *Qua* scientist or historian, neither steps out of the activity he is engaged in, turns back on it, and asks what it is to do science or history. The moment they do this they are no longer scientists or historians but philosophers of science or of history, since 'what is science?' or 'what is history?' are not scientific or historical but philosophical questions. To put this point in general terms, the moment an activity becomes self-conscious and begins to inquire into its nature, the way it differs from others, the concepts it employs, the assumptions it makes and the questions it asks, it ceases to be itself and becomes philosophical. Philosophy on the other hand, is the only inquiry that is not involved in this paradoxical situation, as it can become fully self-conscious without turning into something else.

The third feature of philosophy is that it is a *critical* inquiry. Philosophy aims not only to be radical, not only to be fully self-conscious and encourage others in same direction, but also to be critical. Philosophers question concepts, challenge assumptions, cast doubt on current interpretation of various activities and suggest new ones in their place. Not that they always reject or revise whatever is currently accepted, but rather that their initial attitude is one of questioning, of demanding explanation and of refusing to accept anything, however old and well-established, unless adequate reasons are produced in support of it.

It is this critical character of philosophy that has of late been questioned, or more often, merely ignored on the grounds that philosophy is essentially a descriptive or clarificatory inquiry. Strawson subtitles his very perceptive book *Individuals* ' An essay in Descriptive Metaphysics'; he distinguishes between descriptive and revisionary metaphysics and is concerned only with the former. Conceptual analysts have reached the same conclusion by arguing that philosophy is concerned only with the analysis of concepts which they take to be nothing but *descriptions* of all logically possible situations. Logical positivism, too, has a similar implication, since it divides all statements into tautologies or descriptions. Some phenomenologists have also argued that the task of philosophy is principally to 'eludicate' or 'clarify' the structure of the activity or the inquiry in question.

As I cannot here present a detailed criticism of the view that philosophy is essentially a clarificatory and non-critical activity, I shall simply state my reasons for sticking to the traditional view that philosophy is essentially a critical and revisionary activity. There is hardly a philosopher who has not challenged the credentials of some activity or the way it is practised or understood. Plato attacked the Sophists because he thought their basic assumption that knowledge was teachable was untenable. Bradley and McTaggart questioned the legitimacy of history as a discipline since they thought it rested on the questionable assumptions that time was real and that by taking a position in the temporal process one could divide it into the past, the present and the future. Some nineteenth-century Romantic philosophers and Catholic theologians combined in attacking science on the grounds that it illegitimately split reality into separate parts, 'interfered' with it in the course of examining it, and studied it only in 'distorting' and artificially contrived laboratory conditions. Several other philosophers have questioned the attempt to study human affairs scientifically on the ground that it is either illegitimate, unfruitful or impracticable. Others have shown moral life to be paradoxical on the ground that it assumes both that man ultimately is and is not a perfect being. Yet others[1] have found moral philosophy inherently unstable. In short, there is hardly an activity or inquiry that some philosophers have not attacked as impossible or paradoxical or inherently unstable or meaningless.

Even if one recognizes that some of these philosophers misunderstood the critical nature of philosophy and that they were sometimes mistaken in dismissing an already existing and well-established activity or mode of inquiry as untenable or self-contradictory, one must surely admit that they were right to question and revise it. Unlike some contemporary philosophers who argue or imply that philosophy *must* find some meaning and descriptive capacity in existing concepts and that it should concern itself only with clarifying their meaning, philosophers traditionally have argued, and could not but argue, that the concepts one employs embody one's understanding, and that a different understanding necessarily calls for different concepts and thus for conceptual revision. To philosophise is to offer a certain kind of understanding, and obviously the way one sees and interprets an activity determines, among other things, the concepts one employs, the words one uses and the way one relates them. For example, a philosopher who thinks that all men are ultimately indistinguishable parts of the Absolute and are thus identical may find that he can give no meaning to concepts such as 'I' and 'you', and may therefore feel compelled to dispense with them. Again, a philosopher might feel that if 'I' refers to me as a person and thus includes my body, to talk of 'my body' is a tautology, which should, therefore, be replaced by some other philosophically more appropriate formula. Again, if a philosopher thought that man has no abiding self or underlying substance and that he is ultimately

[1] For example, Oakeshott, *Experience and its Modes*, p. 341 f.

nothing but a series of thoughts, more or less loosely related, he might find himself unable to give any meaning to the expression 'I think', and might instead speak with William James of 'the present thought thinks' or 'the present thought is only the thinker'. Leibniz, for example, could not give any meaning to the concept of space, McTaggart felt the same about the concept of time, and Hegel about the psychological individual. Bradley examined nearly a dozen meanings of the concept of self and found it paradoxical. In short, every major philosopher has found it necessary to offer a new set of concepts, and radically revise traditional ones.

Similarly he might question, and has in the past questioned, not only the way an activity is understood but also the way it is practised; that is, he might question not only *inquiries* like history and science but also *practical activities* like morals and religion. For example, many philosophers have examined the assumptions of religious life and found them untenable. Accordingly they argue that religion is without any meaning or justification and should therefore be rejected. Again, many have argued that moral life lacks all meaning and point unless it is seen in the context of religion, and that the paradoxical moral consciousness finds its ultimate harmony only in the religious consciousness. Even political activity is not exempted as can be seen in the attacks launched on it by philosophical anarchists. Many others like Rosa Luxemburg and Hannah Arendt have offered a powerful philosophical critique not of political life as such but of the way it is organised in the West, and have urged its reorganisation on lines they believed to be compatible with their view of the kind of being man is.

The fourth feature of philosophical inquiry is that it is *interpretative* in character. This view is intended as an alternative to the view that philosophy is essentially a descriptive inquiry. Michael Oakeshott has brought into prominence the idea of philosophical explanation, and he takes explanation to be the most important concern of philosophy. As far as I can see this idea remains inadequately analysed in his writings and raises a number of problems. What, for example, is the philosophical explanation of marriage or monogamy or the independence of the judiciary like? Since philosophy is not a mode like history and science, the logical structure of a philosophical explanation will have to be different from that of an historical and scientific explanation. It seems to me, further, that explanation cannot be taken as the logically ultimate category, since the explanation one gives depends on how one *interprets* the phenomenon one is trying to explain. As I see it, the ultimate concern of philosophy is to *understand*. It does this by offering an *interpretation*. Within the context of such an interpretation *explanation* becomes possible.

The demand for description arises within the context of identification or recognition. If I want to be able to recognise a table or a tree, I want to know what it looks like, and therefore ask for its description. Further, if my demand is to be fully met, the description must be in terms of qualities that I, and others, can perceive; that is to say, it must be in terms of empirical or sensible qualities.

The demand for interpretation, on the other hand, arises within the context of a puzzle or a confusion. I am puzzled by a large number of features that a particular phenomenon displays and wonder if they can all be ordered in some systematic way or explained in terms of one single principle. I can feel this way about a number of things: a picture in an art gallery, several meanings of a word, Hobbes's *Leviathan* or the diversity of moral judgments. In all these cases there is an apparent confusion or chaos or disorder or sheer multiplicity, and one is unable to make any sense of the whole thing in a way that does not leave some important aspect of it unaccounted for. What one is therefore demanding is a manner of conceiving it that resolves the chaos and reduces the multiplicity to order; in short, one is asking for an interpretation.

If an interpretation is to be provided, it cannot be at the same level where the problem arose in the first instance, since there is nothing there but sheer multiplicity. One must probe deeper to a level where one can uncover the sources of multiplicity in some general elements or principles, and thus reduce the multiplicity to a fully satisfactory degree of order. One may, for example, be able to point to some basic meaning of the concept of equality, and show how its different senses arise from the differing character and logic of the contexts in which the concept is applied.

Thus interpretation involves analysis and reduction. At each stage of the inquiry one is moving away from the thing one has started with, and one might even reach a point where it is no longer recognisable. At each stage one lifts the conclusion of the earlier stage onto a new stage, changing it as a result into something different. This something different is nevertheless an interpretation of the conclusion of the earlier stage, and must therefore be related to it. As the entire inquiry is undertaken with a view to interpreting and accounting for the initial given, one must and is able to retrace the steps from the position ultimately reached back to what was originally given. To show the relationship between the point one has finally reached and the starting-point is to offer an interpretation of the latter.

Such a process of moving backwards has a deductive air, and does bear some striking resemblances to the process of deduction, though much depends on what model of deduction one has in mind. It is not and cannot be a straightforward process of deduction as in geometry, since one has suitably to transpose the concepts of one stage in a way appropriate to the other, and this is a highly subtle and complicated exercise as it requires one to elucidate the precise character of the next stage. Moreover, the final stage from where one moves backwards does not come at the start but only at the end of a lengthy process of critical interpretation moving slowly upwards from what is given in experience.

In the light of what I have said so far we can now see some significant differences between description and interpretation. In describing or identifying something one is dealing with empirical qualities, and thus remains pretty close to one's subject matter; that is to say, one never moves away so far from the object of one's description that it is no longer recognisable. Ultimately, of course, description involves interpretation, since everything within experience has, in principle, unlimited properties and stands in an infinite number of relationships with other things, and therefore nothing can ever be fully described: one has always to pick up some features that one considers significant. However, the interpretation involved in any description is minimal, is guided by the considerations of identification, and is such that it keeps one fairly close to one's subject matter. Again, as the purpose and context of description requires that it should be in terms of empirical qualities, description involves induction, since only thus can the empirical qualities common to a number of objects be determined. Finally, as it is words that are used to describe, description is essentially a linguistic activity.

Interpretation, on the other hand, is concerned with understanding and not identification. It involves analysis, criticism and reduction, and therefore a critical or a dialectical, and not an inductive inquiry. In interpreting something one moves away from it, or rather from the way it appears on the first look to its ultimate constitution; and therefore one's ultimate analysis of it can never be useful in identifying it at the phenomenal level. Again, the critical and analytical inquiry is conducted in terms of concepts, not words; that is, logical and not linguistic entities. Though concepts are embodied in words, they need not necessarily be so, and can certainly be studied by means other than the analysis of the linguistic behaviour of the corresponding words.

Let us take a few examples. To say this is a picture with a dark background with a recognisable human figure emerging out of it is to describe it; to say that it symbolises the ultimate futility of human existence is to interpret it. To say that the state is an association of men occupying a definite territory under a government with power to make and enforce laws binding on them all is to describe the institution of the state; to say it is ultimately nothing but a set of ideas in the minds of a certain group of individuals, or that it is the manifestation of the Absolute is to furnish an interpretation of it. In both cases the descriptive formula refers to a class of identifiable objects and is indispensable in identifying the members of that class. If, therefore, someone wants to know which objects to recognise as tables or which human collectivities to recognise as states, the descriptive formula is crucial, while the interpretative formula is simply of no help. Conversely, if someone is puzzled about the phenomenon of a vast number of individuals pursuing their chosen activities and yet constituting a single community, and asks, for example, what the nature of the state is and what ultimately constitutes and sustains it, it is of no help at all to describe to him what states are like. In short, the requirements of identification and the requirements of understanding, though closely connected, are logically different and ought to be kept separate. When we ask for or claim to offer definitions we could mean one or the other, and it is essential to be clear which of these two demands it is that we are trying to meet.

Though interpretation is not peculiar to philosophy and is common to most systematic inquiries like science, history and theology, it is of the very essence of philosophy. In other activities interpretation does not always have a crucial role and can in some cases be replaced by or assimilated to description as, for example, in history; but in philosophy it is indispensable and utterly irreplaceable. Besides, although like all these disciplines, philosophy is interpretative, it differs from them, as argued earlier, in being interpretative in a radical and critical manner.

Philosophy, I have maintained, is a radical, self-conscious and fully critical inquiry. To philosophise about anything thus is to ask what its ultimate structure is, what its essential features are, how they are related, what principles unite and integrate them, what its presuppositions are, whether ultimately it exists and as what, how it can be known and how much can be known about it, whether it is a kind of thing that can be talked and reasoned about and how, whether it can be systematically studied at all, in what different ways and what their limitations are, whether it can be evaluated and critically appraised, and, if so, in terms of what standards and how these standards can themselves be judged and on what grounds, etc. A philosopher wants to examine his subject matter from all sides so that there is no aspect of it that he has left unexplored or has examined only superficially and tentatively; and then he wants to co-ordinate and integrate the various conclusions that he has reached in order to arrive at an understanding of it that is complete and well-rounded.

Although the questions that a philosopher asks, and that I have outlined above, are all philosophical questions, they are not all about the same aspect of the phenomenon under examination. Traditionally, they have been divided into three groups dealing with three different aspects that everything within experience has: whether or not and the manner in which its exists, the kind of knowledge possible about it, and the manner in which it can be talked and reasoned about. The complexes of questions dealing with each aspect have over the centuries become organised into three distinct inquiries called ontology, epistemology and logic. Since a fully philosophical understanding requires asking all the three kinds of questions, these three inquiries are considered to be subdisciplines within philosophy, so that to ask for a philosopher's philosophical system is to ask for his theories in these three fields. They are obviously very closely connected, and one's position in one field limits the range of alternative positions available in the other two. The transition from one to the other is necessary and unavoidable. For example, Aristotelian logic presupposed a certain ontology, and when Hegel denied the latter, he had to work out a new logic. Similarly, the logical theory implicit in the *Principia Mathematica* presupposed a certain ontology which Russell attempted to outline in the *Principles of Mathematics*.

Whenever a philosopher turns his attention to any particular activity or aspect of experience, he is concerned to understand it as it really is and not what this or that form of it is like. In examining the state, for example, he is interested not in a particular state but in the state as such, the state *qua* state. In analysing the concept of justice, he is not concerned with the forms it is believed to take in the bourgeois or the communist states or in the ancient or the modern states but with its essential components. In examining the nature of the family or law or economic activity or religion or language, a philosopher, again, is concerned to determine not what forms they take in his own society or have taken in some past society but instead what they are *qua* family or law or religion or language. He asks what law is and what its inseparable or, to use a rather old-fashioned word, essential features are. One might, for example, describe an existing state exhaustively and yet be nowhere near analysing the essential features of the state. Through indefatigable research one might even produce descriptions of all the existing states and furnish an encyclopaedia of over a hundred volumes, and yet remain as far from a philosophical interpretation of the nature of the state. To parody an old adage, a ton of empirical inquiry cannot yield even an ounce of interpretation and critical anaylsis.

This is not to say that philosophical inquiry is un- or anti-empirical, or that it is formal and deductive. The dichotomy between the purely empirical and the purely formal or between exclusively inductive and exclusively deductive inquiry is misconceived, and provides too clumsy and crude a net from which the fish of philosophy must escape leaving us wondering what kind of a thing this weird animal is and even whether it exists at all. It goes back to Hume's famous polemical remark that if a piece of writing is neither mathematical nor experimental it must be consigned to the flames. Kant enshrined it in his philosophical system in the form of an epistemological distinction between *a priori* and *a posteriori*, and a corresponding logical distinction between analytic and synthetic, propositions. The problem for him and Hume, as for anyone accepting this dichotomy, is how to fit philosophy into it. Philosophical statements must either belong to the category of empirical statements, which is patently absurd. Or they must belong to the class of analytic statements—but this is no more plausible, both because this statement itself, which is surely a philosophical statement, is not an analytic statement, and because the view it expresses makes philosophy definitional and dependent on certain uncriticised assumptions, thus detracting from its critical and radical character. Or philosophical statements must belong to a composite class that is both synthetic and *a priori*, in which case one is involved over again in all the difficulties that commentators have pointed out in Kant. Or, finally, one might so interpret the nature of philosophy that it is seen as a temporary activity that arises only because some philosophers in the past got muddled and that will cease to exist once these muddles are sorted out. Wittgenstein was one of the first philosophers to see the futility of adopting any of the first three alternatives and to have the courage to accept the last one with all its philosophically suicidal implications.

I venture to suggest that these problems and difficulties arise simply because we are approaching the question of the nature of philosophy with the millstone of this false dichotomy tied round our necks. It assumes that empirical information can be dealt with only in an empirical way; that is, that it can be dealt with only in a descriptive manner and is amenable only to the method of induction. My discussion of the distinction between description and interpretation should show the fallacy of this assumption. Besides, the dichotomy between the formal and the empirical inquiry[1] implies that the two are mutually exclusive, and thus fails to take account of the fact that physics, the empirical inquiry *par excellence*, necessarily involves formal inquiry at several stages as Prof. Popper and others have so convincingly shown. Moreover, the dichotomy accommodates and, as the context of Hume's remark suggests, is intended to accommodate, only mathematics and natural sciences and simply ignores a large number of other inquiries. That is to say, the two sides of the dichotomy are not only not mutually exclusive but are not even collectively exhaustive.

---

[1] It will have been noted that I am criticising the distinction both between formal and empirical *statements* and formal and empirical *inquiries*. Ultimately, of course, there can be no distinction between an inquiry and a statement, since every inquiry can only be conducted in terms of, and must result in, certain definite kinds of statements.

I have argued that philosophy is a critical and interpretative or dialectical inquiry that analyses activities with a view to elucidating their essential features. It is therefore neither a deductive nor an inductive inquiry, as it neither begins with any self-evident axioms and works out their implications, nor does it collect as many instances as it can of a particular kind and generalise on their basis. For philosophical purposes an analysis of even one instance might be enough. Though philosophy is not an empirical inquiry either in the sense of going out and collecting its data through a questionnaire or an experiment or an historical investigation, or in the sense of describing and establishing correlations between phenomena, or in the sense of never going beyond the world of sense phenomena, empirical information is, nonetheless, of crucial importance to it. What else but an appeal to 'empirical' information or to experience is made when a philosopher, in the course of an argument, invokes 'the deliverances of moral consciousness' or of 'common sense'; or when he asks what one actually feels and experiences in certain sorts of situations, or whether 'ordinary' men would describe certain situations in this or that way, or how a particular word first originated and whether this can provide a value to its meaning or to a uniting principle in terms of which its various usages and senses can be systematically organised, or how a particular word is used in one's own or other modern or classical languages. A philosopher does not work out his analysis in vacuum or produce his concepts and theories out of his hat; he is not gifted with any special faculty that gives him an immediate access to the essential structure of things. He has to go through the drudgery and painful anxiety of thinking and analysing his own and others' experiences, his own language in all its complexity, the findings of specialised investigations like science and history when they are relevant, and the sorts of judgment he himself as well as others make about the activity in question in both their ordinary and professional capacity.

For example, a philosopher who claims to analyse the nature of time and its relation to space without taking into account what subatomic physics and quantum mechanics have to contribute would hardly be permitted to maintain that his analysis is adequate. Or if he wants to analyse the nature of the state he cannot begin with a definition, or articulate some transcendental and *a priori* insight, but must first examine what goes on in political life. Of course, this does not necessarily entail an empirical investigation, since a philosopher is often in the happy position of having the required information available to him in the ordinary course of life or in 'the common course of the world' as Hume put it. But this is not always so, as, for example, when he inquires how a particular word first originated or what previous philosophers like Plato and Aristotle and Hegel meant by it or how they analysed a particular activity; and then the philosopher has to depend on specialised empirical investigations or undertake them himself.

Thus, though philosophy is not empirical, empirical information is crucial to it. It deals with empirical data in a non-empirical way: it analyses them in order to elucidate their essential structures which it then criticises and relates systematically into a coherent framework. Moreover, once the structure is teased out it is valid for all the various forms of the activity in question, and remains meaningful whether or not the activity continues to exist. Thus Hegel's analysis of the family or Ryle's analysis of mind does not depend on whether or not actual families or minds exist. It is this characteristic of philosophy that philosophers had traditionally in mind when they took it primarily to be concerned with elucidating and criticising 'Ideas' or 'forms' of various activities. However, though concerned with 'forms', philosophy is not a formal activity, as it does not arrive at and deal with them in a formal way.

A philosopher begins his inquiry with any activity or experience that attracts his attention or seems to him significant and worth exploring. Being concerned to penetrate to the deepest layers he goes on to ask and continues to ask the most searching questions about his subject matter. Soon he finds that the answers he has arrived at raise further questions that need to be dealt with if his earlier answers are not to be tentative and *ad hoc*. In the course of dealing with these new questions many more begin to arise that he must examine. The very logic of the inquiry he has embarked upon requires him to carry on till he has reached a point where he thinks no more meaningful questions remain to be asked. The idea of system is thus integrally connected with the idea of philosophy, and the very character of philosophical inquiry entails a *systematic* inquiry, an inquiry that unltimately can end only in a system.

Before I go on to give an example two important points ought to be made. First, a philosopher, on reaching a certain point in his inquiry, might feel that he has sufficiently illuminated his subject matter and has offered a fairly intelligible account of it and that he ought to stop. I do not see any reason why he ought not to, as long as he realises that his inquiry rests on a number of assumptions that he has left unexamined and that it raises a number of other questions and has a number of implications in other areas that he has chosen not to explore. Though ultimately one would wish him to explore and examine all of these, if only for grounding more securely and firmly the analysis he has already offered, it is surely possible to round off the inquiry at this intermediate stage. Those like Sidgwick and Lotze who insist on defining philosophy in terms of a system seem to me to be unduly restrictive, and are involved in the unhappy position of treating many philosophers, particularly many of our contemporaries, as not really philosophers at all. Though they are correct in insisting that a fully satisfactory philosophical inquiry must end in a system, they are wrong to argue that a man is not a philosopher at all unless he has produced a system. When a philosopher stops at an intermediate point in his analysis of a subject he can be said to have advanced a *theory* of that subject.

Second, a philosopher might stop at such a point and not carry on his inquiry with radical and comprehensive rigour, because he might accept as correct the answers given by some other philosopher to most of the general questions that his theory raises. This is, for example, the case with many contemporary philosophers who tend to concentrate only on specific problems, and for the most part take for granted the general validity of the views of the later Wittgenstein. However, once one begins to ask basic questions about their theories, one has to bring in the entire philosophical system of Wittgenstein. What is more, given that philosophy is the kind of activity that I have taken it to be, it is not something that one can take on trust or apply like a technique. There is no place in philosophy either for authorities or for technicians. One can accept another's views only if one is convinced of their satisfactoriness after a careful examination, and then they are no more his views than one's own. In reasoning about and accepting his views one is engaged in the same process as he was, and one is thus as much an independent agent and a philosopher as he. If one's analysis of a particular problem is challenged one cannot take recourse to the argument that one was only following a master, say Wittgenstein. One has to produce one's reasons, defend them by one's own ingenuity, and be ready to abandon them, despite the authority of the master, and the pressure of fellow-faithfuls, if the critic has succeeded in making a dent in the solid-looking armour of the master's philosophical apparatus.

Let us now take an example of a philosopher who finds it necessary to develop a comprehensive system, in order to deal with a problem in a fully satisfactory manner. Take the concept of justice. A philosopher might examine it and show that it involves giving each his due, determined in terms of a general rule, and that it involves a relationship between reward, punishment, office, money or praise on the one hand, and specific human qualities or qualifications on the other. He might go further and seek to develop a theory of justice by distinguishing the concept of justice from cognate concepts like fairness, equality, equity, impartiality and fraternity, by showing its place in the larger moral system and by elucidating its presuppositions. He might, for example, argue that justice is a relationship between men and things while equality is a relationship between man and man, and that while justice determines who should get what, equality determines how one man should be related to another. In analysing the presuppositions of justice he might show that justice is possible only between creatures who are not always altruistic and who expect to be rewarded for services they do to others, who are capable of formulating and acting on general rules, who are separate and distinguishable from others, who can recognise one another as distinct loci of rights and claims, who can understand and communicate with one another, etc. etc. A philosopher who has analysed the essential components of justice, shown their relationships, disengaged it from other concepts and elucidated its presuppositions will undoubtedly have given an intelligible account of justice.

But his account is not fully satisfactory, as it raises a number of general questions that have not been considered. For example, is the principle of justice a satisfactory interpretation of moral life? That is to say, can all our moral judgments be ultimately reduced to and analysed in terms of it? If not, what are its limits? At what stage does such a deontological interpretation of morality break down? Besides, is the assumption of interpersonal communicability valid, since surely one needs to show that men are not beings who can only be engaged in successive soliloquies and that they can therefore understand one another? In general, the concept of justice, like any other concept, derives its meaningfulness and applicability only if certain assumptions are made, and once the latter are challenged it at once becomes of doubtful value. It assumes, for example, that there are many distinguishable and separate persons and that they can make claims on one another. But it is surely possible for another philosopher to understand the nature of the self and its relation to other selves in such a way that he might come to reject both these, and with them the concept of justice itself. He might argue that the body cannot be used as a criterion for identifying, differentiating and defining an individual, and might instead suggest some other criterion which, through a highly complex manoeuvre, requires him to argue that all men are ultimately one. On this basis he might further argue that an individual is nothing but an aspect of a social whole and that whatever he is or has is entirely due to society. This would mean that a man can only have duties and that the notion of claim is absurd.

We can thus see how an analysis of the concept of justice raises highly general questions about the nature of the self and of consciousness. It also raises other general questions that I have not discussed, such as those about the free will, the nature of general rules and the source of their binding power. In discussing these questions a philosopher begins to move away from the theory of justice to a wider moral theory, and from there to still more general philosophical questions that have traditionally been called metaphysics. When a philosopher asks and answers all these and other relevant questions, develops a system, and *then* examines the nature of, say, justice, his account of it leaves no important questions unanswered, does not rest on unexamined assumptions, and is therefore much more satisfactory than that of a philosopher who begins and ends with the concept of justice.

By metaphysics I mean that stage of philosophical inquiry which is concerned with features and principles that are common to all things within experience. For example, everything within experience is in some sense a unity, is subject to change, can be related to man if only in the process of being known and talked about, and involves the ideas of time and space. To analyse and integrate into a well-knit framework highly general ideas like unity, substance, existence, time, space, change and cause, and those principles that underlie all human activities, is the job of metaphysics. It is thus an attempt to give a coherent and general account of all there is. It does not merely elucidate the most basic elements of experience but also asks how it is possible at all and what its presuppositions are.

One of the most crucial problems that any metaphysician is bound to come up against is that posed by the presence of man. Man would seem *prima facie* to enjoy a dual status in the sense that he seems to be both a member of the natural world and thus subject to its laws like its other members, and yet not quite a member of it and thus exempt from some of its laws and subject to some other necessities peculiar to his own nature. There is no metaphysician who has not been baffled by this duality and has not given it most of his philosophical attention and energy. It is this bafflement that has generated a host of problems that have conventionally been recognised as metaphysical problems; indeed, it alone can explain that metaphysics is sometimes defined as an attempt to determine man's place in the universe, a definition that can be shown to be less pretentious and more manageable if taken to mean no more than an attempt to relate man to other members of the natural world by showing how far he can be treated in the same manner as they, and why. Many of the problems generally recognised as metaphysical—free will versus determinism, mechanism versus vitalism, the relation between mind and body, the relation between matter and consciousness, the conflict between science and morality or religion, the distinction between cause and reason—can be shown to spring from the apparently dual status of man. It is not surprising that most metaphysical systems should have ended up in some kind of dualism—transcendental ideas and natural objects of ordinary experience in Plato, matter and form in Aristotle, mind and body in Descartes, extension and thought in Spinoza, phenomena and noumena in Kant, to mention but a few.

Metaphysics is the highest stage of philosophical inquiry. At various other stages philosophy is concerned with specific things, but *qua* metaphysics it is concerned only with the most general and universal questions that, by definition, cannot be asked about specific and narrow areas of experience. At the metaphysical level, specific areas *qua* specific areas disappear—not because they are shown to be illusory but because one is dealing here directly with only universal features which, of course, they all have but not *qua* specific things. This means there can be no such inquiry as political or moral *metaphysics*, though there can certainly be inquiries like political or moral *philosophy*.

When one is confronted with a fully fledged philosophical system—including ontology, epistemology and logic, one might either be interested in it as a whole or in some specific aspect of it, say in its treatment of justice or equality or moral obligation or poetry or art or history. If one is interested in a specific aspect of it one can be said to be interested in its author's *theories* of these subjects. One can then abstract his analysis of them from the larger system and consider them separately. Earlier in the paper I suggested how a philosopher might consider a specific concept or an activity, elucidate its features and presuppositions, and round out his inquiry. He too has advanced a *theory* of these subjects.

One may now ask if both these are theories in the same sense. Obviously there are significant differences between the two. The theory discussed earlier is predominantly analytical and elucidatory but not critical; it rests on a number of assumptions that remain unclarified; it is tentative and lacks the confidence that can come only from an inquiry that has probed its own foundations and assured itself of their basic soundness; it is narrowly based and has not explored the implications of its general position for other activities; it is still pretty close to its subject matter and has not been sufficiently radical; it is philosophising about justice and yet it has not worked out a view of what philosophising means and involves; as a result, it analyses justice in terms of a view of philosophy adopted on trust. The other theory, i.e. the theory that has been abstracted from and that has therefore the backdrop of a fully fledged system, is rather different: it is critical and, what is more, speculative, though it is no less analytical; it rests only on those assumptions that it has carefully examined; it is related to other theories on other subjects; it is not tentative and is not, as it were, suspended in mid-air, but has confidence, firmness and depth, and is able to relate its subject matter to the universal features and principles of the totality of experience.

As long as one bears in mind these and other differences, it would not matter whether one calls them both by the same name or gives them different names. If one likes, one might argue that, since philosophy is always a fully critical and comprehensive inquiry, the earlier, mainly elucidatory inquiry cannot and should not be called philosophy but, say, theory, and that the term philosophy should be reserved only for the other fully critical inquiry. This would mean that there are two distinct kinds of inquiry, viz. theoretical and philosophical, the former being predominantly analytical and elucidatory and never really raising fundamental and universal questions, and the latter being not only analytical and elucidatory but also and mainly critical, constructive and speculative. Personally, though sympathetic to this view, I would like to argue that, though undoubtedly there are significant differences between the two, they are not such as could justify treating them as different in kind, which is, after all, what is ultimately involved in giving them different names. Both, in my view, are *philosophical* inquiries. What is really important is to realise that philosophical theories can be constructed in two different ways, although one of them is more satisfactory and points to the direction in which the other must itself ultimately move.

To sum up what I have been saying in this section. Philosophy is a distinct *kind of inquiry* that differs from all others in being radical, self-conscious and fully critical. It asks a wide variety of interconnected *questions* that can be classified as ontological, epistemological and logical. It can ask these questions about any *subject matter* and this gives rise to various kinds of philosophy like philosophy of politics, of science, of history, and of religion. In its *orientation* it is not only elucidatory and analytical but also critical, constructive, and speculative. In its *level of achievement* it may offer an analysis of a specific concept, or it may offer a theory (of a practical activity like politics or of a systematic inquiry like science or history), or, finally, it may go the whole way and work out a metaphysic. A philosopher may stop at any of these intermediate stages and will undoubtedly have said something worthwhile about his subject matter. In the ultimate analysis, however, the intelligibility he has offered lacks firmness and has no power to resist, and begins to disintegrate under, a much more critical and radical philosophical inquisition. Finally, as for the *manner of reading* a philosopher, one can begin anywhere. All the parts of a philosophical system are mutually related and integrated. One may therefore enter into it at any point, say with its moral or political theory, and move on to examine the way other parts are treated and related to it; or one may begin with the highest principles and concepts and move down to specific parts of it.

IV

The view of the nature of philosophy developed above has certain important implications which may be spelt out.

First, there is no reason at all why philosophy cannot be a first order activity. The distinction between first and second order activity is perhaps ultimately unsatisfactory, and is not, in any case, of a kind that separates the two in such a way that movement from one to the other is completely ruled out. In doing any kind of philosophical analysis one continually finds oneself moving from one to the other, not through naïveté or any lack of rigour but because of the very logic of the analysis. However, this is not the place to outline the various ways in which such a distinction can be drawn and to discuss which of them is the most satisfactory. All I want to suggest is that philosophy can analyse the structure of an activity just as it can analyse the structure of the intellectual inquiry that studies the activity. Thus there can be a philosophy of moral life just as there can be a philosophy of ethics, a philosophy of social life as there can be a philosophy of social sciences and sociology, a philosophy of history as of historiography, of religion as of theology, of nature as of sciences, or politics as of political studies. For example, philosophical questions can be asked both about the way political life is organised and about the way it is studied by political 'science', political history and the history of political thought.[1] Of course, an adequate philosophical analysis of an activity would have to compromise both these kinds of analysis as the two are closely connected. Thus, for example, social philosophy is a study not only of the social life as we live and experience it, but also of the way we talk about it and study it. This is also true of natural philosophy—a more comprehensive term than philosophy of science—and it is worth noting that there is hardly a major philosopher of science who has not gone on to make philosophical observations about the 'world' of nature and thus to intimate, often in a muted form, a philosophy of nature.

There are many philosophers who refuse to regard philosophy as a first order activity, mainly on the ground that this will make it some kind of specialised activity devoted to empirical investigation—like history and science. This view seems to me to be ill-conceived since, from saying that philosophy can be a first order activity, it does not at all follow that it must be an empirical inquiry. I argued earlier that it is possible to deal with empirical information in a non-empirical way. Besides, in order to be able to deal directly with empirical data,

---

[1] I take thought to be a generic term, and ideas, theory and philosophy as its successive levels of achievement. This means that the history of political thought is a generic inquiry, and that the history of political ideas, of political theory and of political philosophy are its three forms.

one need not oneself go out and collect them with specially devised research techniques. One could arrive at them in the natural course of life, or one could accept them from other specialised inquiries. A philosopher, analysing the nature of the state, for example, may borrow from the historian his account of how the word 'state' first emerged and how it was originally used, or of how the institution of the state first arose and what features it then had. This, of course, means that philosophy stands in a relationship of dependence to other inquiries, but it does not require one to say that philosophy could not logically arise at all until they first existed and provided it its subject matter. After all, historically speaking, philosophy existed long before many of the empirical inquiries did.

Secondly, though a philosopher ought to take account of, incorporate and explain the way commonsense sees things, he does not thereby become a 'commonsense' philosopher as Moore sometimes insisted. A philosopher might criticise, correct and go beyond commonsense. He must, of course, show why he finds commonsense unsatisfactory, and explain why it sees things in such a philosophically unsatisfactory way; but he cannot treat it as the authority or the final court of appeal and bow unquestioningly to its commands. Besides, commonsense *qua* commonsense is philosophically irrelevant, and it is only because the philosopher recognises it as embodying philosophically relevant insights that it acquires whatever philosophical authority it happens to have. This means that it is for philosophy to determine when to appeal to commonsense in the course of a philosophical argument and what authority to confer on it. Again, commonsense is not a static given, but is continually refined and sharpened as the findings of sciences and history, or the insights of philosophers and literary figures, filter down to the 'common man' via culture, the intermediate realm between commonsense and the technical inquiries. After all, to be cultured is to be acquainted with these inquiries in a manner and to a degree that educates commonsense while keeping it firmly planted in the ordinary world; that is to say, to be cultured is to be neither merely a 'layman' nor just an expert. To the extent that philosophy contributes to the education of commonsense it hardly stands to reason that it should be judged by the criteria and the demands of the latter.

What has just been said of commonsense is equally true of ordinary language. A philosopher who completely ignores it—assuming that this is possible at all—or introduces new words or uses old ones in an idiosyncratic manner without showing why he must, or who recommends other kinds of changes in the ordinary language without adequate philosophical reasons must certainly be criticised. But that is different from saying that ordinary language is the only thing he is concerned with, or that it is a sovereign authority whose commands he is forbidden to violate. We must distinguish between linguistic analysis, an essential philosophical activity, and linguistic philosophy, an untenable general thesis about the nature of philosophy that makes language, and ordinary language at that, the origin, the solution, and the ultimate boundary of all philosophical activity. Linguistic philosophy and commonsense philosophy deserve much fuller analysis and criticism than is offered here, but I suppose this is excusable in an essay that attempts primarily to outline a certain position.

Thirdly, though philosophy does involve conceptual analysis,[1] the two cannot be identified. Philosophy does not deal with concepts alone but with much besides. For example, it can and does analyse the presuppositions of a specific activity or inquiry or even of experience in general as Kant did. Besides, when it deals with concepts it does not merely analyse them but also relates them and attempts to construct a conceptual framework. Moreover, when philosophy does analyse concepts it is not interested in such an analysis as something intrinsically worthwhile, but undertakes it with a view to understanding the activity concerned; philosophy is a conceptual exploration of experience and uses concepts to interrogate and comprehend experience. Further, philosophy does not deal with all kinds of concepts but only with those that have certain features like generality and abstractness. It analyses, for example, the concept of force but not of mass, the concept of energy but not of heat. In short, to see philosophy as nothing but conceptual analysis is to emphasise only two aspects of philosophical inquiry, viz. concepts and analysis, and to ignore and, what is worse, to distort and misunderstand the rest.

Fourthly, as has been argued earlier, the philosopher, in analysing an activity, does not rely on any transcendental intuition or on any form of *a priori* knowledge but on what is found in experience. This means that he must be sensitive to the appearance of any new aspect of experience or element of knowledge. A political philosopher reflecting on the nature of the state would want to know if the state as it is known to him has always existed, or whether there have been other forms of political and even nonpolitical organisation with different principles of unity. He is concerned to analyse the nature of political life as such and to offer an analysis of it that is applicable to all its various possible forms, and thus his interest in the past forms of political life is a result not of natural curiosity but of the very logic of his philosophical inquiry.

---

[1] Even though various commentators have treated commonsense philosophy, linguistic philosophy and conceptual analysis as different names for the same kind of activity, I would want to argue that they are separate. They may, perhaps, belong to the same family, but they have inherited different traits.

Similarly, in trying to understand what political philosophy is and what sorts of questions it must ask, a political philosopher has to turn his attention to the works of those generally recognised as political philosophers. This means that in the course of doing philosophy a philosopher feels compelled by the very logic of his inquiry to turn to history.

This is not to say that philosophy and history are not logically different kinds of inquiry, or that the philosopher, when he turns to history, can do it in the same way as he does philosophy. Philosophy and history *are* different inquiries, and when a philosopher begins to inquire about the political structure of fifth century Athens or of the medieval common-wealth or about the way Plato or Hobbes or Hegel understood political philosophy, he is certainly taking on a different role—that of a historian —and is subject to different demands. Nevertheless, the fact of their being different does not entail or imply that philosophy and history are separate in practice, or that the same person cannot be engaged in both, or that in the course of doing one, one may not feel logically compelled to do the other as well. The two are organically connected and the transition from one to the other is not an accident or a result of ignorance or, sometimes even, a matter of choice. Not only the knowledge they offer but also the inquiries they involve overlap and entail each other. Those who want to turn the distinction between them into a disjunction and set up barriers between them fail to grasp both the organic inter-dependence of all knowledge and the nature of logical difference.

What is true of the relationship between history and philosophy is no less true of the relationship between science and philosophy. It is in-teresting to note that there is hardly a good scientist who has not at some point in his scientific inquiry felt constrained to raise philosophical questions, and he has done that not because he also happened to be a philosopher, or happened to have an interest in philosophy, but because he felt that his very understanding of science required him to raise these questions. The transition from science to philosophy is often no more than a change of route on the same journey.[1]

Fifthly, as philosophy is concerned with understanding, and as the way one acts in a situation depends on the way one understands it, there is a *logical* connection between philosophy and action or, to put it differently, between philosophy and recommendation. If a philosopher holds that all human activities are traditional and can be carried on only in a traditional manner, in his view it is not just *bad* or *wrong* but

---

[1] See, for example, the frequently quoted remarks of Eddington, Einstein, Heisenberg, Sir James Jeans, Schrödinger and others. Quine observed that 'ontology and metaphysics... constitute boundary areas into which more strictly scientific analysis shades off'. Prof. Hempel shares this view. See *Journal of Philosophy*, vol. 55 (1958), p. 339.

impossible to behave in any other way. A man who insists on acting in a non-traditional way is in the eyes of such a philosopher simply *mad*, just like someone who invests his life's savings in a concern that has already declared itself bankrupt. His enterprise and plans are not *utopian*—a picture of a possible future state of affairs—but *fantastic*—an utterly impossible state of affairs and therefore completely bizarre and abstracted from and opposed to all reality. A revolutionary might, of course, believe that he is wiping the social slate clean and is writing something entirely new, but in effect he is doing nothing of the kind and is as much within the traditional framework as his self-confessed traditionalist compatriots. The philosopher I have been describing will certainly recognise what is generally called 'revolution' as an important phenomenon, but he will reinterpret it as no more than a rather rapid development of a certain aspect of society within the framework of its traditional structure. The common understanding of it as a violent rupture with the traditional structure that ushers in something entirely new and that springs from a consciously and abstractly worked out novel manner of organising society will be rejected as resting on a false epistemology.

A philosopher holding a different view of the nature of human activities and the sort of knowledge they require will offer a different account of what is and what is not possible, of what is and what is not rational, of what is fantastic and what is utopian, and accordingly will advance a different analysis of change and revolution. He too claims to lay bare the ultimate structure of human activities in general, and of specific activities like morals and politics in particular, and insists, and cannot but insist, that our responses to them must be planned in the light of this knowledge. It is only rational to acknowledge what these activities really are and make our responses accordingly; conversely, it is mad or absurd or foolish to behave as if they are otherwise or can be turned into something else.

A philosophical understanding of an activity thus points to its essential and permanent features, and offers criteria for evaluating relevant practical proposals and actions—not, of course, in their specificity but in their general assumptions and orientation. This is no less true of the innocent looking resolutive-compositive method of Hobbes,[1] or of the dialectical method of Hegel.[2] In short, while recognising the logical distinction between philosophy and recommendation and, at a different level, between philosophy and conduct, we must decline the invitation to turn it into a disjunction and set up rigid barriers between them and

---

[1] See, for example, a very perceptive observation by J. W. N. Watkins in *Hobbes Studies*, ed. K. C. Brown (Oxford, 1965), p. 248.
[2] See H. Marcuse, *Reason and Revolution* (London, 1954), pp. 200 f. and 215 ff.

then get into difficulties in a way that earlier philosophers did when they disjoined descriptive and prescriptive or formal and empirical statements or inquiries.

V

We have discussed so far what it is to do philosophy. In the light of it we may now discuss the nature of political philosophy.

Obviously, it means asking philosophical questions about politics with a view to elucidating the kind of activity it really is. As argued earlier this can be done in two ways, one more satisfactory than the other. A political philosopher may explore the internal structure of political life, point to its essential components and relate them. He thus begins and ends with politics and develops a (philosophical) theory of politics. On the other hand, a philosopher may examine all significant areas of experience and develop a comprehensive philosophical system. He may then go on to study politics in terms of the general categories and principles of his system.

The second political philosopher is able to understand political life in a way that does not leave any of the significant questions unanswered. There are no obscure corners in his system and nothing is merely assumed. The first philosopher is in a different position. Though he has made political life intelligible, his theory is inherently unstable and unsatisfactory, as there are a number of crucial questions that he has simply ignored. He might have analysed politics in terms of concepts like purpose, will and rationality, and might not have asked at all whether man is a creature capable of any of these, or whether, instead, he is a mechanistically determined being who can only be understood in terms of pushes and pulls. Besides, he may not have asked, among other things, how politics can be studied at all, how one can go about analysing concepts and defining terms, how one can settle controversies about the uses of words, whether definitions should come at the beginning or at the end, and, if at the end, how one can begin one's inquiry at all. He is thus not able to justify or defend the way he has conducted his inquiry into politics. Again, he may not have asked why politics must exist at all, whether it is a transient human activity that could conceivably disappear under certain conditions or whether it is inseparably associated with human existence, how it is related to other activities and how its structure and components can be assimilated to, as well as distinguished from, theirs, and what its value and place in the general understanding of experience are.

What I have said so far would seem to imply that when one talks of political philosophy one can mean two different things: an examination of the internal structure of politics in a tentative and not fully critical manner, or a thoroughly critical examination of politics in the context of a full understanding of all the significant aspects of experience in a way that integrates its categories with those of other activities. While one begins and ends with politics and is primarily clarificatory, the other sees politics in a wider perspective and is not just clarificatory but also critical and comprehensively constructive. As suggested earlier, one might give them different names, calling the first inquiry political theory, and the second political philosophy. But this may be of doubtful value because, among other things, political theory can be of various kinds, such as empirical, normative and philosophical, and this difference would still have to be brought out. Perhaps, with more justification, one might call the first philosophical theory of politics and the second philosophy of politics, on the ground that the latter, unlike the former, has an entire philosophical system to back it up, and that thus it is able to look at politics from the vantage point of a fully fledged philosophy. In any case the really important thing is to be aware of the two different sorts of writing that pass in the name of political philosophy. I need hardly say that I do not set up any rigid barriers between the two, or disallow any movement from the first to the second kind of inquiry; indeed, my point precisely is that such movement is essential to philosophical thought. All I am suggesting is that these two kinds of inquiry differ in their orientation, in the level from which they consider politics, and in the satisfactoriness of the results they achieve.[1]

I should now like to outline in some detail a fully worked out and ultimately the only satisfactory understanding of politics. As argued earlier, it consists in asking radical and critical questions about politics with a view to understanding it in a way that leaves no important question unanswered. To put the point schematically, political philosophy principally asks three main classes of question: first, those exploring political life from within by eludicating its essential structure and relating its various parts systematically to one another; second, those relating politics to other activities, so as to define its outlines more sharply and clearly and to detect misleading metaphors, analogies, models, assumptions and hypotheses that creep into the understanding of politics; third, those concerning the *raison d'être* of political life. These questions are, of course, closely connected, and the answer to one of them limits the range of answers one can give to the other two. The schematic distinction between them is intended only to disengage the logical type of the questions involved.

[1] The concept of theory raises some extremely complicated questions; in a short essay like this it is not possible to disengage its various senses and trace its fascinating history. It is worth noting, though, that in ordinary as well as professional language we do not use the terms theory and philosophy interchangeably. It is interesting to observe that, though Prof. Berlin does not explicitly distinguish political theory and political philosophy, he

The second class of questions has received a good deal of attention in the current literature on the subject[1] and does not need much comment. The third class of questions, though currently neglected or answered under a different name, has received a great deal of attention in the classical political philosophy. Plato, for example, thought that political life was necessary, since only through it was the Idea of Good actualised in human affairs. For Aristotle, politics is the expression of human capacity for speech and justice, and is thus integral to the existence of man *qua* man, though not to man *qua* God. For Augustine, civitas is natural to man not as God first created him but as he has since become. For Hobbes, the state is the very condition of any organised life and thus of civilisation itself. To be civilised for him is to be civil-ised, to live in a civil society. For Rousseau and Hegel and the Idealists in general, the state is the very essence of moral, and truly human, life. For Marx, it is the expression and perpetuation of man's alienation from himself and his fellow men. For the anarchists like Godwin and Kropotkin, it is a totally unwarranted imposition on man and a hindrance to the rhythmic flow of man's natural impulses and is thus fundamentally anti-human.

Thus there is already a long tradition and a vast literature analysing and answering the second and third classes of question. It is the first class of questions that, in my view, has not been consciously formulated, though, of course, most of these questions are implicit in the political philosophies of all the major figures. It will, therefore, not be unrewarding to spell them out at some length.

To maintain that philosophy involves asking ontological, epistemological and logical questions means that the philosophical exploration of politics results in the development of political ontology, political epistemology and the logic of politics.

Political Ontology

I use the term ontology with great hestitation and considerable misgivings and do so only because I cannot find another word to describe the sort of inquiry I have in mind. Kant dismissed it as a pseudo-science. What roused his fury was the Wolffian view of it, developed most fully

tends to use the latter term when he wants to refer to an inquiry that is general and rests on a comprehensive view of man; but as the distinction is not explicitly recognised, he is sometimes led to talk of political theory 'in the larger sense'. 'Does political theory still exist?' in *Philosophy, Politics and Society*, ed. Laslett and Runciman, 2nd ser. (1962), p. 27.

[1] An article entitled 'Political Action' by Collingwood in *Proc. Arist. Soc.*, New Series, vol. XXLX (1928–9). See also Berlin, *loc. cit.* I cannot understand why Berlin should describe philosophical systems as models; they are intended to interpret the ultimate structure of experience, and thus are descriptions and not models of reality. At places, Berlin psychologises models and equates them with images; at other places, he takes them to be normative in character. See, for example, pp. 15–20 and 25 f.

in Baumgarten's 'Metaphysik'. For Wolff ontology is a purely formal and abstract inquiry into 'possible being'; he deduces his whole system from the most general principle that 'contradictory predicates cannot exist in any subject'. Kant had no difficulty whatever in toppling this view, though he was wrong to argue that he had also thereby knocked down the discipline itself. Since Kant's time ontology has lived a very controversial and uneasy existence. It was the very starting point of Hegel's philosophy[1] in which being was the first category from which others were deduced. For Bentham, 'Necessary to well-being is Being';[2] thus ontology, the discussion of the nature of 'being', became 'the basis' of eudaimonics and so of his moral and political theory. It was also crucial to his theory of fiction. Collingwood wanted 'metaphysics without ontology', though he had earlier suggested that ontology was a part of metaphysics.[3] Strawson[4] sees metaphysics as concluding with highly general ontological propositions. Sartre and Heidegger see ontology as the basis of any sound philosophy, though Sartre sharply distinguishes it from metaphysics,[5] whose possibility and worthwhileness in one of its forms he doubts, while Heidegger tends to identify the two.

As it is not possible to enter into this controversy here, I must content myself with a rather bald assertion concerning what I take ontology to mean. Ontology has generally been defined in terms either of the concept of existence or of the concept of being. The ontic version of it, i.e. one that defines ontology in terms of being, is liable to the criticisms that Professor Ayer and others have levelled against it. Many ontologists start by saying 'X is', and then move on illegitimately to saying 'X exists as a being'—that is, as a unity and as a substance and not merely as a bundle of qualities. Some go even further, and say that 'X has a being', an essentialist statement attributing essence to X. Thus they move from the simple fact of being to the postulation first of substance and then of essence, and thereby perform the miracle of turning existence into essence.

The existential version of ontology, one that defines it in terms of existence and with which I sympathise, is not vulnerable to the criticisms of Kant, Hegel, Collingwood or Ayer. It takes ontology to be an

---

[1] He, too, criticised Wolff's view of ontology on the ground that it did not understand the world 'as a concrete whole but only according to abstract definitions'. *Encyclopaedia*, § 35.
[2] *Works* VIII, p. 83.
[3] *An Essay on Metaphysics* (Oxford University Press, 1940), pp. 14 ff. But also *An Essay on Philosophical Method* (Oxford University Press, 1933), p. 127.
[4] *Individuals* (Methuen, 1959), p. 247. His metaphysical inquiry enables him to notice and 'explain' the close connection between the idea of an individual in the logical sense and the idea of existence, and to find some 'reason' in the view that 'persons and material bodies are what primarily exist'.
[5] *Being and Nothingness*, trans. H. E. Barnes (Methuen, 1957), p. 619; see also the translator's introduction, p. xxxvi.

inquiry into the meaning, kinds and criteria of existence with a view to determining what ultimately exists. This means ontology is concerned with two things. First, it is concerned with the formal determination of the meaning, criteria and kinds of existence. Here various philosophers have suggested that a thing can be said to exist if it can be perceived, or if it has a capacity to produce sensations, or if it can resist an attempt to negate it from outside, or if it has the capacity to subsist and endure in time. Second, ontology is concerned to analyse and interpret objects of experience in order to determine what can be taken ultimately to exist. Here, again, philosophers have come up with different views, such as that it is bodies or matter or sensations or ideas or Ideas or the Absolute that alone ultimately exist. The discussion of the identity and individuality of a thing, the status of universals, and the nature of primary and secondary qualities would thus, obviously, fall under ontology.

If this view of ontology is accepted the precise character of political ontology becomes clearer. It asks what the ultimate and abiding features of political activity are in terms of which various forms of it can be explained, and which must be considered the ultimate and real existents for political purposes.[1] Bosanquet is offering an ontological analysis of the state when he argues in the Idealist vein that the state is nothing more than a certain set of institutions, that these institutions are nothing but certain patterns of behaviour, that these patterns are simply a certain set of ideas in the minds of men, that men come to have these common ideas because of their participation in the Absolute, and that therefore the state is ultimately an expression of the Absolute. Aristotle maintained that the *polis* had no existence independently of its citizens, and that it remained formal, potential and unactualised when they did not participate actively in its life. The *polis*, for him, had a greater being and reality when its citizens did more, and more 'beautiful', deeds. The existence of the *polis* is thus highly personalised, so that Athens is where Athenians are, is of the kind they are, exists whenever and wherever two or more of its citizens meet to discuss its affairs, and is not confined to or located only in the deliberative assembly.

Rousseau, too, offered an extremely perceptive political ontology, though he substituted the idea of public good for the Aristotelian idea of active political participation. As he put it, 'the state...maintains only a *vain, illusory and formal existence* when in every heart the social bond is broken...; and all men, guided by secret motives, no more give

---

[1] What exists for political purposes may not exist for moral purposes. For example, Aristotle was prepared to recommend kindness but not citizenship to slaves; for him they were morally real, but not politically. Similarly, every sentient being, including an animal, has a moral but not a political claim on me; he exists for me at a moral but not a political level.

their views as citizens than *if the state had never been*.[1] The state exists as a state only when, and as long as, the citizens act in a public-spirited manner; when they do so, the result is the general will, which thus has an ontological significance as it constitutes and actualises the state. The social contract creates the state only formally; it is the general will that confers on it a 'real' and 'true' existence. As the transition from the natural to moral life is the very essence of the civil life, which is intended to produce 'a remarkable change in man' and re-form him, the civil life exists, and can only exist, in and through the general will. It may, incidentally, be observed that such an analysis entails a political recommentation: if the state is to exist, which it ought to given Rousseau's analysis of the nature of man, its citizens should act in a public-spirited manner.

In modern times many of the leading political philosophers—Arendt, Oakeshott, Sartre, Strauss and Voegelin—have advanced interesting and highly sophisticated ontological positions. As it is not possible to discuss all of them here, I shall briefly outline Oakeshott's view. For him, activity is the ultimate philosophical category, and everything within experience can be explained in terms of it. What is commonly called self is shown to be nothing but a complex of activities.[2] Institutions, economic, political or social, are all similarly analysed. Every activity, further, has a form or character, and no activity is without it. Its character is tentative and inchoate in the beginning but becomes definite, firm and articulate as it comes to be practised more widely over the course of years. To know an activity fully is therefore to know its character in all its historical complexity. This introduces the idea of tradition, which thus is not just incidental to but inherent in the very structure of activity as Oakeshott understands it. This means, for example, that political 'arrangments' are nothing but the crystallisation of political 'traditions'; what he calls 'literature', too, has no independent status but is the embodiment of a certain 'language'.[3] As he puts it, it is the skill which 'constitutes' the activity.[4] Ontological dualism or cleavage is thus avoided.[5] He is very close to Aristotle for whom also nothing in experience is ever without a form, formless matter and matterless form being only ideal and logically possible limits. Aristotle's theory of natural kinds finds an echo in Oakeshott's unassimilable and autonomous modes of experience. Oakeshott, however, rejects the Aristotelian view that the fully developed form of an activity must already be potentially present in it from the beginning,

---

[1] *The Social Contract* (Everyman's Library), p. 86. Italics added.
[2] *Rationalism in Politics*, pp. 143 and 204.   [3] *Ibid.* pp. 119 ff. and 308.
[4] *Ibid.* p. 137.
[5] For a discussion of Oakeshott's moral ontology, see *Experience and its Modes*, pp. 285 f.

and thus gives greater scope for chance development and human ingenuity.

In addition to the general question of the ultimate constitution and the manner of existence of the state, political ontology also involves a discussion of the question of political identity. What is it that makes a society a single society and different from all others? And what makes it the same society over the centuries? In short, what is the locus of its political identity? Is it the physical person of the ruler as Hegel suggested?[1] Or is it the political person of the representative as Hobbes maintained? Or is it the character of the legislature as Locke argued?[2] Or is it the 'common recognition of a manner of attending to its arrangements' as Michael Oakeshott suggests?[3] Or is it the constitution of a political community as Montesquieu, Arendt and others argue on the ground that it is the constitution that constitutes the political community and thus concretely articulates and embodies its political existence? This last view and its slightly different version in the hands of Oakeshott goes back to Aristotle, who had asked, 'When shall we say that the *polis* is the same and when different?', and answered, 'when the form of the government'[4] or 'the constitution' becomes different, 'then it may be supposed that the state is no longer the same'. For him, this is true not only of the *polis* but also of 'every union or composition of elements' in all of which it is 'the form of their composition' that constitutes their identity.

Aristotle's view would seem to imply that when the established constitutional arrangements are seriously questioned by a significant section of the community, the community concerned is involved in a political identity crisis, and that when this civil war situation is successfully resolved in favour of the contending section and a new constitution is adopted, the community can be considered to have acquired a new political identity. On Oakeshott's view, on the other hand, even a revolution or a civil war cannot tranform completely the identity of a political community, since, however radical, they still remain within the traditional structure of the community. In short, depending on how one analyses the structure and manner of existence of the political community, one suggests different criteria of political identity, and offers different philosophical interpretations of civil war and revolution.

---

[1] *Philosophy of Right*, §§ 279 and 280.
[2] *Second Treatise*, § 212.   [3] *Rationalism in Politics*, p. 123.
[4] *Politics*, iii. 3. 1276b; *De Anima* ii. 1. 412.9. In virtue of form 'a thing is called a "this"'.

Political Epistemology

By political epistemology I mean an inquiry not only into the epistemological *presuppositions* of politics but also into the epistemological *structure* of politics with a view to working out an epistemology that is integral to the very understanding of politics. It involves an analysis of the categories of political cognition—categories like space, time, rationality, intentionality, causality, responsibility and consciousness in terms of which political events are perceived and interpreted.

Take, for example, the ideas of political time and political space. Political activity takes place within the framework of time and space, and every political philosopher feels constrained to take account of them. One of the crucial differences between a traditionalist and a rationalist (of the Cartesian kind) centres round their attitude to time. The rationalist is distrustful of time and, as Oakeshott puts it, hankers after 'eternity' which, in fact, is a 'bogus eternity'.[1] For a rationalist, each unit of time is new and totally unconnected with others, and thus he lacks 'all sense of rhythm and continuity'.[2] Bentham himself said that time was a function of space,[3] that space was everything and time 'nothing', and that, politically speaking, once a constitutional code was worked out in the light of the peculiarities of a particular community it was valid for it for all times.

It is one's view of the nature of time that, along with other things, determines one's views of what is and what is not politically possible, how often to hold elections, when the government should act, when the time is ripe for demanding or conceding reforms, and when the community should go back to its foundations in its task of periodic political rejuvenation or when it should go out in search of new foundations. For Plato, time is unreal and everything involved in the temporal process is inherently unstable and corrupt; therefore, if a political society is to be durable it must be based on transcendental and timeless truths which alone are ultimately and necessarily real.[4] For Aristotle, every moving thing moves in a circle—the symbol of perfection; time, itself a moving thing, is cyclical in nature. Not only political phenomena but even the opinions of philosophers recur in the same form and the same order 'not once or twice nor a few times but infinitely often'.[5] The only way out of the cyclical process of time is to break completely through its barrier and ascend to the world of timeless truths. As this is always and necessarily a personal and not a collective and political affair, political

[1] *Rationalism in Politics*, pp. 2 f, 133 and 170 f.
[2] This is certainly not true of all rationalists. See Popper, *Conjectures and Refutations* (London, 1964), pp. 132 f.   [3] *Works*, I, 189; VIII, 200.
[4] *Symposium*, 211, A–B; *Republic*, VI, 508 and IX, 585.
[5] *Meteorologica*, 339. b. 29.

utopianism on this view cannot but appear naïve and philosophically untenable.[1]

Machiavelli also assumed that time was cyclical in nature, and that the future, broadly speaking, was a return of the past. This made the continuous search into the Roman past for appropriate examples and models of political conduct philosophically necessary. On the Judaic–Christian view time is unilinear so that going back to a past state of affairs is simply impossible. For some other philosophers, time is a flow that periodically explodes, so that that action is 'well-timed' or that reform is 'in time' that comes just before the next point of explosion. Again, political actions require time to mature and show results and thus need a certain amount of time to elapse before they can be judged. On the liberal democratic view, which is embodied in the constitutional arrangements of many European nations, four to five years is considered an appropriate temporal unit for political judgment; and therefore elections, the exercise and expression of political judgment, are held every so many years.

That time is not simply a matrix of political action but enters into its very structure and is thus an important explanatory category of political life can be seen in a number of ways. Several political decisions are taken and several measures are adopted only because of the 'shortage of time'—whether political or specifically parliamentary, and their hasty character and ugly consequences can often only be explained in terms of time. Besides, people engaged in politics continually articulate their understanding of it in terms of time as can be seen, for example, in familiar remarks like 'the time is ripe for reform', 'the time has come to stand up for our rights', 'reforms are long overdue', 'atrocities are forgotten with the lapse of time', and 'time confers authority on individuals and institutions'. The new states, with their acute poverty, formidable problems of 'nation building', and the tremendous expectations and hopes of their peoples, have brought the question of time to the fore, so much so that the style of their politics, the dilemmas they face and the decisions they take can hardly be understood except in the context of time. Even in industrialised societies like Britain where the government tends to concern itself more and more with economic matters, the question of time arises in an acute form, especially as the time-scale required by the political criteria of the accountability of government and the intelligent exercise of political judgment is not always compatible or congruous with that required by the economic

[1] See also Augustine, *Confessions* (Penguin Classics), p. 64. What is permitted at one time may not be permitted at another. 'This does not mean that justice is erratic or variable, but that the times over which it presides are not always the same, for it is the nature of time to change.' By introducing the idea of time he was able to reconcile the eternal validity of moral principles with their changing historical content.

criteria of efficiency and a high growth rate; the unit of time required for economic policies to mature and show results is greater than that permitted by the considerations relevant to political life. This means that political judgment and the choice of government in an election are often no more than an act of faith or hereditary loyalty.[1]

What is true of time is no less true of space, which, too, is not just a form or matrix but of the very essence of politics and enters into its very structure. It is a political truism that the effectiveness of what one says depends on *where* one says it. Modern states and their conflicts would hardly be intelligible without a reference to space. Debates about regionalism and decentralisation are ultimately about the manner of ordering and regulating political space. In most political communities there is a formally organised public space where its representatives meet, deliberate and decide. Often there exist procedures and, in some cases, even ceremonies to fortify and safeguard the political character of public space. There are also procedures for turning private space into political space where public debate can then take place. One of the most important points of debate between the representative and the participatory theories of democracy, in fact, centres round the relationship between the formally organised central public space and the vast number of informal public spaces that invariably spring up in a community that is free and has not yet lost its capacity for political action. The representative theory, with its tendency to equate the political with the parliamentary, concentrates all political initiative in the hands of a central body, with the result that the vitality of the community as a whole tends to be sucked off; and then the community comes to consist of nothing more than a 'flock of sheep innocently nibbling the grass side by side'[2] as J. S. Mill so eloquently put it. The participatory theory of democracy, on the other hand, insists on the participation by all the citizens in the conduct of the affairs of a community, and therefore demands both the dispersal of political space (so that citizens can appear and debate in countless assemblies scattered all over the country), and the integration of these dispersed public spaces with the centrally organised political space in a way that ensures a continual flow of ideas and power between them.

In a very important sense the idea of space is implicit in the ideas of

[1] Though this is not the place to discuss it, it may be mentioned that the idea of time has an important role in the understanding of moral and social life as well. Sidgwick in his *Methods of Ethics* (London, 1962), p. 381, makes time crucial to his moral theory when he formulates the 'Maxim of Prudence' as recommending that the future and the present units of time are to be considered *equally* important and that no moral action should be based on an arbitrary preference of one over the other. For an interesting though rather sketchy discussion of the relation between space and time in his moral theory, see F. H. Hayward, *The Ethical Philosophy of Sidgwick* (London, 1901), pp. 111 and 117 f.

[2] *Representative Government* (Everyman's Library), p. 217.

institution and rationality. Institutions are interposed between individuals; thus they create a space between them, and, in so doing, both relate and separate them. To the extent that political life is governed by institutions, it necessarily creates political space; conversely, when institutions are dispensed with and rule becomes personalised, political space is destroyed, and a mass society, with individuals falling over each other and creating a 'mass' out of a series of unindividuated men, is generated. Similarly, any discussion or argument entails a separateness not only *between* individuals, each of whom has to recognise others as separate beings who cannot be wished away or coerced but have to be persuaded through reasons, but also *within* every individual who has to detach himself from his passionately held convictions and look at them from the standpoint of others. To think is to create a space within oneself, and to argue is to create a space between oneself and others. This seems to be the underlying truth of the remark frequently made that we are too near[1] a particular event to judge it objectively and impartially. It also seems to explain why we associate feelings with lack of objectivity, and consider them a poor precondition for an impartial analysis of a situation; feeling implies identification or fusion with its object, and thus indicates a lack of separateness or distance or space. Such close connection between space and rationality seems also to explain why every totalitarian society is led to appeal to emotions, whether of envy or of fear or of glory or of anything else, in order to create a national hysteria that destroys all elements of separateness and space within and between its members.[2]

Other general questions that political epistemology asks concern the nature of political knowledge. It inquires if knowledge is relevant at all to the field of politics, or whether the latter is merely a matter of hunches or felt needs or momentary impulses or inexplicable skill; and, if politics does require knowledge, it asks what the character of such knowledge is and what it is knowledge of. Plato maintained that political life required the knowledge of the ideally best kind of life. For Burke, it required the knowledge of the intimate details of the institutional arrangements and the history of the community concerned. For Marx, it was the knowledge of the laws of social development that was crucial to politics. Some utilitarians, who were concerned to establish the sovereignty of the political consumer, emphasised the knowledge of what people want, and thus paved the way for market research and public opinion polls with which we have become all too familiar. For

[1] The term 'near', refers, of course, to time, but it is time that has been spatialised.
[2] Among our contemporaries, Oakeshott has taken time to be one of the key concepts for understanding politics, while Hannah Arendt has concentrated on the idea of space. For the way she uses it to define politics and understand its various aspects, see her *Human Condition* (Doubleday Anchor Book, 1959), pp. 175 ff.; and *On Revolution* (New York, 1963), pp. 235 ff.

some theologians, a knowledge of the cosmological and moral intentions of God was most relevant to the conduct of political affairs.

If it is admitted that knowledge of some kind is required in politics, the next question is how it can be acquired. Plato argued that it was the product of a rigorous training that gave one a capacity to intuit the Idea of Good. Machiavelli thought it could be acquired through reading and digesting manuals prepared by perceptive political observers or actors. Burke and Oakeshott suggest that it can be obtained only through long apprenticeship with those who know, and thus imply that, since no knowledge can ever be fully formulated in propositions, political knowledge can only be imbibed and never taught.[1] For some Pragmatists, the way to acquire political knowledge is to be long enough in political life to know one's way around.

As for the general nature of political knowledge, political philosophers, again, have differed. Some think it is epistemic and demonstrably certain, and, therefore, view as misguided the demand for 'a government by public opinion'. They generally tend to look upon political knowledge as knowledge made political; that is, as knowledge that is arrived at independently and outside of politics and then *applied* to politics. Other philosophers take the view that political knowledge is doxic and tentative in character, and look upon it as knowledge that arises from, and is meaningful only in the context of, practical political life.

This brings us to the question that has worried many political philosophers: the question concerning the contribution that political philosophy can possibly make to political life, Nearly every major political philosopher has maintained that a philosopher, himself included, has something worthwhile to contribute to the conduct of political life. Both Plato and Aristotle thought they could point out the ideally or the practically best kind of political life and provide criteria for judging and evaluating various other forms of political life. Hobbes said he had not written *Leviathan* 'without other design than to set before men's eyes the mutual relation between protection and obedience, of which the condition of human nature and the laws divine (both natural and positive) require an inviolable observation', and hoped that it would be taught in the universities so that 'most men, knowing their duties, will be the less subject to serve the ambition of a few discontented persons in their purposes against the state, and be less grieved with the contribution necessary for their peace and defence.[2]

Other philosophers have suggested that the conduct of political affairs

[1] Despite this general similarity, Burke and Oakeshott are poles apart. Though Burke is opposed to 'theories', he is not opposed to the introduction of 'principles' in political life; and seems to believe that faith in the providential arrangement of human history is of immense value both to rulers and subjects.

[2] *Leviathan* (Everyman's Library), p. 391.

requires philosophical knowledge of a different kind. Some have maintained that it needs the knowledge of the significance of political activity
in the general framework of other human activities, so that one neither
overvalues it and makes it the end to which all other activities are sub-
ordinated, nor undervalues it and neglects it as trivial, to be undertaken
only by those who have nothing serious to do in life. Others have argued
that political life needs the knowledge of what politics really is and what
constitutes and sustains it, so that one knows not only what sorts of
actions, attitudes and institutions are likely to sustain or destroy it but
also what constitutes its unshakeable foundation against which no
political action can ever avail. This, for example, is the status that
Hobbes gives to the principle of self-preservation, Bentham to that of
self-interest, and Marx to that of self-expression. For all of them political
life is inherently and necesssarily unstable unles it fully recognises and
accommodates the appropriate principle. Yet other philosophers have
emphasised the need for consistent and clear reasoning in politics, and
have claimed to offer highly general principles by which laws and rules
can be judged, and the limits of political obligation, the nature and
occasion of the citizen's right or duty to resist the government, the moral
strength of diverse claims on his loyalty, the speciousness of a piece of
political reasoning, etc., can be determined.

Granted that philosophical knowledge is needed in politics and that
political philosophy can give it, philosophers have wondered precisely
how it is related to practical knowledge, which, too, is needed, and how
they both enter into the structure of a political decision. Some thought
philosophical knowledge was like a major premise in a political argument from which, given the practical knowledge, a practical decision
could be deduced. Hobbes thought it was a kind of background against
which a political actor, with his practical knowledge, made a decision.
Others like Green and Bosanquet thought it influenced practical knowledge by entering into and determining it from within. For some others
like Aristotle and Hegel, the philosophical and the practical elements in
the structure of a political decision are related in a different, much more
complicated manner.

The Logic of Politics

By the logic of politics I mean an inquiry into a number of questions
that arise concerning the nature and scope of political argument.

An important problem is to clarify what it is that we are doing
when we argue with each other. Are we debating which is the relevant precedent? Or which is the appropriate analogy? Or are we
trying to get into each other's manner of looking at the situation so
as to widen our respective perspectives till they become coincident and
yield a decision that all concerned agree about? Or do we simply go on

talking as we feel or think proper, hoping all along that at some un-expected but definite moment the truth or the right decision will, like a flash, suddenly come upon us? Or do we talk ourselves into an exhausted silence where the still small voice, rendered inaudible by the din and noise of thoughts darting about and words foaming up luxuri-antly, begins to utter and make its utterances heard? In short, what does it mean to talk, debate and discuss? What goes on in these activities? What does it mean and involve to reach a decision? More generally, how is it possible at all that two persons, starting from very different positions, come in the end to a common decision? Or are we to consider the process of agreement a miracle? Or perhaps a mystery, that is, a human achievement and therefore not a miracle, but humanly in-explicable and incomprehensible and therefore a mystery?

Besides, when an agreement or a disagreement is reached the question still remains as to how we are to construe it. We might understand it as the truth and therefore as final and unalterable. Or we might under-stand it as 'the best in the circumstances' and therefore as alterable only when the circumstances change. Or we might see it as 'the least evil' and therefore open to revision if better ideas are later thrown up. Again, we might interpret it in terms of the concept of rationality and insist that it is based on 'solid' reasons that every 'thinking' man must accept; or we might conceive it in terms of the concept of reasonableness, taking it to be no more than a commonly agreed arrangement that has no pretensions of being rationally the best, an arrangement that does not depend for its enforcement on the 'compelling' power of its indubitable logic, but on the participants' willingness to abide by it and to keep going the system that makes possible and is, in turn, continually sustained by such arrangements.

The logical movement of a political argument raises some im-portant questions. Under the impact of the liberal theory of human action, moral and political thinking has come to be dominated by the sharply separated categories of means and ends. This is not the place to inquire whether every or even most human actions have 'ends' and whether the concept of an end is not frequently confused with that of purpose or aim. What we should note is that in almost every human action ends and means are closely connected, and that considerations appropriate to one are invariably relevant to any decision concerning the other. This means that political arguments are never solely about means or ends but about both at once; means cannot be chosen in a purely 'technical' manner but always in the light of ends, and ends cannot be preferred abstractly but always in the light of the means required to achieve them. Besides, when disagreements about ends do arise, they can rarely for long be about a specific end, but soon involve considerations of other ends and thus of a form of life. In short, a political argument tends eventually to escalate into one about an ideally good life. One of the important questions of the logic of political discourse is whether differences about the good life are *sui generis*, or whether they spring from the still more general philosophical differences between the disputants. If the former, the ultimate political choice would seem to be a matter of faith or 'commitment' or of simple unguided preferences; if the latter, as I believe to be the case, it would seem that moral preferences do have a philosophical backdrop and are philosophically arguable.

A political argument cannot usually be stated in a syllogistic form, but involves a number of premises. These premises are not universal and necessary propositions are but of varying degrees of specificity and probability. A political argument, therefore, can lead only to conclusions that are tentative and more or less plausible but hardly ever certain and conclusive. After a careful inquiry Aristotle reaches the same conclusion.[1] A well-educated man, he says, ought to look for as much certitude in reasoning about a subject matter as its nature permits. It is wrong to look for a greater degree of certitude, but it is equally wrong to be satisfied with less. As there cannot be as much certainty in variable and contingent matters as there can be in those that are necessary, we should not expect a conclusive demonstration from a politician any more than we can tolerate a rhetorical argument from a mathematician.

But there have been many philosophers who are not happy with this view. They want political argument to be compelling and conclusive, and want it to reach conclusions that no 'rational' man can ever refuse to accept. They have sought to achieve this end in a variety of ways, the most prominent of which are philosophical, theological, mathematical and scientific. Plato wanted political life to be in the care of philosophers who could reason deductively from necessary truths. Some medieval political theologians thought disagreements and disputes could disappear from politics if only it was conducted on the basis of the infallible will of God. Other philosophers sought to achieve the same end by giving politics a mathematical basis, but disagreed about the branch of mathematics they believed to be capable of yielding most certain conclusions. Leibniz emphasised geometry, Francis Hutcheson emphasised algebra, and Bentham arithmetic. Pursuing the dream Descartes had on the night of 10 November 1619, Leibniz tried to solve complicated political questions by the geometrical method. In his *Specimen demonstrationis politicae*, which was on the same line as his earlier *Specimen demonstrationum politicarum pro eligendo rege Polonarum*, he proved

[1] *Ethics*, i, 3.

that Louis XIV should dispatch his armies from the Low Countries to Egypt to break the power of the Turk. He even sketched out a 'Logique civile' or 'Logique de la vie'.[1] Hutcheson[2] worked out elaborate algebraic formulae to settle moral and political questions. Bentham preferred the arithmetical process of addition and subtraction. Some other thinkers found the mathematical approach barren and unfruitful, and sought to construct a science, whether of society or of politics, consisting of general laws, so that political arguments could be based on an infallible knowledge of the consequences of various courses of action. The failure of these and similar other projects should be a sufficient reminder that political arguments, like those in any other area of practical life, cannot be certain, conclusive and indisputable, though they are not, for that reason, irrational.

The question of political argument leads to that of political judgment. In the Idealist logic, judgment is a central category, and every proposition is the expression of a judgment. With Idealism out of fashion, the concept of judgment no longer occupies a central place, and its analysis is neglected. The Idealists insist that every judgment necessarily involves a universal, though they differ in their views on the nature of the universal involved and the manner in which it enters a judgment. For empiricists the logical step involved in judging a thing is from particular to particular, and a universal, if introduced, is only a synoptic way of expressing a number of particulars. As it is not possible here to undertake a detailed analysis of these and other theories of political judgment,[3] I can only draw attention to some highly complex questions that every theory of political judgment has come up against. Broadly, they concern the nature and structure of political judgment, whether it is always about particulars or whether it necessarily contains references to a class of situations as Kant maintained and enshrined in his universalisability principle, how various apparently unconnected considerations and arguments are interwoven in its formation, and how it resembles and differs from mathematical, scientific, economic, moral and aesthetic judgment—the kinds of judgment with which political judgment has most often been confused. Moreover, as political judgment is formulated in terms of general concepts like proof, cause, leading to, due to, contributing to and consequences, every theory of political judgment finds it necessary to analyse them.

[1] Louis Couturat, La Logique de Leibnitz (Paris, 1901), p. 141. See also J. Maritain, The Dream of Descartes (New York, 1944).

[2] Inquiry into the Original of our Ideas of Beauty and Virtue (1726), pp. 182–4.

[3] The most elaborate theories of political judgment are those advanced by Aristotle, Hume, Kant and Hegel. In recent years Hannah Arendt, for whom the capacity to judge is 'a specifically political ability', has developed and refined Kant's theory. See her Between Past and Future (London, 1960), pp. 220 ff.

Such a comprehensive analysis of concepts entails an inquiry into the nature of political language to which many philosophers have given some attention, though not as much as one would have liked. Nearly all of them considered language to be so essential to politics that they took the capacity for it to be the very presupposition of politics.[1] Aristotle is one of the very few to have also examined the nature and logical type of political statements and the kinds of relationship into which they can enter. None of them, however, asked systematically why and when political language is imperative (as when law is being declared or enforced), emotive (as when a politician is persuading an audience), hortatory (as when a leader is sermonising to his followers about how they should live), rhetorical (as when a politician is addressing an election meeting or is involved in other kinds of competitive situations), inspirational (such as Pericles' funeral oration), or deliberative (as in a legislative assembly or in a cabinet meeting), or of any other kind. None of them, again, analysed systematically the logical structure of a political speech with a view to showing how the argument majestically proceeds to a definite conclusion, what considerations are invoked and in terms of which principles they are interwoven to constitute a unity, and how its different passages display different kinds of language.

To avoid misunderstanding, it ought to be said that, though philosophical understanding of politics involves asking all three kinds of questions, different philosophers may consider them of different degrees of importance, whether in general or in understanding a particular theme. Take, for example, the phenomenon of ideology. Hannah Arendt asks ontological questions about it and analyses its essential character in ontological terms.[2] In her view ideology, the logos of an idea, takes one particular idea as ultimately real, and deductively works out its logical implications on the basis of which it then goes on to reconstruct society. As her analysis is ontological, her criticism of ideology is also ontological in character, and is in terms of her own ontological theory which seems to rest on a rather questionable contrast between events and ideas.[3]

Michael Oakeshott, on the other hand, analyses the nature of ideology from an epistemological angle, and takes its essential character

---

[1] *Politics* i. 2. 1253a. 11. See also the distinction Aquinas drew between 'speech' or 'language' and 'mere voice'. The latter is a sign of pleasure and pain, and is a medium for conveying sensations; language, on the other hand, is 'proper to man', and is a medium for communicating the rational ideas of justice and injustice. *Commentary on the Politics of Aristotle.*

[2] *The Origins of Totalitarianism* (London, 1958), pp. 468 ff.

[3] *Human Condition*, pp. 235 f. and 248 f. She associates ideas with 'originality' and events with 'novelty'.

to consist in its claim to derive practical knowledge from abstract reasoning alone.[1] His main criticism of it, not surprisingly, is in epistemological terms and rests on his view that, as all knowledge—whether of cooking or of gardening or of governing or of philosophising—is ultimately traditional in character, ideals, principles, ideologies and such other general formulations can only be abstractions from an established tradition of behaviour.

The third kind of analysis and criticism of ideology could be from the logical standpoint. It could argue that an ideology is not so much an ontology or an epistemology as a certain manner of reasoning about practical matters, and that it consists in reasoning deductively, universally and in terms of logical necessity about matters that do not permit of deduction, that are specific and concrete, and that are contingent and could have been otherwise.

All these three analyses of ideology are philosophical in character, and none can be faulted merely on the ground that it considers it from only one standpoint. Everything depends on what a philosopher takes to be the essential character of ideology, and here he might reach a very different conclusion to that reached by his fellow philosophers. The proper grounds for criticising a particular philosopher's analysis are whether it is consistent, comprehensive, asks the most searching questions that can be asked about ideology, and whether, since ontology, epistemology and logic are closely connected, it explores the implications of what it says for the other two areas. An ontological analysis of ideology, for example, must be able to show how an ideology derives the knowledge of its central idea, and a logical analysis ought to show what epistemology an ideologist presupposes and how it is faulty.

VI

I have indicated in broad terms what a political philosopher does when he examines political life philosophically. I have argued that he asks ontological, epistemological, and logical questions about politics, and have indicated what types of question they are. Most of them are implicit in the writings of most philosophers, and what I have done is to formulate them much more explicitly so as to show that political philosophy is a distinct and viable inquiry and that it asks questions no other discipline does. To the extent that these questions are worthwhile and in need of discussion in every age, political philosophy remains a worthwhile discipline, even though it may suffer a temporary 'decline'. That

---

[1] *Rationalism in Politics*, p. 118. I think it is a mistake to group ideals, ideology and principles together. Each of them has a different logic and occupies a different place in moral and political life.

these questions need to be asked, that they do illuminate political life, and that we do lose in intelligibility and understanding for not having asked them, can be shown in connection with four important institutions of political life, viz. representative government, property, legislation and the ombudsman, that have been carefully analysed by many writers but not always in a philosophical manner.

It is a remarkable phenomenon in the history of political thought that, even though the representative government has existed in a fairly identifiable form for over a hundred years, and has been considered by many in Britain and America to be the height of political civilisation,[1] it has never been subjected to a full-scale philosophical examination. Mill's *Representative Government* is one of the few systematic theoretical inquiries into the subject, and even he does not ask many of the questions one would like to see asked. In recent years there is a revival of interest in the subject, but even here the concentration is mainly on the various senses of the term 'representative government', the description of how it works, how it can be improved or defended, the conditions under which it can succeed, etc. All this is certainly very interesting and useful,[2] and does illuminate modern European political life.

But there is another side to the question—the philosophical side. One wants to ask how it is possible at all that one man can represent another. *If* it is true that men are solipsistic creatures shut up in the confines of their own subjectivity, no man can ever really understand another, and the relationship of representation just cannot obtain between them. It is then presumptuous and, perhaps, even a fraud for one man to claim that he represents another. That this is not too highminded a question can be seen in the fact that historically, particularly in Britain, the systematic attempt to understand representative government coincided with the dominance of the empiricist epistemology with its emphasis on images as being the representations of objects in the 'external' world. One of the consequences of this has been that some of the philosophical assumptions underlying the representative government are empiricist in character. To the extent that empiricism leads to some kind of solipsism, the question of solipsism has to be faced by any philosophical theory of representative government.

Further, what is it that a representative represents? Opinions? Interests? Desires? Will? Are these the kinds of thing that can be represented? In order that one man can know the desires and interests of another, do we need to assume the uniformity of human nature? And if we do, is it a valid assumption and within what limits? Again,

---

[1] See the controversy between Mabbott and Voegelin in the *Philosophical Quarterly* (1958).
[2] See, for example, A. H. Birch, *Representative and Responsible Government* (London, 1964). It is one of the best studies of this subject.

for desires and opinions to be represented, they must already be fully formed at the moment of representation, so that representatives know what they have to represent and have a point of reference with respect to which to check whether or not they are representing properly. But are human desires, opinions and, even, interests ever fully formed? Are they not vague at the margin? What is more, are they not articulated and defined only in the course of being represented? And if so, does not the representative create what is to be represented in the very process of representing it? What happens then to our ordinary understanding of representative government which requires the prior existence of something to be represented? If we still want to retain the concept of representative government, we will have to redefine its nature in the light of our view of the kind of creature that man is and what can be known about him and how.

The institution of property presents equally interesting philosophical problems. We want to be able to ask what it is that ultimately constitutes the relationship of property, what its essential features are, why it should exist at all and how it is related to man as we know him. Let us take the analysis suggested by the Idealist philosophers. Man, puzzled by the question of his identity, strives to discover it by objectifying himself in the external world. Property is the necessary consequence of this search for personal identity. My property thus has three features. First, it is a part of me and hence partakes of my dignity and sacredness. To violate it is to violate my personality. Second, it is in terms of my property that I discover and define my identity; to interfere with it is to hinder or frustrate my search for identity. Third, it is my property that gives my personality a projection, an extension into the world of matter as well as of other men. In its absence I lack public dimension and remain confined to the perimeter of my own insulated subjectivity. If, therefore, I am denied a right to property, or if my property is taken away from me, I am reduced to a life of illusion and unreality, to idiocy in its original Greek sense.

All this, of course, need not upset a Marxist, since he could argue back in the same philosophical vein that the concern for identity is common to all men, and that therefore not only the right to property but property itself ought to be secured to all. He might also argue that our philosopher has lost his way, in the sense that he starts by asking, 'Who am I?' and ends by answering, 'What am I', surely a very different question.

As for the philosophical analysis of legislation, I may take as an example the analysis implicit in Bentham's political philosophy. For him, man is ultimately a bundle of fleeting and atomic sensations, and, left to himself, lacks a sense of continuity in time. This sense of continuity is achieved through 'expectations',[1] which law makes possible by creating security, stability and a measure of predictability. Legislation, on this view, acquires an ontological significance, since it sets up and attends to the framework within which man can control his environment, 'count on things', build up expectations, 'form a general plan of conduct', and impose a measure of durability and predictability on his fleeting sensations, achieving thereby both a sense of identity and continuity in time. When expectations are shattered, citizens become ontologically disorganised.

Finally, take the ombudsman. We can understand his role in political life in a number of ways, most of which have been explored in the current literature on the subject. But there still remains a manner of understanding it that is recognisably philosophical. A philosopher might argue that a society can be organised in a number of ways, of which two are most important. There is a manner of social organisation where people are interested mainly in their private pursuits—whether of money or of art or simply of amusement—and all they demand of the government is that it should secure them in their chosen areas of action. They have no interest in the conduct of public affairs, and prefer to 'employ' reliable 'servants' to look after the necessary 'chores' of organised life. There is, on the other hand, another manner of social organisation where citizens take an active interest in the conduct of government, and consider politics their own affair and not the 'business' of public servants. Their concern is not so much the security of their interests as the exercise of their capacity for initiative, not so much protection as self-government, not so much economic and civil liberties as political freedom. The first kind of society might be called civil society and the second, political society.

Using this distinction, a philosopher might argue that the most important consideration in the civil society is the protection of the interests of citizens. They should never feel wronged; if they do, an institutional machinery for redressing their grievances should be available to them, since only then can they be kept in a perpetual state of political torpor. As it is in this condition that the government wants the people to remain, it will be eager to guarantee them protection and machinery of redress. What it will not do is to create conditions where they can actively participate in political life and exercise their right to initiate or question proposals and policies. On their part citizens want no more and are content to trade power for security. Of such a society, with its concentra-

---

[1] 'It is by means of (expectations) that the successive moments, which form the duration of life, are not like insulated and independent parts, but become parts of a continuous whole. Expectation is a chain which unites our present and our future existence...' Cited in Robins, *The Theory of Economic Policy in English Classical Political Economy*, p. 63.

tion of initiative and power in a few hands, and the popular desire for nothing but security, a philosopher might conclude, the ombudsman is a necessary expression. He is someone who diligently looks after people's interests, without adding anything to their political power; he redresses their grievances but gives them no additional opportunity for initiative and action.

Thus there are distinct kinds of question that can be asked about every important aspect of political life; to the extent that political philosophy is out of fashion, they remain unanswered and our understanding of political life remains incomplete and unsatisfactory. A political philosopher is someone who asks, and is able to answer, these questions in a systematic way about every important aspect of political life.

VII

It was suggested earlier that a fully satisfactory political philosophy is not possible unless there is a backdrop of general philosophy, and that political philosophy is an exploration of politics in terms of the categories and principles of the system that the philosopher has developed. If a philosopher's understanding of political life is at odds with his understanding of other areas of experience, or if the categories in terms of which he understands political life are not integrated with those developed elsewhere, his analysis of politics, however illuminating and suggestive, is unsatisfactory and deserves to be criticised. For example, if a philosopher comes to the view that everything that exists is necessarily a unity of the universal and the particular, and that reality is essentially dialectical in nature, he must analyse political institutions accordingly. If *all* reality is dialectical, political institutions cannot be exempt from it. Conversely, if *all* activities can best be understood philosophically only in terms of the dialectic and the unity of the universal and the particular, political institutions, too, can best be understood only in these terms. To offer any other analysis of politics is at once to impugn the general validity of his philosophical conclusions, and to introduce a new principle without integrating it into his general system.

That this is not a mistaken demand can be seen in the fact that this is how we discuss or teach the political philosophy of philosophers. We discuss Plato's political philosophy by bringing in his theory of Ideas, his view of the demiurgus, his epistemology and his theory of the soul, and comment on his theory of the *polis* or of the constitution in terms of its compatibility with his general philosophical views. Similarly, we discuss Hobbes's political philosophy in the light of, among other things, his view of what it is to explain anything philosophically, his ontology, his epistemology and his analysis of the human mind. By relating them to his understanding of political life, we are able to show how civil society arises out of man's fundamental desire to preserve himself, how the sovereign is extremely important as he is the only connecting link between the solipsistic individuals, how the entire language of political communication has to be created and defined by the sovereign, how the security of the private space becomes extremely important for the politically castrated individuals, etc. This is also what we do with Aristotle, Kant, Hegel, or Spinoza. We demand that their understanding of political life should be integrated with their understanding of experience in general, and this means that the principles and categories in terms of which political life is explained should be logically integrated with those used for explaining other areas of experience. Every philosopher uses some highly general concepts and universal principles in terms of which he explains and analyses every aspect of experience; to discuss his political philosophy is to discuss how they are used by him to interpret and explain political life. If certain concepts are applicable to everything within experience, which is what a philosopher claims, they must apply to politics as well, and it is his job as a political philosopher to show that they do. Besides, though a philosopher is free to analyse politics in terms of second order concepts with a narrow range of applicability, he must show how they are entailed by and dovetail into his more general concepts.

It seems to me that such a unity has not always been achieved in the writings of philosophers. To illustrate this point, I shall take three works whose greatness is generally admitted, viz. Hegel's *Philosophy of Right*, Hobbes's *Leviathan*, and Mill's *On Liberty*. Hegel's *Philosophy of Right* is the clearest example of a work in which political philosophy is completely integrated with general philosophy, and in which there is hardly any aspect of political life that is not explored in terms of the concepts and principles dominant in the entire system. For example, when Hegel discusses the civil service he does not describe what it is like or how its members are recruited, nor does he content himself with a few general observations. There would have been nothing philosophical if he had done that; almost anyone, whether a philosopher or not, would have done it; and, in any case, one would have been left wondering what had happened to Hegel's general philosophical conclusions and why they were not brought into operation. Fortunately, Hegel does precisely what every philosopher is expected to do: he analyses the civil service in terms of the dialectic, shows how it is a 'universal' class, how it is necessarily entailed by the nature of the state, and how it is a definite moment in the logical development of the Idea of the state. Whether or not one finds this analysis satisfactory is a different question, but that he has subjected political life to a thorough-going philosophical analysis, and that this analysis is of a kind entailed by his general philosophical position, is beyond doubt.

When one turns to Hobbes's *Leviathan*, one is no less struck by the rigorous philosophical analysis of the various aspects of political life. Man is matter-in-motion, and is so constituted as necessarily to want to remain in a certain state of motion. Mind is explained in terms of motion: thinking is understood not as passive contemplation but as the restless darting about of ideas; desires, will, etc., are similarly analysed. As for the process of understanding, it too is interpreted in terms of motion: to understand anything is to see it in motion, in its process of generation. Moral life is also analysed in terms of motion as can be seen in Hobbes's use of the concept of felicity. Now one would expect that when he came to analyse political life, Hobbes would stick to his basic philosophical framework. One is not entirely disappointed. He introduces the resolutive-compositive method and the ideas of the state of nature, of the covenant and of the atomic individual, all of which follow from his general philosophical position. Liberty is seen as freedom to remain in motion, or better, as the absence of any hindrance to motion. Inequality is grounded on the equal capacity to kill; that is, on the equal capacity to terminate motion. Law is seen as the laying down of channels in which citizens' motions are to be directed. Obligation, right, security and such other concepts are analysed along similar lines. However, there are passages in the *Leviathan* where one's expectations are not met. Hobbes's analysis of justice, equity or impartiality, punishment, forms of government and the machinery of administration, to list but a few, is not conducted at a fully philosophical level and is not in terms of the general categories of his system.

When we turn to Mill's *On Liberty*, the lack of unity and continuity is much more striking. In his philosophical works, particularly in *An Examination of Sir William Hamilton's Philosophy*, he analyses the nature of the individual, and concludes that he is nothing but a series of sensations united in a certain way, mainly through memory which Mill cannot reduce any further and takes to be primitive. This leads him to develop, among other things, an interesting theory of consciousness, of the epistemological relationship between individuals, of the nature of reason and of language. But when we turn to Mill's political writings we find ourselves in a different universe with a different vocabulary. Natural concrete individuals begin to appear, and one wonders what has happened to his earlier philosophical analysis of the nature of the individual. What he had said earlier in his philosophical capacity about the nature of consciousness, and the way one becomes conscious of oneself and others, is more or less completely ignored in dealing with civil liberty, equality and the nature and limits of state action. Institutions are accepted as they appear 'on the first look', to use a phrase of Bosanquet's, and are not subjected to philosophical analysis in a way that Plato, Kant, Hegel or Bosanquet had done. It is not asked, for example, if they must be taken as ultimate and irreducible, or if they can be probed further and related to sensation which Mill takes to be one of the ultimate philosophical categories. After all, as we saw earlier, Bentham himself did this in one of his inspired philosophical moments.

This is not to say that there is any inconsistency in Mill of the kind that commentators have discovered between Locke's 'political' and philosophical writings. The charge of inconsistency presupposes a similarity of level, while the point that I am trying to make about Mill is that there is a great divide between his political and philosophical writings, between the way in which the same thing is treated in the two 'kinds' of writings, and that there is, consequently, a diversity of levels. Again, I am not saying that if Mill had analysed political life in terms of the concepts central to his philosophical system, he would necessarily have reached different substantive views on the nature and limits of state action. I am also not suggesting that Mill was not a philosopher. Far from it. He was not only a general philosopher of a high order, but was also concerned to examine political life philosophically. Indeed, it is precisely because of this that one's expectations are great and one's demands high. All I am saying is that in his *Representative Government* important and relevant philosophical questions are not asked, with the result that his level of investigation falls short of the philosophical; and that in his *On Liberty* his general philosophical conclusions and concepts are not integrated with his analysis of political life.

Why Mill and many others should have failed to bring their 'political' and philosophical writings into greater harmony, how the untenable distinction between the 'political' and the philosophical writings should have arisen at all and have misled so many able philosophers[1] into writing 'political' *and* philosophical works but not often works in *political philosophy* raise some interesting and perplexing historical and

---

[1] See, for example, Russell's 'Reply to criticisms' in *The Philosophy of Bertrand Russell*, ed. Paul Arthur Schlipp (Harper Torchbooks, 1963), vol. II, pp. 729 f. He argues that his political and economic philosophy 'deals mainly with matters which I should regard as lying wholly outside philosophy...(on) even a very liberal interpretation of the word "philosophy"'. I did not write them, he goes on, 'in my capacity as a "philosopher"' but only 'as a human being who suffered from the state of the world'. This leads him to insist that, if his books on political philosophy are to be understood, 'my technical activities must be forgotten'. Oddly enough, ethics is differently related to philosophy: while political 'philosophy' 'lies *wholly outside* philosophy', moral philosophy is still 'an essentially different *department* of philosophy', p. 719. Italics added.

philosophical questions that we cannot consider here. What we can do is to observe that what Mill achieved in a lesser degree, Hobbes did in a greater degree, and Hegel in the greatest. It is this satisfactoriness of the *structure*, and not any novelty in or even the tenability of the conclusions reached, that makes the *Philosophy of Right* the best example of a piece of writing, or of a 'text', in political philosophy.

TIME, INSTITUTIONS AND ACTION:
AN ESSAY ON TRADITIONS
AND THEIR UNDERSTANDING

J. G. A. POCOCK

Societies exist in time, and conserve images of themselves as continuously so existing. It follows that the consciousness of time acquired by the individual as a social animal is in large measure consciousness of his society's continuity and of the image of its continuity which that society possesses; and the understanding of time, and of human life as experienced in time, disseminated in a society, is an important part of that society's understanding of itself—of its structure and what legitimates it, of the modes of action which are possible to it and in it. There is a point at which historical and political theory meet, and it can be said without distortion that every society possesses a philosophy of history—a set of ideas about what happens, what can be known and what done, in time considered as a dimension of society—which is intimately a part of its consciousness and its functioning. How these images and ideas of time arise, function and develop may be studied as part of the science of society.

An essential feature of society is tradition—the handing on of formed ways of acting, a formed way of living, to those beginning or developing their social membership—and the transmitter of a message cannot do without some image of a message which he has received and of the way in which he received it. Both images will be, in some way or other, conceptualisations of the mode of activity to be handed on, and it will be thought of as having been received by the transmitter from transmitters before him: his predecessors in a craft, his ancestors in a society, or both. Societies therefore look backward in time to those from whom 'we' received what we now tell 'you'; even the so-called 'timeless' societies described by anthropologists are not really exceptions to this rule. But the variety of the ways in which societies have conceived the transmission of their traditions is very great indeed. This is not surprising when we consider, first, that the image of an activity's continuance must vary both with the character of the activity and with the ways in which practice of it may be thought to be transmitted; second, that any society or social complex envisaging its own continuity must do so in terms of those elements of its structure of which it is sufficiently aware to consider them continuous. Social activities and structures vary widely, and it cannot be predicted with certainty what elements of them will become institutionalised to the point of having stable and continuous images. Even in very simple societies, extrapolation of the image of the social structure in time can produce accounts varying widely, from one society to another, of 'the past', that is of the way in which transmission has been and is being conducted. In complex societies, the past itself is complex; society consists of a number of patterns of behaviour, each of which generates its own 'past' and need not be thought of as continuous in the same way as its neighbour; there may be contradiction between these 'pasts', and even conflict.

Oakeshott has emphasised the extent to which a 'tradition of behaviour' is not conceptualised, whether because its transmission takes place unnoticed or because it would not be appropriate to conceptualise it overmuch, consisting as it does in 'intimations' and 'nuances'. None the less conceptualisation of tradition is constantly going on, as it must if tradition is to function among self-conscious and communicative creatures, and we are beginning to see that it may take place in a variety of ways and give rise to a variety of mental phenomena. The concepts which we form from, and feed back into, tradition have the capacity to modify the content and character of the tradition conceptualised and even the extent to which it is conceived and regarded as a tradition. There consequently arise a wide variety of attitudes and strategies which men may adopt towards society's continuity and the sources of its authority; these are political phenomena, forming part of the organisation and extension of society's consciousness of, and in, its political life. In addition, however, since so large a part of men's consciousness of environment and time is gained through consciousness of the frame of social relationships which they inhabit, the conceptualisation of tradition is an important source of their images of society, time and history. The importance of these visibly transcends the political; we are looking at one of the origins of a distinctively human awareness.

In *The Discovery of Time*[1] Stephen Toulmin and June Goodfield have performed the interesting experiment of taking as their starting-point the consciousness of time to be expected of an archaic villager, limited to awareness of the continuity of his immediate social structure, and examining how this consciousness was progressively transformed by the thought of physical scientists where this raised the question of the time-dimension of the cosmos, by geological, palaeontological and archaeological discoveries, and by changes in social theory occasioned by or occasioning changes in the time-scheme within which human society was conceived to exist. They convincingly show that there was two-way

[1] Volume III of *The Ancestry of Science* series (London, 1965).

traffic between ideas about the character and processes of human society and ideas about the structure and processes of the physical universe; but their thesis is limited by the fact that it does not and cannot deal with ideas about time arising from the self-awareness of particular societies. The 'time' they deal with is geochronic and cosmochronic; thought about society can have contributed to its 'discovery' only to the extent—a very considerable one—that society was considered as a universal phenomenon, a central incident in the history of life, earth and cosmos. But what we call historical consciousness is social and subjective in its origins; it is a developed form of man's awareness of himself as existing and acting in a continuous context of social relationships, and must therefore begin with his awareness of a particular social continuity to which he himself belongs. But we have already seen that this awareness can take forms as many and varied as the social institutions with which it originates. We are following a line of enquiry distinct from that of Toulmin and Goodfield, concerned with an awareness of time that must have been multiple in its origins and its modes; we are forced to recognise that the history of historical awareness is necessarily distinct from that of the discovery of cosmic time, and that no unified 'history of historiography' is likely ever to be written. Since each society has its own mode of conceiving its past, the history of its historical consciousness must in principle be peculiar to itself—even when it becomes conscious of its role within a greater history, even when historical consciousness is imported or imposed from without. We cannot, then, treat the history of historical thought as a unity, a progressive accumulation of insights starting from Hecataeus or Herodotus as the history of science can be said to start from Thales. It is part of the history of social self-awareness, and is as multiple as the social forms and social experiences in which that awareness develops.

We are, then, concerned with the conceptualisation of tradition, with the modes of social self-awareness and the attitudes towards tradition to which conceptualisation may give rise, and with the complex awareness of continuity which we call historical consciousness as one possible outcome of changes in this kind of thought. To understand what happened to the time-consciousness of the archaic villager, we must consider the consciousness of social continuity which the village, the city, the empire, the church or the nation—to go no further—required of their members, and we must enquire after the origins and occasions of changes in that consciousness. When we put it in this way, it is clear that the problem could be studied in the context of social development; the individual's time-consciousness could be looked on as changing in relation to changes in the organisation of society. But an alternative approach, which will be adopted here, is to elaborate and extend the model of a tradition which we have begun to build up, and attempt in doing so to discern the directions which conceptualisation of a tradition may be expected to take, and something of the alternatives, choices and strategies which may confront minds engaged in such conceptualisation.

A tradition, in its simplest form, may be thought of as an indefinite series of repetitions of an action, which on each occasion is performed on the assumption that it has been performed before; its performance is authorised—though the nature of the authorisation may vary widely—by the knowledge, or the assumption, of previous performance. In the pure state, as it were, such a tradition is without a conceivable beginning; each performance presupposes a previous performance, in infinite regress. Furthermore, it may well be that it is the assumption, rather than the factual information, of previous performance that is operative; each action provides the grounds for assuming that it had a predecessor. Traditions of this kind, then, are immemorial, and they are prescriptive and presumptive; and this was pointed out by Burke, who was an acute analyst, as well as an eloquent expositor, of the traditional society and the traditionalist mind.[1] This is perhaps the simplest set of assumptions which we can ascribe to the traditionalist mind, when it is sufficiently self-conscious to have ideas and assumptions about what it is doing and the society it is acting in; but the full exposition of these assumptions requires a sophisticated mind and highly subtle language, as the writings of Hale and Burke bear witness. It can happen, in favourable circumstances, that a society may conceive all the activities of which it is aware, the whole pattern of its structure as it visualises itself, in traditional terms. Such a society will conceive its past as an immemorial continuity, its structure as inherited from an infinitely receding chain of transmitters; timeless societies are those in which the links in the chain are no longer distinguished from one another, each transmitting ancestor being perhaps thought of as the reincarnation of his predecessor, and the process of transmission being compressed into a single timeless act instead of being drawn out into an endless chain. At a more sophisticated level of consciousness, the traditional society may insist that not only are its practices and usages inherited, but its conviction that they are so is itself inherited from an assumed chain of transmitters, so that its knowledge of its past is and can be no more than presumptive. It cannot even know—it can only presume—that it has always based itself on

[1] 'Our constitution is a prescriptive constitution; it is a constitution whose sole authority is that it has existed time out of mind...Your king, your lords, your judges, your juries, grand and little, all are prescriptive; and what proves it is the disputes not yet concluded, and never near becoming so, when any of them first originated.' Burke, 'On a Motion Made in the House of Commons...for a Committee to Enquire into the State of the Representation of the Commons in Parliament', *Works*, ed. Bohn (1866), VI, 146.

presumption, though with this self-validating chain of presumptions many societies have been enviably content.

The traditional conception of society is in several ways of enduring value to social theorists. Any social act does in fact presuppose an antecedent degree of socialisation, and it is conceptually impossible to imagine a social complex coming into existence at any single moment. Both in the seventeenth century and in the twentieth, it has been salutary to be reminded that society is indeed immemorial, and further that our knowledge of the social usages that have preceded us is inherited from those usages themselves, from the assumptions they encourage us to make and the intimations they permit us to pursue. But in the present essay we are concerned less with tradition as an objective fact, a necessary mode of social life, than with the conceptualisation of tradition, with what happens when a society forms an image of itself as a constant transmission of ways of living and behaving; and while it is possible for this self-awareness to take a strictly traditional form, for a society to envisage itself as immemorial, prescriptive, an inherited style of behaviour and thought, this is by no means the only form which conceptualisation of a tradition may take, nor will it necessarily retain the form it has once taken. Now when a change in a society's self-awareness has become at all widely disseminated, that society's styles of thinking and acting have been irreversibly altered. There may still be much in its traditions of behaviour which has not emerged into consciousness and perhaps never will; what has changed, however, is its mode of being and becoming conscious of itself and its existence in time, and once this has happened a society is no longer what it was. We are studying its political and cultural individuality, therefore, when we study the form which its self-awareness has for the present assumed.

Moreover, when we say that a society's image of its own continuous life may take forms other than the traditional, we mean that it may not conceive inheritance as its sole mode of reception, transmission as its sole mode of action, or presumption as its sole mode of knowledge. There are other ways in which behaviour and knowledge may be envisaged, and a society's departures from a purely traditional self-awareness may be enlargements of its political and social, indeed of its human, vocabulary. Nor need human existence in time be envisaged solely as existence in a stream of transmission. Once men are thought of as thinking and acting in ways other than those appropriate to the traditional framework, it becomes possible to envisage their behaviour in social time as a complex series of interactions between different modes of behaviour, of which the traditional is only one. At this point the social framework begins to appear the result or product of human action, instead of merely its matrix; a historical mode of understanding begins to replace a traditional one, and what may be the most far-reaching of changes in a society's style has begun to appear.

A society thinks of itself in purely traditional terms in proportion as it is aware of itself simply as a cluster of institutionalised modes of transmitting behaviour. We may, somewhat in the manner of Victorian anthropologists, envisage a simple kinship society, in which everything is learned from the fathers before the shrines of the ancestors; in such a society, it is evident, everything will be thought of as transmitted, continuous, immemorial and—since each father must speak on the authority of his father—presumptive. It is needless to point out that no society is as simply linear as that; the kind of self-image which the model conveys can be found even in complex literate societies, where the kind and degree of institutionalisation have been favourable to its existence. In pre-industrial England, for example, all social and national institutions could be conceived as bound up with the common law, that law was conceived as custom, and the activity of law-making was conceived as the conversion into written precedents of unwritten usages whose sole authority was that of immemorial antiquity. Consequently, to the end of the eighteenth century it could be argued that the constitution was immemorial, its authority prescriptive and our knowledge of it presumptive. The character of English institutions, in short, was such as to favour the assumption that the only form of action was transmission and the only form of knowledge the inheritance of learning. But in sixteenth-century France we have the case of a complex institutional society where continuity in the past could not be conceived in terms of any single institution, but different institutions suggested the images of different modes of action. The *coutumes*, in force in some regions, suggested the authority of continuous usage; the Roman law, in force in others, suggested that of rational action; the royal jurisdiction and its *cours souveraines*, overarching and co-ordinating all, suggested an authority distinct from the other two but interacting with them; and by the end of the Religious Wars French scholars were saying that their institutions could be understood only in terms of a history of the royal power's expansion at the expense of customary, seigneurial and provincial jurisdictions.[1] *Les rois ont fait la France.* A society's institutions, it is clear, may be either consolidated or discrete, homogeneous or various; it may inherit dialogue, dialectic or conflict between its traditions, and the impulse to replace tradition, first with another image of normative action and secondly with history as the vision of interplay between

[1] The most intensive study of this, written from a historicist point of view, is that of V. de Caprariis, *Propaganda e Pensiero Politico in Francia durante le Guerre di Religione, 1559–1572* (Naples, 1959).

modes of action, may arise from within the inheritance. There are seams, after all, in the seamless web; or it may appear so to those who receive and wear the garment.

Institutionalisation, the necessary cause of traditionalism, may then be the cause of a society's tradition being conceived in terms other than purely traditional. But conceptualisation has a logic of its own, and images and concepts of a non-traditionalist kind may arise from causes lying within the process of giving a tradition conceptual form. So far we have imagined tradition as the concept of an activity's indefinite continuity, arrived at by extrapolating the concept of its continuity in the present and—when this is done rigorously—imagined as immemorial or without a beginning. But the foundation myths of Greek cities, in exploring which Hellenic historiography was obliged to begin, provide us with examples of traditions of a different sort. These do not arise from the extrapolation of institutional continuities, but consist in ascribing a sacred or epic origin to the society conceived as a whole. In the late and sophisticated form which the Greeks gave it, this activity became what is known as historisation; it was the historian's business to discover origins, preferably human inventors, for societies, institutions and arts.[1] But in its more purely mythopoeic form, this kind of 'tradition' has the value of reminding us that a society—whether tribe, city, culture-complex or civilisation—is not necessarily imagined as a whole only in consequence of being imagined as a cluster of institutionalised continuities. There may be an awareness of tradition less precise but equally vivid, and when this occurs society's continuity may not be explicable in institutional language at all. It may have to be expressed in terms of whatever vision of the world human perception and fantasy have been able to conceive by means other than the conceptualisation of institutional or even social traditions, and this vision may entail a very different image of time or none at all; in the great phrase attributed to Australian aboriginals, it may be 'in the dreaming'. But if institutional time and sacred time or non-time are juxtaposed, then society's time-consciousness is already a complex matter.

To describe a timeless existence, a sacred origin or an immemorial continuity, are all ways of conceptualising the continuous existence of society. The more precisely we imagine society as a series of concrete human actions in time, and time in terms of the sequence of such actions, the more we seem to move away from imagining society in terms of the sacred, as our use of the words 'temporal' and 'secular' indicates. Nevertheless, complex interrelations between different ways of envisaging time, society and action are constantly found in the thought of

[1] See M. I. Finley, *The Greek Historians* (London, 1959) and 'Myth, memory and history', *History and Theory*, IV, 3 (1965), 281–302.

societies. In ancient China, for example, there seems to have been equal emphasis on the idea that the *li*, or governing rituals, originated in the creative acts of sacred heroes called the Former Kings, and on the idea that the truth concerning the acts of the Former Kings could only be inferred by presuming their continuity with the traditional character of the *li* as inherited by the present. It is possible at one and the same time to extrapolate the present form of an institution back into a remote antiquity, and to realise (the mythopoeic mind need not even realise) that the beginnings of such an institution are exceedingly hard to imagine, if only because they cannot be conceived in terms of the institution's functioning. A system conceived in none but traditional terms must be conceived as immemorial, since antecedent tradition is necessary in order to account for its existence at any moment; but few societies have been bold enough to assert that they have existed *ab aeterno*, or sophisticated enough to assert that a prescriptive or immemorial tradition is merely one whose beginnings are not to be found in any single moment or moments. Most societies have their culture-heroes or founding fathers; but to imagine traditions of behaviour originating in specific actions is to imagine actions whose creative power is not explained by any antecedent tradition. Hence the charismatic figures who stand at the mythical beginnings of so many traditions—the gods, heroes, prophets and legislators, who abound in the legends even of highly institutionalised societies and provide the inheritors of tradition with occasion to imagine politics and other activities as consisting of charismatic (which here includes rationalist[1]) instead of traditional action, and time as a sequence of such actions instead of as institutional continuity. What stands outside tradition is charismatic; where time itself is envisaged as the continuity of tradition, the charismatic may stand outside time and become the sacred. But if an activity is seen as a succession of charismatic or sacred actions, then a new vision of time may be constructed in terms of moments of creation rather than moments of transmission. This no doubt was what Oakeshott had in mind when he described the ethics of the self-made man as idolatry;[2] such a man must visualise his actions as unendingly creative and charismatic. It may nevertheless happen that the idea of a series of charismatic actions, even the vision of time as composed of a sequence of sacred acts, becomes part of the mental furniture of a society, so worn and domesticated with constant varying use that it may be described as belonging to society's traditions.

'A tradition of behaviour', Oakeshott has truly written,[3] 'is a tricky thing to get to know'; so much so, we now observe, that parts of it must

---

[1] The purely rational founder of a society is always a heroic and miraculous figure.
[2] *Rationalism in Politics*, p. 35.   [3] *Op. cit.* p. 128.

be conceptualised in non-traditional terms. 'The pursuit of the intimations' of such a tradition will not be the simple unfolding of a consistently traditional 'style' of either thinking or acting. It will involve our envisaging charismatic figures, actions and styles of behaviour; these will run counter to the theme of transmission and continuity, setting up alternative images of action and authority. Within tradition there will be dialogue between the non-traditionalist and traditionalist voices with which it speaks, and the pursuit of intimations will involve us in conflict and contradiction, in problems of historical, philosophical and methodological interpretation, even in existential dilemmas of self-determination and self-definition. A tradition may be a turbid stream to swim in, full of backwaters, cross-currents and snags. Nevertheless the dialogue we have begun to depict has its logic and its strategies, and the next stage in our enquiry must be to map some of these.

A tradition, then, may stress either the continuity of the process of transmission, or the creative and charismatic origin of what is transmitted. The two are conceptually distinct and entail different images of action and of time; but they are dialectically related, and are often—perhaps normally—found together within the same tradition. A distinction may be drawn between traditions which conserve highly specific and significant images of the creative actions with which they began and of which they are in some way the continuation, and traditions which depict themselves as sheer continuity of usage or transmission and conserve little or no account of their beginnings. These two types are situated far apart on a spectrum whose ultra-violet and infra-red are, respectively, the sacred, which lies outside time, and the immemorial, which refuses to admit a beginning in or outside it. Burke's 'prescriptive government' which 'never was the work of any legislator',[1] Oakeshott's 'tradition of behaviour' and his 'bottomless and boundless sea', are traditions of pure usage; but we have seen that traditions which admit to no beginning at all are rare and rest, where they exist, on the accident of a society's being very highly institutionalised in a peculiar way. The assumption that everything in English society could be treated as an inheritance from some earlier time was after all a myth —and Burke knew it[2]—resting on the further myth that everything in English law was custom. But if most traditions of usage make some

[1] Burke, *Works*, ed. Bohn (1866), VI, p. 148.
[2] 'In the matter of fact, for the greater part, these authors appear to be in the right; perhaps not always; but if the lawyers mistake in some particulars, it proves my position still the more strongly; because it demonstrates the powerful prepossession towards antiquity, with which the minds of all our lawyers and legislators, and of all the people whom they wish to influence, have been always filled; and the stationary policy of this kingdom in considering their most sacred rights and franchises as an inheritance.' *Reflections on the Revolution in France*, in *Works*, ed. Bohn (1901), III, 305.

acknowledgement to the idea of a creative origin, it is equally true that most traditions claiming to originate in a creative act have to admit that the authority of the initiating charisma has become merged with that of the chain of transmission through which it has been mediated— the well-known problem of the 'routinisation of the charisma'. Traditions once conceptualised are complex mental structures, and in the dialogues that occur within them, what Oakeshott has called the 'abridgement' of tradition into an ideology is only one among a number of intellectual operations that may be carried out.

Ancient Chinese thought (in its Western translations) presents an interesting example of political ideas organised around a tradition more highly and consciously institutionalised than was ever possible for Hellenic thought. The *li* had supposedly been established in mythic time by the Former Kings, and to that extent charismatic figures and creative action formed part of Chinese imagery. But when Confucius, in a time of disorder, set out to intensify the impact of the inherited *li* upon society by eliciting a consciousness of the virtues which they contained, he did not associate these conceptualised virtues with the figures of the Former Kings so much as stress the continuity of their transmission from an ancient time which was known less by contemplating what the Former Kings had done in it than by presuming its continuity with the inheritance of the *li* in more recent times. When he called himself 'a transmitter, not a creator', he was not simply being modest about his own role; he meant that what he was teaching possessed the character of a tradition, whose authority was derived from the continuity of its transmission. But if transmission, not creation, was to be the central social act, then the role of the Former Kings, the creators, was liable to lose its importance. There are several recorded sayings in which Confucius makes it plain that we know what form the *li* possessed under Hsia and Yin, the earliest of the three dynasties which he thought historical, only by inference from our better documented knowledge of the usages of Chou, the most recent dynasty; and if we know Hsia and Yin only by presumption, the same may be true of the Former Kings. His confidence in his ability to know the past by inference and presumption was very high: he held that he could reconstruct what institutions had been like in the past by simple extrapolation from their form in the present, and regretted only that independent evidence did not survive to corroborate him. (In Jacobean England Sir Edward Coke advised antiquarians against venturing to reconstruct the history of institutions without taking the advice of lawyers, who worked on the presumption of continuity.) Confucius is also said to have declared that since we knew what Yin had added to Hsia ritual, and what Chou had added to Yin, we could predict what additions would be made by any future dynasty succeeding Chou—a doctrine which carries 'the pursuit of intimations' to a point where it becomes 'the poverty of historicism'.[1]

It was Mo Tzu, the first post-Confucian thinker to envisage the possibility of governing society by means other than inherited ritual, who declared to his adversaries: 'You are only following the Chou, not the Hsia dynasty. Your antiquity does not go back far enough.' A familiar if important contrast may be erected between the two positions. Confucius was a conservative; he was anxious to invest the present system with authority, and did so by regarding it as an inheritance from the past. Adopting a traditionalist position in a highly traditionalist society, he invested the present system with authority inherited from a former set of practices which themselves acquired it by inheritance from a remoter past...and so *ad infinitum*. In such a scheme of thought it is not necessary to know a lot about the mythical origins and founders; it may even be inappropriate to stress them overmuch. Institutionalisation tends to reduce, if hardly ever to eliminate, the importance of myth; it replaces a mythic dream-time with a secular time of institutional continuity. It is important to have a well-established foundation in the recent past on which to presume continuity with the remoter past; but to attempt independent knowledge of the remoter past is in Burke's phrase 'preposterous' and in the Confucian Hsun Tzu's 'like giving up one's own prince and following another's'. Our knowledge of the past is based on the presumption of transmission, and the subtleties of historical awareness which may arise in this style of thinking consist largely in awareness of how much more there is in a continuous tradition of behaviour than we need or can know.

But Mo Tzu was in the strict sense a radical: that is, he was adopting the posture appropriate to a rebel in a traditional society, which is that of a reactionary. He did not believe it any longer possible to govern society by the inherited means of ritual, and had an alternative set of arrangements to suggest; but it was nevertheless so far from possible in that society to forgo deriving authority from antiquity that he must suggest an alternative version of antiquity which would authorise his alternative arrangements. The appropriate location for his image of antiquity was the remotest accessible past, since there the presumption of continuity with the traditional present would be hardest to apply and, once he had occupied the headwaters of tradition, he would be in a position to maintain that the stream had been diverted from its proper

---

[1] For further treatment, see 'The origins of study of the past', *Comparative Studies in Society and History*, IV, 2 (1962), 222–4, and 'Ritual, language, power: an essay on the apparent political meanings of ancient Chinese philosophy', *Political Science* (published by the Victoria University of Wellington), XVI, 1 (1964), 6–7 (and generally 3–31).

course. Instances of this radical strategy, the advocacy of return to the roots or sources, abound in the history of argument within systems of authority. To take examples from English history, the Levellers opposed to the traditional constitution the image of an idealised pre-Conquest England after which all had been Norman usurpation; and Bolingbroke, followed by the early parliamentary reformers, adopted the Machiavellian tactic of ascribing to the existing constitution 'original principles' on which it had been founded, from which it had degenerated and to which it must be restored. To the latter argument, it is significant, two modes of reply may be detected. In one—represented by Lord Hervey and Josiah Tucker[1]—the past was repudiated as barbarous and no longer relevant; here the conservative's basic concern with the present was pushed to the point of brutal rejection of the appeal to history, a rejection however founded on a developed power of historical criticism. In the other, far more subtly traditional, Burke pointed out that an immemorial constitution can have no original principles, since a system whose knowledge of its own past is based exclusively on the presumption of transmission can never arrive at knowledge of them.[2]

The radical's rejection of the traditional present forces him to adopt new positions. Once he has denied that the present derives authority from a past of which it is the presumptive continuation, three questions confront him. Since his image of the past as he says it was cannot be arrived at by presuming its continuity with a present it is designed to repudiate, how is that image arrived at and maintained? Secondly, since the past as he conceives it does not authorise the present, it cannot possess or transmit traditional authority; what authority does it then possess, or, in other words, why are we obliged to return to it? Thirdly, if it possessed and still possesses such authority, how have matters so fallen out that it is no longer actualised in our institutions? As the radical was, initially at least, a normative writer seeking to give authority to his programme rather than a historical writer seeking to explain what had happened, it is likely to be the second question that concerns him most, but the

---

[1] Hervey, *Ancient and Modern Liberty Stated and Compared* (1734); Tucker, *A Treatise Concerning Civil Government* (1781). The same view was constantly advanced in the *London Journal*, which supported Walpole against Bolingbroke and the *Craftsman* in 1729–34.

[2] *Works*, VI, 146–8. 'To ask whether a thing which has always been the same stands to its usual principle, seems to me to be perfectly absurd; for how do you know the principles but from the construction? and if that remains the same, the principles remain the same...On what grounds do we go to restore our constitution to what it has been at one definite period, or to reform and reconstruct it upon principles more conformable to a sound theory of government? A prescriptive government, such as ours, never was the work of any legislator, never was made upon any foregone theory. It seems to me a preposterous way of thinking, and a perfect confusion of ideas, to take the theories which learned and speculative men have made from that government, and then, supposing it made on those theories, which were made from it, to accuse the government as not corresponding with them.'

means by which he endows his image of the past with authority must be intimately bound up with the means by which he constructs it; since the function of the image is to contain and convey authority, the authority must to a large degree define the image. Mo Tzu indeed seems to have been impelled to open the whole problem of the nature of authority and its place in political society, but he was clearly a man of unusual philosophical capacity. In a traditional society possessing only a highly institutionalised present and the presumption of its continuity in a past, it is likely that the radical desiring a past to return to will be obliged to erect a myth—an image of the past owing most to the creative imagination and heavily endowed with charismatic authority; for if we assume that action and authority conceived as outside the stream of tradition must be conceived as in some way creative, charismatic or sacred, the radical's solution must be dictated by this necessity.

Much obviously depends on whether the tradition already contains images of creative or sacred action[1]—on whether, for instance, it defines the nature of the sacred act with which it began—for then the radical has only to depict the tradition as a departure or degeneration from its own beginnings, and authority may be defined as a recrudescence of the original charisma in the present. It was a weakness in Mo Tzu's position that so little could be said about the Former Kings and the Hsia other than the presumption of their continuity with Chou usages. But great religious traditions in highly literate societies, which begin with detailed written expressions of inexpressible sacred events, will be in a peculiarly interesting position in this respect. Protestant thought, for example, began by making an intensive scholarly and critical endeavour to reconstruct the practices of the primitive church, as possessing the authority of revealed truth over the present, but later generated an increasingly illuminist attempt to attain through inspiration direct experience of the operations of the Spirit not only in primitive times but in all times. In Islam, where the reinterpretation of primitive documents is less possible, the radical Shi'i sectaries claimed that the charisma of the Prophet had passed to the hero 'Ali, and that those who did not give their allegiance to 'Ali were no true Muslims. In such cases as these a sacred charisma, never to be fully contained within the normal mechanisms of transmission, is thought of as awaiting outside time the faithful who seek or expect it within time. Apocalyptics develop elaborate schemes of prophecy, predicting the times and occasions on which the charisma will return to the temporal world; mystics pursue 'the intersections of the timeless with time', regarding their occupation as

[1] On this point—as elsewhere in this essay—I am indebted to correspondence with Mr Marshall G. S. Hodgson of the University of Chicago.

extra-historical. But whether or not the operations of the timeless are conceptualised into a historic scheme, authority has been located outside time, and the strategy of return may end by abolishing its own necessity; 'if a man think to be saved by the report of Christ's dying at Jerusalem, he is deceived'. If the structure of time is the transmission of authority, an authority which may be had by direct contact with the timeless seems to abolish time altogether.

The strategy of return does not depend on the tradition's conserving any image of its sacred or other origins; if 'Ali and the Former Kings do not exist, the radical is often capable of inventing them. English common-law traditionalism repeatedly denied that the origins of tradition could be found at any specific moment,[1] but this did not prevent the Levellers locating in pre-Conquest England 'the birthright of Englishmen', or the Georgian democrats locating at the same period the realisation of 'the original principles of the constitution' and erecting the figure of Alfred into that of the English legislator who had established them. The tradition contained no specified charisma which could be vested exclusively in the Anglo-Saxons, but if we ask what sort of authority English radicals supposed the vanished past to exercise over the degenerate present, we find answers in which the charismatic and the rational are blended. The Levellers identified the inner light of the spirit in every man with his natural reason and the freedom to exercise it; they could both assert with Lilburne that institutions embodying that freedom had once existed in England and assert with Overton that it did not matter if they had not, since the authority of spirit and reason was independent of worldly happenings. The Georgian radicals had abridged the constitutional tradition into a Polybian–Machiavellian 'science' of mixed government, according to which every stable constitution must be founded on certain principles, from which it might degenerate and to which it must be restored.[2] Burke, as we know, contended that theories like these were always distilled from the constitutional inheritance which was then represented as degenerate from them, and that this was 'a preposterous way of thinking and a perfect confusion of ideas'. It might indeed be argued that the element of authority in each case did not belong to the common law and was borrowed from another strand of thought, Puritan or humanist, in the English inheritance; but in each case the authority vested in the past and enjoining a return to it was no longer located in a stream of trans-

---

[1] See Burke, *loc. cit.*, and Davies, preface to *Irish Reports* (1612): 'Neither could any one man ever vaunt, that like *Minos, Solon*, or *Lycurgus*, he was the first *Lawgiver* to our Nation...Long experience, and many trials of what was best for the common good, did make the *Common Law*.'

[2] For details of this abridgement, see 'Machiavelli, Harrington and English political ideologies in the eighteenth century', *William and Mary Quarterly*, 3rd ser., 22 (1965), 549–83.

mission, but consisted in something—whether charismatic or rational—not dependent on time for its validity.

Here we seem to have established some fairly simple cases of 'the abridgement of tradition into an ideology'. The strategist of return, supposed to be making his departure like Mo Tzu from a situation of pure traditionalism, cannot invest the past in which he believes with the authority of tradition. He therefore borrows elements of charismatic or rational authority either from the tradition which he is criticising or from some other strand in his society's inheritance—it is worth noticing that the stream of transmission must already be bearing along elements of charisma or rationality, or elements easily conceptualised as such—and concentrates them wholly in his 'past', in such a way as to deprive subsequent tradition of what now becomes a predominant form of authority, capable of commanding return to the past in which it was once fully actualised. But since traditional thought conceives time in terms of social transmission, an authority which has not been transmitted is not in time and does not depend for its validity on its having been actualised in the past. The strategy of return tends therefore to be self-abolishing.

The phenomenon is familiar enough, being that 'radical', 'rationalist' or 'ideological' thinking which has been criticised from Hsun Tzu to Michael Oakeshott by those aware of the reality and ubiquity of tradition; the outlines of their criticism are also familiar. But there is a fore-shortening of perspective into which a vivid awareness of tradition should not be allowed to lead us. We should beware of supposing that the criticism of tradition by those in search of an alternative basis for authority necessarily leads them into ideological postures, so that every dialogue between the conservers and the critics of a tradition is like that between Burke and Paine. This is simply not so; traditionalism has its own naïvety, which consists in exaggerating its own subtlety and the naïvety of its opponents. It can be empirically shown that the range of strategies open to both the conservative and the radical is greater than we have so far allowed, and that in confrontations between them the awareness of history is by no means all on one side. If the abridgement of tradition is ideology, the criticism of tradition may be history—the ascription to the past of a relation to the present more complex than mere transmission. The ideologist and the historian may be closer partners than seemed likely at first sight.

A tradition in the pure sense consists of a set of present usages and the presumption of their indefinite continuity; the only modes of social action which it conceives or recognises are use and transmission, and the radical critic is therefore driven to invent or import some other mode of action lying outside the tradition. But we have already seen that

traditions of pure usage, containing no other concepts of action or
authority, are on the whole rare. The majority contain some image of
charismatic or other action, which the radical may employ to construct
his strategy of return and develop into the foundations of his ideology.
It further happens that few radicals find themselves confronted with
a traditionalism so pure that it makes no other assertion about the past
than that it is the indefinite antiquity of present usages. Factual statements are commonly made about actions taken or assertions of authority
made in the past, and the basis on which these are made is seldom
exclusively that of presumption. The character of these statements is
all-important to the development of historiography. If they consist
merely of allusions to sacred and timeless events, with no secular or
institutional continuity with society's present, we are in a situation like
that of the Greeks, unable to make any statement about the past which
is not either myth or the rationalisation of myth; if they consist merely
in presumptions of the continuity of present usages, we are in the situation already described, limited to either the presumption of antiquity
or the invention of a timeless myth of charismatic action. But if they
are made in such a way as to facilitate discussion of what happened
and what authority it exerts over the present, then critical discussion
of past, continuity and tradition becomes possible. It is when two men—
who may be the conservative and the radical—begin making contradictory but discussable statements about the past and its relation to the
present that historical thought can begin. We should observe, however,
that it may well be the radical who wishes to initiate such a discussion,
the conservative who denies that it can or should be held. It was the
conservative and traditionalist Hsun Tzu who wrote: 'Abandoned incorrigible people say ancient and present times were different in nature
...The Sage cannot be so deceived'.[1]

At this point literacy emerges as the force modifying the character
of tradition. Should there have existed for a sufficient period the practice of conserving official records or literary expressions of what is taken
to be the tradition's content, the conservative need not rely exclusively
on the presumption of continuity, nor need the radical be confined to the
construction of a charismatic myth. It will be open to the latter to re-
combine and reinterpret the evidences of the past so that they present
an image other than that of the tradition, just as it will be open to the
former to construct an image of society in the classical and canonical
perfection it supposedly enjoyed in some ideal past. The traditionalist,
however, will always distrust the classicist, seeing in him the well-
meaning author of a potentially radical doctrine. Words—the Chinese
philosophers used to point out, referring of course to ideograms—are

[1] H. H. Dubs, *The Works of Hsuntze, translated from the Chinese* (London, 1928), pp. 72–5.

rigid in their form and yet endlessly debatable in their meaning; the tradition is that of the actual practice of the *li* and words should be kept in a subsidiary role; if they become predominant, there must be a ruler with authority to interpret them, and since the basis of his authority must be above words and outside tradition, it must be arbitrary and unintelligible. The fact is that a literate tradition is never a pure tradition, since the authority of written words is not dependent on usage and presumption only.[1] As durable material objects they cut across the processes of transmission and create new patterns of social time; they speak direct to remote generations, whose interpretation of them may differ from that of intervening transmitters of the tradition they express. If the position can be firmly maintained that documents are no more than occasional expressions of an essentially unwritten tradition, the doctrine that equates authority with simple transmission may survive; the concept of English politics we find in Burke is directly connected with the fact that common-law records were assumed to be declarations of an immemorial *jus non scriptum*. But every reader is a potential radical; non-traditional interpretations arise, and with them the question of the authority to be employed in reading and interpreting documents; this authority may be thought of as traditional, rational, charismatic or simply mysterious. Books breed sibyls to read them, and the sibyl's authority, recorded on the various occasions on which it is exercised, now enters the tradition, which increasingly becomes a record of the different interpretations which have been made of items in the social inheritance and the different modes of authority which have been asserted in making them. All these recorded facts are next made available to remote generations in ways that are more than merely traditional, and society's conceptualisation of its modes of transmission—which is to say its image of itself as existing continuously in time—becomes various, subjective and controversial. Documents tend to secularise traditions; they reduce them to a sequence of acts—whether the acts recorded, the acts of those recording them or the acts of those interpreting the records—taking place at distinguishable moments, in distinguishable circumstances, exercising and imposing distinguishable kinds and degrees of authority. They reduce time from a simple conceptualisation of social continuity to that of an indefinite multiplicity of continuities, which— since in the last analysis they represent different ideas of action, authority and transmission—cannot be altogether consistent with one another.

The radical desiring to alter the traditional image of the past has now many strategies open to him besides that of constructing a myth and investing it with a charisma. The past consists of many recorded

[1] See Jack Goody and Ian Watt, 'The consequences of literacy', *Comparative Studies in Society and History*, v, 3 (1963), 304–45.

actions and images of authority, of which the greater part must be acceptable to the conservative as well as to himself; these may be selected and re-arranged so as to provide a new image of the past and the sort of authority it exercises upon the present, counter-interpretations may be put forward and their rival claims may be discussed. Since the discussion of alternative versions of the past and their relation to the present is what we mean by historiography, we may risk the hypothesis that the beginnings of historiography are to be found when, in a literate tradition, an attempt is made to alter not so much the received facts of the past as the kind of authority which they exercise over the present; for this will bring about the discussion of alternative versions of society's continuity as a means of transmitting authority. The concepts employed in constructing and discussing these versions will be various, and will not all seem to us such as historians have any business to be using. Depending upon what modes of authority are supposed to be inherent in the tradition under discussion, there will be timeless concepts of sacred or rational authority; there will be concepts of action and transmission peculiar to the tradition's institutional character, and taken for granted without critical investigation; there will even be uncritical or anticritical employments of the concept of tradition. But the possibility now exists of agreeing, first, that certain acts were performed irrespective of the authority which they exercise, second, that certain forms of authority were asserted and recognised irrespective of whether they are or should be now acknowledged. There now exists the possibility of two further stages in the growth of historical thought. The first is that of a 'pure' or 'objective' historiography, meaning the reconstruction of a past irrespective of the authority which it exercises over the present. This stage, it should be observed, has sometimes been reached by accident; classicists and radicals have discovered, with a sense of shock, that they have reconstructed the past in such terms that it can authorise only itself.[1] The second is the realisation of the complexity of tradition, the discovery that society's past contains and has transmitted all these modes of authority and of action, of which purely traditional authority and the activity of pure transmission form only one conceptualisation, so that the tradition has become a dialogue between its more and its less traditional—a dialectic between its traditional and its anti-traditional—modes of envisaging itself. If the former of these stages is more likely to be reached by radicals and classicists, the latter is more likely to be reached by conservatives and sometime traditionalists.

[1] A *locus classicus* of this sense of shock is Francois Hotman's *Anti-Tribonian* (1566). See Pocock, *The Ancient Constitution and the Feudal Law* (Cambridge, 1957), pp. 11–15, and Julian H. Franklin, *Jean Bodin and the Sixteenth-century Revolution in the Methodology of Law and History* (New York and London, 1963), pp. 46–58.

'The criticism of tradition is history'—a sentence the necessary counterpart of Henry Ford's 'History is more or less bunk. It's tradition'—is now seen to mean that historiography emerges from the context of a discussion of various ways in which the past can authorise the present. In this discussion many concepts by no means appropriate to pure historiography will be constantly in use, and though the tendency to eliminate them and convert the discussion from the level of politics to that of history will be very strong, there is no reason to suppose that it will ever reach absolute completeness. In these circumstances we have to avoid the temptation—which has flawed several brilliant Italian works of the post-Crocean school—to single out those aspects of thought which we consider 'historical' and in their light to condemn others as 'unhistorical' and writings containing concepts of the latter kind as less than 'history'. It is clearly wiser to consider pure historiography as one extreme of a wide spectrum of types of discussion, which will be intensified in proportion as modes of authorisation come to be looked on 'objectively', i.e. in the same light as others. Since what we are concerned with is history, the light in question must be that of a common temporal context, and it should therefore seem—at least *prima facie*— that it will be hard to construct a historiography where the dominant mode of authority is and remains sacred. It is true that one of the main origins of modern historiography is found in the endeavours of sixteenth-century religious reformers to recover the exact text of Scripture and the exact institutional character of the primitive church. This led not only to counter-endeavours in the field of erudition on the part of their opponents, but to discussion of the modes of transmission of authority and the structure of the Christian community. The reformers' posture was radical; they meant to use their recoveries to prove that the historical church had failed to transmit authority and had consequently lost it; and like other exponents of the strategy of return, they faced the question of how to define the authority which had once existed and the authority by which they themselves claimed to know it. Since what was in dispute was an action of the sacred upon the world of time, the reformers claimed the authority of the sacred acting on and through themselves, their acts being conceived as opposed to tradition; they claimed both to interpret the past and to reform the present by personal authority and charisma, and the strategy of return duly proved, in a number of cases, self-abolishing. Their opponents pointed out that charisma was tending to replace transmission altogether, and advocated a return to the accepted modes of interpretation of the sacred origins, which were scholastic reason, institutionalised authority and prescriptive usage. The next step should ideally have been the construction of a vision of Christian history in which all these modes of authority and transmission were seen as acting together; but—apart from the political struggles which discouraged any such eirenic—so long as the Christian world is seen as an interrelation of the sacred and the temporal, the possibility of a Christian historiography depends on the extent to which that interrelation can be defined in terms which permit the temporal to be seen as the product of an inner dynamic. Once the sacred is defined as universal and extra-social, it greatly complicates our task of viewing historiography as the outcome of the secularisation of conceptualised social continuity. We therefore borrow from the great religious traditions such evidence as increases our self-limited understanding of the strategies of tradition.

In the emphasis which Hooker laid on the church as a traditional community, transmitting its interpretations of original revelation in ways which invested them chiefly with prescriptive and presumptive value, we recognise not merely an appeal to tradition as a mode of authority sometimes preferable to charisma, but an intensified awareness of the traditional community which is often considered the ideal conservative response to the strategy of return. To the Shi'i fundamentalism which became a recourse to the charismatic figure of 'Ali, orthodox Sunni Muslims reply by declaring their loyalty to the Ummah, which is the historic Muslim community existing in time, somewhere containing all truth and, though it may contain imperfections and uncertainties as well, not to be broken up by those who are certain of their perfection. Here we have a heightened awareness of transmission as carried on in many modes and asserting many forms of authority; it makes possible—though this seems not to have been realised in Islam—that authentically historical awareness of the complexity of tradition as containing many modes of transmission which was mentioned earlier; and in its realisation that different assertions of authority must be weighed against one another and that a certain relativism attaches to them all, prescriptive awareness of authority and tradition may be renewed on a higher level. This has already been defined as the species of historical awareness which the conservative is especially likely to achieve, but it is important not to credit him with it too hastily and to realise the complexity of the dialogue with the radical that must precede it.

We have so far defined the anti-traditional thinker, not as one who wishes to abolish the authority of the past or to impose a new conception of authority on society, but as one who, having denied that the past authorises the present by vesting it with continuity, is obliged to create a new past and invest it with an authority which easily abolishes the necessity of referring to a past at all. His thought is therefore Janus-faced, but we should pause before emphasising too ruthlessly the contradictions which it may contain. It tends to become unhistorical, in the sense that it devises a mode of authority independent of social continuity; but it contains an equally visible tendency towards the historical reconstruction of the past in a shape which, together with the authority which it possesses for the present, it is the radical's peculiar contribution to leave uncertain and discussable. In a documented tradition his 'past' will be a compost of assertions of fact and authority selected and rearranged from a common inheritance; he cannot help revealing, and leaving open to question, the methods by which he has done this. Furthermore, the more 'factual' and the less 'mythical'—these are not mutually exclusive categories—the past which he claims once existed, the more specific the authority which enjoins that it should exist again, the more he (or his readers, or his adversaries) may feel impelled to ask why it does not exist now: how has the unauthorised present come into being? He may reply, like Plato or Machiavelli, by averring that there exists a general tendency towards instability and degeneration in human affairs; but the more clearly he can differentiate the characteristics of his 'past' from those of his 'present', the more specific he may feel able to make his account of how the latter came to predominate. Boulainvilliers's account of the decline of the *noblesse* is more complex as a piece of historical explanation than his account of their original privileges;[1] the Georgian radicals, having erected the myth of a free medieval commonwealth of landowning warriors, accounted for its decline by tracing the rise of government finance, professional armies and parliamentary influence in ways which passed through Hume to the Glasgow school.[2] The radical reconstructs the past in order to authorise the future; he historises the present in order to deprive it of authority. Both operations may give him a bias in favour of historical explanation, which may emerge almost against his wishes from the very character of his enterprise; as with the radical legal humanists of the *mos gallicus*, who reconstructed Roman law in order to imitate it instead of following the glossatorial tradition, and then found they had reconstructed it in such detail that it could not be imitated. The conservative may profit by such mistakes, but could never have made them.

The repudiation of tradition, and the construction of a mode of authority owing nothing to time or continuity, need not—paradoxically enough—diminish a thinker's interest in the reconstruction of the past. Thomas Hobbes repudiated tradition and constructed a mode of authority which has nothing prescriptive about it. Consequently, it is

---

[1] Comte de Boulainvilliers, *Essais sur la Noblesse de France, contenans une dissertation sur son origine et abaissement* (Amsterdam, 1732).

[2] Andrew Fletcher, *A Discourse on Government in its Relation to Militias* (Edinburgh, 1698). Giuseppe Giarrizzo, *Hume politico e storico* (Turin, 1962).

said, he regarded the study of history as of limited illustrative or prudential value. He denied that the common law was Coke's 'artificial
reason', based upon presumptive awareness of tradition, and said it
was merely the commands of natural reason rendered authoritative by
the sovereign. Yet it is precisely in his writings on English law[1] that we
find him among the advanced historical thinkers of his day, conscious
that the doctrine of immemorial custom could be refuted by recon-
structing the law as it had once been, the feudal law of a feudal society.
Nor did he adopt this line of argument for merely polemical reasons.
There is a visible relation between his denial that the past was a source
of authority for the present and his awareness that it could be explained
as existing in its own right; and his reconstruction of the past was a
piece of serious antiquarian thinking, not a mechanical application of
his abstract theories. Because his thought was unhistorical in one respect,
it could be historical in another. A rationalist approach to authority
and a historical approach to the past may be partners as well as opposites; this is only one of the complexities which follow from the radical's
denial that authority is prescriptive.

In his now well-known reply to Hobbes on English law, Sir Matthew
Hale raised the presumptive theory of custom to a new level of sophistication.[2] He wished to deny that law was a series of simple rational
commands; he contended that law was custom, and that in a given custom nothing could be seen but the fruits of experience, shaped in a
series of concrete situations to which no moment of commencement
could be assigned, and thereafter tested in subsequent situations not
identical with their predecessors but assimilated to them by practice.
The details of these situations had not as a rule been recorded; the content of the law had been constantly refined on the presumption that it
was being preserved; we could say of no item in the law when it had
originated, nor could we trace the succession of contexts in which it
had been shaped and modified. There was only the presumption that
it had answered, and would continue to answer, in all the situations
to which it was exposed; but this presumption was overwhelmingly
strong.

Hsun Tzu had attacked the radical strategy of return by arguing
that the past could not be known by means other than presumption. To
know the ways of the Former Kings we must follow those of the Later
Kings; to know those of the Later Kings we must follow the usages of
Chou; to know those of Chou we must follow Confucius. Hale was

---

[1] *Behemoth* and *A Dialogue of the Common Laws*; in Molesworth (ed.), *English Works*, vi (London,
1839–45).

[2] Printed in Holdsworth, *A History of English Law*, v, Appendix. See Pocock, *The Ancient
Constitution and the Feudal Law, cit.*, pp. 170–81; and 'Burke and the ancient constitution—a
problem in the history of ideas', *Historical Journal*, iii, 2 (1960), 134–7.

attacking a rationalist theory of authority, which implied the possibility of independent knowledge of a past no longer prescriptive, by arguments essentially the same. It is important to observe how the traditionalist strategy shifts under attack. In a system of pure tradition, all knowledge is dependent upon transmission; the validity of transmitted knowledge can only be presumed, but since we have no means of knowledge other than transmission, this presumption must be made of all knowledge; the circle is closed. When therefore the radical, the rationalist or the antiquarian begin to assert that the past can be known by means that do not presume its continuity with the present, that the past does not authorise the present but enjoins another set of political arrangements, that authority can be found by means that do not locate it in the past, or that the past can be studied in ways that do not invest it with authority over the present, the conservative's strategy is—at this stage in the analysis—always the same. Against the rationalist, he avers that nothing can be known of a social institution or its authority which does not stress its continuity with the past to the point where that authority becomes inescapably prescriptive; against the radical, the antiquarian, even the historian, he avers that nothing is known of the past which is not based on transmission and does not compel the presumption of continuity between that past and the present (or between a remote past and a recent past of which the present is the continuation). But both Hsun Tzu and Hale reveal that his position has in fact altered. The radical avers, in one way or another, that the past can be known, and however insubstantial his grounds, he forces the conservative to reply that it cannot be known; it can only be presumed. The radical constructs his image of the past by re-arranging, modifying, and occasionally inverting or contradicting the concepts and documents in which some part of the contents of a tradition is conveyed in easily manageable shapes; and since the elements of his structure are abstracted from a context of which they form part and with the other elements of which they have unstated and presumptive relationships, the conservative is able to point out that the radical's past is a construct, an abstraction, of limited validity. There is of course a sense in which all knowledge in a tradition is of this kind; Confucius may have intended this when he said: 'Shall I tell you what wisdom is? It is to know both what one knows and what one doesn't know.' But in Hsun Tzu the stress on 'what one doesn't know' is the stronger because assertions have been made about the possibility of knowing the past to have been other than the present, and in Hale the stress has become very strong and its expression very sophisticated. The past is a continuity, but a continuity of adaptation; the image of a body changing its cells, of a river changing its water, is more than once used; and we are being told that all we can ever know of the past is that it was unlike the present and yet continuous with it. Even this we cannot know so much as presume, for we cannot know what the past was like at any single moment. Such moments are inapprehensible. The tradition has become a flux, Hale's river that of Heraclitus and Cratylus.

No less than the radical, then, the conservative can think both historically and unhistorically. The radical asserts that the past can be known, but that some elements of it can be known out of their traditional context; the conservative asserts that all knowledge must be knowledge in a continuous social context, but denies to that knowledge any status more positive than that of presumption. It seems to be a sign of un-conscious conservative bias in us, therefore, when we assert that Hale's thinking is 'historical' and that of Hobbes 'unhistorical', or make simi-lar comparisons between Guicciardini and Machiavelli. Hale and Guicciardini certainly possessed a greater sense of the complexity and intractability of historical events, but at the same time they denied that events could be known or governed, if at all, by any but the most rigorously presumptive methods: traditional conservatism in Hale, merging into scepticism and stoicism in Guicciardini. Their opposites in each pair were trying, by the aid of concepts abstracted from their historical contexts, to make history more intelligible and governable. But the conservative's strategies do not end with this union of scepticism and traditionalism, typically conservative though it is. The increasing complexity of non-traditional thought faces him with other challenges, to which he makes other responses.

It may for instance happen that the radicals have captured the past. That is, they may have succeeded in re-arranging concepts about the past so as to form a pattern widely accepted as plausible and containing much that is acceptable and even dear to conservatives, but seeming to authorise in the present only a set of arrangements other than those actually existing. This seems to have happened in Georgian England, where the traditional image of 'the ancient constitution' had been revised to form a quasi-classical image of an 'ancient and balanced constitution', founded on principles from which, it was said, the present constitution was degenerate. In these circumstances there are several replies which conservatives may put forward. There is the traditionalist and prescriptive answer, advanced in this case by Burke, which denies that the principles of the constitution can be known, since they are nothing but continuities of immemorial usage. The more precise, how-ever, the image of the past and its authority to which this answer is opposed, the harder it is to dissolve knowledge into presumption. There is the possibility of constructing a new version of the past, more per-suasive than that of the radicals; but the more striking and original the intellectual means employed to do this, the less likely is it to furnish present arrangements with prescriptive authority. There is the further possibility of drastically denying that the past has authority over the present, and claiming for existing arrangements an authority derived from outside history. It should not surprise us to find this conservative radicalism in close alliance with historical criticism; so at least it was in eighteenth-century England. For the century following the Exclusion controversy, it was a standard tactic of the defenders of the Court—especially when the Court was Hanoverian rather than Stuart—to employ the feudal interpretation to deny the antiquity of the constitution, whether immemorial or balanced, and argue that since the past was mainly darkness and despotism the principles of government, such as they were, must be extra-historical in their location and recent in their discovery. Until the advent of Burke altered the intellectual scene, a classicist appeal to the past was the weapon of English and American radicals, a critical rejection of history that of the Court. Nor is this a peculiarly eighteenth-century phenomenon. Against the 'abandoned incorrigible people' who argued that past and present times were different in nature, Hsun Tzu demanded: 'Why cannot the Sage be so deceived? I say it is because the Sage measures things by himself. Hence by himself he measures other men...by the Way he can completely comprehend things. Past and present are the same. Things that are the same in kind, though extended over long periods, continue to have the self-same principles.'[1]

If Hsun Tzu could pass from traditionalism to essentialism in a few brush-strokes, it might seem that all that has happened is merely a tactical reversion of roles; the conservative desires to defend things as they are, and it is simply an accident of the polemical situation which determines what argument he adopts. But to leave it at that would of course be superficial; there is in the conservative's mind a constancy of belief as well as of interest. His basic position is that the existing arrangements of society contain their own justification, that it is not justifiable to subject them wholly to be evaluated by some standard existing outside themselves; and since it is impossible to cease altogether from visualising the existing arrangements as inherited, the element of tradition never quite disappears from his thought. Hsun Tzu's Sage does not resolve his 'Way' into 'principles' which he proceeds to substitute for it; the Way continues to be the practice of the *li* and the pursuit of the intimations which they contain, and what he is really asserting is that he can find no time in the past in which the *li* were not active and their intimations valid—and intimations constantly present and valid

[1] This translation is that of D. Bodde, in Fung Yu-lan, *A History of Chinese Philosophy*, 1 (Peiping and London, 1937), pp. 282-4.

may be termed principles. In eighteenth-century England the position was more complicated. Ancient and present times were allowed to be different in nature, and the conservative school employed both historical and rationalist criticism to deny that the principles of government were to be found in the past; the same tactic was employed by Voltaire and other defenders of the *thèse royale* in France, against Montesquieu and the lesser advocates of the backward-looking *thèse nobiliaire*. Reversing the strategy of return, it was argued that the true principles of government had been discovered only recently, about 1689, and that once they had been discovered their effect was to render the past irrelevant. If they were of recent discovery they were not contained in tradition, and we seem to be faced by a conservative argument abandoning the appeal to prescriptive sanction. But a pragmatic and a prescriptive conservatism are not as dissimilar in their intellectual style as may at first appear.

If the principles of government were of recent discovery, how had this discovery been made and what was the legitimacy of actions performed before—or indeed after—their discovery? It might be argued that the discovery was made as a result of the developing historical experience of the English people; this seems to be part of the very complex historical thought of David Hume.[1] But if actions performed before their discovery were not to be considered mere folly and barbarism, they must be explained and justified by something other than 'the principles of government', in which case these 'principles' could not be the sole source of authority for political actions. Unhistorical authority alleged by a conservative will be a different matter from unhistorical authority alleged by a radical. It will authorise an existing set of arrangements, whereas its radical counterpart authorises one that must be brought into existence, even if this is to be done by a return to the past; and a consequence is that the authority of the latter must stretch further and do more than that of the former. The conservative demands less of his 'principles' and puts less into them; they will resemble less a comprehensive theory of government than a pragmatic justification of existing arrangements. Indeed, they may turn out on inspection to contain little more than the pragmatic statement that arrangements must be continued if they exist and must be made if they do not exist, and that somebody must attend to continuing or constructing them. There is certainly little more to the conservatism of that admirable eighteenth-century curmudgeon Josiah Tucker.

The conservative in his pragmatic vein is anxious that practical steps shall be taken and existing arrangements upheld, without being subjected to excessive scrutiny in the name of abstract principle. To ensure this he will even repudiate the continuity of past and present, which his

---

[1] Giarrizzo, *op. cit.*

prescriptive and traditionalist brother is so anxious to maintain. But prescriptive action is undertaken on nothing more than an assumption, which its defenders are memorably reluctant to see replaced by an abstraction; and that assumption is no more than the presumption of its continuity with earlier action, which must also be presumed—as a matter of practical necessity—of the majority of actions undertaken in a purely pragmatic spirit. A pragmatic action must have a context and make sense in that context. A prescriptive style, which appeals constantly to precedent, may have much in common with a pragmatic style, which appeals only to necessity; this is how it was that the conservatism of the eighteenth century could reflect the thought both of those who thought the Revolution justified by precedent and of those—the so-called *de facto* Tories —who thought it justified only by necessity. Burke was able to unite these lines of thought by demonstrating that neither entailed, and each rejected, the establishment of an abstract and recurrent principle of dethronement. Pragmatism is the establishment of a continuous style of behaviour which cannot any longer be presumed; this is the sense in which it is conservatism without traditions.

We may now see how it is that the conservative can unite the extremes of traditionalist veneration for a past and sceptical denial of the past's relevance for the present. He believes wholly in an established and continuous mode of behaviour, which contains within itself all the criteria by which it can be judged and so cannot be judged by any standard outside itself. The radical attempts to establish such a standard in the past, the rationalist outside it. The appeal to tradition can be used against the rationalist, to return all thinking to the context of a given social continuity. But the radical is in one way a more formidable opponent, because he has an alternative version of the prescribing past, and as soon as traditionalism becomes a means of denying that such a version can be reliably constructed, it becomes a mode of scepticism differing only in degree from outright denial that the past can be known or relevant. Historical scepticism becomes a conservative weapon when it becomes a means of denying that the present act or arrangement can be judged by some standard located as existing and emanating authority in the past. An act concerning which nothing can be said with certainty except that it must be presumed continuous with some antecedent act is not so very unlike an act of which not even that can be said, given only that it is our agreed purpose that a social continuity must be established and maintained. At this point it becomes a conservative interest to emphasise the discontinuity of history, its character as a series of discrete actions, where previously it was to his interest to emphasise the presumed continuity with which it transmitted authority and legitimation. If each act is unique it cannot be judged by comparison with any of its predecessors; but if its intent is to establish authority and continuity, it should be accepted as such and not condemned. A series of such acts will re-edify a presumptive tradition; and neo-conservative and neo-Burkean historians are seeking to reduce history once more to an esoteric and disenchanted narrative of the almost inscrutable acts of statesmen.

There is here an antinomian and anarchic strain in conservatism. Distrusting recurrence and regularity, it reduces history to a river into which one cannot step twice, with the consequence that it becomes difficult to step into it even once. It is interesting that the 'abandoned incorrigible people', against whom Hsun Tzu declared the steadfastness of the Sage's self-discovered nature, were probably not radical heirs of Mo Tzu but Taoists; since an affinity between Oakeshott's thought and Taoism has been detected by some critics. The assertion that 'past and present times are different in nature' is certainly to be detected in some Taoist writings,[1] but it does not seem to mean that the past may be reconstructed by historical technique and seen to be different from the present. 'Footprints', we are told, 'are made by shoes, but they are far from being shoes'; an utterance which seems to indicate that history escapes our knowledge. The Taoist insistence on the undifferentiated unity of all reality led them, it appears, to repudiate all attempts to pin exact definitions on it. If then you tried to assert that the present was known and properly governed, the river would slip through your fingers as you tried to net it. But this argument goes from Cratylus to Heraclitus: if you cannot step into the river once, you cannot step into it twice either; and no more than Hale did the Taoists believe it possible to determine the state of the tradition at single moments, past or present. They therefore abandoned the use of all concepts in government, even the concept of government itself. This view shocked Hsun Tzu, who was inclined to regard the transmitted contents of tradition as a body of authoritative institutions and dogmas, but it is a natural if extreme development of an integral part of the traditionalist style; indeed, it seems likely that the Taoists reached their belief that no moment in the Way was the whole of the Way, and that consequently no moment was like another moment, partly through reflection on the nature of tradition. Because the intellect cannot grasp the full meaning of any act in the sequence of a tradition, it cannot grasp the whole meaning of the tradition; and consequently it is very easy to think of action as the carrying on of a style, the continuation of a mode of behaviour whose character can be apprehended but never analysed, and which in turn is realised in action rather than in conceptualisation. From this the Taoists went on to regard the whole of reality as a style—

[1] Arthur Waley, *Three Ways of Thought in Ancient China* (London, 1939), pp. 32, 37–8.

the Way—and to take that delight, which Oakeshott shares, in telling stories of craftsmen who could perform their tasks perfectly because they did not consider how to do them, who were perfect in their style because they did not conceive it as a style. But if politics is to be the practice of a pure style, the practical is in fact being absorbed by the contemplative, the pragmatic by the aesthetic; where the traditionalist legitimised his acts by presuming them continuous and the pragmatist acted to institute a continuity, the aesthetic statesman acts so that the continuous style of his actions may be contemplated and enjoyed. All three share a conservative style; they presume a tradition.

Disinterested historiography is possible only in stable societies, where the present is fortified by means other than the writing of histories. It is therefore part of the conservative style to emphasise that history is studied for its own sake, and in a well-known passage Oakeshott has compared the impure historian who expects the past to teach him something, with the pure historian for whom the past is dead, a beloved mistress whom he does not expect to talk sense. But if the past can be considered dead, this can only mean that society's relation with its past, which we have seen to be society's continuing structure and its own inner self, has been stabilised by means other than those of the historian. In less stable societies, Oakeshott's historian is an impossibility. For Machiavelli, who makes significant use of erotic imagery as regards the past, history is Fortune, a treacherous and savage virgin whom we can never fully possess, but who may well devour us if we do not master her; and the river may burst its banks in devastating flood.[1] Even in a stable society, there is a certain cosiness about the Oakeshottian *ménage*. The point about a mistress is that we are not obliged to live with her; Oakeshott's historian and his past maintain separate establishments. But once we define society's awareness of its structure as its awareness of its continuity, of the complexity of its relations with its past, the occasionally enjoyed mistress begins to assume more serious, more terrible and more moral possibilities. To the Florentines she was the maenad Fortune, an irrational and irresistible stream of happenings. To the Romantics she was (and is) the Goddess History, of their relationship with whom they expect a final consummation, only too likely to prove a *Liebestod*. The conservative style leaves her in the role of mistress, but it has been the aim of this essay to show that traditionalism and its refinements form only one voice in a dialogue with and within tradition, out of which arises a constant discussion and redefinition of the modes of continuity and authority which link past to present and give the present its structure. In that dialogue the past is to the present something more like a wife: an other self, perpetually explored.

[1] *The Prince*, ch. 25.

IS THERE REASON IN TRADITION?

SAMUEL COLEMAN

In recent years at least two papers have appeared that proceeded from a discussion of tradition to a discussion of unintended consequences.[1] And as a result of the difficulties of modernisation of underdeveloped nations, tradition has increasingly come to be the subject-matter of social scientific essays on the problems of rapid industrialisation and of many intended and some distressing consequences.[2]

This essay[3] begins with an analysis of the nature of tradition, proceeds to a brief exposition and history of traditionalism as an ideology, and then enters upon an examination of unintended consequences, particularly the explanation of these offered by Robert K. Merton.[4] In the course of this paper I shall discuss some important elements of conservative thought.

TRADITION

What characterises traditional practices and beliefs? Acton[5] asserts that a tradition is marked by: '(a) its chronic character, (b) its continuity and (c) its authoritativeness. Clearly, (c) is its most important feature. There is a tradition only when the belief or practice is handed on unquestioned.'

The chronic character of a tradition must first be distinguished from habit, which is personal and singular, whereas tradition is social and cultural. Even if a tradition regulates the behaviour of only a single person, e.g. the President of the United States, the tradition is socially known. The President's traditional conduct has been handed down

---

[1] Karl Popper, 'Toward a rational theory of tradition'. This paper first appeared in 1949 in *The Rationalist Annual* and has been reprinted in *Conjectures and Refutations* (London: Routledge and Kegan Paul, 1963), p. 121. The second paper is H. B. Acton, 'Tradition and some other forms of order', Presidential Address, *Proceedings of the Aristotelian Society, 1952–1953*, N.S. vol. 53 (London, 1953).

[2] See Ralph Braibanti and Joseph J. Spengler, *Traditions, Values and Socio-Economic Development* (Durham, N.C.: Duke Univ. Press, 1961), as one among several such collections. Also, articles like David Apter, 'The role of traditionalism in the political modernization of Ghana and Uganda', in *World Politics*, vol. 13, October 1960; Adam Curle, 'Tradition, development and planning', *Sociological Review*, N.S. 8.

[3] I am indebted to Professor S. Morgenbesser for many fruitful discussions and ideas. Professor Dorothy Emmet, Professor Arthur Collins and Mr Kenneth Winston have read the manuscript and made helpful suggestions. They cannot be blamed for what I have made of their ideas.

[4] Robert K. Merton, *Social Theory and Social Structure* (Glencoe: The Free Press, 1957).

[5] *Art. cit.*

[239]

to him; it is regular and predictable conduct within the defining circumstances. Traditions attach to roles, rather than to individuals apart from their roles. Habits belong to the individual apart from his role.

Thus, investigation may reveal that a gentleman always adjusts his tie while waiting for the doorbell to be answered when he attends a party. It may be even disclosed that for generations now every gentleman has predictably adjusted his tie as he is about to appear before some group. It is nevertheless a habit, not a tradition. What is traditional is the normative requirement of neatness the habit subserves. If the gentleman should fail to touch his tie as he is about to join a group, no one will notice. But if he joins the group with the knot of his tie under his ear it will elicit notice if not comment. Traditional behaviour is behaviour by some maxim, formulated or not, that one has learned. It implies some normative power in the tradition: '...and as all medieval society was dominated by the idea that what was customary was also right, breach of these customs...soon became a wicked thing; and after that, a crime.'[1]

The normative character of traditional practices has been challenged and the following instance offered in refutation: On a sweltering day at an academic meeting in New York, attended by many German academics forced out by Hitler, one brave innovator broke the tradition by removing his coat. He was applauded and his example followed by many others. Had the tradition been normative, it is asserted, he should have been rebuked. It may happen, however, that a tradition changes or comes to an end when altered circumstances render it inconvenient and an alternative is at hand. Certainly in this instance the circumstances were greatly altered from those of German climate and academic rigidities. The applause seems to have been for the innovator's courage in breaking with the normative behaviour. Had there been no normative property in the tradition of wearing a jacket in academic precincts, his removal of his jacket would have elicited no comment at all.

How is tradition distinguished from that which is not habitual, but is observed to be statistically both chronic and continuous, like the large number of deaths on the highways on long summer weekends? Migration from the cities, for example, is traditional. But the record of 'chronic and continuous' traffic accidents, traditionally compiled by the police and traffic safety organisations, does not make the accidents traditional. For these casualties are not in accord with any maxim or traditional manner of behaviour: they are accidental, not intended; they are a statistically predictable consequence of the traditional flight from the city to the countryside.

Is it true that 'there is a tradition only when the belief or practice is

[1] Marc Bloch, *The Rise of Dependent Cultivation*, Cambridge Economic History, vol. 1, p. 241.

handed on unquestioned'? Professor Acton cannot mean *any* questioning, for, as Radin tells us, a great deal of questioning and philosophising goes on in pre-literate societies about these beliefs and practices. Evans-Pritchard was 'struck by the intellectual force shown by the primitive African in upholding his beliefs against evidence which to the European seemed flagrantly to refute him'.[1]

Where a traditional practice becomes oppressive, it may be angrily questioned and yet be maintained by superior power and authority. Some roles are more comfortable and desirable and others are quite undesirable in any stratified society.[2] The insistence on the maintenance of traditional feudal relationships; the stubborn retention of jim-crow arrangements throughout the United States; the dogged conservatism of the Party hierarchy in the Soviet Union; the resistance to technological innovation and the struggle to keep the traditional work customs by trade unions: in each of these cases the clinging to traditional arrangements safeguards material advantages. Almost all social roles that are regulated by tradition may express or imply power and status relationships; changes will often entail decrements and increments of power and status. Has a tradition become something else if, when questioned and resented, it is then retained by force? Is it still a tradition if maintained by persuasion?

There are further difficulties. Acton continues:

When a traditional belief has been questioned investigation may show it to be true or false. Those who after such an investigation, accept a traditional belief because there is now conclusive evidence for it, are no longer mere adherents of a tradition, for they have considered and overcome the arguments against it. They no longer accept the belief on its own authority, but because of the evidence that supports it.[3]

Not all traditions are susceptible of empirical investigation. Popper tells of hearing a recording of Mozart's Requiem, conducted by an American who was 'untouched by the tradition that has come down from Mozart. The result was devastating.'[4] Here the authority of the traditional performance cannot be empirically tested, for it is aesthetic (although its authentic descent from Mozart can in principle be verified).

---

[1] Quoted by Michael Polanyi, *Personal Knowledge* (Harper Torchbook edition, 1964), p. 287.

[2] *Gorgias*, 484 b. Cf. Novalis: The stronger has the stronger right. Pascal's discussion of Justice runs along the same lines. Also '...material interests may be tied up with the maintenance of a tradition. When for example in China, the attempt was made to change certain roads...the perquisites of certain officials were threatened'. Max Weber, *General Economic History*, tr. by Frank H. Knight (1961), p. 261.

[3] Acton, *art. cit.* Although Acton here speaks of belief, I assume that it would apply to practices, for if the wants of the practitioners remained unchanged, they would act on their beliefs. If these change, so will the practices, *ceteris paribus*. Earlier he joined beliefs and practices (in the quotation above).

[4] Karl Popper, *Conjectures and Refutations*, p. 122.

Most questions about traditional beliefs are answered by appealing to other traditional beliefs rather than to scientific investigation; many traditional beliefs are not even amenable to such investigation. However, let us suppose that the traditional belief that man's span of years is three score and ten, stemming from the Bible, is challenged. If it is supported by appealing to the authority of the Bible, it remains, according to Acton, traditional. Suppose it is confirmed in another by now traditional manner: statistical investigation, and it receives a high degree of confirmation. Man's span of years is indeed, it is discovered, three score and ten. If then it is taught and passed down, it seems to me it remains a traditional belief, though in another tradition—say, the actuarial rather than the Biblical.[1] The belief itself becomes traditional when it is handed down and taught to succeeding generations of students.

Investigation, says Acton, can transform a traditional practice or belief to a rational practice or belief by confirming it. And practitioners are converted from 'mere adherents of a tradition' to, presumably, rational agents. Disconfirmation would leave the practice merely a tradition. Now, take the following instance: Turkish farmers leave the stones on their cultivated fields. When asked why, they say that is the way it has always been done and that it is better that way. In point of fact, it is. When U.N. agronomists, after considerable exhortation, persuaded some young Turks to remove the stones from their fields, their crops suffered. Apparently the stones help condense and retain the dew in the arid climate, but this was unknown. It may have been known to the originators of the custom, for there is evidence that it was known in biblical times. This apparent fact had been forgotten, while the practice persisted.

Now, was leaving the stones on the ground not a tradition when the reason was known and passed down from generation to generation? Did it become a tradition when the reason was forgotten? The young Turks whose crops were poor because they departed from the traditional practice probably reverted to it. Were they no longer 'mere adherents of a tradition', as Acton implies, when they continued the traditional practice, because they now had evidence for doing it? The others had continued to leave the stones on the fields in the traditional way, because they had believed all along that it helped the crops. For them, had the tradition ceased to be a tradition and been converted into a rational practice, as Acton implies? Obviously, if it is handed on unchanged, and the practice is no different from what it has been for

---

[1] The belief should be distinguished from the object of the belief—the proposition 'man's life span is three score and ten years, in the West currently'. The object of the belief is not traditional.

thirty centuries, it would be misleading to say that it was no longer the traditional practice. It is now a rational practice, Acton would say, for he opposes reason to tradition, which persists because the practitioners are lazy.

Is a 'traditional air', or a folk tune whose composer is unknown, a tradition, while Mozart's music and manner of performance are not? What of Stravinsky's music? It seems to me that we would avoid all sorts of muddle if we did not speak of traditions being transmuted into non-traditions by confirmation of the proposition believed or the practice followed; we could instead speak of the traditional character of a song, a practice or a belief. A folk song, Mozart's music and Stravinsky's are all traditional in varying degrees. And a practice becomes less traditional as innovations are made in it.

Acton goes on to say:

Now liberal societies are societies in which free scientific enquiry is highly valued and in which the free exchange of commodities promotes new divisions of labor. It follows that liberal societies are also societies in which new circumstances and ways of life must constantly emerge. Traditional societies, on the other hand, are less given to critical scientific enquiry, and tend to remain in whatever division of labor they have reached.[1]

There are many traditions that are maintained without being subject to the scrutiny of reason or scientific inquiry: that one wears formal clothes to a formal affair; that one's last name is inherited from the father, and others of which I cannot think. 'The really important things to know about a society is what it takes for granted.'[2] Acton speaks as if in a liberal society traditions are constantly being examined for rationality, in a sort of continuous Cartesian enterprise. Was not Redcoatism[3] examined and altered because the environment changed from European to American? If there is no change, why would anyone examine the traditional practice? Changed circumstances may render traditional beliefs and practices inconvenient, disfunctional, or lethal, as in Redcoatism, and diminish their normative character. And even then people will endure traditional practices made oppressive by a changed environment if no alternative seems feasible, no live option apparent. The process of change thrusts traditional ways up for scrutiny as they

---

[1] Acton also brackets liberal, innovating and rational. But China and the Soviet Union are innovating and illiberal and attempt to rationalise traditional behaviour more than any other societies. And what will automation mean for the division of labour?

[2] A. L. Kroeber and Clyde Kluckhohn, 'General features of culture', *Man and Contemporary Society* (New York: Columbia Univ. Press, 1955), 1, 197.

[3] Redcoatism is the name given by Harold Rosenberg in *The Tradition of the New* (New York: Horizon Press, 1959) to such unreasoning clinging to tradition as exhibited by the first Redcoat soldiers to fight in America, when their traditional close-order parade style made them easy targets for the guerrilla tactics of Indians and colonists.

become unsuited to the altered circumstances. To say that 'traditional societies[1]...are less given to critical scientific enquiry, and tend to remain in whatever division of labour they have reached', or to say 'it is almost axiomatic that the majority of countries that most need development are the most devoted to tradition'[2] is to say that the most static societies are those that change the least: to be tautological at best, and at worst literally preposterous. Societies usually remain traditional, i.e. static, as a consequence, not as an antecedent condition, of the lack of change initiated by contact, conquest, natural calamity or growth or technological innovation. A traditional society, as the phrase is used, applies to one that retains almost all its practices and beliefs unchanged over a particular time span, and has no built-in traditional mechanism for instituting change.[3]

The fabric of tradition is torn not nearly so brutally by the application of reason and scientific inquiry as by the roads and radios that enlarge horizons, the penicillin that makes for the spurt in population size, the factories that demand the introduction of time precision and force a change from the traditional mid-morning and mid-afternoon meals. In some respects the traditional arrangements of Africa and Asia are passing even more swiftly than those of some countries in the West; and it is not because these emerging nations are more liberal, more given to rational examination or that they practise scientific inquiry more widely.

If we take the traditional to be that aspect or attribute of any belief or practice which is repetitive, normative for a given context or set of circumstances, handed down either in writing, orally or in practice, that is, taught by example or by precept, then what is opposed to traditional? Acton, in the tradition reaching back to Max Weber,[4] counterposes rationality to tradition, or rational to traditional. Weber uses rational in the sense of an efficient means to an end, and recognises that it is possible to have a rational means for traditional ends. Economists and other social scientists mean by rational, efficient, or

---

[1] All societies are more or less traditional. Edward Sapir calls attention to the viscosity of traditional arrangements in his article on 'Custom' (*Encyclopedia of the Social Sciences*, New York: Macmillan, 1930–35): 'Belief in the rapidity of change of custom is exaggerated, however, because it is precisely the comparatively slight divergences from what is socially established that arouses attention. A comparison of American life today with the life of a medieval English town would in the larger perspective of cultural anthropology illustrate rather the relative permanence of culture than its tendency to change.'

[2] Adam Curle, 'Tradition, development and planning', *Sociological Review*, N.S. 8, p. 223.

[3] In an epistemological sense, a scientific outlook based on empirical testing of beliefs and practices implies a disposition to discard disconfirmed beliefs or practices that are inefficient in the light of available knowledge. Such a higher order disposition makes for change.

[4] Paul Diesing in *Reason in Society* (Urbana: University of Illinois, 1962) discusses utility and rationality.

'maximum output to input ratio'; in the jargon of social scientists the rational is also that which 'maximises expected utilities'.

People's utilities vary: no single 'rational' way can be found of maximising the 'expected utilities' of the members of a group even in the pursuit of an end common to that group. I shop for food in the supermarket because the speed and convenience of a single stop for shopping 'maximises my utilities'. My wife achieves the same end—but by shopping for food quite differently. She shops in a series of small stores: the meat market, fruit store, dairy, bakery and grocers. She likes the tradesmen; she likes to meet her friends there; she also claims that it is cheaper. It would be irrational for me to shop in small stores, because I wish to save time. But it would be equally irrational for my wife to shop in the supermarket, since she finds it not only impersonal, but expensive. If my prime goal were to save money, then it might be 'rational' for me to shop in small stores. If my wife's prime goal were to save time, then it might be 'rational' for her to shop in the supermarket.

The meaning of rational is uncertain. This problem arises constantly: should the road be absolutely straight, which appears most rational, or should it curve to preserve the shrine where the Founding Fathers deliberated over the Declaration of Independence? One might have to decide (rationally) to have the surgery performed with a 95 per cent chance of a cure, and a 5 percent chance of living out one's life as a vegetable and in pain. Does one 'maximise the expected utilities' or 'minimize the possible losses'? Which is rational?

Except in some vague sense, one does not speak of ends as rational, but only of means. If an action cannot be distinguished from its end, as in writing a poem or shaking hands, then the concept of rationality becomes inapplicable. If an action in principle is distinguishable from its goal, but in practice it is often or always impossible to do so, then the concept loses much of its practical meaning.

If rational conduct is conduct which achieves its goal, then going to a physician to be cured of an illness may be no more rational than the Hopi rain dance. The order of magnitude of the efficiency of both actions is probably the same. And if rational is used to mean 'in accord with the evidence', we get into the difficult problems of confirmation of hypothesis and so on.

The rationality of a certain means to an end becomes hard to judge. A student wants to become rich as a professional and sees that surgeons, say, are the richest group of professionals; he knows he can get into a good medical school; should he become a surgeon even though he swoons at the sight of blood? Would that be rational? Who has only one goal or an ordered hierarchy of discrete values without competing or concomitant goals and values? Alternative courses of action must always be weighed to find one which does not conflict with one's other values or desiderata. Any action taken toward 'maximizing expected utilities' constantly threatens to arouse latent, unexpected values and wants. When these surface, they are likely to get in the way of the set 'rational' course of action which then no longer 'maximizes the expected utilities', for it will lead to collisions with the newly found wants.

In an atomised society in which economic rationality, the maximum ratio of output to input, is demanded by competition, external dis-economies such as air and water pollution undermine the notion of rationality.[1] Economic rationality becomes socially irrational, that is, costly and inefficient. It is also quite appropriate to speak of a tradition of 'rationality' in capitalist countries; and the conduct of members of traditional societies, given their wants, beliefs and utilities, may be considered quite rational.

Deliberate has been counterposed to traditional: one either does the traditional thing or one deliberates. But one may well, and probably does, deliberate as between two traditional courses where they overlap, or when unwonted circumstance has intruded upon the routine. In an open and changing society more opportunities for choice, and more deliberation, occur than in a static society. Changes create new, unfamiliar circumstances which the traditional responses do not suit unambiguously.[2] For in an unchanging society, the norms are set; conflicts between traditionally defined roles are unlikely; and usually but not exclusively the unexpected or catastrophic gives rise to situations to which the traditional behaviour does not apply unambiguously. A choice must then be made; moral reflection or deliberation occurs.

Traditional is the opposite of innovatory, or new, or unique. The 'rational' can be repetitive, taught, and normative, in other words, the traditional thing to do.[3] What will displace the traditional after deliberation is the *new* course of action that is not traditional.

Since innovation takes place in a small portion of all practices, what else is non-traditional then? For instance, it is described as a tradition in certain parts of Germany for the father to cut the loaf of bread for the evening meal. However, that is not all that was traditional: that it was bread and not rice or cassava; that it was baked in the shape of a round loaf and not flat as in the Near East; that it was cut and not torn apart;

---

[1] But, with the decline of competition, this criterion of rationality changes. All sorts of practices which reduce the ratio of output to input become standard. Cf. Alan Harrington, *Life in the Crystal Palace* (New York: Knopf, 1959). Cf. also Kenneth Boulding, *The Skills of an Economist* (Cleveland, 1958), pp. 74 ff.

[2] Cf. Dorothy Emmet, *Rules, Roles and Relations* (New York: St Martin's Press, 1966).

[3] See *Rationalism in Politics*, pp. 80 ff. (London: Methuen, 1962). Oakeshott asserts that the traditional *is* the rational: the term rational is relative to the traditional arrangements and conduct.

that a steel knife was used, not one of flint or bone; that metal utensils and not chopsticks or fingers were plied; that the meal was at evening time; that they sat at a table rather than at a mat on the floor; that they sat on chairs rather than squatted; that they ate together rather than the children with their own mothers in separate huts, and so on. Only the actual ingestion of nutriment was not traditional, but biological.

In all that we do there is an element of the traditional. How then do we distinguish traditions and the traditional from culture and cultural items? 'Cultural phenomena are shared acquired dispositions, all of them dispositions of specific human beings.'[1] Or, we may define 'a "cultural object"' as a "learnable from" item, that is, a cultural object belongs to the class $\hat{\alpha}(\exists x)\ (\exists y)\ (x \neq y$ and $\Diamond(x$ learns α from $y))$ (i.e. belongs to the class of those things α, such that for distinct x and y, it is *possible* that x learns α from $y) \dots$ ' or 'Culture = def $\alpha\ (\exists x)\ (\exists y)\ [x$ learns α from y and $x \neq y]$'.[2]

By this definition $E = mc^2$ is a cultural item before anyone has read it, for it is possible that it be learned from its originator. It could hardly, at that point, be called traditional. To be traditional, a cultural item would also need to be standard for a given reference class, though it would not need to be the only standard practice or belief for that class in those defining conditions; e.g. there are several traditional marriage ceremonies in the United States.

Further, a traditional practice or belief is handed down by one generation of the reference class to the next, which need not be the case for a cultural item. Additionally, the cultural item need have no normative property, whereas traditions do have, in widely varying degreees, a normative character. Without carrying the distinction any further, it is clear that the relationship of a person to a cultural item can be different from his relationship to a traditional practice or belief. All traditional items are cultural; not all cultural items are traditional.

In addition to the learned normative components in any traditional practice, there is an element of the idiosyncratic, unique and personal. Each of us performs the traditional hand-shaking rite differently. Each of us is unique, different from all who have lived, are living, and, very likely, will live. This uniqueness is the result of our infinite constitutional variety and the infinitely diversified things we learn by example or precept. The unique, however, can be more than merely the idiosyncratic. There may also be a creative component; and of these creative

[1] Sidney Morgenbesser, 'Role and status of anthropological theories', *Science*, 8 August 1958, vol. 128, p. 286.
[2] Alan Ross Anderson and Omar Khayam Moore, 'Formal analysis of cultural objects', *Boston Studies in the Philosophy of Science*, 1961/62 (Dordrecht, Holland, 1963), pp. 132, 137.
    Kayaks and yo-yos and other things would be called cultural products, whose manufacture and use are learned.

responses 'It would be naïve to insist that they were only learned and conditioned, although they are caused, and previous learning and conditioning are part of their causes'.[1]

Our beliefs, clothes, activities are all personal combinations and permutations of what we have learned. What we alone have excogitated creatively and taught others, either in equations, or in prose or art forms, is on the whole a small part of all we do and say and are, though it be the most meaningful. Although they are related, the element of the idiosyncratic should be distinguished from the creative, in the sense that Newton, Einstein, Plato and Whitman are creative: their creativity alters the traditional belief or practice. They innovate in the traditions they have received. The idiosyncratic leaves the traditional practice or belief unchanged.

What of matters like 'generational struggle'? The forms of struggle are passed on; the clash is between the traditional, normative behaviour of an adolescent as set by his 'peer group', or his choice of comrades on the one hand, and the parental norms pressed upon him. The clash itself may be inherent in the process of coming to maturity, a sort of psycho-biological recurrent need, shaped by the social environment. For instance, the period of adolescence becomes prolonged with advancing industrialism; at the same time, the environment changes swiftly and differs from one generation to the next. The forms of the struggle, and the issues involved, represent a clash of two sets of traditions, differing more sharply the greater the difference in the environment of the two generations at the period of their maturation. As in eating, there is a recurrent, biophysical as well as social and traditional component.

There is also a tradition of innovation, where what is perennial is change itself in a given social item. The tradition calls for changes in women's clothes and the annual models of automobiles from Detroit. Even the changes themselves seem to follow a tradition.[2]

The model changes in automobiles in the United States are peripheral; seldom is there a large innovation, affecting, for example, front-wheel drive, or the position of the engine. There is, however, a tradition of innovation and of change in the United States where the labels 'old-fashioned' or 'traditional', particularly in technological affairs, imply that their referents 'stand in need of improvement'.

In one of its meanings, tradition refers to the entire process of passing a practice or a belief down, of teaching the young shared and acquired

[1] Morgenbesser, *op. cit.* p. 286.
[2] See Melville Herskovits, 'The processes of cultural change', in Ralph Linton (ed.), *The Science of Man in the World Crisis* (New York: Columbia Univ. Press, 1945). He refers to H. Richardson and A. L. Kroeber, 'Three centuries of women's dress fashions; a quantitative analysis', *Anthropological Records*, v (1940), 111–53.

dispositions to behave, analogous to the process called 'enculturation' by anthropologists. In a correlative usage, tradition refers to the entire bundle of all the arrangements of a society, including speech, food-taking and so on, analogous to the 'culture' of a society, in the anthropologists' sense. In these general meanings, tradition is that which makes us human.[1] However, tradition is also employed to mean a single product of the process of enculturation, or a single strand or component of the culture—say, shaking hands, or academic processions. Not infrequently, failure to distinguish the general from the specific or the process from the product gives rise to a lurking ambiguity in the discussions of tradition.

Professor Oakeshott slips from the employment of tradition to refer to the entire culture or the process of enculturation of a society to the meaning which refers to a single tradition of that society. Thus, '...a society's tradition of behaviour' refers to the 'body of tradition', the culture; similarly in '...a traditional manner of behaviour', the reference is to the manner of behaviour being enculturated. But '...existing traditions of behaviour' refers to traditions, organised collections of individual components of the society. That a society's political arrangements are related to its culture is descriptive, and can be formulated as an empirically verifiable proposition. That a society ought to adhere to a specific tradition—'knowledge, as profound as we can make it, of our tradition of political behaviour' (*Rationalism in Politics*, pp. 123, 128–9) implicitly prescribes a specific tradition, and is something else again.

Professor Oakeshott sometimes uses traditional to refer to the tiny bits and pieces of culture, or of learned dispositions to behave, such as individual components of words, or words themselves, and 'molecular actions' or 'actones'. At other times by 'traditional' he refers to the beliefs and practices composed of these bits and pieces.

Furthermore, that behaviour is culture-bound is one assertion. That the culture is such-and-such is quite another matter. Particular traditions are variegated by socio-economic, regional, religious, and ethnic differences within a nation, especially within a nation in change. There would be no agreement as to what any particular tradition prescribes;

---

[1] 'Man is not born human. It is only slowly and laboriously, in fruitful contact, cooperation and conflict with his fellows, that he attains the distinctive qualities of human nature'. Ernest W. Burgess, Harvey J. Locke and Mary N. Thomas, *The Family* (New York: The American Book Co., 1953), p. 148. Quoted from R. Park and E. W. Burgess, *Introduction to the Science of Sociology* (Chicago, 1921).

An example of the use of 'tradition' in its first meaning by an anthropologist is: 'We are dealing with human beings reacting to situations they continuously project against the body of tradition to which they have been enculturated from the moment of birth.' Melville J. Herskovits, 'Economic change and cultural dynamics' in Braibanti and Spengler, *op. cit.*

certainly only in the broadest (and vaguest) terms could an agreed-upon definition of a political tradition be achieved. What is the traditional American attitude toward education? From the traditionally greater (by far) number of institutions and students of higher education than in other countries, it might be inferred that it is one of appreciation and respect. On the other hand, is it not one of derogation and contempt, as the derisive term 'egg-head' and aspects of the McCarthy movement might suggest? Any tradition is ambivalent, manifold, ambiguous in formulation and prescription. This is not to suggest that Professor Oakeshott is unaware of these distinctions, merely that he sometimes fails to observe them.[1]

When David Hume called custom 'the great guide to life', he included in it the inherited arrangements which order our activity. These traditions govern our activity because we are taught from birth to be active within these patterns. However, changing circumstances render the relevant traditions incoherent, disfunctional, inconvenient or ineffectual; live options are sought, and when discerned, the attempt is made to alter or supersede the no longer functional tradition. Thus, in rural circumstances a large family (particularly sons) provided not only additional means of production, but also security, especially in old age, and was therefore a traditional desideratum. However, industrialism and its attendant urbanisation and population growth gave rise to circumstances in which the traditional large family was disfunctional. Similarly, new conditions give rise to new wants and outlooks; thus with advancing wealth the hedonistic Christmas celebration has replaced the traditionally austere Puritan Christmas.

When John Stuart Mill complained, a century after Hume, that 'the despotism of custom is everywhere the standing hindrance to human advancement', he had in mind the same traditional arrangements that make social (and therefore human) life possible. For the persistence of the traditional attitude toward procreation and the hostility to birth control might well be seen in India today, as a hindrance to human advancement. Since, in a changing society, some traditions are continually being rendered disfunctional by changing circumstances, until over many generations almost all have been altered either slightly or greatly, the same customs which are our great guide to life may, when they persist into changed conditions, become the standing hindrance to human advancement.[2]

---

[1] Cf. Michael Oakeshott, 'A reply to Professor Raphael', *Political Studies*, January 1965.

[2] 'We should be anxious, terrified and frustrated, and we could not live in the social world, did it not contain a considerable amount of order, a great number of regularities to which we can adjust ourselves. The mere existence of these regularities is perhaps more important than their peculiar merits or demerits. They are needed as regularities and are therefore handed on as traditions, whether or not they are in other respects rational or necessary

Because traditional practices are often retained for other ulterior ends, it has been generalised that people cling to tradition always for other, concealed, desiderata; never *qua* tradition. If an individual tradition is meant here, what of the following case? A young man comes to dinner without tie and coat. His mother sends him back to dress properly, and he demurs: 'Why do I have to wear a coat when it's more comfortable this way?' If she answers: 'Because we are not labourers or immigrants', then the tradition of wearing tie and coat to dinner is instrumental to the extent that it enables the family to claim a socially eminent status. However, if his mother answers: 'Because we always come to dinner clothed', isn't the tradition valued *qua* tradition? No justification is offered except that it is what we do because it has been done, as in moral matters into which such matters of etiquette shade.[1] Most of the individual strands of our everyday conduct, individual traditions, like our names or our foods are not reflected upon or justified as if there were live options to them. There are many traditions that each of us enjoys—Christmas dinner, for instance—but do we enjoy them *qua* tradition?[2]

One enjoys the meal, another takes pleasure in the festivities in the bosom of the (extended) family; commercial establishments enjoy the merry jingle of their cash registers at the sale of Christmas gifts; bakeries appreciate the crowds buying the traditional fruit cake. These are all valuing the tradition for other desiderata. There are (even) some who value Christmas as celebrating the birth of Christ; these seem to cherish Christmas as a single religious tradition.

But there may well be Mr T., who inevitably suffers gastric discomfort after the meal; loathes some of the relatives who attend and is an atheist. Yet he nevertheless attends because it is traditional to do so, and insists that his children continue this disagreeable tradition. Such a person would value tradition *qua* tradition, as that which is passed down because it is passed down. He would value not the individual tradition, as almost all of us enjoy some particular traditions, but the process of handing down, and the totality of the received arrangements. He justifies a particular belief by pointing out that it is the received belief; he holds that a practice is valuable because it was followed in the past and handed down to us.

We all obey traditional patterns in the great bulk of our daily activity,

---

or good or beautiful or what you will. There is need for tradition in social life.' Popper, *op. cit.* p. 130. See Oakeshott's description of a body of tradition, or culture, in *Rationalism in Politics*, p. 128.

[1] Etiquette or protocol are traditions which are highly normative, formalised, and even formulated as rules. Traditions such as Christmas dinner are not.

[2] For a statement of the position that tradition is always retained for other, concealed desiderata, see Harold Weisberg, 'Tradition and the Traditionalists', in *Philosophy and Education*, I. Scheffler (ed.) (Boston, 1958).

for they are the arrangements we have learned; most of us honour the forms of propriety and enjoy traditional occasions. However, most of us are readier than Mr T. to alter or abandon the received tradition to suit our convenience or interest, while Mr T. simply sticks to the tradition because it is the tradition.

Mr T., like Hume (and Popper), values tradition (in general) *qua* tradition (not for other desiderata—i.e. *how* it orders affairs). It is a tradition, it imposes order. Are Hume and Popper therefore to be considered traditionalists like Mr T.?

I think not. For they do not resist change; they understand that new arrangements may issue in a more acceptable order. Hume suggests that his perfect commonwealth be attained by such gentle alterations that would not disturb society. And Popper, though not utopian, proposes piecemeal social engineering. A traditionalist opposes all change, clings to traditional arrangements, and formulates his traditionalism 'almost always [as] ideological and extremist'.[1] A traditionalist considers a belief or practice justified because it has been held and practised by those from whom he or his contemporaries have learned it; he believes a practice or a belief has intrinsic utility just because it is the received practice or belief.

THE RISE OF IDEOLOGICAL TRADITIONALISM

We may consider traditionalism, as opposed to tradition, as an ideology which seeks to halt social change and to cling tenaciously to every traditional belief and practice, in the way that a very correct or insecure person might hold fast to the practices prescribed by etiquette or protocol. Ideological traditionalism arose in reaction to the French Revolution.[2] Justus Möser valued tradition because it was a storehouse of wisdom:

> When I come across some old custom or old habit which simply will not fit into modern ways of reasoning, I keep turning around in my mind the

[1] 'Traditionalism is conscious, deliberate affirmation of traditional-norms, in full awareness of their traditional nature and alleging that their merit derives from that tradition, transmitted from a sacred origin. Traditionalism, which is a form of heightened sensitivity to the sacred, demands exclusiveness. It is content with nothing less than totality...Traditionalism is almost always ideological and extremist.' Edward Shils, 'Tradition and liberty: antinomy and interdependence', *Ethics*, vol. LXVIII (April 1958). The notion of sacred origin narrows the definition.

[2] 'Historicism...arose everywhere as a political argument against the revolutionary breach with the past. A mere interest in history becomes historicism when historical facts are not merely lovingly contrasted with the facts of the present, but where "growth" as such becomes a real experience. This is the common meaning of Burke's "continuity", French traditionalism, and German historicism.' Karl Mannheim, 'Conservative thought', *Essays on Sociology and Social Psychology* (New York: Oxford University Press, 1953). Also see Hans Georg Schenk, *Die Kulturkritik der Europäischen Romantic* (Wiesbaden: I. Steiner, 1956).

idea that 'after all, our forefathers were not fools either' until I find some sensible reason for it.[1]

For Burke, the wisdom contained in tradition was more nebulous, but he stands near Möser:

We are afraid to put men to live and trade each on his own private stock of reason; because we suspect that this stock in each man is small and that the individuals would do better to avail themselves of the general bank and capital of the ages and of nations...Only with trembling hand and the greatest of caution will he venture to touch the social institutions in which reason and prejudice are so strongly blended.[2]

One did not need to examine each tradition for the knowledge or wisdom it embodied; Burke assumed that even when indiscernible, that deposit of reason was there and that all that has survived has come down to us because of this content. We should approach social institutions with the greatest caution because excising a traditional practice or institution may yield unintended consequences, for we cannot always see what knowledge resides in the tradition:

In states there are often some obscure and latent causes, things which appear at first view of very little moment, on which a great part of the prosperity or adversity may most essentially depend.[3]

Thus, although the Turkish farmers did not know the wisdom of leaving the stones on the cultivated fields, their adherence to the tradition was a latent cause of successful crops.

Recoiling 'with earnest horror [at] the appearance of unselfish crimes'[4] the bright young men of Europe, and particularly Germany, withdrew their support from the theories of the Enlightenment and the politics of the French Revolution, welcomed Burke's arguments and put them to use to counter the assumption that society and political institutions were mechanisms, to be repaired as one might a clock—by taking it apart and putting it together again. Perhaps the Newtonian world-machine model gave rise to or nourished the notion that society could be understood as a mechanism; perhaps the swift growth of technology fostered mechanical analogies for society. At any rate, the romantics made this mechanical conception of society their target.

Herder had already developed an organicist approach to nature as

---

[1] Justus Möser, *Works*, vol. v, 260. Quoted in Mannheim, *op. cit.* p. 140. Mannheim considers Möser as standing 'completely in the atmosphere of the Enlightenment. His grandfatherly wisdom is sober, practical, rational' (p. 139).

[2] E. Burke, *Reflections on the Revolution in France.*

[3] *Ibid.*

[4] Friedrich Schlegel, *Signatur des Zeitalters* (Wien: Concordia, 1820), p. 9. Quoted by H. G. Schenk, 'Leviathan and the European Romantics', *Cambridge Journal*, vol. i, no. 4 (January, 1948).

well as to society, so that such theories were ready to hand when Gentz's translation of Burke's *Reflections* appeared in 1794. It was not much later that Novalis wrote: 'Society is but communal life; an indivisible thinking and feeling person. Every human is a small society.'[1] No portion of society could therefore be abstracted without affecting the entire organism; radical excisions imperilled the Whole. Neither science nor intellect could disassemble this growing and living, veined and tendoned One into its component Many and their logical relationships. For Adam Müller, the most distinctive of the German Romantic political philosophers,

The state is not a mere factory, a farm, an insurance, an institution or mercantile society, it is the intimate association of all physical and spiritual wealth, of the total internal and external life of a nation into a great, energetic infinitely active and living whole. Science can reproduce neither a lifeless, stationary picture nor a concept of this whole, for death cannot represent life, nor can stagnation represent movement.[2]

But who would call the state a machine, and its members cogs and gears? Who would compare the state with a structure, and its tender, sensitive constituent members with cold masses of stone?[3]

Among the German romantics, society was always in motion, growing, in process though not in progress. The French counter-revolutionaries, expelled by the Revolution, sought regress; the terminus of change was the *status quo ante*. For them tradition hardened into immobility. De Maistre is the distinctive figure here. For him, duration is often the chief criterion by which to evaluate any traditional practice. Man, being evil, corrupt and full of pride, can accomplish nothing by himself: it is his arrogance that leads him to fancy that he can plan and shape human affairs. His endeavours are foredoomed.

Not only do I doubt the stability of the American government, but the particular institutions of English America inspire no confidence in me...it has been decided to build a new town as the seat of the government. The site was chosen on the banks of a great river; it was decided that the town should be called Washington; the situation of all the public buildings was marked out; the work has been set in hand and the plan of the capital city is already circulating throughout Europe. In essentials, there is nothing in this beyond human powers; a town can very easily be built: nevertheless, there is too much deliberation, too much of mankind, in all this, and it is

---

[1] *Novalis Schriften*, herausgegeben von J. Minor (Jena, 1923), Zweiter Band, s. 120, Fragment 44. Tr. mine.

[2] Adam Müller, *Elemente der Staatskunst, zweite Vorlesung*, Tr. in H. S. Reiss, *The Political Thought of the German Romantics* (New York: Macmillan, 1955), p. 150.

[3] Adam Müller, *Elemente der Staatskunst, erste Vorlesung*, Herdflamme edition (Jena, 1922). Tr. mine.

a thousand to one that the town will not be built or that it will not be called Washington, or the Congress will not sit there.[1]

From the view that the traditional contains a wisdom, however obscure, one proceeds to consider with awe that men stored this wisdom in their practices without intending to and unknowingly; then a short step takes one to the notion that men act in accordance with some Super-Individual Wisdom or Society's Purpose; and from there one passes over to the notion that men are God's tools, subserving His Divine wisdom and Design. Any attempt to repudiate The Divine for a human design will not lead towards heaven but will inevitably land men in hell.[2] De Maistre pointed out that the French Revolution, the most ambitious undertaking by men to shape their society, showed that the men who sought to direct events were themselves helplessly swept along by them.[3] Men were the tools of a majestic force. Time shapes events, though its hands are human rather than those of a clock. For Time is 'God's Prime Minister in this World'.[4] An ideological traditionalist who uses duration as his chief criterion of value thinks that nothing should be done for the first time. God and his Prime Minister, Time, have done whatever deserves to be done; men possess no more than a tool's ability to plan and design.[5]

So the reaction to the French Revolution forked in two directions. Burke's emphasis on tradition as a store of social wisdom merged with organicism in the romantic politics of Novalis, Adam Müller and others. These romantics accented the movement and growth of society and their emphasis led to the development of German historicism and organic social and political theory. De Maistre represents the end of the other road: Burke's prescription of change in order to preserve was ignored and his reliance on traditions was converted into an inflexible regressive traditionalism, sterile though understandable in the circumstances.[6]

[1] *The Works of Joseph de Maistre*, edited and translated by Jack Lively (New York: Macmillan, 1965). Considerations on France, Chapter VII, p. 85.

[2] Pascal, Hölderlin and many others have said this.

[3] 'It has been said with good reason that the French Revolution leads men more than men lead it...The very villains who appear to guide the Revolution take part in it only as simple instruments; as soon as they aspire to dominate, they fall ingloriously. Those who established the Republic did so without wishing it and without realizing what they were creating; they have been led by events; no plan has achieved its intended end.' de Maistre, *op. cit.* p. 49.

[4] *Ibid.* p. 161. See also Isaiah Berlin's discussion of de Maistre in *The Hedgehog and the Fox* (New York: New American Library, 1957).

[5] 'Yet it is a truth as certain in its way as a mathematical proposition that no great institution results from deliberation, and that human works are fragile in proportion to the number of men concerned in them and the degree to which science and reasoning have been used a priori.' de Maistre, *op. cit.* p. 82.

[6] Burke's *Thoughts on French Affairs* ends: 'If a great change is to be made in human affairs, the minds of men will be fitted to it; the general opinions and feelings will draw that way.

THE TRADITIONAL AS THE RATIONAL

Tradition, it is sometimes argued, functions in profound and unfathomable ways to serve men; yet the wisdom that lies concealed in traditions, to follow the view affirmed by Möser and Burke, was placed there unwittingly by men as they went about their tasks.[1] De Maistre similarly affirmed this unconscious wisdom: 'Nothing great has great beginnings...no human institution can last...if it [be] not...self-generated, without any previous or known deliberations...it must grow in secret, like a tree'.[2] A century and a half after de Maistre, Friedrich Hayek rephrases the same idea:

By tracing the combined effects of individual actions, we discover that many of the institutions on which human achievements rest have arisen and are functioning without a designing or directing mind; that, as Adam Ferguson expressed it, 'nations stumble upon establishments, which are indeed the result of human action but not the result of human design'; and that the spontaneous collaboration of free men often creates things which are greater than their individual minds can ever comprehend.[3]

De Maistre asserts that men are instruments for the realisation of God's plan; Hegel says that Reason cunningly utilizes men and their passions for its own design; Hayek and Ferguson imply that no design exists at all. However, in *The Constitution of Liberty* Hayek speaks of 'that higher, superindividual wisdom which, in a certain sense, the products of spontaneous social growth may possess'.[4] This seems to offer, by implication, a bridge from the unplanned consequences of the spontaneous actions of men to that of a consequence embodying Society's

---

Every fear, every hope, will forward it; and then they, who persist in opposing this mighty current in human affairs, will appear rather to resist the decrees of providence itself, than the mere designs of men. They will not be resolute and firm, but perverse and obstinate.' If traditions embody wisdom, then whatever traditions exist have survived because of that wisdom. Survival and success then measure the rightness of human endeavour. *Die Weltgeschichte ist das Weltgericht.* And in the *History of the Communist Party of the Soviet Union* Stalin was merely 'fixing' the judge to ensure a favourable verdict.

[1] Oakeshott expresses this unintended function of traditions: 'Consider the view that unless you expressly aim at something it will never be achieved. Nothing could be more manifestly false as a generalization. Those who look with suspicion on an achievement because it was not part of the design will, in the end, find themselves having to be suspicious of all the greatest human achievements. The doctrine that a thing either does not exist or at least is worthless if it is not planned, and that unforeseen consequences are a sign of failure, is a piece of extravagance.' *Cambridge Journal*, vol. II, no. 9, p. 532.

[2] De Maistre, *op. cit.* pp. 158, 172.

[3] Friedrich A. Hayek. *Individualism and Economic Order* (Chicago: University of Chicago, 1948), p. 7. The Ferguson quotation is from *An Essay on the History of Civil Society*, 1st ed., 1767, and is cited along with many other similar quotations in an excellent footnote on p. 7. All quotations from Hayek, unless otherwise noted, are from this essay.

[4] *The Constitution of Liberty* (Chicago: University of Chicago, 1960), p. 110.

Purpose, and from there it is but a short step to divine purpose and back to de Maistre.[1]

Karl Menger, the Austrian economist, had pointed out:

> ...it is obvious that we have here a certain analogy between the *nature and the function* of natural organisms on the one hand and social structure on the other.
>
> The same is true with respect to the *origin* of a series of social phenomena. Natural organisms almost without exception exhibit, when closely observed, a really admirable functionality of all parts with respect to the whole, a functionality which is not, however, the result of human *calculation*, but of a *natural* process. Similarly we can observe in numerous social institutions a strikingly apparent functionality with respect to the whole. But with closer consideration they still do not prove to be the result of an *intention aimed at this purpose*, i.e. the result of an agreement of members of society or of positive legislation. They too present themselves to us rather as 'natural' products (in a certain sense), as unintended results of historical development.[2]

Menger discusses both the formation and operation of these practices and institutions, like 'money, law, language, the origins of markets, of communities, of states, etc.' which reveal 'a really admirable functionality of all parts'. The formation of these institutions fills him with wonder:

> How can it be that institutions that serve the common welfare and are extremely significant for its development come into being without a common will directed toward establishing them?[3]

From the formation of such institutions, Hayek draws these conclusions among others:

> The necessity of the individual submitting to the anonymous and seemingly irrational forces of society.
>
> The fundamental attitude of true individualism is one of humility toward the process by which mankind has achieved things which have not been designed or understood by any individual and are indeed greater than individual minds.[4]

Are these conclusions justified? From the statesment: (a) '...we discover that *many* of the institutions' and (b) '...the spontaneous collaboration of free men *often* creates things which are greater than

---

[1] In this connection: Dorothy Emmet, *Function, Purpose and Powers* (New York: St Martin's Press, 1958), provides interesting and illuminating reading.

[2] Karl Menger, *Problems of Economics and Sociology*, tr. by Francis J. Nock, edited, and with an introduction by Louis Schneider (Urbana: University of Illinois, 1963), pp. 130, 146. The original was published in 1883. Schneider's introduction discusses Hayek and Menger's views on social formations as unintended consequences. The basic works are Robert Merton's paper, 'The unanticipated consequences of purposive social action', *American Sociological Review*, 1 (1936), 894. Also Merton, *Social Theory and Social Structure* (Glencoe: The Free Press, 1957), chapter 1 and *passim*.

[3] Karl Menger, *op. cit.* p. 146.   [4] Hayek, *op. cit.* p. 24.

their individual minds can ever comprehend' [my italics] we are now committed not only to some institutional processes and certain of their consequences, but to these processes in general and to whatever they may produce—such as war, Highland feuding, jim crow, mendicancy and so on. Menger considers this process of social evolution analogous to that of natural evolution.[1] This analogy leads us to a view which is close indeed to that of the traditionalists.

If the analogy with evolution and natural selection is pursued, then most institutions, like most new mutations, would have harmful effects and would not serve the common welfare. Secondly, to see if an institution is injurious or beneficial, we would need some criteria, applicable over a long period of time. Certainly, many institutions have caused their practitioners to decline.

Furthermore, many institutions have been imposed and maintained by a minority whose material interests these institutions served. Not to get too close to home, Chinese civilisation as described by Weber, Wittfogel and others, offers a long documentation. Nor can it simply be stated that, e.g., slavery was a product of many choices, a sort of freely chosen institution. Certainly it did not arise by natural selection from the countless choices of slaves themselves.

Hayek goes even further than awe in his contemplation of these unconscious social processes. He considers that a functional harmony obtains in society ordaining who shall do what in accord with preordained talents and abilities properly distributed:

> If all men were completely equal in their gifts and inclinations, we should have to treat them differently in order to achieve any sort of social organization. Fortunately, they are not equal; and it is only owing to this that the differentiation of functions need not be determined by the arbitrary decision of some organizing will but that, after creating formal equality of the rules applying in the same manner to all, we can leave each individual to find his own level.[2]

There is no reason to believe that the right number of college professors, carpenters, politicians are born. And what is the right number

---

[1] Cf. '...the operation of what Pepper has called "natural selective" systems. The ultimate agency of the selection is the human being; not the expert, however, but the unconscious choice of countless people.' Paul Diesing, *Reason in Society* (Urbana: The Univ. of Illinois, 1962), p. 6. The reference is to S. C. Pepper, *The Sources of Value* (Berkeley: Univ. of California, 1958).

Oakeshott describes this process thus: '...[communal activity] is the product, not (of course) of design but of numberless, long forgotten choices.' *Rationalism in Politics*, p. 249.

These accounts ignore the existence of unequal clumps of power, and the likelihood that the choices were made, if the accounts have any validity, by a relative few who had the power and position to make choices that were accepted by or imposed upon the rest. 'The strong did what they could, and the weak suffered what they must.'

[2] Hayek, *op. cit.* p. 15.

for the 'jet set'? In fact, the free market, whose operations have so impressed Hayek, uses inducements and penalties to distribute people so that jobs get done. Hayek stretches Adam Smith's notion of the invisible hand to the point where it ensures that no 'mute, inglorious Milton' or village Hampden will remain so.

Adam Smith was speaking of the *operation*, not the *formation*, of the *market*, not of *all* institutions, when he said that people, as they go about their self-interested business, seem to be guided by an invisible hand to promote the common welfare.[1] Smith did not think that all traditional arrangements served the common welfare: charters of monopoly, which were traditional if not natural, were restrictive. Merchants' conspiracies, which were natural as well as traditional, were also evil, impeding the spontaneous, self-interested pursuits of free men. They were, by design, eliminated by positive action.

In fact, however, the operation of the economy and the free market has had many undesired results:

Crises occurred approximately every ten years—in 1815, 1825, 1836, 1847, 1857 and 1866 in England—and in about the same sequence in all capitalist countries...In the age of mass production after 1870, depressions became longer and more severe.[2]

Would Menger have marvelled so at the glories of the economy if he had seen Vienna in the Thirties? Partly as a consequence of the Thirties, the processes of the market are today by no means so undesigned. The spontaneous activities of men in pursuit of their self-interested business are constrained by factory legislation; by governmental agencies (in the United States) like the FCC, FTC, SEC and many others; pricing and quality regulations; government subsidies, as in transport, and government competition, as in housing; welfare state provisions; unions; minimum wages and maximum hours, all of which impede the free play of the labour market, and numerous other interventions that have made the market a very different affair from the one Adam Smith observed. These positive laws were designed to alter the operations of the market to eliminate its most distressing effects, and certainly fit Menger's definition of design, i.e. the result of an agreement of members of society or of positive legislation. So far, since the most elaborate interventions in the economy in the Thirties, we have had the longest period in our history without economic crisis.

There is, understandably in Menger, a nineteenth-century evolutionary approach strongly reminiscent of Spencer and social Darwinism.

---

[1] In *The Wealth of Nations*.
[2] Dudley Dillard, 'Capitalism after 1850' in *Chapters in Western Civilisation* (3rd ed., New York: Columbia Univ. Press, 1961), II, 297.

The market economy served not the general or common welfare, but the welfare of those able to shape the economy to suit their own needs and able to maintain it thus until those for whom it was disfunctional attained enough power to force alterations. Similarly, it is questionable whether language can be considered so perfect a formation if criteria more exacting than those of Menger be applied. Menger also marvels at the law; but between the Sophists and Marx, there are many like Novalis and Pascal, who point out that the law, far from serving the common welfare, serves the welfare of the stronger groups.[1] How common is the welfare that an institution serves? This is one question the Menger–Hayek theory must answer. The other question is: how *perfect* are those institutions, like language, which do serve the common welfare? Are they more admirably functional than our bodies and all the ills they are heir to? Our backs, so poorly suited to erect posture; our eyes so nearsighted when compared to those of birds; our inferior sense of smell and hearing; our musculature and coordination so botched compared to those of cats; out inept structure, compared to ants. These flaws of our physical evolutionary development find their poorer counterparts in all the institutions whose analogous functionality Menger and Hayek find so awe-inspiring. Further, Hayek asserts that

Man, in a complex society can have no choice but between adjusting himself to what to him must seem the blind forces of the social process and obeying the orders of a superior.[2]

This is the choice between subordination to the social process made up of individual spontaneous actions which leads to progress, and subordination to the planned or purposeful social action which, like the spontaneous process, also involves coercion. In addition, however, the planned or purposive action retards 'social advance':

...for advance to take place, the social process from which the growth of reason emerges must remain free from its control....

...We are not far from the point where the deliberately organized forces of society may destroy these spontaneous forces which have made advance possible.[3]

To 'plan' or 'organize' the growth of mind, or for that matter, progress in general, is a contradiction in terms.[4]

---

[1] *Novalis Fragmente*. Herausgegehen von Ernst Kamnitzer (Dresden, 1929), p. 481.

[2] Hayek, *op. cit.* p. 24.

[3] Friedrich Hayek, *The Constitution of Liberty* (Chicago: Univ. of Chicago Press, 1960), p. 38.

[4] Friedrich Hayek, *The Road to Serfdom* (Chicago: Univ. of Chicago Press, 1944), p. 165. Cf. 'It may indeed be said that it is the paradox of all collectivist doctrine and its demand for "conscious" control or "conscious" planning that they necessarily lead to the demand that the mind of some individual should rule supreme—while only the individualist approach to social phenomena makes us recognize the super-individual forces which guide the growth of reason. Individualism is thus an attitude of humility before this social process...' *Ibid.* p. 166. The terms 'progress' and 'advance' are Hayek's.

Hayek implies here that *all* consequences, good and evil, in social affairs are unintended by men. If the action be purposively social, the social consequences are unintentionally harmful. If the action be individual and spontaneous, the social consequences are unintentionally beneficial. The message resembles the advice attributed to a Chilean politician: 'Some problems are insoluble; the rest solve themselves.'[1]

Because the formation of *some* institutions that were useful took place without social design, the conclusion is drawn by De Maistre and Hayek that *all* institutions that arise without social design are useful. From this it is inferred that *all* institutions thus formed operate for the common welfare so long as men use them without social design, i.e. spontaneously. The further implications are that an institution that is *designed* by agreement or legislation will be disfunctional; that an institution that is altered by agreement or legislation will run counter to the common welfare; and that *all* social action by agreement will harm the general welfare by retarding 'progress'. The passage is made in a series of non-sequiturs from *some* beneficial unintended consequences of men's social inaction to the ineluctably injurious unintended consequences of *all* deliberate social action. Hayek's outlook is close to that of the romantic traditionalists. It was, after all, the unintended consequences of the French Revolution that first disenchanted the bright young men of Germany; Burke warned against such consequences. And to explain these unintended 'unselfish crimes' the romantics elaborated the notion of society as organic, as a natural growth in which all parts are interrelated and functional as in a living being.

The connection between the beneficial unintended consequences of spontaneous individual action (u.c. 1) and the injurious unintended consequences of men's planned social action (u.c. 2) is provided by Professor Robert K. Merton.[2] The institutions of which Menger speaks

---

[1] Another view of the matter is offered by Cowling, who considers politics '...an uncertain, broken-backed activity which is saved from triviality chiefly by the ambition of politicians, the continuity of habits and institutions and the permanent interests of persons and groups; and that almost all public discussion, from our ignorance of the future and the difficulty of anticipating the accidents of political decision, decides not what is to be done (although that is the conventional pretence maintained), but which party or group shall command sufficient support to make the decisions.' He contends that unintended consequences make a mockery of *all* political activity. 'Politicians [pretend] that they intended the consequences.' Maurice Cowling, *The Nature and Limits of Political Science* (Cambridge Univ. Press, 1963), p. 119.

'Thus, whenever there is innovation there is the certainty that the change will be greater than was intended, that there will be loss as well as gain and that the loss and gain will not be equally distributed among the people affected; there is the chance that the benefits derived will be greater than those which were designed; and there is the risk that they will be offset by changes for the worse.' Michael Oakeshott, *op. cit.* p. 172. See also p. 124.

[2] *Social Theory and Social Structure*, chap 1. This chapter on unintended consequences follows Merton's earlier and fuller discussion, 'The unanticipated consequences of purposive social action', in the *American Sociological Review*, 1 (1936), 894.

as serving the common welfare and the wisdom the Romantics saw embodied in traditions are for Merton 'latent functions' unrecognized and unintended by its practitioners, 'social windfalls'.[1] The Democratic Clubhouse may have among its manifest functions the election of candidates and the distribution of patronage. Prominent among its latent functions, however, is the provision of an unofficial means of communication between the economically important underworld and the city officials. If purposive social action seeks to eliminate the corrupt party clubhouse, it will produce unintended consequences (U.C. 2) because it has not provided a functional alternative by which the latent function[2] of the clubhouse is performed.

The lineage from Burke and the Romantics, who saw every tradition as fulfilling some function, even if undiscerned, to the traditionalists like de Maistre, to Oakeshott and to current functional analysis which holds that society is an organism whose practices and institutions are interrelated functionally, is clear. Organicism and the functional interrelationships of cultural items is common to the divergent outlooks held by conservative liberals like Burke, romantic politicos like Adam Müller, traditionalists like de Maistre, contemporary conservative liberals like Hayek, liberal conservatives like Oakeshott and liberal supporters of social planning like Merton.[3]

Merton proposes that we forestall unintended consequences by searching out the latent function of a practice or institution we want to dismantle or change. Do you wish to replace the small grocers in a poor neighbourhood by chain stores that will presumably offer better wares at lower prices? Merton advises one to seek out the latent function (U.C. 1) of the small grocer—he may offer needed credit to his impoverished customers, which the chain store will not do, with the unintended result (U.C. 2) that there will be hunger and emergency calls for welfare toward the end of the week; or possibly the small grocer offers shelter during inclement seasons in a community (e.g. Puerto Rican) whose subculture calls for the men to gather in the evening. These latent functions must be provided for, although, of course, they are latent neither to the grocer, nor to his customers. Perhaps they are to the Housing Authority.

Before continuing, it may be useful to tidy up our usages. An action

---

[1] *Social Theory and Social Structure*, p. 129. 'Latent functions' and 'social windfalls' are UC. 1.

[2] Latent functions therefore, for Merton, are the wisdom embodied in seemingly irrational practices. (*Ibid.* p. 64.)

[3] 'To seek social change, without due recognition of the manifest and latent functions performed by the social organisation undergoing change is to indulge in social ritual rather than social engineering.' Merton, *op. cit.* p. 81. Merton and Oakeshott, however, do not share the conception of tight integration of society that some of the organicists, particularly Novalis, Müller, and anthropologists like Malinowski (mainly students of pre-literate societies), seem to hold. See Merton, *Social Theory and Social Structure*, chapter 1.

has many ramifying consequences that we can roughly classify as follows. (1) Direct or primary are those immediate consequences of the action which bear upon the aims of the agents. These promote or retard the achievement of the goal of the agents. (2) Secondary consequences bear upon other related objectives of the agents; that is, secondary consequences may promote related goals and be welcome to the agents, as the entrance into teaching of Peace Corps graduates promoted a secondary objective of the Administration. On the other hand, secondary consequences may also be injurious to other related goals and be undesirable and unwelcome to the agents, like the growth of gangsterism during Prohibition. More remote consequences, which are never all in, may be ignored for the purposes of this discussion.[1]

A consequence is intended only if it is the aim or goal of the agents. A medieval church decree forbade raising the price of grain during a famine. The primary consequence—which was to keep grain off the market—was unanticipated and unintended. What had happened was that those who had the grain feared to violate the decree, yet refused to sell it at prices below what the grain could command. Thus, the consequence was directly contrary to the aim of the agents, since the famine was intensified rather than alleviated. (If the decree had been ignored, and the prices been raised, that should not be considered an unintended consequence in our usage. Many acts are inconsequential or ineffective in respect to the intention of the agents.)

Primary consequences may be anticipated and intended, as in the case of Unemployment Insurance. A primary consequence cannot be unanticipated and intended, although it may be anticipated and unintended, as in the case of death following risky surgery. Secondary consequences also may be anticipated and unintended, as in the case of the WHO physicians who eradicate a disease endemic to a land by using penicillin, although they are aware that a secondary consequence will be a swifter rise in population than in food supply, resulting in widespread hunger. The drop in the rate of crimes committed by Negroes in Montgomery, Alabama, during the bus boycott was an unanticipated, unintended and welcome secondary consequence. In the case of

---

[1] Any action will have unintended consequences. A. C. Bradley points out that tragedy may be viewed this way (*Shakespearean Tragedy*, Cleveland: World Publishing Co., 1955, p. 32). If I speak loudly to my companion in a restaurant, I may make it impossible for a waitress to hear a patron's request, as a result of which the dyspeptic patron creates a scene and the waitress is dismissed, with weighty consequences for her. Similarly, purposive social action may have countless unintended consequences which are, however, neutral to the intentions of the agents. As a result of the institution of free higher education, thousands of young couples have met in class, fallen in love and married. If, however, there should be a staggering rise in the number of out-of-wedlock children born to students, this may prove to be a secondary, rather than a remote or neutral, consequence bearing on the related goals of the agents, particularly in the United States.

gangsterism during Prohibition, we have an unanticipated, unintended and unwelcome secondary consequence.

Before a consequence can be labelled as unintended, it is important to know what the actual consequence is. The primary consequence would be the end aimed at, if achieved. Thus, although Prohibition is often cited as an example of legislation whose consequence was perverse to the intention, the fact is that the primary intention of its vociferous proponents was to reduce heavy drinking among the poor and working classes, and that this was the primary consequence of their activities. The increase in the consumption of alcohol among the middle and upper classes was one of many unintended, secondary consequences: such as widespread violation of the law; an increase in criminal and gangster activity; death from toxic liquors; and the corruption of government officials. But the primary consequence was not unintended since the primary intention was attained: the evidence shows that there was a sharp decline in drunkenness among the poor.[1]

It is important to know the intention, as well as the consequences. Soviet agriculture is cited as a terrifying example of intervention in the natural economic processes. But what was the intention of the Communist Party rulers when they collectivised agriculture? The best opinion is that the intention was not to raise agricultural production, but to facilitate the collection of grain and produce from the peasantry; to break up the traditional form of peasant life; to impose stronger control over the peasants and so on. Collectivisation did achieve these ends.[2]

Sometimes unintended consequences arise because of sheer ignorance that could have been remedied. Countless stories told by UN experts recount these instances: experts thought to improve the inadequate village diet by fattening the cattle. Upon their return six months later they found the cattle fatter but the people leaner, for they had given their food to the cattle: they refused to eat their cattle because they considered them members of the family, more kin than kine. Such unintended consequences are avoidable.[3]

Sometimes the consequence is anticipated though undesired by the agent, but the considerations are overriding, as in the example above of eradicating endemic diseases.

The intentions of the agent are not clear when more than one aim is held. Two aims—subsidised housing for the poor and urban renewal—appear in the preamble to the first federal Housing Act in the United

[1] Martha S. Bruère, *Does Prohibition Work?* (New York and London: Harper Bros., 1927), p. 18.
[2] I. P. Halpern: *Stalin's Revolution: The Struggle to collectivize rural Russia, 1927–1933.* Ph.D. dissertation, Columbia University, 1965. Publication forthcoming.
[3] Margaret Mead, *Cultural Patterns and Technical Change* (New York: Mentor Books, 1955).

States. City officials tended to emphasise the urban renewal aims of the Act, for it removed eyesores and raised real estate values. This, however, led to the demolition of more dwelling units than new construction provided for the displaced slum dweller, so that the housing purpose of the Act was frustrated. Mutually frustrating intentions not infrequently result from compromises made in committee of legislative bodies. Inevitably some unanticipated, undesired consequences will follow. And since politics is carried on by coalitions in many countries of the West, a variety of goals compete in legislative committee majorities.[1]

Do the consequences attributed to the social action of the agent to effect stipulated purposes really result from that act?

Social Security measures were enacted to make receipt of assistance a matter of right, to eliminate the need for direct relief and assistance. Millions now receive social security benefits. Yet the relief rolls grow and the sums spent on direct assistance mount.[2]

The social intention was to make people insure themselves against destitution in old age and in the event of disability. Has it successfully achieved this? To the extent that adequate insurance payments are made to the aged and survivors, yes. Do the relief costs to people receiving social security payments grow more than, as much as, or less than they would have grown had there been no social security payments? That requires investigation, but *prima facie*, the rolls are reduced by the amount of the insurance payments. But Friedman implies that the relief rolls grow as a *consequence* of social security payments. The swelling of the relief rolls is primarily the result of racial discrimination and the growing unemployability of the unskilled because of the upgrading of skills in the job mix in the northern cities at a time of growing immigration of unskilled workers from rural areas in the South and Puerto Rico. The rise in the cost of living and in acceptable standards of living has also led to a rise in welfare costs. And whatever relief is paid to recipients of Social Security is to eke out inadequate payments.

Frank Knight points out that in social action one must be able to say what the effects would have been of social inaction as well as of social action. The problem lies in knowing what would have happened had a course other than the one pursued been followed. In Friedman's example, it is incumbent upon him to say what the results of not having the Social Security self-insurance programme would have been, in our urban industrial society. Those consequences, with a growing proportion

---

[1] See Milton Friedman, *Capitalism and Freedom* (Chicago: Univ. of Chicago Press, 1962), pp. 178 ff.

[2] *Ibid.* See especially the last chapter. He describes as unintended consequences a series of effects of social welfare legislation.

of the elderly, might well have been the least desirable of all. We might indeed have been overwhelmed by Hayek's natural processes, as we were during the Thirties. The enormous changes set in motion by our runaway technology, by our shift from a rural to an urban environment, the rise in the expectations of the citizenry, and their widening political participation, make it clear that, if social action leads to unintended consequences, social inaction may lead to much graver ones.

FUNCTIONAL ANALYSIS OF UNINTENDED CONSEQUENCES

Merton's explanation of unintended consequences is a sophisticated functionalism: u.c. 1 arise as items performing functions 'unrecognized and unintended' by its practitioners. u.c. 2 arise when u.c. 1 are eliminated without otherwise satisfactorily providing for the performance of the latter's latent functions. The general functionalist thesis asserts that cultural items are interrelated in such a way that they operate to maintain a homeostasis in the society, much as a thermostat operates to maintain a room at a given temperature or within a given temperature range.

When a disturbance in one or more of a series of factors threatens to throw an essential variable outside the range 'necessary' for the stability of the system, other compensatory factors come into operation to restore that important variable within the range that enables the system to remain at homeostasis. Thus, in the instance of the small grocer in a poor neighbourhood, the food supply of his patrons would be cut off when their money ran out, thus throwing this important variable (food supply) below the limits necessary for the stability of the system. But the small grocer, by extending credit, restores the quantity of food supplied within the range necessary to maintain the homeostasis (u.c. 1). Now, if the small grocer is eliminated and no satisfactory alternative is made available, then, when money runs out, the variable of food supply will fall below the value necessary to sustain the ongoing system and there will be no compensating mechanism to restore it: an unintended consequence (u.c. 2).

Unlike many functional analysts, Merton does not consider all social formations, institutions and items as functional. Thus he eliminates any general teleological theory, like Malinowski's, that every 'cultural or social item' serves a function necessary for the maintenance of society.[1] Such a statement is either a tautology or impossible to falsify, for if the

---

[1] Bronislaw Malinowski, 'Anthropology', *Encyclopedia Britannica* (New York and London, 1936), supp. vol. 1, pp. 132–3. For other functionalist points of view, see Paul Collins's forthcoming book on *Functionalism in the Social Sciences* (New York: Random House). Also, Don Martindale (ed.), *Functionalism in the Social Sciences* (Philadelphia: Academy of Political Sciences, 1965). A collection of essays pro and con functional analysis.

function is not apparent, it is said to be merely hidden but nevertheless there.

There are, however, other difficulties with Merton's analysis of unintended consequences. The notion of latency in the function is not wholly satisfactory. A function of a social item is latent if the 'objective consequences [of that function] contributing to the adjustment or adaptation of the system are neither recognized nor intended by the participants in the system'.[1] The function that is latent is recognised by the sociologist; it is unrecognised by the participant. Can the latent function of extending credit be said to be unrecognised by the small grocer's needy patrons? Is the latent function of the Democratic Clubhouse—to serve as a means of communication between underworld and City Hall—not recognized by the underworld characters or the club leader? Or is the participant the rank-and-file member from whom the 'objective consequences contributing to the adjustment or adaptation of the system' are hidden? (If the participant is one for whom the institution serves a latent function, then the definition is merely circular.) It is not likely, however, that a rank-and-file club member, a genuine 'participant' in the club, will be unaware that a club leader, on being given a list of telephone calls he has been asked to return, usually telephones the underworld leader on his list first, before getting around to the Congressman or Mayor.[2] This function of the clubhouse, as a needed channel between a large, though illicit, economic activity and the city officials, may be latent from other members of the whole system, but not from the participants in the operation of this institution or those whom it serves.

Obviously it is the participant in the practice or item that is meant. For instance, the rain-dance among Southwest Indians is not a satisfactory meteorological device. It is continued we are told because it performs the latent function of a pre-Spring-sowing festival. The rain dancers are genuine participants in an institution which serves only a latent function—its manifest function is to bring rain. However, I am told that anthropologists in the field will often find, upon interrogating members of the society they are studying, that these members are aware of the latent function the anthropologist has assigned to a particular practice.

The propriety of the term 'latent' is questionable where the sociologist intends by it that the participant is unaware of some subsidiary purpose which the function serves.[3] It might be countered, however,

[1] Merton, *op. cit.* p. 51.
[2] Fred J. Cook and G. Gleason, 'The shame of New York', *The Nation*, vol. 189 (31 October 1959).
[3] When Merton refers latent function to purpose, he makes it clear that he refers to the failure of other participants to recognise what purposes are fulfilled. See below. George M.

that the participants are not aware how the 'objective consequences' of their activity contribute to the adjustment or adaptation of the system; that, in other words, the participant does not see the 'latent function' as it operates in a chain of interlinked factors maintaining the stability of the system. Such an explanation, it seems to me, would confuse the perspective of the observer-sociologist with the perspective of the objects of his study. Nor is it established that every consequence of every item affects the system as a whole.

Further, 'unrecognized and unintended' are separable notions. A consequence or 'function' may be unintended but recognised at once when it appears. Many combinations and permutations are, therefore, possible. For instance, we can discern three separate actors in this matter of unintended consequences, or latent functions. There are the participants in an item: the grocer and his poor customers, or the leaders and members of the Democratic Club. There are the agents of social change: those who have the power to effect alterations in an item. (The City Housing Authority is an agent but not a participant. Reform politicians and movements, however, may be participants as well as agents.) Lastly, there may be observers, or social scientists, who are neither participants or agents. Some observers, however, as in the case of economists in the employ of the legislature, may be agents as well as participants. A function therefore may be recognized by participants, and latent from agents and observers; it may be intended by one and unrecognised by the others, and so on. 'Objective consequences' are what the observer is expected to discern. They will often seem 'irrational' to him, and to the agent who is not a participant, if the item is embedded in a different culture or subculture. To leave stones on the cultivated field was 'irrational' to the UN agronomists. 'Functional' or 'disfunctional' 'objective consequences' depend upon the purpose assigned to the system containing the item as the system is individuated by the assessor.

There are instances in which a practice fulfils functions which are unrecognised by the practitioners. Thus, in one family the chore of washing the dinner dishes fell to the father and daughter. When a dishwashing machine was installed, the father came to be aware that the one period of the day in which he engaged in talk and common activity with his daughter had been eliminated. Dishwashing had served not only the manifest function of cleaning the dinner dishes; it had offered a time for visiting between father and daughter. Another function of

Foster, *Traditional Cultures and the Impact of Technological Change* (New York: Harper Bros., 1962), offers many instances in which unintended consequences arise because the functions fulfilled by a practice, e.g. washing clothes in the river, are latent from the sociologist and other technicians.

the arrangement may have been to enable the mother to rest and the brother to do his school work. In other words, items serve more than one function; some of these functions *may* be latent to some of the practitioners.

However, in the instance just mentioned, the manifest function was being fulfilled. The dishes were being washed. Merton and Hayek, however, emphasise those items in which the manifest function is not being fulfilled, or is being 'irrationally' done, so that the practice seems irrational because in fact the important function is latent. Thus, retaining the small grocer seems 'irrational' when he can easily and profitably be replaced by a glittering supermarket. In that case, however, the function that is latent, i.e. extending credit, is latent from and seems irrational to the observer, not the participants. If the father and daughter insisted on washing the dishes manually while the machine was left idle, that 'irrational' practice would soon enough need to be explained.

Merton also relates function to the purpose of the participants: a manifest function serves the 'avowed purpose' of the participants. It is implied that a latent function, on the other hand, serves the unavowed purpose of the participants. Why do people fail to avow their purposes?[1]

Two reasons for the failure to avow a purpose may be distinguished: first, the participant may himself be unaware of his purpose. It remains in his unconscious, repressed by the 'super-ego'. The purpose then is unavowed even to the agent himself. The second reason is that the participant is aware of his purpose, but will not publicly avow it. In this event, the avowal is relative to the public to whom the avowal is made or from whom it is withheld.

Merton uses as an example of latent function the case of Veblen's conspicuous consumption, in which possessions are bought because they are expensive and will be recognised as expensive by those to whom they are displayed. A patently expensive car displayed by someone raised in the Puritan tradition serves as a sign of his pecuniary achievement, as an index of his likelihood of being among the elect as well as of his success as an American. His desire thus to proclaim his status may be unconscious, for it has been thoroughly repressed by his Calvinist super-ego. Even to himself he may explain his purchase of the Rolls-Royce by reference to its superior merit. Or it may be that he is aware

---

[1] Merton describes a latent function as one which is unrecognised and unintended. As I have mentioned, an unintended function may well be recognised; and a function unintended by the founders (e.g. of the Democratic Party Club) may well come to be recognised. Some of the founders may even come to intend that function for the club of serving as intermediary between underworld and Officialdom.

As to unavowed: a purpose may be intended and unavowed. It may even be unintended and (later) avowed, as Cowling points out above. And a recognised function may remain unavowed.

of the purpose of his purchase, but explains it to his mother or his minister as in the long run inexpensive, because of its superlative construction. He is violating moral norms. His explanation to his mother is hypocritical: the tribute vice pays to virtue. It may also be that our affluent Puritan avows his purpose quite freely to his wife and close friends: 'That will knock them over', he gloats, but only to a small group. Is this still an unavowed purpose?

In social and political matters purposes may also be unavowed. The arrangement may be so thoroughly seen by the agent as the way things ought to be that the fact that the arrangement serves *his* purpose is rendered invisible. The agent then has a false consciousness, an ideology in Marx's sense.[1] Thus, the tacit assumption in the Debates in the Army Council is said to have been that servants could not vote because they had sold their independence to their employer. The debaters were not aware that this unspoken assumption served their own social purposes by keeping workers employed by them politically as well as socially powerless. The latent function of this arrangement served the unavowed (even to themselves) purpose of the debaters. Many similar instances could be found in the field of relations of whites with Negroes in the United States. However, a white trade unionist who opposes the admission of Negroes to his union because he dislikes Negroes or fears their competition for the limited jobs in the craft dare not say so publicly. He will justify their exclusion on the grounds of their inability to qualify for the status of journeyman. This unavowed purpose is one of which the agent is quite aware.

Unavowed purposes of which the agent is unconscious may be expected to decline as hedonistic values are more widely accepted and as men's desires and purposes become more recognisable and acceptable by a more sophisticated, Freud-oriented, self-aware society. Purposes that were previously suppressed by the super-ego are allowed to emerge into consciousness and may be unashamedly avowed. In such a situation, both u.c. 1 and u.c. 2 arising from unavowed purposes may be expected to decline.

Similarly, if the inversions of ideology are dissipated in an affluent society in which the gap between rich and poor has been narrowed, poverty eliminated, and some sort of tentative social scientific approach to social and political matters has become pervasive, we may even expect a decline in the purposes unavowed to oneself because of 'ideological' suppression, as well as a reduction in the number of instances

---

[1] Marx means by ideology taking the idea to be the independent variable; it is a 'false consciousness'; an inability to understand the 'true' factors at work, a 'mystification of the real' economic factors. See the *Introduction to the German Ideology*; also *The Eighteenth Brumaire of Louis Napoleon*.

of conscious but unavowed purposes.[1] The avowal of purpose is relative to the time, place and the public to whom the avowal is made or from whom it is withheld. So also are the unintended consequences which are thus engendered because the unavowed purposes lead to functions 'latent' from the public from whom the purpose is concealed.[2]

A MARXIST ANALYSIS OF UNINTENDED CONSEQUENCES

Merton offers another approach to the terms functional and disfunctional by suggesting that rather than seeing the functions or disfunctions as the 'objective consequences' of the item for the system, functions and disfunctions relate directly to people:

persisting cultural forms have a net balance of functional consequences either for the society considered as a unit or for subgroups sufficiently powerful to retain these forms intact, by means of direct coercion or indirect persuasion.[3]

It hardly seems likely that a practice maintained by coercion or persuasion is 'latent' from both subgroups of practitioners. But with this suggestion Merton offers us a path into an alternative theory of unintended consequences, or, with enough polishing and fitting, a complementary theory. For if items are maintained by coercion, or come to be recognised as disfunctional for some and functional for others, conflict will probably arise between the groups. And, whether it be in an organisation or a village or a state, the conflict is likely to be political in the broad sense of that word. And in politics, Tocqueville remarked,

men mutually push each other away from their respective plans...the destinies of this world proceed as the result, but often as the contrary result, of the intentions that produce them....[4]

Engels, like most traditional functionalists, was a monist; he explained unintended consequences as Tocqueville did:

[1] Such a society is envisioned by Herbert Marcuse in *Eros and Civilization* (New York: Vintage Books, Random House, 1962).

[2] Of course, it may also be possible that a practice fulfilling 'latent functions' may be eliminated and no functional alternative established. The unavowed purpose goes unfulfilled, or is simply dissipated. Thus, when a change of schedules made the subway line inconvenient as a bedroom, one subterranean resident gave up altogether his life as someone who had contracted out and returned to the over-organised 'normal' world of job and home. See Edmund G. Love, *Subways are for Sleeping* (New York: New American Library, 1958), last chapter.

[3] Merton, *op. cit.* p. 32. The entire discussion makes it clear that these are latent functions, functional for some subgroups and disfunctional for others.

[4] *The Recollections of Alexis de Tocqueville*, edited by J. P. Mayer (London: The Harvill Press, 1948), reprinted in part in *Introduction to Contemporary Civilisation in the West* (New York: Columbia University Press), 3rd ed., II, 517.

history is made in such a way that the final result always arises from conflicts between many individual wills...thus there are innumerable intersecting forces, an infinite series of parallelograms of forces which give rise to one resultant—the historical event...For what each individual wills is obstructed by everyone else, and what emerges is something that no one willed.[1]

This explanation is related to the unintended consequences which arise in purposive social action when there is a conflict of goals as in the first housing law.[2] Purposive social action, as commonly used, is on a very restricted scale: the planning of a housing project, or the elimination of a corrupt political club. But the problem of conflicting wills enters into the failure to abolish political corruption: the goals and intentions of those for whom an item is functional, e.g. the political boss and underworld operator, collides with the goals and intentions of those for whom an item is disfunctional, e.g. the reform movement. And in such events, the result may not be intended by any participant.[3]

In addition to conflicting wills, Engels also offers the explanation that if the consequences of an action are unintended, it may be that 'these ends are from the outset incapable of realization, or the means of attaining them insufficient'.[4] Ends are from the outset incapable of realisation when the necessary conditions for a goal are in principle impossible: that everyone should have a mountain top of his own to which he can retire for contemplation. The means are insufficient for a goal when the necessary conditions are not present, but are in principle attainable. *The Communist Manifesto* offers the instance of early proletarian movements as being foredoomed because the material conditions were not yet present for success.[5]

---

[1] Letter of Engels to Joseph Block, in *Selected Works*, ii, 489 ff. For Engels, the problem was to fit these unintended resultants with the preordained march of history. He accomplished this by making the sum of the consequent resultants follow a path set by the hidden laws of history.

[2] 'I think that you and I, with our heavy responsibilities for the maintenance of peace, were aware that developments were approaching a point where events could have become unmanageable.' *New York Times*, 28 October 1962. At the close of the Cuba missile crisis, President Kennedy to Soviet Premier Krushchev.

[3] It has been suggested that Engels, in discussing conflict, and Adam Smith, in discussing economic processes, may be referring to the same process. Engels, however, implies that men are pushed away from their goals in conflict, and to that extent fail, so that the consequence is intended by no one, and marks defeat or failure.

    Smith seems to mean that when the market operates so that people reach their individual goals, are successful in their investments and exchanges, the invisible hand guides them to promote the common welfare. Engels would point to the depressions, when the invisible hand seemed to be a mailed fist, for evidence of the unintended consequences of economic conflict. The process of aggregating microunits into macrounits, the aggregation of individual utilities and actions, is one I am not prepared to examine here.

[4] Engels, *Selected Works*, ii, 457 (Ludwig Feuerbach). See the discussion of unintended consequences in Friedrich Engels, *Ludwig Feuerbach and the End of Classical German Philosophy*, in Karl Marx and F. Engels, *Selected Works* (Moscow: Foreign Language Publishing House, 1962), ii, Section iv. Also A. D. Lindsay, *Karl Marx's Capital* (London: Oxford University Press, 1931).   [5] Opening section of Part iii, section 3.

This formula is a variation on another statement of Marx: he asserts that the hand mill gives us society with the feudal lord; the steam mill gives us capitalism with the industrial capitalist. By implication, then, any attempt to establish capitalism based on the hand mill, or feudalism based on steam, will fail. For one is manipulating the 'dependent' variable: the political or legal relationships. Marx might therefore explain the unintended consequences of the attempt in Russia to erect socialism on pre-capitalist productive forces in the same manner as in the *Manifesto* he explained the failure of the Conspiracy of the Equals.[1]

Merton explains those unintended consequences which arise when one of these presumed 'social windfalls' is dismantled and no functional alternative is provided. There are still many instances of items functional to some and disfunctional to others around which conflict may develop; such functions and disfunctions are not 'latent' to the contending groups. And if such conflicts do arise, results will also be unintended.[2] It is one of the chief omissions of functionalist-type discussions that they do not take conflict into account as a factor in politics or social operations.

A third explanation of unintended consequences is that they arise when an attempt is made to manipulate the 'dependent variable'. But both the many pitfalls of Merton's explanation and the lacunae in the Marxian explanations seem to me to be avoided in a rather simple fourth type of explanation.

A TENTATIVE EXPLANATION OF UNINTENDED CONSEQUENCES

Purposes, whether avowed or not, are all comprised in a person's wants. A purpose unavowed to and unrecognised by the agent himself will nevertheless be reflected in his desires; it will be a purpose he unconsciously or unwittingly seeks to suit. He is likely therefore to use or bend some practice ready to hand in order to fulfil this unconscious and unrecognised purpose. The function the practice fulfils will, for him, be somewhat different from the function it manifestly or ostensibly fulfils. Thus, commerce and the market were considered by the medieval church as institutions whose purpose was to enable men mutually to exchange goods that were needed, not as institutions to enable men to become wealthy or to profiteer. This purpose may well have been, among some fledgling merchants, a purpose unavowed even to them-

---

[1] What actually followed the Revolution in Russia was an attempt at rapid industrialization, i.e. turning to the independent variable.

[2] See Philip Selznick, *TVA and the Grass Roots* (Berkeley: Univ. of California, 1949). Merton's suggestion that some items are functional to one group and disfunctional to another allows for conflict as a source of social change; this might then be the way in which in actuality the 'net of functional over disfunctional consequences' is cast up—in votes or bargains, and so on. Merton, *op. cit.* pp. 51 ff.

selves, for, as Pirenne somewhere comments, a good Christian could not see a money-box without envisaging the devil squatting on the iron lid. Nevertheless, these same fledgling merchants used the market to make money, though they concealed this spring of their activity even from themselves.

But the purpose of acquiring wealth must for most merchants have been a conscious purpose quite early in their careers. The inhibiting moral or legal sanctions would only mean that the merchant failed to avow his purpose, at its most inhibited, to himself; or, somewhat less inhibited, to any other, though conscious of his secret purpose; or still less inhibited, he shared his secret with his immediate family, or with other merchants who understood each other's motivations. For a long time merchants were unable to avow their purpose to the priest and even to the sovereign. So that there were always subgroups in the society from whom the purpose was concealed: to these subgroups, by and large, the function of the market in fulfilling the unavowed purpose of profiteering was meant to be latent. That it may have been latent seems to be supported by the naïve church decree mentioned above, whose effects were so disfunctional.

In another instance, a pickpocket will not avow his purpose in riding the subways to the public at large. Yet his purpose can be known beyond the subgroup—his wife, fellow felons, and his lawyer—to whom he avows it. It may also be well known to the police and any alert and observant fellow passenger. And the purpose has been unavowed to other subgroups because it can only be fulfilled at their expense; to these subgroups it is a latent disfunction, and is an anti-'social windfall'.

Thus may arise the u.c. 1 type of unintended consequence, like the market; u.c. 2 will arise similarly because the existing items are put to different uses by people with different utilities. All the consequences of a change or elimination of an institution or practice will be difficult to track down and will thus prove unintended and unanticipated because many of the uses to which an item is put are unexpected and even bizarre. For many of its votaries, the Thanksgiving Dinner provides an occasion for family gatherings and festivities rather than giving thanks to God for blessings enjoyed. Should it be suppressed by a militantly atheistic regime, there may well be a proliferation of Cousins' Clubs to to satisfy the latent (to the regime) function of festive family reunions. The temporary shutdown of the subway system by a strike will deprive derelicts of their dormitories, perverts of their pleasures, pretzel vendors of their patrons and pickpockets of their pelf, and therefore give rise to all sorts of consequences—the crowding of the public libraries with sleepy derelicts, or an infestation of commuter trains by pickpockets— unintended by the Transit Authority or the strikers.

The bizarre uses to which an item is put and the unintended consequences entailed are perhaps best illustrated by the story of the *New York Times*. The newspaper itself is an illustration of u.c. 1: started as a journal of news and opinions over a century ago, it has acquired more and more latent (from most readers) functions until it may be said to be a 'social windfall', or 'the product of superindividual wisdom', because it does so much more than its founder ever intended that it should. The unsuspected uses of this social item to fit the diverse utilities of different subgroups were revealed by the strike which shut the paper down in 1962–1963, leading to u.c. 2.

The *New York Times* during the period of rapid industrialisation of the United States was by contemporary American standards a skimpy paper: it ran ten or twelve pages per issue, of which a small proportion was advertising. With the growth of the consumption economy—among other similar consequences the conversion of the austere Puritan celebration of Christmas into a hedonistic celebration[1]—advertising proliferated to account for an average of about 80 pages daily in the *New York Times* of 1964; the skimpy paper of a hundred years ago swelled to a paper weighing almost seven pounds on some Sundays.[2] Observe the 'functionality': at the same time the numbers and activities of men grew and new nations emerged so that now there are more than a hundred national capitals from which news is transmitted to the *Times*; were it not for the expansion of the paper because of the advertising, there would be no room for the vast amount of news now skittering over the wires from every cranny of the six continents. This news not only has space in the larger paper, but it is in fact needed to act as lures to the readers, guiding them like Ariadne's threads among the masses of advertising, which it is hoped they will read.

Thus the consumers' society serves to make us aware of the transformation of the world from one of 'five hundred million people and one and a half billion natives'[3] into one which increasingly becomes a unity; and the proliferation of news from a hundred capitals helps the consumer society sell its wares. This social item was eliminated temporarily by a strike.

During the strike, funeral directors complained of poor attendance at the unannounced services; employment agencies languished; sales plummeted at department stores; New Yorkers remained in euphoric ignorance of the mimeographed proclamations of government and their agencies; actors' voices echoed as acoustics deteriorated in half-empty

---

[1] A classical example of Weber's *Paradoxie des Folgen*.
[2] In the autumn up to Christmas, some Sundays before Easter in the spring.
[3] J. P. Sartre, Preface to *The Damned*, by Frantz Fanon (Paris: Présence Africaine, 1963) p. 7.

theatres; plays postponed their openings, since they would get no notices; politicians saved their gestures, for they would be seen only by the immediate audience. The most latent of all functions proved to be quite affecting, illustrating the functionality of an item, and the internal relations of our society: it is all One, as Hegel says.[1]

The same marvelous technology that has given us the consumer-oriented economy that brought about elephantiasis of the *Times* has also provided us with the means of extending life expectancy. Things like better and varied food at all seasons and medical technology have raised the proportion of elderly persons in our society. Now, when one partner in a marriage dies, the other—usually the widow—may have years to live, not in a farmhouse with relatives but in an apartment alone. To mitigate her loneliness 'man's best friend' has been pressed into service, while incidentally providing protection against the apparently more frequent attempts at purse-snatching and burglaries. A boom in dogs is under way.

However, dogs must be trained for urban living; the first stage is paper-training the puppies. Providentially at hand to fill this (latent) function, we find that almost ten absorbent pounds of the *New York Times* are hardly more costly than the newsprint itself at retail.[2] And it offers the additional advantages of news; advertisements; accounts of dog shows; a special section of classified advertisements called Dogs and Cats. It is understandable that a plangent telegram from a dog breeders association entreated the union to end the strike.

People make do with whatever is at hand to fit their various sets of desires. The underworld character in Merton's illustration sees the political club as it meets his wants: a channel of communication with City Hall, a means of protection from the police. The politico sees the club as a means of attaining power. The precinct worker sees it as a way of getting a soft, politically distributed job; the zealous Democrat reformer sees it as an instrument to be captured for cleaning up the city, or turning the rascals out (and himself in); the reformer of the opposition party sees it as The Enemy to be liquidated. The institution has not so much manifest and latent functions, but more helpfully, a multiplicity of uses, consequences and effects which need to be searched out in order

---

[1] *Rechtsphilosophie.*

[2] That is, six daily and one Sunday paper each week. The (manifest) function of the absorbency is to take the ink in the high-speed presses. The weight of the paper varies with the shopping season, and must come close to ten pounds for all but the summer months. This weight includes the ink. The cost is ninety cents per week for the seven issues. At current costs in half-ton lots the blank newsprint would come to about 70 cents. Newspapers are sold to the dealers in most cases—and certainly before the recent price rise—well below the cost of production, as television and radio programmes are to the American public. A large circulation did the *New York Daily Mirror* in, for it lacked the advertising necessary to make up the loss sustained on each copy.

to foresee all the consequences of change. Nor did the founders of political parties and branches intend or foresee all these uses to which others have put their creation, nor the forms others would impose on their creations to adapt it, however little or much, to the use they had for it.

In the same way, U.C. I arises as the product of various shapings by individuals and groups of whatever formations are at hand. The evolution of mental institutions can be considered a U.C. I, the result of the spontaneous actions of many groups and invididuals. Menger and Hayek might well consider these institutions as an instance of the product of unplanned action which serve the common welfare. Goffman points out that the institution is organised to fit the utilities of the 'true clients' of the hospital: inmates' relatives, police and judges, and the staff which runs the hospital. As a consequence:

mental patients can find themselves in a special bind. To get out of the hospital, or to ease their life within it, they must show acceptance of the place accorded them, and the place accorded them is to support the occupational role of those who appear to force this bargain. This self-alienating servitude, which perhaps helps to account for some of the inmates becoming confused... [1]

The institution of mental hospitals serves a welfare common to all except the ostensible recipient of that welfare: the inmate, whom the stay in the hospital is presumably aimed to cure—i.e. enable the patient to return to normal daily living. The consequence seems to be perverse: the stay unfits him for a return to normal life; the better he adapts to the life in the hospital, the less does his stay in the hospital 'cure' him.

This case of a perverse U.C. I is deceptive. The intentions, the utilities of those who hold the power, relatives, police, judges, staff, are on the whole fulfilled: the patient is incarcerated; the motions of medical services are gone through to salve consciences, and so on. This illustrates one set of answers to the questions asked above about U.C. I: how common *is* the welfare served? and how effectively does it promote that welfare?

A person's wants are on a continuum ranging from those hidden even from himself to those that are known to himself, known to his closest friend, known to his family, known to a subgroup and publicly proclaimed. His preferences are many and shifting. Preferences of people and subgroups are diverse and the diversity is also on a continuum. For they vary from a coincidence of the utilities of some to a divergence all the way to the point of direct conflict. And it is these variations and diversities and conflicts that produce unintended consequences. [2]

[1] Erving Goffman, *Asylums: Essays on the social situation of mental patients and other Inmates.* (Garden City: Doubleday Anchor Books, 1961), p. 386.

[2] Professor S. M. Lipset remarks that the greatest unintended consequence of purposive social action may well be the phenomenon described by Robert Michels as the iron law of

The large number of cases of u.c. 2 arising from the elimination of 'functions' latent from the agents of change could be greatly reduced if participants themselves were the only agents of social change. Full participation in thoroughly candid discussion of an item and the proposed alteration would preclude many of the u.c. 2 that take place, in, e.g., housing programmes. Differing utilities would then result in compromise, perhaps, or in defeat for some and success for most. And the achievement of a change might well be one that pleased no one fully.

CAN UNINTENDED CONSEQUENCES BE ELIMINATED?

Economics has been able to predict roughly the unintended consequences of certain socio-economic actions, e.g. of price fixing a commodity in short supply. The black market price can be more or less accurately predicted if the demand curve is known.[1] Economics is a field in which unintended consequences seem to flourish like the green bay tree: both the formation and operation of the market are discussed as unintended consequences. Popper occasionally writes of the market as operating to produce unintended consequences: the single buyer or seller, by putting his house up for sale, or by seeking to buy a house, thereby alters the market price against his intention by altering the ratio of supply to demand.

Under conditions of scarcity the provisioning activity of men provides a field for varying and conflicting wants and purposes. There is a constant clash of buyer with seller, competitors (either those making the same product, or making competing products), employers and employees, and so on. Would abundance eliminate unintended consequences by ending the scrabble for scarce goods?[2]

oligarchy, that is, the oligarchical control developed in organisations formed to promote democratic control by the members, e.g. trade unions, Social Democratic parties and similar organisations. Here is a clear case of the operation of the utilities of the leaders who concentrate control in their hands: the gathering of power so that they may keep their preferred positions is an unavowed purpose, perhaps even to themselves. The quest for esteem, once they have won it among their members, tends to turn to other and more influential subgroups of the population, e.g. the politicians or the middle class. This desire for prestige among other and even hostile strata of the population is unavowed (to themselves, to their families, and certainly to the membership); yet it may well be conveyed wordlessly to these subgroups. If, as has been suggested, the desire for esteem is central in social behaviour, analogous to the maximisation of profits in the economic behaviour of entrepreneurs, then it will significantly shape the utility curve of individuals and subgroups.

[1] Economists concerned with the unintended consequences of tampering with the free market sometimes seem to mean by unintended not unanticipated, for they claim to be able to predict, but undesired by themselves rather than the agents.

[2] Abundance and scarcity are relative to wants and appetites. The achievement of abundance requires social control. For if, under conditions where abundance is possible, new inventions mother new necessities, and these are available to only a few for a long while, then in a

In the field of economics, perhaps. Marx and Engels thought that only proletarian dictatorship could usher in a state of abundance, for which social measures would be required to provide another necessary condition. If the United States should succeed in narrowing the gap between rich and poor by measures adumbrated in the anti-poverty programmes, it will only have made it possible to eliminate economics as a source of unintended consequences.

Political and social matters would still find people with differing and colliding utilities making do with the institutions about them, adapting them, impressing their own uses upon them. Different, unexpected and conflicting uses and effects of these manipulated social formations would give rise to consequences unanticipated and undesired, anticipated and undesired, unanticipated and welcomed, as well as anticipated and intended by different agents and subgroups at different times. What can be done here? We could avoid all change, and thus avoid unintended consequences in social matters, as Plato sought to do in *The Republic*. But in order to forestall all change we would have to arrest our technology. And we cannot arrest our technology because the lower organisms, like roaches or bacteria, constantly mutate into new strains resistant to the old exterminators and antibiotics.[1] Fuel depletion and the effects of using certain fuels over protracted periods also engender problems that only technological development can solve. And it is highly improbable that we will agree to trammel our medical technology short of a painless life and immortality for our youthful selves. Since technological change will continue, social and political changes will have to be effected; the problem of unintended consequences will continue to trouble us.

Of course, we are sometimes urged not to make social changes lest change lead us where we would not go: unintended consequences can be avoided by making 'slow, small changes'[2] or none at all. In a rapidly changing environment, unintended consequences will follow more surely from deliberate inaction than from deliberate action. Thus, urbanisation was attended by the growth of slums, disease, housing shortages, new problems of the elderly, and a multitude of social ills which became the more severe and undesirable as nothing was done to bring them under control. Conservatives often stand pat because they

stratified society these new commodities will imply superior status in the possessor. Then abundance will continue to recede, like utopia. Nor can any flood of goods from technological cornucopias ever end poverty without narrowing the gap between top and bottom of the standard of living scales.

The evidence here seems to show that the technology can be plied quite effectively even in a class society, and that the motion toward a classless society may prove to be a consequence of, rather than a condition for, the full exploitation of the technology.

[1] Richard LaPière, *Social Change* (New York: McGraw-Hill, 1965).
[2] Oakeshott, *Rationalism in Politics*, p. 49.

have an affection for the past or the present, whose affection in turn they may be simply requiting. In that case it is not the undesirability of the unanticipated consequences of change that deter them from action, as much as the desirability of retaining existing arrangements, or arrangements that approximate as closely as possible to those conceived to have obtained in the past.

Can the social sciences enable us to eliminate unintended consequences? Cannot such methods as polls[1] enable us to avoid them? One problem is that human beings can react to laws or predictions about themselves, resulting in such well-known phenomena as the self-fulfilling prediction (there is going to be a shortage of furniture juice, whereupon everyone rushes to stock up on furniture juice, creating the predicted shortage) and the self-defeating prediction (it is announced that a poor potato crop is expected, whereupon farmers plant more potatoes to take advantage of the high prices a poor crop is expected to bring, leading to a big potato crop and low prices). Human beings can also behave contra-predictively, out of sheer contrariness.[2]

It may be feasible to iron out this sort of contrariness and varying utilities among humans by various means: terror, lobotomies, or Skinnerian 'conditioning', and create in this manner a harmony among all so that everyone employs all social items only in a directed way; everyone acts on a single set of wants and utilities, and social scientists can trace out the consequences of any move and obviate unintended consequences.[3] Short of such an imposition of a single set of utilities, can we not learn to predict accurately the effects of a planned social change? Not likely, for it may prove that the applicable laws of human behaviour ultimately have a statistical form: If A, then, in 72 per cent of the cases, B; in 28 per cent of the cases, C. If the prediction is statistical, then there is no way of avoiding anticipated but unintended and undesired consequences.[4]

---

[1] Daniel Bell, 'Twelve modes of prediction—a preliminary sorting of approaches in the social sciences', *Daedalus*, vol. 93, no. 3 (1964), p. 845.

[2] Michael Scriven, 'An essential unpredictability in human behavior', *Forum Philosophy of Science Series*, Voice of America. Similar instances of self-fulfilling and self-defeating predictions can be offered outside the field of economics, so that an end to scarcity would not bring an end to all self-defeating and fulfilling predictions.

[3] Technological developments have made possible all these methods, and they have been and are being tried. If American advertisers are eager to use subliminal messages, it is not impossible that governments will turn to them. Nevertheless, the current purge in China, the failure of the Great Leap Forward, and the Sino-Soviet rift, show that even where the greatest centralised control is exercised consequences cannot be all anticipated and intended.

[4] Acton, 'Tradition and some other forms of order', *art. cit.*, contends that either conflict of wills or error lead to all unintended consequences. It is possible to eliminate error and conflict, and to find that the theory may never ultimately be such that we can deduce the consequence from it. If Acton's omniscience refers to knowledge of the ultimate knowable by humans, then it may be possible to know these ultimate laws, and the initial conditions,

This does not mean that we are ever at the mercy of unintended consequences. Careful scrutiny of all the uses to which an item is put, full participation of *all* the users of the item (and they alone) in making the change, and the use of pilot projects and the many approximations that can be made by social scientists, can all reduce the number of unanticipated consequences of social action. Some consequences will still prove to be unintended but not unanticipated to some of the participants because of conflict and compromise. Not to act will inevitably bring on unintended consequences. Action after ordered inquiry and full democratic deliberation of all participants can sharply reduce unintended consequences.

CONCLUSION: REASON IN TRADITION

The reason in a traditional practice or social item is a function of the extent to which that practice meets the wants of its practitioners. At some time, traditional practices satisfy the desires of all, or most, or some (powerful) practitioners. When an item is oppressive to any subgroup of participants, that is, does not fit its utilities, the subgroup will attempt to alter it if it acquires enough social and political leverage.

Traditional practices become disfunctional, i.e. cease to meet the wants of a subgroup of its practitioners, when the utilities of that subgroup have changed as a result of changed environment or any other reason.[1] When that happens, it is possible that the practice will be retained in some adaptation to satisfy other wants. Thus, the traditionally religious Thanksgiving and Christmas holidays have become increasingly hedonistic occasions for reunions with family and friends and extensive party-going.

Different subgroups in a population adapt traditional practices to fit their own changing utilities, so that a practice may superficially seem to be unchanged, but serve different purposes for different subgroups. This sort of development is illustrated in the growth of the *New York Times*, which in effect, though not noticed by the public, has been transformed from a newspaper that was sustained almost entirely by its income from sales into a commodity subsidised by the advertisers. Observations by a non-participant may not reveal the changing utilities an item serves, or the varying manner in which it fits the utilities of different subgroups of its participants.

and to have a probabilistic prediction. But if Acton means a God-like omniscience, then we can retain conflict of wills, because such omniscience would enable us to know the resultant anyhow, and still avoid u.c.

[1] T. Scitovsky, 'A note on profit maximisation and its implications', in *Readings in Price Theory*, George Stigler and Kenneth Boulding (eds.) (Chicago: Richard Irwin, for the American Economic Association, 1952).

Since ongoing practices are adapted, it may often be the case that although there is reason in the practice, it is not 'rational', if by 'rational' one means greatest output to input ratio in satisfying culturally determined wants. 'Rationality' is itself relative to the time, culture, place, state of knowledge, and so on. The tradition as it is practised is very likely to be a makeshift, an adaptation, and not optimally efficient for its practitioners. Foster[1] describes women washing their clothes laboriously in a river, scorning the newly installed, convenient, *individual* washtubs because the clothes washing enabled the women to visit with each other, gossip, and serve utilities other than the cleaning of clothes. Communal washtubs would have provided a much more efficient manner of meeting all the utilities involved. As it was, hauling the wash down the hill to the river, kneeling on its banks to scrub, and labouring back up the hill with the load of wet wash was a practice in which there was reason (it was the only *communal* way available for clothes washing) but which was not 'rational' (in the sense of obtaining the greatest possible efficiency). However, had it been open to the women themselves to choose between the new types of plumbing made available to them, their full discussion would most likely have prevented the installation by non-participant agents of useless individual washtubs, and would very probably have led to a system of communal washtubs that would more efficiently have served all the utilities involved.

The perfectly 'rational' is a function not only of the mores of the society, but of the available knowledge. In our society, our scientific findings and their applications are rocketing ahead of our changing mores and viscous traditional practices. These traditional practices can be shown to have 'reason': they provide satisfactions to some, at least. Yet, in time, they usually fall short of the criterion of 'rationality' made more volatile by our racing science and technology.

[1] George Foster, *Traditional Cultures*.

REVOLUTION, TRADITION AND POLITICAL CONTINUITY

K. R. MINOGUE

POLITICAL DISCONTINUITY

My theme is the cultural struggle between the idea of a process, and that of a starting point. Starting points are prominent in all fields. Every English schoolboy knows that English history begins in 1066, just as every Roman schoolboy heard about Romulus and Remus. I find my own starting point unforgettable because civil servants, insurance companies and clubs all seem to have an unquenchable thirst to discover when I began. School histories of science are accounts of who discovered what, when.[1] In more sophisticated circles, we find academics trying to discover the origins of totalitarianism or of the idea of democracy. And on my packet of cigarettes, I read, 'suppliers of fine tobacco since 1839'. Historians go to work undermining these naïve discontinuities. Told that the industrial revolution may be dated from 1760, the historian is happy to show that the seventeenth century exhibits many of the characteristics thought erroneously to be the monopoly of the late eighteenth century. Historians undermine and destroy starting points, as infallibly as philosophers transpose what other men believe to be fundamental.

This cultural struggle is found at its liveliest in the field of politics, and one of its particular skirmishes is Burke's *Reflections on the Revolution in France*. The issue raised by that book may be simplified into the question: is revolution or tradition the idea by which the process of politics may be best understood? Burke was confronted by a body of men who sought in every possible way to create an unbridgeable gap between the *ancien régime* and the new order being unfolded in France during the 1790s. They renamed streets and months, abolished the historic provinces of France, and set up temples for the new cults they espoused. Burke argued that this was both unwise and impossible, insisting on the ubiquity of tradition in a manner similar to that in which he had previously insisted upon the ubiquity of law in the case of Warren Hastings. We are all, Burke argued, the products of tradition, and the illusion that we can escape from our past is entirely crippling. The melodramatic turbulence with which men attempted to break out

---

[1] On the problem of dating scientific discoveries, which is illuminating in the study of revolution, see T. S. Kuhn, *The Structure of Scientific Revolutions* (Chicago, 1962), ch. VI.

of their pasts appeared merely as a colossal folly. It is clear from this argument that the whole idea of tradition is a cannibal; it will eat up any concept of political change. It will exhibit the evolution of the Russian state, for example, as a steady onward march from the Kiev *Rus* to the Duchy of Muscovy, and on to Czarist St Petersburg as one continuous process in which the changes modify but do not disrupt the thread. Time is tradition's ally, for what today seems strikingly new tomorrow will have sunk to familiarity; each passing year makes the purges of Stalin more of a piece with the *oprichnina* of Ivan IV.

In a less plausible way, the idea of revolution will play Heraclitus to tradition's Parmenides. These days when revolutions are daily announced in activities as varied as housebuilding, dish-washing and philosophy, the concept of revolution often seems to belong merely to the vulgar hyperbole of self-promotion. The lines of thought which culminate in the cliché that we live in a revolutionary age have crystallised for the social sciences into the composite problem of modernisation, or how (i.e. by what revolutions) we came to be so beautiful. It is clear, I think, that any suggestion that we live in an entirely new world, totally severed from the past, would not survive serious consideration; nor has any such theory of the modern world been advanced. But the cumulative effect of so many piecemeal emphases might well suggest such an idea to uncritical minds. Further, there is in our culture a passionate desire, if not to believe in a total modern revolution, at least to wish that there were one, and to bring it about. The entire science of psycho-analysis is devoted to releasing men from their past; and there are people who regret living in (to use Houseman's self-pitying phrase) 'a world I never made'. In the field of politics, the followers of Marx are striving to reach a situation in which politics, seen as the heritage of an imperfect past, will wither away.

Revolution and tradition are, then, terms which expand into each other's territory. To explore the relation between them, we must first give a brief account of political tradition—a subject which is, for all its currency, little analysed. Politics we may indicate briefly as the activity which leads to decisions of state, and a series of distinguished writers, from Aristotle to Hannah Arendt and Sheldon Wolin, have taught us to see it as the realm of public things in which men are pre-eminently free. This public realm is to society as the nucleus is to a jellyfish, and at any given time we may indicate fairly clearly who are the people who participate in it. Kings, representatives, squires, party leaders and party managers are typical inhabitants of the public realm, whilst housewives, children, the peasantry, and domestic servants have seldom in these roles participated in it, and never affect it without making a disproportionate amount of fuss.

Now it is common to assume that the public realm of any state has, over very long periods of time, the continuity of a style and a tradition. Each country characterises itself by the description it gives of its own political style. In Britain, the elements of political continuity are both obvious and often described: insularity, a common language, a respect for legality, a preference for trusting people in public life, the tendency to adapt an existing institution to a new task rather than create a new one. A political tradition is a manner of dealing with problems, based like all tradition on imitation of predecessors. The imitation is that of children, beginning with externals and growing inward to a modified recurrence of the same types of emotion and calculation found in earlier times. Political types abound; men of principle debate with men of compromise, and a Tom Paine lives again in his biographer Michael Foot. Since we are dealing with a self-characterisation, we have to beware of an element of self-flattery. The role played by the English working classes in politics has often been assimilated to the political tradition and commended for its moderation. But Edmund Wilson once described the same disposition as spiritless, and the whole tradition has often been condemned as incapable of dealing with twentieth-century situations. But on examination, these criticisms always turn out to be attacks—usually from *within* the tradition—upon a limited part of it. And this, as we shall see, is necessarily so. And within a political tradition individuals change, and many, like Coleridge, put away their squeaking trumpets of sedition in the attic of youth; but those who fought in the International Brigade find successors in those who march in protest against atomic weapons, looking back, within the tradition, to Lollards, Levellers, and Chartists.

The range of the concept of a political tradition becomes evident when people try to get outside it. Clearly it is possible to regard a tradition as a resource at one's command; and a writer like Burke will be glad of the fact that the British political tradition has within itself the materials for its own evolution. Each new political crisis draws out a set of responses which become inevitably another move in the evolution of the tradition. We need, of course, to keep our attention fixed upon the 'inevitability' of this fact, because what is inevitably true is always likely to be vacuous. But the reason for inevitability here is that we *are* our traditions. The British political tradition is no more than the British political character, operating over time and studied historically.

This becomes evident when, as commonly happens, an attack upon a political tradition becomes a move in the tradition itself. What is attacked is necessarily only a part of the whole tradition, and further, the tradition has to be turned into a source of political guidance in order to be worth attacking. And this requires that alternative sources of political guidance be established. God, and Reason, have both been called upon to play this role. Now experience suggests that God in British politics is an Englishman; it also suggests that what Englishmen find rational is significantly different from what men of other traditions find rational. The reason is, of course, that rational prescriptions always have gaps which, though often unnoticed, can only be filled by making assumptions or espousing values which arise uncriticised from the culture itself. But apart from these empirical considerations, there remains the logical one: to appeal to God or reason is itself part of the British political tradition. Any political tradition throws up many criteria of political action, and God and Reason can only seem to be escapes from the tradition if the tradition itself has first been demoted to (what it cannot be) one source of political guidance among others. This results from an equivocation about the term 'source'. A source may be 'that out of which all political action emerges' or it may be simply a criterion of political action.

To say that we cannot escape from tradition is, then, simply another way of saying that we cannot be other than we are—a statement which would indeed be entirely vacuous were it not that the illusions of practical life so constantly tempt us to think differently. It is not surprising, however, that many people experience a kind of intellectual claustrophobia when confronted with this understanding of political tradition. The mistake they have made is to confuse considerations of explanatory plausibility with those of practical possibility. And in trying to escape from tradition conceived of as a prison, they attempt to distinguish within British politics (or indeed those of any other state) various independent traditions such as the radical or the conservative.[1] The advantage is, of course, that it then seems possible to choose one's tradition, or even to combine strands of different traditions into dazzlingly new combinations. The result of this understanding is to establish both a broad and a narrow sense of 'tradition'. There is no serious confusion in talking of such entities as 'the radical tradition in British politics', but it does appear to involve us in a false belief about the character of tradition generally. Tradition is necessarily a bundle of diverse elements; if it were not, it would be static. It develops as these elements react to new situations and interact with each other. It ought, therefore, to be understood in Oakeshottian terms as a conversation; and interchange of voices in the whole point of it. The narrow sense turns a tradition into a monologue rather than a conversation, and makes the relations between one narrow tradition and another external. This is a mistake. It is certainly true that there are 'external' relations between political traditions, as exemplified by the reception of English

[1] See on this point Michael Oakeshott, *Rationalism in Politics* (London, 1962), p. 137.

constitutional ideas into France during the eighteenth century—but in each case, the influenced tradition must convert foreign material into its own terms. And the elements of one country's political tradition lean heavily on each other and form part of a single political experience.

France balanced her intellectual payments after 1789 by exporting back to Britian (and over the world) the idea of revolution. British rulers had always been aware of the danger of revolt, rebellion and disturbance; now they had to worry about this rather new-fangled idea whose realisation would no doubt produce guillotines in Trafalgar Square. In politics as in private life, one man's anxiety is another man's opportunity. The philosophical radicals, seeking an extension of the franchise, yoked their cause to the fear of revolution. As befitted a mechanical age, they had a boilerhouse theory of political tension: if the pressure of discontent (steam!) could be shown to be increasing in the country, then parliament would have to supply some release, or risk blowing up the works. But James Mill and his fellow-radicals drew a much more amusing inference from the model: if you want a piece of legislation passed, you must present it as a release of pressure, by the device of building up appropriate quantities of steam in the country. This appears to have been just what they did.[1] It was a game which had its dangers, especially for men who were not in the least revolutionary. It appears to have been successful because, in spite of a certain amount of hayrick burning and rioting, the mood of the country was profoundly unrevolutionary. Even the huge crowds who turned up to watch the public execution of condemned rioters in Bristol in February 1832 remained, in spite of fears, orderly.[2]

Nineteenth-century Britian passed three Reform Bills and did not experience a revolution. Yet British politics *were* 'revolutionised' in the nineteenth century, for the extension of the franchise changed the constitution from oligarchy to democracy, and brought in its train a host of consequent adjustments. The justification for the use of 'revolution' here lies in the practice of historians. Two random examples of that practice will suffice. We read that in the fourteenth century military technique 'had already been revolutionised by the archer, and a second revolution was taking place...by the introduction of artillery'.[3] Here 'revolution' means the process, triggered off by an event, which fairly rapidly transforms an activity. Here is another example concerned with the growth of a system of public credit: 'The rise of this system in the six decades before the Seven Years War was rapid enough, and important enough in both its main and secondary effects, to deserve the

---

[1] Joseph Hamburger, *James Mill and the Art of Revolution* (New Haven, 1963).
[2] *Ibid.* p. 259.
[3] A. L. Morton, *The Matter of Britain* (London, 1966), p. 30.

name of Financial Revolution. Its effects on the country's life, social attitudes and historical developments resemble on a smaller scale those of the Industrial Revolution which followed it, and which it arguably helped to make possible.'[1] In historical writing, big revolutions beget little revolutions, as grandiose trends are split up into their components. Along these lines, then, we may say that the Reform of the franchise was a revolution in British politics. We derive, indeed, the superficial paradox that British politics did, and did not, have a revolution in the nineteenth century.

The interest of this contradiction is not that it presents any logical difficulties—it depends simply upon confusing the political concept of revolution with the historical use—but in what it implies about the idea of a tradition. As we shall see, the idea of a political revolution only developed fully in France in the late eighteenth century. The model is the French Revolution, and there were many further examples in 1830, 1848, etc. The intellectual problem is to discover just what it is that goes to make up a revolution. We may well decide to reject the melodramatic circumstances of Paris in the 1790s—the Madame Defarge view of the matter—because such turbulence has been common to many other kinds of situation. Searching for a more reliable criterion of revolution, we may point to the social reconstruction which took the *ancien régime* apart and put in its place the rationalised France of the *Code Napoléon* and the metric system. By directing our attention to these supposedly deeper changes, we have moved the idea of revolution away from political up- rising towards social transformation—an idea of revolution which has proved serviceable both to historians and to political theorists. 'Revolu- tion' has turned into a process linked to some supposedly initiating event. Further, this initiating event may have few if any of the obvious characteristics of a revolution; even contemporaries may have missed its significance, yet it may be seen as the source of significant transforma- tion. And by this line of thought the First Reform bill may be taken as a revolution in British politics, one whose implications simply took a rather long time to emerge.[2] A revolution has become 'that after which things were never quite the same again'.

It would seem, then, that the term 'revolution' was pressed into the service of registering our awareness of living in a world of rapid change. Eugene Kamenka has acutely pointed to one interesting consequence— the fact that political revolutions seem now to be the old-fashioned devices by which backward countries try to catch up with the West— 'the more men see such revolutions as part of the regular life of their

---

[1] P. G. M. Dickson, *The Financial Revolution in England* (London, 1967). Quoted *Times Literary Supplement*, 20 July 1967, p. 641.
[2] Maurice Cowling, *1867: Disraeli, Gladstone and Revolution* (Cambridge, 1967).

country, the less prone they seem to be to turn to political revolutions for salvation'.[1] The more we have revolutions, the less likely we are to have a Revolution.

A further consequence of this extension of the idea of revolution is that it has led to a mistake about the character of tradition: for it is only sensible to talk about so many revolutions if we assume that tradition is something fixed and static, a set of habitual responses which do not vary from generation to generation. So static an idea of tradition has been embraced in two areas. First, it is a standard part of the rhetoric of those who, wishing to persuade us to make some particular change, begin by recommending the virtues of change in general as a dynamic element of life. Secondly, sociologists have embraced the conception of a 'traditional society' which exists largely for the purpose of being the starting point of an account of the social process of modernisation.

However, unless the idea of a tradition has already been emasculated by being identified with externals such as ceremonies (e.g. Britain is a traditional country because of the changing of the guard at Buckingham Palace) this account of it is mistaken.[2] Further, outside the crudities of political propaganda, there is no serious question at issue. We might either restrict the idea of revolution to that of the illegal overthrow of a government resulting in widespread social transformation[3] (in which case a revolutionary process is merely a metaphor); or we might incorporate the idea of a revolutionary process into our account of how a tradition works. That British politics during the nineteenth century were, in certain respects, 'revolutionised' will therefore not contradict the fact that the British political tradition remained intact and unviolated throughout the period. But the fact that we have these alternatives illustrates well the aggressive way in which the ideas of tradition and revolution invade each other's territory.

THE IDEA OF REVOLUTION

The first and—as I shall argue, in a sense—the only revolution began in France in 1789. The novelty of this event was such as to require, if not an entirely new word, at least an important modification of an existing one. The Greeks had had a variety of words to indicate what we call a revolution—*metabole* and *metastasis* cover a change of govern-

---

[1] Eugene Kamenka, 'The concept of a political revolution', in Carl J. Friedrich (ed.), *Revolution* (New York, 1966), p. 123.

[2] See the essay 'The Tower of Babel', in Oakeshott, *Rationalism in Politics*, p. 59, and especially around, p. 64 (cf. p. 31).

[3] See the account of Revolution given by Paul Shrecker, 'Revolution as a problem in the philosophy of history', in Friedrich, *op. cit.* p. 34.

KPA

ment; but *kinesis*, a more general word which contrasts movement with repose might be used. Polybius used *anakuklosis* to indicate the cyclical overturning of a state.[1] The word *peripetia*, which Aristotle used in the *Poetics* to describe a change in the fortunes of a hero from one state to another (from happiness to despair in tragedy, for example), is also relevant, because Collingwood[2] argued that it was from literary criticism translated into French, that the political use of the term 'revolution' arose. Italian writers in the late middle ages, however, used *rivoluzione* in a political context to indicate an overwhelming change.[3] The Italian word may be related to the late Latin *revolutio* which St Augustine used for the migration of souls.[4] During the middle ages the word had come to signify in astronomy the circular motions of the heavenly bodies. Copernicus's work *De revolutionibus orbium coelestium* turned out to be a revolutionary (modern sense) book on revolutions (old sense). But in politics the late medieval cult of astrology rather than the science of astronomy is the significant source, for the idea of revolution steadily expanded from its connection with the idea of the wheel of Fortune.

Herein lies the ambiguity of talking of the English Revolution in the seventeenth century. This seems first to have been done, in the modern sense, by the French historian Guizot in his book *Histoire de la Révolution d'Angleterre* (1827).[5] But three events in seventeenth-century English politics were currently thought of as revolutions—the establishment of the Protectorate, the Restoration of Charles II, and the Revolution of 1688. In each case the term is used to indicate a return to an earlier condition. The Protectorate was a return to English liberty—'by God's grace restored,' the Restoration of Charles II was a return to monarchy, and the expulsion of James II was commonly interpreted as a return to an earlier, better condition symbolised by the maintenance of English liberties in the destruction of the Armada a hundred years before in 1588. The idea of a return to an earlier state was extended by Burke to mean simply the maintenance of a traditional state; this allowed him to pinpoint the differences between 'Glorious Revolution' and the events then taking place in Paris. Indeed, the classical view of political turbulence had been well stated by Spinoza: 'In fact, I am fully convinced that every form of commonwealth which can be devised to secure human concord, and all the means required to guide a people, or to keep it within definite bounds, have already been revealed by experience.'[6] Politics is a matter of reshuffling a fixed pack. But that was not what the French revolutionaries thought they were doing; and the reason was

---

[1] Liddell and Scott's Greek Lexicon.
[2] R. G. Collingwood, *The New Leviathan* (Oxford, 1942), p. 199.
[3] Arthur Hatto, 'Revolution', *Mind* (1949), p. 495.   [4] *Ibid.* p. 509.
[5] *Ibid.* p. 505.   [6] Spinoza, *Tractatus Politicus*, 1, 3. Wernham's translation.

that the doctrine of progress—a linear image replacing a circular one—had grown up in the century intervening between Spinoza and the French Revolution.

It has been persuasively argued that the American War of Independence was the first, and indeed the purest, of modern revolutions. Certainly Condorcet and many of the *philosophes* believed it a revolution, though many were not satisfied that it was sufficiently radical. Further, if social upheaval be taken as the criterion of a revolution, then the American case may be seen as a genuine instance. Yet the entirely political style of the Americans, which so commends it to Hannah Arendt as the perfect case, might just as well be a reason for disqualification. It seems to me that Burke's conservative instinct was right at least in seeing the French and American cases as distinct kinds o political event. And the crucial point, which makes it unnecessary to argue the case, is that the mythology of revolution has ignored the American case and taken all its leads from the French.

How, then, does a revolution look to those who make it? It appears first as a short, sharp struggle between Revolution and Reaction. Revolution is the work of the vast majority of people struggling against the entrenched privileges of a few—king, aristocrats, perhaps the very rich, and such hirelings as servants and policemen. It is commonly imagined as a movement of the young against the old. This is partly because it is the young who man the barricades against the supporters of ageing politicians; partly because the revolution is dominated by hope, the virtue of the young, in contrast with the cynicism, compromise and despair of the reactionaries. The image of youth and novelty leads to metaphors of birth, and just as pain is associated with birth, so terror and violence come to be seen as a natural part of revolution. But terror and violence are transfigured by confident hope so that suffering becomes noble and necessary, the condition of bringing something new into the world. And in this sense of novelty, we have the element which decisively marks off the French Revolution from any other precedent of political turbulence.

Revolution appears as a spontaneous bursting forth of an elemental force. It is the voice of the common man finally entering into a political life from which he has long been unjustly excluded, and Hannah Arendt has written that 'one may suspect that Marx's effort to rewrite history in terms of class struggle was partially at least inspired by the desire to rehabilitate posthumously those to whose injured lives history had added the insult of oblivion'.[1] Revolution tolls the knell of an unnatural and ultimately doomed situation of injustice. The injustice seems to be imagined as a kind of cumulative disequilibrium; it becomes increasingly

[1] Arendt, *On Revolution* (New York, 1963), p. 64.

absurd and intolerable with every passing year, and thus generates inevitably the irresistible force which will overthrow it.

These thoughts culminate in the pressure-cooker theory of revolutions; and the necessity which is part of the grandeur of revolutions appears as a mechanical necessity produced by a build-up of the force of resentment. Translating this image back into the social life from which it came has led to the simple view that revolutions are made by a spontaneous uprising of unbearably oppressed masses. It is sometimes convenient in propaganda to present this picture, but its implausibilities have made it quite untenable. Most men, as Yeats remarked, lead lives of quiet desperation; what must be explained is why at a particular time this desperation leads (if it does) to political action rather than, for example, to religious quietism. It has further been observed that the masses compose colourful crowd scenes on the periphery of any revolution, but that the actual decisions are taken by an experienced political class. And it has also been observed that revolutions arise not from the desperately impoverished but from people whose lives have been materially improving. The pressure-cooker theory of revolutions has therefore been abandoned, at least in its crude forms, even by revolutionaries themselves, for they have come to be more impressed with the role of a revolutionary vanguard. But the pressure-cooker image is kept in the background to support the idea that revolutions result from an irresistible buoyancy coming from outside the ordinary sphere of politics.

Our concern in this section is simply to explore the idea of revolution as understood by revolutionaries themselves. But we may digress to observe that Marx, the greatest theorist a revolution ever had, was bewitched by the whole idea. No doubt his intoxication was intellectual; he was hardly the man to spend his days dreaming of naked-breasted liberty advancing the tricolor, as in romantic paintings. He gave an account of historical processes which culminated in a final revolution. But the fact that revolution comes at the end of this expository sequence need not lead us to conclude that it was a late arrival in his processes of thought. For it is logically possible to begin with the idea of revolution, rather as a novelist may begin with his climax, and then work backwards to discover a plausible set of hypothetical processes which will generate the required ending. This logical possibility appears to be also a plausible description of how Marx actually thought, the more so in view of the steady diminution of the role of revolution in his mature thought.[1]

The idea of revolution, whether in Marxism or any other version, has

---

[1] Robert C. Tucker, 'The Marxian revolutionary idea', in Carl J. Friedrich (ed.), *Revolution* (New York, 1966), p. 217.

enormous cultural resonance in western experience. The element of fashion in western life, the search for novelty, the cult of originality, even the persistent conflict between one generation and another can all find expression in a revolutionary situation. Further, one of the standard themes of Western political and social thought has been that the technical innovation and inventiveness of science must in some way be matched by similar progress in the moral and political spheres. The indispensable Robespierre, a radical litmus-paper, sums it up: 'Tout a changé dans l'ordre physique; et tout doit changer dans l'ordre moral et politique.'[1] But it is above all religion which revolution has tapped as a source of vitality. The French Revolution was for many an attempt to take the heavenly city by storm; and the Christian philosophy of history appears secularised in the eighteenth-century doctrine of progress. The revolutionary as a social type resembles nothing so much as a puritan, sharing a distrust of ordinary men, a devotion to a theory, and ruthlessness about means. With the era of revolutions, a new kind of moral athlete came into the world, and as revolution became a way of life, men of such disparate temperaments as Lenin and Nkrumah went into training for it, regarding their lives merely as a preparation for the decisive moment. It is above all the sense of living at history's decisive hour which made revolutionaries impatient: the present was a time of darkest iniquity, the future a rosy dawn.

Passions of this kind generally required beliefs of corresponding force. Revolutionaries, like puritans, are dogmatists, and Burke, when he takes time off in the *Reflections* from slating the moral character of the French leaders, turns to attack their abstract dogmatism. This style of thought can be seen, at its most sweetly reasonable, in a pamphlet Condorcet wrote in 1788.[2] It recommends a set of rational principles to Louis XVI in the reforms arising from the calling of the Estates-General. Although published anonymously in London, Condorcet denied that his caution arose 'par cette circonspection timide ou honteuse qu'inspire la crainte d'être l'objet d'une vengeance inique ou d'un châtiment merité'. It arose merely, he confessed, from *amour-propre*, for he knew that others could put into better words the principles he so sincerely held.[3] He addressed the king as *monarque vertueux* and cast him for a reforming role. 'Courra-t-il jamais aucun danger en quittant un moment le Trône pour descendre auprès de [son peuple]? Un bon père est-il, nulle part, plus en sureté qu'au milieux de ses enfants? Ah! cette place est la plus digne d'un Roi vertueux: elle convenait à Louis XVI.'[4] The striking thing about such pamphlets—for this one belongs to a class of writings all exhibiting the same tone—is that the most ample,

---

[1] *Arendt, op. cit.* p. 39.
[2] *Reflexions d'un Citoyen sur la Révolution de 1788.*
[3] Condorcet, p. 5.
[4] *Ibid.* p. 8.

indeed flowery, sentiments of submission, are combined with a serene confidence in the entire rationality and good faith of the king. Above all, Cordorcet has no doubt what rational government amounts to. The difficulty is that this rather charming tone of voice is liable to turn sour very rapidly when the object of devotion fails to conform to the writer's will. Clearly, though quite inexplicitly, political obligation is made entirely conditional upon the rational behaviour (conceived of as not seriously controversial) of the king and the administration.

Condorcet exhibits enormous confidence in his judgments; and it is characteristic of revolutionaries to feel a strong sense of the necessity about what they do. In the next section, we shall be concerned with the question of necessity in sociological terms; here it is merely relevant to note the various sources of this feeling of revolutionary certainty. It is an essential part of the political concept of revolution. In the *philosophes* we find rational necessity. Each revolutionary act may be presented as logically necessary because it is thought to have been deduced from rational premises. The actual details of the deduction are, of course, asserted rather than made explicit; that they could never be. Nonetheless, the claim is made. Another sort of necessity comes from conceiving of society as an engine in which injustice builds up the steam of resentment; we have already met this as the pressure-cooker view of revolution. A rather similar view would hold that the element of necessity comes from the overriding priority of feeding the poor, and from this, no doubt, other necessities, such as maintaining in power the regime which recognises this imperative, would flow. Many of the revolutionaries have felt that the necessity of their actions arose from their status as actors in a grand historical drama; and it may well be suggested that a rhythm of aesthetic necessity—a pattern of rising tensions, climaxes, dénouements—has at time gripped those participating in these stirring events. Certainly a revolution provides scope to play roles—orator, martyr, mouthpiece—which are seldom possible in the humdrum of day-to-day politics. So far as the political concept of revolution is concerned, the important point is the attempt to combine a sense of freedom with a sense of necessity.

What I have been describing is the revolutionary myth as it came definitively into being in the decade after 1789. As an account of reality, it has some evident faults; but even as a revolutionary myth, it came to be regarded as unsatisfactory and unrefined. Generations of men from that day to this have pored over the events of the French Revolution and produced a vastly more refined theory. What stimulated them was failure, for by 1799 the revolution, as a revolution, was virtually dead. It had been killed by (to use the esoteric shorthand) the events of Thermidor and Brumaire. It seemed as if the abstract egalitarianism of the initial ideas had been halted in its application at just that point where egalitarian principles were producing advantages for a distinct class of men called, in revolutionary thought, the bourgeoisie. The Thermidorean reaction was interpreted not as a revulsion against the Terror by men who had begun to regard it as pointless brutality, but as the reaction of a social class which now had got what it wanted from the revolution, and had begun to fear that its newly gained privileges would disappear if the revolution should continue its course. From this point of view, the Babouvist Conspiracy of the Equals in 1796 was the last flicker of the true revolutionary spirit. It was Marx who produced the most satisfactory modification of the revolutionary myth to deal with this difficulty. He presented the revolution not as a single once-and-for-all convulsion, but as a series of convulsions on the instalment plan. Each instalment would be arrested by a new class, establishing a new and onerous set of privileges—until the final instalment imminent in his lifetime, wherein there would be no Thermidor because there would be no social class with an intelligible need to bring about such a reaction.

Brumaire presented a different problem. The revolutionaries consisted of leaders and followers, and there is an inherent element of servility in all leader-follower relations, an element which tempts the leaders to despise the followers in spite of all the abstract flattery of 'the people'. The emergence of Napoleon suggested that all historical revolutions were in danger of succumbing to some tyrant-surrogate emerging, like Napoleon, from the ranks of the revolutionaries themselves. Such a man could appeal to the boredom and exhaustion most people experience after a few years of revolutionary turmoil. That the people were unsatisfactory as revolutionary instruments had to be recognised and many revolutionaries came to agree with their conservative critics that centuries of tradition and deference could not be eradicated in a hurry. The revolution was therefore caught in a difficult choice. To eradicate all traces of the past required a dedicated concentration of power during the transition period; but this very concentration of power tempted its holders to exploit the revolution and set themselves up as rulers on an old pattern.

This difficulty raised even more fundamental problems. The classic nineteenth-century idea of revolution envisaged it as a dynamic interval between two radically different conditions of mankind: before, the miseries of the current condition, after, the bliss of the new order. Marx had been extremely cautious about predicting the future, fearing that too much concern for tomorrow would become bourgeois reformism. But even Marx, it later seemed, had held too static a view of the revolution. The classic idea, it now seemed, had substituted pie on earth for pie in the sky, but it was still pie, still (even at times in Marx) a consumer's idea of paradise. Revolutionaries came to diagnose a worship of false gods in such utopianism; they moved from the idea of revolution to that of revolving. The revolution must become, not a single discontinuity between different states of affairs, but a continuous discontinuity, a manner of life always devoted to uprooting the weeds of habit, and reforming the lapses into superstitious idolatry, the comfortable but insidious drift towards bureaucratic routine. This line of thought grows naturally out of the idea of revolution; it was strikingly explored by Sorel, and its effects may be seen in the conduct of revolutionary affairs in China and Cuba. The idea of revolution has ceased to be a means towards the attainment of some ideological end, and has become a struggle conducted for its own sake.

The notion of a revolution in permanence needs to be carefully distinguished from similar ideas. Within Marxism, for example, Trotsky suggested the notion of a 'permanent revolution' which would spread over the borders of Russia and involve other countries, leading to a single socialist world community. It was this notion that Stalin rejected with the slogan of socialism in one country. But Trotsky was concerned, not with the general slowing down which is likely to afflict any revolution, but rather with certain particular barriers (for example, the backwardness of Russian industry, the attitudes of the peasantry) which in Marxist thought might delay the final consummation. Again, American journalists, as a cold war device, interpreted the constant social and technical change in American life as a true 'permanent revolution' besides which Stalinist Russia appeared frozen in Byzantine immobility. This is an assertion, couched in propagandist terms, of the fact that America is a modern society—with all that modernisation has come to mean to sociologists. Can we then say that the idea of a revolution going on all the time is the same as the notion of modernity? In spite of clear parallels, the answer is clearly no, and contemporary leaders of revolution are quite decisive on the point. For the genuine revolutionary idea is moral. It seeks a condition in which men are fully human because fully free. And revolutionaries argue that the social mobility and technical inventiveness of modern society are entirely compatible with the irrationality of privilege and widespread submission to impersonal social forces.

Any attempt to discover the principle of revolution must clearly take account not merely of the idea at any one point, but of the way in which it has changed in reaction to circumstances. But from Marat to Mao Tse Tung, the idea of struggle has persisted, and the problem is to discover the terms of the struggle. At first sight, the new order confronts the *ancien régime*. But what in the *ancien régime* imperatively demands overthrow? Is it the political contrast between monarchy and democracy?

Salvemini, who ended his history of the French Revolution with the overthrow of the monarchy in 1792, would seem to imply that the issue is constitutional, but the whole history of the idea of revolution suggests that this contrast is superficial. Is the struggle in social terms one between privilege and underprivilege? Radical cartoons of the eighteenth century often picture an obese collection of aristocrats round a board groaning with food, whilst starvelings look on from the streets. There is no doubt that such images concentrate the sense of injustice which appeared to make revolution morally irresistible; they fill in the details obscured by abstract principles like equality and the rights of man. To take privilege as fundamental carries us half-way to the pressure-cooker theory of revolutions, and seems to link up with the Aristotelian view that inequality is the cause of all turbulence. But while this idea of what revolution is about has usually been tactically advantageous in mobilising indignation against an established order, it is also the source of the consumptionist heresy—what is known in some revolutionary circles as goulash communism. The revolution is fundamentally a moral idea, and any suggestion that the revolution will have been consummated when the national cake has been equitably distributed is thought to be a betrayal of the cause.

A more general formula which sums up all revolutions is that something which ought to be changed is swept away by something which cannot be resisted. And, in the language of the social criticism which preceded 1789, the real impetus of revolution seems to be found in the artificiality of the *ancien régime*—the superstructure of special barriers that impeded 'natural' movement, human activity and human intercourse within the French nation. The French nation is taken here as the paradigm of a country undergoing revolution, and the localism of that particular *ancien régime* is reproduced in other times and places by social and cultural splits with a people. The central image of revolution is of a Laocoon figure, struggling to be free of numberless restrictions, and the inevitability of revolution is the bursting forth of a nature too long crippled by artificial impediments. At the root of revolution lies the contrast between nature and artifice, and Rousseau is revolutionary precisely because he is most sensitive to that contrast. In many respects, the revolutionary is exactly the reverse of the Christian, and especially of the Puritan, who spends his life wrestling with his nature and trying to subdue it; the revolutionary seeks to release what the Puritan would repress, and to create a society responsive to the prompting of 'nature'. Rousseau is here a crucial figure, because he turned Calvin on his head a century before Marx did the same to Hegel, and in a more fundamental way. In the revolutionary tradition, the bourgeois individualist, who supplies our idea of personality, the man who creates out of the elements of his nature a *persona* by which he lives in society and necessarily represses many of his impulses—such a man is morally crippled. We necessarily develop such a *persona* as we grow up, and growing up may be represented as a move from nature to artifice. Robert Lowell, in a nostalgic poem about grandparents, expresses the same idea:

> Even at noon here the formidable
> *Ancien Régime* still keeps nature at a distance.

The distinction between nature and artifice belongs to the philosophy of the Enlightenment; stated baldly, it seems unconvincing once men have become historically minded. But nature and artifice are not, in this context, absolutes sullenly contemplating each other's irreducibility. A revolution is a process in which a vicious duality turns into a happy and virtuous unity. Nature and artifice were both, in the nineteenth century, turned into processes, and even, in the hands of Marx, 'artifice'—the state—was made a lever of history and accorded a certain kind of necessity before its ultimate disappearance from the stage of history. Marx sophisticated the thought of the *philosophes* in allowing the artifice of the *ancien régime* a limited release from its earlier status as an inexplicable accident of human villainy. For if we press the untenable distinction between nature and artifice one stage further, we shall discover that nature is that which needs no explanation because it bubbles up out of the necessities of human nature; it is what may rationally be deduced from the character of human beings. Artifice, on the other hand, is fundamentally inexplicable, depending upon a series of mere contingencies of human history, compounded by endless acts of greed and folly. Those who conceive of the matter in this way are understandably provoked to rage if the *ancien régime* fails to fall at the first blast of Reason's trumpet. And in their rage, they are likely to diagnose force and fraud as the only reasons left why the revolution does not immediately succeed.

Burke recognised this point, and met it head on by insisting that artifice *was* human nature. 'We have real hearts of flesh and blood beating in our bosoms. We fear God; we look up with awe to kings; with affection to parliaments; with duty to magistrates; with reverence to priests; and with respect to nobility. Why? Because when such ideas are brought before our minds, it is *natural* to be so affected...'[1] Indeed, in prefacing these rhetorical remarks with 'We preserve the whole of our feelings still native and entire, unsophisticated by pedantry and infidelity' he attempted to reverse the criteria of nature and artifice, so that it was the revolutionaries who appeared corrupt and artificial.

This reversal is a simple thing to do, and would seem to point to a

---

[1] Edmund Burke, *Reflections on the Revolution in France* (Everyman edition), pp. 83–4.

crucial instability in the revolutionary principle. For nature, being necessary, turns into Reason. A revolutionary like Paine looks forward to a new society which he can recommend indifferently as either natural or rational, and the two terms come down to the same thing. Correspondingly, the artificial is the irrational. But revolution is also recommended as spontaneous, and contrasted with the repression involved in the artificial privileges of an *ancien régime*. Once again, we have an inversion of the Puritan position, for the Puritan fears spontaneous impulses as irrational, and calls the repressive element in his personality 'Reason'.

It would seem, then, that the idea of revolution is an attempt to have things both ways, to have both rationality and spontaneity; and this can only be done by the simple assumption that in some final condition they will not conflict. This assumption is summed up in the revolutionary concept of nature.

ACTIVITY AND PASSIVITY

We may bring some degree of order into the question of freedom if we mark off the three principal parties to any revolution: the revolutionaries themselves, the masses, and the guardians of the *ancien régime*, who might as well be called the reactionaries. The revolutionaries regard themselves as free, since they are consciously taking the initiative; yet they are also necessitated because they are part of an inevitable process. Marx took a hint from Hegel and dialectically embraced this contradiction in the formula that freedom is the recognition of necessity. To have been merely a tool of some historical process would derogate from human dignity, but historical processes appear to be invincible—here the temptations of the contradiction are evident in that the idea of revolution must be shown both as morally superior and as inevitable.

In sophisticated revolutionary writings, the reactionaries have to be presented as puppets on historical strings. They are diminished both by their lack of freedom and their inevitably losing role. There is, however, a strong temptation to regard them as free in order that they may also be regarded as wicked. It is clearly absurd to be indignant at the behaviour of kings, aristocrats, bourgeoisie and foreign colonialists if they are merely playing roles that cannot be changed. Rather similar considerations apply to the masses. Whether they are seen as the victims of bad education, or as sharing a consciousness determined by their position in a class-divided society, they are generally seen as effects rather than as causes. But they do have the option of choosing freedom by joining the revolutionary movement.

Freedom and necessity in Marxist terms are matters of sociological causation, and Marx himself was acutely aware that a satisfactory theory must be rigorously consistent on this point. He attacked earlier socialists for the inconsistency of explaining the people deterministically as the product of their environment, but implying that the socialist thinkers themselves were the miraculous product of some special pipe-line to Reason, unaffected by social circumstances. Yet this question was never solved in Marx's theory. 'The coincidence of the changing of circumstances and of human activity can be conceived and rationally understood only as *revolutionizing practice*',[1] he wrote in 1845. This seems to amount to revolution being understood as a kind of freedom-in-necessity, but it hardly clarifies the question. Forty-five years later Engels wrote: 'We make our history ourselves, but, in the first place, under very definite assumptions and conditions. Among these the economic ones are ultimately decisive. But the political ones, etc., and indeed even the traditions which haunt human minds also play a part, though not the decisive one.'[2] Here the question is begged by the word 'ultimately', and by the conception of conditions playing 'decisive' and 'non-decisive' parts. For how can the 'non-decisive' affect the 'decisive'?

This particular question is certainly insoluble so long as revolutionary theory remains attached to the distinction between fundamental and non-fundamental 'causes' in history. In supposedly scientific revolutionary theory, explanation is taken to mean giving an account of the causes of a thing; such a structure of causes and effects is a historical process, and all appearances of human deliberations and choice must be shown as terms in such a causal sequence. Hence, if freedom is taken to be what is not part of a causal sequence, it simply cannot appear in such a theory. Yet the revolutionary tradition places a considerable emphasis upon freedom, and unless this tradition is utterly incoherent, we must find some place for it. In Condorcet's famous words, 'the word "revolutionary" can be applied only to revolutions whose aim is freedom'. The freedom he meant is convincingly construed by Hannah Arendt as participation in the political realm; more generally, it means having a part in determining the laws of the society in which one lives.[3] Such an understanding of freedom is unexceptionably liberal. In particular, freedom meant a release from the arbitrary oppressions of the *ancien régime*. This is a purely political matter; the theory of revolution soon advanced into social questions. In Marx's words (in which 'materialism' means what we are discussing as the revolutionary tradition): 'The standpoint of the old materialism is "*civil* society"; the standpoint of the new is *human* society, or socialised humanity.'[4] This means a

---

[1] Karl Marx, *Theses on Feuerbach*, III.
[2] Frederick Engels, Letter to J. Bloch, 21–2 September 1890; in Karl Marx and Frederick Engels, *Selected Works* (London, 1950), II, 443.
[3] Arendt, *op. cit.* p. 21.   [4] Karl Marx, *Theses on Feuerbach*, X.

great deal, much of it cloudy, but what it has at least to include under freedom is release from a condition of poverty which it was assumed reduced the proletariat to a form of slavery entirely determined by the necessity of keeping alive. Freedom meant a fully human condition of life, in which men are conscious of choosing what they do.

But the main point remains implicit in Condorcet: freedom is primarily something for the future. The more scientific a theory of revolution tries to be, the more it seeks to exhibit the structural necessity of the processes leading to revolutions, at least under present circumstances. It happens that 'revolution' is an important concept both of political ideology and of a good deal of sociological theory. The common ancestor is, of course, Marx, and something like a joint endeavour has built up a theory of revolution which commands widespread assent. Thus among the necessary conditions of revolutions are to be found a certain economic advance, a situation in which real wages have risen and men, especially in cities, have advanced a good way beyond a subsistence standard of living. It appears to require entrenched social inequalities no longer regarded as part of the order of things by the vast majority of the people. Politically it requires a ruling class which has lost confidence in the old ways, but continues to rule oppressively. In addition, the actual outbreak of a revolution requires certain types of events to trigger it off. One suggested trigger is said to be a sudden brief economic reversal following on a long period of economic advance. A war or a riot commonly helps to precipitate matters.

This type of general theory has produced a tolerable picture of most of the political events we call revolutions. It is only tolerable, however, because of the extreme vagueness of most of the terms involved. To the extent that we can identify these conditions in some historical situation, we shall often find that revolutions either failed or were not attempted. Further, the social dimension of the idea of revolution makes it difficult to judge whether, say, the Iraqi overthrow of the Hashemite monarchy in 1958 should be counted as a revolution or a *coup d'état*. These matters are details, however, because we find here the same kind of split-realm difficulty we found in the Marxist theory of social causation. We are required to distinguish between two radically different classes of facts— structural facts, around which we can construct a general theory, and 'accidental events', which may have a decisive bearing upon the occurrence or non-occurrence of revolutions, but cannot be subsumed under any general theory. Or, we may put the same point in another way: the general theory might, if sufficiently articulated, discover the hypothetical causes which would necessarily lead to *a* revolution, but not to *this* revolution. To talk of the inevitability of the Russian revolution is to conclude more than the historical facts themselves could possibly tell us;

and an episode like Lenin's crossing Germany in a sealed train provided by the Germans remains a weed in a tidy landscape.

There is another crippling difficulty which is even more germane to our discussion of political discontinuity. There has, as we suggested in the last section, only ever been one revolution without a direct model, and that was the French Revolution of 1789. Every revolution since then has been made by men either imitating that revolution directly, or working with a theory of political change based upon those crucial events. These ideological preoccupations with the idea of revolution are clearly important parts of a revolutionary situation which cannot be assimilated into a structural analysis. Marx once remarked that the French Revolution was played out in Roman dress; the revolutionaries of subsequent times have been taking off their trousers in order to play *sansculottes*. Sometimes the existence of a model to imitate has been a valuable aid to the conduct of events by insurgents. On other occasions, it has had a baneful effect. Proudhon summed up the effect in Paris in 1848:

une masse confuse apporte une petition à l'Assemblée: souvenir de 1793. Les chefs du mouvement s'emparent de la tribune et propose un decret: souvenir de Prairial. L'émeute se retire et ses auteurs sont jetés en prison: souvenir de Thermidor...Cette manifestation inintelligente, impuissante, liberticide et ridicule, ne fut, du commencement jusqu'à la fin, qu'une pastiche des grande journées de la Convention.[1]

It is just this element of imitation which allows us to talk in what might otherwise be paradoxical terms of a revolutionary tradition. For if we now turn to try to locate tradition, as we have located 'revolution', in an intellectual context, we shall find that it is a term whose function is to combine freedom and explicability. The actions of a man working within a tradition are not even in principle predictable, yet they are 'all of a piece with' the tradition. We have here a criterion of explicability which does not require any kind of rational necessity; it is, in other words, a historical criterion. We saw that 'revolution' is a term arising in political ideology, history, and sociological theory; 'tradition' too is common to these fields and it is from its historical usages that it takes its main conceptual characteristics. It has no beginning and no end. A tradition can be designated, but it cannot be defined, because any definition would be a formulation of the tradition, and there are any number of possible formulations, none of which can limit or explain its future career. It is both complex and continuous over time, with the consequence that many discernible elements of it will exhibit discontinuity. And like an electrical charge, it may jump over gaps.

[1] J. L. Talmon, *Political Messianism* (London, 1960), p. 454.

Given such a flexible idea, can we find any kind of situation which would prohibit us from assimilating a political revolution to tradition? Can we, in other words, discover in revolution a discontinuity so complete that we might conclude that a political tradition has come to an end? It would help if we could show that revolutions produce unique kinds of social consequences. This is certainly what revolutions are intended to do, but it is difficult to discover any that have. The commonest explicit aims of revolution are liberty and equality; but (however we define them) these things exist as fully in Sweden and Britain, which had no revolution, as in France or Russia. Indeed, the immediate consequence of revolutions has often been a severe contraction of liberty, at least for a short time. Or, it might be thought that revolutions are necessary to break down the rigid and artificial barriers within an outmoded traditional society. Yet many countries have evolved from feudal to modern without such violent upheavals. It might, of course, be said that in some countries such as France or Russia, nothing but a revolution would have succeeded in achieving the same result. But this is again the argument from necessity, and such arguments fail because they go beyond any evidence history could possibly provide, collapsing into the assertion that revolutions were necessary where revolutions occurred. In another version, we shall meet this argument when discussing the possible exhaustion of a tradition.

In certain obvious respects the continuity between a revolutionary regime and its predecessor is very obvious indeed. In Russia, the Ochrana is replaced by the much more efficient MVD. In France, a century of opposition to Hapsburg Austria is rapidly followed by the same policy more energetically pursued. Ironically enough, it is often just the most hated characteristics of the *ancien régime* which reappear magnified in the new order. 'Thus we see that the true historical function of revolutions is to renovate and strengthen power... The peoples erect scaffolds, not as the moral punishment of despotism, but as the biological penalty for weakness... Revolutions rend the air with denunciations of tyrants. Yet in truth they encounter none in their beginnings and raise up their own at their ends.'[1] Here Bertrand de Jouvenel is driving home a paradox, but the facts of the case make it easy for him. And we have already noted that as time passes the revolutionary regime appears increasingly to be no very remarkable continuation of a much longer tradition.

The deliberate and relentless attempts made in revolutions to break all connection with the past might well be seen as an implicit admission of continuity. Like the Anabaptists at Münster, revolutionaries work hard to obliterate all traces of the regime that went before. They try to make the revolution approximate as closely as possible to the foundation

[1] Bertrand de Jouvenel, *On Power* (Boston, 1948), ch. IX, 2, 3. pp. 218–19.

of an entirely new state. The foundation of states is commonly a matter of military conquest, the clamping of a new and alien ruling class upon a conquered country. This is essentially different from any revolution we know. The dispersion of the *émigrés*, the expulsion of some millions of more or less wealthy Russians was a violent breach with the past; yet the events of the revolution had been preceded in each case by a lengthy debate between all the articulate sections of French and Russian politics; and the revolutionaries, whose attitudes had been affected by that debate, were now placed in the same position of responsibility as their predecessors. Much had changed; but a very great deal had not.

We might, however, salvage the belief that a revolution is a radical discontinuity which establishes an entirely new tradition if we were to argue that the very fact of a revolution demonstrates that the antecedent tradition had become exhausted. In this extreme form, the argument falls because it is another variant of the argument from necessity; it is, in other words, historicist. But if we turn it into a loose generalisation that revolutions generally only succeed where the political tradition has become exhausted, then we are forced to consider that it might mean to say that a tradition is exhausted. We might certainly take the view that governments become exhausted; it is commonly said that they lose confidence and 'run out of ideas'. We might also believe that a regime had become 'exhausted'. A constitution, or a class of men, might well keep coming to decisions consistently disliked by most of those who thought about politics; or it might be that disaster in war led people to believe that the regime was unsatisfactory. Under such circumstances as these, we shall find new constitutions being adopted, kings going into or coming out of exile. But governments and regimes are very particular products of a political tradition, and we ought not to take the part for the whole. The argument may become more serious, though also much less precise, if exhaustion is attributed to a political tradition taken as a certain quality of imagination, or a set of principles whose implications had been fully explored and consequently exhausted, or a set of habits and expectations which no longer 'corresponded' to a new situation—particularly in modern times a new situation created by rapid economic change.

Exhaustion may be construed as rigidity: the political tradition refuses to change its habits because to do so would involve the importation of foreign ideas. This suggestion is rendered plausible by the fact that the ideologies of revolution are almost always rationalisations of a foreign way of conducting politics. The *philosophes* had drawn many of their ideas from England, and in Russia Marxism was a vehicle of western ideas. The underlying metaphor here is again biological: revolutions are the convulsions produced by the assimilation of foreign political ideas into a political tradition. Yet once more it is the case that there is nothing reliably regular. The Czarist regime in the decades before 1917, far from remaining rigid, was busily equipping itself with a modern apparatus of representative government. Sometimes, as in the case of Japan, such modifications avert a violent seizure of power, sometimes they don't; and biological metaphors do not greatly help us to distinguish the one case from the other.

It would seem, then, that any attempt to argue that revolutions happen because traditions have become exhausted commits two important mistakes. The first is the fallacy of mistaking the part for the whole; and this fallacy is present no matter how grandiose may be our characterisation of the tradition—even when we are talking of its 'quality of imagination' or the fundamental principles underlying it. For, to lay aside other objections, until a tradition is finished, we must always be generalizing from only a part of the evidence. Secondly, the use of the metaphor of exhaustion reveals the fact that this argument is illicitly turning a tradition into a process (and, metaphorically, a biological process) and this robs the men whose actions are thus explained of that very freedom which it is the essence of the concept of tradition to preserve.

Modern political revolutions are not, then, historically necessary, nor are they the inevitable effect of certain socio-economic structures. On the other hand, it would be absurd to believe that they arise merely from the random wilfulness of wicked men. How may we understand them? In the last section, we explored the revolutionary idea as understood by revolutionaries themselves. Here we may observe that the term 'revolution' is also useful to historians. The historian begins with the actual political insurgence, but his interest soon expands to take in what went before and after. Loosely speaking, the historian is interested in a revolution and its causes; what, he will ask, disposed men to overturn their constitution and set up a new one? In answering this question, he will no doubt pay some attention to the 'causes' suggested by the revolutionaries themselves. But he will suspect that this particular set of causes constitutes a justification of the revolution, and he is not interested in justifications; a set of grievances may be useful but cannot explain why the revolution occurred. He will in fact be more interested in why this particular set of conditions was taken to be a set of grievances. And here, I think, the historians of the French Revolution have come across a disposition, which first grew up in France, to resent a passivity due to social restrictions. Men felt hemmed in, and explained this feeling to themselves in terms of the restrictiveness of the society they lived in.

This revolutionary disposition explains all resented things not as the punishment of God, nor as the niggardliness of nature, but as the effects of a bad society. And what is resented is passivity; not being fully in control of one's destiny. This passivity is a way of characterising all evils—war servility, violence, superstition, criminality, prostitution, commercialism, or (more recently) insanity. In France in the late eighteenth century 'privilege' was supremely the emblem of this restrictiveness which pinned men down to a station and robbed them of their full powers. The demand for equality was a demand for the abolition of privilege; but what it produced was the career open to talent, which released the active potentiality of some who had been resentful (called, in revolutionary theory, the bourgeoisie) but enslaved others. Equality of opportunity is clearly not a possible resting place for such a principle, because it merely changes the incidence, not the fact, of privilege. For talent itself is a social product, partly because society itself determines what is talented and untalented, and partly because it is impossible to put everyone in an equal starting position. It is for this reason that the revolution cannot stop; it must be a ceaseless assault upon the stopping-points supported by those who seem to benefit from the current equilibrium. The fact that the conception of social necessity lies at the centre of the revolutionary disposition is further suggested if we look at the kind of character most anathematised in the revolutionary tradition. This is the philanthropist, the man who benefits from the social structure but tries to nullify the consequent discontent by free acts of generosity. The one doctrine quite intolerable within revolutionary thought is that the only real change in the human situation will arise from a change of heart. This is, of course, a perfectly pragmatic recognition of the fact that the hearts of the rich are touched more easily than their pockets; but change of heart doctrines are resented by the revolutionary disposition not because they are in error, but because they directly threaten the central assumption of social necessity.

It is evident that the revolutionary disposition has a good number of rationalist features. It is addicted to the Cartesian illusion that one can clear the ground and start all over again—the most extreme kind of assertion of activity against mere passive continuity. And as the basis for its political activity, it seeks and believes that it has found fundamental truths which no one but an evident rogue can rationally deny. It prefers 'what has been made to what has grown', for making appears to be a more active process than growth. And it dislikes the past, because in the perspective of time the pressures and conditions of human activity appear inescapable; the actions of past men are always inadequate, aways far from any ideal.

Once we have observed this revolutionary disposition as a modification of European rationalism, we shall also see clearly why the ideas of freedom and necessity are so freely used in rationalist thought. They stand for activity and passivity, understood as the extreme good and the extreme bad in human life. European politics has, in the last two centuries, been strikingly modified by the revolutionary disposition, and by the myth it created out of the French Revolution.

REVOLUTION AND SELF-TRANSFORMATION

If the happiest end of an intellectual inquiry is to discover a single principle of unification, then we have ended in the shallows of misery. For we began with two concepts and ended up with six. The ideas of revolution and tradition arise in three fields—in political discussion, in history and in sociology—and in each field it amounts to a different idea. The field of sociology is, for our purposes, the least complicated, for we found there that the idea of revolution, as a term of social causation, appeared to promise a good deal more than it fulfilled. We found logical confusion in the idea of social causation, and we also found that no regularities appeared to connect a revolution and its causes, unless they were protected by such vagueness of specification as to render the theory suggestive rather than rigorous. And the idea of tradition, as used by sociologists, seemed to stand for an unchanging way of life, existing, like the destined victim in a murder novel, merely to be destroyed by the process of modernisation.

The real confrontation between the ideas of revolution and tradition came in the fields of history and political theory. In politics we found the concept of revolution to be a prolific generator of starting points and, consequently, new identities. 1789 and 1917 are merely the best-known models of revolutions presumed to have introduced a new order into the world, or at least into the nation. The novelty of the political situation was reinforced by the giving of new names, and by exhortation a complete social transformation was attempted, a break with a bad past, in which every national activity became attuned to the new order.

Such attunement was thought possible because a revolution was no ordinary change of government or regime, but, as it were, a philosophical *coup d'état*, philosophical in the sense of claiming to have a method and an understanding of reality behind it. The political triumph therefore seemed no more than the first step to a comprehensive change creating a new identity; and the dates of upheaval were celebrated as a promise and an aspiration, rather than naïvely as the moment when the world was turned upside down. Further, the existence of a philosophy promised what had never previously seemed possible of achievement: the the union of action and thought, or, in the Marxist terminology, the unity of theory and practice. The dream of Plato had come down into the streets. Philosophers had always been recognised as unworldly men, who purchased their clarity and intellectual comprehensiveness at the cost of withdrawal from responsible political action; by contrast, action was something always done rather in a fog, based not upon axioms but upon maxims, generalisations often sufficient to the purpose but inevitably of limited worth in a world of constant surprises and accidents. The onset of philosophical, and consequently (it was hoped) infallible, political action would certainly justify its claim to novelty.

The political idea of tradition could hardly match this headstrong fancy. Conservatives could, of course, point to the glories of the past and insist upon its value; further, if, as often happened, revolution was rapidly followed by civil or external war, then revolutionaries would often discover a reservoir of pride in the past accomplishments of the people; but this could still be done in revolutionary terms. Revolutionaries could plunder tradition without embracing traditionalism. Most fatal of all, the appeal to tradition resolved itself into little more than a timid appeal to caution. Conservatives faced a dilemma: either they rationalised their tradition, in which case it ceased to be tradition and became one more political programme, or else they refused to rationalise it, in which they appeared no more than the upholders of a mystical trust in an existing political arrangement widely regarded as bankrupt.

The political uses of each term seem to have arisen from a sense of confusion in a world without landmarks; and the appeal to tradition, like the appeal to revolution, is an attempt to restore landmarks. The conservative is prepared to abandon perfection and tries to find at least a certain number of reliable bearings in his political tradition; the revolutionary, seeking something more ambitious, attempts to locate his landmarks in the future.

The historical idea of tradition—by contrast with the political—is of much greater range simply because it does not have to be a basis for action. It cannot seriously be eroded by the idea of revolution because it contains within itself the assumption that in time the continuities which have been deliberately, indeed brutally, suppressed in a political revolution, will re-emerge. It is a manner of asserting, within the world of history, the indispensable condition of continuity.

The intellectual confusion so prominent in revolutionary theory is the result of transposing into intellectual terms the conditions of an impossible endeavour. Whereas the historian enjoys the past for its own sake, the revolutionary finds in it little more than the cause of present miseries. And, like a dog chasing its own tail, he seeks actively to get to work on the inaccessible cause of the pain. More than that, he seeks to transform himself into the kind of animal who does not trail this passive and disagreeable organ in his wake. The past must drop off, and the world be remade; and in the idea of revolution man cultivates his romance with the project of self-transformation.

RATIONALISM TRIUMPHANT:
AN ESSAY ON THE
KIBBUTZIM OF ISRAEL

DOROTHEA KROOK

On a working holiday at one of my favourite kibbutzim, in the leisure hours that spring like a heavenly balm from the hot, toiling life of the kibbutz, I found myself re-reading Michael Oakeshott's writings on morals and politics. As I read, recalling and re-living the passion of excitement first induced by those marvellous essays,[1] two questions, seemingly separate and disconnected, kept on crossing and re-crossing my mind. *Is* there an answer to *Rationalism in Politics*? Was there anything in the life of this country that could conceivably interest a mind like Michael Oakeshott's?

The difficulty, I could see, was that everything in this country is in a sense incredibly simple. The simplicity is obviously a function of its smallness and newness—the smallness of its space, numbers and resources, the newness to the job of its politicians, diplomats, civil servants, technologists. Yet (I reflected) it was anything but a toy-state—another Luxembourg, only without the benefit of secure borders. It was a modern state, in the full meaning of the term: small indeed, but complete; containing all the necessary parts of a modern state; each component part a complex little organism; and the whole exceeding the sum of its parts to make a properly national state. It was not even really small (I argued). Rather, it was decently, reassuringly *man-sized*. Bigger than Periclean Athens or Renaissance Venice; but not uncomfortably big, like Great Britain, not an outsize monster, like the United States or Russia or China. Everything here was cut down to human size: visible to the naked eye, reachable by the human hand, graspable by the human mind. In such circumstances, the study of political life and institutions becomes peculiarly attractive and rewarding. The simplicity is encouraging enough, the complexity challenging enough, the errors and follies maddening enough for any imagination; and the precariousness of the whole miraculous artifact makes the game of observation and analysis one of the most serious one has ever engaged in. Add to this a conspicuous absence of social forms (open-necked shirts and the rest), which doubles and trebles the ease of access to almost everything

[1] *Rationalism in Politics and Other Essays* (London: Methuen, 1962).

[309]

that matters in the country—and the exhilarating illusion of being in touch, and (more) of being able to *do* something about almost anything one chooses, is complete. I remembered Michael Oakeshott's doctrine of the reality of such illusions; and was further encouraged by the thought that his generous mind had never been too superior to be interested in simple things. I therefore decided that to honour his greatness I could perhaps do worse than set down the thoughts that have shaped themselves in my mind about the curious little communities, unique to this country, which some sober people have acclaimed as a light for revelation to the Gentiles and the glory of thy people Israel.

With Oakeshott's *Rationalism in Politics* in mind, the light and the glory, I shall want to argue, are in their being the very things that the Oakeshott doctrine proclaims to be impossible. According to this doctrine, no social or political institution which is 'rationalist' in its origin and inspiration, which is founded in ideology and consciously sustained by ideology, can have the character of a natural, living thing—a thing of organic growth, self-perpetuating and self-renovating. For Oakeshott, the 'consciously planned and deliberately executed' is the logical contradiction of that which 'has grown up and established itself unselfconsciously over a period of time'.[1] The first absolutely precludes the second, the second can never issue from the first; where there is conscious planning and deliberate execution, there can be no unselfconscious growth. Again, 'a training in ideology' is radically incompatible with 'an education in behaviour'.[2] Those who have only 'the morality of the self-conscious pursuit of moral ideals'[3] have a 'technical knowledge' but not a 'practical knowledge' of morals and conduct; they have the formulas, but not the skills; they behave according to the book, not according to 'a customary and traditional way of doing things'.[4]

What I want to suggest in this essay is that the kibbutzim of this country effectively disprove these striking contentions. There can be few social communities in the world, present or past, which have been more consciously planned and more deliberately executed; yet their growth, over a period of some fifty years, has been as organic, as spontaneous, and in that sense 'unselfconscious', as that of any society innocent of ideological intention or design. Moreover, though only fifty years old, they give the impression of being as *permanent* as any of the old traditional societies of Europe. Their power to endure seems somehow to be assured by their flexibility and adaptability, by their capacity for self-correction and self-renovation. Again, there can be few young

---

[1] *Ibid.* p. 21. [2] *Ibid.* p. 35.
[3] *Ibid.* p. 35. [4] *Ibid.* p. 10.

people who have ever been subjected to a training as ideological as have those of the kibbutzim, or have had more systematically and relentlessly inculcated into them a morality of the conscious pursuit of moral ideals. Yet this has not prevented them from acquiring an 'education in behaviour'. Nor surprisingly has it prevented the emergence of precisely the kind of moral life Professor Oakeshott recommends. He calls it 'the unselfconscious moral tradition of an aristocracy who, ignorant of ideals, [have] acquired a habit of behaviour in relation to one another and [have] handed it on in a true moral education'.[1] What I will try to show in the last section of this essay is that it is *mutatis mutandis* just such an aristocratic tradition and habit that the kibbutzim of modern Israel appear to be producing.

The rationalist origin and inspiration of the quasi-political movements from which at the turn of the century the kibbutzim sprang are already reasonably well documented.[2] The ideological doctrines of its founding fathers varied considerably, and over an apparently wide range. Many, but by no means all, were Marxist Socialists. Some were Anarchists (usually of the mild Kropotkin variety), some were Tolstoyans, some were influenced by the *Narodniki* (Russian Populists). A few were neither socialist nor non-socialist, but simply apolitical individuals whose imaginations had been kindled by the vision of a perfectly egalitarian, democratic community of workers and peasants in the historic land of the Jews. Viewed in a larger perspective, the seemingly wide range of variation was in fact narrow, being confined for the most part to the radical-revolutionary wing of modern political doctrine when it was not specifically Labour–Socialist. From the standpoint of *Rationalism in Politics*, however, what they all had in common is obvious. They were all uncompromisingly, ferociously, intransigently ideological. They believed unquestioningly in the power of ideology to create a new and better society; and they were resolutely determined to create such a society, which should not only be good and just, but good and just for the

---

[1] *Ibid.* p. 35. The young people of the kibbutzim are of course not literally 'ignorant of ideals'; but nor are those of Oakeshott's historic aristocracies; and I will want to argue that here as there a consciousness of moral ideals is not incompatible with their being practised by inherited custom and tradition, so long as the condition Oakeshott mentions (*ibid.* p. 36) is satisfied—namely, that the ideals are 'a sediment, suspended in a religious or social tradition,...belonging to a religious or social life'.

[2] Mainly in books and articles in Hebrew, most of them not available in English. An article by Dr Shlomo Avineri, 'Israel in the Post-Ben Gurion Era' (*Midstream*, September 1965), discusses these movements in a slightly different context. The topic is also briefly treated in the excellent book on the kibbutzim in general, *The Other Society* by H. Darin-Drabkin (London: Gollancz, 1962). This book contains a full bibliography of works on the kibbutzim available in English, French and German. *The Kibbutz* by Dan Leon (Israel Horizons and World Hashomer Hatzair, 1964), also very good, contains a short bibliography of works in English.

right reasons—that is, consistent to the last detail with the basic doctrines of the chosen ideology.

The more utilitarian reasons for the founding of the kibbutzim have sometimes been used as an argument against the attribution of a solely ideological foundation. Where is the ideology (it has been asked) in going in for the type of settlement which happened to have been, in the conditions of colonisation of the place and time, merely the most economical form of social organisation and the best suited for purposes of defence? Given the small numbers of the colonists, it was obviously economically intelligent to do what they did: the women could be released for an eight-hour work-day by having the children brought up communally in separate children's houses, by communal eating, laundering, clothes-making; the pooling of economic resources (modest farming experience, modest supplies of tools and implements) made subsistence farming just possible; a twenty-four hour guard could be kept against Turkish and Arab marauders. Economic necessity and physical survival were the real causes; ideology only helped to sugar the pill—made the grinding labour and the human deprivations (the sacrifice of personal freedom, the close communality of the life) more endurable.

The answer to this argument is I think obvious. Why in conditions of colonisation not essentially dissimilar did (say) America, Canada, South Africa, Australia *not* go in for this kind of settlement? Why did it not occur to them; or if it had, would have been vigorously rejected (one may safely suppose that a South African Dutch Voortrekker family would sooner have died a hundred times at the hands of their Zulu enemies than give up the smallest scrap of their independence as a family unit); or, when it *did* occur (to Coleridge, Southey and their fellow-Pantisocrats, for instance) it met the usual fate of such utopian schemes? If it did occur to the Jewish settlers in Palestine in the period immediately before and after the First World war, it was because certain potent ideological movements of the later nineteenth century put the idea into their heads; and if it worked, and has continued to work for nearly half a century, it is because they believed that they were creating a new and better society, which was to be a model to all mankind and a pride and joy to every participant in the great work. The utilitarian reason reinforced the ideological, but never replaced or displaced it; and if the thing is a triumph—which has still to be shown—it is distinctly a triumph of ideology.

Ideology (I first want to argue) is their life's blood. The ideological passion that brought them into being; the unsleeping consciousness of ideological ends, purposes, tasks to be pursued and accomplished; the consistent reference to fundamental principles of every 'issue', every decision, big or small, affecting the life of the community, or that of an individual member, or that of the kibbutzim as a whole in their relation to the political life of the country: all this has persisted through the half-century of their existence, and continues virtually unabated to the present day. Ideological bonds have sustained them in a fellowship of mutual responsibility and service such as the western world has probably not known since the time of the primitive Christian churches; ideological differences have brought them, over and over again, to the edge of self-destruction; and the tension between the bonds that sustain them and the differences that threaten to tear them to pieces defines the very essence of their passionate life.

The ideological issues that have preoccupied them have been, broadly speaking, of two kinds: the strictly internal, that is, those bearing exclusively or almost exclusively on the internal organisation and life of the kibbutz; and the external, or those concerned mainly with the relation of the three principal federations of kibbutzim to the national political parties that represent them in the Knesset (parliament) and in the coalition government. These parties are historically closely connected with the kibbutz federations, if not actually their offspring, and the kibbutzim exercise a powerful influence on their national policies.[1]

[1] There are three principal federations, and the majority of kibbutzim (93·4%) belong to one of these. Moving from Right to Left, there are the kibbutzim of the *Ichud* group, affiliated to *Mapai*, the Labour party roughly corresponding to the Gaitskell–Wilson centre of the British Labour Party; those of the *Meuchad* group, affiliated to Ahdut Ha'Avoda, roughly corresponding to the Left, formerly Aneurin Bevan, wing of the British Labour Party; and those of the *Artzi* group, affiliated to *Mapam*, which formally corresponds to the extreme Left (Silverman–Brockway) fringe of the British Labour Party but is in fact closer in character and spirit—and in historical importance—to the old Independent Labour Party of Keir Hardie. (The full titles of the federations are, respectively, *Ichud Hakvutzot Vehakibbutzim, Kibbutz Meuchad* and *Kibbutz Artzi Hashomer Hatzair*.) According to the most recent figures published, of a total of 222 kibbutz settlements, seventy-nine belong to the Ichud (Mapai) federation, seventy-three to the Artzi (Mapam) group, and fifty-six to the Meuchad (Ahdut Ha'Avoda). The Ichud group, however, includes about five kibbutzim affiliated to the Liberal Party. There is also a small number of religious kibbutzim, eleven in all, nine of these affiliated to the *Hapoel Hamizrachi*, the Labour wing of the religious political parties, and two to the extreme religious *Poalei Aguda* party. The Communist party has one kibbutz settlement; and there are just two kibbutzim with no political affiliations. Until the recent (1968) unification of the separated Labour parties, Mapai was the biggest single party, without however commanding an absolute majority. It formed coalition governments with one or both of the other two Labour parties, with the more moderate of the religious parties (the National Religious Party), and sometimes also with the whole or part of the Liberal Party (corresponding very closely to the British Liberal Party). In the present National Government, Mapai, Ahdut Ha'Avoda and Rafi, a right-centre splinter of Mapai, have formed a united Labour Party, which Mapam has as yet refused to join. The corresponding kibbutz federations, however, have remained separate.

I ought to mention that the kibbutzim of which I have personal knowledge are confined to the Kibbutz Meuchad (Ahdut Ha'Avoda) group. In respect to their ideological commitments, they are firm but rather less rigid than are those of the Kibbutz Artzi (Mapam) group, and rather more rigid than are those of the Ichud (Mapai) group.

Of the internal issues, one of the most sharply divisive in the past ten years and more has been that of the use of hired labour in the kibbutzim, precipitated by the mass immigrations from 'oriental' (non-European) countries in the early 1950s. With few exceptions, the immigrants from North Africa or Iraq or Persia did not want to become members of a kibbutz. Unaccustomed to a routine of work, they viewed with horror the idea of working an eight-hour day six days of every week of every month of every year. They disliked and feared, so far as they understood it, all the business about the communal ownership of property. Moreover, they did not at best feel at ease with their European brethren, at worst felt themselves despised and discriminated against; and they generally preferred to set up a wretched kiosk in an over-crowded Tel-Aviv street sooner than become free and noble tractor-drivers or tomato-growers in a kibbutz. Failing the kiosk, they were however prepared to work as hired labourers in the kibbutzim; and given on the one hand the kibbutzim's chronic shortage of labour, and on the other the national problem of finding employment for the masses of unskilled new immigrants, it could be reasonably argued (as Ben-Gurion and other supporters of the hired-labour policy did vehemently argue) that to give employment to the unemployed was both the patriotic duty of the kibbutzim and a useful, indeed necessary, means to their own economic survival, and that it was folly and wickedness to refuse. Some of the kibbutim did not refuse; but the majority did: on the sound ideological[1] ground that the habitual employment of hired labourers[1] violated a fundamental principle of their society, that of the common and equal ownership of the community's property and means of production, and of the fruits of its labour; and that it invited the creation of what they called an 'employer's mentality', whose demoralising effects on the prized egalitarianism of their social structure was justly to be feared. Their opponents called them fanatic purists, anti-patriots, anti-Zionists, accused them of loving their dogmas better than their fellowmen, prophesied their deserved economic ruin. They retorted that economic ruin was as nothing compared with moral ruin; that their opponents had no care for the true socialism, which ought to be their most sacred trust; and that they (the opponents) would be better employed in prevailing upon the recalcitrant Oriental immigrants to join the kibbutzim as full participating members.

The argument continues to the present day—even though the ex-

---

[1] The emphasis is on the 'habitual'. Almost all the kibbutzim have at one time or another employed hired labour for certain essential kinds of work, mainly building and teaching, when they have not been able to produce from among their members the number of building workers or teachers urgently needed. But (they argue) there is all the difference between taking hired labour only in emergencies and habitually employing it; and this, it seems, was not seriously disputed by the opposition.

perience of the past ten years appears to favour the opponents of hired labour, and the most recent solutions proposed proceed from the view that the hired-labour policy has failed. The kibbutzim which did not take hired labourers have pointed out that the kibbutzim which did have been demoralised in exactly the way they said they would be. The employers' mentalities among them have increased and multiplied, and are a horror to see; their economic expansion has not been so spectacular as to give them even the base utilitarian justification they hoped for; and the situation has produced other ironies. For instance, the hired labourers appear to have been left completely unmoved by the inspiring example of employers working not for private profit but for the communal welfare. They have resented having to take orders from an employer who doesn't look like an employer but only like another worker; they have demanded the rights and privileges of members of the kibbutz, and have complained of 'discrimination' when these were refused; they have tended to do bad, sloppy work. Labour relations, in short, between employer and employed in these kibbutzim have been no better, and in some respects a shade worse, than they are in the rest of the country; and this has led the critics of the hired-labour policy to moralise about what happens to people who have had a long and expensive socialist education when they slip into shady capitalist practices. A recent decision of the Kibbutz Meuchad group has been to forbid the starting of new kibbutz enterprises (factories mainly) which are so big as to require hired labour: they are to be kept small enough to be run by a labour force drawn exclusively from the membership of the kibbutz; and if this means a slower rate of economic expansion and a freezing of, if not a drop in, the standard of living, so much the worse (they say) for the standard of living.

In the sphere of education, the disputed issues are especially numerous, even though (or perhaps because) there is the widest general agreement about the value and importance of education. The reasons for the agreement about principles are easy to see. Being Jews and having the Jew's traditional reverence for learning for its own sake, the kibbutzim attach the greatest importance to the kind and quality of the formal education given to their children and young people. Being socialists and egalitarians, they believe in the doctrine of the equality of opportunity for the enjoyment of all the good things of life, and in the benefits of a decent education as among the best of these good things. Being socialists and egalitarians in the modern world, and knowing that their survival as self-supporting economic communities depends on a high standard of literacy among their members, they recognise the utilitarian value of a good general education.

However, pedagogic truth is not always easily reconciled with ideological truth; and one of the main recent disputes has been about the introduction of 'streaming' into the kibbutz secondary schools. That the question should have arisen so relatively late is due to the simple fact that, until the last ten years or so, the number of children of secondary school age even in the biggest kibbutzim was so small as to make streaming economically unthinkable. But as the numbers have grown, it has become economically feasible—on condition that certain changes in established attitudes and practices were accepted; and it is the proposed changes that have raised the ideological storms.

Pedagogically speaking, the best solution was obviously to scrap the small secondary schools of the individual kibbutzim, and to establish large schools of the 'comprehensive' type, preferably large enough to serve each group of kibbutzim on a nation-wide scale. The first experiment in this kind of school was made by the Kibbutz Artzi group, which long ago set up and to this day maintains a single big boarding-school for all its secondary-school pupils. (The pupils include a substantial number of non-kibbutz children from the cities and towns.) The experiment was judged to have been a failure by the other groups of kibbutzim, for two principal reasons. The first, the economic, was that the removal of the bigger children deprived the kibbutzim of their much-needed labour. The second and more important was moral and ideological: the absence of the older children impoverished the social and cultural life of the kibbutz; threatened to undermine a traditional function of the older children, that of acting as 'instructors' and leaders to the younger children; and violated that basic principle of kibbutz life which attaches the highest value to the actual physical presence of every member and his direct and continuous participation in the life of the community.

The idea of national comprehensive secondary schools was therefore abandoned in favour of the 'regional' secondary school—that is, a school just big enough to serve all the kibbutzim in a given region; and this did appear to solve the main problems created by the national boarding school, especially if the regional schools were day-schools. As the school was very close to most of the kibbutzim in the region, the problem of the loss of the young people's labour was solved: they could go home every day and work on their own kibbutzim in the normal way; or, alternatively, by a rotation-and-exchange system, they could give their labour to other kibbutzim (especially for seasonal work), which would in due course 'repay' the labour they had received. The moral problem, turning on their physical absence from their own kibbutzim, appeared likewise to be solved. If they could go home to their kibbutzim every day, the loss to the social and cultural life of the community was reduced to a minimum; and even if the schools were boarding-schools (there would be very few of these, as day-schools were distinctly preferred), they could still remain physically much closer to the life of their kibbutzim—by going home for the Sabbath, for instance—than they could if they were at a national boarding-school at a great distance from their own kibbutzim.

Such regional schools have in fact been established by the Ichud group of kibbutzim, and a few also by the Kibbutz Hameuchad group. But the struggle continues, especially in the Kibbutz Hameuchad; and the resistance, coming mainly from the smaller kibbutzim, has not yet been broken down. These small kibbutzim still passionately believe that their older children ought to form an integral part of their own kibbutz community; therefore they still prefer a small secondary school of their own to a regional school. They are willing, indeed eager, to have children from 'outside' (from the cities, towns and villages) attending the school, to augment the numbers to a size which makes streaming economically possible. But if these reinforcements are insufficient, they are willing it seems to sacrifice the pedagogic value of streaming for other social and moral values. Under pressure, indeed, they are liable to reveal a deep distrust of the whole idea of streaming, on the grounds of its supposed inegalitarianism. Where there is no streaming (they argue), the young people enjoy a sense of equality, the absence of a sense of 'discrimination' (however objectively justified), the corporate spirit induced by a common class-room experience, the comradely help of the weaker by the stronger; and these together (they claim) are worth more for the communal life of the kibbutz than the presumed educational benefits—which in this mood they may go so far as to doubt—of the streaming system.

Thus up to the present, at least in the Kibbutz Hameuchad, the die-hard ideologues have on the whole had their way. And to the extent that they have, they are (their opponents say) allowing to go to waste a valuable resource of the kibbutzim and of the country as a whole. According to one intelligent view, the regional secondary schools of the kibbutzim are peculiarly favoured to become the Etons and Winchesters of the country: by the prestige the kibbutzim as such enjoy with the public; by the general recognition of the superior moral calibre of young people brought up on a kibbutz; and even (a point not as trivial as it seems) by certain lucky physical features—that they can readily offer boarding facilities to young people from every part of the country, and that they have the traditionally right setting, being situated generally in the depths of the country, often in the midst of magnificent natural scenery. Etons and Winchesters in the Emek, the Galilee, the Carmel! Scaled down, of course, to the proportions appropriate to a population of less than three million instead of fifty million;

but aiming at scholastic standards as high (and why not, if the Jews are, as everyone says, the most intellectual people in the world?); providing the training in leadership which the kibbutzim have anyhow provided for nearly fifty years; and (best of all) improving upon their great models by the infusion of the socialist-egalitarian light—being the English public schools stripped of whatever class-consciousness, snobbism, false social privilege they still retain. It is no wonder that my interlocutor gazed wistfully at the vision, and execrated the kibbutz ideologues whose eyes are sealed to it.

In my attempt to argue the ubiquitous presence of the ideological in the life of the kibbutzim, I have chosen two examples which I hoped could make their point without an excess of particular detail. For the true flavour and savour of the thing, however, the particularity is of course essential; and there is nothing more fascinating, as one goes deeper into one's study of the phenomenon, than the repeated recognition of the general-ideological lurking in the most minutely particular of the 'issues' one hears publicly and privately discussed. There would not be room in an essay of this length to give even the first ramifications of the ideological considerations involved (for instance) in the controversy, still not settled, about the proper *size* of a kibbutz: whether kibbutzim should remain small, deliberately limiting themselves to 300–500 souls, or should expand to the limit of their physical capacity (a thousand souls or more), and which is the more fully consistent with the principles and ideals of kibbutz life. Or again, there is the problem that exercises some of the new kibbutzim in particular—whether the basic principles and ideals of kibbutz life require separation of parents and children, or whether the children may be permitted—once the kibbutz can afford it economically—to live with their parents; and if they may, for which part of their lives—from infancy to the beginning of school-life (up to the age of 6), or during the elementary-school years (6–12), or later.[1] The practical questions are of course answered with the help of non-ideological psychology; but the rights and wrongs of the principle are argued in the light of the communal ideal, and its prescriptions (in this instance) about the values of a literally common, equal upbringing in the communal children's houses. At the other end of the educational process, there is again the difficult and delicate

[1] In the great majority of the kibbutzim—more than 90%—the children live entirely in their separate children's houses, and never (except as a special treat on Friday nights, for instance) sleep in their parents' houses. In many of the newer kibbutzim, however—which may not yet have built their permanent houses, and can therefore more easily make the physical arrangements required—there is pressure from the mothers to have their children sleeping at home for a given period of time, as the children do in a few of the older kibbutzim. This is one reason why the question is constantly being discussed, in all its ideological and psychological bearings; and it seems likely that more and more kibbutzim may adopt the practice already prevailing in some.

question of a university education for the academically gifted young people. Of these—alas for the peasant-and-worker ideal of the kibbutz—there is, as in every Jewish community, a significantly high proportion; and the problem they create is, like so many other kibbutz problems, at once and almost inseparably economic and ideological. Should a young man capable of being a brilliant lawyer or research scientist or (worse) philosopher or literary critic be allowed to become one, even though once he has completed his professional training the kibbutz can make no use of him—in which case he leaves the kibbutz, and some twenty-four years of expensive keep and education have, from the book-keeping point of view, gone down the drain? Or, ignoring the budgetary side and looking only at the moral-ideological: is it really a good thing (ask some of the older comrades, remembering the European Jewish café intelligentsia of the first world war period) to foster the intellectual powers at the expense of the physical and manual; and if we do, are we not slipping back into the unnatural condition of Jewry in dispersion, which was all lawyers, doctors, and philosophers with not a tractorist or tomato-grower to offset them? On the other hand, if as we claim we regard learning and the life of the mind as a supreme good, are we not bound to rejoice in the intellectual gift above all others, and—following the immemorial tradition of our people—do all we can to stimulate and develop it? The task of deciding between these conflicting claims is obviously not an easy one; and this is why no doubt they constantly return to the problem in the various forums of debate in which the ideological battles of the kibbutzim are conducted.

These are, principally, the General Assembly (the *assefa klalit*) of each individual kibbutz, held once a week, generally on Saturday nights; the meetings of the Central (Executive) Committee of each federation of kibbutzim, which take place once every 5–6 weeks; and the Plenary Conference of the federation, held every 4–6 years. These together, but especially the Conferences, offer a rich return to the interested observer —an innermost window into the ideological life of the kibbutzim. At a typical Conference, the platform is dominated by members of the first and second generations—that is, the founding fathers and their sons and daughters; the third generation (the oldest are 19–25) are still too young to take the lead, and come mainly as audience, to listen and learn. The visitor marvels first at the fluency of the speakers: they never seem to hesitate for a moment, never have to search for a word, never emit those gentlemanly um's and ah's which no English public speaker would dare to appear without. From this he rightly infers two things: first, that they are so fluent because they are so single-minded in the pursuit of the object—they keep their eyes firmly fixed on the object, trusting it to supply them with the words they need; second, that they are wonderfully *at ease*—with their ideas, with themselves, with their audience. The style of debate tends to follow that of the Russian revolutionary leaders, who were often in fact the mentors of the first generation of kibbutz leaders. The speeches are often immensely long: an address of three hours or more is, or was until recently, considered a reasonable norm. They are sometimes a trifle deficient in form, and may lack a clearly defined beginning, middle and end. There is plenty of natural elo- quence, but when this fails, the favourite modes of achieving the sublime are the high-rhetorical and the visionary-prophetic. These however are reassuringly mingled with homely parable, unembarrassed jokes, and a mass of anecdotage, some of it—especially that of the oldest kibbutz leaders, who really were there and remember exactly what Ussishkin said to Herzl about Uganda at the Sixth World Zionist Congress of 1903—a treasure-mine for the historian. The younger part of the audi- ence generally listens attentively, and appears to be curiously forbearing about the flowers of rhetoric and the prophetical afflatus—neither responsive nor irresponsive, neither pleased nor irritated.

The visitor cannot help noticing other things, too. The violence of extreme partisanship, for instance; the sense of proportion often lost or misplaced—the little made great and the great little; a vast deal of parochialism; and, for the Jewish observer, the faint, persistent scent, not wholly agreeable to refined nostrils, of the Jewish *Kleinstadt* of Eastern and Central Europe, from which most of the founding fathers came—its way of viewing and doing things, which are not always the ways of a free and sovereign people. Presently the disagreeableness passes off; and then he sees only how profoundly, unalterably charac- teristic it all is. As he looks and listens, he finds himself remembering Matthew Arnold's famous definition of the Hebraic spirit.[1] He recog- nises its earnestness, its tenacity, its assurance, its intensity, as it bears down on him, like the columns of hot wind that blow in from the Sea of Galilee on an August afternoon, from the speakers on the Conference platform.

Turning briefly to matters bearing on the relation of the kibbutzim to the larger political life of the country, one discerns the same kind of ideological warfare, conducted with the same earnestness, tenacity, assuredness and intensity. Every student of the short political history of the country knows the story of the bitter ideological conflicts that have split and re-split the Labour parties, and the kibbutzim's intimate connection with these. In the past twenty-five years alone there have been no fewer than four major splits. These were the Great Split of 1944, of the original Mapai and Ahdut Ha'Avoda parties; in 1952, the split

---

[1] Matthew Arnold, *Culture and Anarchy* ('Hebraism and Hellenism').

of the kibbutzim of the Meuchad group, into the present Ichud and Meuchad groups; in 1954, the Second Great Split, this time of the Mapam party, into the present Mapam and Ahdut Ha'Avoda (the latter having joined Mapam after the 1944 split from Mapai); and in 1965, the further split of Mapai, into the Rafi party, led by Ben-Gurion, and the present Mapai, which has been joined by Ahdut Ha'Avoda to form a new 'Alignment' party. One cannot help remembering Winston Churchill's penetrating observations about the irrepressible contentiousness of the Jews:

No matter how forlorn their circumstances or how grave the peril to their country, they are always divided into many parties, with many leaders who fight among themselves with desperate vigour...[They] have shown a capacity for survival, in spite of unending perils and sufferings from external oppressors, matched only by their own ceaseless feuds, quarrels and convulsions...Centuries of foreign rule and indescribable, endless oppression leave them still living, active communities and forces in the modern world, quarrelling among themselves with insatiable vivacity.[1]

To make these splits fully intelligible would require an account of their complex causes more detailed than any I can attempt here. I will therefore only mention the main disputed issues. In the 1944 split, when the country was still under British Mandatory rule and the Jewish community in Palestine had suspended its struggle for independence to support the Allies' war against Nazi Germany, they turned upon whether a sovereign Jewish national state was or was not a necessary condition for the accomplishment of the great Zionist aim of 'the ingathering of the exiles'; whether, consequently, Partition was a good or a bad thing; whether, in the circumstances of the time, the Jewish national state was more likely to be achieved by 'political' means—that is, by Great Power support, and diplomatic activity directed to that end—or by the building up of the 'independent strength' of the Jewish community in Palestine—that is, by illegal defence, illegal immigration, and continual, unremitting settlement; whether in the pursuit of the 'political' method, it was or was not desirable to seek alignment with the Western powers, at the possible cost of alienating Soviet Russia; and, finally—the most bitterly disputed issue, and the immediate cause of the split—whether 'factional freedom' was or was not to be permitted: whether minority views were to be allowed full freedom of expression in their own separate publications, or whether they were to be suppressed in the interest of party unity. The split of 1954, taking a stage further one of the issues of the 1944 split, turned principally on the proper attitude of a Jewish socialist party towards Soviet Russia: whether it should be 'sympathetic'

[1] Winston Churchill, *History of the Second World War*, vol. v.

(because we were socialists, and the Soviet Union was the centre of the socialist half of the world), or 'cool' (because Russia was anti-Zionist, and at that time actively persecuting Jews); and, again, on the question of freedom of expression of minority views. The Mapai split of 1965 is still too close, and its causes—ideological, practical and personal—still too entangled, to admit of a summary statement. What can safely be said is that at least some of the ideological issues were not new, being a development or outcome of disputes leading to the earlier splits, and that the kibbutzim were involved in this as they were in the previous ones.

The historic split of the kibbutzim of the Meuchad federation in 1952 appears to have been an indirect, and so to speak delayed, consequence of the Great Split of Mapai in 1944. The kibbutzim generally sympathetic to Mapai policies left, to form their own separate federation (the Ichud); the kibbutzim generally supporting Ahdut Ha'Avoda (which was then still a part of Mapam) remained in sole possession of the Meuchad federation. The act of separation was a bitter and protracted affair. It affected some of the oldest, biggest kibbutzim; agreement about the division of communal property it entailed was often difficult to reach; and while the negotiations were in progress—sometimes continuing for a period of years—the former fellowship of labour and love was violently disrupted. One heard dreadful tales of families divided; of communal dining-halls, in which comrades had eaten together for thirty years, literally separated into two sections, each party eating on its own side, with faces averted from the other; and almost all the normal activities of an established kibbutz—fresh building, planting of new trees and grass, even re-painting of houses and trimming of gardens —brought to a halt. I remember a visit to one of these old kibbutzim in 1958, when the division had only just been completed, and the impression I received of a great estate fallen into neglect and desolation: unkept and untidy, still, inactive, stifled by a deathly sort of languor. It has since become one of the most beautiful kibbutzim in its region, all trees, lawns and roses, its former intense human life fully restored, its ideological quarrels (new ones) resumed and proceeding at the General Assemblies each Saturday night with unabated vigour. I think of it as a paradigm of the mysterious workings of ideology in the life of the kibbutz: its power alternately to devastate and to restore, perhaps— remembering Winston Churchill's prophetic words—in an unending cycle.

Some may think that I have over-proved my case about the kibbutzim and their ideological entanglements. Does anyone who knows anything about the matter really dispute it? The answer, surprisingly, is that people do; and still more surprising are the people who do. I have been told by a distinguished professor of economics of the Liberal school that, whatever they may have been in their glorious past, the kibbutzim are now thoroughly, irredeemably 'bourgeois, conservative and conformist'. They are bourgeois in having long ago given up the ideal of plain living and high thinking, and in now caring about the material amenities of life—the 'standard of living'—quite as much as the rest of depraved modern humanity. They are conservative in nevertheless clinging to and propagating—muddle-headedly or disingenuously or both—their Marxist-socialist dogmas about the divine election of the proletariat, the millennial virtue of the public ownership of the means of production, and so on, without a care for modern social and economic realities. They are conformist (of course) in caring nothing about the liberty of the individual—demanding the kind of rigid conformity to the standards of life, thought, speech, dress prescribed by the community which crushes individuality out of existence. The professor represents a point of view widely held in Liberal circles in the country. This is that the kibbutzim have 'played an important historic role' in the development of the country, but have 'had their day': they are now out-dated, nonfunctional bodies, out of step with the times, an economic liability, a moral nuisance, and interesting chiefly as museum-pieces, for the use of the historian and social anthropologist.

On the other side, I have heard the nationalist-ideological foundation of the kibbutzim fiercely denied by a famous old kibbutz leader, who was one of the chief architects of the whole wonderful structure, and still, at the age of over eighty, exercises a formidable influence on the national policies of his kibbutz 'movement' and thus on those of the country. I had been telling him, in a social sort of way, about the little essay I was planning to write about the kibbutzim as a triumph of rationalism, in the complacent expectation of receiving nothing but praise for the virtuous enterprise, and of course full confirmation of my view. Instead, to my astonishment, I got a kind of Hegelian–Bradleyan–Oakeshottian tirade against the vicious abstractionism of ideologies in general, and a passionate repudiation of the idea that the kibbutzim were ideological or 'rationalist'. They were *a way of life* (he shouted), not an idea; they were concrete, palpable, tangible realities, not a tissue of doctrines and dogmas in somebody's handbook of socialism; they were designed—and succeeded in their design—to express and fulfil the intuitive, non-rational, non-conscious depths of man's nature, not just the rational, conscious, intellectual side of it; it was *the whole man*, including in particular his physical, corporeal being, that was committed to the business, not just his shallow little mind; and if I had *lived* in a kibbutz for forty years as he had I would know what he was talking about, and wouldn't want to make such a song and dance about the ideology. Knowing that he had also spent the forty years in ceaseless exposition, in speeches, writings and 'seminars', of the ideological foundations of the kibbutz movement, and was at that moment still the head of the avowedly ideological training-college of his group of kibbutzim, I had reason to be dismayed and amused at his act of rejection. I could see, however, that it was the word 'rationalist' that had upset him, and I tried to explain that 'rationalist' in this particular argument (Oakeshott's) was used synonymously with 'ideological', but of course needn't be; that 'ideological' could (and in my opinion should) be used in a more inclusive sense, to take in the intuitive, non-rational, non-conscious side that he minded so much about, as I did; and surely he didn't deny that the ideological in this inclusive sense *was* the foundation, heart's blood, etc., of the kibbutzim. But he seemed not to be interested—seemed to find the super-subtle distinctions wearisome, kept on repeating, 'It's a way of life, a way of life'; and I went away without the blessing I had come for, almost convinced that he was right, and almost did not write the essay.

Luckily, this same group of kibbutzim soon afterwards held a Conference, whose proceedings resolved any last lingering doubts about the ideological issue, restored confidence in my project, and added substantially to the store of impressions from which the idea, or Idea, of the Kibbutz finally shaped itself.

Stripping it to the bone, I think the idea in its Platonic essence is composed of the following irreducible elements. They are (1) the common ownership of all material goods; (2) the equal distribution of all material goods; (3) equality of opportunity to enjoy all the non-specialised (general, human) cultural and spiritual goods, opportunity according to ability for the more specialised; (4) the democratic administration of the life of the community; (5) the simplicity or modesty of the material arrangements of life; (6) the principle of example and leadership, yielding the principle of aristocracy.

I have judged these to be the necessary and exhaustive conditions. A kibbutz must satisfy each and all to be a kibbutz; if it does not, it is not a kibbutz, or at best a 'degenerate' one (like the degenerate workers' state of Trotsky's theory about the U.S.S.R.). All the more specific ideals, aims and objects of the kibbutzim, all their existing institutions, habits and practices are either subsumed by them, in which case they are essential; or, if they are not thus subsumed, they are not essential—though the inessential may, in special circumstances, and with the weaknesses of human nature in mind, be desirable, helpful, even necessary.

I propose to pass briefly over the first five points, some of which are self-explanatory, and to linger over the last, whose meaning and implications are I think least obvious.[1]

About the common ownership of all material goods—the land, buildings, equipment, productive labour and services of the whole community—all that need be said is that it is a fixed, unalterable belief of every member that the private ownership of property is the *radix malorum* in human life, and that it is futile to talk about a good and just society where the basic condition of goodness and justice—the absolute proscription of private ownership of property—is absent. It is, for such a bunch of 'idealists' as the world thinks them, a curiously realistic position, implying a pessimistic view of human nature. They do not say that private ownership 'as such' is bad; they only say that men, being the greedy, possessive, competitive, prestige-loving creatures they are, cannot be allowed to have this instrument of power for the domination and exploitation of their fellow-men put into their hands. If we want them to be 'good' that, is, to behave decently, *the least* we have to do is to deprive them of the possibility of accumulating wealth. This alone won't ensure their goodness, but without this nothing else will avail. Accordingly, this principle is rigidly observed by the kibbutzim, without significant exception.[2] No member of a kibbutz owns anything as his personal property, every member so long as he remains a member owns everything the community possesses; and on the whole they behave like owners of everything, not like owners of nothing. But of their attitude and stance in respect to property and money I shall have more to say presently.

There are some who, standing upon the letter of things, have denied the absolute equality of the distribution of the material goods and services of the commune. They will point to the fact that the grandmothers and grandfathers might have such amenities as refrigerators (or electric fires, fans, kettles) while their sons and grandsons have not; that some members have the use of a 'private' motor-car while the rest have not, and so on. The answer is that these seeming irregularities are in fact strictly regulated. They are derived from what are believed to be considerations of reason, justice and humanity which do not violate the

---

[1] For an excellent account of the democratic administration, see H. Darin-Drabkin, *The Other Society*, ch. 4; 'Management and Democracy' (pp. 98–112).

[2] A test-case was the German Restitution payments, made for the most part in the late 'fifties. Members of kibbutzim who received such payments handed over the money to the kibbutz treasury; and where the total sum was big enough, it was used for some special purpose, like the building of a library or lecture-hall or the erection of a memorial building or foundation. Those who did not want to do this left the kibbutz, taking their money with them. In some kibbutzim, members were allowed to keep a small sum (not more than IL. 1,000—£125—at most), on condition that they used it only as they would their normal cash allowance, that is, for small personal purchases, gifts, etc. Even this concession, however, was regarded as a deviation from principle by the majority of kibbutzim.

principle of the equal distribution of material goods and services; and they (the considerations) are agreed to be thus and not otherwise by the democratically determined consent of the community as a whole. Thus, given a scarcity of refrigerators (or electric kettles, fires and fans), it is agreed to be just, reasonable and humane that the oldest, 'veteran' members shall have them before the rest. Given a scarcity of motor-cars, it is just and reasonable that someone who is a Member of Parliament and has to make regular and frequent journeys to Jerusalem shall have the first the kibbutz can afford (if it can't afford even one, the M.P. has to travel by train or coach); that a veteran member who is not an M.P. but is crippled, and does administrative work entailing journeys on kibbutz business, shall have the second the kibbutz can afford; that a member who is not an M.P. and not crippled but needs it for an 'outside' job shall have the next,[1] and so on. Apart from these regulated exceptions, the rule concerning the distribution of material goods is: No one shall have a refrigerator, an electric kettle, an electric fire— or for that matter, at an earlier stage, a mattress, a cupboard, a table and chair—until everyone can have one.

I think the thing that first struck me as matter for reflection in the kibbutz set-up was the combination of a conspicuous simplicity in the material arrangements of life with a remarkably high level of education, culture, and, in general, preoccupation with these things. In modern Western society, there have of course always been individuals or families who, from choice or necessity, have lived very simply while dedicating themselves to the things of the spirit; and poets in Parisian garrets and Bohemians in chilly London bed-sitters are a class familiar enough. Yet, broadly speaking, Western society leads one to associate refinement of mind and taste with a certain refinement in the material arrangements of life. One thinks of Oxford and Cambridge colleges, of the great libraries in the great English country-houses (perhaps not as much used these days as they used to be, but still there), of the Huxleys, the Stracheys, Virginia Woolf, Abinger Harvest, and one feels that there has always been a significant correspondence between the two, and somehow ought to be.

[1] In the older, bigger kibbutzim there are members, especially those with professional training, who work outside of the kibbutz in non-kibbutz establishments (hospitals, research institutions, engineering firms) for normal payment, which they hand over to the kibbutz. They are often people who have become members of the kibbutz late in life, e.g. by marrying into it, and have come with professional skills which the kibbutz itself is unable to use. The general feeling of the kibbutzim is, however, that the number of members working 'outside' should be kept as small as possible. They attach the greatest importance to the physical presence of their members, and their direct, physical participation in the life of the commune, and are on the whole reluctant to see them working outside—except in administrative jobs for the kibbutz, or in the central offices of the kibbutz federation, or of course in government and army services.

This is the expectation which the kibbutzim disappoint. It is hard to reconcile the little two-roomed dwelling-houses with the often splendid museums, galleries, culture-halls,[1] and occasional open-air theatres which the older kibbutzim have and the newer ones aim at having; nor the gruelling physical labour by day with the regular expeditions by night, in the huge open trucks which are the standard means of communal transport, to theatres, concerts, exhibitions in the towns. Systematic education is if possible even more highly valued than general culture. The appetite for instruction is insatiable. The most precious gift a Hebrew-speaking guest can bestow on a kibbutz is a 'lecture': on anything he pleases—Shakespeare, Henry James, the principles of the British parliamentary system, the causes of the American Civil War, will all draw excellent audiences any evening after nine o'clock. There are adult night-classes, given for the most part by teachers of the kibbutz, in almost every subject in which working adults may be excused a deficiency of expert knowledge: foreign languages, especially English; history; 'geography of Israel' (a special indigenous study which takes in, besides the geography, also the flora, fauna, history, archaeology of the country); mathematics and physics; Hebrew literature and philosophy; European literature and philosophy; and of course Bible studies, which remain inexhaustibly interesting to people who have already had some eighteen years of it at school and are not religious—often doctrinal atheists and violently anti-clerical. I know something about W.E.A. classes in England, and I would be hard put to it to define the difference between the spirit and atmosphere of those classes and these. It is not that those were not serious, but that these are more so: the lectures seem here to answer to a deeper, older, more imperative need. Nor is it that the W.E.A. students did not enjoy what they were learning, but that the kibbutz people enjoy it with a peculiar intensity, whole-heartedness and whole-mindedness of enjoyment. There is a kind of recognising intelligence at work, as if they had somehow known all along it was like this, were expecting it to be like this, and rejoiced to find it so. The rejoicing is always uppermost: they look what they feel—that they are at this moment in possession of absolutely the best thing life can offer, and would think the world well lost for it. I think they must be among the most rewarding pupils there are to teach.

Returning briefly to the simplicity of the material arrangements, and remembering the economics professor's charge about the bourgeois affluence of the older kibbutzim, it seems that some definition of the term 'simple' (or 'modest') is called for. It is, of course, up to a point

---

[1] The name, universally used for the building or complex of buildings containing library, lecture-halls and club-rooms, sounds less corny in Hebrew than in English.

a relative term. A two-roomed cottage, the present standard dwelling-house, is less simple and modest than a wooden shack, the dwelling which preceded the two-roomed cottage (and is still often given to young men and women before they marry); and a wooden shack is less simple and modest than a tent, which preceded the wooden shack. Yet I don't suppose that a normal British working-class family, let alone a middle-class family, would quarrel with the proposition that a two-roomed family house is modest; and the middle-class parents, with their sound, civilised ideas about one room, however small, per child, would certainly shudder at the thought of one room for two, three or even four children. Their horror would no doubt be mitigated by the knowledge that in the kibbutzim in which the children live for a period with their parents (of which there are still very few), they spend most of their time, for study and play, in their own communal houses and club-rooms, and really only sleep in their parents' houses. Also, even though there may be four or five children in the family, the room in practice rarely holds more than two at a time because of the limited period they live with their parents. Thus, in a kibbutz in which the children are with their parents from the ages of 6 to 12, the younger children will be living entirely in the under-6 children's houses and the older children in their 13–18 quarters; and in this way a manageable rota is maintained. However, there must be cases where the rota system breaks down, and then there would seem to be no alternative to having all the children in the precious second room. Moreover, the whole family tends to assemble in the parents' house on the Sabbath and holidays; and when there are four or five children, and a constant stream of other people's children calling in to see them, and their parents dropping in to see the parents, and hordes of visitors as well (the kibbutzim are inexhaustibly hospitable to guests, and there seems no limit to the number of beds that can be produced for people wanting to spend the night), one feels that a two-roomed house is about as modest a space as could be conceived for the exercise of so much human good-will and gregariousness.

For the idea I am exploring, however, the abstract definition of the terms 'simple' and 'modest' in respect to the material arrangements of the kibbutzim is, I believe, less important than the basis of any definition, either relative or absolute, that may be proposed. The basis is that of *minimum need*. To each according to his need, but no more; and what in the total circumstances, especially the economic-budgetary, of the kibbutz is the minimum need of anybody for anything is, as usual, determined by the consent of the community. Thus, if and when the kibbutz can afford it, people will get extra rooms for special purposes: the member engaged in full-time literary work (publishing and editing for the kibbutz movement, poetry or novel-writing of his own) will get a study, the resident sculptor or painter a studio, the teachers a common room, and so on. If the kibbutz can't afford it, they have to do without, using their living-rooms or the wide open spaces of the estate.

The application of the minimum-need principle in this connection also neatly solves the problem—which is, or could be, a serious problem for a society aiming at an absolutely egalitarian distribution of material goods—of the accumulation of personal possessions, mainly by gifts from the rich American fathers, uncles and grandfathers who are always wanting to 'do something' for their poor relations, as they see them, in the kibbutzim. Some families have rich American relations, others have not; and if the families who have keep on receiving from them pieces of Regency furniture or Persian rugs or expensive china coffee-services, this might theoretically produce a qualitative difference between one family-house and another sufficient to cause uneasiness. The families with the rich relations generally refuse the gifts: on sensible grounds of utility—that a Regency chaise-longue, for instance, would not be nearly as useful for putting up guests as is the convertible sofa it would have to replace; and on the grounds of taste— it would not after all go very well with the cottage-weave rugs and the wicker arm-chairs. The point is, however, that even if a kibbutz woman with a secret hankering for the bourgeois splendours of life took some of the proferred gifts, the quantity she could take would be strictly limited. She could have *one* Regency sofa, not a half-a-dozen of its kind, one or two Persian rugs, not a house full of them. There is obviously a physical limit, reached very soon, to the personal possessions one can accumulate in a two-roomed house; and this is how the regulated simplicity and equality of the basic items (like the house) in the material arrangements ensure a corresponding simplicity and equality in the rest, effectively preventing acquisitiveness, even on the smallest scale, while allowing scope within the limits fixed by the wealth of the community for the expression of individual taste.

In this connection, too, I have been struck by the absence of either a primitivist or a puritan spirit in the attitude of the kibbutzim to their material conditions. They never *preferred* to live in tents and wooden shacks; they did while they had to, and stopped as soon as they could. Nor is there any doctrinal-Puritan suspicion of beautiful things, or the aesthetic as such: there is the usual whole-hearted appreciation of this art-loving member's collection of prints or that musical member's collection of records or another's copper bowls or Persian enamels. Even less is there any Puritan resistance to the modern amenities of life (the refrigerators and electric kettles) as demoralising, weakening to the pioneering spirit, and so on. The attitude is, rather, that we want all these things, and shall have them as soon as we can afford them; but we want them and shall have them only on the strict, literal egalitarian basis. Until every one can have a refrigerator, no one shall have one; and everyone shall always have exactly the same amount of money to spend on prints or records or copper bowls or whatever.

It is only fair to the Liberal opponents or critics of the kibbutzim to say that it is not the limitation of the individual's freedom of choice in the matter of curtains and carpets they have in mind when they speak of 'conformism' or (more violently) the 'regimentation' of the kibbutzim. They are thinking of something more serious and fundamental— namely, the intolerableness of having to submit to the Central Committee for their approval and consent almost every act of choice, including the most personal, the members may wish to make. They cannot go on the shortest holiday, they certainly cannot go abroad, they cannot take study leave, they cannot change their jobs, cannot decide what their children are going to do, sometimes cannot even marry whom they please without the approval and consent of the Central Committee. The fact that their comrades on the C.C. are generally as sympathetic, understanding and humane about all reasonable requests as may be desired, and only anxious—sometimes over-anxious—to ensure the greatest happiness of the greatest number in the kibbutz does not alter the other stubborn fact, that they *have to ask*. An intelligent, vivid young woman, born and brought up in one of the oldest kibbutzim, daughter of a brilliant, brave pioneering father who was killed in Nazi-occupied Europe while attempting to save Jews from extermination, left the kibbutz at the age of thirty principally (she told me) for this reason. I hear her saying vehemently: 'I had thirty years of it, and I just couldn't *stand* any more. I just couldn't stand having to ask permission for every blessed thing I wanted to do. I got sick of having my personal affairs discussed and weighed and considered by everybody, having to hear other people's personal affairs discussed, weighed and considered by everybody. It just became too much for me, the endless communality, the constant exposure, the lack of privacy.' She may have been exaggerating, as disenchanted people will, the extent and intensity of communal control; and even if it is as she says, it is heartening to think that there are at least some 90,000 people in the world who do not find it oppressive, or at least endurable, or at worst a blessed yoke. But that it is a yoke few people of the kibbutzim will deny, nor that it is perhaps the most rigorous sacrifice the kibbutz society exacts—and, of course, necessarily exacts—from its members, compared with which living in a wooden shack or doing without a refrigerator is a minor deprivation indeed. It is no doubt also the final reason that the majority of freedom-loving, choice-exercising men and women will never consent to join

a society which they may—for other people ('those who can take it')—
exalt and admire.

I have already intimated that whatever reservations people may have
about the kibbutzim, no one denies their 'great historic role', as they
call it, in the development of the country before and since the establishment of the State. Given their tiny numbers (they form 4 per cent of the
population), they have produced a significantly high proportion of the
nation's heroes and leaders, particularly in the military and political
spheres. On the military side, the *Palmach*, the famous striking force of
the *Haganah* (the illegal defence army of the Jewish community in
Mandatory Palestine), has become the symbol of the Heroic Age in the
birth of the nation. Its troops and commanders were drawn almost
exclusively from the kibbutzim, and its units based on and effectively
maintained by the kibbutzim. With a force of some 3,000 young men
and women at the start of the War of Independence, and a brilliant,
daring combination of guerilla and regular methods of warfare, the
Palmach won some of the most vital victories of the War, without which
the country would certainly have fallen to the invading Arab armies.
Its exploits have already become legendary, and are the basis of a
developed folk-lore in the kibbutzim. This does not prevent it, or rather
its spirit, from exercising an active, non-legendary influence on the
present life of the nation. Many of its commanders are still alive, some
of them not yet 50, holding leading positions in military or political
life. Most of the Chiefs-of-Staff and senior officers in the Israel Defence
Forces since 1948 have been men who received their military training
and first experience of war in the Palmach.

In the political life of the country it has been the same story. The
Labour Party, which dominates the Coalition Government, has the
closest links with the kibbutzim, indeed, to a large extent, directed if
not dominated by them, and naturally draws its leaders from them.
Of the three Prime Ministers the country has had, two have had their
homes in kibbutzim. The present Speaker of the Knesset is a member of
a kibbutz; so are some 40 per cent of the Cabinet; so is a good part of
the leadership of the Histadrut, the Trades Union Council of the
country, which however is a much more complex body, with more
complex national functions, than the T.U.C.[1]

---

[1] 'The General Federation of Labour (Histadrut) is not only a trade union organising about
80 per cent of the country's workers, but also has its own affiliated economic enterprises
which include the kibbutzim, the moshavim (smallholder's cooperative settlements, about
equal in population to the kibbutzim), urban industrial co-operatives, Solel Boneh (Israel's
largest contractor for building and public works), banks, etc. This sector accounts for about
a quarter of the national economy and for 60 per cent of agriculture' (Dan Leon, *The
Kibbutz*, p. 43). Mr Leon calls it a 'trade union', but I think it is more accurately described

Reflecting on this dominance or predominance of the kibbutzim in the military and political life of the country, and finding it suddenly interlocking in my mind with other features which had made a powerful impression, I found an unexpected hypothesis taking shape. Was it possible, against all appearances and probabilities, that the kibbutzim were producing something in the nature of an aristocracy? And if so, what was the definition of aristocracy that could accommodate so unlikely an instance?

It was obviously necessary first to disengage from the notion, and treat as inessential, certain features of historic aristocracies which were especially (and rightly) repellent to the liberal-democratic, and still more of course the socialist, mind: their privilege, their 'class-consciousness' (contempt of social inferiors, snobbery, etc.), their exploitation of others, their non-productive lives, their pursuit of pleasure. These were to be seen as secondary or contingent features of aristocracies, which came into being and flourished in historical circumstances that gave special opportunities for the development of these, so to speak, pathological malformations. They were not, it seemed to me (with my new example in mind), of its essence; its essence was in its primary social functions, and the primary characteristics which enabled it to perform those functions.

A rapid review of the historic aristocracies of Western Europe, thus disencumbered, yielded the following essential features.

(1) Inalienable possession of, and rootedness in, landed property ('great estates').

(2) Complete freedom from the basic material cares and preoccupations.

(3) An ideal of public service and public leadership (made practicable, in the first instance, by the freedom from material cares).

(4) Association, by family or social group or both, with the *great things* in the history of the nation: with events, exploits, achievements, at once in the highest degree heroic and romantic and historically decisive.

(5) A sense of superiority, based on past and present, but especially past, merit, taking the form of exclusiveness, inbreeding, a certain disdain of others, a certain arrogance and *hauteur* (especially in the young).

The case under review seemed to fit and fit, though in unexpected ways. If the traditional aristocracies were free of material cares, they were so because of their vast material possessions, which were, of course, their private and personal property. Like Bertrand Russell's grand-

as a kind of T.U.C., since the 80 per cent of the country's workers it organises are in fact, as in other countries, for the most part organised into separate trade unions (Electrical Workers', Railway Workers', Port Workers', etc.) and are as unions affiliated to the Histadrut.

mother, they had the indifference to money which only those have who have always had enough of it. But, astonishingly, the people in the kibbutzim had it too—exactly the same sort of indifference. What this seemed to prove was that the relevant, the decisive, thing was not the private and personal *ownership* of the property. Rather, it was the absolute, inalienable *security* in the use of it. If it was *yours* in that sense, it didn't matter that you didn't actually, literally, own it, or owned it in partnership with 900 other people. You felt about it, behaved towards it, and acted as a consequence of it exactly as if you owned it; and one had only to watch an adult male member of a kibbutz walking about the fields or orchards or vineyards of his kibbutz estate to have visible proof of his sense of inalienable ownership.

The same appeared to be true of the money aspect. Certainly complete freedom from material cares is ensured by the possession of illimitable or almost illimitable quantities of money. But it seems, paradoxically, that essentially the same kind of freedom may be ensured by a total lack of it. The kibbutz aristocrat, like his European counterpart, never in effect handles money.[1] He never in all his life has to conduct a serious financial transaction, never has to keep accounts of income and expenditure: all this is done for him by the kibbutz treasury, which acts as his bailiff, banker and broker rolled into one. He has all, literally all, his needs provided for, all his 'expenses' paid; and the fact that the needs and the expenses are modest, not lavish, makes no difference in principle: the effect is the same, that of a sense of complete freedom from material cares—from petty financial worries, from the bourgeois preoccupation with money-making and money-keeping. Consequently, he too is as indifferent to money as only those can be who have always had enough of it: witness the indifferent readiness with which kibbutz Cabinet Ministers or M.P.s or engineers or research scientists hand over their earnings to the kibbutz. They don't need it, therefore don't want it and don't care about it. In this connection, indeed, the new kibbutz aristocracy has a positive advantage over the historic European aristocracies. If a member of it should suddenly, fatally, find himself gripped by the itch for money and private possessions, it won't help him to marry a rich brewer's daughter; for her fortune will only go straight into the kibbutz treasury, and he will get nothing out of it. He can in that case do only one thing, and this is to opt out of the aristocracy, permanently and irrevocably—that is, leave the kibbutz and go and seek his fortunes in the great bourgeois world. In this way, the 'purity' as to

---

[1] The cash allowance a member of a kibbutz receives for purely personal expenses (gifts, etc.) varies between about £10 (IL. 80) and £20 (IL. 150) a year. Everything else—clothes, books, holidays, travel and so on—is paid for by the kibbutz treasury from the appropriate budget.

values and standards of the kibbutz breed of aristocracy is preserved more completely and more certainly than the historic aristocracies have generally succeeded in preserving theirs.

The freedom from material cares is the condition, here as there, of the exercise of the activity pre-eminently characteristic of aristocracies, in particular those (like the British) which have been in the main a living, participating force in their society, not (like the post-Napoleonic French) self-immolated and withdrawn. I refer to leadership in public life, and especially in the political and military departments of it. This function in turn presupposes an ideal of public service, inculcated with due consciousness but practised as an 'inherited' tradition. There is perhaps a temerity in speaking of traditional practices in a society hardly fifty years old. Yet that which has the quality, the stamp, the 'feel' of the traditional is so, whether it is fifty or five hundred years old; and this is the case with those acts and practices of the kibbutzim which express their ideal of public service.

What they have contributed to the political and military leadership of the country has already been mentioned. The greatest of these acts of leadership (I have also indicated) were accomplished in the heroic age of the modern nation in the years immediately before and during the War of Independence, the most critical, exciting and inspiring in its history. This, too, has its significance. There is no aristocracy whose past is not more great and glorious than its present: the present distinction of the Cecils is not to be compared with their greatness in the time of the first Elizabeth; and (violently adjusting the time-scale) so it is with the Norman and Tudor political families of the kibbutzim. They are honoured and revered mainly for their glorious past, and themselves live partly on it; and this is as it should be if it is an emergent aristocracy we are talking about.[1]

The spirit of the heroic age, if not its irrecoverable glamour, persists in certain traditions of national service which have come into being since. The famous Youth Movements of the country have been formed, and are directed and supported, by the kibbutzim. These train and send to the Youth Movements a constant stream of 'instructors', whose task it is to inspire the young people to the pioneering efforts which the country—with more than half of its total area, the Negev, virtually uncolonised—still desperately needs. One of the direct outcomes of this moral–ideological education provided by the kibbutzim is the volunteer division of the Israel Defence Forces called NACHAL (Pioneer Fighting

[1] In this fancy, the families who came to the country in the 'Second Alya' (about 1904–12) would be the Norman, those who came in the 'Third Alya' (in the early 1920s) the Tudor. *Alya* in Hebrew means literally 'ascent', and is the word habitually used for 'immigration' (to Israel).

Youth), composed of young men and women who have elected for the period of their Army service to go to dangerous border areas and there form settlements of the kibbutz type. These generally become permanent settlements, and in this way the territorial defence of the country is constantly strengthened in the places where it is most needed.

Again, there is the practice of the kibbutzim of requiring each and every one of their young men and women who has completed the normal period of compulsory military service—at present two and a half years for the men, twenty months for the girls—to put in another complete year of national service, generally in a new border settlement. They live there as members for that year, giving their labour in the normal way, while at the same time helping to guard the settlement. Or again, the kibbutzim, which still produce the highest proportion of reserve officers, periodically give up members to become officers in the regular army, even though their shortage of man-power makes the loss of a member, especially of this calibre, a real sacrifice. (The same is also true, of course, of the young people who are sent away for the third year's national service: the kibbutz loses their much needed labour for that year.) In the same way, and at a similar cost of manpower, they regularly send instructors or 'leaders' to the Jewish youth movements abroad, with the object of bringing young people to settle in the country in the first instance, and in particular, if possible, in a kibbutz.

These are some of the ways in which the tradition of national and public service established in the heroic age is carried forward. If they are not already more numerous and more spectacular, this is because (say the kibbutzim, with some bitterness) they have been prevented from giving more by hostile vested interests in the State, which fear the 'socialist' influence of the kibbutzim and its encroachments on liberal (or Liberal) territories. A powerful king, Ben-Gurion, resolved to create a single, unified national state, and determined to this end to subdue and if necessary crush what he saw as 'partisan' interests, has (they say) stupidly spurned the help of his most loyal and disinterested barons, and as a consequence squandered one of his most valuable moral resources for the building of the national state. The particular problems crowding this area of dispute, the arguments and counter-arguments advanced over more than a decade, are too complex and controversial to be taken up here, even in outline. From the point of view I have been advancing about the kibbutzim, what can be said is that it is part of a larger problem belonging characteristically to the present stage of their—and the State's—development. This turns upon the finding of a viable relation between the kibbutzim as self-supporting, autonomous communities and the national state: the reconciliation of their needs—economic, social, political and moral—with its (the State's) needs; the renunciation on both sides of attitudes and habits inimical to such reconciliation. In the years that have passed since the establishment of the State, the problem has not been settled, or indeed yet fully recognised; the blame for the failure, if there is blame to be apportioned, does not rest entirely with the ruthless king and his cynical court; and while it remains unsettled, the range and scope of the nobility's disinterested services to the commonwealth are bound to remain limited. But this, exactly, is to be expected of an emergent aristocracy and an emergent state. They are still all becoming, not yet being; and no doubt only time, the maker of all established things, can effect the settlement which will give the ideal of public service of the kibbutzim the conditions for maximum growth.

Why, finally, do I insist on calling it an 'aristocracy', and not (for instance) an 'élite', or—following Coleridge and T. S. Eliot—a 'clerisy'? The choice was considered, not arbitrary. An élite, I think, is basically a meritocracy. Its members are persons of distinctively intellectual endowments, with a specialised, quasi-professional 'training of the mind'. It is associated with an urban, not a rural, culture; and it tends to reject as superstitious ('obscurantist') the notion of hereditary virtue. A clerisy may allow more to the hereditary; but it, too, supposes in its members developed intellectual and spiritual powers; and it puts its emphasis on moral and spiritual leadership to the exclusion of other kinds.

Having before my mind's eye certain representative young men and women of the third generation of the kibbutz-born—the sons and daughters of the heroes of the War of Independence, the grandsons and granddaughters of the founding fathers who came in their immigrant ships from the small towns and villages of Eastern and Central Europe —I see them as neither élite nor clerisy but as a plain landed aristocracy still (following Matthew Arnold's nomenclature) in the Barbarian stage of their evolution.[1]

I pause to emphasise that my hypothesis is based almost exclusively on my observation of this third generation—the first generation to be wholly native born, and the first therefore in whom the lineaments of aristocracy could be discerned, supposing them to be there to be discerned. It is not intended to apply to the fathers and grandfathers, who are generally as innocent of any pretension to the aristocratic as were their fathers and grandfathers in their native towns, villages and hamlets. Nor, in saying this, do I forget the great rabbis, scholars, and good pious men and women whom these same towns, villages and hamlets produced in impressive numbers, who might in an extended sense of the word be called an 'aristocracy'—of the spirit, the mind, the charac-

---

[1] Matthew Arnold, *Culture and Anarchy* ('Barbarians, Philistines, Populace').

ter. But it is precisely not an aristocracy of the spirit I am speaking about. I am speaking about a 'territorial', landed aristocracy, produced in and nurtured by a particular physical habitation (the kibbutz estate), and deriving most of its virtue from its physical rootedness in this habitation: from the sense of its permanence (that their children and their children's children to the tenth generation will be there, in the same place, the same air, looking out towards the same Carmel, Gilboa, Kinneret); and from the sense, powerful though only felt in the blood and felt along the heart, that almost everything that is great and heroic in the life of the nation has somehow sprung from, or is deeply associated with, that particular plot of land.

To return: the young Barbarians of the third generation are intelligent, but not distinctively intellectual. Indeed people who don't like them say they look 'stupid'; and this is false, but even it if were true would be an argument for, not against, the aristocratic title. As in the historic aristocracies, the 'stupid' look is the product of the tranquility, the composure, the absence of anxiety which springs from their absolute, never-questioned security in their material surroundings. That the surroundings are in the country, not the city, contributes massively to the tranquillity and composure, and also of course to the 'stupid' look: the squire and the peasant, brought up in the stillness, monotony, absence of distraction of the deep countryside, both tend to look stupid compared with their urban counterparts. As to the security, it is something quite different from that of the sons and daughters of the propertied urban bourgeoisie. They have never had the consciousness of 'working for a living'; yet they have always worked, exceedingly hard, by what is for them already simple custom and tradition, on the estate on which they were brought up. They have never been anything but active, busy, fully employed: first in play and study, then study, physical work, and youth movement activities, then Army service, then post-Army service, then back to their life's work on the estate or in public life or both.

They have had a decent general education (up to the age of eighteen), but generally no higher education, only the specialised professional training they require for their work on the estate (wheat-growing, cow-keeping, chicken-breeding, factory-running, teaching, nursing, child-rearing). Their normal pursuits are pre-eminently practical, rather than intellectual: their work on the estate is physical or practical (tractor-driving or estate management: the sedentary administrative work is almost always done by elderly members no longer capable of other work); they may read books for pleasure and instruction, listen to music, study pictures, but only after working hours. Their amusements are predominantly physical and outdoor: they don't go in for blood-sports or fast cars, but they love to go on long rambles, strenuous excursions, archaeological expeditions; and they would travel the world ten times in a life if they were allowed to. On Friday nights and feast nights, in the great dining hall, they love to sing their modern folk-songs and dance their modern folk-dances into the early hours of the morning; and when they are not singing or dancing, they are talking, joking, yarning their heads off in their communal houses and club-rooms.

Their manners are not unlike those of the early-feudal nobilities of Europe, before the ages of taste gave them the fine surface with which their descendents are now habitually associated. Their manners are not refined. They generally do not speak beautifully: their speech tends to be rough, unmodulated, quarrelsome in pitch and tone. They generally don't eat beautifully, don't sit and stand gracefully. In company, they tend to be too silent or too noisy. They can be charming to pretty young women and kind to old people; but to almost everyone else they tend to be brusque, off-hand, over-direct, often wounding. They are distinctly in the Barbarian phase: not yet the glass of fashion and the mould of form, the observ'd of all observers.

Of the manners in a wider sense of these young men and women of the third generation, I have heard the burghers of Jerusalem and Tel-Aviv speak with furious indignation. 'They're insufferable. Arrogant as they come; haughty, disdainful, as if they were the lords of creation. Think no one but their own kind good enough for them: don't mix with outsiders, look as if they don't want to be touched by them. Exclusive, oh *dear*, yes. They don't intermarry, not they. Marrying some one who isn't a member of a kibbutz is like marrying out of the faith: they're worse than the religious, they are. Such snobs, such high-and-mightinesses, with their shorts and their shirts and their *kova tembels*!'[1] Or, if they are of a more intellectual cast: 'They're an *in-group*, that's what's the matter with them. Treat the rest of the world as if it didn't exist; just scorn and despise you if you don't "belong". Everybody else is a mean little bourgeois, who cares about nothing but money and possessions; only they're noble and free.' And, significantly: 'It's not as if they themselves have *done* all that much. Their grandfathers made the decision which put them there, and now they're being proud and haughty about it—taking all the credit without having done anything to earn it.'

I laugh, and say, 'You're only, you know, showing the typical bourgeois reaction to a hereditary aristocracy. It's true it's only three generations old; but it's bad enough already, it seems, to get right under

---

[1] *Kova tembel* is the name given to the cloth cap, usually blue in colour, worn by members of kibbutzim for outdoor work. It is considered a characteristic part of the kibbutz uniform, though widely worn also by the rest of the population.

your sensitive republican–revolutionary skin.' And so I believe it is; the reaction is nice circumstantial evidence for the hypothesis. The young people are indeed somewhat arrogant, disdainful, exclusive. They do hold their heads rather high, do turn a rather blank, inexpressive face to the outsider. It is also true that they personally, individually, have not 'earned' their presumed superiority. Their grandfathers made the crucial decisions which created the society into which they were born. Their fathers were the leaders, heroes and martyrs of the great age in which the national state was created, threatened with extinction, and miraculously saved. They are conscious of being directly associated, through their immediate families or the social group or both, with the greatest—the most heroic, romantic, decisive—events in the history of the nation. And they are conscious of this as an example and an inspiration: they will do as their fathers did, not because or not chiefly because they have judged it to be the 'right' thing to do, but because their fathers did it, and they know their fathers to have been great men. In this way, 'ideological' instruction is being reinforced, and gradually displaced, by the direct, immediate power of the personal example: of a personal ideal of honour and virtue, commanding an allegiance which no ideology by its nature can command.[1] This is the sense in which their virtue is, or is becoming, 'hereditary'. It does not exclude a full consciousness and appreciation of what is inherited; and it positively demands the active, personal, individual re-creation of the heritage. But it is not *self-made*: it is not solely or chiefly the product of the individual's intelligence and effort; and in this sense it is not 'earned', and therefore not the virtue of an élite or meritocracy. And because it is not directed exclusively to the moral and spiritual guidance of the community, but loves to exercise itself also in the active, practical spheres of government and national defence, it is not, or not distinctively, the virtue of a Coleridgean clerisy.

If the view I have proposed is valid, its interest as an historical and moral phenomenon is surely great. If what we are witnessing is indeed the emergence of an aristocracy, it will be the first aristocracy the Jewish people has ever produced which is at once secular, land-rooted, and wholly indigenous. The priests of the Temple periods may have formed an aristocracy of a kind; but their inspiration was wholly religious, and their leadership nourished solely by the temple, not by life and work on the land. The sporadic aristocracies of Jewry in

---

[1] This process of the reinforcement and gradual displacement of pure ideology by the personal example may, of course, be confused with such modern bugbears as the 'cult of personality', or whatever; and muddle-headed counter-indoctrination ('You must do the thing *for its own sake*, not because your father did it') may check it, perhaps permanently. It would be a great pity if this happened.

dispersion have all been foreign and imitative: either an assimilated part, usually minute, of the aristocracy of the host nation; or a separate social group, consciously Jewish, yet *qua* aristocracy hardly to be distinguished from that of the host. Never before this in the history of the Jews will there have been a case of a secular aristocracy of the European type, based on landed property inalienably possessed in the historic land of the Jews, and wholly indigenous in having been created and nurtured solely by the history and culture of the land.

It will be, moreover, by the queerest paradox, an aristocracy springing from a peasant-and-worker community of the kind which has been ideologically the bitterest foe of historic aristocracies; and if it knows how to value its uniqueness, and guards it accordingly, it will remain to the end a community of this kind: implacably egalitarian, democratic and socialist. It will in that case be the most paradoxical thing of all—an aristocracy with the prestige of a traditional aristocracy, and its power of leadership and example in the national life, but without privilege, without 'class-consciousness', without the will or the means to exploit others with the weapons of its prestige and power. And, most remarkably, it will be an aristocracy without private wealth. Poorer than the meanest tradesman in the matter of private property, possessions, money: yet rejoicing in, indeed cherishing, its poverty as the condition of its service to the community and the nation. Its motto might suitably be the words of the Jewish sage, 'Poverty becometh a Jew as a scarlet saddle a white horse'.

AN IDEOLOGICAL FALLACY

PRESTON KING

IDEOLOGY: THE WORD

For words are wise men's counters, they do but
reckon by them; but they are the money of fools...
HOBBES (*Leviathan*, 1, 4)

The word 'ideology' was coined towards the end of the eighteenth century by the French philosopher Destutt de Tracy. He meant by it undistorted truth. Napoleon, however, imposed upon the expression a negative intent when he denounced as '*idéologues*' those philosophical speculators whose lucubrations he assumed to be subversive of the order enshrined in his person. This contrast reflects the indeterminate meaning of the term. For 'ideology' openly converses in terms of conscious purpose, scientific guidance, objective decisions and progressive advance, while simultaneously brooding over (and possibly presupposing) the reality of irrational commitment, partial interests, and subversive inclinations.

Marx's use of 'ideology' is ambivalent. On the one hand, he condemns ideologies as distortions; at the same time, he implicitly supports ideology, if it is the right sort. Marx, of course, was very far from rejecting the negative connotation put upon the term by Napoleon. For, with Marx, an 'ideology' was very often a mask, or a reflection or even perhaps a reification of partial material interests; and to the extent that it meant this, it inevitably implied a falsity, the alienation of truth.

'Ideology', for academics in general, has tended to acquire a negative connotation, while, for political activists, the expression tends to be used in a highly favourable sense. Various scholars, taking up the matter where Marx the scholar left it, have tended to use the word in such a way as to suggest an inherent limitation upon, or alienation of, the truth. Karl Mannheim,[1] for example, drew attention to Bacon's warning against the deceptions of the *idola*: they were phantoms and preconceptions; 'sources of error derived sometimes from human nature itself, sometimes from particular individuals'; 'obstacles in the path of true knowledge' (p. 55).

Mannheim, Sombart, Troeltsch, Weber and many others have been especially interested in the character of ideology. Mannheim accepted that interests affect the elaboration of systems of belief; although he supported the view that intellectuals as a group are freer from this sort

[1] Karl Mannheim, *Ideology and Utopia*, trans. Wirth and Shils (Routledge, 1954).

of prejudice than other classes. Weber drew attention to the fact of ideology as a heuristic tool: it was important to study the manner in which interests have historically determined or conditioned patterns of belief. This was the primary interest reflected in his *Die protestantische Ethik und der Geist des Kapitalismus* (1904–5) as well as in such related studies as Tawney's *Religion and the Rise of Capitalism* (1922)—studies attempting to relate patterns of thought to material interests and economic conditions. Such work was primarily influenced by the academic Marx, and later by Freud; and most of it today is referred to as 'sociology of knowledge'.

It is possible to argue, of course, that research into the sociology of knowledge completely by-passes any concern with bestowing praise or blame upon ideology. But this is not true. The sociology of knowledge is generally regarded in at least two ways: as an *alternative* to ideology, and as an objective means of *studying* ideology. In either case, there is a suggestion of the inadequacy of ideology, and the implication of some form of censure upon it. In fact, with most academics, this censure is applied quite openly. Werner Stark,[1] for example, believes it best to allow 'ideology' to imply distortion while substituting 'sociology of knowledge' where what is intended is merely a general outlook, inevitably dependent in some degree upon one's condition and position (pp. 48 ff.). What is implied in this sort of formulation is either the distinction between an acceptable and an unacceptable general outlook, or the distinction between an acceptable way of looking at (or investigating) a general outlook, and the unacceptability (or distortion) of the general outlook investigated. In the case of either of these distinctions, ideology is indicated as the diseased valve, and the sociology of knowledge as either a satisfactory cure or substitute. In fact, what one generally finds is that anyone today in search of 'truth' tends to be suspicious of 'ideologies'. It is typically for the academic, viewing ideology as an obstacle to truth (because assumed to be intrinsically distorted), that the expression retains its negative significance.

It is usually for the activist, by contrast, that the word ideology loses its negative significance. Whereas the academic's primary objective is the determination of truth, the activist's is the realisation of a particular aim. Thus, an ideology may obstruct the academic in his work, while it may be essential to the activist in his. The practice of politics requires an understanding of circumstances, conjoined with a programme of action; and an ideology will contain both of these things. In a settled political order elaborate programmes of action are not so necessary, because what is to be done, and what is accepted as having to be done, is largely ingrained in the habits of a people, in the legal system which

[1] Werner Stark, *The Sociology of Knowledge* (New York, 1958).

engirdles them, in the tacit relations of deference and command which may relate one class to another. In an unsettled political order very little may be taken for granted; in a polity in crisis there are few publicly recognised guidelines that can be followed; and it is typically in such circumstances that political leaders worry that they have no adequate overall understanding of the situation and no truly appropriate programme of action; and so they demand an ideology, or regret the absence of one, and *possibly* with reason in either case.

It is necessary to insist upon the difference in standpoint between the academic and the activist; but to insist also that in practice any particular individual, like Marx, may in fact prove to be both. It would be absurd to insist, moreover, that an academic ought not to be an activist; equally, that an activist cannot be an academic. To do this is to compartmentalise human capabilities in too crude a fashion. From this, however, the major point to be retained is that it is not particularly helpful to regard an ideology as being in itself either good or bad. It will be one or the other, depending upon one's perspective; and given that one's perspective is rarely unilinear, it may well be both. An ideology tends to be regarded as negative when it obstructs the attainment of truth. It tends to be regarded as positive when it assists in the implementation of programmes of social and political action. Thus ideologies will be regarded as erroneous and as bases of distortion which must be guarded against. They will equally be regarded in certain circumstances as providing a necessary framework for the conduct of political life and thus as deserving to be promoted. In short, a very important area of disagreement about ideology relates not merely to what it means, but to whether it is good or bad.

Nonetheless, one reason why people disagree about the merits of ideology is because they do not impress upon it an identical meaning. Although it is inevitable that one should discuss the merits of definitions provided by others, it is equally necessary that such disputatiousness not be too prolonged and that it culminate in and be abridged by some statement of what it is that the writer has in mind as forming the factual substance of his concern, as opposed to what he conceives to be the essentially correct meaning of a term.

It is necessary to deal first with some conventional meanings ascribed to the term because so many of them are short-sighted. 'Ideology' is usually regarded as a recent phenomenon; but the basic political reality referred to is by no means so. It is usually regarded as a secular phenomenon; but secular ideologies constitute a recent development, and even now do not hold the field alone. It is usually regarded as being, or as pretending to be, scientific. But it may simply be the case that 'science' is generally what we contemporaneously conceive to be objective or correct, which in a previous age would quite as acceptably have been labelled 'theology'. Moreover, viewing ideology literally, in terms of the 'logic of an idea', there is no reason why a 'scientific' political view should be considered intrinsically more ideological than one that is 'theological'. An ideology is generally regarded as being revolutionary or reformist. But Marx and Engels did not regard the 'German Ideology' as revolutionary; nor have we any particularly good reason for assuming than an ideology cannot be conservative or reactionary.

Reinhard Bendix[1] sees ideology as a scientific and non-theological development. Following Carl Becker, he sees the major break between a pre-ideological and an ideological world as emerging somewhere between the thirteenth and eighteenth centuries. The pre-ideological, for him, is characterised by belief 'in the supreme deity'. The ideological he sees as characterised by a view of nature (human and otherwise) which conceives it as ultimately reducible to comprehensible and 'discoverable laws' (p. 295). It is of course useful to distinguish between the Middle Ages and the Renaissance, as well as between theology and science; but it is another matter to suggest that the distinction between the ideological and the pre-ideological can best be distinguished by reference to these differences. If ideology is not in fact scientific, at least in the way that, say, physics is, then it is no more impossible for an ideology to borrow from the philosophical and practical trappings of theology than it is for it to borrow from those of science. If we say tentatively that the business of ideology is to provide an integrated understanding of the world, together with a programme of social and political action, it is clear that the acceptability of any particular ideology will vary with time and place; and as its primary objective is the organisation of a society, the variety of its intellectual accoutrement (whether scientific, theological or otherwise) must be imputed a purely secondary and inessential significance.

Hannah Arendt,[2] too, tends to see the development of ideology as a recent phenomenon—in fact as 'a very recent phenomenon' (p. 468). But the actual content which she assigns ideologies does not impress one as being particularly recent. She writes, for instance, that ideologies 'explain everything and every occurrence by deducing it from a single premise': but it is far easier to reduce Christianity to a single premise (the existence of God) than it is to perform similarly radical surgery upon Marx. Arendt explains (p. 469) that an ideology

is quite literally what its name indicates: it is the logic of an idea. Its subject matter is history, to which the 'idea' is applied; the result of this application

---

[1] Reinhard Bendix, 'The age of ideology: persistent and changing', in D. Apter, *Ideology and Discontent* (Glencoe, 1964).
[2] Hannah Arendt, *The Origins of Totalitarianism* (London, 1958).

is not a body of statements about something that *is*, but the unfolding of a process which is in constant change. The ideology treats the course of events as though it followed the same 'law' as the logical exposition of its 'idea'. Ideologies pretend to know the mysteries of the whole historical process—the secrets of the past, the intricacies of the present, the uncertainties of the future—because of the logic inherent in their respective ideas.

Much of this may be plain hyperbole; it is certainly exaggerated. The passage which avers that ideologies pretend to know the mysteries of the whole historical process is probably more applicable to Judaism, Christianity and Islam than it is to Marxism and racialism. The passage which insists upon the extreme *logical* coherence of ideology is also slightly exaggerated. It is possibly because Arendt insists upon the novelty and explicit coherence of ideologies that she can find so few of them, all of recent vintage. In effect, she reduces the field to two; she does not say that there are no others, but merely that racialism and Marxism are the most important (p. 159). But liberalism is probably equally important, and as ideological, although there may be less awareness of it as an ideology because it is found more acceptable. Also, racialism is not very coherent at all, as compared for example with liberalism. (The point here of course is not to make a moral judgment.) Moreover, whether or not Marxism, socialism, racialism, and liberalism are deducible from a single logical premise, they are certainly committed to gaining or protecting single political goals: as for example the dictatorship of the proletariat, improvement in the conditions of life of working people, the supremacy of one race over others, or an 'open society'. It is at least as much the commitment to an exclusive goal, as the deduction from a single logical premise, which leads into the distortions with which ideologies are usually associated.

Arendt (p. 208) is aware of Christianity as offering 'the most powerful and all-inclusive legendary explanation of human destiny'. But she promptly dismisses it from the court of her concern: 'Legends', she explains, 'are not ideologies.' Thus she toes the line drawn by writers like Bendix. Of course it is true that legends by themselves are not ideologies. But in what sense would it be true to say that Christianity is nothing more than a legend? It is for too many people a way of life, a basis of organisation and a hope for the future; and all of this can, as in some countries it does, have great political significance. The point about a legend is that it is really supposed to have no significance, certainly not contemporaneously, not politically. A legend is merely *legenda*, what is written, and, perhaps, forgotten; what is legendary is suggestive of what is ancient, mythical and, probably, historically untrue; a legend is certainly not a mode of organisation, suffused with a directive purpose and associated with a concrete view of the way in which the world works and is structured. The conclusion to be drawn from this is that Arendt is mistaken: Christianity cannot be dismissed as a 'legend'; and it cannot be discounted as non-ideological. It has had far greater significance ideologically than racialism, for example, could ever pretend to have. And this is supported by the fact that so many racialists, as in South Africa and the southern United States, are inveterate theologists as well, who demonstrate the correctness of *apartheid* and segregation by reference to biblical passages which demonstrate that the sons of Ham were intended by God to be hewers of wood and drawers of water. The point of all this is merely to indicate that a commitment to religiosity may be ideological just as a commitment to ethnicity may be; and that the two may be combined to constitute a composite religio-ethnic ideology, as has happened in the Dutch Reform Church, among the Mormons, and elsewhere.

C. J. Friedrich and Z. K. Brzezinski[1] tend to see ideology as a secular and reformist phenomenon. They define an ideology to be (p. 74) 'a reasonably coherent body of ideas concerning practical means of how to change and reform a society, based upon a more or less elaborate criticism of what is wrong with the existing, or antecedent, society'. This sort of statement is generally satisfactory, although attended by marginal difficulties. For example, an ideology might well involve an elaborate argument *against* change; for where an established mode of life is challenged by a rigorous, systematic and ideological formula, the response may be to lift the concern with that mode of life from the mere level of behaviour onto the level of systematic and ideological reflection, so that, in this form, it constitutes a viable counter-argument to its challenger. Thus it is necessary to weaken the stress that tends to be placed upon ideology as a means of effecting change and reform exclusively; so that it becomes meaningful (that is, neither contradictory nor redundant) to speak of a 'conservative' ideology and of a 'reformist' ideology. Thus, if it is possible to call Marx an ideologist, it becomes equally possible to say the same of Hegel. The central element is present in both: a concern with total explanation, and an attempt to relate it to certain essential types of political and ethical behaviour. From one important standpoint, there is in any case no great difference between attack and defence, reform and conservation. The central question, ethically, is, what is one to do? Either to attack or to defend is to act—and systematic reflection may at any time become relevant to the act, whether it be conservative or reformist. Certainly it is easier not to reflect if one decides to do nothing, than it is to avoid reflection if one decides upon aggressive measures. But this scarcely warrants the

---

[1] C. J. Friedrich and Z. K. Brzezinski, *Totalitarian Dictatorship and Autocracy* (Harvard University Press, 1956).

conclusion that the radical is intrinsically more likely to become an ideologist than the reactionary. For the most radical of activists, the anarchist, is intellectually among the least systematic, and, in this sense, among the least reflective. In regard to systematic reflection, the De Maistres of this world will always win hands down over the Kropotkins and Bakunins. So one returns to the view that 'reform' should not be considered intrinsic to the meaning of ideology, but merely as one variant form of ideology. Friedrich and Brzezinski, as already noted, tend to attribute to ideology a purely secular character. But if we return to their basic definition it is clear that the element of reform it indicates is in no way contradictory to religion: Christianity and Islam, from the very beginning, were reformist in the extreme. And as for the question of the extent of change that ideologies demand, certainly no more apocalyptic change could be imagined than that prefigured in the second coming. In short, Christianity, as one religion, easily fits into their basic and original definition of an ideology: it is quite coherent; it wishes to change society, although primarily by improving upon the morality of its members; and, as in St Augustine, it contains an elaborate criticism of the antecedent society. The only significant difference here is that Christianity holds out some promise of reward (for moral reform) in another life; whereas communism, for example, does not. The question is whether the presence of an other-worldly element on the one side and its absence on the other is sufficiently significant a consideration to warrant the differential classification of communism as ideological and of Christianity as non-ideological. It is difficult to think that it would. Early Christianity was primarily concerned with utilising the instruments of church and state to save, or contribute to the salvation of, souls, and force (when Christianity became a state religion) was in no way excluded as a means of achieving this end. The communistic salvation of individuals must be read in a more materialistic fashion, since it has utilised the state as a means of increasing economic production and eliminating class oppression—without in any way excluding force as a means to this end. The tentative implication that forms the point of all this is that the term 'ideology' cannot be usefully restricted to imply 'recent' or 'secular'.

Friedrich and Brzezinski, like Arendt, in discussing ideology in general are in fact more concerned with certain recent historical phenomena—namely, communism and fascism—rather than with anything else. They tend not so much to begin with ideology conceived as a central and *continuing* political experience, as with ideology conceived as a unique and *limited* political experience; they begin, in fact, with recent historical experience, from which they extract an ideological essence which is assumed to be recent and unique, although it is not. It is from this mistakenly foreshortened perspective that some writers have anticipated the end of ideology.

To cope with this confusion it is essential that we distinguish between forms of political organisation and types of political belief-system. From this it follows that the recognition of novelty among the former will not necessarily entail an equal novelty among the latter. A new form of political organisation, such as federalism, can easily make do with an older type of political belief-system such as liberalism. Similarly, a totalitarian form of government could quite easily, in principle, make do with any one of a number of belief-systems—such as Calvinism (including innumerable other variant Christianities), Islam, Judaism and so on.

Friedrich and Brzezinski are actually more concerned with the concept of a totalitarian ideology than with that of ideology *per se*. They see a totalitarian ideology as one which is concerned with total destruction and total reconstruction, involving typically an acceptance of violence as the only practicable means of achieving these ends. It is, they write, 'a reasonably coherent body of ideas concerning practical means of how totally to change and reconstruct a society by force, or violence, based upon an all-inclusive or total criticism of what is wrong with an existing or antecedent society'. This concern with *totalitarian* ideologies should not, in principle, detain us—except for the question it raises as to whether in this case it is the ideology that is different or the totalitarianism. Most probably it is the latter. Totalitarianism does not so much seem to be made possible by novel ideas or idea-systems, however much it may be accompanied by these, but by radical advances in technique as regards communications, transport, production, and weaponry. These not only make it easier to supply the wants of vast populations, but also to control, persuade and manipulate these populations.

At this stage we may omit further comment on the various meanings ascribed to ideology in the current literature. The writers so briefly discussed are reasonably representative. But from all this two primary areas of disagreement emerge. The first relates to the question whether ideology is good or bad. The second relates to the question as to what it actually means. All that has been established, in a preliminary way, is (a) that ideology may reasonably be considered both good and bad; and (b) that the meanings attributed to it, however contradictory among themselves, and however arbitrary they must ultimately and necessarily be, tend on the whole to be too restricted to provide a proper understanding of the phenomenon to which they relate. The rest of this paper is primarily concerned to broaden the meaning of ideology and to suggest one sense in which it involves (from an academic perspective) an error which it were better to avoid.

IDEOLOGY: THE FACT

Excelling all whose sweet delight disputes
In heavenly matters of theology;
Til swoln with cunning, of a self-conceit,
His waxen wings did mount above his reach...

MARLOWE (*Doctor Faustus*)

If we distinguish between systems of political organisation and systems of political thought, it is clear that an 'ideology' is usually classified under the latter. At the same time, however, it is clear that we do not mean the same thing by political thought, or political philosophy, as we mean by ideology. If we take ideology literally and intend by it 'the logic of an idea', this meaning will not prove sufficient to distinguish it from any form of systematic political reflection. In all such cases we are confronted with ideas, and with the logic of these ideas. The difference between a political philosophy and an ideology does not relate to any quality logically intrinsic to either. Both relate to politics in a comprehensive manner and attempt to explain and even to direct it. Arguments which attempt to demonstrate why one should obey the state in general, or that certain types of state are best, obviously relate to politics in a directive manner; and these represent one typical sort of argument (although not the only kind of argument) advanced by political philosophers. Despite all this, one still tends to regard political philosophy as somewhat more objective than ideology. The reason lies not so much in differences of logical structure as in the different uses to which they are put. It may be that Marx has been viewed as an ideologist while Hegel has not, because Marx's ideas rather than Hegel's have been utilised by parties and governments to explain, justify and direct their activities. Marx himself of course helped to make this possible, since he deliberately intended his ideas to be used as weapons: the point was not merely to understand the world, but to change it. It is generally at this point, where ideas are used to conserve and change the world, that they become capable of assuming an ideological character.

An ideology, therefore, is not understood here as a system of political thought—but not as a system of political organisation either. It involves a system of political thought as systematically and coherently applied by and to a particular group whether the latter be the government of a state, or a subordinate group, class, or estate within it. The notion of a system of political thought being 'applied' (to a group) is intended to carry the sense of its providing a framework within which, and a set of principles by which, the activities of the group (or the decisions of its representatives) are explained, justified and directed. No one will dispute the assertion that an ideology is not a system of government. It is more difficult to slip past unchallenged with the suggestion that it is not a mere system of political ideas either. Ideologies are generally accepted as systems of thought. The reason, however, why this acceptance is unsatisfactory is because we generally view a political philosophy as a system of political ideas, and yet find that ideology and political philosophy are in some sense mutually repugnant. Without immediately elaborating upon this 'repugnance', which we might refer to more neutrally as a 'difference', attention may simply be drawn to the fact that an 'ideology' is usually conceived as an idea in action or as an idea that seeks to be activated; the fabric of a 'political philosophy', by contrast, is less inclined to wear in this way. 'Ideology' is more likely to imply commitment and action; 'political philosophy' evokes reflection and understanding. While commitment and action are as important as reflection and understanding, it is as well to record the difference and, indeed, the mutual repugnance. This does not so much lie in logical structure as in intended or actual application. Accordingly we must recognise that ideology involves more than the conception of a system of ideas; it is a conception of a system of ideas in action. Although it is true that 'ideology' is often used to indicate a system of political ideas, it is equally true that it is used to indicate a coherent programme of political action. In this paper it will be used to imply a combination of the two.

In order to accommodate the ordinary usage of those who intend ideology to convey nothing more than a system of political ideas, a distinction may be drawn between 'ideology by purpose' and 'ideology by function'. By the former may be understood a system of ideas which has not been organisationally activated (or 'applied' in the sense previously intimated) but which is either designed for this purpose or which is conceived (by anyone) as a potential means of fulfilling it. By the latter may be understood a system of ideas which has been organisationally activated. An ideology by purpose, then, is a system of ideas which is *intended* (by its author or by certain of its admirers) to serve as an ideology. An ideology by function is a system of ideas which actually serves this purpose. To conform to an important aspect of ordinary usage, and at the same time to abbreviate, an ideology by purpose could simply be called an 'ideology'. An ideology by function could simply be called an 'ideological system'—an ideology as 'applied' to a system of government. In either of these senses ideology will carry the suggestion of application—as either an existent application or as an intended application.

An ideology, then, will either involve the *actual* application of a coherent system of political ideas to a political system in such a way as to direct its activities, or it will involve the serious *intention* of making this application. Ideology is ordinarily used to convey both the notions of intended and of actual application. One may speak of 'the' or 'a' Marxist ideology when merely intending reference to a theoretical system. One may speak of the Soviet ideology when intending the actual application of such a system to the government of a particular state. Application, intended or actual, is involved in both cases. So the word 'ideology' may be used to cover both. It happens occasionally, however, that one wishes to keep the distinction in mind. When that is intended, the term 'ideological system' will be used in the sense previously indicated. 'Ideology' itself will inevitably be used in both ways.

Given that an ideology involves the actual or intended application of a coherent system of ideas to a system of government, in both an explanatory and a directive (or normative) sense, it will follow that an ideology will not merely be a political point of view or outlook (*Weltanschauung*) or philosophy or metaphysic. A political point of view may not be integrated or coherent; it may only relate to a particular issue and not constitute a general outlook. A political outlook, although more coherent than a point of view, may nevertheless fail to transcend a purely declaratory (more degenerately, a 'declamatory') stage and so remain unreasoning. A political philosophy, although more coherent than a political *Weltanschauung* and although thoroughly reasoned, may not be applied and may not be so intended *vis-à-vis* the direction of a group's activities. Whereas the absence of such an intention and application is possible in the case of a political philosophy their absence is probable in the case of a political metaphysic, since the concern of this category of reflection is not only not to recommend, but altogether to escape concern with recommendation as a category.

The operations of every government involve some concept of right and wrong, of rules to be obeyed, of law; and laws are ideas which can be regarded as being both explanatory and directive. It is possible to argue that a system of law, like an ideology, can hold a society together. But it is equally possible to argue that the unity of a society otherwise held together can be reflected in a system of law, or rationalised in an ideology. A system of law, like an ideology, can be conceived abstractly as only being intended for application, or concretely as an actual procedure or practice. A law can be conceived as a rule written in a book or as a recurrent type of behaviour of which no one (who actually instances such behaviour) is consciously aware. Law, since it need imply nothing more than a recurrent mode of behaviour, may involve the recurrence of any type of behaviour and so may be good or bad. Just as law may diminish social tensions by drawing attention away from them, so it may exacerbate these tensions by drawing attention to them. An ideology is more encompassing than a system of law, but the latter can certainly be treated ideologically. Attention could be drawn to its assumptions, these collated, possibly reduced to a single assumption, premise or ground, this then presented as an object of faith as well as a type of logical axiom whence the activities of a government are intended, or made, to unfold. In the same way that a system of law can protect or promote the partial interests of a social group, so may an ideology. In the same way that some laws may promote the interests of some groups within a society more than others, so may some ideologies. Although there will be only one system of law, there may be a variety of conflicting ideologies. The system of law as a whole may basically reflect the interests of a dominant group. The ideology of the government, if the government has one, may equally reflect those interests. But there may be other groups whose interests are violated by the law and obfuscated by the governmental 'ideology', and so they may concoct rival ideologies *vis-à-vis* one another as well as the government with a view to promoting their interests by incorporating them into the present or a projected system of law. Thus, within any society, governmental and any other groups may wield ideologies. It should be noted, however, that we have not asserted that ideologies are mere refractions of group interests. Nor has it been suggested that all governments and interest groups have ideologies.

That this is so, however, must turn upon an ultimately arbitrary distinction. An ideology, according to what has been said above, involves the application of a coherent system of ideas to political activity in order both to explain and direct it. Thus, whether or not we are actually confronted with an ideology in any particular case, will depend upon how coherent we shall insist that an applied system of political ideas must be before it is magically reconstituted as an ideology. In Russia and China, for example, systems of political thought are applied much more thoroughly and coherently than, say, in France or England. The question is how precisely this line can be drawn.

All governments, parties and other such organisations have some point of view; but this will merely mean that they will have a point of view about something, and not necessarily about everything or even most things. Thus not every political organisation, however superior or inferior, need be expected to have a systematic outlook upon all those matters which potentially fall within its range of concern, enabling it to utilise that outlook as a framework within which to explain and direct all of its activities. Some political organisations, like some individuals, will conceive of their activities much more coherently than others. (Although the question cannot be discussed at this stage, it is probably a mistake to regard the attempt at a coherent approach to political decision-making as bad. What is bad is when one assumes one is being systematic while being, in fact, merely circular.)

One would not say that an ideology was a 'truth'. It contains some conception of truth, but it also contains, beyond that, some conception of right. What is true and what is right are not necessarily compatible categories. If it is right to save the life of X, then it may be wrong not to lie in respect to his whereabouts. An ideology contains an inherent tension between a conception of right and conception of truth, and cannot be reduced to either. An 'ideologist' who sees himself to be concerned exclusively with the 'truth' can no longer be described as an ideologist; nor can one be so described if exclusively concerned with right. For an ideology involves a conjoint picture of truth and right. A complete devotion to truth renders one at best a scientist, at worse a vegetable, and in either case divorces one from the universe of moral discourse. A complete devotion to right renders one at best a politician, at worst an aerated utopist, and in either case divorces one from the universe of factual inquiry. Of course it may be thought that the commitment to truth is somehow superior to the commitment to right. But such a thought is probably mistaken. It is no more the case that to establish truth necessarily advances right than that an established right necessarily advances truth. Any outlook is composed of tensions, and so is any political ideology. The tension between truth and right is one of these.

An ideology involves both some manner of deduction from an overriding principle and some sort of commitment to an exclusive goal. It may involve more of one than the other, but more of either one, rather than of any one in particular. It involves deduction as part of a philosophical process. It involves commitment as part of a political process. It is not necessary that we should attempt to establish the manner in which an ideology is assembled. It is not likely that we would discover anything more novel by pursuing this line of inquiry than we would if we were concerned with the history of ideas in general or, more narrowly, with the sociology of knowledge. In so far as an ideology attempts to marshal a group to attain a particular aim, its adoption necessarily represents a commitment by the group sharing it. The word (aim) may be quite rigidly confined, to mean more a projection than a reality; but, if it is so confined, it should not be overlooked that the *preservation* of a reality may equally be projected, and thus become the object of an ideology. The point of all this, however, is that an ideology does not possess an exclusively logical or philosophical character at all. It possesses equally a political character without which it cannot be ideological. Still, the sort of political commitment revealed in an ideology usually assumes a specifically logical character. This consists in the translation of the ideology into one or a few basic principles, whence one may deduce not only what is correct in the objective mathematical sense, but also what is correct in the subjective ethical sense. It is this procedure which, as we shall later see, creates some difficulty. It is impossible to characterise as fallacious in general any commitment to an exclusive goal; such a commitment might be perfectly right in the circumstances of the moment. But the assumption, by contrast, that certain types of true logical deduction are necessarily politically right will not stand up to inspection. (But this is a question which cannot be further discussed at this stage.)

An ideology not only provides an understanding of a condition of fact together with a recommendation of action, but it also provides a focus for the general loyalties of an individual. One's understanding of reality, since the latter constantly changes, must constantly be re-interpreted. Agreement upon a broad objective may be too broad to cover the innumerable intermediate decisions that must be taken to achieve, and to avoid aborting, that objective. Thus, within an institutional context, there stands the need for some sort of arbiter between the individual, on the one hand, and the correctness of his grasp of the ideology and its goals on the other. Since an ideology is a coherent system of ideas applied to a group, the ideology will be the focus of the individual's loyalty within that group. But since a coherent system of ideas does not altogether apply *itself* to the group, it is important to see one way in which this is done by human agents. The formal loyalty demanded by an ideology is not, in the first instance, to an individual, nor is it to a set of individuals. It is, instead, to an idea or a principle: such as freedom, equality, justice or salvation. These are ideas, but they are also goals: they can be aimed at, one can seek to achieve them. The difficulty is, that they are intrinsically abstract goals—and this is not affected if we say they are generalisations from experience, or abbreviations of experiences or if we say that they are rationalisations of selfish economic interests; or that what ought to be done can be deduced from them; or that they reflect a pursuit of intimations. As abstract goals, whatever the historical process through which they have become established as goals, they require a more concrete form if they are to hold a group together. Thus there must be priests, scribes, intellectuals, even lawyers, who manipulate these ideas in such a way as to demonstrate that the concrete practices of the group, or its concrete aspirations, are consistent with the general conceptions and abstract aspirations embodied in its ideology. And this is one of the factors that accounts for the highly intellectual character of an ideology: its official interpreters must explain the appropriateness of concrete aims by reference to abstract goals, and not by reference to the simple demands, commands or directions of some whimsical individual.

Devotion to an ideology is slightly different from mere devotion to a group or to a person, though it may begin within the context of such devotion. One may be devoted to a group or to a person merely because this expression of loyalty is mutually profitable. Within the context of American politics the acceptability of loyalty in terms of a mutually profitable arrangement is often called 'log-rolling'. (More universally the invitation, 'you scratch my back, I'll scratch yours', reveals its nature.) Loyalties can be traditional, materialistic or merely based upon familiarity with associates. There are by contrast ideological loyalties, where one's commitment to the group is expressed in terms of one's commitment to the *ideas* which are conceived (in receiving the loyalties of all other group members) to bind the group together, to make it a whole. As suggested, however, devotion to an idea can begin in the form of devotion to a group. If one is an American or an Englishman or a Russian, it is quite possible for one to begin as a nationalist, out of simple familiarity with one's country, or for other reasons and then, on reflection, to extract some element which one thinks is peculiar to the particular national temperament of one's country, so that the loyalty which was originally and directly bestowed upon the group is now transferred to the distinctive idea or virtue with which the group becomes identified. One might still be called a nationalist, but then one's nationalism would have assumed a more pristine ideological form, as expressed in terms of one's devotion to the ideal of freedom embodied in the Constitution, or devotion to the concept of inflexible, undogmatic moderation embodied in the commitment to muddling through, or devotion to the construction of a communist society as originally projected in the works of Marx and Engels and furthered by the Revolution of 1917. But just as it is possible to move from commitment to the familiar to commitment to an ideology, so it is possible to reverse this process. For there are many people who have deserted their own lands to settle in the United States, in the United Kingdom and in the Union of Soviet Socialist Republics, because they thought they would find it possible to institutionalise and objectify their own otherwise abstract loyalties to such ideals as 'freedom', 'moderation' and 'communism'.

Ideologies are not necessarily restricted to governments. For a government is merely one type of social group, however distinctive its character. Ideologies may be wielded by any group or sub-group within a society. It is possible that a government might always adopt an ideological style; it is conceivable that it might never do so. It is possible that a government might or might not wield an ideology, permitting other inferior groups the same latitude. It is possible that a government might or might not wield an ideology, while refusing other, inferior groups the right to wield an ideology contrary to that held by the government, or to wield any ideology at all. All of this is possible. The distinction between an ideology as held by a government, and as held by other subordinate groups, is not—for our purposes—of any immediate importance. It is only important in so far as a government will, at least formally, possess more power than any other group internal to the same society. Thus, again formally, it will be able to impose its will upon these groups and so be able to permit or refuse them the right to operate in an ideological manner (however the government itself may operate).

An ideology as applied by a sub-group or a government is not necessarily tyrannical, although it may be. An ideology is tyrannical when it stipulates that some particular person or body has the exclusive authority to declare its implications in all or most cases. When that happens, even though the ideology itself places greater emphasis upon loyalty to itself than upon any interpreters of its meaning, the point is nevertheless reached where the interpreters are de facto supplied with the loyalty of members so that it is they personally who are obeyed. In this case the form of politics remains ideological, but the content is personal. What is personally determined cannot be questioned but it is justified by the proponent as ultimately stemming, not from himself, as it does, but directly from the ideology.

An ideology is not tyrannical when there are no serious limitations placed upon the rights of its adherents to discuss freely its implications and possible applications. This may happen within a one-party state which wields a particular ideology, as seems presently (1968) to be the case in Tanzania, for example. And it may happen even more obviously in a situation where the government either has no determinate ideology or applies what it has sporadically (as in the United States). Of course, governmental groups may wield ideologies with varying degrees of deliberation, inflexibility and coherence.

Ideological parties, like ideological governments, can be organised around the principle of open debate as well as by reference to a structure of quasi-military command. It is not true of course that parties and governments structured by reference to open debate and deliberative accord will necessarily prove unequal to those structured by reference to command and obedience. For although quick and firm decisions may be obstructed through tedious debate, sure and convinced support may be alienated through arbitrary commands. Of course it will happen that individuals as well as governments who know what they want, when confronted with others who do not, will necessarily be better placed (ceteris paribus) to succeed. But it is the easiest thing in the world for a group to know, politically, what it wants, without being 'ideologically' oriented to its achievement. It is not necessary to have a systematic understanding of the world in order to want to conquer it (perhaps one may refer to Alexander or to Genghis Khan), or develop or destroy or control it or (as perhaps with Switzerland) to profit from the world while keeping it at a distance. 'Singlemindedness', in short, is not a part of the meaning of 'ideological politics', since it will not always be found in an ideological system and will frequently be found in non-ideological systems. One factor which requires to be considered is the deliberate smokescreen effect so often encountered in ideological systems when they claim to embody the loyalties of group members while in fact they do not. An ideology is not likely to involve the smokescreen effect when members' adherence to the group which the ideology engirdles is truly voluntary. But governments are often most hysterical in their manipulation of ideologies, not when the states they control are cohesive, but when they are or become fissiparous; so that often the ideological formulae, ubiquitous as they are, do not so much represent a unity, as a tenuous and final effort to constitute a unity. Put to such use, ideology achieves a smokescreen effect. And behind the smokescreen one may find little more than an estranged membership on the one side, with corrupt and bickering politicians on the other. There need be no singlemindedness at all as regards the implementation of policy, however well concealed the actual programmatic incoherence may be beneath an extraordinarily lucid, but irrelevant, flow of ideas. Typically, tyrannical ideological systems are those applied to groups, but openly or tacitly rejected by them, and where the possibility of elaborating alternative ideologies is suppressed. It is also typically in these circumstances that an ideology becomes a smokescreen and the political consciousness it embodies becomes 'false'. Here the 'official' ideology does not accurately reflect the outlook and commitments of the group members (the citizens or subjects); and therefore the official consciousness becomes a 'false' consciousness. It is clear that this may happen within any ideological system, whether communist, socialist, capitalist or otherwise. The official democratic ideology in the United States, for example, is regarded by many Negro Americans as embodying, for them, a false consciousness. Similarly, the official socialist ideology of Ghana was regarded by many Ghanaians as embodying, for them, a false consciousness. A 'false' consciousness may be so in so far as it does not reflect the outlook and commitment of the community or sub-communities towards whom it is beamed. But it may also be false in so far as it is simply and vigorously rejected, by the national community or by certain of its sub-communities. As we have seen, an ideological system is not merely an outlook, but a commitment, and not merely the idea of a commitment, but its practice. Thus the rejection of an ideological system is not just the rejection of an idea, nor of a practice, but of an idea as practised, or of a practice as idealised. So the rejection of 'socialism' in Ghana cannot be read as the rejection of a noble idea wrongly abused, but of a particular ideological system, in form and content, as it stood. The partial Negro rejection of democracy in America cannot be read as the rejection of a noble idea shamefully despised but of a concrete ideological system, both in form and content, as it stands. In these circumstances, the most extreme form which the repudiation of a 'false' ideology can take is its violent rejection. Ideological politics, especially open, permit sophisticated stratagems and superb argumentative subterfuges. But once it is assumed that this system of argument is really closed, then one may withdraw altogether and subject it to physical attack.

Short of physical attack, a great deal of argument can take place within any ideological system. The reason for this is not too difficult to see. First, however, it will be necessary to remark that the type of ideological system presently assumed is that of an 'official' kind—expressing or embodying the cohesiveness, outlook and purpose of a governmental group. This does not prejudice the applicability of the general conclusions of this discussion to all ideological systems; it merely advises that our immediate concern and examples will relate to governmental ideologies. A governmental group, with its member-citizens, may operate as an ideological system. If this is to mean anything at all it must imply that there are governments (as suggested earlier) which do not wield ideologies. Such governments exist. However, as between all governments, it may well be to draw attention to one common factor (there are of course several others): this is decision-making. The difference between ideological and non-ideological systems very much hangs on a difference in the character of decision-making. The point of this, however, is not to suggest that non-ideological decision-making is of one type (no more than non-human forms of life are of one type). In taking a decision for any group the decision may be explained or justified by reference to a common end that is supposed to bind the group together. A head of state may do this, no less than the head of a corporation or union or cultural society. He may explain or justify what he has done by reference to a common end which is supposed to express the shared purpose of all members. In the case of voluntary associations this operation is usually easy to execute. That is because these associations are almost always of the sort where their purpose is actually spelt out in a charter or contract or constitution; and thus the officers generally know quite concretely what aims they are to pursue and the members know by what yardstick their performance may be measured. In the case of associations where membership is involuntary, as with governments, explanation and justification by reference to a common purpose is rather more difficult to achieve (for various reasons which I do not wish immediately to touch upon). Nonetheless this is often done, typically by governments which themselves have constitutions. Now the difference between ideological and non-ideological decision-making is a difference of kind; and yet it is a difference that must be measured in degrees. For example, in an ideological system the common purpose stated cannot be restricted to a particular time and place; it must be unending and its application illimitable. Also, it cannot be shared among individuals or groups who have conflicting understandings of the actual nature of the world and of history; the specific purpose cannot be divorced from the general outlook. Thus 'democracy' is an ideology, but 'home-rule' is not; 'peace' can be promoted ideologically, but a Korean (or Vietnamese) truce cannot be. These examples suggest differences of kind—and yet, at the same time, they reflect differences of degree. For the political abstraction is always burdened with institutional encrustations. (Why else do we speak of a given country as being, for example, the 'birth-place' of parliamentarism or the 'home' of the free?) And the concrete political aim can always be viewed as a particular expression of an enduring purpose (such as 'self-determinination for all peoples'). Communism and capitalism, democracy and aristocracy, can be viewed as ideological systems, by contrast with personal autocracy or enlightened despotism, which are basically non-ideological.

But even here, the quarrel between differences of degree and differences of kind re-emerges. If democracy and aristocracy can be admitted as ideological systems, then why not monarchy? And if monarchy, why not personal autocracy? And if this, why not any other system at all? This argument is not convincing, but it is plausible; what it really reveals is the continuity in degree between all systems of government. Of course a monarchy could be ideological if it invoked a highly coherent world-view conjoined with a commitment to a highly general and exclusive goal. It just so happens that most monarchies do not. Monarchy is usually just another name for hereditary one-man rule. And although it could in principle be turned into a sophisticated ideological system it usually is not. There may of course be a reason for this that is intrinsic to the nature of monarchy: that it is simply too personal. We have already seen that an ideological system may indeed reduce to personal rule *de facto*; but that it can only do so to the extent that the ruler (refusing to justify himself *qua* himself) poses as an intermediary between the citizens and the achievement of their common goal. It is more difficult to alter this relationship in such a way that the ideology is made to consist in, as oppposed to merely camouflaging, personal rule. Still, despite the difficulty, such an alteration remains possible.

Any particular group may be transformed into an ideological system or deflated into one that is not. Any given government can project an abstract goal for the society as a whole—such as freedom—and justify, or attempt to justify, all of its activities as flowing from the pursuit thereof, not only in domestic policy but in foreign as well. Foreign wars may be consistently justified and explained as an attempt to protect or extend liberty both at home and abroad. The refusal to establish a public health system, to provide more government scholarships, to initiate slum clearance schemes, can all be justified and explained as an attempt to protect the liberty of physicians in their practices, of universities and scholars in their researches, and the liberty of all individuals to buy, sell, build and destroy their own homes as and when they wish. There is no limit that can be placed upon the ways in which an abstract goal can be utilised by a government to justify and explain the unending series of concrete decisions which it must take. What becomes ideological about this is the way in which an abstract idea is consistently and coherently used to justify and explain to a group the directing decisions which impose upon it its apparent and active character *qua* group.

Now it is clear that this ideological activity may be engaged upon more or less coherently, consistently, unyieldingly, extensively and consciously. That is why it becomes so difficult to point to any particular *government* or society or group organisation, and say (except in extreme cases and even then for only limited periods of time) that it operates entirely as an ideological system. That is why it is difficult to maintain that democracy is an ideological system and monarchy is not or that 'communism' is and 'democracy' is not. Thus we must stop looking for easy examples of ideological systems and ask, instead, *when* it is that a system is operating ideologically. This assumes, then, that any system can do so and, further, that virtually no system does so all the time. Our criterion of an ideology thus becomes more dynamic and less static, and more similar to our disposition to ask, let us say, when it is that a man is behaving badly, rather than how we determine that a man is evil.

So much has been said about communism and socialism as ideologies that there is no need to rehearse these arguments here. It may be more interesting to explore, however briefly, the way in which a society not conceived to be ideological can and does operate in an ideological manner. When a government operates in an ideological manner it justifies or explains itself by reference to general principles or abstract goals which it assumes that all citizens share and which are supposed to be continuous and overriding. Either the government can operate in this way, or other groups can do so, while attempting to impress their outlook upon the government itself. Take a situation where a government operates in theory according to a constitution. The latter can be said to embody the ideals, purposes and procedures of the state. Whatever the government does that is right is 'constitutional'; whatever it does that is wrong is 'unconstitutional'. The constitution of the state comes to be viewed as the axiomatic ground of its organisation and activities. Thus it cannot be questioned, except in ways which it itself permits, and it must be regarded as being politically sacrosanct. When one becomes a subject of a monarchy, one swears axiomatic allegiance to the monarch. When one becomes a citizen of such a constitutional state as has been described, one swears allegiance to the constitution, declaring thereby one's intention to uphold and support it. The constitution, like the scriptures and political philosophies, is interpreted, but it is interpreted by judges, rather than by priests and intellectuals. Further, these interpreters do not declare, or do not intend to declare, their will but merely that of the directing document whose meaning they do no more than elicit. A constitution can therefore be treated as the framework of an ideological system. 'Life, liberty and the pursuit of happiness' might well be its abstractly intended goal.

Now of course it is true that under most constitutional systems the general assumption is merely that the constitution provides a framework for governmental activity, not a directive clearly stipulating what must be done. And a framework of this kind cannot be ideological in that it is clear from the start that it is not so much intended to tell the government *what* to do, but *how* to do it; not as an axiom that will bear the weight of deductions, but as a mere launching pad, solid and unsinkable, whence any number and variety of group initiatives may be fired. The point is, however, that all depends here upon how the constitution is regarded. And for many segments of the community it will not be regarded as a mere framework, but as in fact stipulating what must be done, however abstractly, and as embracing an entire range of assumptions thought to inhere in the document itself. If the constitution in its relation to governmental decisions is regarded as an axiomatic principle, which fairly precisely determines all governmental initiatives as opposed to a stable pad whence various and even contradictory initiatives may be launched, then one is confronted with an ideological outlook; and if that outlook is adopted by a group, then that group becomes an ideological system; and where the government is that group then it, too, becomes an ideological system. But the important point is this: it is only *to the extent* that a government adopts this outlook, and explains and justifies itself in the appropriate manner, that it becomes an ideological system. Thus it becomes reasonable to say of a government that is not ordinarily thought to be an ideological system that it becomes one to the extent and for as long as it operates like one.

Within any group there will be certain tensions, within all states certain conflicts of interest. Typically, under an ideological system what will be posited is a common, if abstract, goal. The attempt to resolve tensions and to settle conflicts—where this attempt is made argumentatively—primarily consists in stating an overriding principle or common purpose whence may be deduced a correct settlement. Typically, under a non-ideological system no such attempt is made. But this leaves open several possibilities, and this implies that, in fact, there is no 'typical' non-ideological method of resolving basic social tensions or conflicts of interest. Competing groups may simply attempt to get as much as they can before others stop them. Others may operate on a *quid pro quo* basis in the sense of making a concession for every concession made. Others may frankly assume that there is no common purpose or principle and that the only way to advance or protect one's interests is by forcibly removing or restraining those who happen to get in the way. And others still may simply have no idea whatever as to what common principles they should adopt, or whether it is possible meaningfully to adopt any at all.

Now a constitutional system begins to operate as an ideological system when it is no longer treated as a mere changeable framework, but as an object of belief and devotion. The constitution, formally the framework of action, becomes instead the distilled, guiding principle of action. It does not matter that a mere constitution cannot effectively guide a state over the shifting sands of foreign and domestic policy. It is only necessary to recognise that the actual conduct of a government can always be 'explained' or rationalised or commended by reference to what is supposed to be the spirit of the constitution or the intentions of those who initially devised it. The ideologist who wishes to convert a constitutional into an ideological system typically commences by insisting that all or certain classes of citizens formally swear allegiance to the flag or to the country or to the document which broadly stipulates how that country's government operates.

One instance of this sort of activity comes from New York State in the form of an act called the Feinberg Law. The purpose of this law was, according to its supporters, to guard against the subversion of the state constitution. This the law attempted to do by making it mandatory that all teachers and lecturers in the schools and universities of the state sign a loyalty oath. One of the interesting aspects of this sort of approach is the importance that is attributed to a generalised statement of intent and the sorts of consequences that can be deduced from it. Every state, of course, recognises treason as a crime, and disloyalty towards the state, when translated into legal terms, would basically mean treason. New York State, however, at the time the Feinberg Law was passed, was not bereft of a law of treason. Thus the Feinberg Law did not add anything, in this respect, which was not already there. This reinforces the sense of redundancy attaching to the law. However varied the reasons may in fact have been for passing it, one of them, certainly, was to protect the community's 'right of self-preservation'—as one U.S. Supreme Court Justice put it. How was the community to protect itself? Not simply by punishing those who, in law, betrayed it, but by insisting upon a declaration by a certain class of community members that in effect they would never betray it. This approach is typical of the ideological style and in this we have one instance of it as it emerged within a particular constitutional system. There is a conflation of moral duty with legal duty. There is an initial insistence upon the word, rather than the deed. There is involved an excessive kind of moral abstractness without reference to time, place or propriety.

Ideological systems can be particularly pernicious (especially in an authoritarian tradition) because of their moral abstractness, which does not in fact permit the kind of precision in application that is expressly intended to be imposed by such systems. In January 1967 the U.S. Supreme Court held the Feinberg Law to be 'unconstitutional' (which is what the law aimed to prevent everyone else from being) precisely because of its rigidity of form on the one hand, and vagueness of content on the other. For if anyone swore an oath of loyalty and then violated that oath, such a person clearly laid himself open to prosecution: thus the formal rigidity of the law. But at the same time, since the law did not adequately stipulate what loyalty consisted in, this automatically became subject to endlessly varying interpretations, thus the law's vagueness of content (and therefore the illimitable range of its applicability). Consequently, one could violate one's oath of loyalty by doing anything which one's superiors might consider disloyal—as perhaps by undressing publicly or (the actual example presented to the Supreme Court) by displaying publicly a copy of the *Communist Manifesto*.

But in the same way that an ideological system can be legally pernicious, so it can be logically vacuous. The latter, in fact, is the ground of the former; but it is also its trapdoor and escape hatch. For if an ideology can be manipulated by those in power so as to lead to such conclusions as they desire, it can also be amended by those who are out of power to lead another way. If a government claims a commitment to liberty, and enters upon foreign wars to extend it and internal censorship to protect it, there will always be those to argue that liberty cannot be imposed and that censorship defeats and routs it. If a government claims a commitment to socialism, and enters upon foreign wars to extend it and internal censorship to protect it, there will similarly be those to argue that socialism cannot be imposed and that censorship stifles and destroys it. Even a government which invokes the superiority of one race as a justification for trampling others underfoot, will be met with the objection that the genius of the race was not to destroy, but to build, not to dispossess the weak, but make them secure. Any ideological system is subject to such manoeuvring, for and against, since there is always an unintended gap between the general goal, principle or belief which it stipulates and the variety of specific causes the ideology can be made to serve.

As we have seen, a great deal of argument can take place within an ideological system. To shut off such argument these systems can become closed; but they may also be open; they can, in short, vary in the degree of tolerance or authoritarianism that they permit or require. But despite the degree of debate that can be permitted within an ideology, one essential feature of such systems is a demand for some form of belief. In much the same way that geometry demands axioms, an ideology demands a belief. The political application of a coherent system of ideas to a group is really nothing more than the elaboration of a commitment —a commitment of that group to the particular system of ideas. One is 'committed' to an idea, basically, when one cannot demonstrate its validity, or simply when one is inclined to accept it without such demonstration. Within a deductive system of argument, of course, one always reaches some fundamental position which cannot be demonstrated. The fundamental position, the axiom, must then simply be accepted. But usually it is accepted simply because it is believed to be 'obvious' or 'self-evident'. In short it is believed to be true, but it is not believed that its truth can be demonstrated. In this sort of case one must treat the fundamental position as an object of faith, of belief, or one must circularly attempt to demonstrate its truth by reference to all the other propositions which it has already presupposed. An ideology, therefore, when 'applied' to a group, formally commits them to it in the form of a belief (its validity could not be *logically* demonstrated). The ideological system *as a whole* is not an object of belief. (If it were, there could be no argument within it.) But certain of its quintessential elements are: such as liberty or equality or self-realisation or majority rule or the people's will—and so on. Any one of these can be advanced as a fundamental principle, out of which the logic of the system may be held to unfold, imposing a 'necessary' connection between the general principle(s) and the most important of a government's (or a group's leaders') particular decisions.

The area of commitment demanded by an ideology locates the fundamental belief(s) required of its adherents. Beliefs, of course, are of different sorts and involve commitment to different perspectives and goals. Different ideologies will invoke different fundamental beliefs.

But not all systems of government (as previously indicated) are ideological and, therefore, not all systems of government operate by reference to the holding of some fundamental, explanatory, justifying and directing belief. Some governments operate by reference to openly and recognisably contradictory 'beliefs', which may be invoked at will in any manner found suitable at the time. This sort of procedure will only be called ideological to the extent that the different 'beliefs' involved are treated as fundamental and exclusive when invoked. But it is not necessary that they be so treated, since it is quite possible to regard them not as guides, but as brisk summations of what in the circumstances it was thought the government might best do. If, for example, a government explains and justifies itself by reference to the principle 'unity is strength', it may not really mean this universally, as a principle whence it deduces the need to merge its own administration with that of another state. It might simultaneously and quite consistently demand, and posit as its goal, 'Freedom now!', implying the end of its administrative absorbtion into another polity (as under colonial rule, for example). If it were merely positing in the present the principle of unity, whereas in the past it had supported the principle (in effect) of disunity, then it would clearly be operating contradictorily. But what is more probable is that the general 'belief', 'principle' or 'universal aim' is not so much that, as a formula which does no more than briefly summarise the highly particular reasons for taking a certain decision at a given time. So to repeat: governments often operate by reference to openly contradictory 'beliefs'—but this is not necessarily to operate ideologically, since the 'belief' may not really be regarded as such by anyone, but merely as an essay in instant communication (a summarisation of a much more involved and detailed argument whose conclusion was not apparent at the outset). In short, what appear to be contradictory 'beliefs' may be nothing more than slogans and maxims to be invoked at will. Such an approach is not ideological.

Not all systems of government are ideological, and thus not all societies are tied together by reference to a common belief system. An imperial polity, for example, is not so much tied together by belief as it is by conquest or force. (To obey a government because one fears it is not the same as obeying it because one shares its outlook and aims.) Under such circumstances rule does not tend to be legitimated by reference to values held in common between conquered and conqueror, but (in so far as they are held at all) by reference to values or beliefs restricted to the conqueror. In the same way that one group may conquer another without a discernible belief system operating commonly between them (and thus legitimating for both the act of conquest), so is it possible to make of several units (e.g. conqueror and conquered)

one group (certainly administratively) without any common belief
system uniting them. In so far as a system of government can be non-
ideological, this must mean that a society can be tied together without
reference to any common belief system. A non-ideological system must
either be characterised by the total absence of belief systems or by the
presence of more or less equal and competing belief systems. The
presence in societies of competing belief systems is an historical commonplace; the absence from societies of all belief systems seems merely con-
jectural, nothing more than a logical and futuristic possibility. (But
by 'belief system' is not intended any particular belief about any particular matter, but about a belief system in the sense of an 'ideological
system', or a general and directive system of ideas that embraces some
general conception both of what is and what ought to be as applied
either to a sovereign or sub-sovereign group. Such a system can be conceived to flow from one or a limited set of principles or axioms, which
then become objects of belief.) 'The absence from societies of all *belief
systems*' is not intended to imply 'the absence of all *beliefs*'. For one may
believe that one's redeemer liveth, or that one could have defeated
Botvinik had one really tried, without in any way being able to prove
either proposition, while divorcing both—entirely—from any political
purpose, goal or consideration. What is intended is a *political* belief
system (naturally a religion is capable of supplying this) or, in other
words, the ideological direction and organisation of a social group,
whether the latter be sovereign or voluntary.

A group, however, that has many belief systems is in the same position
as one that has no belief system—from the perspective of its highest or
sovereign point of organisation. It follows as a matter of course that
a society without a common belief system—which is so in the sense that
it either has *none* at all or *diverse* belief systems—cannot be directed by
reference to a single ideology. Where there is no consciousness of, nor
an ability to refer to, a single belief system, no one can pretend to deduce
(at least the governing or directing agency cannot deduce) what ought
to be done from some prior and exclusive principle which is regarded
as transcending all others. In these circumstances, of course, a government might make much ado about 'the common good'. If it approached
such a good as a fundamental reality impervious to all considerations of
fact, then 'the common good' will have been transformed into an
a priori principle, an article of faith, and therefore into the basis of an
ideological system. The position would be otherwise if it merely accepted
that there *might* be a common good, which it could seek to elicit as a
basis of general agreement. The hypothetical society which is entirely
free of all ideological groups and movements must, so long as it remains
in this state, equally remain free of all prospect of the government

reverting to or assuming an ideological style. The society which contains diverse ideological groups and movements, however, can always entertain the prospect of its governing agency assimilating such a style (either by imitating an inferior group or by an inferior ideological group becoming the government).

A fundamental political belief, forming the spearhead of an ideological system, is not the same as a political programme. It is possible for a government to have no ideology, and yet to have a programme. The latter may be more or less rigorously pursued, realistic, realisable or consistent. But it need not imply commitment to any specific metaphysic nor need it be abstract. It is possible to test the extent to which a concrete programme has been implemented, and not by reference to an exclusive and fundamental principle. *The* programme will change, since the degree of its realisation eliminates *pro tanto* as a goal its projections; and *the* programme, in historical retrospect, can always be regarded as *a* programme, which was only relevant to a particular time and place.

An ideology is often viewed as repugnant to a political programme. But in so far as an ideology stipulates as a part of its meaning the relating of a system of ideas to a programme of political action, some form of programme is always subjoined to an ideology. The point about this subjunction, however, is that it is always treated as dependent, not otherwise, because flowing somehow logically from initial premises. It is in this sense that an ideology and a programme can be viewed as mutually repugnant—in the situation where either is regarded as prior, or where both are regarded as independent. A political ideology turns a political programme into the consequence of a premise. A political programme turns a political ideology into either an 'abbreviation' of an experience or into a rationalisation of a commitment. It is in this way that the two become mutually repugnant, although they may share a very similar defect, labelled in an ideology 'doctrinairism' (impracticality and rationalisation) and in a programme 'dogmatism' (rigidity or inflexibility). All the same, whereas an ideology is intrinsically doctrinaire, a programme is not necessarily dogmatic.

Dogmatism tends to assume the form of mere stupidity. A doctrinaire stance, by contrast, is infinitely more subtle and intellectual. Dogmatism posits belief, but basically an unreasoning belief. The doctrinaire position posits belief, but of the type conceded to the initial phases of a mathematical proof. But we are here concerned with political ideologies, not with political programmes. Within an ideological system, what is *politically* required of members is commitment to the stipulated—if abstract—goals of the group. Similarly, what is *logically* required is belief in the basic premise or premises of the ideology (or the general system of ideas). Belief in these premises will not only afford to the government (or directing agency of a group) the means whereby, and the framework within which, it explains, justifies and generally pursues its activities. It will also serve as a criterion by which is at least partially determined the status of members—and possibly even whether they are regarded as members at all.

We have seen that, where the organisation of a group is translated into an ideological system, there is posited and presupposed some fundamental agreement upon an abstract goal, which takes the political form of commitment and the logical form of belief. It is clear that the presence or absence of this belief can be viewed as the distinguishing characteristic of a group member. And where a person can be recognised as a member of a group by virtue of his belief, so can he in fact become a member by accepting the condition that he believe. Not all groups or systems of government accept or reject potential members by reference to belief, however. Nor do all ideological systems do so *exclusively* on this basis. Members (whether of an ideological or non-ideological system) might be rejected, accepted and promoted by reference to other criteria, such as consanguinity (as in tribalism and racialism), accomplishment (as in a meritocracy), and location (as, theoretically, in most nationalisms)—not merely by reference to belief (as often in Christianity, Islam and communism). The more an ideological system universalises its principles, and permits belief in them alone to stand as an earnest of one's adherence, the more pristine it becomes. For this reason, racialism does not provide an entirely satisfactory example of an ideology. Apart from the fact that there is no very coherent system upon which it can depend (as some ideologies do upon figures like Augustine and Marx), racialism is accompanied by a limiting condition. Adherents of a racial ideology must not only meet the condition of believing in the superiority of a certain group, they must also be biologically affiliated to it. Adherents of a nationalist ideology must not only believe in the superior virtue, etc., of a national group, but they must also be located within it, either by birth or residence. It is for this reason that racialism and nationalism are not as good examples as can be offered of ideologies: it is difficult to be a racialist or a nationalist without somehow belonging to the race or nation one vaunts. For this reason the possibility of adherence to these types of ideology is more complicated than in other cases (such as communism, socialism and liberalism), for what is required is not merely commitment to some abstract goal and the acceptance of some fundamental belief, but the possession, too, of some characteristic feature which neither belief nor disbelief—of whatever kind—will affect. Such additional criteria of community inclusion lessen the force of an ideology. They deprive it of a purely logical character, and focus as much attention upon an individual's condition (race, location and function) as upon his belief.

Elaborate ideologies of a racialist or nationalist kind are little more than half-way houses between tribalism and true ideology. For this reason I believe it mistaken to lump communism and fascism together indiscriminately, as most recent writers are inclined to do. Too much attention has been directed to the brutality of which both systems are extraordinarily capable: of brutality all systems are capable. What it is important to draw attention to here is the ideological difference, or the degree thereof: communism is far more *ideo*-logical than nationalism or racialism. It will not do merely to argue that communism's primary concern is class, while racialism's is with race (although this is true). For within a communist system it is possible for an adherent to shed his class identity; indeed, one of the basic goals posited is the shedding of all class identities. But within a racialist system it is impossible for just anyone to become assimilated to the group in this way: without the necessary genetic qualifications his beliefs will count for little; and thus the logic of this system, as a device designed to assimilate membership by reference only to a fundamental belief or principle, is inhibited. It will not do to conflate the ideological character of communism with that of racialism: *qua* ideology, the latter is more primitive and less developed than the former. Communism is a much purer example of ideology.

In the application of a system of ideas to a group, where the system is intended to convince by the strength of its consistency, and to secure as substantial support for government policy as is possible, and in this sense to unite a group in as complete a fashion as can be, there can be no doubt that he whom the system designates as an enemy must be treated as essentially assimilable in order to add to the strength of the system. The ideological system which does not do this automatically weakens itself, since, although it is designed to convince, it becomes intrinsically restricted to the possibility of only convincing some. An ideology is designed to convince, but if it posits conditions for affiliation which transcend conviction itself, it automatically limits itself to a particular audience. Ideology in its pristine form does not do this. Its appeal transcends all particularities. Thus it invites affiliation on the basis of belief alone. And this must mean that whoever opposes it will be regarded as a potential convert (not merely as an enduring enemy). Such is the character of its logic and, so conceived, the potential breadth of its appeal becomes universal. The logic of the idea expands outward without obstruction. Where the enemies of the system cannot be absorbed, then the logic of the system cannot embrace them. Where the logic of the system cannot embrace them, its political energy *qua* ideology is exhausted. It would be foolish to conclude from what has been said, however, that socialist governments, for example, are more powerful than nazi or fascist governments. All that is intended is that their *logic* is more powerful, because the range of their potential application is greater.

There are religious ideologies and secular ideologies, totalitarian ideologies and piece-meal ideologies, authoritarian, materialistic, and aesthetic ideologies, ideologies that appeal to blood, ideologies that appeal to class, ideologies that appeal to territoriality and ideologies— the most pristine of all—that appeal exclusively to belief. Ideologies are not just systems of government and they are not merely sets of ideas. An ideological system may exist for a moment, it may exist for years. When it exists it exists in the form of a particular relation between a coherent system of ideas and a system of government (or of any sort of organised group); it exists as a coherent set of ideas, both normative and factual, which gives shape, or which is assumed to and is presented as giving shape, to the activities of a government. It is not merely a programme set in motion; for this may not be, and may not be presented as being, a deduction from a principle. It is not merely a principle, since a principle need not, while an ideology must, yield a programme of action. It requires of those who embrace it not just a belief, but a political belief, and not just any kind of political belief, but one that is fundamental. Since ideologies do not exist in books, no writer may be called an ideologist who may not also reject this label. Marx is, and Marx is not. Hegel is, and Hegel is not. Aquinas is, and he, too, is not. It will depend on how they are interpreted and the uses to which they are put. Perhaps every writer who is comprehensive enough, and who is actually read, could both accept and discard this tag.

Hobbes and Hegel, for example, usually are not utilised, and there-fore are not understood, ideologically. It is often said of course that every government has an ideology and that every political philosopher is an ideologist. (Such assertions are usually intended to convey nothing more than that (*a*) every government has a general outlook or policy and (*b*) that no political philosopher altogether escapes the activity of recommending.) But this is not in fact so. The works of every political philosopher are not adopted by sovereign or sub-sovereign groups to explain and direct their activities. Political philosophers are ideologised only rarely; as in the case of Marx or (possibly) Aquinas. Also, not every ideology has a political philosopher (as with racialism), although this lack may tend to weaken the coherence of the ideology. And further, not every group has an ideology (whether elaborated by a single political philosopher or not), since many groups (whether sovereign or not) have very limited objectives (like most families and, indeed, most states). Also, an abstract objective (like justice) is not necessarily associated with any coherent world view at all.

Following on this discussion of ideology, the following is offered as a general definition:

a coherent system of ideas of whatever kind, involving some understanding of man and the world, and which attempts to relate this understanding to a programme of political action, so that the understanding does not remain abstract but is (or is intended to be) applied, and is not (or is not intended to be) simply applied to an individual but to a group, and is so applied as to lead towards the achievement of an exclusive goal, but a goal formulated in a very general way.

Ideology, if it is a discernible fact, must have a discernible history. It will not merely be a history of ideas, nor will it be a mere history of institutions. (Let us not here debate the question whether institutions are reducible to ideas.) It will be a history of ideas in a particular relation to organised, institutional activities. The history need not be 'continuous'; there may be gaps. It need not be inevitable; there is much room for accident. The history provided in the following section will be potted, yet smooth enough, it is hoped, to convey the reader to the particular conceptual destination the writer intends. History is necessary to lengthen perspective, and that is the aim of the next section. Christianity may be taken as the first and most pristine form of ideology to emerge in the West. It is very much aware of itself as a dramatically new beginning. It is in fact obvious that our own methods of dating reflect the importance which we ourselves attribute to it as a new beginning. We may accept as appropriate the line of demarcation which it itself describes between past and present. Of course all such lines involve a geometry of myth. With this in mind, one may be allowed to ape the Christian division, very much due to the attraction of its neatness, thereby separating the ideological from the pre-ideological at the year zero.

IDEOLOGY: A HISTORY

There is neither Greek, nor Jew, circumcision, nor incircumcision, Barbarian, or Scythian, bond, or free, but Christ is all, and in all.
Acts x. 34

The year zero effectively demarcates because—as the name suggests—it marks the absence of something. This something is almost literally a 'logical' formula for the recognition, and therefore the inclusion and exclusion, of community members. Among the early Greeks and Romans the basic principle of inclusion was kinship. The emergence of Epicureanism and Stoicism resulted in the diminished importance of ties of kin, partly due to their displacement by the new concept of Humanity, of the brotherhood of all men.

Kinship can serve as the basis of an ideology, but only with difficulty: its criterion of recognition and acceptance is not sufficiently logical. It is true that a kinship system can always be hypostatised. Adoption is an example of this process. Where an individual does not meet certain basic biological demands for assimilation and internal status, the system's demands can always be disregarded in their strict, literal sense and stretched (indeed, abstracted) so as to allow one who is not in fact a son or whatever to be designated 'son', etc. Thus, 'son', 'father', 'mother' and other such terms can acquire a legal, rather than a biological, sense. A *complete* change of front along these lines, however, is a difficult feat to achieve. But where it is achieved, the kinship system has really become ideological. The identity of the kin has been transferred from a biological to a principled basis.

One's brother may become such because he is *recognised* as a brother. There need be no particular reason for this recognition. It may simply be that he works well or is helpful or likeable or has no family of his own. To treat a stranger like a brother means no more than to treat him well —but within a system where it tends to be assumed that the necessary qualification for receiving such treatment is actual brotherhood, or kinship; so that when a person is shown friendship this will not merely be described as friendliness, but as 'brotherly' love, or something of the sort. This idea of kinship as a uniting factor can be pushed so far that prospective friends may even feel that no genuine fellowship and loyalty exists between them unless their wrists have been slashed and their blood has actually mingled. But where one reaches the stage that a 'brother' can become such by recognition, it is possible to move on to the point of completely locating brotherhood as a function of a shared principle, belief or faith, rather than as a function of a biological relationship. This movement is not inevitable; we need only remark that it has frequently occurred. Where this transpires, one's kinsmen become, perhaps, all good men, or all honest men, or all moderate men, or all freedom-loving peoples everywhere. When the transformation is as complete as this, it is clear that the kinship system remains no longer in any way intact. It has tended to become purely ideological. The focus of identity is no longer a biological relationship, but either the attainment of a general belief, or some other qualification. The sharing of the belief or quality can relate one to others, and at the same time assume the form of a goal to be attained. The goal is of a kind, however, that cannot be precisely defined, which must mean also that it can never be exactly or definitely reached.

Christianity incorporated the concept of universal brotherhood, and in fact employed it as a basis for conversion irrespective of condition, kin or location. This transition, for simplicity's sake, can be dated from the death of Aristotle (322 B.C.) to the conversion of Constantine (A.D. 303). This places an arbitrary line between the Antiquity of Kinship and the Modernity of Belief at the Year O. This date theoretically coincides with the birth of Christ as well as being intermediate between the eclipse of official paganism and the official sanctioning of Christian thought.

Ideological politics, in short, noticeably began with Christianity. The latter offered a mythological vision of the past, of the advent of the future and of a community of believers united in their acceptance of this vision, which was essentially untestable and irrefutable. Theoretically, condition, kin and location were irrelevant. But belief was not. Wealth, intelligence and skill were important, but secondary. What was immediately essential was not being a good *man*, but a good *Christian*, i.e. one who thoroughly and unquestioningly accepted the historical and futuristic vision of the truth as enshrined in Christian doctrine.

Of course it will be remarked that Christians are and were as much concerned with practising and living up to their beliefs as with accepting them. But this is only partly true. Christians were not equally concerned with these matters at the same time and in the same way. What was always asserted was the absolute necessity of belief for salvation. The qualification that only *some* believers would be saved followed after. The attainment of salvation depended, then, upon the individual meeting several conditions. But all of these were in principle possible for anyone, and the first of these was belief in Christ. If only practice were necessary, then it would become possible to lead a completely satisfactory life without declaring any faith at all. But in the same way that Christians have commonly assumed that a world without God must be immoral, so have they commonly assumed that an individual devoid of belief in God must be sinful. The initial belief is the foundation stone of (what is explicitly designated) The Faith, or The True Faith.[1]

It is true that many Christians have been greatly and almost exclusively concerned with practice. But it is equally true that many have tended seriously and immediately to insist upon faith alone. When this happens, the formal pronouncement of ideological allegiance may be made within a context where competing allegiances are possible, and possibly less dangerous. The formal pronouncement becomes a first and essential step; for the adherent, it may possibly be an act of bravery. Merely to *declare* (quite apart from considerations of practice) that one is a Christian (in Rome) or a Jew (in medieval Christendom) or a

---

[1] Cf. J. N. Figgis, *From Gerson to Grotius* (Cambridge, 1907, 1931), p. 20: 'The Holy Roman Empire...did indeed attempt to realise the ideal of an all-powerful State, but that state was the Church...It has been said that there was no Austinian sovereign in the medieval State. That is true of the individual kingdoms. It is not true of the Church...Baptism was a necessary element in true citizenship in the Middle Ages, and excommunication was its antithesis.'

capitalist (in the U.S.S.R. or China) or a communist (in the United States), could be positively dangerous. This was why the famous disciple, after all, denied his lord, despite the crowing cock and the scornful judgment of succeeding generations. At such a stage, the basic demand is not that one practice one's preaching, but that one declare one's faith.

'I will tell them how to show their true faith: let them act according to their words.' So wrote Seneca. But this protest is more appropriate to a settled order. The declaration of belief, where it creates no dangers, and generates no consequences, becomes trivial. One form of this gulf between belief and practice is encompassed by the expression 'hypocrisy'. The term describes it and condemns it. But the condemnation tends to run in two directions: towards the notion that one should cease to camouflage one's actual behaviour, and towards the other notion that practice should be amended in the direction of the ideal. The trouble with this condemnation of hypocrisy, where intended to imply that one should ape the ideal, is that there may be no concrete or logical or otherwise ascertainable path leading thereto. The ideal (which is the principle or belief or faith when conceived as a goal) may simply be vacuous or inapplicable. From it may be adduced completely contrary activities, so serving to indicate its bankruptcy. Not only may ideals be too vague to lead logically to any concrete activity, but, even where they do, it may be wrong to follow them there. The gulf between belief and practice tends to become inevitable where the former reaches its apogee of abstractness and universality. When this happens, criticism which intends practical reform becomes, logically, pointless. The ideal itself can provide no guide. And, indeed, the continued acceptance of a vacuous, inapplicable or irrelevant belief may make the hypocrisy inevitable.

Our immediate concern, however, as well as being a logically prior concern, is not with the hypocrisy predicament, as sketched in the preceding paragraph, but with the belief predicament, where one feels forced or inclined to choose between rival ideologies. The representatives of an established order, whether ideological or non-ideological, may suppose that they can protect that order either by inducing individuals to abjure their beliefs or to accede to new ones. Early Christianity, as a non-sovereign ideology, was threatened and tested in this way; later, as an official or state ideology, it similarly threatened and tested others. What all of this was designed to produce was the voicing of fundamental principles and pieties, together with a display of icons and meditative gestures.

The fundamental belief essential to adherence to Christianity related of course to the divinity of Christ: 'but Christ is all, and in all'. This belief can be viewed as involving little more than absolute loyalty to a particular individual, combined with an inclination to accept as true whatever pronouncements he might make. In this there is nothing ideological. But as Christianity evolves, Christ is stripped of such irrelevant appurtenances as his whims, tastes, fantasies and body. He reaches a level of hypostasis where he no longer exists as a man at all but only as his 'essential' self—which is a principle. Thus, belief in Christ is translated from loyalty to an individual to loyalty to a set of principles—such as love, non-violence, etc.—which have been fixed within a doctrinal mould. To declare a belief in Christ then would not merely involve an acceptance of these principles individually, but their acceptance within a particular, interrelated pattern, and capped by a special metaphysic and science, as regards, for example, the notion that the universe is controlled by a godhead, and that the latter is benevolent, and that he devised the world in a certain way and according to a particular time-schedule.

A community united in fundamental acceptance of such a system of ideas could be called Christian, and its doctrine Christianity or Christism or even Christianism (like Buddhism from Buddha and Calvinism from Calvin and Lutheranism from Luther and Marxism from Marx). This doctrine might acquire sufficient logical coherence, basic simplicity, explanatory sweep, and political relevance to qualify as an ideology. And it might be classified as a *religious* ideology, not because it is non-political but because of its particular metaphysic—which posits the existence of a controlling godhead, etc.

A community of believers implies the existence of non-believers. Some non-believers may not have been blessed with the opportunity of learning, but others may have first embraced and then rejected the true faith. In the first category would fit, for the Roman Church, such groups as Muslims, heathen and Jews. Into the second would fit heretics and apostates. For these, pardon was impossible since they, knowing the truth, evilly refused the grace of inclusion which the acceptance of this truth would entail. It was the opinion of so wise and mild a Catholic as Aquinas that such persons should not only be excommunicated but executed as well.

This same writer, in *De Regimine Judaeorum*, accepted that the Jews were to be excluded from ordinary concourse with Christians because of their sin, which, of course, was unalterably connected with their disbelief. Aquinas, addressing himself to the Duchess of Brabant, wrote:

whether it is correct that all Jews in your realm should be obliged to wear some special sign to distinguish them from Christians. To this the answer is easy and in conformity with the decision given by the General Council. Jews of both sexes and in all Christian lands should on all occasions be distinguished from other people by some particular dress.

Christianity opposed particularism in every regard except that of belief. This was the basis of its universalism, its proselytising zeal, its optimism, and its well-intentioned terrorism.

The emergence of the modern nation-state set the stage for a transition away from Christianity as the dominant ideology. Basic to this secular development was the late medieval rediscovery of Aristotle, which made possible the revival of the classical conception of the state. The Aristotelian ideal of the *polis* entailed an autonomous and autarchic state based on kin. This formula was consonant with the political and economic developments of the late middle ages, involving the overthrow of verbal adherence to the mystical *Imperium Mundi*, the diminution or rejection of the belief in *unus populus christianus* and the displacement of the power of the *corpus mysticum Ecclesiae*.

The modern nation-state disrupted the medieval synthesis. We need not, however, be concerned to refute the contention that this much vaunted synthesis was no more than a myth. We know that the Holy Roman Empire was neither holy, nor Roman, nor an empire. But it must be said that a myth, for all that, is not necessarily devoid of power. Ideologies as a whole are largely little more than myth. When, therefore, we speak of a medieval synthesis, we are not to be understood to speak of an actual unity, whether economic, legal or political. The medieval synthesis referred to here is basically ideological, nothing more. What this means is that the literate European of the Middle Ages probably thought himself to be a member of a universal body of Christian people, that this body was subject to the political control of the Holy Roman Emperor, that the Emperor was a member of the holy body of the church, and that this entire structure was spiritually supervised by the incumbent of the Holy See. Explanation and justification of political acts would presuppose the existence of God, and would take the form of a proof that what was done flowed from or was permitted by his will. Disputes between emperor and pope, and later between monarchs and popes, would primarily be directed towards demonstrating that they really had received their authority from God, and thus that their political acts, whether supervisory over or independent of the other power, were legitimate. Whether or not God actually existed would not even matter. It was assumed, of course, that he did. But this was posited as a matter of faith, and need not have been argued within the system at all (although occasionally it was), since the real argument related to the train of deductions that could be made to follow from this initial axiom. So many of the extraordinary political arguments advanced by writers like John of Salisbury and Dante were only intended to prove who it was that God intended to exercise authority.

No ideological synthesis is ever complete—which is to say, lacking in a certain degree of incoherence. This is true of the medieval synthesis. When we speak of the 'breakdown' of such a synthesis, we only refer to such a convincing demonstration of an area of incoherence that it becomes impossible to continue to regard the given ideological framework as viable; the consequence being that it is eventually deserted. The emergence of the nation-state, however, is not coincident with the desertion of Christian ideology. The nation-state, after all, was not at first inclined to justify itself outside a Christian framework, but merely to claim, within that framework and against the pretensions of the Papacy, a divine right of rule by kings, independent of papal interference. But the nation-state, in winning its argument for independence from papal control, contributed at the same time to the trivialisation and dismissal of the ideological structure within which it sought its justification. How could one take seriously an argument from divine right, when it could be made to demonstrate, equally convincingly, the justice of papal supervisory authority, and the justice of monarchical independence from such supervision? One could not obey both Henry VIII and the Pope. One could not be both Protestant and Catholic. And yet it was necessary to choose. Was this choice not, perhaps, somewhat arbitrary, when set against the background of a belief in Christ and God, which was shared by both Catholic and Protestant? The reply of a Hobbes is yes. The percipience of such an observer leads him to regard Christian belief, and arguments leading from this, as basically trivial, in so far as they relate to the determination of the locus of legitimate authority. This is not to say that he attacks the belief, but that he begins to ignore it. But of course, Machiavelli had already ignored it—and this would define the almost inevitable trend of the future. The emergence of the modern nation-state particularised Christian ideology. It did not displace it. But this particularisation constituted an essential step towards its elimination since it trivialised the entire ideological framework of Christian belief.

There is no intrinsic incompatibility between a national and a religious ideology. National ideologies are often religious. Typically, under a religious ideology, it is assumed *either* that enemy states have not the same god, and that the weakness (or strength) of these states is a function of the weakness (or strength) of their god(s), *or* that you share a common god, and that the opposition (as in war) of the other state to one's own (or vice versa) is a function of error, a miscalculation regarding the intentions of the divine will. In the first case there is assumed a plurality of divine wills; in the second, that there is only one such will. Where it is assumed that there is only one divine will, this becomes a common will, and logically legitimates purely rational disputes between nations relating to the determinations of this will, particularly in respect of the rights and wrongs of conflicting national causes. But, as already suggested, where everyone invokes the same god to justify wildly divergent aims and policies, it may eventually happen that sophisticated persons will no longer find the basic axioms, principles or beliefs particularly useful in explaining or justifying the propriety of their actions especially to opponents who invoke the same initial beliefs. Thus, consciously or unconsciously, they may tend to discard them (as a basis of political argument). They might begin instead, for example, from the principle of natural right, rather than from that of divine will. Or they might begin from the axiomatic assumption that they must promote the specific interests and common good (materially defined) of the nation. But when that happens the ideological framework begins to shift radically.

As new types of fundamental social axioms and modes of argument attain the ascendancy, the reigning Christian ideology (*qua* ideology, not outlook) is either displaced or replaced (an ideology can be displaced without being replaced). In early and medieval Christianity, it is not so much total disbelief that is feared, but a disbelief in Christianity assuming the form of a belief in something else (such as paganism, Manichaeism, Arianism, Palagianism, Judaism, Islam and so on). But from about the sixteenth century the danger no longer stemmed merely from the possible adherence to rival beliefs, but equally from the serious possibility of an atheistic denial of belief altogether. It is often precisely at that point in time where an ideology is least tenable—i.e. in greatest danger of eclipse—that the most strenuous efforts, involving considerable logical acumen, may be expended to save it. We witness such an effort in *le pari de* Pascal (1623–62), where the brilliant and devout mathematician is even prepared to resort to an argument from probability in order to place faith on a sound footing.[1] The interesting aspect of such an attempt is the fact that it indicates a new awareness of the intrinsic weaknesses of Christian ideology. It is precisely because important writers simply began to ignore a fundamental tenet of Christianity (the existence of God) that such exemplary attempts were made to reaffirm its central position. But without success. Christianity as a religion was not dead. But Christianity as an official ideology was

---

[1] Pascal notes that there are two ways by which we are persuaded of the truth of religion: by reason and by authority. He remarks that no one utilises the latter any more, which he thinks a mistake: '*on dit qu'il faut croire par telle et telle raison, qui sont des faibles arguments, la raison étant flexible à tout.*' In a sense he was right: reason can prove anything. But if one is stuck with a system which insists upon a connection between certain fundamental principles and an illimitable string of specific political decisions, then one is stuck with a system of rationalisation—within which anything can be proved. Cf. Blaise Pascal, *Oeuvres* (ed. 1926–7), t. 3, p. 56.

dying. The demise of the ideology would go hand in hand with the rise of Protestantism, the tendency to regard religion as a private indulgence, the increase in tolerance and individualism and the resistance to ideological formulae in political argument (as, notably, in Machiavelli, Hobbes and Locke).

Protestantism and the Catholic Counter-Reformation represent a sort of ideological interregnum. Either no dominant ideology exists, or it has assumed no precise and recognisable form. Luther opposed the Pope, and supported the power of the local princes. Machiavelli opposed the Papacy and supported the vision of a unified Italy. The nationalistic slogan 'My country right or wrong' would suit neither of them. There is less of an overall ideological consensus. The safe shores of belief are in sight, but they are rival beliefs, and so men set themselves a certain direction without collectively attaining the security of land. The nation-state, subsequently and increasingly, becomes the important focal point of decision-making. But although the framework within which states explain and justify their activities loses much of its former coherence, what remains a commonplace right up to the eighteenth century is the assumption that a universal moral principle of right political conduct is possible.

Despite Hume and Montesquieu and the modifications allowed by Kant, this view was even to persist into the nineteenth century. The existence or continuation of a belief in universal moral principles is essential to the existence or continuation of ideologies. In a theological age such principles may be declared to flow, more or less self-evidently, from the supposed nature or will of God. In a more secular age, they may be said to stem more or less directly from Nature itself—so that we increasingly confront the concept of natural, rather than divine, law. In a more technological age, discussion of what we ought to do may simply be regarded as a science. The nineteenth century produced no end of treatises on 'moral science', much ethico-political writing being influenced of course by Social Darwinism. (Later, one was even to hear of *Christian* Science.) Of course, scepticism about the validity of universal moral principles goes as far back as Thrasymachus. But where such scepticism exists, ideologies are not likely to do so as well.

Probably the most important ideological force to succeed political Christianity was nationalism. *Nationality* is not the same as this. Nationality is a fact, a condition. Nationalism is a belief, a guide. One is a national by birth, by law. One is a nationalist by conviction or faith. The growth of nationality as an identity is intimately associated with the growth of the nation-state as an entity. Nationality generally involves an overlapping of kinship and territorial ties. Nationalism evolves when this identity becomes an exclusive object of pride. As such, it binds together all classes, it provides a common outlook, it establishes an object of veneration; and this incorporates the interests of the state, projected as a goal, to which commitment is invited, unquestioning, like a faith.

It takes a considerable time for nationalism to emerge as a full-blown ideology. Elie Kedourie, perhaps too precisely, describes it as 'a doctrine invented in Europe at the beginning of the nineteenth century'.[1] Its many forms project various elements, such as racial identity, territorial identity, historical destiny and so on. We have already noted, however, the way in which a political system becomes decreasingly ideological in the degree that it projects an increasing number of discrete elements, seen either as axioms or as objects of faith, since this increases the difficulty of reasoning from a single abstract premise to a particular practical decision. In this respect, nationalism is not as purely ideological as, say, Christianity (conceived in a theocratic mould and not merely as a 'private' faith) or socialism or communism. Even in its purest forms nationalism projects more discrete items of belief than the latter; and it places extraneous limitations upon the assimilation of membership—and therefore upon the doctrine's persuasiveness—which the other doctrines do not. This is one reason why nationalism is usually more popular than Christian theocracy or socialism or communism: all the latter are considerably more rigorous, intellectually, than the former.

Nationalism, however, was from the start—unlike Christianity—in some degree regarded as an expedient, as a means of promoting the cohesion and interests of a particular group. This was particularly true of the German version. As F. O. Hertz writes: 'In no other country has such a vast literature on the national character been produced as in Germany, and its aim has mainly been to exhort the German race and mould the national character to a model purporting to be the only true one.'[2] The quantity of this material must be viewed (1) in direct relation to the extreme national disunity which obtained in Germany until well into the nineteenth century and (2) in relation to the conscious insistence upon the need for a German ideology. From this use of belief to achieve a goal flows the imperviousness of nationalisms to logic and the evidence of experience. In this regard, it will generally become impossible to argue with a convinced nationalist in so far as he will usually refuse to consider or reflect on any fact that tends to run in a direction contrary to his original ideological presuppositions. Nationalist ideologies, therefore, seen in terms of their instrumentalist function, do not merely reflect a national or racial character, dogmatically

---

[1] Elie Kedourie, *Nationalism* (Hutchinson, 1961), p. 9.
[2] F. O. Hertz, *Nationality in History and Politics* (London, 1944), p. 46.

conceived. More importantly, they attempt to persuade that this character exists and provides a basis for unity or a focal point of group loyalty. An important assumption of nationalist theory is in fact the *diversity* of member nationals. It might be *said* that they were all one, but this was largely in order to make them so and diminish feelings of separateness. Indeed, the fact of diversity, which is to say, the popular and psychological perception of barriers between peoples within the state, often increases the felt need for an ideological identity.

Nationalism was necessarily self-conscious because its primary purpose was to achieve a particular type or degree of social cohesion; ideas were intended entirely to serve this purpose and so assumed a subsidiary function. National ideologies offered a glorified vision of the nation, of both its being and becoming, and usually not as an aggressor but as a victim, or as an inoffensive—but virtuous—power, always mindful of justice or, at the very least, almost always right, demanding the citizen's sympathy and belonging, urging upon him the suspension of judgment. In the case of nationalist ideologies, what is important is service to one's country. As Christianity's ideal adherent was not a good man, but a faithful believer, so nationalism's ideal was not justice, but patriotism—not good men, but loyal patriots.

The nineteenth and twentieth centuries especially have witnessed a multiplicity of ideologies competing for favour. One need only refer to liberalism, socialism, communism, racialism, nationalism, anarchism, syndicalism, corporatism, existentialism and conservatism to bear this out. The fact that there are so many is itself witness to the difficulty of any one of them becoming dominant. Even the two that we might be inclined to label 'dominant' seem to show signs of disintegrating: here I refer to socialism and communism.

Of course it might be argued that nationalism is really the dominant ideology of our century. Although this is largely true of the nineteenth century, it would be difficult to maintain that it is so today. It must be remembered that nationalism is not the same as promoting the interests of the persons embraced within a particular territorial area—otherwise referred to as a nation. It involves this, but is not exhausted by it. An ideology is not defined simply in terms of the interests which it promotes, but in terms of the argumentative framework within which these interests are explained and justified. Thus, the Soviets and the Chinese, for example, have distinct and conflicting national interests, of which they are inevitably aware. But the disputes between them have not been conducted by reference to these interests, but by reference to the deviation of the one or the other from communist principles. Thus their ideology is communist, not nationalist. There is no overt parallel to the American nineteenth-century concept of a nationalistic Manifest

Destiny or anything of that kind. The Sino-Soviets, in *Novy Mir* and *The Peking Review*, have couched their debates neither in terms of national interest nor even in terms of what is right or appropriate as such. Instead, they argue in terms either of who is (or is not) a *true* Marxist–Leninist or in terms of who conforms most (or least) closely to the spirit of Marxism–Leninism. It is not necessary here to explore the question whether the ideology involved is an opiate or smokescreen or superstructure—or whatever—but merely to note what the ideology is. It is communist. And those ideologies which today receive the widest currency appear to be either communist or socialist. In the third world, for example, those leaders who bother to profess an ideology at all tend most frequently to profess one that is socialist. It is necessary to see that an ideology may very well have an effect upon practice, in a predictable way, for what one does may well be affected by the way in which one discusses it. But the more a particular ideology is invoked to explain incompatible activities by separate and even opposed groups, the more likely it is that it will either die out or be superseded by a different ideology. The ideological force of Christianity is spent when the Catholic can take the Protestant seriously and see the reasonableness of his position. Here he recognises the arbitrariness of his own, and not only of the other's belief. Similarly, the ideological force of communism is spent when one party's line has to be accepted as more or less equal to another's. The overall doctrine no longer seems to produce any particular, predictable type of action in practice. Thus, if the doctrine is retained at all, it has to be superseded, for otherwise it simply ceases to be taken seriously.

Ideology emerged in Europe most dramatically with the birth of Christianity. This doctrine offered a criterion of community exclusion and inclusion on the basis of belief. There is no doubt that Christians thought their God the only true God and that there was no limitation upon any man's admission to His temple of belief, apart from the requirement of belief itself. Early Christians, however, were not consciously aware that their belief was ideological.

With the emergence of nationalism, however, theocratic Christianity was definitely eclipsed and the new dominant ideology became—albeit in a glass darkly—remarkably conscious of itself as such. Christian apologists, however, had already begun to set the example. No surer evidence of the muddied waters of Christian belief, of a new, awkward, artificial self-consciousness of the form of belief demanded, can be provided than that of Pascal's wager.[1]

Here a primitive acceptance of Christian truth had been routed. In

---

[1] Pascal, *op. cit.* t. 4, pp. 39 ff. William James provides an excellent summary account in *The Will to Believe*.

its stead stood the self-conscious probabilism of probability. The argument suggests that even doubt affecting the *central* assumption of religious belief—viz. the existence of God—should be dismissed, not so much because unfounded, but because prejudicial to the possible attainment or protection of one's future interests. This in no way suggests that Pascal was in the slightest degree atheistic, but that he had to tailor his recommendations to suit the increasingly materialistic outlook of his times. In doing so, it became possible to view Christian belief as a function of material interests, and not merely as a function of truth. In this way belief takes the place of truth, self-consciously, and the essential matter becomes that of accepting, not questioning, or of accepting as beyond question, an ideology or set of assertions, the acceptance of which involves some notion of utilitarian advantage, one such advantage being immediate admission into a *corps de croyants*. In Pascal, therefore, the precursor of contemporary Christian existentialism, we have some evidence of the fact that a waning theocratic Christianity, too, tended to become *self-consciously* ideological.

Consciousness, however, comes in degrees. There is very little or no self-consciousness about early Christian ideology. This is a claim which nationalist ideology cannot quite make. And in the modern age we are confronted with what one might call 'the Sorelian crisis', where beliefs may in no wise be viewed as embodying truth, but, instead, may be consciously manipulated in order to marshal the activities of people to achieve a frankly unquestioned goal. Ideologies often have a genuine strength when accepted as actually true. They lose this strength when consciously conceived as tools, or instruments of control (at least for those persons who consciously view them as such).

The status of ideology reaches a peculiar impasse with Marxist socialism. For, on the one hand, Marx condemned ideologies as distortions. And, at the same time, he implicitly supported ideology if it was the right sort. The materialist conception of history, for Marx, served the purpose of unmasking sinister interests lurking behind the effulgence of flowery words. And, at the same time—according to Engels's 1883 preface to the German edition of the *Manifesto*—he believed that a time would be reached when the displacement of a class interest (the bourgeoisie's) would lead into the emancipation of the whole of society from partial interests, when (in short) ideology would be at an end.

Marx, of course, never fully clarified his position and this has produced difficulties. Nevertheless, the position he advanced need only be regarded as self-contradictory if one insists that he was a strict historical materialist. Engels denied that either of them was. However that may be, if Marx were a strict materialist, then it would clearly prove contradictory to view one ideology as a distortion and another as somehow 'legitimate', 'just' or 'true'; to insist on the one hand that all thought is determined by interest and, on the other, that this would eventually cease to be so.

In any case, there remains in Marx this vagueness, this lack of clarity. Full blown, his might be called the Sorelian crisis. Georges Sorel (1847–1922) assumed the thoroughgoing truth of historical materialism (combined with the facile pragmatism of William James). And he believed that the triumph of a particular (i.e. the proletarian) interest would constitute the generalised triumph of justice. Sorel viewed ideologies (seen as the intellectual refractions of interest) as myths. They were not 'true' ('truth' being somehow irrelevant) but only 'real' or existent. Sorel's point was not that they were false, either. In regard to ideologies, truth and falsity were both irrelevant. Myths, or ideologies, he regarded as impervious to truth.

Sorel sought to propagate an ideology for the trade union movement in Europe. He set out an apocalyptic vision of the development and triumph of a group. He consciously and deliberately insisted upon the prior importance of belief itself, and argued that the holding of the belief, quite apart from criticism, inspection, probing, probability or validity, was the only essential factor in the assurance of this belief's triumph. This belief related to the triumph of a working-class order, through adherence to the myth of the general strike which formed a vision of the action to be taken by this class, unthinkingly, unquestioningly, grouping its members in absolute distinction from the members of the opposed class.

In Sorel, ideology attained the full flower of self-consciousness. Ideology, as has been suggested, may be seen to involve the acceptance of an unquestioned belief as the criterion for affiliation to a body of believers. Questions such as: *Is* Jones a socialist?, or *is* Jones *really* a liberal?; and assertions such as: Smith is a *true* Christian or communist, etc., usually reflect an ideological bias. The test of what Jones *is* or of what Smith *is*, is what each believes. One may fail, or one may not live up to, one's beliefs, but the important thing in determining the ideological orientation of a man is the doctrine he professes. From this one supposedly deduces how he will or (at least) how he wishes to live.

For Sorel, all major social movements effected reform only by representing 'their future action in the form of battle images assuring the triumph of their cause'. A myth cannot be refuted since 'it is... identical with the convictions of a group', since it is the expression of these convictions in terms of movement and since, consequently, it cannot be broken into parts. The myth of the general strike would form in the workers' minds a battle image which would assure 'the triumph of their cause'.[1] Sorel, therefore, became the first political writer to place his entire emphasis (as opposed, e.g. to a Platonic aside) upon the need for consciously elaborating a doctrine which is deliberately distorted in order to secure widespread popular adherence.

Given the feeling that people must believe in something, a bridge of quite narrow span suffices to convey us to the notion that any belief at all will do. Sorel's theory provides the basis for our crossing over into the twentieth century of indiscriminate belief in belief, and commitment for its own sake, irrationally conceived. Sorel is our bridge to nazism and to fascism, to voluntarism and to existentialism in politics. But he is also a bridge which may help to take us beyond these beliefs and, possibly, in some sense, beyond ideology itself.

One of the essential maladies of our time springs from the desire to promote belief even when it cannot be believed; from the desire to trumpet faith even when it is indifferent to truth. One reason why the desire is so strong upon us to promote belief is because we feel that society will collapse without it. But belief we always have, assumptions we cannot escape; yet to be critical of our beliefs, though this may constitute a danger, entails as well as this a ground for hope. Because we *do* believe, it is not necessary to infer that we *should* believe.

IDEOLOGY: A FALLACY

> The point is that the rules of morality are not of the nature of eternal truths, immutable in their authority—but only rough statements of what in ordinary cases is man's duty.
>
> J. N. FIGGIS[2]

Figgis was only mistaken in supposing that Christian ethics, to the exclusion of other types, was possessed of this flexibility. Any moral rule can be handled both flexibly and rigidly. There is nothing intrinsic to the nature of any rule which will in practice enable us to predict whether it will be applied in one way or another. In the case of Christianity there is of course ample evidence of strictness of application. What it is necessary to realise, however, is that looseness of application becomes a function of scepticism towards the absolute legitimacy or appropriate applicability of the rule applied. The danger is that any moral rule will be applied strictly where it is assumed to be possessed of a universal rightness.

Now there are at least two problems that may arise in the application of a rule: one is that it may be applied too strictly (e.g. 'never steal') and the other is that it may be too vague to entail any specific

---

[1] Georges Sorel, *Réflexions sur la violence* (Paris, 1907, 1912), pp. 32, 46 and 168.
[2] Figgis, *op. cit.* p. 92.

application at all (as perhaps, 'be moderate in all things'). Most of the Ten Commandments, for example, are capable of strict, and overly strict, application. But the Categorical Imperative, The Golden Mean and the Golden Rule may be very difficult to apply in any determinate way whatever. This presupposes that the latter type of statement is intended as a guide to conduct, of course. Naturally, it might not be so intended. It is possible that Aristotle's conception of the mean was not meant as a guide to judgment but as a statement of what good or bad conduct consists in. It is equally possible that Kant's concept of the Categorical Imperative was not intended to tell us how to behave but to indicate what good behaviour consists in. But this is improbable, judging from the texts, and certainly does not conform to the prescriptive reading generally placed upon these texts.

Now such moral items as those contained in the Ten Commandments tend to be discrete and reflect no logical coherence. The argumentative moral systems of an Augustine, however, and more especially of an Aquinas, entirely transcend such a purely declaratory phase. The latter in short become more purely ideological: which is to say, more argumentative, more coherent, and more capable of being applied in a deductive fashion in the explanation and justification of political activity, thus tending to acquire more the guise of a science than a dogma. This sort of reflective activity takes us well along the way to reducing discrete principles to some one in particular whence all the rest may be deduced. Typical examples of this reduction in ethics are those general principles already mentioned: the Golden Rule, the Golden Mean, the Categorical Imperative, each of which may be viewed as containing the whole of morality, reduced to a particular formula. The point about these formulae, however, is that they cannot really tell one how to behave; they can be seen as varieties of an ethical Rorschach test, permitting the agent to read into them whatever behaviour he favours. How one applies the Golden Rule depends upon how one expects to be done by. And the intermediate point between one principle and another (such as anarchy and tyranny) is rarely clear or determinable.

There are several aspects of what I shall refer to as the ideological fallacy. One is the tendency to assume that there is always a rule to cover every particular case. Another is the tendency to believe that every given rule, where it can be indisputably applied, should be. And a third is a tendency to believe that a universal principle relating to moral conduct can be applied in any specific case. The first, however, is more characteristic of the pettifogger, the second of the bureaucrat, and the third, more particularly, of the ideologist. The ideologist is really a kind of refined pettifogger. His general attitude is that there is or ought to be a rule, or that we must act as if there were one, which can and ought always to be abided by. But when we return to the conclusion that no rule, nor any set of rules, is broad or precise enough to cover all contingencies, it is clear that anyone who insists that there must be a rule (or indeed a 'line' to be deduced from a system) is forced to regard any specific injunction or decision as being necessarily entailed by a universal proposition. This sort of mentality, when transplanted to the centre of political decision-making, reveals itself as being basically ideological, if coherent enough, and as merely pettifogging if 'consistently' ad hoc.

Now it is clear that an ideology is not merely a system of ethics, as we saw earlier. Thus the fallacy to which one refers cannot merely relate to a deficiency in ethical reasoning. It contains such a deficiency, but primarily as related to a political context. When dealing with this context, we are broadly concerned with two sub-categories: political science and political philosophy. These categories are not opposites. They are mutually dependent and in some sense presuppose one another. The difference between them, however, is not that the one is descriptive and the other recommendatory. Political philosophers recommend; but they also describe. Political scientists describe; but they also recommend. The value/fact disjunction does not quite catch the philosophy/science disjunction. Perhaps it would be better to think in terms of logical considerations as distinct from descriptive considerations. Both political science and political philosophy are explanatory, but they involve different *types* of explanation; or different *areas* of explanation. The question then to be considered is this: what arguments can be levelled against the supposition that the primary and distinguishing characteristic of political philosophy is its concern with logic (assumptions, implications, contradictions, deductions, etc.)? If this supposition can avoid being punctured, then we can say that the political philosophy/political science distinction should be viewed in terms of the distinction between a primary emphasis upon logical analysis as against an emphasis upon descriptive analysis. This does not automatically exclude 'ought' from either category. But it does leave us with three possibilities *vis-à-vis* the normative aspect. (1) It has nothing to do with either category. (2) It overlaps both categories. (3) It exclusively overlaps with the 'science' category, the descriptive, the practical. (The fourth possibility—roughly, that philosophy is recommendatory to the exclusion of science—is probably not worth considering.)

Let us say that one cannot ascend from a purely factual statement to a recommendation. To do so affords an example of the naturalistic fallacy. Let us also say that one cannot descend from a purely logical proposition to a recommendation. To do so probably affords—in its purest outline—an example of the ideological fallacy. None of this is to imply that prescription is completely autonomous *vis-à-vis* logical and descriptive statements or analyses; that implication would be erroneous. But it does suggest that prescription, as opposed to explanation (whether logical or descriptive), involves a different procedure, approach, emphasis or concern. A prescription, when *recommendatory* in form (it could be hortatory, imperative, etc.), can fall back upon logic and description in support of itself; but no piece of logic or description can, in itself, entail a recommendation.

Now one might deduce from the above that the political philosopher or scientist, *qua* philosopher or scientist, cannot recommend (i.e. the first of the three possibilities mentioned two paragraphs above). But this would be mistaken. Given that recommendatory argument depends upon (i.e. has to fall back upon) a knowledge of both facts and logic; and assuming that the philosopher and scientist are better equipped with this knowledge than others; then it follows (certainly) that they are in a better position to *assess* recommendations than others and (less certainly) that they are in a better *position* to recommend than others. From this it does not follow that philosophers and scientists are simply and legitimately in a position to *tell* people what to do; it only follows that (*qua* philosophers and scientists) they are in a better position to argue with people regarding what might best be done; and this, of course, usually only relates to the public rather than to the private sphere, since a philosopher or scientist need not be expected to know the psychology, disposition, mood, interests, ambitions, aspirations, etc., of any particular person whom he happens to encounter (while all such considerations are presumably relevant to what any particular individual 'ought' to do).

Tentatively, therefore, one is inclined to opt for the second possibility mentioned three paragraphs above, i.e. that as a matter of fact and as a matter of appropriateness, normative discussion insinuates itself both into scientific and philosophical discourse; it is only important to be clear about when we are recommending and when we are explaining (or at least that we try to be clear). If an incisive argument cannot be marshalled against this position, then normative discussion could be said to overlap both philosophical and scientific analysis. In drawing attention to the ideological fallacy, one would only be ruling out the particular procedure to which it refers as a legitimately recommendatory one. Thus, it would not entail any statement about how we may or might or should proceed, but only one regarding a procedure to be avoided. It is difficult to say anything in general about how we *should* proceed (except in a negative sense), since this would imply that an ethical criterion of truth was available to us.

Political science and political philosophy one can primarily distinguish by reference to the distinction between logical and empirical analysis. Both of the latter are involved in any discussion of what is and of what ought to be. Descriptive and logical thinking primarily involve, in political science, correspondence with the facts, and, in political philosophy, the internal coherence of an argument. These two elements can never really be divorced from one another. A political philosophy achieves whatever relevance it has from refusing to be entirely divorced from matters of fact. And the initial condition of a political science is that it not accommodate logical inconsistency. As for the discussion of matters of fact and the testing of argumentative consistency, these activities can be conducted in an entirely non-recommendatory framework, although the question of whether and when that framework is non-recommendatory is difficult and perhaps ultimately impossible to determine. One can say, however, that in so far as there is a distinction to be made between explanation and recommendation it is essential to see that the offer of an explanation is not the same as the offer of a recommendation. For when we 'recommend' an explanation we are not, in the ordinary sense, recommending anything at all—but are instead merely indicating what we think to be true.

Recommendation, although not necessarily a part of political analysis, whether scientific or philosophical, does necessarily entail, when it obtains, the utilisation of both of these categories. Although they may possibly exist without it, it cannot exist without them. But although theory can be divorced from recommendation, practice cannot. The need of recommendation for theoretical analysis is not reciprocated by the latter's need for it. The mutual necessity, therefore, does not obtain between recommendation and theory, but between recommendation and practice. Action without recommendation is impossible. Recommendation not intended to be acted upon is futile.

Ideologies, as we have already seen, are not merely intended as theories, but as guides to action. Therefore we must consider them as a species of recommendation, and therefore of ethical thinking—but, again, not within the private, but within the public, the political sphere. The ideological fallacy, therefore, will relate to an analytical error involved in the marshalling of a political recommendation. Although a political philosophy, conceived in terms of its predominantly logical emphasis, is not necessarily ideological, an ideology *is* necessarily political philosophy, conceived from this same logical perspective. For the ideology falls back upon philosophy (or logic) and science (or facts) in marshalling its recommendations. The fallacy that I am here concerned with, however, is more logical or philosophical than scientific or factual.

A particular recommendation may be described as right or wrong, as worthwhile or useless, etc. What we must seek to do is to improve our understanding within this category. And one of the means of doing this consists in saying that procedure x is erroneous, even though we may not be able to say that any other procedure is absolutely valid. A major contribution of the Greeks was to indicate a certain range of avoidable errors which, when kept in mind, would permit one to escape the more obvious risks of intellectual adventure. When we espy verbal floats and buoys which read *non sequitur, petitio principii*, and the like, we know to steer clear. Our collection of these devices constantly expands in size to include, for example, Moore's comparatively recent definition of the naturalistic fallacy.

The ideological fallacy merely accounts for one instance wherein this general recommendatory activity comes to grief and must be rejected. The matter of importance is not the word, though 'ideology' seems most apt, but the condition or error referred to. One may refer to an 'ideological' fallacy because the term ideology has never, since Napoleon's use of it, lost its negative character, nor did it do so in Marx (or especially not in Marx) and not even in Sorel. 'Ideology' has usually suggested the distortion of an assumed truth, and the most important reason why people have come to express a need for it in principle is because they deny the possibility of truth, while nevertheless demanding a directional belief to synthesize an ordered, progressive and non-ritualistic society; and because they view ideology as advertisement, as deliberate propaganda, as a necessary cheapening of intellectual coin in order to secure the unquestioning support of the masses for a particular cause.

We may now approach ideology more directly. The acceptance of it creates an identity, and is intended to promote action. It is prescriptive or recommendatory. Yet there is an important distinction to note between prescription, in the strictest sense, and recommendation. 'Prescription' is more suggestive of dictation and command; and the least argumentative way in which information can be communicated is by propaganda; and this, too, may be seen as one of the more sophisticated forms that a prescription can assume. Dictation, commands and propaganda may all be needed at times, but it is clear that there is a difference between these and recommendations. The difference is, that where recommendations require justification, reasons, submission to proof and refutability, the character of a prescription, in the strictest sense, rules out the possibility of it being brought into question. Ideology, in so far as it rules out the possibility of such disputes, arguments and questions as would put its *basic* tenets to some form of (what one might call) objective or rational test, neither explains nor recommends (in so far as this requires and implies argument) anything at all. The condition for an ideology actually serving as a guide to conduct is that it be in effect hortatory and prescriptive. If it is not, then it does not in fact *guide* conduct, but merely provides an innocuously formal framework, which is not actually deductive, within which guidance is executed, but upon which the latter does not distinctly depend.

Every recommendation of a political move assumes the possible choice of distinctly alternative moves. Since possibility inheres in what is given, informed recommendation must depend on informed acquaintance with the latter. Because, if we do not know what a given situation involves, we cannot know what possibilities it contains, and the degree of defect in our knowledge on this head is simply a corollary of our ignorance of what we are choosing between. To say that a particular choice is to be recommended, is to say that it is good. The logic of argument here is based on comparisons between the alternative possibilities. Any recommendation which is universal is non-rational, or illogical. Because rational argument about choice depends upon the assessment of alternatives, assessment depends upon a knowledge of the alternatives, and the latter depend upon the specific situation. This always changes with time and thus alters the ground upon which all arguments, for and against any recommendation, must depend. But a recommendation which is universal rules out the possibility of particular circumstances making it inapplicable, while it does not rule out the fact that circumstances change. It therefore claims to be true irrespective of any context, which valid arguments for recommendation, however, must necessarily depend upon. Its claim, then, is *a priori*, analytical, arbitrary. And its logical form becomes not at all that of a recommendation, but that of command: its very nature proscribes discussion. Its truth can only then be psychological: i.e. emotional, intuitive, based perhaps upon a 'moral sense'.

We must not insist upon an *identity* between ideology and soap-box oratory or propaganda. There is a difference of tone and mode. What is distinctive about an ideology, as opposed to a straightforward command, is that it does not claim to be propounding an order but a truth. And here resides its inherent illogic, that it claims some universal recommendation (e.g. 'Stealing is [always] wrong'—'Irrespective of circumstances, one should never steal') is right, *a priori*, in any context, whereas the 'rightness' of any choice logically depends upon the comparison of specific alternatives which a changing situation throws up.

So that to 'recommend' liberty, class stratification, equality, centralisation, decentralisation, etc., *universally*, as divorced from a context, is not to *recommend* at all, but to express a preference or pronounce a command. *Recommendation* we may agree to have a built-in demand for supporting reasons. And any recommendation, which of itself implies no particular context, eliminates the very possibility of there being such reasons. For these depend upon a context, in terms of the specific possibilities which it provides. In the degree that one specifically rules out an accounting for possibilities, to that degree one rules out the possibility of a recommendation being in any sense *rational*. Thus it becomes contradictory to assume that any recommendation is capable of truth when one eliminates the very grounds which are necessary to make it rational (i.e. capable of truth).

We may define the Ideological Fallacy as consisting in *a universal, non-contextual recommendation which claims to be true, but the possibility of whose truth is eliminated by virtue of its claim being non-contextual—both in space and time.*

For many people the question arises as to whether there is any alternative to ideologies. In short there is the question whether there can be assertions of truth within the category of recommendation. If there can be no truth, then there are only alternative visions which, though 'distorted', constitute the only 'truths' available. It is this question which I now wish briefly to discuss. And by way of preface it should be noted that truth, for the writer, subsumes two sub-categories of objective statement: characterisations of assertions as 'true' and 'false' and as 'right' and 'wrong'.

Some people say that truth is absolute; others say that it is relative. But to say what truth is—whether absolute or relative—seems to be quite impossible, and this because of entirely logical considerations.

If one says, for example, the first, one will—and rightly—be asked for examples. And the difficulty in such an event, is that so many assumed truths of past years have been found to be inadequate later on, that the universal propositions of today, even though not *proved* inadequate, are only accepted as provisional, particularly in the field of science.

However, if one says the second—that truth is relative—the statement traps, perhaps condemns, its maker. For if the truth of all statements *is* relative, then this very statement must also be relative—which is to say that it cannot be entirely true.

Now, there is a commonplace variant on the idea that the truth of all statements is relative. This is the idea that all statements, or systems of statements—for example, 'ideologies'—are 'determined' by the environments whence they emerge.

The trouble with the assertion that systems of ideas are socially determined is that it says too much and too little. Determined in what *way*? Plato and Aristotle, for example, were contemporaries. Yet one urged the benefits of monarchy, the other the benefits of aristocracy, while both lived under a system of government which was in form more nearly democratic than anything else.

The notion that social and economic conditions determine ideas is imprecise. But even it if were assumed to be precise and valid, it would again be necessary to test the logic of this assertion against itself. In which case the necessary conclusion would be that the very assertion that ideas are socially determined, or conditioned, is itself socially determined or conditioned. But this conclusion only reinforces the impression of imprecision attaching to the concept of social determinism. Determined in what *way*?

The reason why the notion X (that ideas are socially determined) constitutes a variation on the notion Y (that the truth of all ideas is relative) derives from the following fact. Both suggest that no assertion can possess a universal validity. And, again, we may see that this assertion is vitiated by the necessarily entailed implication that it, itself, can contain no such validity.

We may note one last relevant variation on the notion that truth is relative. This is the belief that all ideas are *reflections* of a social order or that they *spring from* the same. Such a formulation suggests that material conditions are, in some sense, 'prior', and that ideas are derivative or 'secondary'. Apart from the fact that this may not mean very much, it is, to the extent that anything is, certainly false. There is no more reason to believe that facts produce ideas than that ideas produce facts. We only know that the world, for us, does not exist apart from ideas, or consciousness. This neither entails that ideas or facts are either prior or derivative. The two categories are simply inseparable from the dual process of knowing and being known.

The notion that 'ideas merely reflect a given social order' may be considered a variation on the notion that 'the truth of all assertions is relative' because the former implies that *no* assertion can be universally true.

We thus return to the apparent logical impossibility of characterising truth—as either absolute or relative (whether determined, reflective or otherwise). Truth and falsity are categories *within*, not *above* which, we operate.

If we say that truth is absolute and then take any particular assertion as evidence of such absolutism, it is always possible to step back from the assertion, to re-examine it, and, in short, to ask whether it *really* is true. The fact that such a procedure is never considered self-contradictory (though it may reveal stubbornness) suggests that no universal assertion about the world is ever self-evident—whereas self-evidence is an essential characteristic of what we mean by 'absolute truth' (in the sense that a thing is so totally, obviously and self-evidently true that its truth cannot even be doubted).

If we say that all truth is relative—as we have already shown—this very formulation must be applied to itself, producing the result that even it cannot be quite true. Thus, again, the discussion of the nature, or basic character, of truth is necessarily left open.

Not only does it seem impossible to say that truth is absolute or that truth is relative. Equally, it is impossible to say that there is no truth. One cannot say what it is, or describe it, as a whole, as a category, as such; *and* one cannot deny it, as such, as a category, as a whole. For the very assertion that there is no truth—as Aquinas has shown—presupposes its own validity, and thus contradicts what it assumes.

It is because we cannot say that truth is absolute or relative or impossible that we must accept it as an inescapable category. We cannot get above it. We cannot get out of it. It is simply the category within which we must conduct our affairs when we try to see, to assess and to report upon the world as it is or as we think it is and ought to be. Since we have at hand no certain means by which we can ever say *what* is true, and since we cannot affirm, without self-contradiction, that there is no truth, the logic of our predicament imposes upon us a certain humility.

The definition of the ideological fallacy neither presupposes that truth is absolute or relative. It only presupposes it as the ultimately indefinable category of assertion within which we conduct our affairs, and from which we only really escape in death. We cannot avoid assertions of true and false, nor of right and wrong. As long as we are concerned with the nature of the world, and as long as we remain alive and conscious to operate within it, we unceasingly weigh facts and assess or judge acts. The stipulation of the fallacy fundamentally presupposes nothing more. What it expressly designates is an error in political argument. But it cannot be ignored that what is an error for many will, for some, constitute an intentional act of stealth and cunning. We cannot judge the propriety of ideology universally. That sort of judgment we have already seen to be an error characteristic of ideologies themselves. We can only do what we have done: and that is to take note of a logical fault.

POLITICS AND LITERATURE:
JOHN ADAMS
AND DOCTOR JOHNSON

DONALD DAVIE

Professor Oakeshott has argued that poetry makes an irreplaceable contribution to the conversation of mankind; but that it can be seen to be irreplaceable only if the conversation of mankind is understood as something distinct from, because more comprehensive than, the sustained enquiry of the human mind into 'ourselves and the world we inhabit'.[1] Poetry, he argues, is irreplaceable in the conversation of mankind to just the degree that it does *not* contribute to that enquiry.

Although Professor Oakeshott conducts this argument with wonderful grace and amenity, and although his essay is directed mainly against the crass philistine who believes that poetry is ultimately (or sooner) replaceable, yet in my view no serious devotee of the poetic can afford to accept his civil compromise. For such a devotee of poetry (a term which, as Professor Oakeshott uses it, comprehends all literature and all the finer arts), it is essential to maintain that the poetic activity contributes not just to the conversation of mankind but to its enquiry also, that the poetic is a mode of that enquiry, and that a devotion to poetry entails 'a belief in the pre-eminence of enquiry, and of the categories of "truth" and "reality"'.[2]

In respect of this disagreement, a crucial case is the large class of writers who conceived of themselves, and are conceived by others, as contributing to an established field of enquiry; who nevertheless can be seen to be 'making images of a certain kind and moving about among them in a manner appropriate to their characters'[3]—that is to say, acting poetically in the very course of their enquiries. Certain enquirers into politics are particularly interesting from this point of view, if only because, as Professor Oakeshott reminds us, 'in ancient Greece... "politics" was understood as a "poetic" activity in which speaking (not merely to persuade but chiefly to compose memorable verbal images) was pre-eminent, and in which action was for the achievement of "glory" and "greatness"—a view of things which is reflected in the pages of Machiavelli.'[4]

[1] Michael Oakeshott, *The Voice of Poetry in the Conversation of Mankind*, (London 1959).
[2] *Ibid.* p. 35. [3] *Ibid.* p. 31. [4] *Ibid.* p. 15 n.

I propose to consider, as a political writer of this kind, John Adams, the second President of the United States. And I shall suggest, first, that Adams indeed combines perceptiveness in politics with poetic activity, in the same way, if not to the same degree, as a Bacon or a Burke; secondly, and more immediately to the point, that there is a limit to his political sagacity as to his poetic capacity, a limit which appears when we compare him with Doctor Johnson, an author who (it turns out) meant more to him than he ever cared to acknowledge; and thirdly that his fallings short in political sagacity and in poetry are related, so that we may vindicate common sense and common usage, and speak simply of a single failure of imagination. By this stage of my argument I shall be suggesting that properly to read John Adams as an ornament of American literature is not different from reading him as a shrewd observer of the political arena; and this is to reject, as untrue to the experience of reading John Adams vigilantly and with sympathy, the distinction which Professor Oakeshott asks us to make between 'conversation' and 'enquiry'.

The work by Adams which I shall consider is his *Discourses on Davila*. These appeared at intervals through the year 1790, in the *Gazette of the United States*, a federalist periodical published in Philadelphia. They appeared between hard covers in Boston in 1805, and when C. F. Adams a half-century later reproduced them in Volume VI of the *Life and Works* of Adams, he incorporated some valuable marginalia, dating from as late as 1812–13, found in John Adams's library copy. The Davila whom Adams is discoursing upon is Enrico Caterino Davila, whose *Historia delle guerre civili di Francia*, published in Venice in 1630, was known to Adams not in the English translation by W. Aylesbury (1647), though that folio was in Adams's library, but in the French translation of 1757 by the Abbé Mallet. Adams may well have been led to the work in the first place by Bolingbroke's commendation of it in the fifth of his *Letters on the Study and Use of History*.

Zoltan Haraszti, in his invaluable *John Adams and the Prophets of Progress*,[1] says of those parts of the *Discourses* which are not straight translations from Davila (as are eighteen out of the thirty-two papers), 'The papers are striking, and reading them one has at first the feeling of having discovered a literary treasure.' Unfortunately, he goes on, this feeling cannot be trusted, since 'the entire group is based upon a single chapter of Adam Smith's *Theory of Moral Sentiments*'. The logic of this is unacceptable unless we have very simple-minded and mechanical ideas of plagiarism on the one hand, originality on the other. Shakespeare himself would not scape whipping if we counted all his borrowings against him. And Mr Haraszti allows that Adams's phrasing is often

[1] Cambridge, Mass., 1952, p. 168.

more powerful than Smith's, and that 'his passion for stringing together epithets and metaphors makes his presentation particularly vivid'.

However, it is worth examining in some detail Haraszti's case that Adams is heavily indebted to Adam Smith, if only because this will bring us to what interests us more—Adams's indebtedness to Dr Johnson. We find to begin with that Section II of the *Discourses*, with epigraph from Voltaire, though it is not at odds with anything that Smith says, is a genuine elaboration of it—and in a direction (hence in a tone) quite alien from Smith's:

Of what avail are all these histories, pedigrees, traditions? What foundation has the whole science of genealogy and heraldry? Are there differences in the breeds of men, as there are in those of horses? If there are not, these sciences have no foundation in reason; in prejudice they have a very solid one.

There is nothing in Smith's chapter to approach this implication that if the philosopher's reason permits him to do nothing with such a deep-rooted prejudice but merely deplore it, *so much the worse for him, and especially for his politics*. (This section quotes Young's 'Love of Fame', and aptly.)

Section III, with epigraph from Voltaire, begins with a passage which, as Haraszti shows, has a parallel on the first page of Smith's Chapter. But it soon changes. One may usefully compare a passage about the poor man in Adams (a passage, incidentally, which is much wrenched by Hannah Arendt in her *On Revolution*)[1] with the no less good but quite different development by Smith. And what follows, beginning, 'Is there in science and letters a reward for the labor they require?' has no source in Smith; it recalls rather Dr Johnson's

> When first the college rolls receive his name,
> The young enthusiast quits his ease for fame;
> Through all his veins the fever of renown
> Burns from the strong contagion of the gown;
> (*Vanity of Human Wishes*, ll. 135–8.)

At the end Adams shifts from the learned profession to the military, just as Johnson does in his poem.

And sure enough, Section IV has an epigraph from the *Vanity of Human Wishes* about martial glory (of which Smith says nothing):

> Such bribes the rapid Greek o'er Asia whirl'd,
> For such the steady Romans shook the world

---

[1] New York, 1963. Miss Arendt quotes the passage with long *lacunae*, and this alters the force of it, since Adams allows as Miss Arendt does not that the emulous appetite can be satisfied *socially* (e.g. by the man who keeps a dog to 'look up to him') as well as *politically*. Miss Arendt ignores the source in Adam Smith.

Compare Johnson's version of these 'bribes' ('The festal blazes, the triumphal show') with Adams's taunting interrogations: 'A ribbon? a garter? a star? a golden key? a marshal's staff? or a white hickory stick?' After a remarkable passage on death-beds, and a grandly eloquent paragraph on marks of distinction in the Roman republic (entirely his own), Adams approaches Smith only in his last paragraph, with the example of the triumph of Paulus Aemilius.

Section V has a four-line epigraph from *The Vanity of Human Wishes*, ll. 177–8 conjoined with ll. 183–4 (with no acknowledgement of a *lacuna*). But it is in respect of this paper that comparison with Smith is most in order, and most damaging to Adams. Smith writes:

To those who have been accustomed to the possession or even to the hope, of public admiration, all other pleasures sicken and decay. Of all the discarded statesmen who, for their own ease, have studied to get the better of ambition, and to despise those honours which they could no longer arrive at, how few have been able to succeed! The greater part have spent their time in the most listless and insipid indolence, chagrined at the thoughts of their own insignificancy, incapable of being interested in the occupations of private life, without enjoyment, except when they talked of their former greatness, and without satisfaction, except when they were employed in some vain project to recover it. Are you in earnest resolved never to barter your liberty from the lordly servitude of a court, but to live free, fearless, and independent? There seems to be one way to continue in that virtuous resolution; and perhaps but one. Never enter the place from whence so few have been able to return; never come within the circle of ambition; nor ever bring yourself into comparison with those masters of the earth who have already engrossed the attention of half mankind before you.

And Adams:

Ministers of state are frequently displaced in all countries; and what is the consequence? Are they seen happy in a calm resignation to their fate? Do they turn their thoughts from their former employments, to private studies or business? Are they men of pleasant humor, and engaging conversation? Are their hearts at ease? Or is their conversation a constant effusion of complaints and murmurs, and their breast the residence of resentment and indignation, of grief and sorrow, of malice and revenge? Is it common to see a man get the better of his ambition, and despise the honors he once possessed; or is he commonly employed in projects, intrigues after intrigues, and manoeuvres on manoeuvres, to recover them? So sweet and delightful to the human heart is that complacency and admiration, which attends public offices, whether they are conferred by the favor of a prince, derived from hereditary descent, or obtained by election of the people, that a mind must be sunk below the feelings of humanity, or exalted by religion or philosophy far above the common character of men, to be insensible, or conquer its sensibility. Pretensions to such conquests are not uncommon; but the sincerity of such pretenders is often rendered suspicious, by their constant conversation and conduct, and even by their countenances.

Adam Smith is much superior to Adams here, for Adams, once he has committed himself to rhetorical questions, seems unable to break the habit; and Johnson is not in the picture at all. He can be brought into it if we recall that the disappointed statesman probably in Smith's mind as well as in Adams's was *Bolingbroke*, whom Jefferson and Adams both admired (though not uncritically). Johnson had written, in his review of Soame Jenyns's *Free Enquiry*, of 'the contemptible arrogance, or the impious licentiousness of Bolingbroke'.

Section VI has an epigraph from Juvenal and also from Johnson's imitation of him, in a couplet from *London* that was never far from Adams's lips, nor from the tip of his pen:

> This mournful truth is everywhere confess'd,
> Slow rises Worth, by Poverty depressed.

This section owes nothing to Smith (if only because it is wholly and specifically *political*) and it owes nothing to Johnson, though it has one curious parallel with him:

The Romans allowed none, but those who had possessed curule offices, to have statues or portraits. He who had images or pictures of his ancestors, was called noble. He who had no statue or pictures but his own, was called a new man. Those who had none at all, were ignoble.

Compare Johnson, *The Vanity of Human Wishes*, ll. 83–90.

> From every room descends the painted face,
> That hung the bright Palladium of the place,
> And smoak'd in kitchens, or in auctions sold,
> To better features yields the frame of gold;
> For now no more we trace in ev'ry line
> Heroic worth, benevolence divine:
> The form distorted justifies the fall,
> And detestation rids th' indignant wall.

The similarity here is presumably a matter of Johnson and Adams having a common source in Juvenal.

Section VII appears to owe little to Smith and nothing to Johnson. It has an epigraph from Pope's Moral Essays:

> Tis from high life high characters are drawn,
> A saint in *crape* is twice a saint in *lawn*.

And in Section VIII, which is given up almost entirely to a barely acknowledged verbatim quotation from Smith, the epigraph is again from Pope:

> Wise, if a minister; but if a King,
> More wise, more learn'd, more just, more everything

Section IX however has an epigraph from Johnson:

> Heroes, proceed! what bounds your pride shall hold?
> What check restrain your thirst of pow'r and gold?
>
> *(London, ll. 61–2)*

Adams begins: 'The answer to the question in the motto...' And this prepares us for the Section to stay quite close to Johnson. So it does, in a curious way; when Adams says, 'Consider the story of the ambition and the fall of Cardinal Wolsey and Archbishop Laud; the indignation of the world against their tyranny has been very faint; the sympathy with their fall has been very strong', he can hardly *not* be reproaching Johnson, or urbanely sneering at him, for treating both these characters in just this way—not in *London* however, but in *The Vanity of Human Wishes*:

> For why did Wolsey near the steeps of fate,
> On weak foundations raise th' enormous weight?
> Why but to sink beneath misfortune's blow,
> With louder ruin to the gulphs below?   (ll. 125–128)

and

> Rebellion's vengeful talons seize on Laud.   (l. 168)

And Adams indeed could claim, when he goes on to quote and praise from Juvenal's Satire III and from Johnson's imitation of it in *London* ('Although the verse, both of the Roman and Briton, is satire, its keenest severity consists in its truth'), that the poet of *London* castigates in others just that thoughtless veneration for eminence which the poet of *The Vanity of Human Wishes* fell into himself when he wrote so mournfully of Wolsey and of Laud. It would be no more than natural for Adams to applaud the young firebrand Johnson, friend of the reprobate Richard Savage, who wrote *London* against the establishment of Walpole, and to deplore the older and mellower or perhaps more politically timorous Johnson who wrote *The Vanity of Human Wishes*.

In the four papers which remain of the *Discourses on Davila* I detect no traces of Doctor Johnson, unless indeed it was Johnson, in his capacity as editor and commentator on Shakespeare, who brought to Adams's attention the passages from Shakespeare's *Troilus and Cressida* which make up Section X of the *Discourses*. It is at any rate quite impossible to accept Zoltan Haraszti's insinuation that the 70 lines of Shakespeare, to which of course there is no parallel in Adam Smith, are merely 'padding', an embellishment or amplification of the source only in this discreditable sense. On the contrary Adams's citation of Ulysses' speech on Degree is perhaps the most astonishing and admirable thing in all the *Discourses*. It is common form nowadays to take this as the key passage in the understanding of Shakespeare's political philosophy (the understanding in particular of how undemocratic Shakespeare is); but the passage was first given this central importance only thirty years ago, by the late E. M. W. Tillyard and the late Theodore Spencer. Adams's citation of it thus has the force of a startling anticipation of modern opinion, which that opinion has vindicated.

And yet this ought not to startle us. Twenty-five years ago Alfred Van Rensselaer Westfall in his *American Shakespearean Criticism 1607–1865*,[1] quoted an entry in Adams's Diary for 1772, which consists of a comment on some lines from *The Merry Wives of Windsor*, and declared: 'What may be called the first American Shakespearean comment, if not criticism, began with this man who became the second president of the United States.' Adams in fact was quite exceptional among men of affairs of his age, not just in the United States but in Britain also, in having a mind stocked with literary experience, and in drawing upon that experience not just for flowery embellishments but as a repository of moral and political wisdom. We are accustomed to think of the Founding Fathers as representing, not just a high level of social responsibility and political astuteness, but as representing also, more generally, a high level of civilisation. And this is surely right. But when we think in this way we think pre-eminently of Jefferson, and of his sensibility to pictures, statuary, music, architecture. Jefferson read widely in the classical literatures, and undoubtedly he had the best library of all the early Presidents. But of all the Presidents, with the possible exception of Lincoln, the only one to outstrip John Adams as a Shakespearean was his son John Quincy Adams, 'who read the plays on his mother's table when he was twelve years old'. The conclusive evidence of the literary civilisation of the elder Adams is not after all in such a full-dress instance as this use of Shakespeare in the *Discourses on Davila* but in the extent to which Shakespeare and Milton, Prior and Pope, Swift and Young, are ever present in his prose on whatever subject, in the fully assimilated aspect of submerged and unacknowledged quotation and allusion. And Johnson is there too, in just the same way.

In this matter, as in much else, John Adams was at pains to obscure his own tracks. In his old age at least he was ready to blow many a blast on a Philistine trumpet. To Jefferson in 1816 he declared:

Style has governed the Empire. Swift, Pope and Hume have disgraced all the honest Historians. Rapin and Burnet Oldmixon and Coke, contain more honest truth than Hume and Clarendon and all their disciples and Imitators. But who reads any of them at this day? Every one of the fine Arts from the earliest times has been inlisted in the service of Superstition and Despotism. The whole World at this day Gazes with Astonishment at the grossest

[1] New York, 1939, pp. 193–5.

Fictions because they have been immortalized by the most exquisite Artists, Homer and Milton, Phidias and Raphael. The Rabble of the Classic Skies and the Hosts of Roman Catholic Saints and Angells are still adored in Paint and Marble, and verse.[1]

In the next year he is still haranguing Jefferson on the same score:

Eustace is a Supplement to Dupuis; and both together contain a compleat draught of the Superstition, Credulity and Despotism of our terrestrial Universe. They show how Science, Litteratur, Mechanic Arts, and those fine Arts of Architecture, Painting, Statuary, Poetry, Musick and Eloquence: which you love so well and taste so exquisitely, have been subservient to Priests and Kings Nobles and commons Monarchies and Republicks. For they have all Used them when they could, but as the rich had them oftener than the poor, in their power, the latter have always gone to the Wall.[2]

And less than three weeks later he asks another correspondent:

Is it possible to inlist the 'Fine Arts', on the side of Truth, of Virtue, of Piety, or even of Honour? From the dawn of History they have been prostituted to the Service of Superstition and despotism. Read Herodotus, Pausanias, Plutarch, Lucian, and twenty others, not forgetting several of the Christian Fathers and see how the fine Arts have been employed. Read Eustace's classical Tour of Italy.[3]

But this is rather different, is it not? The question is neither rhetorical nor frivolous; and we know the answer to it no better than Adams did. Certainly I cannot answer it, who would never have read Adams at all, nor Jefferson either, but for the recommendations of that frequently exquisite and always honest poet, Ezra Pound, Fascist and anti-Semite. *Is* it possible to enlist the Fine Arts? We know how to do so no more than Doctor Johnson when he deplored, in the finest of all tributes to Shakespeare, that Shakespeare's plays did not uniformly punish wicked characters and reward the virtuous.

And this is Adams's dilemma. It is not that he does not know what the arts are about, or that he cannot respond to them; what puzzles him, as it puzzled Johnson and puzzles all of us in some degree, is how to square with his conscience the fact that he does respond to them, intensely. This is very clear from another letter written to Waterhouse twelve years earlier:

I have heard, as you insinuate, that Sterne was a wicked man; and there are traits of a false Character, in his Writings: yet Benevolence, Generosity, Simpathy and Humanity that fill the Eyes and bosoms of the readers of his

---

[1] *The Adams–Jefferson Letters*, ed. Lester J. Cappon (Chapel Hill, 1959), II, 502–3.
[2] *Ibid.* p. 507.
[3] *Statesman and Friend. Correspondence of John Adams with Benjamin Waterhouse, 1784–1822*, ed. W. C. Ford (Boston, 1927).

Works, will plead forever for their immortality. Virtues and Vices, Wisdom and Folly, Talents and imbecility, Services and demerits are so blended in most of the distinguished Sons of Men, that there is no knowing what Judgment to form of them, or what to do with them. Julian, in that ingenious Fable, The Caesars, throws headlong into the gulph of Tartarus, all the Tyrants; Alexander, Caesar, Augustus, Trajan and Constantine, are made to acknowledge that Fame, Power, or Pleasure were their Objects; Marcus Aurelius alone was confessed to have aimed Singly at the good of the People. I know not whether the number of pure Characters among Mankind in general will bear a greater proportion. The Number of unexceptionable Romances is not greater. Most of the fashionable ones, deserve to be slighted more than Sterne. Yet I own myself to be childish enough to be amused with their fictions....[1]

'Virtues and Vices, Wisdom and Folly, Talents and imbecility, Services and Demerits are so blended in most of the distinguished Sons of Men, that there is no knowing what Judgment to form of them'—because Adams believed this, we need not be surprised to find that Johnson, some of whose writings were never far from the surface of Adams's mind, should nevertheless never be spoken of by Adams except with marked hostility.

For instance, in Mr Cappon's admirable edition of the *Jefferson–Adams Letters* there are two entries in the index under 'Johnson, Samuel, lexicographer'. One of them sends us to Adams declaring in 1815, 'Johnson and Burke were more of Catholicks than Protestants at Heart and Gibbon became an Advocate for the Inquisition'. The other, no more amiable, of date 1813, is much more interesting:

The fundamental Principle of all Phylosophy and all Christianity is 'REJOICE ALWAYS IN ALL THINGS. Be thankfull at all times for all good and all that We call evil.' Will it not follow, that I ought to rejoice and be thankful that Priestley has lived? Aye! that Voltaire has lived? That Gibbon has lived? That Hume has lived, though a conceited Scotchman? That Bolingbroke has lived, tho' a haughty arrogant supercilious Dogmatist? that Burke and Johnson have lived, though superstitious Slaves or self-deceiving Hypocrites both. Is it not laughable to hear Burke call Bolingbroke a superficial Writer? To hear him ask 'Who ever read him through?' Had I been present I would have answered him 'I, I, myself, I have read him through, more than fifty Years ago, and more than five times in my Life, and once within five Years past. And in my Opinion the epithet "Superficial" belongs to you and your Friend Johnson more than to him.' I might say much more. But I believe Burke and Johnson to have been as political Christians, as Leo 10th.

The interesting name here is that of Bolingbroke. For Mr Haraszti has confirmed that the influence of Bolingbroke on Adams was as great as it is here asserted to be. (It was even greater on Jefferson.) Yet Adams

[1] *Ibid.* pp. 29–30.

finds no inconsistency—nor, given his view of human nature, is there any—in declaring Bolingbroke 'a haughty arrogant supercilious Dogmatist'. But the letter goes on to more interesting matters:

I return to Priestley, though I have great Complaints against him for personal Injuries and Persecution, at the same time that I forgive it all, and hope and pray that he may be pardoned for it all, above. Dr. Broklesby an intimate Friend and convivial Companion of Johnson told me, that Johnson died in Agonies of Horror of Annihilation, and all the Accounts We have of his death corroborate this Account of Broklesby. Dread of Annihilation! Dread of Nothing? A dread of Nothing I should think would be no dread at all. Can there be any real substantial rational fear of nothing? Were you on your deathbed, and in your last moments informed by demonstration or Revelation that you would cease to think and to feel at your dissolution, should you be terrified? You might be ashamed of yourself for having lived so long, to bear the proud Mans Contumely.

('The proud man's contumely'—a good example of how intimately Adams's mind is impregnated with Shakespeare.)

You might be ashamed of your Maker, and compare him to a little Girl amusing herself her Brothers and Sisters by blowing Bubbles in Soap Sudds. You might compare him to Boys sporting with Crakers and Rocketts: or to Men employed in making more artificial Fire Works; or to Men and Women at Farces and Operas, or Sadlers Wells Exploits; or to Politicians in their Intrigues; or to Heroes in their Butcheries; or to Popes in their Devilisms. But what should you fear? Nothing. Emori nolo Sed me mortuum esse nihil estimo.

'I have no wish to die, but that I be dead I consider as nothing.' Brave words! But what have they to do with the piously barbed hope in the same paragraph that Joseph Priestley, for his injuries to Adams, 'be pardoned for it all, above'? At any rate, one of several other places where Johnson figures in Adams's letters (but unnamed and unacknowledged in the index), reveals Adams not quite so stoical at the approach of death. This is in 1814:

I am sometimes afraid that my 'Machine' will not 'surcease motion' soon enough; for I dread nothing so much as 'dying at top' and expiring like Dean Swift 'a driveller and a Show' or like Sam. Adams, a Grief and distress to his Family, a weeping helpless Object of Compassion for Years.[1]

Swift comes into Adams's head out of Johnson's *Vanity of Human Wishes*:

> In life's last scene what prodigies surprise,
> Fears of the brave, and follies of the wise?
> From Marlb'rough's eyes the streams of dotage flow,
> And Swift expires a driv'ler and a show.

[1] *The Adams–Jefferson Letters*, II, 435.

As the latest editors austerely explain, 'Swift was intermittently insane before his death in 1745. Servants are said to have shown him to tourists for a fee.'

At this point we have reached the inflammatory question of how far either Adams or Jefferson died a Christian. There seems to be little doubt that the two old men conceived themselves to be in some sort Christians, though aware that their Christianity was too sceptical and conditional for them to afford to be frank about it, except to each other. But Adams at least, with his ferocious anti-clericalism, was quite incapable of understanding how Johnson, particularly in such a work as *The Vanity of Human Wishes*, rested his whole view of life on a very bleak and agitated but unshakeable faith in the Christian God. Adams and Jefferson, in their letters, are still locked into historical time—Adams like his later admirer Pound convinced that only sinister destruction of records has lost the clue which lies somewhere in the historical past; Jefferson, more sanguine and with a more successful career behind him, looking still, though with chastened eyes, for fulfilment in the future. In each case the deistic approval of the Christian ethic simply overlooks the great claim of Christianity—to have redeemed history, and made it meaningful once and for all, by the historical event of the Incarnation. No unitarianism, not any Jeffersonian admiration for Jesus as a great moral teacher, could come near to satisfying what a mind like Johnson's in *The Vanity of Human Wishes*, weary of mere historical process and iteration, looked for in Christian faith.

And this is why, to speak for myself, Adams in his Letters pleases more after a hundred pages than after five hundred. At first one is delighted by his tough-minded and humorous cordiality, his unflagging curiosity, the strong savour as well as the flexibility of his writing. But the suspicion grows that Adams's scepticism is not after all tough-mindedness but the product of a conspiracy theory of history (whence, too plainly alas, some of Ezra Pound's liking for him); the curiosity is (Adams almost admits as much) the running wild of a still hungry intelligence, operating irresponsibly because his conspiracy theory has got him to the stage where every speculation has as much and as little point as any other; and the humour even is irresponsible and after a while leaves a bad taste. A scepticism so thorough as Adams's was by 1812, even if it had firmer bases than it has, leaves a man nothing with which to face the future; and of course Adams was so old by this time that, as he acknowledges, he has really no future to face. It is his age—that is, the age he grew up in, which formed him, the age of the Enlightenment—which gives to all this the unexpected, and undoubtedly quite genuine, good humour.

The Discourses on Davila are another matter. And I hope I have shown that when Zoltan Haraszti had 'the feeling of having discovered a literary treasure', he ought to have trusted that feeling. His discovery that the *Discourses*, when they depart from Davila, rest on a chapter of Adam Smith which Adams amplifies out of Johnson and Shakespeare and others—this, which Haraszti thinks reveals the treasure as fool's gold, in fact does nothing of the kind. He is misled by a mistaken and out-dated notion of what originality is, in literature. The *Discourses on Davila*, at least the fourteen essays of useful reflections embedded in them, are a literary masterpiece. One is tempted to enforce this judgment by quoting a sustained passage, for instance the paragraph from Section IV beginning, 'Has there ever been a nation who understood the human heart better than the Romans...?' But it is better to avoid giving any impression that great literature is a matter of detachable purple passages. On the contrary, what makes the *Discourses* an achievement of the literary imagination is something much more nearly connected with what makes them also a penetrating and perennially relevant examination of political behaviour.

Accordingly, Adams's limitations as an observer of politics are also his limitations as a writer; for in both cases what we have is a failure of imagination. If we now define the place where that failure comes, it is by no means to deny that the *Discourses* are a great imaginative achievement; it is on the contrary to define that achievement by setting bounds to it.

In the *Discourses* Adams is arguing for political institutions as a way of harnessing the allegedly universal passion of emulation. In fact I believe we have to deny that this passion *is* universal: for there are cultures of the unprivileged which elevate 'solidarity' as the highest value, and condemn as betrayals of that principle the distinctions achieved by individuals. Such is the culture of the Trades Unionist, which Adams had no opportunity to observe. But I find that his argument fails in another way, for instance in Section V:

Emulation really seems to produce genius, and the desire of superiority to create talents. Either this, or the reverse of it must be true; and genius produces emulation, and natural talents, the desire of superiority; for they are always found together, and what God and nature have united, let no audacious legislator presume to put asunder.

The concession which Adams makes here—when he envisages 'the reverse' proposition—reaches much farther than he seems aware of. For if it is only talented men who are emulous, then emulation and the desire for distinction are not such universal appetites as he elsewhere in his treatise supposes. But in any case there is a more horrifying possibility, which Adams does not envisage. What if the *untalented* are emulous? An apparition like Lee Oswald, or other pathetic killers who seem to kill only so as to be caught and 'get their names in the papers'— these suggest that the wish to be distinguished, while not universal, is distributed at random, among talented and untalented alike.

Adams is saved from envisaging this because he still confides in a providentially determined harmony between the desire for distinction and the deserving of distinction—'what God and nature have united'. And this is characteristic. Although it seems to be true that for Adams 'nature' as a providentially ordained order is less tightly organised than for Jefferson,[1] still he shares with him the conviction that there is such a providential order in nature, and that human reason can discern it. This is indeed the force of the epigraphs he takes from Pope, particularly the motto on Section XIII:

> First follow nature; and your judgment frame
> By her just standard, which is still the same.

For Adams as we might expect seeks authority from the Pope of *Essay on Man* and *Moral Essays*, from the poet whose horizons are bounded by the precepts of Bolingbroke, not from the greater poet who in *The Dunciad* envisaged all providential order swept away and chaos come again.

Now Johnson on the other hand could share the experience behind the last lines of *The Dunciad* no less than the experience behind the *Essay on Man*. It is Johnson the devout Christian of Augustinian temper (also Pope the Roman Catholic) who can envisage that God moves in mysterious ways, above and perhaps athwart the natural order which He ordained; it is Adams the sceptic who cannot afford not to believe that God guarantees a beneficent harmony in Nature and human nature. There is one more place where Johnson appears in the *Discourses on Davila*, which brings this out clearly. In section XV, where Adams is in effect denying the contention of the Declaration of Independence that 'all men are created equal', he declares:

Nature, which has established in the universe a chain of being and universal order, descending from archangels to microscopic animalcules, has ordained that no two objects shall be perfectly equal.

And in the marginalia which Adams subsequently wrote to his own work, he notes against this passage:

This is not a chain of being from God to nothing; *ergo*, not liable to Dr Johnson's criticism, nor to the reviewer's.

The reviewer is identified by Zoltan Haraszti as Arthur Maynard Walter (1780–1807), and his review appeared in the *Monthly Anthology*

[1] See Daniel J. Boorstin, *The Lost World of Thomas Jefferson* (1948).

of Boston, where I have been unable to consult it. Johnson's criticism of the alleged 'great chain of being' appeared in his review in 1757 of Soame Jenyns's 'Free Enquiry into the Nature and Origin of Evil'—a review which is one of Johnson's greatest works:

> The scale of existence from infinity to nothing, cannot possibly have being. The highest being not infinite must be, as has been often observed, at an infinite distance below infinity...
> Between the lowest positive existence and nothing, wherever we suppose positive existence to cease, is another chasm infinitely deep; where there is room again for endless orders of subordinate nature, continued for ever and for ever, and yet infinitely superior to non-existence.
> To these meditations humanity is unequal. But yet we may ask, not of our Maker, but of each other, since on the one side creation, wherever it stops, must stop infinitely below infinity, and on the other infinitely above nothing, what necessity there is that it should proceed so far either way, that beings so high or so low should ever have existed? We may ask; but I believe no created wisdom can give an adequate answer.

Adams, it may be, *does* just escape by the skin of his teeth from Johnson's unanswerable objection. But Johnson goes on to explode the whole image of 'the great chain'. In famous words, which have been vindicated by A. O. Lovejoy in his standard work on this topic, Johnson declares:

> This scale of being I have demonstrated to be raised by presumptuous imagination, to rest on nothing at the bottom, to lean on nothing at the top, and to have vacuities from step to step through which any order of being may sink into nihility without any inconvenience, so far as we can judge, to the next rank above or below it.

And Adams cannot escape the charge of 'presumptuous imagination'. In the *Discourses on Davila* Adams is a very great writer. But Johnson is greater—not by virtue of greater facility in the management of language but simply because Johnson's imagination could comprehend abysses and exaltations beyond the compass of that Enlightenment culture which Johnson transcended whereas Adams, restive and sceptical though he was, remained in the end bounded by its assumptions. This is not the place to examine Johnson's political writings. But if we were to do so, we should have to find, either that Johnson's mind and imagination were not so fully engaged in this field as in others, or else that his writings on politics were superior to Adams's—more profoundly imagined, and *therefore* more sagacious.

A BIBLIOGRAPHY OF
MICHAEL OAKESHOTT[1]

The following abbreviations are used: *CJ—Cambridge Journal*; *CR—Cambridge Review*; *JTS—Journal of Theological Studies*; *S—Spectator*.

BOOKS, ESSAYS AND REVIEW ARTICLES
ON PHILOSOPHY, POLITICS, ETC.

1927

Religion and the Moral Life (The 'D' Society Pamphlets, no. II; Cambridge), pp. 13.

1928

'The importance of the historical element in Christianity', *The Modern Churchman*, XVIII (1928–9), 360–71.

1932

'John Locke', *CR*, LIV (1932–3), 72–3.
'The new Bentham', *Scrutiny*, I (1932–3), 114–31.

1933

Experience and its Modes (Cambridge University Press), pp. vii + 358.

1935

'Thomas Hobbes', *Scrutiny*, IV (1935–6), 263–77.

1936

'History and the social sciences', in the Institute of Sociology, *The Social Sciences* (London: Le Play House Press), pp. 71–81.

1937

'Dr Leo Strauss on Hobbes', *Politica*, II (1936–7), 364–79.

1938

'The concept of a philosophical jurisprudence', *Politica*, III (1938), 203–22, 345–60.

[1] Compiled by W. H. Greenleaf, University College, Swansea, who would be glad to hear of any other items. Essays marked with an asterisk [*] are reprinted, or printed for the first time, in *Rationalism in Politics and Other Essays* (1962), where they may most conveniently be consulted; though it should be noted, perhaps, that some alterations and additions were there made to the texts originally published.

1939

The Social and Political Doctrines of Contemporary Europe (Cambridge University Press), pp. xxiii + 224.

The same, with additions and corrections, pp. xxiii + 241.

'The claims of politics', *Scrutiny*, VIII (1939–40), 146–51.

1941

The Social and Political Doctrines of Contemporary Europe, 2nd edition (Cambridge University Press), pp. xxiii + 241.

1942

The same, with five additional prefaces by F. A. Ogg (Cambridge University Press; New York: Macmillan), pp. xxiii + 241.

1946

Hobbes's *Leviathan* (edited with an introduction; Oxford: Blackwell), pp. lxvii + 468.

1947

'The "collective dream of civilisation"', *The Listener*, XXXVII (1947), 966–7.

*'Rationalism in politics', *CJ*, I (1947–8), 81–98, 145–57.

1948

'Scientific politics', *CJ*, I (1947–8), 347–58.

'Contemporary British politics', *CJ*, I (1947–8), 474–90.

'Science and society', *CJ*, I (1947–8), 689–97.

*'The Tower of Babel', *CJ*, II (1948–9), 67–83.

1949

*'The political economy of freedom', *CJ*, II (1948–9), 212–29.

'The universities', *CJ*, II (1948–9) 515–42.

'J. D. Mabbott: *The State and the Citizen*', *Mind*, LVIII (1949), 378–89.

1950

*'Rational conduct', *CJ*, IV (1950–1), 3–27.

'The idea of a university', *The Listener*, XLIII (1950), 424–6.

1951

Political Education (Cambridge: Bowes and Bowes), pp. 28.

'Mr Carr's first volume', *CJ*, IV (1950–1), 344–52.

'The B.B.C.', *CJ*, IV (1950–1), 543–54.

1954

'The idea of "character" in the interpretation of modern politics' (a roneoed paper presented to the Political Studies Association Conference at Cambridge).

1955

'The customer is never wrong', *The Listener*, LIV (1955), 301–2.
La Idea de Gobierno en la Europa Moderna (Madrid: Ateneo), pp. 33.

1956
*'On being conservative'.
Political Education [reprinted with some minor alterations and additions in P. J. Laslett (ed.), *Philosophy, Politics and Society*, 1st series (Oxford: Blackwell), pp. 1–21].

1957
'Die Massen in der repräsentativen Demokratie', in A. Hunold (ed.), *Masse und Demokratie* (Erlenbach-Zürich und Stuttgart: Rentsch), pp. 189–214.

1958
*'The activity of being an historian', *Historical Studies I*, ed. T. D. Williams (London: Bowes and Bowes), pp. 1–19.

1959
* *The Voice of Poetry in the Conversation of Mankind* (London: Bowes and Bowes), pp. 63.
'Nazism', in *Chambers Encyclopaedia*, IX, 737–9.

1960
*'The moral life in the writings of Thomas Hobbes'.

1961
*'The study of "politics" in a university'.
'The masses in representative democracy', in A. Hunold (ed.), *Freedom and Serfdom: An Anthology of Western Thought* (Dordrecht, Holland: Reidel), pp. 151–70.

1962
Rationalism in Politics and Other Essays (London: Methuen), pp. 333.
The same (New York: Basic Book Publications), pp. 333.
Hobbes's *Leviathan*, ed. M. Oakeshott with an introduction by R. S. Peters (New York: Collier Books), pp. 511.

1964
'Political laws and captive audiences', in G. R. Urban (ed.), *Talking to Eastern Europe* (London: Eyre and Spottiswoode), pp. 291–301.
R. Bassett, *The Essentials of Parliamentary Democracy*, 2nd ed.; edited with an introduction (London: Cass), pp. xxiv+214.

1965
'Rationalism in politics: a reply to Professor Raphael', *Political Studies*, XIII (1965), 89–92.

1966
'Historical continuity and causal analysis', in W. H. Dray (ed.), *Philosophical Analysis and History* (New York: Harper and Row), pp. 193–212. [A reprint with minor deletions of *Experience and its Modes* (1933), pp. 126–45.]

Experience and its Modes (Cambridge University Press), pp. viii + 359. [A reprint of the 1933 edition.]

Rationalismus in der Politik (Neuwied und Berlin: Luchterhard), pp. 362. (Translation into German by K. Streifthau.)

1967

'Learning and teaching', in R. S. Peters (ed.), *The Concept of Education* (London: Routledge and Kegan Paul), pp. 156–76.

BOOK REVIEWS

1926

J. Needham (ed.), *Science, Religion and Reality*, *JTS*, xxvii (1926), 317–19.

A. C. Bouquet, *The Christian Religion and its Competitors Today*, *JTS*, xxvii (1926), 440.

E. Griffith-Jones, *Providence—Divine and Human*, *JTS*, xxvii (1926), 440–1.

1927

C. Gore, *Can We Then Believe?*, *JTS*, xxviii (1927), 313–16.

E. G. Selwyn (ed.), *Essays Catholic and Critical*, *JTS*, xxviii (1927), 313–16.

W. R. Bowie, *The Inescapable Christ*, *JTS*, xxviii (1927), 313–16.

P. Gardiner, *Modernism in the Church of England*, *JTS*, xxviii (1927), 316.

T. Whittaker, *The Metaphysics of Evolution*, *CR*, xlviii (1926–7), 230.

R. B. Perry, *General Theory of Value*, *CR*, xlviii (1926–7), 408.

R. W. Sellars, *The Principles and Problems of Philosophy*, *CR*, xlviii (1926–7), 429.

F. J. E. Woodbridge, *The Realm of Mind*, *CR*, xlix, (1927–8) 93.

A. A. Jascalevich, *Three Conceptions of Mind*, *CR*, xlix (1927–8), 93.

A. G. Widgery, *Contemporary Thought of Great Britain*, *CR*, xlix (1927–8), 156.

1929

P. S. Belasco, *Authority in Church and State*, *JTS*, xxx (1929), 426–8.

J. S. Mackenzie, *Fundamental Problems of Life*, in *Journal of Philosophical Studies*, iv (1929), 264–6.

1930

J. Marteau, *Clémenceau*, *CR*, li (1929–30), 332.

J. C. Powys, *The Meaning of Culture*, *CR*, li (1929–30), 367–8.

G. E. G. Catlin, *The Principles of Politics*, *CR*, li (1929–30), 400.

K. Feiling, *What is Conservatism?*, *CR*, li (1929–30), 512.

Ll. Powys, *The Pathetic Fallacy*, *CR*, li (1929–30), 512.

H. Rashdall, *God and Man*, *CR*, lii (1930–1), 39.

G. G. Atkins, *The Making of the Christian Mind*, *JTS*, xxxi (1930), 203–8.

H. H. Farmer, *Experience of God*, *JTS*, xxxi (1930), 302–3.

1931

H. Driesch, *Ethical Principles in Theory and Practice*, *JTS*, XXXII (1931), 326–7.
F. J. Sheen, *Religion without God*, *JTS*, XXXII (1931), 434–5.
K. Heim, *The New Divine Order*, *JTS*, XXXII (1931), 434–5.
E. Holmes, *Philosophy without Metaphysics*, *JTS*, XXXII (1931), 434–5.
L. P. Smith, *Afterthoughts*, *CR*, LII (1930–1), 287.
F. H. Bradley, *Aphorisms*, *CR*, LII (1930–1), 287.
L. Britton, *Love and Hunger*, *CR*, LII (1930–1), 357.
J. B. Pratt, *Adventures in Philosophy and Religion*, *CR*, LII (1930–1), 511.

1932

F. J. C. Hearnshaw (ed.), *Political and Social Ideas of the Age of Reaction and Reconstruction*, *CR*, LIII (1931–2), 332.

1933

M. Ruthnaswamy, *The State*, *CR*, LIV (1932–3), 359.
J. Macmurray, *Interpreting the Universe*, *CR*, LIV (1932–3), 395.
C. R. Morris, *Idealistic Logic*, *CR*, LV (1933–4), p. 152.

1934

M. Grant, *A New Argument for God's Survival*, *CR*, LV (1933–4), 332.
L. Curtis, *Civitas Dei*, *CR*, LV (1933–4), 450.
O. Gierke, *Natural Law and the Theory of Society, 1500 to 1800* (tr. Barker), *CR*, LVI (1934–5), 11–12.
H. Levy and others, *Aspects of Dialectical Materialism*, *CR*, LVI (1934–5), 108–9.
A. N. Whitehead, *Adventures of Ideas*, *JTS*, XXXV (1934), 73–5.
C. D. Burns, *The Horizon of Experience*, *JTS*, XXXV (1934), 75–6.
G. Michaelis, *Richard Hooker als politischer Denker*, *JTS*, XXXV (1934), 76.

1935

H. G. Wood, *Christianity and the Nature of History*, *CR*, LVI (1934–5), 248.
E. F. Carritt, *Morals and Politics*, *CR*, LVI (1934–5), 449.
M. B. Foster, *The Political Philosophies of Plato and Hegel*, *CR*, LVII (1935–6), 74.
W. Tilly, *Right: A Study in Physical and Moral Order*, *JTS*, XXXVI (1935), 322–3.
H. G. Wood, *Christianity and the Nature of History*, *JTS*, XXXVI (1935), 323–4.
J. C. McKerrow, *Religion and History*, *JTS*, XXXVI (1935), 323–4.

1936

W. Brock, *An Introduction to Contemporary German Philosophy*, *CR*, LVII (1935–6), 195.
L. Strauss, *The Political Philosophy of Hobbes*, *CR*, LVIII (1936–7), 150.
F. H. Bradley, *Collected Essays*, in *Philosophy*, XI (1936), 114–16.
B. Pfannenstill, *Bernard Bosanquet's Philosophy of the State*, in *Philosophy*, XI (1936), 482–3.

1937

K. Mannheim, *Ideology and Utopia, CR*, LVIII (1936–7), 257.
F. Birch, *This Freedom of Ours, CR*, LIX (1937–8), 55.
L. Strauss, *The Political Philosophy of Hobbes*, in *Philosophy*, XII (1937), 239–41.
M. Roberts, *The Modern Mind*, in *Scrutiny*, VI (1937–8), 208–10.

1938

R. G. Collingwood, *The Principles of Art, CR*, LIX (1937–8), 487.

1939

J. Marshall, *Swords and Symbols*, in *Philosophy*, XIV (1939), 493–4.

1940

E. F. M. Durbin, *The Politics of Democratic Socialism, CR*, LXI (1939–40), 347–50.

1941

G. Wallas, *Men and Ideas*, in *Philosophy*, XVI (1941), 95.

1946

B. Croce, *Politics and Morals*, in *Philosophy*, XXI (1946), 184.

1947

R. G. Collingwood, *The Idea of History*, in *English Historical Review*, LXII (1947), 84–6.
J. Bowle, *Western Political Thought, S*, CLXXIX (1947), 626.

1948

C. E. M. Joad, *Decadence, S*, CLXXX (1948), 290–2.
R. B. Perry, *Puritanism and Democracy*, in *Philosophy*, XXIII (1948), 86–7.
H. D. Lasswell, *The Analysis of Political Behaviour, CJ*, I (1947–8), 326, 328.
L. Whistler, *The English Festivals, CJ*, I (1947–8), 382, 384.
J. Lavrin, *Nietzsche, CJ*, I (1947–8), 450, 452.
W. T. Jones (ed.), *Masters of Political Thought* (vol. II), *CJ*, I (1947–8), 636–7.
K. B. Smellie, *Why We Read History, CJ*, I (1947–8), 766–7.
S. Campion, *Father, a Portrait of G. C. Coulton, CJ*, II (1948–9), 116, 118.
The Earl of Lytton, *Bulwer–Lytton, CJ*, II (1948–9), p. 188.

1949

A. Koestler, *Insight and Outlook, S*, CLXXXIII (1949), 20, 22.
F. Williams, *The Triple Challenge, CJ*, II (1948–9), 313–14.
J. D. Mabbott, *The State and the Citizen, CJ*, II (1948–9), 316, 318.
F. Sternberg, *How To Stop The Russians Without War, CJ*, II (1948–9), 435–7.
G. C. Field, *Principles and Ideals in Politics, CJ*, II (1948–9), 444, 446.
Sir E. W. Whittaker, *The Modern Approach to Descartes' Problem, CJ*, II (1948–9), 629–30.

S. M. Jacobs, *Notes on Descartes' Règles*, *CJ*, II (1948–9), 629–30.
P. Valéry, *Descartes*, *CJ*, II (1948–9), 629–30.
H. Selsam, *Socialism and Ethics*, *CJ*, II (1948–9), 692–4.
E. Dudley, *The Tree of Commonwealth* (ed. Brodie), *CJ*, II (1948–9), 763–4.

1950

G. Ryle, *The Concept of Mind*, *S*, CLXXXIV (1950), 20, 22.
J. Godley, *Tell Me the Next One*, *S*, CLXXXIV (1950), 734.
J. W. Watmough, *Cambridge Conversations*, *CJ*, III (1949–50), 252–4.
J. Plamenatz, *The English Utilitarians*, *CJ*, III (1949–50), 312–313.
Sir R. Filmer, *Patriarcha and other Political Works* (ed. Laslett), *CJ*, III (1949–50), 384; *Philosophy*, XXV (1950), 280–1.

1951

G. J. Renier, *History, its Purpose and Method*, in *Philosophical Quarterly*, I (1950–1), 284–5.
C. Morgan, *Liberties of the Mind*, *S*, CLXXXVI (1951), 419.
G. Santayana, *Dominations and Powers*, *S*, CLXXXVII (1951), 578.
T. Wilson, *Modern Capitalism and Economic Progress*, *CJ*, IV (1950–1), 504–6.
J. H. S. Burleigh, *The City of God*, *CJ*, IV (1950–1), 567–68, 570, 572.
R. H. Barrow, *Introduction to St Augustine*, *CJ*, IV (1950–1), 567–8, 580, 572.
T. H. Marshall, *Citizenship and Social Class*, *CJ*, IV (1950–1), 629–30.
N. Machiavelli, *The Discourses* (ed. Walker), *CJ*, IV (1950–1), 698.

1952

E. von Kuehnelt-Leddihn, *Liberty or Equality*, *S*, CLXXXVIII (1952), 338–40.
Lord Radcliffe, *The Problem of Power*, *S*, CLXXXVIII (1952), 451–2.
W. H. Walsh, *An Introduction to the Philosophy of History*, in *Philosophical Quarterly*, II (1952), 276–7.
E. M. Forster, *Two Cheers for Democracy*, *CJ*, V (1951–2), 436–8.

1953

M. Cranston, *Freedom*, *S*, CXC (1953), 579.
T. D. Weldon, *The Vocabulary of Politics*, *S*, CXCI (1953), 405–6.
D. Forbes, *The Liberal Anglican Idea of History*, *CJ*, VI (1952–3), 248–51.

1954

H. Read, *Anarchy and Order*, *S*, CXCII (1954), 593–4.
J. Bowle, *Politics and Opinion in the Nineteenth Century*, *S*, CXCIII (1945), 66, 69.
M. Duverger, *Political Parties*, *S*, CXCIII (1954), 92–3.
R. Kirk, *The Conservative Mind*, *S*, CXCIII (1954), 472, 474.
E. Benes, *Memoirs*, *S*, CXCIII (1954), 639–40.
A. Dru (ed.), *The Letters of Jacob Burckhardt*, in *Encounter*, II, no. 6 (1954), 69–70, 72–4.

1955

H. Marcuse, *Reason and Revolution*, S, CXCIV (1955), 404–5.
K. C. Wheare, *Government by Committee*, S, CXCV (1955), 129.
H. Butterfield, *Man on his Past*, S, CXCV (1955), 595–6.
P. Bloomfield, *Uncommon People*, S, CXCV (1955), 871–2.

1956

G. Barraclough, *History in a Changing World*, S, CXCVI (1956), 220–21.
C. Rossiter, *Conservatism in America*, S, CXCVI (1956), 451–2.
A. J. Ayer and others, *Studies in Communication*, S, CXCVI (1956), 502.
J. Bowle, *Minos or Minotaur?*, S, CXCVII (1956), 31–2.
G. Salvemini, *Mazzini*, S, CXCVII (1956), 459–60.
J. Brooke, *The Chatham Administration*, S, CXCVII (1956), 746.

1957

Lady Stenton, *The Englishwoman in History*, S, CXCVIII (1957), 459–60.
H. Warrender, *The Political Philosophy of Thomas Hobbes*, S, CXCIX (1957), 198.
G. Heckscher, *The Study of Comparative Government and Politics*, S, CXCIX (1957), 490–1.
J. Lewis, *Marxism and the Open Mind*, S, CXCIX (1957), 654.
H. Butterfield, *George III and the Historians*, S, CXCIX (1957), 718.
B. de Jouvenel, *Sovereignty*, in *Crossbow*, I (1957), 43–4.

1958

M. Polanyi, *Personal Knowledge*, in *Encounter*, XI, no. 3 (1958), 77–80.

1961

J. Chiari, *Realism and Imagination*, in *British Journal of Aesthetics*, I (1960–1), 198–9.

1962

P. Laslett (ed.), *Locke's Two Treatises of Government*, in *Historical Journal*, V (1962), 97–100.
R. Shackleton, *Montesquieu: a Critical Biography*, in *Modern Language Review*, LVII (1962), 442–4.
H. Arendt, *Between Past and Future*, in *Political Science Quarterly*, LXXVII (1962), 88–90.

1965

P. Laslett and W. G. Runciman (eds.), *Philosophy, Politics and Society* (2nd series), in *Philosophical Quarterly*, XV (1965), 281–2.
The Bow Group, *The Conservative Opportunity*, in *New Society*, VI (1965), 26–7.

1966

J. C. Holt, *Magna Carta*, in *Government and Opposition*, I (1965–6), 266–71.
J. Lively (ed.), *The Works of Joseph de Maistre*, in *New Society*, VII (1966), 28–9.

1967

K. Brown (ed.), *Hobbes Studies*, in *English Historical Review*, LXXXII (1967), 123–5.

J. R. Lucas, *The Principles of Politics*, in *Political Studies*, xv (1967), 224–7.

1968

F. H. Hinsley, *Sovereignty*, in *English Historical Review*, LXXXIII (1968), 441–2.

MISCELLANEOUS WRITINGS

1930

'The 55th Exhibition of the Cambridge Drawing Society', *CR*, LI (1929–30), 417.

1931

'Scutari' (a poem), *CR*, LIII (1931–2), 67.

1932

'Cracow' (a poem), *CR*, LIII (1931–2), 266.

1936

'The servant girl who burnt Carlyle's MS', *The Listener*, xv (1936), 459–60.

'Robert Jenkins'.

[Both of these items appeared in *Imaginary Biographies* by A. Bryant and others (London: Allen and Unwin, 1936), pp, 61–81.]

(With G. T. Griffith), *A Guide to the Classics, or, How to Pick the Derby Winner* (London: Faber), pp. 136.

1939

Obituary Notice of Geoffrey Rossetti, *CR*, LX (1938–9), 166–7.

1947

(With G. T. Griffith), *A New Guide to the Derby: How to Pick the Winner* (London: Faber), pp. 133.

1951

'A reminder from "Leviathan"', *The Observer*, 29 July 1951.

INDEX